Changing Patterns

Changing Patterns:
Women in Canada
Second Edition

≈≈≈≈≈≈≈≈≈≈≈≈≈≈≈≈≈≈≈≈≈≈≈≈≈≈≈≈≈≈≈

Edited by Sandra Burt, Lorraine Code,
and Lindsay Dorney

M&S

Canadian Cataloguing in Publication Data

Main entry under title:

Changing patterns: women in Canada

2nd ed.
Includes bibliographical references.
ISBN 0-7710-2854-7

1. Women – Canada – Social conditions. 2. Women – Canada. 3. Feminism – Canada. I. Burt, Sandra D., 1947– . II. Code, Lorraine. III. Dorney, Lindsay.

HQ1453.C53 1993   305.4'0971   C92-095000-0

McClelland & Stewart Inc.
The Canadian Publishers
481 University Avenue
Toronto, Ontario
M5G 2E9

Typesetting by M&S
Printed and bound in Canada

Contents

≈≈≈≈≈≈≈≈≈≈≈≈≈≈≈≈≈≈≈≈≈≈≈≈≈≈≈≈≈≈≈≈

Preface

≈≈≈≈≈≈≈≈≈≈≈≈≈≈≈≈≈≈≈≈≈≈≈≈≈≈≈≈≈≈≈≈≈≈≈≈≈≈

In the early 1980s Michael Harrison of McClelland & Stewart initiated discussions with a group of feminist scholars, who were then working in southwestern Ontario, about producing a collection of articles suitable for Canadian students of Women's Studies. The text would, at the same time, introduce informed and interested non-academics to issues central to women's lives in Canada. The group met regularly for several months, comparing notes and suggestions about what was required to produce a readable and informative book, until, in the early spring of 1986, an editorial committee was established, consisting of the three present editors. We concluded that we wanted to produce a book that would tell the story of recent changes in Canadian women's lives, set against a historical background. We were concerned that the book should not be merely a collection of previously published articles. Hence we asked contributors to take this opportunity to integrate their new research with a review of recent work in their area of expertise. The chapters in the first edition of *Changing Patterns* were written in response to that request.

One particularly valuable aspect of the production of the book was an all-day conference meeting of the contributors held in autumn 1986. Each contributor prepared an early draft of her chapter, which was circulated before the meeting in preparation for discussion by the entire group. The meeting gave us the opportunity to integrate the chapters in a way that is unusual for an edited collection. It became clear, for example, that some central topics, such as the status of women in the work force, or women's political participation, were being addressed by several authors as aspects of their research. This integrative treatment of these and other aspects of women's lives reflects our conception of the best approach to Women's Studies as an area of study, teaching, and research.

The first edition of *Changing Patterns* has been widely used across the country, in Women's Studies courses and general introductory courses in the humanities and social sciences. Pleased with this development, we solicited reactions to the book from people who had taught and studied it. This second edition marks our attempt to incorporate as many of their suggestions as possible, without compromising the integrity of the project and within a volume of manageable size and scope. Contributors to the first edition have revised their original chapters to address more recent developments in feminist theory and practice. We have added three chapters that treat the topics most frequently requested by people who have used the book. These revisions and additions will, we hope, ensure that *Changing Patterns* will continue to count as a pertinent text for feminist scholars in the 1990s.

We thank Michael Harrison for his continued enthusiasm for this project, Lealle Ruhl for her capable editorial assistance, Jacqueline Code for her excellent work in preparing the index, Joanne Voisin for her patience with changes, and the anonymous referees who read the first manuscripts.

Introduction

≈≈≈≈≈≈≈≈≈≈≈≈≈≈≈≈≈≈≈≈≈≈≈≈≈≈≈≈≈≈≈≈≈≈≈≈≈

The women's movement has touched the lives of many Canadian women, radically transforming the nature of their everyday experiences. Inspired by these transformations, feminist scholars are developing critiques of old social orders and are challenging long-standing assumptions about social structures and how people are located within them. In this collection feminist scholars writing from a variety of perspectives discuss women's positions in Canadian society, both historically and in the present. That society has a long history of implicitly endorsing androcentric points of view. Positions of power and prestige have been occupied primarily by white, affluent, educated, and propertied men; and Canadian society has been built around the values that these men stand for. As in other industrialized societies in the twentieth-century Western world, Canadian social structures and institutions have been shaped by capitalist production with its competitive market economy and technological commitments.

Throughout the twentieth century, and most notably since the 1960s, Canadian women have been engaged in vigorous efforts, both practical and theoretical, to contest these systems of power and to challenge patriarchal structures and values. Their successes have been so remarkable that many young women in the 1990s have begun to think in post-feminist terms, arguing that measures like pay equity and affirmative action have achieved the goals that feminists had set for themselves, and hence that nothing urgent remains on the feminist agenda. In this book Canadian feminist scholars take issue with that new-found complacency. While the writers celebrate women's achievements over the past thirty years, they also note how, and seek to explain why, women continue to be marginalized and disempowered. They examine some of the historical constraints on opportunities for women in Canada and consider how those constraints have been differently experienced by women in anglophone and francophone Canadian society, by Native Canadian women, by women of diverse social, cultural, and ethnic origins, and by women situated in different social and economic strata. The authors show how fixed assumptions about an essential female 'nature' have historically shaped all aspects of women's lives, influencing their psychological, physical, and social well-being. They introduce feminist analyses of these assumptions and examine some of the changes that those analyses have generated.

One of the first assumptions that feminists have challenged is the belief that women and men should and do in fact live in separate social spheres: men in a public world of competitive political and marketplace activity; women in a private world of domestic, caring activity. Feminist analyses of this traditional public/private dichotomy have revealed it to be a contrived division, perpetuated to maintain patriarchal power. There is nothing 'natural' about it. And although its terminology of 'public man/private woman' seems to refer to all men and all women, historically the dichotomy has only ever referred to a division of labour that is typical of a select population. Even within relatively affluent, two-parent, heterosexual families, some women have chosen or needed to participate in the paid labour force or have given their labour to voluntary organizations. Women of the working class, unmarried women, women who are single mothers, and lesbian mothers in co-parenting relationships have often had neither the means nor the desire to live as the dichotomy would dictate. When women have worked in the home, the structures and assumptions of their lives have rarely followed the public/private pattern. Nor has the domestic sphere been a uniformly happy place, even for the affluent women who have been expected, or have chosen, to spend their lives caring for a traditional home and family. Women's work in the home is persistently undervalued; and an increasing awareness of the prevalence of domestic violence, in all classes and racial groups, has dispelled any residual impression that the traditional patriarchal household is always a place of harmony and peace. Women's greatly increased labour-force participation in the decades since the end of the Second World War further underlines the inaccuracy of any suggestion that women are confined to a private sphere of the home, away from the 'public world' of politics and work.

Patriarchal societies have held the expectation that the home provides men with physical and emotional comfort and offers women a secure place to fulfill their 'natural' destinies. According to the doctrine of separate spheres, the important business of any society is conducted in the public domain, where men and reason rule, and society's frivolous and less significant activities take place in the private sphere, where women dwell. Yet feminists have shown that the ideology of sanctity and domestic bliss that surrounds the home has worked to conceal and condone male despotism. That same ideology has disadvantaged women who have entered the work force, who have needed or wanted to be productive, competitive labour-market participants.[1] It has thwarted their efforts to obtain good child care, restricted their employment opportunities, condemned them to unequal pay for work of equal value, and been the source of blame when they do not perform all of their many duties to an unrealizable standard of perfection.

The boundaries between public and private domains, activities, and expectations in Western industrialized societies have never been as rigid as allusions to the public and private dichotomy imply. The boundaries have shifted historically, culturally, racially, and according to class and geographical region. Women's suffrage rights, legislated federally in 1918, provide one of the earliest and most noteworthy examples of boundary shifts. With suffrage women won the right to participate in the public political realm and to increase pressure on politicians for legal changes. In some respects women's achievements, especially in gaining access to employment, have far exceeded what many of the suffragists envisaged. Yet suffrage alone has not provided a complete solution to the inequalities and oppressions that women experienced in the past and continue to experience in the 1990s. In her contribution to this book, Jane Errington examines the circumstances that led to the suffrage victory. Her chapter reveals how both reformist and conservative forces contributed to the final outcome.

Errington's analysis demonstrates that the breakdown of the boundaries between the public and the private can also bring new problems for women. It can result, for example, in increased public intervention in matters such as personal health and sexual behaviour, which were once believed to be of private, personal concern. She observes that in pre-Confederation New France, where the family was the basic social and economic unit, home and workplace were usually the same. In that society, "the division between the public and the private spheres, both within the walls of the homes and within the minds of its residents, was ill-defined and sometimes non-existent." Yet by the time of Confederation, women in British North America were expected to confine their activities to the domestic sphere and to be the guardians of an entrenched ideology of family virtues.

Errington notes that even in the early part of this century there was an active network of women's organizations such as the Young Women's Christian Association and the Women's Christian Temperance Union in Canada. These groups were responsible for providing social services well before governments took on the task. They helped immigrants find jobs and shelter, they set up soup kitchens for the unemployed, and they provided health care for isolated farm families and the elderly. They worked to relieve the burden of loneliness for prairie families and generally made Canada a more humane place to live. Yet in spite of women's increased visibility in the public sphere, with the expansion of industrialization in Eastern Canada an ideology of public versus private gathered new strength. At the same time, settlers moving to the Canadian West found that the patterns of their lives more closely resembled those of the residents of New France, where the boundaries between the different areas of home and work were either indistinct or virtually non-existent. Industrialized Western Canadian cities, by contrast, were to repeat the pattern of separate spheres manifested in capitalist industrialized societies elsewhere.

The blurring of the public/private dichotomy has not occurred uniformly throughout Canadian society. One lesson to be learned from Roxana Ng's chapter is that women of diverse circumstances have been affected differently by this blurring. The discriminatory social mechanisms that Ng describes have meant that in many immigrant nuclear families only the men have reasonable access to the labour force. The women are frequently confined to a doubly private world of home and/or ethnic community, partially in consequence of their limited access to English- or French-language instruction. Even those women who do enter the paid labour force are normally employed in domestic service or in sewing, child minding, and related work. In this way many women remain confined to the home, even when some of them are engaged in paid labour – and so they are excluded from the social and economic benefits of labour-force participation.

Women have a long history of wisdom and expertise in providing health care. Yet in the domestic realm, women's provision of health care for their families, according to their designated role, was gradually supplanted in the move away from home care to hospitalization around the beginning of the twentieth century. 'Medicalization,' which Wendy Mitchinson discusses in her chapter on the medical treatment of women, is a process in which matters that appear to be of private, personal concern become occasions for public intervention and control. Mitchinson documents the success of physicians in claiming for themselves an exclusive, esoteric expertise and in establishing their monopoly over health care. Historically, women found it difficult to gain admission to medical schools; and even though formal barriers have virtually disappeared in recent decades, subtle patterns of systemic discrimination against women in medicine persist. Moreover, the male-doctor/female-nurse dichotomy tends to perpetuate a version of the traditional public/private dichotomy both in the kinds of work that doctors and nurses do and in the differences in the authority and esteem accorded to them. The long period during which the practice of midwifery was illegal in Canada affords a striking example of public (legal) appropriation of a practice where women's (private) experiential knowledge and skill had made it possible for them to participate co-opera-tively and empathetically in other women's lives. Childbirth, increasingly, became an event that was not to take place at home, but in the hospital.

The point of these observations is not to paint a nostalgic picture of premedicalized, preindustrial society, nor is it to underestimate the bene-fits that progress in science and medicine has brought to Canadian women. The gains for women include decreased care-giving burdens and responsibilities and increased freedom and capacity to engage in other, non-domestic activities. But progress does not come without its costs. Work that used to be done in the home tends now to be regarded as public; and some of the costs are evident in a diminished scope for personal, fami-lial health care and in a trivialization of patients' reported experiences of their own state of health. The gains have to be balanced against these losses and costs.

Many feminists who are fully aware of the advantages of state-run health insurance and welfare programs are nevertheless concerned that the costs of making women's gynaecological and reproductive health into matters of public concern have been too great. Wendy Mitchinson details innumerable 'expert' interventions into women's pre-reproductive, repro-ductive, and post-reproductive lives. These interventions range from advice about how much exercise a prepubescent girl should have, through advanced technological control of childbirth, to hysterectomies and estro-gen treatments for menopausal women. Doctors have traditionally offered controlling advice about proper, normal female sexuality; and controver-sies surrounding abortion, birth control, and other forms of reproductive technology count as further evidence that Canadian society has not been content to regard a woman's biology as her own. Women in the past were constrained to remain in the home to produce and reproduce the labour force. Yet a woman's biology, which allegedly provided the rationale for confining her to the private sphere, has not been left in her own (private) control. Women's recent efforts to establish health collectives and to legal-ize midwifery attest to their desire to regain control of their bodies.

The fact that so few of a woman's allegedly private activities remain her private concern reinforces feminists' conviction that the ideology of public and private is an artificially constructed mechanism of control. Joanna Boehnert shows how psychology has produced ideals of what it is to be a good woman and has judged women who fail to conform to these ideals to be abnormal and deviant. Such condemnations range over numerous areas of seemingly private concern: sexual expression and 'proper' sexual response; ideas about 'gender-appropriate' activities, education, and occupation; and advice about how a woman ought to mother her children and interact with her husband or partner. Clearly there are many respects in which the domestic domain is only nominally private. This point is strikingly borne out in Rona Achilles's analysis of reproductive technology. The fact that motherhood remains central "to women's identity and self-esteem" attests to the social pressures that a woman still feels to fulfill her 'natural' biological role. Although there is no doubt that new developments in reproductive technology have made it possible for infertile women (and couples) to have 'their own' children, it is also true, as Rona Achilles points out, that these new possibilities often exert pressures that restrict women's reproductive freedom and choices. Moreover, these technologies are unevenly available in Canadian society in ways that reinforce racial, cultural, and economic inequalities.

As women have crossed the mythical boundary between the public and private domains of Canadian society, it has become increasingly clear that no aspect of social or personal life can easily remain untouched by change. Susan McDaniel gives some indication of transformations in family structure and child-raising practices that follow upon women's increased labour-force participation. Both Naomi Black and Sandra Burt show how issues such as sex discrimination and equal pay for work of equal value become crucial in a labour market in which women are becoming full participants. The impact of women's voting patterns in federal and provincial elections and the implications of women's lobbying in matters connected with the Charter of Rights and Freedoms show some of the effects women are having on the patterns of Canadian life, as well as the significance of Charter-based thinking for women's strategies and goals.

Women's changing labour-force participation further illustrates the changing patterns of their lives. In 1901 only 16 per cent of Canadian women were working for wages.[2] Most of these early female workers were either domestic or factory workers. Sandra Burt notes in her chapter on public policy how even this minor intrusion by women into what men regarded as their territory was viewed with alarm by many legislators who firmly believed that women belonged at home. Between 1907 and 1951 there was only a gradual increase in the percentage of women in the labour force. Susan McDaniel discusses aspects of this increase. But by 1989 there were nearly six million women in the Canadian labour force (representing 58 per cent of all women of employable age within Canada).[3]

Nonetheless, women's increased participation in paid labour has not succeeded in eradicating ideological support for women's and men's traditional roles. The labour force has been and continues to be highly segregated by gender. Particularly outside the professional classes, women and men usually work in different kinds of jobs with different financial rewards and promotion opportunities; and within the professions, even the most 'successful' women may bump up against a glass ceiling that cuts them off from possible promotion. In other areas of the segregated labour force, women continue to be the disadvantaged group – and differently disadvantaged because of age, race, and ethnicity – partly because affirmative action measures have not been sufficiently forceful. Recent pay-equity legislation in Ontario may alter the situation, but some women are critical of this initiative for institutionalizing male definitions of value. Women generally have held less prestigious jobs than men, with fewer decision-making opportunities, lower pay, and fewer possibilities for advancement; and all of these diminished opportunities are more acute for women of marginalized ethnic and racial groups. Women who enter the labour force at an older than presumed average age (when average is based on a typical male career path) face further economic and status disadvantages. Still today women, on average, earn only about 65 per cent of what men earn. Their jobs tend to remain concentrated in the clerical, sales, and service sectors. And while women's union membership has increased in the past few years, women still make up only 40 per cent of all unionized workers (an increase from 39 per cent in 1984).[4] Hence, even though women have become increasingly visible in the public world of paid labour during the past four decades, they have often been expected to bring with them into the workplace the attitudes, skills, and aspirations that attached to their traditionally private roles.

Another negative development has been an increase in the number of jobs women are expected to accomplish. Susan McDaniel, in her examination of the changing Canadian family, shows not only how labour-force participation has resulted in additional work for most women, but also how there has been no corresponding reduction in domestic labour. Many of the new recruits to the labour force are married women with children. By 1981, 51 per cent of Canadian married women were working outside the home for wages, an increase from 10 per cent in 1950. There has also been an increase in the proportion of women at work who have young children at home. As recently as 1968, in a special labour-force study conducted by the Dominion Bureau of Statistics, the authors concluded, "The presence or absence of a young child remains, in the aggregate, the most important single attribute affecting a wife's participation in the labour force until age 33."[5] Yet by 1984, 57 per cent of Canadian women whose youngest child was between three and five years old were in the labour force. In that same year, 64 per cent of women with school-aged children were working outside the home, compared with 74 per cent of women with no children.

Women's second-class status in the labour force has persisted for a variety of reasons. Researchers cite employer discrimination, discriminatory job descriptions, a lower incidence of unionization among female workers, and choices by women to limit their job commitments in order to facilitate child-raising. One compelling explanation, which is derived from the persistence of traditional conceptions of women's roles, is the 'reserve army' thesis.[6] According to this thesis, women make up a large group of potential workers who normally stay at home, but may be called in to the labour force in times of need. The demand for women's work may be short term, as it was during the two world wars, or it may be longer term, as it tends to be when the economy is expanding and new workers are required. Until the end of World War II women were viewed as a temporary labour reserve. Yet when men returned to claim their jobs, women were expected to retreat to their proper place, and a new ideology of scientific housework evolved to make their retreat appear to be a clear choice. In the context of the recession of the 1990s, unemployment is a growing problem for women, concentrated as they are in the least secure job sectors. Also, more women are opting to work part-time, either by choice or necessity. In 1989 nearly one-quarter of all women in the paid labour force were working part-time.[7]

These changing social and economic patterns have had remarkable consequences for women's lives. In the late 1960s, as women's responses to social upheaval were politicized by the growing rift between idealized versions of life in the home and the real conditions that had developed after the end of World War II, women became increasingly vocal about their positions in patriarchal societies. Labour-force participation, changing family forms, the spirit of rebellion on university campuses, and the civil-rights movement in the United States prompted the emergence of consciousness-raising groups, which provided crucial inspiration to the emerging women's movement. Its development is charted in Naomi Black's account of some of these events, and Lorraine Code details the theoretical assumptions that were generated and produced out of that development. The 1960s and 1970s were witness to an unprecedented increase in the number of women's groups in Canada, united in their call for action in what were defined as women's issues. In setting up rape crisis centres and shelters for abused women, largely financed by government grants, women let it be known that they intended to continue to play an active part in the development and administration of programs affecting family life. The need for such centres was apparent in the 1960s, but it is increasingly obvious in the 1990s with our new knowledge of widespread family violence, much of it directed at women. At the same time, as Joanna Boehnert notes in her review of psychology, women began to reject men's diagnoses of their successes and their failures, and new forms of feminist psychotherapy began to evolve in response to widespread demand.

Yet in the 1990s, even as women are demonstrating their capacities to participate throughout the political and labour-market arenas, and even as highly qualified, independent professional women are becoming increasingly visible in every area of Canadian society, the ideology of home and family as part of an anti-feminist backlash is constantly reinvoked to thwart women's efforts and restrict their freedom. The anti-feminist impact on policy has been strengthened by the emergence of a neoconservative, pro-family agenda within the federal government. The inadequacies of both day care provisions and long-term care facilities for aged and ailing relatives and spouses attest to the persistent assumption that it is up to women to provide such care. Not the least of the systemic social practices that rely on a misinformed conception of the sanctity of the domestic domain is a continued social reluctance to intervene in marital violence. Women who attempt to leave abusive domestic situations frequently discover that all of the available spaces in women's shelters are occupied. Women who succeed in leaving unsatisfactory marriages commonly enter a cycle of poverty and despair as men fail to keep up support payments, and the years away from paid work take their toll in the fact that such women are usually considered ill-qualified to re-enter the job market. All of these practices demonstrate the force of the radical-feminist claim, elaborated in Lorraine Code's chapter, that the personal is political.

In the final decade of the twentieth century it has become apparent that the personal is differently political for women in different circumstances in Canadian society. Although it is true that all women are disadvantaged and marginalized in capitalist, patriarchal societies, it is also true that these processes work quite differently in the various layers and sectors of the society. Native women, women of colour, affluent and poor women, heterosexual and lesbian women, anglophone and francophone women, all experience different forms of marginalization and oppression. The sisterhood that was the vision of the early years of the second wave cannot be taken for granted. Women's commonalities and differences have always to be discussed, determined, and negotiated. Questions of difference have moved to the top of the feminist agenda.

Part of the political impact of women's writing and cultural production in Canada, traced for us variously in the chapters by Michèle Martin and Shelagh Wilkinson, is that readers, listeners, and viewers often find access, there, to some of the commonalities and differences of women's lives across a widely varied social spectrum. Such experiences give content to the 'personal is political' slogan by making possible a peculiarly intimate form of communication across, and through, the differences between and among women. They show how women are disadvantaged in the most minute aspects of their lives, yet how those minute aspects differ quite dramatically from one place in society to another.

NOTES

1. We have retained the language of "choice" and "need" in this discussion, recognizing that these are contested terms in the present-day feminist climate.
2. Frank Denton and Sylvia Ostry, *Historical Estimates of the Canadian Labour Force,* 1961 Census Monograph (Ottawa: Dominion Bureau of Statistics, 1967).
3. Labour Canada, Women's Bureau, *Women in the Labour Force, 1990-91,* 1.
4. Ibid.
5. Canada, Dominion Bureau of Statistics, *Women Who Work,* Part 2, December 1968, 21.
6. Michele Barrett, *Women's Oppression Today: Problems in Marxist Feminist Analysis* (London: Verso, 1980).
7. *Women in the Labour Force, op.cit.,* 7.

Chapter One

Feminist Theory

≈≈≈≈≈≈≈≈≈≈≈≈≈≈≈≈≈≈≈≈≈≈≈≈≈≈≈≈≈≈≈≈≈

Contemporary feminism, which came into being with the student and civil-rights movements of radical protest in the 1960s, is an active, evolving, politically engaged movement. As such, it has been instrumental in effecting fundamental social changes. Feminism is also a theoretical project whose purposes are to understand the power structures, social practices, and institutions that disadvantage and marginalize women, and to devise innovative strategies of social transformation that will promote women's emancipation. British feminist Juliet Mitchell observes that feminism is "an ideological offspring of certain economic and social conditions. Its radicalism reflects the fact that it comes to prominence at points of critical change and envisages it with an imagination that goes beyond it."[1] Mitchell's observation points to the close connections between feminist practice, which works to transform material and social conditions, and feminist theory, which develops out of that practice and informs it. Theory is constantly modified by what proves effective in practice, and practice is shaped by theory; so any apparent separation between theory and practice in this chapter will be made only for purposes of analysis. This account of changing feminist theories is intended to describe the theoretical context in which the emancipatory practices that are detailed in subsequent chapters have evolved in Canadian society.

Feminist theorists work to develop critical analyses of how, in patriarchal societies, women and men tend, generally, to live different lives and have different experiences. These experiences can be differentiated along sex-gender lines even as they differ also according to class, race, age, ethnicity, religion, and numerous other attributes and variables. Patriarchal societies are those in which men have more power than women and readier access than women to what is valued in the society or in any social subgroup. In consequence of this power and privilege differential, men in such societies or groups occupy positions that permit them to shape and control many, if not most, aspects of women's lives. Most known societies are patriarchal to a greater or lesser degree, although they exhibit specific variations in how power is distributed and manifested. Feminist theorists seek to understand this uneven distribution of power and privilege: to examine how it came into being, how the oppression of women by men is related to other forms of social oppression, such as racism, classism, and homophobia; and to develop strategies to eradicate it. The point of studying the situations and ideologies that oppress women is to work towards producing social change.

Feminists differ in how they identify the primary feature(s) of women's oppression, in the theoretical questions they place high on their agendas, and in the strategies they develop for challenge and change. Yet, although these issues are approached from different angles and with varying estimations of their significance, there are several common feminist themes. In particular, feminists want to understand how the organization of production, reproduction, sexuality, and socialization, in their shifting manifestations, has determined women's circumstances throughout history and across cultural, class, and racial boundaries.[2]

Production, in this context, includes all of the processes that go into producing and distributing food, clothing, shelter, and the other material necessities of human lives. It is primarily, but not solely, an economic category, for it also includes political and cultural activity. Reproduction refers not just to conceiving and bearing children, and giving birth, but also to raising children, ministering to the physical and emotional needs of husbands, lovers, and children, and caring for the elderly and the sick. The boundaries between reproduction and socialization, and between reproduction and sexuality, are not rigid ones, for women are socialized to use their reproductive capacities in certain approved ways. They are expected to socialize their children to perpetuate acceptable sexual reproductive behaviour. In patriarchal societies, women's sexuality is subject to strict censure and control by social pressures that define and enforce permissible modes of female sexual expression. Hence, for feminists, both sexuality and socialization are political matters, although different ideological strands within feminism accord these various structures and activities differing importance. Likewise, the structures and practices identified as oppressive to women have changed throughout history and been variously shaped by class, race, culture, and other social positions.

The starting point of feminist theory, then, is in women's lives: in the varied experiences of women; and in the concrete situations where they live and are differently marginalized and disadvantaged. Theoretical analysis is integral to feminism, because women's experiences do not speak for themselves. For this reason, consciousness-raising was crucially important in the early years of the current women's movement. Women needed to learn from each other how to see and name their experiences of oppression and how to recognize the commonalities of their circumstances. Theory – and consciousness-raising – are still fundamental to the movement in its self-critical project; revising its initial assumptions of female sameness (sisterhood), deriving ever more subtle analyses of the effects of patriarchy, defining and redefining the problems that have to be faced, and evaluating new strategies for change.

Marilyn Frye develops a useful image to show why it is so difficult to see the minuscule oppressive structures of everyday life in an allegedly democratic, free society.[3] Frye notes that if one examines one wire of a birdcage, one can neither see the other wires nor understand why the cage is so confining. One might wonder why the bird would not just fly around that wire and go free. The same thing would happen if one were to inspect each wire separately – it would not be apparent why any single wire would constrain the bird. It is only by stepping back to examine the entire structure – the interconnected and mutually enforcing system of barriers – that one can see why the bird is trapped. Similarly, it is necessary to stand back from particular oppressive social practices to see their mutual reinforcement; to see, as a feminist, how patriarchy is constructed out of practices that, considered singly, may not seem to be particularly significant or oppressive. Yet together these practices form an intractable structure.

Over the last two and a half decades, there has been a major shift within feminism from an earlier focus on women as a caste, class, or homogeneous group to a concentration upon differences among women. It can no longer be assumed that there is a single, essential 'women's experience' out of which universal analytic categories can be developed. Differences of race, class, and sexual practices are just a few of the differences that have become primary focal points of theoretical discussion. Contemporary feminist theorists face the tasks of accounting for differences among women's experiences and, simultaneously, of discerning common threads and themes that make these experiences specific to women. The task, now, is to develop theoretical tools that will make it possible to examine the samenesses and differences in women's lives without losing sight of the boundaries of commonality or of specificity. These are delicate tasks, for experience is always structured and mediated by a complex of material, social, cultural, historical, and unconscious forces. There is no 'pure, untainted' experience; and the forces that shape it are often complex and difficult to understand. Furthermore, it is always just as important to account for the absence of women from social practices and institutions as it is to produce analyses of visible oppression. Thus feminists have to learn to see how standard theoretical analyses of social practices often justify, or mask, women's absence. Finally, in performing these tasks a theorist faces a curious paradox: consciousness of the effects of sex-gender seems to be *necessary* to the very existence of feminism, even though feminists are committed to eradicating the oppressive consequences of sex-gender expectations.[4] And all of these tasks must be performed without losing sight of the fact that sex-gender-specific exclusions and oppressions work differently across the social order. The goal of these projects is not only to produce knowledge about women – to make women visible – but also to develop informed, critical analyses of the structures of power and privilege that keep women in their socially assigned places and are stubbornly resistant to change.[5]

Women in the industrialized Western world grow to womanhood in circumstances where it is assumed that (to quote Adrienne Rich):

> women are a subgroup, that "man's world" is the real world, that patriarchy is equivalent to culture and culture to patriarchy . . . that generalizations about "man", "humankind", "children", "blacks", "parents", "the working class" hold true for women, mothers, daughters, sisters, wet-nurses, infant girls, and can include them with no more than a glancing reference here and there, usually to some specialized function like breast-feeding.[6]

Patriarchal assumptions about the appropriate places for women to occupy in 'man's world' are so seamlessly woven into the ideologies and policies of most Western cultures that they seem to dictate the 'natural' way for things to be.[7] Because of the persistence of these beliefs, it is especially important for feminist theory to maintain its continuity with the consciousness-raising practices of the late 1960s and early 1970s. Women need to go on learning how to see their personal and seemingly idiosyncratic experiences as the effects of systemically oppressive beliefs and practices.

No feminist theorist could take on all aspects of patriarchy at once. Yet Frye's birdcage image stands as a reminder that concentrating on any one aspect may cause one to lose sight of the interwoven patterns of oppression that patriarchy perpetuates. Feminists have to develop a "doubled vision"[8] so they can at once challenge specific patriarchal practices and step back to see how those practices reinforce and are reinforced by the whole social structure. They have to see what else needs to be tackled for any practice really to be changed, and to estimate how changing one practice might affect the whole.

Biological Determinism: *Ancient Views*

Many of the ideas and practices that have worked to maintain women's disadvantaged social positions have their roots in the history of Western thought. The belief that a woman's nature and all of her possibilities are determined by her biology – specifically her reproductive biology – is one of the most ancient and persistent of these ideas. It has long been used to justify a range of social practices designed to keep woman 'in her place.' Assumptions about 'woman's nature' have not only described what that nature allegedly is, but have also prescribed what a woman should be.

Biological determinism has its best-known ancient formulation in the philosophy of Aristotle (384-322 B.C.). Despite vast increases in the sophistication of biological knowledge, which make the 'facts' on which Aristotle based his normative claims look quite naive, views remarkably similar to his have persisted even throughout the twentieth century. In their political, revisionary projects feminists repeatedly find themselves required to counter modern versions of Aristotelian beliefs to the effect that women are not capable (physically, intellectually, or emotionally) of holding certain kinds of jobs, or that placing children in day care is a violation of a mother's *natural* role.

Woman's place in the Aristotelian scheme of things is defined purely by her essential function, which is seen as a biological, reproductive one. Her rational capacities are declared to be underdeveloped and inferior in comparison with those of men. Hence men are to rule over women, in whom the irrational element of the 'soul' tends naturally to overrule the rational element. Aristotle writes:

> The male is by nature superior, and the female inferior; and the one rules, and the other is ruled; this principle, of necessity, extends to all mankind. Where there is such a difference as that between soul and body, or between men and animals . . . the lower sort are by nature slaves, and it is better for them as for all inferiors that they should be under the rule of a master. [9]

In Aristotle's view, neither women, children, nor slaves can be citizens. Because only citizens can participate in the political life of the Greek city state, women are barred from such participation, as are children and slaves. Furthermore, because virtue, through which the best human qualities are realized, is achievable only through participation in political activity, virtue, too, in its highest forms, is inaccessible to women (and to slaves and children).

Aristotle maintains that even in respect to their own essential function – the reproduction of the species – women play an inferior part. The male parent's contribution to the offspring is the soul: that which makes it essentially human. The female parent contributes only crude physical matter in the form of menstrual blood (catamenia). According to Aristotle, hers is a passive contribution, by contrast with semen, which he regards as an active substance, "for the catamenia have in their nature an affinity to the primitive matter."[10] This unformed matter, then, awaits insemination by the male parent to endow it with human form and human capacity. Women's contribution to reproduction is merely to provide the material that is to be acted upon and to offer a place of incubation to the future infant. Hence, both with respect to rationality, which distinguishes human beings from other Aristotelian 'natural kinds,' and with respect to reproductive function, women are inferior to men. Their inferior position is biologically determined, according to the natural order of things, and no further explanation for their civic status is required.

Aristotle's philosophy underpins most Western theories about human nature from classical times up to the eighteenth century. As Beverley Baines shows in her chapter in this book, Aristotelian conceptions of the biologically determined inequality of women and men can even be discerned in the assumptions that underlie much of nineteenth- and twentieth-century legal practice.[11] Yet it was by no means inevitable that Aristotle should develop the functionalist, biological-determinist ideas that he did. From the earliest days of developing theories of human nature there were well-known alternative possibilities, which might have opened up quite different ways of thinking about women and about the relations between women and men. In fact, Aristotle seems to have articulated his position partly in reaction to a startling and innovative proposal about the social relations between the sexes that was developed by his own teacher, Plato (427-347 B.C.).

In the *Republic,* Plato has *his* teacher, Socrates, describe an ideal society in which every citizen will perform the function best suited to his or her 'natural' capacities. Future merchants, craftspeople, and tradespeople will receive training appropriate to the acquisition of the skills they need for their occupations; and those who are to form the military forces will receive an education designed to make them suitably courageous, yet neither rash nor cowardly. The ruling, guardian class will be responsible for maintaining harmony within the state and governing it wisely. Its members will receive a rigorous training in music and the arts, gymnastics and athletics, mathematics, and all of the highest arts of reason.

Remarkably for his time and even for ours, Socrates intends that the guardian class should be composed of both women and men, who will receive exactly the same education. He maintains that there is *nothing* in female nature to prevent women's participation, arguing, "There is no pursuit of the administrators of a state that belongs to a woman because she is a woman or to a man because he is a man. But the natural capacities are distributed alike among both creatures, and women naturally have a share in all pursuits and men in all – yet for all the woman is weaker than the man."[12] Hence, "Women of this kind . . . must be selected to cohabit with men of this kind and to serve with them as guardians since they are capable of it and akin by nature."[13] Socrates explicitly states, then, that there are no specifically female traits, either biological or psychological, that would naturally exclude women from these pursuits. So that child-rearing will not interfere with the education and other activities of women of the guardian class, Socrates establishes a set of social arrangements in which there will be no conventional family structures. Children, who will be born as a result of brief periods of co-habitation in designated marriage festivals, "will be taken over by the officials appointed for this, men or women or both" and raised communally.[14]

It would be a mistake to claim, on the basis of this radical proposal, that Plato was a feminist. He puts forward a proposal quite different from Aristotle's of how women might live in a 'man's world,' but there is little doubt that it is a man's world, and it is unlikely that the kind of equality he advocates would be acceptable to twentieth-century feminists. The guardians' educational system is modelled upon an extension of educational practices designed for the *male* citizens of the Greek polis. The proposal is that women should participate equally in men's activities and pursuits, devised and elaborated so as to bring out the best in masculine nature. Women might become guardians, but only by becoming honorary men: by having men make room for them within male-defined structures. Present-day variations on this theme, where women are admitted to business and other high-status occupations on the (often implicit) condition that their 'femininity' not be permitted to count, are only too familiar.

In any case, it is Aristotle's conceptions of women's nature that provide the basis for virtually all of Western theory up to the eighteenth century, and they offer the principal rationale for maintaining patriarchal social arrangements. Even later Platonists, who were influenced by other aspects of Plato's philosophy, did not take up his novel ideas about women or about equality between the sexes. In fact, it was not until the development of liberalism in the eighteenth century that the first serious challenges to biological determinism were articulated.

The Liberal Challenge

Liberal political theory, especially as it developed in Britain and France in the eighteenth and nineteenth centuries, prepared the way for a fundamental challenge to biological determinism. The early liberal feminists' contention that women's inferior social status was a consequence of their lack of education and opportunity, and not of their nature, opened the way for a re-examination of traditional assumptions about 'women's nature.' Moreover, the social and economic upheavals that accompanied the Industrial Revolution undermined the idea that women's natural, biologically determined place is in the home. As women began to work in factories there was a growing differentiation between the activities that they performed at home and at work. In the face of such practical evidence, it could no longer so easily be maintained that women were fitted only to perform a biologically determined role. These challenges and alternatives are significant feminist milestones, for they undercut the sense of inevitability that feminists often feel in the face of deterministic arguments. If women's circumstances can be explained by their limited access to education, opportunity, and other social resources, rather than by their 'nature,' it is possible that if the 'goods' of the society are more equally available, then women's emancipation will follow. (More recently, feminists have begun to show that biology, too, is shaped by environmental and other circumstances.)

The eighteenth century witnessed the widespread development of liberal, egalitarian political ideals, which challenged fundamental social and political beliefs and inspired the American and French revolutions. Most significantly, liberal thinking gradually came to displace the belief that political authority was based in inherited title, and that rulers, by natural right, stood in benevolent patriarchal relations to their subjects. Thomas Hobbes (1588-1679) and John Locke (1632-1704) argued that society should work as though it had been established by a freely entered contract among free and equal individuals. The role of government was to ensure the personal safety and protect the property rights of citizens who had demonstrated their capacity to know their own interests by opting into the contract. In an age when people had unquestioningly believed that members of lower social orders should simply submit to the greater wisdom of their natural superiors and rulers, these were novel ideas.

The argument that all members of a society are free and equally participating individuals led feminists to contend that equality should be enjoyed by women, too. They could see no reason for it to remain a masculine privilege. Feminists had to demonstrate the limited scope of the new-found ideals of equality, for it certainly was not true that all of the early liberals were feminists or that they were united in rejecting biological determinism. Most early male liberal theorists unthinkingly assumed that the liberal 'individual' about whom their theories spoke would undoubtedly be male; and many of them clearly believed that women were inferior beings.

It was to take issue with such assumptions about female inferiority that Mary Wollstonecraft (1759-1797) wrote her famous treatise, *The Vindication of the Rights of Woman*, completed in 1792. Wollstonecraft maintains that if women were to have the same education and opportunities as men, they would be men's equals in every respect. Only because of their inferior education, she argues, do women appear to be merely emotional creatures, lacking in rationality; they are not so by nature. It is women's rights to education and equal treatment that Wollstonecraft is concerned about vindicating.

Wollstonecraft wrote her *Vindication* largely to refute the position developed by Jean-Jacques Rousseau (1712-1778) in *Emile,* his treatise on education. Rousseau is, in a sense, the liberal individual *par excellence.* He comes across in his political writings as a man deeply committed to values of freedom, individualism, independence, and equality. Rousseau envisages a transformation of civil society into a moral society in which all men are citizens and equals, while women are virtuous wives and mothers. In *Emile* he advocates an education for young men that would develop their reason to its fullest potential and train them to tame nature and understand its secrets. Women, in Rousseau's view, are much closer to nature than men because they have a different intellectual character – they are less able to engage in abstract thought, to reason well, and to form universal judgements. But they are well endowed with taste, practical sense, and feeling. Hence, he believes, they should be educated to *complement* men, adorn their lives, raise their children, and obey them. Like nature, women must be tamed, kept in check. In particular, their sexual passions must be controlled so that men can be free from enslavement to female sensuality.

Like Aristotle, then, Rousseau is a firm believer in biological determinism. Several issues that have become contentious for twentieth-century feminists are foreshadowed in his work. Most present-day feminists reject the complementarity thesis that is implicit in Rousseau's work, according to which women and men are declared to be different but equal and complementary; and many feminists take issue with the idea that women should be the guardians of morals, particularly of sexual morals. In helping men to control their reputedly more robust natural sexuality, women are required to suppress or deny their own sexual desires. These expectations generate a paradoxical and oppressive view of women as both chaste and wanton, defined wholly in relation to men, and required to subordinate their self-expression to men's ideas of what they should be.

Wollstonecraft takes Rousseau to task on many of these issues. Her arguments in favour of equal education for women occupy the greater part of her treatise: she attributes all aspects of women's disadvantaged situation to their circumscribed intellectual opportunities in a patriarchal society. When women are trained to prefer and are expected to occupy themselves with trivial tasks, they cannot help but appear feeble-minded and deficient in rational capacity, she argues.

According to Wollstonecraft, women and men are created alike both in sexual feeling and rational capacity. Rather than accepting the claim that it is women's responsibility to curb excessive masculine sexual interest and indulgence, she argues that female chastity is impossible without equivalent male chastity, both practised according to a single rather than a double sexual standard. Wollstonecraft plainly regards sexual constraint as preferable to free sexual expression. She believes that reason, equally developed in both sexes, should rule over passion, which is equally strong in both sexes. The passion in which marriage begins should evolve into a rational, passionless friendship where sexuality is carefully controlled. It is her belief that such a relationship between equals can serve as a model for the structure of civil society.

Yet Wollstonecraft does not reject complementarity outright, for she believes in the maintenance of a family structure in which women would be responsible for child care. Employment outside the domestic sphere is not one of the primary rights she claims for women. If women are to perform well in the important task of mothering, she maintains, they must be educated just as men are educated. Otherwise they will be unable to give their children a rational upbringing. Her larger point is that only when women are educated so that they too can be ruled by reason will they be able to share in the opportunities of the new egalitarian society. She evidently expects that most women will enjoy these opportunities at home. Yet Wollstonecraft sees such a clear continuity between domestic and civil life that there is no stark public/private dichotomy in her work. She believes that domestic life is part of civic life and that the same capacities and virtues are appropriate to each.

In later developments of liberal theory, women's potential for intellectual achievement and their right to the franchise came to be recognized as interconnected issues. Because the franchise could be claimed only by educated property owners, women had remained effectively disqualified as potential voters. John Stuart Mill (1806-1873) was mindful of these obstacles when he wrote *The Subjection of Women,* so his arguments in favour of education and equal rights for women are, in this respect at least, directed towards a goal somewhat different from Wollstonecraft's. Nonetheless, like Wollstonecraft, Mill believes that educated women will be more likely to choose a domestic life than a career. The major change he envisages, apart from their qualifying for the franchise, is that women will be better able to share in their husbands' intellectual pursuits and to raise their children intelligently.

Equality is the dominant theme of Mill's essay: the need for "a principle of perfect equality, admitting no power or privilege on one side, nor disability on the other" to govern the relations between the sexes.[15] Like Wollstonecraft, he believes that women and men are equally rational, intelligent beings, and that the contention that women are not rational simply ignores their lack of opportunity to develop their reason. Mill is convinced that society as a whole will benefit if women are granted all of the educational opportunities available to men.

Harriet Taylor Mill (1807-1858) proposes much more radical social changes when she argues that there should be no laws concerning marriage and that a woman should retain guardianship of, and take financial responsibility for, her own children.[16] Hers was a radical challenge to patriarchy at a time when wives and children were regarded by law as the property of the father. Taylor's proposals were intended to ensure that the issue of providing for children would be irrelevant in divorce proceedings and would not be used to tie a woman into an unworkable marriage for fear of losing custody of her children. She contends that a woman should consider carefully how many children to have, rather than having a great many in order to strengthen her tie to the man who feeds her. As well, Taylor believes that if women are not to barter their persons for bread, they must not only be educated but also be permitted to enter any occupational field they wish. Clearly, Taylor would have applauded many of the successes of present-day feminists in restructuring women's participation in the work force and in bringing about reform in family law. Higher education for women, which is taken for granted as an opportunity today, was an unknown possibility when she was writing.

This early liberal emphasis upon equality of opportunity has carried over, if in a different guise, into contemporary feminist thought. And liberal rejection of deterministic explanations for women's situation has become a constant feminist theme. But original formulations of liberal theory require modification for contemporary feminist purposes. Liberal theorists write of 'men' and 'women' as homogeneous groups: they rarely address questions about how their theories could bear upon the circumstances and interests of women or men who are less well situated, socially and economically, than the theorists themselves. In short, they believe that their experiences are representative of human experience as such. Furthermore, most early liberal theorists take for granted that women's concerns will, as a matter of course, be covered by analyses of men's situations and interests. Contemporary feminists have rightly insisted that analyses of men's social circumstances usually gloss over or obscure women's experiences, and that these experiences require separate analysis.

The Marxist Challenge

Liberal ideology is just one of several sources of present-day feminism. An equally important ideological landmark for understanding the origins of feminist theory is the development of Marxist thought in the nineteenth century. Early Marxism was primarily an analysis of the modes of production and the social relations that accompanied the Industrial Revolution and the rise of capitalism. Although Marxist and socialist thinkers do not concentrate upon developing explicit refutations of biological determinism, their work assumes that biology cannot provide the sole explanation for social inequality and the oppression of one group of people by another. Economic factors are at least as important, if not more so. Furthermore, liberalism, despite its apparent classlessness, is very much a bourgeois or middle-class ideology. Marxism, by contrast, is class conscious above all. In its later feminist formulations, Marxist socialism opens possibilities for analysing the connections between class oppression and women's oppression.

According to Karl Marx (1818-1883), culture and society are rooted in material, economic conditions, and human beings are essentially social creatures, shaped by material and social circumstances. These claims contrast sharply with the liberal idea of the abstract, self-realizing individual, freely opting for membership in society. Whereas in liberal thought it is necessary to understand the individual in order to understand society, in Marxist thought the reverse is true: it is necessary to understand society in order to understand the individual. Because Marx regards human nature as essentially historical, he maintains that it cannot be investigated in abstraction from specific historical circumstances. More specifically, human nature cannot be understood in abstraction from the organization of material productivity in the society.

Under capitalism, which is the focus of Marx's critical analysis, the two main classes are the working class (the proletariat) and the ruling class (the bourgeoisie), which owns the means of production. Members of the same class participate in similar kinds of productive activity and live in similar social and material circumstances. These circumstances shape the physical development and the personalities, attitudes, and consciousness of members of each class. The greater health and life expectancy of the ruling class, contrasted with that of the proletariat, is one example of how these processes work. Not only does the ruling class dominate the mode of production, it also determines the development and circulation of knowledge and values. Hence it generates perceptions of human nature and social reality that are distorted by its own perspective so as to make the status quo seem like the 'natural' way for things to be. It is clear, however, that capitalist social arrangements are designed to serve the interests of the ruling class. So members of the proletariat who accept the received view as 'natural' are living in a state of 'false consciousness,' which makes it difficult for them to see the world from the perspective of their own class interests.

Marx's theory of alienated labour is particularly significant for feminists. Marx argues that the root cause of such alienation is to be found in the structure of industrial production, where workers have no say in the conditions of their work or in the design of its products and are cut off from its final use. As Marx puts it: "The *alienation* of the worker in his product means not only that his labour becomes an object, assumes an *external* existence, but that it exists independently, *outside himself,* and alien to him."[17] In consequence of being constantly engaged in alienated labour,

Marx believes, members of the working class are deprived of any sense of participation in the processes in which they spend most of their waking hours. They experience their work as meaningless and unfulfilling and their place in the social order as insignificant.

One of the roots of alienation is in the division of labour into isolated, minutely specialized tasks. Marx would replace this divisive situation with collective ownership of the means of production and a reorganization of the labour process that would reintegrate mental and manual labour. Alienated labour would be supplanted by the conscious, purposeful activity that Marx calls "praxis." This term refers to a co-operative social activity that does involve some division of labour, but only through drawing upon the knowledge, experience, and skills of workers themselves. By contrast with alienated labour, praxis would develop in awareness of collective human needs and of the place of each person's endeavours in the scheme designed to satisfy those needs.

Marx's distrust of biological explanations is apparent in his contention that the division of labour in capitalist society is rooted in the division of labour and of power within the family. The claim is that those familial divisions are based purely on physiological factors: on differences of sex and age. Yet Marx maintains that the enslavement of a wife and children within the family is the first form of private property; and for him, private property is one of the fundamental social evils. It is an evil that cannot be rationalized by spurious appeals to biology. It is an evil that is perpetuated by capitalist social arrangements.

A more sustained analysis of women's oppression under capitalism is developed by Marx's associate, Friedrich Engels (1820-1895), in *The Origin of the Family, Private Property and the State,* published in 1884. In the nuclear family of capitalist society, Engels sees a microcosmic mirroring of the larger, macroscopic social structure, with the husband occupying the role of the bourgeoisie and the wife the role of the proletariat. Engels attributes the privatization and denigration of household labour to the development of the nuclear family, where "the wife became the head servant, excluded from all participation in social production."[18] The solution he envisages would be for women to refuse to remain confined within the sphere of private domestic labour by entering the public world of productive work. To make this transformation possible, domestic labour and child care would have to become public, collective responsibilities.

In short, in the Marxist view, women are oppressed under capitalism because of a sexual division of labour that serves the interests of men directly. That same division of labour serves the interests of capitalism indirectly, through serving the interests of men. Women are responsible, without pay, for child-raising, cooking, attending to all of the mundane family needs, and looking after the sick and the aged, leaving men free to devote themselves fully to productivity in the public world of waged labour. Under such an arrangement, capitalist society need not pay for the reproduction of the labour power upon which it depends.

In the early years of socialist fervour there were differences of opinion among socialist women about whether 'the woman question' would be dealt with by the revolutionary changes that socialist thinkers and activists were proposing. The contrasting views of some of the leading socialist women illustrate this point. Radical German socialist Rosa Luxemburg, for example, believed that her sex was irrelevant to the issues for which she was campaigning. She saw women's oppression as one of the many miseries of capitalist society that would no longer exist after the socialist revolution. By contrast, Luxemburg's friend Clara Zetkin believed that women's issues had to be dealt with separately, in recognition of women's dual oppression by both capitalism and patriarchy. Zetkin helped to found the International Socialist Women's Congress, and it is she who, in 1910, declared March 8th as International Women's Day. That day, which is still celebrated annually in Canada and throughout the world, was set aside to commemorate a 1909 strike by female garment workers in New York, who were protesting overcrowded, poorly ventilated, dangerous working conditions and very low pay. From related motives, Russian feminist Alexandra Kollontai campaigned for a special bureau in the Russian Social Democratic Labour party to devise ways of addressing women's concerns and argued that a commitment to promoting the liberation of women should be included in the stated aims of the party. She had noted that the Social Democratic Labour Party in pre-1914 Russia showed little interest in the circumstances of working-class women.[19] Although Kollontai's initial efforts met with little success, she later managed – at least temporarily – to place women's issues on the agenda of the Bolshevik revolution. Kollontai and Zetkin both realized that patriarchy exerts a kind of oppression all of its own. It is true that its manifestations have much in common with other forms of oppression; but feminists who have focused on the forms of oppression that patriarchy creates have ensured that the distinctive features of the oppression of women receive separate analysis.

Today socialist feminists continue to debate the issue of whether Engels's scheme to deal with the 'woman question' is the best solution. It still has not been determined whether women's participation in the work force, together with the collectivization of domestic tasks and child-rearing, could work to end women's oppression.[20] What is clear, however, is that no explanation in biological terms alone can account for the ways in which women are disadvantaged and marginalized in most known societies. Material and economic factors are instrumental in perpetuating the oppression of women by men. Feminists have worked, with notable success, to transform these circumstances: campaigning for affirmative action programs, insisting on equal pay for work of equal value, and demanding safe, affordable child care arrangements.

The Freudian Challenge

A third and equally important source of inspiration for modern feminism has come out of the analyses of sexuality and psychosexual development initiated by Havelock Ellis (1859-1939) and Sigmund Freud (1856-1939) in the late nineteenth and early twentieth centuries. It is interesting that this line of inquiry should have come to be so significant in feminist thought, because Freud himself stated unequivocally that "anatomy is destiny": as clear a statement of biological determinism as anyone could make.[21] Indeed, Freud and the early Freudians had no doubt that psychosexual development was biologically determined. Hence feminists in the early years of the current movement were highly critical of Freud, characterizing psychoanalysis as a form of brainwashing designed to keep women quiet, passive, and in their place – especially sexually. The well-adjusted woman, in Freudian terms, was one who had learned to accept her patriarchally defined role of passive dependence in a heterosexual marriage, schooling herself to please her husband. Sexual maturity was her goal. Evidence of its achievement was the ability to achieve vaginal orgasm, to recognize male supremacy in all things, and to be content with her place in life. Kate Millett argues in *Sexual Politics* that the primary effect of Freudian discussions of female sexuality was to convince "the dispossessed that the circumstances of their deprivation are organic, therefore unalterable."[22] In short, Freudian doctrine, literally read, stands as a strong rationalization of women's subservient position in sexual relations, with its claim that their situation is biologically determined, natural. Joanna Boehnert suggests in her chapter on the psychology of women that the intellectual and scientific respect Freud's theories commanded made it seem unnecessary to criticize any of the social and institutional restrictions on women's lives. Freudian explanations of psychosexual development seemed to be adequate and definitive.

In the light of these events, it may appear preposterous to claim Freud as one of the inspirations of contemporary feminism. Freudian theory seems to reinstate a form of determinism that can only lead women to blame themselves if they are unable to accept their natural place in the world. But psychoanalytic theory, especially since the late 1970s, has been an immensely fertile area of feminist discussion. The very need to criticize Freud's views because of their discrepancy with women's experiences opens a vitally important debate about aspects of women's lives that most political theorists ignore. In its emphasis upon sexuality, desire, primary process, and creativity, psychoanalytic theory addresses private, disorderly, and non-rational aspects of personal experience. It emphasizes the central significance of sexuality in human lives and creates space for an affirmation of female sexuality, defined and practised in women's own terms. It gives impetus to analyses of the social implications of sexuality and desire, of the relations between repression and social organization, and of the interplay between individual psychic formation and the production and maintenance of the social order.

Through analyses of the effects of parenting and socialization in producing sexual identity, feminists have developed critical readings of classical psychoanalytic texts and have explored the implications of drawing a distinction between sex and gender.[23] Second-wave feminists tended, initially, to work with a clear distinction, using the term 'sex' to refer to the biological differences in genitalia and reproductive function between male and female human beings; and 'gender' to refer to the social and psychological creation of masculine and feminine people, socialized to fulfill a complex set of requirements and expectations about what it is to be a woman – or a man. More recently feminists have hesitated to maintain so clear a distinction. Recent work on sex and sexuality has made clear that sex cannot be accepted as a simple physiological given, then to be embellished by gender. Sex, too, is to a significant degree a social construct.[24] Some feminists have argued that the sex/gender distinction merely repeats the old body/mind, nature/culture distinction, which tended to denigrate bodily, physical powers and pleasures that many feminists now want to affirm and celebrate. And 'gender' seems to divide too neatly into two, thus obscuring different manifestations of gender in different cultures, subcultures, and sexual orientations.[25] Yet despite these new debates, there is still evidence that a sex/gender-order (which varies across historical, cultural, and racial lines) dictates how people should live their sexual being. Hence questions about the psychosexual construction of masculinity and femininity are central to current feminist discussion.

One of Freud's most articulate early feminist critics is Simone de Beauvoir (1908-1986), in her pathbreaking study, *The Second Sex*. This work stands as a milestone in the development of contemporary feminism: even those who criticize it do so within a frame of reference that de Beauvoir has created. Her observation that "one is not born, but rather becomes a woman"[26] connects directly with later feminist analyses of patriarchally constituted psychological and sexual being. At least as influential is de Beauvoir's characterization of women as "the second sex," thus designated by virtue of their creation as Other, with reference to a masculine norm. De Beauvoir writes:

Just as for the ancients there was an absolute vertical with reference to which the oblique was defined, so there is an absolute human type, the masculine. . . . Thus humanity is male and man defines woman not in herself but as relative to him; she is not regarded as an autonomous being. . . . She is defined and differentiated with reference to man and not he with reference to her; she is the incidental, the inessential as opposed to the essential. He is the Subject, he is the Absolute – she is the Other.[27]

Many of the best-known present-day feminist writings amount, in effect, to a set of variations on this theme.

De Beauvoir believes that the relegation of woman to 'otherness' derives from received conceptions of female biology, and women's psychological inability to transcend it. Women are commonly portrayed as immersed in the material realm, dragged down by their physical being, slaves to the reproduction of the species. Influenced by Jean-Paul Sartre's claim that conscious beings are distinguished from material beings in their capacity to define themselves, to *transcend* their material being, de Beauvoir maintains that this capacity belongs to men but not to women. In this failure to transcend, primarily, women are Other. Because de Beauvoir seems to accept this pessimistic picture of female biology, and of women's psychological inability to come to terms with it, many feminists have taken exception to her description of what it is to belong to the second sex. They argue that her ideas are fundamentally misogynist and that her evident horror at the 'messier' aspects of female anatomy and biological functioning places her in the camp of male detractors of femininity.

The Second Sex presents a detailed descriptive analysis of the social and psychological processes through which a female baby becomes a feminine woman. It offers a marvellous account of the construction of femininity on the basis of biological determinism. De Beauvoir's analysis covers such previously unmentionable aspects of female existence as puberty, menstruation, sexual intercourse, and childbearing. The simple fact that so much could be written about the physical, phenomenological details of what it means to live as a woman in a male-defined world astonished de Beauvoir's early readers. Their astonishment alone attests to the pathbreaking character of her work.

It is worth noting that when she wrote *The Second Sex*, de Beauvoir did not consider herself to be a feminist. Like many of the socialist feminists, she believed that revolutionary socialism would bring an end to the oppression of women along with all other social injustices and that the class struggle had priority over the feminist struggle. Although she remained a socialist throughout her life, de Beauvoir later came to believe that socialist and feminist issues required separate treatment. She commented, "Feminists are women – or even men, too – who are fighting to change women's condition in association with the class struggle, but independently of it as well." She declared herself a feminist after all, "Because I realised that we must fight for the situation of women, here and now, before our dreams of socialism come true." [28] De Beauvoir remained politically involved throughout her life. She became a member of the group "Choisir" in 1971 to protest against the illegality of abortion in France. In 1977 she became editor of a new radical-feminist journal, *Questions féministes,* devoted to theoretical texts that dealt with women's oppression. In this capacity she was closely allied with the new French feminists, even though she wrote none of the texts now considered pivotal to their thinking.

Feminist theory could not have advanced as it has since the 1960s had the ground not been prepared by all of these intellectual and social developments. Even feminists who have taken issue with aspects of these lines of thought have found in them a necessary critical focus. In proceeding, now, to discuss some of the forms that feminist theory has taken in the last decades of the twentieth century, my intention is not to suggest that all was quiet in the feminist world between the early growth of liberalism and socialism and the feminist resurgence in the 1960s. Feminist activism in campaigning for the suffrage alone would attest to the falsity of such a suggestion. And the concerted activities of cultural feminists and social-reform feminists at the end of the nineteenth and the beginning of the twentieth centuries were remarkable in their social impact. Jane Errington details the activities of Canadian suffragists and Canadian social feminists in her chapter in this book. Naomi Black shows, too, how wrong it would be to claim that there were no feminist issues before the emergence of the contemporary women's movement. But the purpose of this chapter is to give an idea of some principal strands of present-day feminist theory. Certain historical movements in which these strands originated have been described in order to locate current feminism within a broader intellectual history. The next task is to examine contemporary feminism in some of its many guises.

Contemporary Theory: *Liberal Feminism*

Contemporary feminist theory draws upon the entire spectrum of ideas, causes, and political agendas discussed so far – adding to, elaborating upon, and engaging critically with them. Some twentieth-century feminists have concentrated on adapting classical political theories to feminist ends. Thus, against the background of classical liberal theory, contemporary liberal feminists argue for women's rights to enjoy the freedom and equality of opportunity claimed by the autonomous liberal individual.

Betty Friedan, who is probably the best-known spokeswoman of post-1960 liberal feminism, observes in *The Feminist Mystique*: "My definition of feminism is simply that women are people in the fullest sense of the word, who must be free to move in society with all the privileges and opportunities and responsibilities that are their human and American right."[29] Feminism, as Friedan understands it, is less a theory of women's oppression by patriarchy than it is a theory of human rights.

According to liberal feminists, sex discrimination is unjust primarily because it deprives women of equal rights to pursue their own self-interest. Justice and fairness require equal opportunities for each individual, regardless of sex. Liberal feminists deplore the informal discrimination, with its roots in biological determinism, that is generated by the assumption that women are not suited to certain kinds of work, or that they are especially suited to other – peculiarly 'feminine' – kinds. Liberals also oppose the formal discrimination that produces an asymmetry in the legal rights of women and men in capitalist societies. Liberal feminists maintain that women's inferior social status is not freely chosen; rather, bias and discrimination block their access to equal participation with men in occupations that confer a high social status. Women's relegation to low-paid clerical and service work, for example, and their (often sole) responsibility for child care and housework diminish their freedom and autonomy in other areas of their lives. Their poverty relative to men often makes it impossible for them to exercise their legal rights or to enjoy their social rights. Women's lack of equality in public life is exacerbated by oppressive sexual standards according to which they are viewed primarily as sex objects. Hence they are limited in their freedom to dress and act as they would like, for fear of inviting unwanted sexual attention; and in their freedom to move about in public spaces, for fear of sexual assault.

Liberal feminists aim to free women from their dependent status in patriarchal society, and their efforts have met with notable success. In her chapter in this book Sandra Burt gives an account of some of the successes that Canadian liberal feminists have realized. Yet liberal feminists retain some ideological commitment to the belief that political decisions are the decisions made within the formal political process – that the term 'politics' should be restricted to what takes place in the public sphere. For this reason they have been less assiduous than socialist and radical feminists in their analyses of the daily politics of the 'private,' domestic sphere, and hence in their analyses of sexual power and privilege. Liberal feminists argue persuasively that women must be included equally within existing public decision-making structures. Yet they often assume that the structures themselves need no modifications beyond those that would automatically come about if women were included on an equal basis with men.

Friedan claims to have located the root of all sexist evils in the "feminine mystique," which defines woman in terms of her femininity and judges her solely according to her performance as a wife and mother. Women, in her view, must claim an identity of their own in order to shake off the effects of this mystique. Although large numbers of middle-class white American women recognized themselves in Friedan's analysis and tried to change their lives accordingly, the problem as she presents it is clearly specific to these reasonably affluent women living in the stability of a continuing marriage. Now it is true that all women are constrained by the ideology of femininity. Yet the self-realization Friedan urges is by no means equally available to all women in all economic and social circumstances. Like most liberal feminists, Friedan advocates individual solutions, taking scant account of the extent to which patriarchal capitalism sustains women's oppression. By contrast, socialist feminists, across a wide spectrum of positions, argue that oppression cannot be treated as an individual problem. It can be understood only by seeing women against the background of the social and economic circumstances that shape their lives and can be eradicated only through collective action. Whether abstract equality, or equality with men, could achieve all that is necessary for women's emancipation remains a question with no easy answer. Perfect equality could well create a set of problems all of its own, derived from a requirement to live as equals, but on men's terms. Hence, although equality would undoubtedly be preferable to subservience and oppression, many feminists argue that it would only be for want of a better solution that a feminist would be a liberal. [30]

Liberal theory can, at best, define an area of public life in which women would have unlimited formal opportunities. It offers no indication of how access to that area would, in practice, be achieved. Feminists who are critical of liberal solutions point out that autonomous, freely participating citizens need wives at home to mind the children and attend to domestic matters. Because liberal theory works with a model of society in which feminist change would merely require men to move over to make room for women, it does not challenge the extent to which those structures are defined and constructed to promote masculine well-being, understood according to a narrowly stereotyped conception of masculinity. Liberal feminism leaves masculine values intact and does not address the systemic injustices fostered by the patriarchal relations that sustain women's sexual and economic dependence.

Contemporary Theory:
Marxist and Socialist Feminism

Marxist and socialist feminists are critical of liberal theory because they believe that there is no point in arguing for political liberalism unless one has a theory to show how people can achieve the economic means, and the power, to enjoy it.[31] They argue that equality of legal rights will have minimal impact upon actual social inequalities unless there are far more fundamental economic and social changes. Drawing, then, upon a Marxist analysis of class oppression, socialist feminists maintain that the capitalist economic system oppresses women as a group, just as it oppresses the working class as a whole. Yet within capitalist patriarchal society, women are subjected to additional forms of oppression that relate specifically to their sex. First, within the labour force women's work is alienated labour in the same ways that men's work is: women own neither the means of production nor the products of their labour. Second, women in the labour force commonly find themselves in positions where they are subordinate to men whose superiority is by no means obvious: hence they are doubly alienated from realizing their potential. Third, women who work at home, as housewives, are in an even more powerless position: their lives are devoted to serving others, their labour is accorded no material value, and they have limited access to the activities of the 'public' world.

Under capitalism women are the primary producers of goods and services for use within the family, yet because their labour has no monetary exchange value, it is considered worthless. But feminists differ on the question of whether domestic labour is alienated labour in the same sense that capitalist productive labour is. Some feminists maintain that the menial, non-creative, and isolating nature of household tasks marks them as alienated labour.[32] Others claim the household as the only unalienated work space in capitalist society. There, women know that what they do is useful, for they see the importance of their labour in caring for those they love and sustaining family values.[33] In the home women have more control over the pace and use of their work than office or industrial workers do. Yet these positive features have to be weighed against the fact that women's labour is undervalued. Hence some socialist feminists have argued that there should be wages for housework; and most of them maintain that women's invisible domestic labour needs to be revalued to acknowledge its vital role in reproducing the labour power upon which economic productivity depends.

These analyses have demonstrated the extent of capitalism's dependence upon women's unpaid, invisible labour. But it needs to be remembered that capitalist societies are not alone in oppressing women. Notable among socialist feminists who remind us that women's oppression cannot be fully explained by the sexual division of labour under capitalism are Michele Barrett and Gayle Rubin. Barrett observes that the sexual division of labour was not a capitalist creation: capitalism may have refined and elaborated it, but the ideology of a gendered division of labour was there to be elaborated.[34] And Rubin outlines a spectrum of patriarchal practices that oppress, subdue, and denigrate women, yet are quite independent of capitalist economics. She observes: "No analysis of the reproduction of labour under capitalism can explain foot-binding, chastity belts, or any of the incredible array of Byzantine, fetishized indignities, let alone the more ordinary ones that have been inflicted upon women in various times and places."[35] Yet Barrett also notes significant structural differences between precapitalist and capitalist modes of production, which are apparent in social arrangements that have direct consequences for women's lives. Capitalist society is marked, in particular, by an emphasis upon competitive mass production and by that specialized, and alienating, division of labour into minute, isolated units that is a focus of Marx's critique.

These features of capitalism recall Engels's contention that the disempowering effects of the sexual division of labour would be nullified if women could enter the paid labour force as full participants. Socialist feminists have pointed out that entry into the work force does not automatically count as a liberating experience for women. Rather, many women simply find themselves doing double duty: they work for wages in the labour market and continue to do just as much unpaid domestic labour at home. Without radical social restructuring that would make good child care readily available and effect a redistribution of other household tasks, Engels's solution cannot be the ideal one.

Its problems are exacerbated by the fact that, more often than not, women in the work force earn considerably less than men do. Even in the early 1990s women commonly earn sixty-seven cents for each dollar that men earn. Some socialist feminists see this wage differential as the primary cause of women's ongoing powerlessness and oppression, even as they gain increased access to waged work. The wage differential used to be rationalized by claims that the father's income is the 'family income,' which is equitably shared within the family. This argument has been used by employers, who contend that women work only to *supplement* the family income. Yet the ideology of liberal capitalist society allows no 'interference' in 'private' family matters to ensure that the man's income really is distributed as it is thought to be: too often the ideology works to conceal the genuine poverty of women and children. Moreover, the 'family wage' argument could only apply to women who have heterosexual, patriarchal living arrangements. Single mothers and lesbian couples have no such family wage at their disposal. Feminist efforts to transform these unjust practices are achieving some success, at least in current efforts to legislate wage equity.

Women have tended to enter the labour force in temporary, unskilled jobs that offer them no security. Some socialist theorists have characterized these women as a 'reserve army of labour,' which capitalism can draw upon at times of need and dismiss into unemployment when economic circumstances dictate.[36] Such women do not achieve economic independence from men, and those who have no man tend to become dependent on social welfare. When one adds the fact that, in capitalist society, women who are 'liberated' from domesticity into the labour market are often engaged, like men, in alienated labour, it is easy to see that Engels did not have the perfect solution to women's oppression.

Moreover, just as assumptions about the family wage often mask women's inferior economic status, so too assumptions about the class to which 'the family' belongs often conceal a woman's inferior, or equivocal, class membership. A Marxist division along class lines does not offer an obvious way of designating a woman's social class. She can sometimes be identified according to the class of her husband or of the man on whom she is dependent, but for a divorced, single, or independently employed woman, or for women in permanent lesbian relationships, class identification has to work quite differently.

Socialist feminists have addressed these issues by advocating alternatives both to capitalist modes of production and to the patriarchal organization of families and other social institutions. Socialists see the nuclear family as a cornerstone of women's oppression. It keeps women socially powerless, enforces compulsory heterosexuality,[37] and reproduces masculine and feminine stereotypes in the next generation. Capitalist society seems to require stereotypical feminine women to nurture men to manhood and to help them fulfill the demands of adult masculinity. As Heidi Hartmann observes, "Sexist ideology serves the dual purpose of glorifying male characteristics/capitalist values, and denigrating female characteristics/social need."[38] In sustaining a high level of demand for consumer goods and inculcating in children the competitive, free-market ideology of capitalism, the nuclear family is effective in perpetuating women's subordinate and marginal positions.

Contemporary Theory: *Radical Feminism*

Radical feminists would be in general agreement with socialist-feminist analyses of women's social and economic circumstances and with many of their strategies for change. But radical and socialist feminists differ on a fundamental question of emphasis. Whereas material, economic, and social factors are primary for socialist feminists, radical feminists contend that the oppression of women by men is the root cause of all oppressions (radical = at the root).

Radical feminism was born out of women's disillusionment with New Left politics in North America, Britain, and France in the late 1960s. Women in the United States who were fighting for equality and justice in the civil-rights movement and against the war in Vietnam found themselves treated as subordinate members of these organizations and exploited as sex objects and servants (making the coffee, doing the secretarial chores) for their male co-workers. Such experiences prompted Robin Morgan to write, "Sexism is the root oppression, the one which, until and unless we *up*root it, will continue to put forth the branches of racism, class hatred, ageism, competition, ecological disaster, and economic exploitation."[39] Sexism, as manifested in patriarchal families, gender stereotyping, pornography, wife and child abuse, and rape, became the focus of radical-feminist analysis.

The radical-feminist dictum 'the personal is political' declares that patriarchal society structures personal experiences and social relations in ways that disadvantage women. For example, the liberal slogan that the government has no place in the bedrooms of the nation, which Canadians (echoing Pierre Trudeau) proudly intoned in the late 1960s, improves upon the belief that society can legislate permissible sexual behaviour between adults. But it screens from public scrutiny such common and damaging practices as rape and sexual abuse within marriage and families. In fact, many of the everyday practices that perpetuate women's oppression occur within the home, a place that is protected by an ideology of sanctity and privacy that maintains the invisibility of women's domestic and childrearing labour.[40] Before radical feminists placed it on the public agenda, domestic violence passed as a private matter in which the law ought not to meddle. Radical and socialist feminists emphasize the systematic difference in power between women and men, which manifests itself in men's socially and legally sanctioned control over women's sexual, procreative, and emotional lives. The ideology that supports this control produces the consequence that when things go wrong in the domestic sphere, the woman is held accountable for not being appropriately obedient and submissive. Such power relations need to be undermined if women's emancipation is to be possible.

Many radical feminists maintain that any male-female relation will necessarily be oppressive to the woman; hence they conclude that female separatism is the only option. Notable among them is Mary Daly, who claims: "For men . . . life has meant feeding on the bodies and minds of women, sapping energy at the expense of female deaths. . . . It is men who have sapped the lifeforce of women."[41] Daly maintains that women under patriarchy live in a condition of "robotitude," a term that refers to "the state of servitude of women in a phallocratic world."[42] This condition is induced by a system of myths devised by men and internalized by women to the point where they live unthinkingly by them. Radical feminism, for Daly, is a voyage of "woman becoming,"[43] fuelled by "gynergy" (women's energy),[44] and moving toward a full affirmation of woman-centred values.

It is a voyage toward developing a separate and self-affirming women's culture.

Contemporary Theory: *Sexuality and Reproduction*

Socialist and radical feminism developed out of quite distinct concerns, but they have been mutually influential, with many common themes and agendas uniting their interests. One important issue of concern has been women's sexual and reproductive freedom. Feminists have been active, vocal, and often successful – although their successes are still fragile – in claiming women's right to abortion on demand, insisting upon reliable birth control, affirming women's sexual freedom in relationships – either lesbian or heterosexual – that refuse patriarchal norms and challenge male control over childbirth and child-raising.

In *The Dialectic of Sex,* one of the first radical-feminist texts, Shulamith Firestone names biological reproduction as the primary source of women's oppression. [45] She believes that women can escape from the traps of biology only through reproductive technology and communal living arrangements that supplant the nuclear family. So long as women bear children, their biology will be their destiny. In the years since Firestone made these claims, however, the revolutionary promise that she saw in reproductive technology has been seriously contested. Rona Achilles shows in her chapter here how these technologies threaten women's reproductive autonomy. Firestone urges women to reject the ideology of romantic love that encourages them to live as sex/love objects for men, deluded in the belief that romantic (heterosexual) love is the route to happiness.

Adrienne Rich focuses somewhat differently on women's reproductive lives, contending that their experiences of motherhood have been co-opted by "motherhood as institution." A complex power structure produced by the interlocking forces of law, medicine, culture, and professional expertise works to create an "invisible institution" of male control over women's bodies and minds. [46] Rich celebrates women's strengths in keeping much of the experience of motherhood for themselves despite the power of institutional control. She is impressed with some women's abilities to preserve, "even within the destructiveness of the institution: the tenderness, the passion, the trust in our instincts, the evidence of a courage we did not know we owned." [47] Women's capacity to resist patriarchal power draws upon these strengths.

In like vein, Mary O'Brien argues that men have endeavoured to negate their alienation from the reproductive process by appropriating children as their own (giving them a name and a place in the social structure). Thus they claim "ownership of the woman's reproductive labour power in a sense recognizably similar to . . . the sense in which capitalists appropriate the surplus labour power of wage labourers."[48] Yet, she observes, "Embedded in the child is the alienated reproductive labour of the mother"[49] – alienated because patriarchal societies do not permit her to call the child her own. O'Brien maintains that this appropriation needs to be understood in dialectical relation to woman's reproductive consciousness. A woman knows that the child is hers, and it grows with her love, yet she must nurture it to be a labourer or a producer of children in its turn. Out of the strength of female reproductive consciousness, O'Brien also sees a possibility for developing a unified social consciousness that could transform the social structures that perpetuate the alienation of both reproductive and productive labour.

The belief that male-female relationships are inevitably oppressive to women has led many feminists to advocate alternatives either of the separatist kind that Mary Daly advocates or of some other variety. Some feminists recommend celibacy as the only solution, for they believe that sexual relations, whether lesbian or heterosexual, always generate dominance and oppression. Separatist lesbian feminists contend that sexual expression between women is the only acceptable sexuality for women who are seeking freedom from the exploitative requirements of patriarchy. Separatists contend that male domination is sustained by heterosexuality, which ties women to men socially, economically, and emotionally. The only way to break free, they maintain, is through female separatism. Lesbianism has an impressively subversive political potential in a society where women are defined, primarily, as sex objects for men. Adrienne Rich characterizes compulsory heterosexuality as a "*political institution*" created "to enforce women's total emotional, erotic loyalty to men." She says that heterosexuality wrenches "women's emotional and erotic energies away from themselves and all other women and from woman-identified values."[50] Rich believes that the pain a growing girl experiences in transferring her affections from a woman – her mother – to a man shows that this is an unnatural choice into which women are coerced by the patriarchal order. She urges scholars to explore the continuum of lesbian experience past and present, so that women will realize that heterosexuality is not the only option.[51] Separatist feminists believe that lesbianism offers a place for a radical restructuring of sexuality in a woman-culture founded on non-hierarchical, mutually affirming female values.

Contemporary Theory: *French Feminism*

Contemporary French feminism stands as a distinct and original contribution to feminist theory. French feminists are ideologically closer to socialist and radical feminists than they are to liberal feminists. They share with English-speaking radical and socialist feminists an activist origin in the student revolt in Paris in 1968. Yet French feminism has its roots in French and German philosophical traditions that are markedly different from the traditions that have shaped feminist theory in the English-speaking world. French feminists are not so much political theorists as intellectuals in a society where an intellectual can play a vociferous political role, attacking the arrogant assumptions of entrenched institutions. Perhaps in consequence their theoretical work focuses on literary and psychoanalytic theory, creativity, and sexuality. The reinterpretation of Freud by French psychoanalyst Jacques Lacan has become one of the focal points of feminist writing in France.

For Lacan, the Freudian story of human psychosexual development is a story of the 'fall' from one-ness with the mother into consciousness. That fall is, at the same time, a fall into language, which Lacan refers to as the symbolic realm. Language is the bearer of the patriarchal social order. It exists prior to the moment when a child learns it, yet it is the primary mode of expression available to any maturing child. It is through language that a preconscious child becomes a conscious human subject. Central to Lacan's discussion is the belief that entry into the symbolic order brings with it an awareness of separation-alienation from mother, self, and world. Men endeavour to overcome that separation through a (phallic) mastery, partially manifested in the (patriarchal) power of language. It is through language that a child learns of the greater value accorded to maleness in a world where femaleness signifies otherness.

It is small wonder, then, that language both as the subject-matter of linguistics and as the substance of literary texts has become a primary concern in French feminist writings. Julia Kristeva, for example, asserts that the conception of language itself, as it is studied by linguists, is riddled with political implications. She explores the arbitrariness of meaning, the artificiality of separating 'speaking subjects' from their context, and the power inherent in the application of linguistic labels.[52] Her aim is to understand the overweening power of masculine rationality, which privileges "reason, order, unity and lucidity," doing so "by silencing and excluding the irrationality, chaos and fragmentation that has come to represent femininity."[53] Above all (and following Lacan), Kristeva sees in language a means of designating sexual difference: a fundamental difference that manifests itself "in the relationship to power, language, and meaning,"[54] which is radically different for women and for men. With other French feminists, Kristeva is critical of feminist efforts to minimize the significance of biological, sexual difference. Women, she believes, should affirm and rejoice in their difference. In it they have a means of subverting the patriarchal order. They should use it to advantage, even if it results in their relegation to a marginal status, beyond the written text and the limits of public discourse.

Femininity, sexuality, and discourse are central topics of analysis in the works of two other French feminists: Hélène Cixous and Luce Irigaray. Characterizing traditional discourse as essentially phallocentric, Cixous speaks "about women's writing: about *what it will do.*"[55] She believes that conceptions of 'masculine' and 'feminine' imprison thinkers within oppressive binary oppositions. Yet she, too, maintains that the solution is not to *deny* sexual difference, as advocates of androgyny have done, but to emphasize, write, and celebrate the feminine. Such writing, as she conceives of it, does not "annul differences but stirs them up, pursues them, increases their number."[56] Hence no one 'pair' of differences, such as the traditional male/female dichotomy, is privileged, yet difference is always a central topic of discussion.

French feminists read texts, then, to see what is left out: they read the gaps and exclusions in a text as manifestations of power in discourse. Rather than concentrating their critical attention on modes of material production, they examine cultural production to discern what its artefacts say – and resist saying – about their creators. French feminists draw upon the potential of the comic, the ironic, the mimetic, to reveal the arbitrariness of patriarchal assumptions by 'making them strange.' Irigaray advocates a subversive feminine discourse that 'writes from the margins' to displace (phallocentric) male discourse.[57] In miming the masculine, this writing points to the ephemerality of masculine power with its exclusive claim to occupy the dominant speaking positions. It celebrates the power of female sexuality, pleasure, and desire. There is no question, here, that women should try to be just like men: rather, the point is that their strength is in their difference. French feminists displace the univocal voice of the masculine tradition with a plurivocality that constantly affirms difference. Since women's most visible difference is bodily, it is the female body that is to be foregrounded, as a source of disruptive female desire and creativity.

In their writings on sexuality, feminine creativity, and power structures that are constructed around sex and class privilege, contemporary French feminists examine many of the same physical and psychological implications of being a woman in a man's world that de Beauvoir analyses in *The Second Sex*. Yet contemporary French feminists differ markedly from de Beauvoir in their celebration of bodily femininity and in the challenges they pose to the theories and cultural artefacts that systematically devalue it. They expose standard analyses of the 'human condition' as androcentric and heterosexist; maintaining that even the word 'human' refers only to *men's* theories and inventions. It is but one small example of the entrenched phallocentricity of language and discourse, which needs to be

unmasked, ridiculed, and subverted. Elaine Marks and Isabelle de Courtivron remark that French feminists, fittingly, have "stolen the intellectual
tools of patriarchy and, in many cases, [have] turned them against their
inventors."[58]

Contemporary Feminism:
Diversity and Commonality

Distinctions among the separate strands that have, historically, gone into
the making of feminist theory tend to obscure the commonalities that initially united feminists of seemingly disparate ideological persuasions.
Feminists of the early years of the 'second wave' rallied around a common
cause in their opposition to patriarchy. They focused on their new-found
similarities and celebrated the sisterhood of all women. In the 1980s difference became the most pressing item on the feminist agenda. Groups of
women who could not see themselves as the 'women' that feminism
claimed to be speaking for criticized the early second-wave theorists for
assuming a falsely universal category of 'woman.' The fact is that, for all its
ideological differences, early second-wave feminism was primarily the creation of white, middle-class, affluent, educated, and usually heterosexual
women. Its generalizations about the experiences of women took for
granted a homogeneous female position in society that could not capture
such specificities as race, class, culture, age, or sexual preference, in whose
terms women's experiences were as different from one another as they
were similar in virtue of their 'femaleness.' Feminists of the 1990s are
attempting to work through issues of commonality and difference, to
determine the extent to which it is legitimate to claim a common feminist
cause in the face of the exclusions and marginalizations within feminism
that assumptions of sisterhood tended to produce.[59]

Black feminists have been especially articulate in pointing out how consistently feminist discourse, articulated out of white middle-class experience, has arrogated to itself the right to speak for all women, black or
white, rich or poor, heterosexual or lesbian. Women of colour have been
particularly critical of an analogy that was drawn by white feminists in the
1970s, between the social positions of women and blacks. This so-called
equation attests to an implicit racism both in the language and in the
presuppositions of early second-wave theory.[60] In producing this analogy,
white feminists simply ignored the enormous power differential, in predominantly white societies, between black and white women. They failed
to take into account the effects of institutionalized racism in maintaining
black women in poverty relative to white women, and in situations of more
acute marginalization and differently restricted options. Moreover, in
claiming the feminist cause as the primary political cause, white feminists

could not see the urgency, for black women and other racially marginalized women, of making alliances with the oppressed men of their own racial or ethnic groups, in their struggles against forms of oppression whose effects often were more acute than patriarchal oppression. 'The patriarchy,' too, has usually been white and middle-class; relations between women and men in other classes and races cannot adequately be analysed on the same patriarchal model.

Issues of universality and diversity have generated a paradox at the centre of feminist theory in the 1990s. Feminism seems, still, to require the consciousness-raising that enables women to claim some measure of unity 'as women,' even while they concentrate on understanding differences. There is something persuasive, still, about Nancy Cott's observation: "The value accorded to 'sexual difference' in feminist theory has increased at the same time that the universality of the claim for sisterhood has been debunked. Ethnic, racial, and sexual diversity among women is stressed more than ever before in feminist theory, but so is the emphasis on how women (as a whole) differ from men (as a whole)."[61] But these urgent issues that centre around differences within feminism have the effect of problematizing the very idea that it is possible to refer to 'women as a whole' in any but an unjustly reductive way. Hence the historical goal of achieving equality for women has to be refined and redefined if it is to retain any legitimacy as a feminist project.

Equality and Difference

The question of equality forms a thread that runs through most of the early feminist texts and is highly contested in the pluralistic feminisms of the 1990s. Few feminists would deny that there is still some force in the (primarily liberal) claim that social justice demands equality before the law, with respect to opportunities for education and employment, to property ownership and remuneration for work, and to all matters of human rights. Plato's proposal in the *Republic* draws feminist attention because of the equality of educational opportunity he proposes for women and men. The early liberal preoccupation with issues of equality was one of the principal inspirations of contemporary feminist thought; and feminists still claim, and dispute, the value of working toward equality. Yet arguments to the effect that achieving equality *between the sexes* is the primary feminist goal are highly problematic. Both feminists and anti-feminists (albeit for different purposes) read such claims to mean that women want to be just like men. Yet it would be a rare feminist, today, who would name equality with men as the aim of her efforts to promote women's causes. Plato's scheme in the *Republic*, with its reliance on a masculine model, indicates why this idea is problematic.

The liberal vision of equality is similarly contentious. It provides ready support for a claim that women and men are equal, but different, and hence should occupy different but complementary places in society. Hence it translates too easily into a belief that women – even enlightened and educated ones – are best suited to be wives and mothers. Mill's belief that an equally educated woman will be prepared – and pleased – to share in her husband's pursuits shows that the equality he envisages is to be understood strictly on male terms, and that it derives primarily from the experiences of an affluent and propertied class of men. None of the arguments in favour of equality between the sexes has been able to show how the unalike can be treated equally; for 'equality' tends to mean sameness of goals, rights, and opportunities.

To state the goal of feminism as one of achieving equality with men amounts to approving of how men are and claiming that women want to be like that too. But the question "Equality with *which* men?" could never be answered, "Oh, of course, with all men." Women would never have claimed equality with men who are oppressed because of race, class, religion, ethnicity, or any other attribute. They do not want equality with coal miners, or with industrial workers sterilized by the chemicals they work with, or with men infected with cancer from pollutants in asbestos mines. [62] Modern (liberal) feminists who campaign for equality with men forget that men themselves are not equal under capitalism. Setting out to achieve equality with men requires opting into a utopian myth according to which all men can in fact (not just in theory) achieve success in proportion to their natural initiative, intelligence, and energy. It takes no account of the structural social impediments that locate men quite differently in relation to the powers and privileges that affluent societies appear to hold out to everyone.

Now, in a formal, abstract sense, women probably do want the freedom to achieve such status as *their* initiative, intelligence, and energy allow. But in patriarchal, capitalist societies, equality is more abstract than it is real. Women are not likely to achieve any real emancipation from the oppressions that have shaped their lives, as long as the structures of such societies remain intact, simply stretching a little to make space for women. If neither the rhetoric nor the practice of equality can accommodate differences between women, between men, and between women and men, then its value is questionable. As long as putative labour-market equality can (even implicitly) require women to conceal evidence of pregnancy, to work until labour begins, or to refrain from having children, then women's relevant differences from the (masculine) labour-market norm are not being taken into account. [63]

Questions of difference have never been adequately addressed in liberal capitalist societies, whose moral theories and common wisdom agree in declaring that it is both immoral and unjust to treat individuals differently. In the rhetoric of democratic societies it is simply taken for granted that all should be treated alike and equally. And traditional moral theories emphasize the importance of impartiality and equality in moral decisions, arguing that these values will be preserved only if moral decisions are based on reason alone, with no appeal to emotions. If the differences that are now central to feminist analysis are to be taken adequately into account in moral and political decision-making, then different ways of thinking about difference have to be developed.

A productive and controversial debate about sexual differences in moral consciousness was stimulated by Carol Gilligan's 1982 book *In a Different Voice*.[64] Analysing the responses of a group of male and female subjects to Lawrence Kohlberg's tests for measuring moral development, Gilligan concluded that there are two moral systems. One system, which she perceived in the responses of her male subjects, approaches morality as a complex of rights and principles that provide a basis for making moral decisions. This approach to moral problems contrasts with a kind of response more common in her female subjects, according to which human lives are a network of social relationships and judgements of 'right' and 'wrong' depend upon the kinds of response, and care, that a specific situation demands. Traditionally, moral philosophers have believed that rights and principles are the proper issues for moral debate, for they can yield universally valid solutions. Questions about feelings and caring have been relegated to a realm of sentiment that is so idiosyncratic and particular that it does not lend itself to moral analysis.

There is a persistent belief in the history of Western thought that it is *reason*, rationality, that distinguishes human beings from other living creatures. According to this belief, the best realization of human possibilities will be achieved through the cultivation of reason. Now the emphasis upon rights and principles in moral theory derives from this veneration of reason. The argument goes that it is only through the use of reason that moral principles and rights can be discerned. Hence in the historical examples discussed earlier in this chapter, the education of the 'reason' is a constant theme. It was in consequence of their allegedly inferior rational capacities that women were deemed inferior to men. Wollstonecraft's claims for equal female access to the domain of reason can be understood in light of this belief. In the theories that inform the moral ideology of late twentieth-century capitalist societies, as Gilligan shows, the belief persists that rationally discerned, universal, impartial moral principles constitute the proper 'stuff' of moral judgements. The capacity to act upon such principles is heralded as the mark of achieved moral maturity; and it is commonly believed that women are deficient in this capacity.

There is a still more subtle problem about reason for feminists.

Genevieve Lloyd shows that reason itself, both as a distinguishing human characteristic and as a character ideal, is defined, throughout history, by exclusion of the traits that are traditionally associated with women and femaleness. [65] Lloyd demonstrates the near-impossibility simply of revaluing and celebrating these undervalued traits to claim for them a value equal to that accorded to 'masculine' traits. Much more radical deconstructions and reconstructions are required. In Gilligan's work, then, although she claims that both moral 'voices' are available alike to women and men, it is still not clear how such a sex-undifferentiated interplay could work, in practice. The 'different' voice that Gilligan hears has been associated with lesser female preoccupations, throughout a long and oppressive history. Her work appears to suggest that both voices should be permitted to speak freely and both sets of concerns accorded equal worth. But much more needs to be done in identifying the specificity of these voices – not just to women and men, but to a small and fairly homogeneous group of subjects – before the transformative potential of her work can be assessed. Meanwhile, Gilligan's research is remarkable for the sheer volume of productive, innovative debates it has generated around issues of rights and care.

Feminists are faced with the necessity of transforming a social system that has been constructed and informed by the assumption that what a select and privileged group of men do is the normal *human* thing to do, as Simone de Beauvoir's analysis of female Otherness makes clear. In the history of Western thought, 'humanness' has been androcentrically defined; when women – or members of other races and cultures – think, speak, or act differently, their behaviour is judged deviant because of its divergence from that norm. Attributions of difference tend to lose sight of the fact that difference is a symmetrical relation. If women are different from men, or blacks from whites, or lesbian women from heterosexual women, then men, and whites, and heterosexuals are, by the same token, different from women, blacks, lesbians. If members of any one of these groups speak in a 'different' voice, then they all do. The different voice in which the morality (and rationality) of the white male tradition has long been speaking – and drowning out all other voices by calling them 'different' – is itself but one voice among many. It may have legitimate things to say: it has gone to some lengths to ensure that its pronouncements count as the only respectable ones. But the other voices that are insisting on their share of the speaking places in the 1990s are emphasizing the partiality, the narrow specificity, of that masculine voice.

North American culture has been built on an ideology of sameness and conformity, which has produced the effect that when differences are noted, they tend to be noted judgementally, as deviant from a norm. An observed difference, in this conformist context, often provides a pretext for condemnation. Indeed, the history of woman's place in patriarchal society is a history of judgements to the effect that woman is different from man, and *hence* inferior (Other). The consequences have been apparent in the exploitative and oppressive practices that feminists have been working to displace.

In the process, many early feminist theorists concentrated upon de-emphasizing and/or defusing difference, arguing in favour of 'gender-blind' laws, policies, and practices. They believed that this would be the best route to equality. These feminists claimed that taken-for-granted polarities are less stark than they seem to be; and they argue in terms of difference-in-sameness, sameness-in-difference, with a goal of understanding and tolerance. Such a program has never seemed to offer enough to the feminists who have maintained that women's differences from one another, and from men, have to be affirmed and celebrated. That program is unacceptable to feminists who believe that social structures and institutions have to be reformed so that they can deal adequately with all of the myriad differences between and among people.

Gilligan's work was inspired by a difference she perceived between her experiences as a woman and the theory she was teaching. She comments: "I was teaching the theory of adolescent development based on the view that maturity was being autonomous and independent. But I had never experienced that. It was clearly based on the male development cycle."[66] Gilligan did not just notice a difference and conclude that it must be sex-based: she cites evidence to support her conclusions. But what she does with the discrepancy between her *experience* and the accepted *theory* is particularly feminist. It tends still to be assumed, in 'malestream'[67] thought, that if experiences fly in the face of established theory, then so much the worse for the experiences. Theories are granted an intellectual authority that overrides experiences, so that if certain experiences do not 'fit' the theory, then the assumption is that there is something wrong with the experiences, not with the theory. Women, and other marginalized people, are familiar with the coercive power of theory and expertise in scientific, technological societies. But, like Gilligan, growing numbers of feminists are asking the revolutionary, subversive question: "What is wrong with this theory that it cannot explain my experience and the experiences of other women?" These are the questions feminists are asking as they work both in theory and in practice to undermine the silencing effects of theoretical, patriarchal power structures.

Lorraine Code

NOTES

1. Juliet Mitchell, "Reflections on Twenty Years of Feminism," in Juliet Mitchell and Ann Oakley, eds., *What is Feminism?* (New York: Pantheon Books, 1986), 48.

2. These are the four constant structures of women's oppression designated by Juliet Mitchell in the title essay of her *Women: The Longest Revolution,* first published in 1968 (London: Virago Press, 1984).

3. Marilyn Frye, *The Politics of Reality: Essays in Feminist Theory* (Trumansburg, N.Y.: The Crossing Press, 1983), 4-5.

4. Nancy Cott draws attention to this paradox in her "Feminist Theory and Feminist Movements: The Past Before Us," in Mitchell and Oakley, *What is Feminism?* 49.

5. For feminist analyses of power, *see:* Anne Ferguson, "Motherhood and Sexuality: Some Feminist Questions," and Jana Sawicki, "Foucault and Feminism: Towards a Politics of Difference," both in *Hypatia: A Journal of Feminist Philosophy* 1, no. 2 (1986); Kathy Ferguson, *The Feminist Case Against Bureaucracy* (Philadelphia: Temple University Press, 1984); and Sandra Lee Bartky, *Femininity and Domination* (New York: Routledge, 1990).

6. From Adrienne Rich's remarks at the Columbia University Seminar on Women and Society, 1976. Quoted by Hester Eisenstein in her *Contemporary Feminist Thought* (London: Allen & Unwin, 1984), 74.

7. Joan Kelly observes: "It has been a strength of patriarchy in all its historical forms to assimilate itself so perfectly to socioeconomic, political and cultural structures as to be virtually invisible." In Joan Kelly, *Women, History, and Theory* (Chicago: University of Chicago Press, 1984), 61.

8. *See:* Joan Kelly, "The Doubled Vision of Feminist Theory," in Kelly, *Women, History, and Theory.*

9. Aristotle, *Politics,* trans. Benjamin Jowett, in Richard McKeon, ed., *The Basic Works of Aristotle* (New York: Random House, 1941), 1254b.

10. Aristotle, *De Generatione Animalium,* trans. Arthur Platt, in McKeon, *Basic Works of Aristotle.*

11. *See:* Judith Hicks Stiehm, "The Unit of Political Analysis: Our Aristotelian Hangover," in Sandra Harding and Merrill Hintikka, eds., *Discovering Reality* (Dordrecht: Reidel, 1983), 31-43.

12. Plato, *Republic,* trans. Paul Shorey, in Edith Hamilton and Huntington Cairns, eds., *The Collected Dialogues of Plato* (Princeton, N.J.: Princeton University Press, Bollingen Series, 1961), 455d-e.

13. Ibid., 456b.

14. Ibid., 460b.

15. J.S. Mill, "The Subjection of Women," in John Stuart Mill and Harriet Taylor Mill, *Essays on Sex Equality,* ed. Alice Rossi (Chicago: University of Chicago Press, 1970), 125.

16. *See*: John Stuart Mill and Harriet Taylor Mill, "Early Essays on Marriage and Divorce" (1832), in *Essays on Sex Equality*.

17. Karl Marx, *The Economic and Philosophical Manuscripts of 1844* (New York: International Publishers, 1964), 96.

18. Friedrich Engels, *The Origin of the Family, Private Property and the State* (New York: International Publishers, 1972), 65.

19. For an extended account of the contribution of women to the early socialist movement, *see*: M.J. Boxer and J.H. Quataert, eds., *Socialist Women: European Socialist Feminism in the Nineteenth and Early Twentieth Centuries* (New York: Elsevier, 1978).

20. These issues are debated in the essays collected in Lydia Sargent, ed., *Women and Revolution: A Discussion of the Unhappy Marriage of Marxism and Feminism* (Boston: South End Press, 1981).

21. Sigmund Freud, *Sexuality and the Psychology of Love,* ed. Phillip Reiff (New York: Collier Books, 1963), 181.

22. Kate Millett, *Sexual Politics* (New York: Avon Books, 1971), 187.

23. Noteworthy among texts that approach this task are: Juliet Mitchell, *Psychoanalysis and Feminism* (New York: Pantheon Books, 1974); Dorothy Smith and David Smith, *Women Look at Psychiatry* (Vancouver: Press Gang Publishers, 1975); Nancy Chodorow, *The Reproduction of Mothering: Psychoanalysis and the Sociology of Gender* (Berkeley: University of California Press, 1978); P. Susan Penfold and Gillian Walker, *Women and the Psychiatric Paradox* (Montreal: Eden Press, 1983); and Hannah Lerman, *A Mote in Freud's Eye: From Psychoanalysis to the Psychology of Women* (New York: Springer, 1986).

24. See, for example, Thomas Laqueur, *Making Sex: Body and Gender from the Greeks to Freud* (Cambridge, Mass.: Harvard University Press, 1990); and Suzanne J. Kessler, "The Medical Construction of Gender: Case Management of Intersexed Infants," *Signs: Journal of Women in Culture and Society* 16, no. 1 (Autumn 1990).

25. See in this connection Judith Butler, *Gender Trouble: Feminism and the Subversion of Identity* (New York: Routledge, 1990); and Denise Riley, *'Am I That Name?' Feminism and the Category of 'Women' in History* (Minneapolis: University of Minnesota Press, 1988).

26. Simone de Beauvoir, *The Second Sex,* trans. H.M. Parshley (New York: Knopf, 1953), 301.

27. Ibid., xviii-xix.

28. Simone de Beauvoir, *Simone de Beauvoir Today: Conversations with Alice Schwartzer, 1972-1982* (London: Chatto & Windus, 1984), 32.

29. Betty Friedan, *The Feminine Mystique* (New York: Dell, 1963), 317.

30. *See,* for example, Marion Tapper, "Can a Feminist Be a Liberal?" *Australasian Journal of Philosophy,* supplement to Vol. 64 (June 1986). These last points are paraphrased from Tapper's paper, 47. See also Lorraine Code, "Simple Equality is Not Enough," in the same volume.

31. Some theorists distinguish between Marxist and socialist feminism, arguing that Marxist concerns are more purely economic whereas socialist feminists are concerned to effect more wide-ranging social reforms. But Josephine Donovan, for example, claims, "Contemporary 'Marxist feminism' is more appropriately called 'socialist feminism' to point up that it no longer represents an undiluted Marxism but a Marxism modified . . . by radical feminism." In Josephine Donovan, *Feminist Theory* (New York: Frederick Ungar, 1985), 66. The term 'socialist feminism' will be used in the rest of this chapter.

32. *See*: Sheila Rowbotham, *Woman's Consciousness, Man's World* (Harmondsworth: Penguin Books, 1973); and Zillah Eisenstein, "Developing a Theory of Capitalist Patriarchy and Socialist Feminism," in Z. Eisenstein, ed., *Capitalist Patriarchy and the Case for Socialist Feminism* (New York: Monthly Review Press, 1979).

33. *See*: Susan Sontag, "The Third World of Women," *Partisan Review* 60 (1973).

34. *Cf*: Michele Barrett, *Women's Oppression Today: Problems in Marxist Feminist Analysis* (London: Verso, 1980).

35. Gayle Rubin, "The Traffic in Women: Notes on the 'Political Economy' of Sex," in R. Reiter, ed., *Towards an Anthropology of Women* (New York: Monthly Review Press, 1975), 163.

36. This thesis is advanced, for example, by Iris Young in "Beyond the Unhappy Marriage: A Critique of the Dual Systems Theory," in Sargent, *Women and Revolution.*

37. *See*: Adrienne Rich, "Compulsory Heterosexuality and Lesbian Existence," in A. Snitow, C. Stansell, and S. Thompson, eds., *Desire: The Politics of Sexuality* (London: Virago Press, 1983), for a superb and extensive radical-feminist analysis of the political implications of compulsory heterosexuality.

38. Heidi Hartmann, "The Unhappy Marriage of Marxism and Feminism," in Sargent, *Women and Revolution,* 28.

39. Robin Morgan, *Going Too Far: The Personal Chronical of a Feminist* (New York: Random House, 1977), 9.

40. There have been significant changes in the workings of this ideology in Canada in the 1980s, largely in response to feminist political pressure. (See Sandra Burt's chapter in this book.) But feminists in Britain continue to express concern at the reluctance of the law to intervene in domestic disputes. *See*: Katherine O'Donovan, *Sexual Divisions in Law* (London: Weidenfeld & Nicholson, 1985).

41. Mary Daly, *Gyn/Ecology: The Metaethics of Radical Feminism* (Boston: Beacon Press, 1978), 173.

42. Ibid., 53.

43. Ibid., 1.

44. Ibid., 34.

45. Shulamith Firestone, *The Dialectic of Sex: The Case for Feminist Revolution* (New York: Bantam Books, 1970).

46. Adrienne Rich, *Of Woman Born: Motherhood as Experience and Institution* (New York: Bantam Books, 1981), 58.

47. Ibid., 285.

48. Mary O'Brien, *The Politics of Reproduction* (London: Routledge & Kegan Paul, 1981), 58.

49. Ibid.

50. Rich, "Compulsory Heterosexuality," 217.

51. Ibid., 227ff.

52. Perhaps the most accessible of Kristeva's many works to those unfamiliar with the French tradition is *About Chinese Women* (London: Boyars, 1977).

53. Toril Moi, *Sexual/Textual Politics* (New York: Methuen, 1985), 160.

54. Julia Kristeva, "Women's Time," *Signs: A Journal of Women in Culture and Society* 7, no. 1 (1981), 21.

55. Hélène Cixous, "The Laugh of the Medusa," in Elaine Marks and Isabelle de Courtivron, eds., *New French Feminisms* (New York: Schocken Books, 1981), 245.

56. Ibid., 254.

57. Irigaray's two most frequently cited works, *Speculum de l'autre femme* and *Ce sexe qui n'en est pas un,* have been translated into English and published by Cornell University Press.

58. Marks and Courtivron, *New French Feminisms,* 35. The tools referred to are those developed by such French theorists as Jacques Derrida and Michel Foucault, but the reference could apply to the entire French intellectual tradition, with its emphasis on reason and the suppression of the body. See also Toril Moi, ed., *French Feminist Thought* (Oxford: Basil Blackwell, 1988).

59. For a good analysis of some of these issues, see Elizabeth V. Spelman, *Inessential Women: Problems of Exclusion in Feminist Thought* (Boston: Beacon Press, 1988).

60. *See:* Bell Hooks, *Ain't I a Woman? Black Women and Feminism* (Boston: South End Press, 1981), 102; Bell Hooks, *Feminist Theory from Margin to Center* (Boston: South End Press, 1984); and Patricia Hill Collins, *Black Feminist Thought: Knowledge, Consciousness, and the Politics of Empowerment* (London: Unwin Hyman, 1990).

61. Cott, "Feminist Theory," 59.

62. These are Zillah Eisenstein's examples in *The Radical Future of Liberal Feminism* (New York: Longman, 1981), 231.

63. Explicit requirements of this sort are less commonly evident than they were prior to contemporary feminist challenges. In 1960, for example, a woman scientist in the United States was told in the early days of her employment, "If you become pregnant, you'll get fired." She reports, "So I got pregnant, and they never knew it. I just wore a lab coat one size larger. . . . I came back two days after the baby was born, and I never told a soul there that I had had a child." Vivian Gornick, *Women in Science* (New York: Simon & Schuster,

1983), 102. Such overt prohibitions are not so common in the 1990s, but workplace discrimination of a subtler sort is documented almost every day.

64. Carol Gilligan, *In a Different Voice: Psychological Theory and Women's Development* (Cambridge, Mass.: Harvard University Press, 1982).

65. *See*: Genevieve Lloyd, *The Man of Reason* (Minneapolis: University of Minnesota Press, 1984). Recent feminist work in the philosophy of science endeavours to explain the invisibility of women and 'the feminine' in scientific practice, with its ideals of rational objectivity. *See*: Ursula Franklin, "Will Women Change Technology or Will Technology Change Women?" CRIAW *Papers* (1985); and Sandra Harding, *The Science Question in Feminism* (Ithaca, N.Y.: Cornell University Press, 1986).

66. *The Guardian* (U.K.), April 1982.

67. This is Mary O'Brien's term, introduced in *The Politics of Reproduction,* and now a widely accepted term in feminist discourse.

SUGGESTED READINGS

Bartky, Sandra Lee, *Femininity and Domination*. New York: Routledge, 1990.

Birke, Lynda, *Women, Feminism and Biology*. Brighton: Harvester Books, 1986.

Code, Lorraine, *What Can She Know? Feminist Theory and the Construction of Knowledge*. Ithaca, N.Y.: Cornell University Press, 1991.

Eisenstein, Hester, *Contemporary Feminist Thought*. London: Allen & Unwin, 1984.

Eisenstein, Zillah, *The Radical Future of Liberal Feminism*. New York: Longman, 1981.

Frye, Marilyn, *The Politics of Reality*. Trumansburg, N.Y.: The Crossing Press, 1983.

Gilligan, Carol, *In A Different Voice: Psychological Theory and Women's Development*. Cambridge, Mass.: Harvard University Press, 1982.

Harding, Sandra, *The Science Question in Feminism*. Ithaca, N.Y.: Cornell University Press, 1986.

Keller, Evelyn Fox, *Reflections on Gender and Science*. New Haven, Conn.: Yale University Press, 1985.

Lloyd, Genevieve, *The Man of Reason: 'Male' and 'Female' in Western Philosophy*. Minneapolis: University of Minnesota Press, 1984.

Marks, Elaine, and Isabelle de Courtivron, eds., *New French Feminisms*. New York: Schocken Books, 1981.

Moi, Toril. *French Feminist Thought*. Oxford: Blackwell, 1988.

Okin, Susan Moller, *Women in Western Political Thought*. Princeton, N.J.: Princeton University Press, 1979.

Segal, Lynne, *Is the Future Female? Troubled Thoughts on Contemporary Feminism*. London: Virago Press, 1987.

Weedon, Chris. *Feminist Practice and Poststructuralist Theory*. Oxford: Basil Blackwell, 1987.

Chapter Two

Pioneers and Suffragists

In 1828 a newspaper editor in Upper Canada commented, "The estimation in which woman has been held in various ages of the world and in different countries may be regarded among the most indicative 'signs of the times' denoting with almost unerring precision the state of civilization or the advancement of the people toward that state. . . . As knowledge increased, or as civilization was promoted, the rank of woman was correspondingly promoted and her condition proportionately meliorated." Throughout the ages, Hiram Leavenworth of the *Farmers Journal* continued, woman has always been the subject of "deep intense affection" and essential to the happiness and salvation of man. Now, he asserted, in these progressive and civilized times, woman, by reason of "her delicacy of perception," her "feminine purity and serving dependence," and that "elevation of character which distinguishes and endears her sex," has finally attained her rightful place beside man. [1]

One wonders how Canadian women of Leavenworth's time, and those of an even earlier period, themselves viewed their situation. Only in the past fifteen years have a few scholars begun to consider the woman's point of view and to realize that there is an important story to tell about women in New France and Acadia, in British North America, and, after 1867, in Canada. In the exciting process of discovering this history, Canadians, particularly Canadian women, are recognizing an essential part of their heritage – a past that gives meaning to the present and offers a deeper appreciation of their own circumstances.

Our knowledge of the history of women and of the evolution of a women's culture in Canada remains woefully incomplete. The discipline is still in its infancy and is complicated by the need to find new ways of re-creating and interpreting the past to unravel the complex experiences of often invisible women. Few women recorded their thoughts or daily activities, and only a minority signed petitions, drew wills, or paid taxes.

Traditional histories have avoided this problem of sources by denying that women have a history. Most often, only major actors (always men), 'momentous' political events, or 'significant' social, economic, and political national developments are considered worthy of attention. Even social historians are only now beginning to discover that the working man had a wife, a mother, a sister, a daughter, and often a working woman at his side. Though there remain many more questions than there are answers, it is now possible to tell at least part of the story and to identify a number of factors and trends that shaped women's experiences.

The following is by no means a thorough history of women in Canada and cannot possibly provide the richness of detail that is necessary for a real appreciation of women's experiences. Moreover, although Canadian women's history is but one part of the larger story of the history of European and North American women, space precludes all but passing reference to those vital links. This chapter will provide only a basic overview of the history of Canadian women from the mid-seventeenth century, when Europeans first arrived, to approximately 1960. In so doing it attempts to take 'women's time' into account; for while the Conquest, the American Revolution, the War of 1812, and Confederation affected *all* Canadians' lives, Canadian women, like women throughout the world, more often measured their lives by the more personal events of birth, marriage, and death, and by the demands of day-to-day existence.

As well, it should be kept in mind that there were, and were seen to be, large differences in the experiences of the mistress and the maid, the wife and the spinster, and the teacher and the working girl. But, as Veronica Strong-Boag and Anita Clair Fellman note, "In some ways women's lives resemble each other's as much or more than they resemble those of the men with whom they are closely associated."[2] All women were in some way or another subordinate to men, and this often brought them together.

Subordination did not mean automatic submission, passivity, or loss of all personal autonomy, however. Throughout the last three centuries, Canadian women have taken an active part in shaping their own lives and the lives of those around them. All played an essential role in the establishment and development of their communities, and there were a number of women who pushed beyond the bounds of institutionalized restraints and implicitly – sometimes explicitly – challenged the public and personal mores of their times. At the same time, in many respects women shared a common culture,[3] which was often perpetuated over a number of generations. It is likely that despite differences of language, location, time, and technology, the peasant women of New France would have had a real understanding and sympathy with the women of mid-nineteenth-century rural Upper Canada and with western farming women of the twentieth-century Canadian West.

For this reason, the early colonial period must be included in any general history of Canadian women. The year 1867 was a watershed in the political development of the country, but it heralded little change for the nation's women. While Canadians celebrated union, women's daily lives and expectations continued in their colonial patterns. It was not so much the political but rather the economic and social developments – the transformation from an agricultural to an industrial economy, and the movement from a rural to an urban society – that provided the rough benchmarks in the history of women. Moreover, these developments influenced women's lives at different times and in varying ways, and women's responses to these new situations were patterned by tradition and custom. An appreciation of the post-Confederation history of women, therefore, must be firmly rooted in an understanding of colonial lifestyles and traditions.

New France

European women first made their appearance in what would become Canada in the mid-seventeenth century. In 1637 a few well-educated and relatively wealthy women of the Catholic orders of the Ursulines and Hospitalières landed at Quebec, determined to carry the message of God to the New World. Shortly after Marie de l'Incarnation founded the Ursuline convent in Quebec, the religieuses were joined by lay women who arrived with their fathers, husbands, employers and, after 1663, under the protection of the King to make a new life for themselves and their families. [4]

From the very beginning, the lives of both lay and religious women in New France differed quite significantly from the lives they would have led in Europe. There is no question that many of the religious, political, and social institutions in the new colony were patterned after those in France. But the economics of the fur trade, the importance of the military, the demands of life on the frontier, and the overabundance of men provided some women of the Ancien Régime with a unique opportunity to exercise considerable influence on colonial life and development. It should be noted, however, that such opportunities were not shared by all. Native women, in particular, derived very little, if any, benefit from the European presence.

In New France and Acadia between 1650 and 1750 all roads for lay women led to matrimony. The physical dangers of the frontier, the economic difficulties of existence, and the scarcity of women prompted them to become wives and mothers, a role that the government, the church, and tradition encouraged. Particularly in the early years of settlement, French-Canadian women married young, often at thirteen or fourteen years of age, bore children, and, in the frequent event of widowhood, remarried quickly.[5] Marriage and motherhood did not, however, imply a complete submergence into obscurity or total dependence on and subservience to one's husband.

Women, by reason of their sex, were expected to bear children, see to their upbringing and education, and maintain the home and the garden. Yet dwellings in New France were relatively small, simple, and utilitarian, and childhood lasted only until the child was old enough to contribute to the household economy. In the pre-industrial society of New France, like that in Europe, the family was the basic social and economic unit, and the home and the workplace were often the same. By necessity, women, men, and, when old enough, children, worked side by side in the fields and in business. As a result, the division between the public and the private spheres, both within the walls of the home and within the minds of its residents, was ill-defined and sometimes non-existent.[6] Although women were subordinate to the male head of the household by law, in practice marriage was more like a partnership, with women and men assuming joint responsibility for the family and the household economy.

The primary importance of the family in New France and the challenge of frontier society provided women with a latitude of movement and occupational opportunities largely denied them in Europe or later in British North America. Married women often took an active part in the marketplace. Some opened taverns next to their artisan-husbands' shops; others acted as laundresses for the local garrisons. It was not unusual for wives to accompany their husbands to the fur-trade posts in the wilderness, where a few managed the canteens or became directly involved in trading. And when the need arose, a number of women undoubtedly stood beside their husbands in hand-to-hand combat with the Iroquois.

The fur-trade economy of New France also meant that women who stayed at home carried on the family business in their husband's absence. Some became fur traders themselves; others managed property, oversaw extensive mercantile establishments, or 'minded' the store or workshop. As Jan Noel concludes, the wives of absent fur traders and military men played an invaluable role in the day-to-day running of the colony's economy.[7] Particularly during the early years of the eighteenth century, when New France was more settled and the proportion of women to men was more balanced, a number of widows chose not to remarry, but to carry on family businesses alone and as trustees for their children.[8]

As well as those women who played an active part in the economy, there were others who were influential in its religious and political life. Throughout the seventeenth century, French nuns were one of the most prominent and influential groups in New France, providing religious leadership and establishing charitable services essential to the fledgling colony's survival. The religieuses provided not only leadership for the faith

– building missions, hospitals, and schools for the colonists – but they often also had the ear of the royal administration and helped shape local and colonial policy. By establishing schools for both elite and peasant girls, they "endowed the colony with an educational tradition" that was unique, and they consciously encouraged women to contribute to their own and to their colony's development. The curriculum of the Ursuline schools for the elite at Quebec and Trois Rivières, for example, though apparently weak in housekeeping skills, emphasized the importance of needlework because this skill would enable women to produce trade items for the fur trade. These schools also taught elite women the "requisite skills for administering a house and a fortune."[9] The schools for the popular classes taught basic literacy and provided an education suitable for 'a young lady,' a curriculum that some influential Frenchmen felt was potentially disastrous, for it encouraged girls to move to the towns, causing a "depopulation of the countryside."[10]

The presence of self-reliant, strong, religious women in positions of prominence and influence symbolized the colony's acceptance of women's active participation in all aspects of colonial life. Even the law was forced to recognize the favoured position that women gradually attained. Women who were insubordinate to authority or who committed adultery were dealt with much less harshly than women or men offenders in Europe. Property law carefully protected the rights of a woman as well as her children. Under the Custom of Paris, the foundation of law in New France, a widow was frequently appointed guardian of her children; she also inherited equal shares with her children in her husband's property and often managed the family business until the children came of age.[11]

In hindsight, the French society that was painstakingly established on the Canadian frontier in the seventeenth and eighteenth centuries seems to have been remarkably progressive for some European women. The relative openness and freedom that these women experienced did not protect them, however, from the trials and miseries of pioneer life. Disease and endless physical toil only added to the burdens of frequent pregnancy and childbirth. Although apparently healthier and better fed than their sisters in France, the women of the new colony also faced the problems and tensions resulting from enforced separation from their husbands and families, early widowhood, and the periodic calamities of Indian and European wars. In the latter half of the eighteenth century, all French colonists found themselves in a particularly devastating situation.

In the 1750s, with the expulsion of the Acadians by the British, the women of the Maritime region were uprooted, often separated from their families, and forced into exile. In 1760, after the British Conquest of Quebec, a number of women in New France were also forced to abandon their homes and to return to a France in which they were strangers. Most stayed in Quebec after the capitulation, however, and having survived the bitter conflict, the heartache, and the deprivation of the British-French colonial wars, discovered that British rule threatened not only the way of life of French society as a whole, but also the unique place that women had attained within it.

Little is known about how the first few years of British rule changed women's place in Quebec society. By the turn of the century, however, although the civil code remained, the arrival of increasing numbers of English-speaking settlers from the thirteen American colonies and from Britain helped to provoke a radical change in Quebec society. Moreover, the expulsion of the Acadians, the Conquest, and shortly thereafter the American Revolution signalled the introduction into Canada of what would become a new and quite divergent view of women and their 'properly appointed' roles.

Families of New Englanders moved to the recently vacated lands of Nova Scotia in the 1760s. In 1784, British-American loyalist families fled north after the American Revolution, and in Upper Canada they were joined by an increasing number of restless Americans in search of land and expanded opportunities. By 1800 this northward migration was augmented by the arrival of a few immigrants from Britain, whose numbers substantially increased after 1815 and the conclusion of the Napoleonic Wars. Like their French-Canadian sisters, most of the English women who came to Canada at the end of the eighteenth and in the first half of the nineteenth centuries came as wives, mothers, or daughters. They had to confront a wilderness frontier and were part of a preindustrial rural economy. But these women had quite different expectations and experiences than did the women of an earlier New France. Those who arrived in the Maritimes and north of the St. Lawrence and the Great Lakes tried as much as possible to recreate the patterns and traditions of their old homes – whether in the Old World or the anglo-American community. As well, the rapid development of British North America after 1815 and the gradual acceptance of the Protestant Victorian view that a woman's proper place was in the home soon imposed restrictions and limitations on English women's lives that had not existed in the Ancien Régime.

Pre-Confederation Canada

The years between 1790 and approximately 1850 were a time of transition for Canadian women. In the early years the settlers of Upper Canada and the Maritimes were preoccupied with establishing viable British communities. The family remained the most basic and important social, economic, and political institution, and family members were bound "together in a single body in a common enterprise of subsistence" and survival. Women were a necessary part of this unit and contributed materially to "the corporate family economy." In addition to looking after the affairs of the home and the garden, women were also responsible for "almost every aspect of social reproduction,"[12] including the medical, spiritual, and educational welfare of the family and community. As well, some women found themselves managing property, opening a tavern, and, if widowed, running the family business.

Such an extensive role for women was from the very beginning under attack, however. Under British common law, women, particularly those who were married, were subordinate to men. Moreover, as Mary Ryan notes in her work on U.S. pioneering communities of the same time, the frontier society and the interdependence of family members it encouraged were "by definition, temporary" and "doomed to extinction within the space of two generations."[13] By 1820 the Upper Canadian and Maritime colonies were relatively secure and increasingly developed. Frontier practices and attitudes were perpetuated by newly arrived immigrants and old settlers who were moving to the back country. But in the older parts of the colonies the economy was becoming diversified, and society as a whole was increasingly institutionalized and stratified. As a result, although British North America was still preindustrial, the division of labour on the basis of sex became more exact, as distinctions began to be drawn between public and private spheres of activity. As these distinctions became more defined, women throughout North America were increasingly confined within the physical and psychological limits of the private world of the home and the hearth.

This was not just a linear progression developing over time. From the beginning of this period there were women who, because of their wealth, training, and high position in society, had already accepted the 'dictates of domesticity' or what U.S. historian Barbara Welter has called "the cult of true womanhood."[14] Like most new arrivals, Elizabeth Simcoe (wife of the first lieutenant-governor of Upper Canada), Anne Powell (wife of the Chief Justice), Hannah Cartwright (wife of one of the colony's leading merchants), and other wives, daughters, and mothers of the newly formed colonial elites attempted to recreate the patterns of their old lives. For these women, who were attached to influential and prominent colonists, the patterns of the old thirteen colonies and Britain rested on the acceptance of two separate and distinct spheres of life for women and men. A woman was presumed to be emotionally and intellectually, as well as physically, different from a man. By virtue of her sex, she was most suited to be a wife and mother. Her natural sphere of endeavour and influence was, therefore, within the home, which was now expected to be a haven and sanctuary from an increasingly volatile and hostile world. It was a woman's special responsibility, these gentle folk of wealth and standing believed, to guard the home and make it a place of virtue for the family and thus the foundation of a virtuous and civilized nation. Having embraced such beliefs, it is not surprising that members of the upper class of colonial society actively resisted the levelling endemic to frontier existence and tried to impose their acceptance of a hierarchy of class and sex on those around them. [15]

From the very beginning, therefore, women in British North America were subject to two conflicting views of a woman's place – a climate that persisted throughout the century. Yet even this interpretation, of two life-styles and expectations existing simultaneously, must be qualified to recognize the diversity, contradictions, expectations, and also the commonalities that existed within and between each group. Increasingly throughout the first half of the century, women of all levels of society lived in male-dominated households, and their character and indeed their very existence were defined by the significant men in their lives – father, husband, or son.

The vast majority of women in Canada at this time were wives or widows, mothers, or young girls waiting to attain such 'exalted' and 'natural' positions. "To be female and alone" was "to be confined to the lower ranks of the social order." [16] For elite women, a good marriage was particularly essential to secure or to better their own status in society and the future status of their children. For these women, occupational opportunities outside marriage were very limited. This is perhaps best illustrated by the story of Anne Murray Powell's three daughters in early Upper Canada.

The youngest Powell girl, Mary, married at the age of twenty-seven. The middle daughter, Eliza, apparently popular and well-loved although a spinster, conformed to social expectations by serving her parents and her sister within their households, as a companion, nurse, and general helpmate. But the plight of the oldest daughter, Anne, highlights the severe restrictions of upper-class colonial society after 1800. Perhaps the most intelligent and stubborn of the three, Anne's repeated wilfulness brought her into repeated conflict with her family. And, as Katherine McKenna notes in her work on the Powell family, Anne's refusal to accept the social norms of her class eventually resulted in complete ostracism. [17]

Most women in British North America did not have the financial means to stay at home indefinitely, patiently awaiting marriage. They either married young or were obliged to support themselves from an early age. The most accessible and, in the first half of the nineteenth century, a quite respectable means of self-support was in domestic service. Women of 'good character' and 'sober and steady habits' who were willing to work were in constant demand. Young girls and widowed women easily attained posts as maids, cooks, laundresses, and farm help. But most girls did not expect to spend their lives in service. They married or remarried quickly, leaving their mistresses and masters to find a replacement. Unmarried or widowed women of some means, skills, or training found even a short time of drudgery as a servant unappealing. Particularly in the early years of the century, it was quite respectable for a single woman to open a boarding house or tavern or a millinery shop. Some women took their goods on the road and toured the British colonies as itinerant peddlers. The choice of some widows not to remarry, but rather to carry on their husbands' businesses, though relatively unusual, was also socially acceptable, as attested to by the appearance in the colonial press of notices from women running saddleries and taverns, who hoped that their deceased husbands' customers would continue to patronize them. [18]

As the century unfolded, an increasing, though still relatively small number of single and widowed women of some education took up teaching. Initially these women, many recently arrived from Britain, opened up academies for young girls to teach the daughters of the upper and middle levels of society their three Rs and all those matters "necessary for a person of their sex" and rank: needlework, housekeeping, embroidery, French, and penmanship. With the growth of the public-school movement after 1840, the acceptance of women as teachers became institutionalized. Public trustees quickly realized the economic and social benefits of hiring women teachers to work under male supervisors. Women, it was asserted, were "ideally suited to the instruction and governance of the young." It was said that "By the law of nature and revelation" women, who already had "a position of subordination and dependence," [19] could best instill those qualities in their students. More importantly, trustees soon found that women could be employed at substantially lower wages than men, and they encouraged unmarried women to take up their duties in the growing number of public schools.

The feminization of the teaching profession after the mid-century provided colonial women with an occupational option in a world that was becoming progressively closed to them. The nature of their involvement in teaching, however, reflected the quickly solidifying attitudes towards a woman's role in the workplace, an attitude that would prevail for the next hundred years. Women did and, it was asserted, *should* have subordinate positions, and they required and deserved less wage for equal work. This view was readily learned by Canadian children, who were daily exposed to "this powerful symbol of women's inferior position in society." [20]

It was not just in teaching that the nature of women's work changed radically. Between 1820 and 1860, as British North America developed economically and became socially more stratified, economic opportunities for single and married women outside the home constricted. Many in rural areas continued to work in partnership with their husbands on the family farm. In colonial towns and cities, however, not only did fewer women engage in 'male' occupations in the marketplace, but their involvement in even those occupations traditionally reserved for women lessened. The midwife, for example, once the only and fully accepted help for the pregnant woman, was disappearing, fast being replaced by trained male doctors, as Wendy Mitchinson discusses here in her chapter on the medical treatment of women.

By the time of Confederation, the transition from pioneering communities to a stratified Victorian society was largely complete. All women were expected to remain within the private sphere of the home, and those who could not were allowed to pursue only those endeavours that were considered natural extensions of a 'true woman's' place – teaching, nursing, and domestic service. Fewer and fewer women were running businesses; rather, they were at home, pursuing 'woman's work.' By example they were to protect the hearth, the family, and the children of the nation from the evils of the public world. Ironically, as the ideology of domesticity became increasingly entrenched, the industrialization of British North America was simultaneously encouraging the complete division of public and private spheres and forcing a growing number of unskilled women into the factories as poorly paid wage labourers.[21]

It must be noted that, although they were expected to remain in the private sphere, some women in British North America did become involved, to a limited degree, in the community at large. Between 1800 and 1860, middle-class and upper-class women, like their sisters in the United States and Great Britain, organized and joined various Bible and charity societies. The need for such organizations was increasingly evident to colonial elites after 1820, as thousands of immigrants and destitute and unemployed residents began to move to the towns and villages of British North America. For women like Eliza Powell, Christian duty and traditional involvement in church affairs, a high rank in society, and a fear of growing social disorder encouraged, even demanded, that they protect their families by looking after the deserving poor, orphans, destitute mothers, and unlettered and ungodly families.

Organizations such as the Female Benevolent Society of Kingston, Upper Canada, the Dorcas Society, and various Orphan's Homes and Widow's Friends Societies were formed to give help to the needy. Although often but not always subsidiary to male organizations, these women's groups did provide many of the colonies' earliest social services.[22] As well, they provided some wealthy women with contacts outside the home, with opportunities to learn and to practise leadership skills and with a sense of community that was exclusively female. Through such activities there evolved a distinct woman's culture and a consciousness of women's concerns that crossed class lines. The givers of charity, those women of the upper levels of society who were attempting to preserve and strengthen the family, most often concentrated their attention on the plight of homeless, needy, and abandoned women and children. Nonetheless, these group activities were limited and were considered to be of secondary importance to a woman's primary duty to her own family.

By 1867, when the older colonies united, the public/male, private/female dichotomy was seemingly entrenched. Yet, as women moved into the Canadian West with their husbands and fathers, the pioneering cycle of Canadian life was perpetuated. In the West, however, the old ideas were reshaped by the new conditions of settlement, the isolation of frontier existence, and the new technology at hand.

Confederation Canada

Canadians and, later U.S. and European immigrants, were propelled west between 1867 and 1920 by the accessibility of land and opportunities and by their own rising ambitions and expectations. Women were an integral part of this migration and played a vital role in the settlement and establishment of a new society. This was not the first time that women had played a significant role in the development of the West. Before the arrival of white women in the Red River and the Hudson Bay Company lands, the fur trade had been largely dependent on the labour and co-operation of Native people, particularly Native women who had provided white fur traders with an essential personal link between the indigenous and the European commercial cultures. Until well into the nineteenth century Native women were "remarkable economic partner[s]," whose skills and "wilderness know how" materially aided the Europeans' physical and economic well-being.[23]

The arrival of the first white women in 1811 had little initial impact on the practice of mixed marriage or on white-Indian personal and trading alliances. But as their numbers increased, white women added a new and divisive element to the fur-trade society. They brought with them expectations and assumptions of a genteel life and Victorian attitudes towards race and family, which encouraged these wives of Hudson Bay factors and traders and Protestant clergymen to demand that European-Canadian social customs and mores prevail.

The influx of Ontario farmers and entrepreneurs and their wives and daughters reinforced the growing belief in Anglo-Saxon racial and social supremacy and added another level to the existing social order, one based on a sedentary, pioneer, farming lifestyle. The new women in the West worked beside their husbands in the fields and contributed to the family economy by tending the garden, raising chickens, and often taking sole responsibility for the dairy, as well as coping with the demands of the household and the children. Gradually, these women also "set about to reproduce the traditions they had left behind, the missionary societies, the bible classes . . . temperance organizations, women's institutes and the less formal networks through which medical knowledge and the craft skills of domestic life were shared."[24]

Life in the Canadian West was quite different from that in rural Ontario. Particularly during their first years there, farming families were often distant from each other and from the conveniences of schools, shops, and close neighbours. Such isolation made new emotional and physical demands on farm women. After 1900, as a national market system, a wheat economy, and mechanization encouraged cash-cropping and increased specialization, the role of the farm wife changed radically. Larger farms and larger farm households all encouraged a sharper division of labour based on sex. Many of the tasks once considered a woman's responsibility became too extensive to remain part time. As Marjorie Cohen notes, "As long as any aspect of production involved the farmhouse, it remained within the female domain, but outdoor activities gradually became the preserves of men."[25] For example, the founding of cheese factories and creameries, the increased size of herds to meet new market demands, and the introduction of new machinery to separate and process milk all encouraged male farmers to assume responsibility for the dairy, which had traditionally been controlled by women.

Nonetheless, prairie wives continued to contribute to the overall economy. In addition to working in the home, a number of women after the turn of the century also took (or were forced to take) employment off the farm, supplementing the household economy with wages earned from working as teachers, shop clerks, or employees of the growing service industries of the region. Despite this diversification of occupational activity, the primary role of married women in the Canadian West continued to be as partners of their husbands. They also continued to share a distinct sense of a rural, western farming identity that was quite different from that of the East. This became evident toward the end of the century as women began to pressure first for increased involvement in the political process and then for the right to vote.

Not only married women were on the move west. Single Canadian and immigrant women joined this migration in growing numbers, attracted by the demand for farm help, domestic servants, teachers, and wives. Yet between 1870 and 1920, as the Canadian economy became industrialized and urbanized, women were also drawn to the growing towns and cities of the new nation, where factories, shops, and mills promised adventure, greater personal and economic independence, and relief from the seeming monotony and drudgery of farm life. As Susan McDaniel shows in her chapter here, the effects of this movement from farm to city were felt particularly strongly by women. Those who remained on the farms found that their traditional activities outside the farm house were increasingly marginalized. The women who left the farm, either with their families or on their own, found new opportunities in the cities but also new restrictions. The realities of city life and factory work also brought new insecurities, made new demands on women's time and skills, and raised apprehensions in the minds of many Canadians about the future of the family. Both women and men became alarmed that the family unit was disintegrating before the industrial onslaught.[26]

Industrialization did provide young, single, and widowed women, particularly in Ontario and Quebec, with an attractive occupational alternative to domestic service, which throughout the period continued to employ most women workers. Even the least skilled girl had hopes of securing what seemed to be a well-paid job, which, with its set hours, allowed her to leave the demands of the workplace at the end of the day. After 1900 the economy expanded and women could find work as clerks, stenographers, typists, telephone operators, nurses, and workers in a variety of factories. But work in the factories, the burgeoning service industries, the stores, the telephone exchanges, and the textile and needle trades also entailed long hours, unhealthy working conditions, and boredom. There was no protection from arbitrary pay cuts, periodic speed-ups, demands for more production, or layoffs. Women workers soon discovered that the industrial system, and the male workers within it, erected almost impenetrable barriers to attaining either skills or advancement. A general acceptance of scientific-management techniques and specialization of tasks meant that a hierarchy of occupations and responsibilities was increasingly institutionalized. Women were carefully relegated to subordinate positions, to well-defined 'women's work' (which often demanded patience and dexterity) or to semi-skilled and unskilled tasks. Men established and managed the new businesses, which were creating increasingly restricted and poorly paid work ghettos for women.[27]

A large proportion of the female work force seemed unconcerned about the implications of many of these developments. Few of them expected to stay in the workplace for any length of time. Work provided the single girl with a wage, perhaps some training, and an opportunity to contribute to the family income. Work outside the home was expected to and usually did end upon marriage, and few women appeared to have any personal commitment to their jobs. Attempts by a few concerned women to organize segments of the female work force met with resistance not only from male co-workers, unions, and employers, but from many women. There were exceptions to this. Women telephone operators in Toronto organized and struck for better wages and hours in 1907; women needleworkers unionized; and some women were admitted as members of skilled craft unions.[28] But the weakness of the union movement in Canada before

World War I and the prevailing assumption by women and men of all classes that a woman's true work was as wife and mother together deterred the transient female work force from organizing and agitating for better wages and conditions. Their very presence in the workplace in such numbers seemed to be revolutionary.

By the turn of the century there were a few Canadian women who challenged quite vehemently both their domestic roles and their limited place in the work force. Choosing to pursue a career rather than, or perhaps in addition to, marriage, some daughters of middle-class and upper-class families, like their counterparts in Europe and the United States, began to demand entry into universities and into the new professions. Augusta Stowe-Gullen, Emily Stowe, and Amelia Yeomans, for example, breached the walls of male exclusivity in the medical profession. A few others pursued legal careers. Most middle-class women, however, continued to gravitate to teaching or to the new professions of the progressive age, particularly nursing and social work. Yet to the discerning few it was evident that, even in the so-called professions, women were relegated to the bottom rungs or were segregated because of their sex. Women medical candidates in the 1870s met with resistance from established schools and had to go for their training to the United States or, eventually, to attend special women's medical colleges affiliated with Canadian universities. This segregation carried over into later medical practice. The few women doctors in Canada became obstetricians or entered mission work, where "their unique nurturing instinct" was utilized.[29]

Most women attracted to the medical profession were encouraged to train as nurses, an occupation that most people, certainly doctors, believed was far more suited to their nature. Within institutions, nurses almost always played a subordinate role. Only the few public health nurses had any independence from the tyranny of constant supervision, submission to doctors' orders, and the rigid moral code that prevailed in a hospital. Nurses, like teachers, discovered that the mystique of femininity, which regulated their lives, also meant lower wages. Attempts by the growing numbers of nurses and teachers to gain some semblance of control over their own work and training by forming professional organizations were adamantly resisted. It was only after World War II that the Federation of Women Teachers of Ontario and nursing associations gained any control over the admission and certification of their members.[30]

Despite the continuing segregation of work by sex and the continuing subordination of women, rapid industrialization between 1900 and 1920 ushered in the 'new woman' – a woman who was increasingly educated, apparently independent (many claimed they were too independent), and unquestioningly in the public workplace. A few Canadian women dared to suggest that this 'coming out' was but the first step towards attaining full political and economic parity.

The Reform Movement

Canada's industrial development furnished many women with outlets for their skills and energies in addition to the home and other workplaces. Improvements in transportation and communications, the growth of cities, and the availability of new consumer goods provided by the coming of industrialization heralded an age of national growth and excitement. Yet the expanding economic horizons also brought with them social and economic tensions and problems, which seemed to jeopardize the nation's continued physical and moral development. Canadians of all classes were concerned about the presence of 'alien' immigrants, the growing crime rate, and the visible poverty that plagued Canadian cities. Antagonism between the interests of owners and workers seemed to threaten the very foundations of the nation. This new awareness of society's ills was accompanied, however, by an optimistic belief that by identifying and classifying problems, by organizing like-minded citizens, and, where necessary, by enacting legislation to redress specific ills, the nation and the world could be reformed to ensure progress and the continuance of a moral, civilized, virtuous society. [31]

The progressive-reform impulse that gripped North America between the years 1880 and 1920 sanctioned an increased activism and awareness among Canadian women. Across the country, but particularly in the cities, thousands of upper-class and middle-class women, increasingly educated, with their children in schools and new labour-saving devices and servants in their homes, joined the movement to reform. They were propelled out of the isolation of their homes by a sense of religious duty and a spirit of expanding opportunity, which combined with their growing apprehension about the state of Canadian society and their special place within it. First at the local and then the provincial and national levels, Canadian women came together to redress a host of social ills, campaigning for, among other things, temperance, religious instruction, improvements in the workplace, better housing, facilities for single women, and state-run public health and child welfare programs. Eventually their activities compelled them to press for direct involvement in the political life of the nation.

Many of the first of these women's organizations were denominational. Methodist, Presbyterian, Baptist, Congregational, Catholic, and Anglican women established women's auxiliaries, institutes, and missionary societies to spread the word of God and, in some cases, make provision for the needy.[32] These groups were soon joined by a number of secular, although still religiously motivated, organizations, which took their mandate from parent organizations in Britain and the United States. In 1870 the first Canadian branch of the British Young Women's Christian Association was established in Saint John, followed shortly by the appearance of local YWCAS, which provided housing, domestic training, and religious instruction for young girls in Montreal and Toronto. Over the next twenty years other groups coalesced and joined the forces of reform. The Anglican Girls' Friendly Society, the Dominion Order of the King's Daughters, and the Fédération nationale Saint-Jean-Baptiste in Quebec were among the most prominent.

The Girls' Friendly Society (GFS), a branch of a British organization, was established in Canada in 1882. With its primary objective of providing shelter and support for single immigrant girls in a family-like setting, this Anglican group sponsored "labour bureaus, adult education classes, lunch rooms, recreation centres, vocational homes and sick funds."[33] In 1886 the U.S.-inspired Dominion Order of the King's Daughters (DOKD) was also organized to assist young single girls in Canada's cities. A broadly based Protestant group, the DOKD, like the YWCA and the GFS, attempted to guard the spiritual, social, and personal integrity of the working girl. After the turn of the century, the Fédération nationale Saint-Jean-Baptiste provided Catholic francophone lay women in Quebec with similar services. Founded in 1907, the Fédération was a loose alliance of some twenty-two women's groups that had emerged to address specific problems created by the industrialization of the province. Unlike the YWCA, the GFS, or the DOKD, the Fédération, although concerned about individual girls, primarily concentrated its efforts on broad social and economic issues affecting all Quebec women: housing, child welfare, working conditions, the need for vocational education for women, and prohibition.[34]

The largest and perhaps the most influential women's organization of the time was the Women's Christian Temperance Union (WCTU), founded in Owen Sound, Ontario, in 1874. Formed expressly to stop the liquor trade, it had attracted thousands of members by the time it became a national union in 1883. Inspired by temperance movements in the United States and men's organizations in Canada, the women of the WCTU believed that alcohol was the root of all society's ills. It caused crime, poverty, sexual immorality, and, most insidiously, it invaded the nation's homes and destroyed the lives of innocent women and children. The only solution, the WCTU declared, was complete prohibition, legislated by the state. The liquor trade was not the only target of the WCTU, however. The struggle to preserve and strengthen a moral society also prompted members to form Protestant missions, to agitate for stronger drug laws and anti-tobacco legislation, and, in the end, to demand female suffrage.[35]

Most of those whom Veronica Strong-Boag refers to as "club women" believed that they had not only a right but also an obligation to participate in the public sphere. As mothers it was their particular responsibility to preserve the sanctity of the Canadian family. They held that "those special nurturing qualities which were common to all women,"[36] when organized and aimed at society's ills, would not only improve men and their actions in the public sphere, but would also bring society back to its virtuous roots in the family. Thus most women reformers were essentially conservative. But as a result of their participation in reform organizations, many Canadian women gained valuable leadership and organizational skills and gradually began to act independently of their men. A new interdependence among Canadian women and a respect for their own abilities developed, which reinforced their collective confidence and encouraged a growing public assertiveness. These middle-class women, by their very participation in organized reform, were also challenging the private/female and public/male dichotomy. Yet, they did so only because they believed it was absolutely essential to infuse the public world with a domestic, female morality.[37] Most continued to accept the middle-class belief that women were best suited to be wives and mothers. It was to protect this view of the world and to ensure the continuance of the family and, thus, of the race and civilized society that an increasing number of women became involved in national affairs.

Most Canadians gradually accepted women's participation as agents and promoters of social reform, particularly as the "social feminist"[38] impulse that was embraced supported the public view of a woman's rightful place as being in the home. There *were* a number of citizens, mostly men but also a few women, who feared this new woman who was organized, forceful, and increasingly vocal in pressing her concerns. By her very presence in the public arena and her unseemly demands for recognition as the nation's conscience, the new woman, some argued, was challenging, indeed threatening, the family and those traditional values she was claiming to strengthen. This attitude was particularly evident in Quebec. Nationalists like Henri Bourassa and conservative Catholic clerics generally considered that French-Canadian feminists and the Fédération were tainted by foreign, alien, anglo influences. Although all three groups – Quebec feminists, nationalists, and the church – were committed to preserving the family, they were divided on how best to achieve this. The nationalists and the church were agreed, however, that active Quebec women were a particular threat to traditional authority and social values, and clerics and nationalists in Quebec and ultra-conservatives throughout the country mounted vehement attacks on the new woman.[39]

In the early years of the reform movement, few reform-minded women advocated a revolutionary change in the social or political order or desired any involvement in politics. Even after the turn of the century they were divided over the question of female suffrage. In the 1880s and 1890s, only a few in Canada were so radical as to assert that "the insidious distinction of sex is an arbitrary and artificial one, having no foundation in reason or common sense."[40] There were only a handful who, like the members of the Toronto-based Dominion Women Enfranchisement Association (DWEA), demanded equality and the vote as a natural right. Most women involved in reform recognized and welcomed the innate differences between the sexes. And most of the nation's mothers began to agitate for the vote only after it became clear that the reforms so necessary to their society's regeneration would not be enacted without it.

By the early 1890s, several of the female reform organizations had active support across Canada. The WCTU had almost ten thousand members, scattered throughout the countryside and in the nation's towns and cities. The Girls' Friendly Society, the Dominion Order of the King's Daughters, the YWCA, and the missionary societies all continued to attract new members. The differences in purpose and intent were offset by considerable duplication of ideas, methods, problems, and members among the many organizations. By 1893 the growing self-awareness and self-confidence of women, together with their realization of the need to expand their scope, prompted the creation of one national body to bring the various national associations into co-operation and common action.

Under the strong influence of Lady Ishbel Aberdeen, wife of the Governor General, the new National Council of Women of Canada (NCWC) became a clearing house and a strong lobbying group for women's reform activities across the country. Declaring itself non-partisan and non-sectarian in an effort to defuse the potential conflicts arising from differing religious and political beliefs, the NCWC also asserted its commitment to "the homes and the Nation . . . the family and the State." Its intention was to extend "feminine influence over the operation of Canadian society" and to promote "national enthusiasm and affection." The formation of the NCWC "set the stage" for "feminine nationalism, reform and ambition," and for the first time gave the Canadian women's movement a sense of national unity and group identity.[41]

The formation of a national organization did not resolve, however, the varied and, at times, conflicting views held by women of various regions of the country and of differing income levels towards the issues of the day. Most 'club' women lived in the nation's cities, and their proposed reforms were, not surprisingly, concerned with urban problems. Women in the Canadian West did share the national desire for prohibition and concern for the problems presented by the arrival of large numbers of immigrants.

Indeed, the WCTU was particularly strong in the West. As farmers' wives, however, living on the political periphery of Canada, rural Western women did not share many of the Eastern concerns for municipal and factory reforms. Many members of the women's auxiliaries of the United Farmer's Associations of Manitoba, Saskatchewan, and Alberta distrusted the intentions of the urban-based, middle-class reform groups, believing that they were but appendages of the industrial, political interests of the East. The growth of Western cities and the increasing diversity of classes, races, and occupations in the West tended to exacerbate such division among Canadian women. As Carol Bacchi has pointed out, "Although these women managed to cooperate for several female-oriented goals, ultimately they identified with their class rather than their sex."[42]

With their commitment to middle-class values, the city women's thrust for reform also tended to ignore the real, daily problems of the large numbers of women who worked in factories and shops. Such organizations as the YWCA, the WCTU, and increasingly the NCWC were concerned only that working girls be protected from the immoral, unhealthy, and seemingly unwomanly aspects of the workplace. With their distrust of labour and labour organizations and their view of women as future mothers, not members of the work force, middle-class women advocated piecemeal reform of the physical and moral environment of the workplace. Although their proposals did include better hours and wages, the establishment of nurseries to care for the children of the working woman, and new safety and training regulations, the progressive impulse accepted without reservation the hierarchical organization of the social and economic order and that the needs of women were essentially different from those of men. For the most part, equal pay and questions of promotion and advancement for women within the system – issues that many working girls considered essential – were not considered.[43]

The Suffrage Movement

These differences in concerns and, indeed, in ideas about how women could best achieve the necessary reform of society became evident when some women extended their activities from the social to the political realm. Initially the call for female suffrage was sounded by a small number of women. Before the turn of the century most women involved in the auxiliaries, missionary and charitable societies, and groups like the YWCA and GFS believed that moral suasion and the justness of their causes would ensure reform. It became increasingly clear, however, that though women's concerns and suggestions for change were often applauded, politicians, legislators, and businessmen were not inclined to provide legislative support. Gradually, during the late 1880s and the 1890s, women across the country began to realize that while petitions, pamphlet campaigns, mass meetings, and even the newly granted right for some women to vote at the municipal level raised Canadians' awareness of national problems, they did nothing to redress them and ensure economic and social justice. The answer, it seemed, lay in getting the vote, so that through women's voice in the democratic process, Canadian society could be saved. [44]

The battle for women to get the vote was by no means a triumph of equality, of women's rights broadly defined, or of the union of Canadian women for a great cause. Even at the height of the campaign, just before and throughout World War I, many women vocally disapproved of the proposal, asserting that politics was no place for a mother. Those who supported the campaign did so for a variety of reasons and chose a number of different vehicles to press their claims. For the 'club' women of the East and the cities, suffrage was merely the means to ensure the success of various reforms, particularly prohibition, protection of women in the workplace, and care of the nation's children. The female preoccupation remained the home and the family. Working women who supported the cause did so to promote the practical concerns of equal pay and equality in the workplace. For the farm women of the West, though no less committed to reform, the vote also came to be viewed as a means of placing particular regional interests on the national political agenda. [45] And the few women of Quebec who actively campaigned for female suffrage did so cautiously because of constant pressure from the church and public opinion to abandon their cause.

The movement for the vote, like that for reform, began at the local and provincial levels. Between 1880 and 1900 most municipalities granted the franchise to all property owners, regardless of sex, thereby affording first unmarried and then married women the means to promote their reform ideas in the communities and the school system. Canada's problems, however, were national in scope, and a number of women began to agitate for the franchise provincially and then nationally. The first suffrage organization, the Toronto Women's Literary Club, founded in 1876, was a small group of middle-class, educated, professional women, who lobbied not just for the vote but also for the opening of schools and universities to women. It was not, however, until the WCTU endorsed the suffrage campaign in 1893 and the Dominion Women's Enfranchisement Association (DWEA) was founded in 1889 that the issue really entered the public sphere.

Between 1895 and 1910, suffrage or political-equality leagues were formed in each province, with branches in all major urban areas. Farm associations in Ontario and the West and some labour groups, including the Toronto Labour Council and the B.C. Federation of Labour, supported women's demands for the vote, and increasingly members of the press supported the cause. Yet even after the National Council of Women endorsed women's suffrage in 1910 (after a heated debate and only by a vote of seventy-one to fifty-one) there was little unity among women on if or how this reform could be achieved. While the middle-class 'club' women worked within provincial and national branches of the NCWC and the DWEA (renamed the Canadian Suffrage Association in 1907), Western farming women most often chose to combine their efforts within the Grain Growers' Associations of Manitoba and Saskatchewan and the United Farmers of Alberta.[46]

The WCTU was one of the few, perhaps the only organization, that managed to bring diverse and potentially conflicting groups of women into common action. In large part this was because its primary objective was prohibition. The demand for the vote, although a key concern, was merely the means to attain social and political reform. The WCTU, because of "its appeal to women's maternal role"[47] and its avowed purpose to strengthen the home and the family, was able to galvanize support from both men and women who remained fearful of the social and political upheaval that might result when women were granted the vote. Moreover the WCTU developed skilled leaders through the battles of the suffrage movement. One of the best-known activists for suffrage and for women's rights in general, Nellie McClung, got much of her inspiration and early training in the WCTU. As her biographer, Veronica Strong-Boag, concludes, "Nellie McClung represents that generation of women who were active in both the reform and the feminist communities. As such, she was in the mainstream of turn-of-the-century feminism."[48]

It was in the West – Manitoba, Alberta, and Saskatchewan – that women first received the provincial franchise in 1916. Within the next six years, all of Canada's provinces, with the exception of Quebec (where women did not receive the vote until 1940) had granted women the vote and also what many Canadians considered was the even more contentious right of running for public office. The provincial franchise did not ensure the triumph of prohibition or other national reforms, however, and the suffragists turned their attention to the Ottawa campaign. The federal government had assiduously avoided the question for some time. But in 1917 political necessity and the demands of wartime policies finally prompted the Borden government to take action.

The Military Voters Act of 1917 and the Wartime Elections Act were blatant attempts by the new coalition government led by Borden to ensure its success in the crucial upcoming national election. The first act granted the vote to all British subjects, female and male, who were actively participating in the Canadian armed services. The second act disenfranchised

conscientious objectors and naturalized Canadians born in enemy countries and enfranchised women who had close relatives serving in the armed
forces of Canada or Britain. The intent of this partial female enfranchisement was to ensure that the views of men in the service could be heard, if
only through their next of kin. There was certainly no assumption by the
government that women had a natural right to participate in political
affairs. It was not until March 1918, when Prime Minister Borden introduced the Women's Franchise Act, followed two years later by a new
Dominion Elections Act, that all women were granted the right to vote.
Yet even after Agnes Macphail of Ontario was elected to the House of
Commons in 1921, Canadian women were still denied full participation in
Parliament. Only after the Judicial Committee of the Privy Council con-
firmed that women were 'persons' in 1929, was that last institutional bas-
tion of male prerogative, the Canadian Senate, at least in theory, forced to
open its doors to women. As Beverley Baines shows in her chapter here on
women and the law, the decision in the Persons case rested solely on evidence that women were not specifically excluded from Senate membership in the British North America Act.

The victory at the federal level and the judgment in the Persons case did
not resolve the question for all Canadian women. Those in Quebec,
although able in the 1920s and 1930s to vote for representatives to the
House of Commons and to participate at the municipal level, were denied
this right provincially. In the early years, the Fédération nationale Saint-
Jean-Baptiste, the English-speaking Montreal Local Council of Women,
provincial chapters of the WCTU, and various affiliates of the NCWC campaigned for equal political rights for women within the province. Fierce
resistance from influential Quebecers and the church forced the Fédération to abandon its support of female suffrage in 1922.[49] A few courageous
French-Canadian women nonetheless continued to agitate as members of
the Montreal Council of Women. Unfortunately, however, throughout
the 1920s the women of Quebec were divided along class and cultural
lines. This was particularly true after 1927 when a second francophone
organization, L'Alliance Canadienne pour le Vote des Femmes du
Québec, was established. Over the next few years, many activities, representatives, and membership and educational campaigns were duplicated
by the two groups, and as a result efforts to pressure the government and
the Quebec people to obtain the vote were weak and uneven.

It was not until the end of the decade, when Thérèse Casgrain became
president of the Provincial Franchise Committee, that the feminist movement in Quebec became a force to be reckoned with. Reorganized into the
League of Women's Rights and with a strong leader, Quebec women made
suffrage a critical issue in the public press and the National Assembly. In
1940 the new Liberal government of Premier Joseph-Adélard Godbout,

despite renewed and intense resistance, finally gave women the vote and the ability to hold provincial office.

The triumph of Canadian women in gaining full political rights did not bring with it equality. As Sandra Burt shows in her chapter on public policy, the exercise of female franchise did not initiate revolutionary changes in the political process. With few notable exceptions the provincial legislatures, Senate, and House of Commons have remained male preserves. Getting the vote and being recognized in law as equal participants in the political affairs of the nation were significant and necessary victories, but they did little to change the place of women in the home and in the workplace or to alter community attitudes about the 'other' sex. In the 1920s women found these battles much more difficult to fight and, indeed, they have yet to be won.

The War Years and After

There is no question that the outbreak of war in 1914 and the manner of Canada's participation in it were instrumental in securing many progressive reforms, including female suffrage. Canadians expected that this momentous battle for the Empire and for Justice would be the beginning of a new and better era of national and global development. And throughout the war years there seemed to be indications that a new era of real equality was at hand for women.

Particularly after 1916, as the economy was fully mobilized to meet wartime demands, women moved in large numbers into the nation's factories, replacing the men who were fighting overseas or had transferred to war industries. Throughout 1917 and 1918 women became an essential part of Canada's wartime labour force. To meet new demands, the Imperial Munitions Board encouraged employers to accept women workers, who received wages 20 to 30 per cent lower than a man's for the same work.[50] Industry, it seems, welcomed their new employees.

The presence of so many women in the workplace was accepted by Canadians as part of the great patriotic effort. But public opinion held that only single women should be so engaged in industry – and only on a temporary basis. At the end of the war women would move back into the home to resume their real work as wives and mothers. And in 1919, though some women did continue to work in the industries that had employed them before the war – textiles, tobacco, appliance, and service industries – many found themselves unemployed, forced out of their workplaces by returning men.

The end of the war did not herald a new, enlightened age. Indeed, an immediate postwar depression and mounting social and labour unrest prompted a new conservatism in Canadian society. Women, rather than being "beneficiaries of a reorganized and updated capitalist order," continued to be subject to "inequality in the workplace . . . merely modernized [in] its forms."[51] As in the pre-war years, most working women continued to be in domestic service. Nevertheless, a perceived shortage of servants prompted the governments to establish training programs in the domestic arts for young girls and to promote the immigration of single women as domestic workers.[52]

Certainly, there were some changes in circumstances and attitudes as a result of the war and industrialization. Women's magazines, clerics, employers, and the middle class now accepted that single women had a valid role to play in the paid work force. But women in the work force were still underpaid and relegated to the least skilled and most mundane tasks. For the most part, it continued to be assumed that girls would only work for a limited time. Marriage automatically meant the end of a 'career,' and the new matron was expected to retreat to the home to look after the husband and children. Perhaps unconsciously aware that many girls might not welcome leaving the work force, the media and the schools began to stress that homemaking was a career in itself, one that demanded skill and determination. In the 1920s motherhood was raised to the level of a profession, supposedly essential for the development of the nation.[53] And as the prosperous 1920s gave way to the terrible 1930s, women found themselves under increasing pressure to embrace this 'new' profession of homemaker and leave the public workplace to men, who now more than ever needed to earn a wage.

After the federal victory for suffrage, what has come to be known as the first wave of feminism lost much of its drive and receded from the public political arena. But discrimination in the workplace and the prevailing social acceptance of real differences between the sexes did arouse some women activists in the 1920s and 1930s to try to redress the balance. At both the provincial and federal levels, representatives such as Agnes Macphail, Nellie McClung, and Mary Ellen Smith joined with other social and economic reformers to enact protective legislation for women and children, at home and at work. In the 1920s most provinces passed married women's property acts and minimum-wage legislation for women and took measures to protect the nation's children. The NCWC, the YWCA, professional organizations like the Federation of Women Teachers' Associations of Ontario (FWTAO), and nursing associations and other groups did continue to work quietly, but their activities received little public attention. For many working-class women, the continued acceptance by many of these groups of Victorian, middle-class values and of the primary virtue of motherhood failed to address the real concerns of the workplace.[54] For some working-class women, the answer lay in political parties of the left; others turned to unionism.

In 1902 the Socialist Party of Canada had been the first political party to admit women as full members, and after that time all the various tendencies within the Canadian socialist movement had championed the cause of women's suffrage. [55] The impact of this support seems to have been negligible on the final decision to grant women the vote, but it did open the door for women's participation in political parties of the left. After the 1921 federal election a growing number of women began to assume "an auxiliary or supportive role" within the traditional structures of all political parties. As well, a number of women remained influential within the progressive farmers organizations, while still others continued to support socialist platforms. By the 1930s some working-class women, rejecting "both the conventional feminist mode of moderate social reform as well as the traditional partisan model of women as ancillary political workers and primary social and fund raising organizers," [56] established a women's committee in the new Co-operative Commonwealth Federation, the forerunner of the New Democratic Party, to promote leadership training and other programs to assist Canadian women. Even today, however, at both the provincial and federal levels, the number of women candidates and sitting members is grossly unrepresentative of the female population.

In the 1920s, many working-class women concluded that a rather more direct and more immediately effective means of gaining economic equality was through unionism. Despite opposition from employers and working men, such groups as the International Ladies Garment Workers Union of America (ILGWU), the Amalgamated Clothing Workers of America (ACW), and the Industrial Union of Needle Trades rallied their constituents. [57] Through a number of well-publicized strikes, such as that in 1924 by the ACW against the Society Brand Clothing Company in Montreal or, in 1931, when the ILGWU of Toronto walked out for better wages, the working woman's concerns were brought to the attention of the public. Economic gains were limited at best, however. It was not until the outbreak of World War II that the aspirations of women workers to achieve real equality seemed about to be fulfilled.

As in the first war, between 1939 and 1945 women took an integral part in the great patriotic effort, a part co-ordinated this time by the national government. [58] In 1942 the National Selective Service registration identified Canadian women as part of a large labour reserve, and shortly thereafter the government began to draw selected groups of women into war-related industries. First young girls, then married, childless women, and, finally, women with children were recruited into all aspects of Canada's industrial war effort. From the outset it was clear that this policy was only to meet the wartime emergency. Women did receive some training through various government-sponsored programs for specific jobs, but the training was designed to meet the immediate needs of industry, not to enhance women's labour skills.[59] The tasks women performed in the munitions industry, for example, were sex-linked, demanding the dexterity, acceptance of repetition, and patience deemed 'natural' to women. The temporary nature of their employment was quickly brought home to women at the end of the war when government-sponsored facilities for child care closed and the tax concessions granted to married women came to an abrupt halt. Married women were clearly expected to return home; single women were expected to marry and make a home to raise their children. And though many women resisted, it was clear that the long-hoped-for new day of equality was not at hand.

Throughout the 1940s and 1950s, ideas of femininity, of fundamental differences between the sexes, and of a 'woman's place' persisted and were actively espoused by that stratum of middle-class women who had embraced maternal feminism at the turn of the century. But the war had given a significant number of women, for a time at least, economic independence and personal autonomy. While their husbands were overseas, many had worked and maintained the family single-handedly. Others had joined the services and had taken an active part in the war effort in Europe. Economic prosperity in the 1950s and a quiet new self-confidence in their own abilities encouraged a growing number of women to question and to challenge society's expectations.

After 1950 more and more girls completed high school, attended university, and demanded admittance to professional programs. Women's occupational organizations like the FWTAO and nursing associations renewed their efforts to gain control over training and certification of their members. An ever-growing number of women entered the work force, including married women who often chose to work part-time as well as to raise a family. And, increasingly, middle-class women became directly and actively involved in the political process.[60] Problems of inequality persisted, however. In the 1950s women worked in rapidly expanding work ghettos within factories, service industries, and offices. They sought part-time work not only from choice but also to provide the family with sorely needed income to make ends meet. Part-time work also gave employers a way to improve productivity and profits without the expense of a full-time worker's benefits.[61] Throughout the economy women's wages were, and still are, well below those of men performing comparable tasks. In addition, although more girls were in school, they were usually directed into fields considered appropriate for their sex, and their overall numbers in schools continued to be well below those of boys. And throughout the postwar period, society's ambivalence and, at times, outright hostility, particularly towards married women working, were evident in the lack of social and legislative support available to them. Nonetheless, the groundwork of education, increased affluence, and awareness resulted in a growing self-confidence and a rise in personal expectation during the 1950s, which laid the foundations for a new wave of feminism to emerge in the 1960s.

The Voice of Women (VOW), founded in 1960 to oppose nuclear-weapons testing and proliferation, is considered by some to be the first self-conscious women's group in English Canada of the second wave of Canadian feminism, as Naomi Black discusses in her chapter on the second wave. Despite internal political divisions, which appeared in 1963 after the Pearson government decided to allow BOMARCS on Canadian soil, and an apparent lack of public credibility, the VOW did provide leadership training for future status-of-women activists. [62] It also illustrated the political tensions and opposition that any campaign for women's rights could and did generate in Canadian society. Middle-class women in Canada, increasingly frustrated by the lack of opportunities and basic institutional inequalities in national life, continued to demand action throughout the early 1960s. By February 1967 they had successfully pressured the federal government to establish a royal commission to study the status of women in Canada. The commission did not solve the problem; however, it did provide women with a forum to articulate their grievances.

By 1967, although the division between the private and public spheres persisted, advanced industrialization, changes in the structure of the family, and rising expectations among all Canadians blurred and complicated an easy distinction between women's and men's roles. While many Canadians continued to assume that a woman's real work was still as a wife and mother, economic necessity, ambition, and personal circumstance continued to force and to encourage both married and single women to work.

To a casual observer, it might also have seemed that the history of women in Canada had come full circle. The women of New France and early-nineteenth-century British North America had also been responsible for looking after the home as well as taking an active part in the marketplace. But there were significant differences in the two situations. For the first time a significant proportion of women in Canada in the 1960s was questioning the very basic tenets of a paternalistic, male-dominated society. And although divisions based on occupation, class, and location persisted, there now existed a sense of unity among an increasing number of Canadian women, one that would have been impossible in the eighteenth or nineteenth centuries. In 1967, women, as they had done for hundreds of years, presented radically differing solutions to their problems. Nonetheless, most were agreed that traditional assumptions of a woman's place and woman's work had to change.

Jane Errington

NOTES

1. *Farmers Journal,* July 16, 1828, 4.
2. Veronica Strong-Boag and Anita Clair Fellman, eds., *Rethinking Canada: The Promise of Women's History* (Toronto: Copp Clark Pitman, 1986), 2.
3. A term used by Margaret Conrad in her work on Maritime women's diaries, "Sundays Always Make Me Think of Home," in *Rethinking Canada,* 67-81, and "Recording Angels: The Private Chronicles of Women from the Maritime Provinces of Canada, 1750-1950," in Alison Prentice and Susan Mann Trofimenkoff, eds., *The Neglected Majority,* Vol. 2 (Toronto: McClelland & Stewart, 1985), 41-60. Conrad writes of that separate women's world, with its distinct experiences, values, and identity.
4. For a brief overview of women in New France, see, among others, Jan Noel, "Les Femmes Favorisées," in *Rethinking Canada,* 23-44, and Lilianne Plamondon, "A Business Woman in New France, Marie-Ann Barbel, the Widow Fornel," in *Rethinking Canada,* 45-58.
5. Isabel Foulché-Delbosc, "Women of Three Rivers: 1651-63," in Susan Mann Trofimenkoff and Alison Prentice, eds., *The Neglected Majority,* Vol. 1 (Toronto: McClelland and Stewart, 1977), 14-26. She notes that widows remarried within an average of eight months after bereavement. *See also*: Noel, "Les Femmes Favorisées," 25, 33, for examples of remarriage and the legal provisions that accommodated and encouraged this.
6. *See*: Noel, "Les Femmes Favorisées." *See also*: Philippe Aries, *Centuries of Childhood* (New York: Random House, 1962); Peter Laslett, *The World We Have Lost,* 2nd. ed. (Cambridge: Methuen, 1979).
7. Noel, "Les Femmes Favorisées," 39.
8. *See*: Noel, "Les Femmes Favorisées." *See also*: Plamondon, "A Business Woman in New France," in which the extensive business activities of Marie-Ann Barbel after her husband's death in 1645 are described. *See also*: Louise Duchêne, *Habitants et marchands de Montréal au XVII siècle* (Montreal: Plon, 1974). Laurel Thatcher Ulrich, in *Good Wives: Image and Reality in the Lives of Women in Northern New England, 1650-1750* (New York: Vintage Books, 1992 [1980]) chronicles similar situations in the American colonies. *See also*: Louis A. Tilly and Joan W. Scott, *Women, Work and Family* (New York: Routledge, 1987).
9. Noel, "Les Femmes Favorisées," 32.
10. L. Franquet, *Voyages et mémoires sur le Canada,* quoted in Noel, "Les Femmes Favorisées," 33.
11. For discussion of the legal position of women in New France, *see*: Plamondon, "A Business Woman in New France"; Noel, "Les Femmes Favorisées"; Foulché-Belbosc, "Women of Three Rivers."
12. Mary Ryan, *Cradle of the Middle Class: The Family in Oneida County, New York, 1790-1865* (New York: Cambridge University Press, 1981), 19, 24.

Unfortunately, the history of women in early British North America is woefully incomplete. *See*, however, Marion Fowler, *The Embroidered Tent: Five Gentlewomen in Early Canada* (Toronto: House of Anansi, 1982); Beth Light and Alison Prentice, *Pioneer and Gentlewomen of British North America 1713-1867* (Toronto: New Hogtown Press, 1980); Katherine McKenna, "Options for Elite Women in Early Upper Canadian Society," paper given at the CHA (Winnipeg, 1986); Naomi Griffiths, *Penelope's Web: Some Perceptions in European and Canadian Society* (Toronto: Oxford University Press, 1976).

13. Ryan, *The Cradle of the Middle Class*, 20. For a discussion of the legal position of women in nineteenth-century Canada, see Constance Backhouse, *Petticoats and Prejudice: Women and Law in Nineteenth Century Canada* (Toronto: The Women's Press, 1991).

14. Barbara Welter, "The Cult of True Womanhood," *American Quarterly* 18 (1966), 150-174. See also: Nancy Cott, *The Bonds of Womanhood: 'Woman's Sphere' in New England, 1780-1835* (New Haven, Conn.: Yale University Press, 1977); and Leonore Davidoff and Catherine Hall, *Family Fortunes: Men and Women of the English Middle Class* (Chicago: Chicago University Press, 1987).

15. For biographical material on these and other women, *see*: McKenna, "Options for Elite Women"; Fowler, *The Embroidered Tent*; Patrick Brode, *The Bone and the Sinew* (Toronto: University of Toronto Press, 1986); Katherine McKenna, "Anne Powell and the Early York Elite," in S.F. Wise et al., eds., *None Was Ever Better* (Cornwall: Ontario Historical Society, 1984), 31-43. See also: Barbara Maas, *Helpmates of Man: Middle Class Women and Gender Ideology in Nineteenth Century Ontario* (Bochum: Universitatsverlag Dr. N. Brockmeyer, 1990).

16. Peter Russell, "Attitudes Towards Social Mobility in Upper Canada," Ph.D. thesis, Carleton University, 1981, 315.

17. McKenna, "Options for Elite Women," 23, 21.

18. This comes from preliminary work I have done with Upper Canadian newspapers 1793-1830. See also: Leo Johnson, "The Political Economy of Ontario Women in the Nineteenth Century," in Janice Acton et al., eds., *Women at Work: Ontario 1850-1930* (Toronto: Women's Educational Press, 1974); Russell, "Attitudes Towards Social Mobility"; Jane Errington, "The Softer Sex: Rhetoric and Reality of Women's Experiences in Upper Canada," unpublished working paper, 1986. In *Women's Work, Markets and Economic Development in Nineteenth Century Ontario* (Toronto: University of Toronto Press, 1988), Marjorie Griffin Cohen discusses the significance of women's labour to both the maintenance of the family and the accumulation of capital.

19. Alison Prentice, "The Feminization of Teaching," in *Neglected Majority*, Vol. 1, 52. See also: Ruby Heap and Alison Prentice, eds., *Gender and Education in Ontario* (Toronto: Canadian Scholars Press, 1991); Alison Prentice and Marjorie R. Theobold, eds., *Women Who Taught* (Toronto: University of Toronto Press, 1991); Susan E. Houston and Alison Prentice, *Schooling and*

Scholars in Nineteenth Century Ontario (Toronto: University of Toronto Press, 1988).

20. Prentice, "Feminization of Teaching," 65.

21. Johnson, "Political Economy of Ontario Women." For a discussion of some of the alternatives to marriage open to Quebec women, *see*: Marta Danylewycz, *Taking the Veil* (Toronto: McClelland and Stewart, 1987).

22. *See*: P. Malcolmson, "The Poor in Kingston, 1815-1857," in G. Tulchinsky, ed., *To Preserve and Defend* (Montreal: McGill-Queen's University Press, 1976); S. Houston, "The Impetus to Reform," Ph.D. thesis, University of Toronto, 1974.

23. Sylvia Van Kirk, "The Role of Native Women in the Fur Trade Society of Western Canada, 1670-1830," in *Rethinking Canada*, 61. Van Kirk notes that Indian women made the moccasins worn by all in the West at the time, ensured an adequate supply of pemmican, and were frequently called upon to assist in paddling and steering traders' and explorers' canoes. For a full discussion of the fur-trade society, *see*: Van Kirk, *Many Tender Ties: Women in Fur Trade Society* (Winnipeg: Watson and Dwyer, 1980).

24. Beth Light and Joy Parr, eds., *Canadian Women on the Move 1867-1920* (Toronto: New Hogtown Press and OISE, 1983), 3. *See also*: Sara Brooks Sundberg, "Farm Women on the Canadian Prairies Frontier," in *Rethinking Canada*; The Corrective Collective, *Never Done: Three Centuries of Women's Work* (Toronto: Women's Educational Press, 1974); Linda Rasmussen et al., eds., *A Harvest Yet to Reap: A History of Prairie Women* (Toronto: Women's Educational Press, 1976). For examples of women's activities in the U.S. West, *see*: Sandra L. Myers, *Westering Women and the Frontier Experience, 1800-1915* (Albuquerque: University of New Mexico Press, 1982); and Julie Jeffrey, *Frontier Women: The TransMississippi West, 1840-1880* (New York: Hill and Wang, 1979).

25. Marjorie Cohen, "The Decline of Women in Canadian Dairying," in *The Neglected Majority*, Vol.2, 73.

26. For a brief overview of the impact of industrialization on Canadian society and its women, *see*, among others, Light and Parr, *Canadian Women on the Move*; Acton et al., *Women at Work*; Wayne Roberts, *Honest Womanhood: Feminism, Femininity and Class Consciousness Among Toronto Working Women* (Toronto: New Hogtown Press, 1976).

27. Alice Klein and Wayne Roberts, "Besieged Innocence: The 'Problem' and Problems of Working Women," in *Women at Work*; S.M. Trofimenkoff, "One Hundred and Two Muffled Voices," and Graham S. Lowe, "Women, Work and the Office: The Feminization of Clerical Occupations in Canada, 1901-1931," in *Rethinking Canada;* Pat Armstrong and Hugh Armstrong, *The Double Ghetto* (Toronto: McClelland and Stewart, 1984).

28. Joan Sangster, "The 1907 Bell Telephone Strike: Organizing Women Workers," in *Rethinking Canada*; Klein and Roberts, "Besieged Innocence," in

Women at Work; Roberts, *Honest Womanhood*; Gail Cuthbert Brandt, "Weaving It Together: Life Cycle and the Industrial Experience of Female Cotton Workers," in *The Neglected Majority*, Vol. 2.

29. Veronica Strong-Boag, "Canada's Women Doctors," in Linda Kealey, ed., *A Not Unreasonable Claim: Women and Reform in Canada, 1880s to 1920s* (Toronto: Women's Educational Press, 1979).

30. Judi Coburn, "I See and Am Silent: A Short History of Nursing in Ontario," in *Women at Work*.

31. The progressive age, as it is known in the United States, is ably described in Robert Weibe, *The Search for Order* (New York: Hill and Wang, 1967). For the Canadian context, *see*: Robert Craig Brown and Ramsay Cook, *Canada 1896-1921* (Toronto: McClelland and Stewart, 1974), and the introduction to *A Not Unreasonable Claim*.

32. Veronica Strong-Boag, "Setting the Stage: National Organization and the Women's Movement in the Late 19th Century," in *The Neglected Majority*, Vol. 1, 88.

33. Ibid., 92.

34. Marie Lavigne, Yolande Pinard, and Jennifer Stoddart, "The Fédération Nationale Saint-John-Baptiste and the Women's Movement in Quebec," in *A Not Unreasonable Claim*. For a history of Quebec Women, see *Quebec Women: A History* written by the Clio Collective and translated by Roger Gannon and Rosalind Gill (Toronto: The Women's Press, 1987).

35. Strong-Boag, "Setting the Stage"; Wendy Mitchinson, "The WCTU, 'For God, Home and Nationhood': A Study of Nineteenth Century Feminism," in *A Not Unreasonable Claim*.

36. Kealey, *A Not Unreasonable Claim*, 8.

37. Ibid.

38. Social feminism in this context is sometimes also referred to as "maternal feminism." *See*: Kealey, *A Not Unreasonable Claim*, 7-8.

39. Susan Mann Trofimenkoff, "Feminism, Nationalism and the Clerical Defence," in *Rethinking Canada*, 136; Lavigne, Pinard, and Stoddart, "The Fédération"; Trofimenkoff, "Henri Bourassa and 'The Woman Question,'" in *A Not Unreasonable Claim*, 79.

40. Emily Stowe to Premier of Ontario, 1889, quoted in Wayne Roberts, "Rocking the Cradle for the World: The New Woman and Maternal Feminism," in *A Not Unreasonable Claim*, 20.

41. Strong-Boag, "Setting the Stage," 101-103.

42. Carol Bacchi, "Divided Allegiance: The Response of Farm and Labour Women to Suffrage," in *A Not Unreasonable Claim*, 106-107.

43. Roberts, "Rocking the Cradle for the World"; Klein and Roberts, "Besieged Innocence"; Lori Rotenberg, "The Wayward Worker: Toronto's Prostitutes at the Turn of the Century," in *Women at Work*; Trofimenkoff, "One Hundred and Two Muffled Voices"; Christine Simmons, "'Helping the Poorer

Sisters': The Women of the Jost Mission, Halifax, 1905-1945," in *Rethinking Canada*; Lavigne, Pinard, and Stoddart, "The Fédération;" Mitchinson, "The WCTU."

44. For the most comprehensive account of the fight for the vote, *see*: Catherine Clevedon, *The Woman Suffrage Movement in Canada,* 2nd edition (Toronto: University of Toronto Press, 1974).

45. *See*, for example, Roberts, "Rocking the Cradle," 40-41; Strong-Boag, "'Ever a Crusader': Nellie McClung, First Wave Feminist," in *Rethinking Canada*; Bacchi, "Divided Allegiances"; Lavigne, Pinard, and Stoddart, "The Fédération."

46. Bacchi, "Divided Allegiances," 102.

47. Mitchinson, "The WCTU," 159.

48. Strong-Boag, "'Ever a Canadian,'" 182.

49. Lavigne, Pinard, and Stoddart, "The Fédération," 80.

50. Ceta Ramkhalawansingh, "Women During the Great War," in *Women at Work.*

51. Veronica Strong-Boag, "The Girl of the New Day," in Michael Cross and Gregory Kealey, eds., *Readings in Canadian Social History 4* (Toronto: McClelland and Stewart, 1985), 169.

52. Ibid.; Marilyn Barber, "The Women Ontario Welcomed," in *The Neglected Majority,* Vol. 2; Genevieve Leslie, "Domestic Service in Canada, 1880-1890," in *Women at Work*; Barbara Roberts, "A Work of Empire: Canadian Reformers and British Female Immigration," in *A Not Unreasonable Claim.*

53. Mary Vipond, "The Image of Women in Mass Circulation Magazines in the 1920s," in *The Neglected Majority,* Vol. 1; *see also*: Strong-Boag, "Girl of the New Day."

54. Sylvia Bashevkin, "Independence versus Partisanship: Dilemmas in the Political History of Women in English Canada," in *Rethinking Canada,* 254.

55. Roberts, "Rocking the Cradle," 43-44.

56. Bashevkin, "Independence versus Partisanship," 262.

57. Catherine MacLeod, "Women in Production," in *Women at Work*; Anne Woywitka, "A Pioneering Woman in the Labour Movement," in *Rethinking Canada*; Strong-Boag, "The Girl of the New Day"; Gail Cuthbert Brandt, "Weaving It Together."

58. For an account of women in World War II, *see*: Ruth Roach Pierson, *"They're Still Women After All": The Second World War and Canadian Womanhood* (Toronto: McClelland and Stewart, 1986).

59. Pierson, "Women's Emancipation and the Recruitment of Women into the Labour Force," in *The Neglected Majority,* Vol. 1, 144.

60. Bashevkin, "Independence versus Partisanship," 263.

61. Julie White, "It's Good, It's Bad: The Contradictions," in *Rethinking Canada,* 226.

62. Bashevkin, "Independence versus Partisanship," 264.

SUGGESTED READINGS

Armstrong, Pat, and Hugh Armstrong, *The Double Ghetto: Canadian Women and Their Segregated Work,* 2nd edition. Toronto: McClelland and Stewart, 1984.

Cohen, Marjorie Griffin, *Women's Work, Markets, and Economic Development in Nineteenth Century Ontario.* Toronto: University of Toronto Press, 1988.

Gorham, Deborah, "The Canadian Suffragists," in Gwen Matheson, ed., *Women in the Canadian Mosaic.* Toronto: Peter Martin Associates, 1976.

Griffiths, Naomi, *Penelope's Web.* Toronto: Oxford University Press, 1976.

Kealey, Linda, ed., *A Not Unreasonable Claim: Women and Reform in Canada, 1880s-1920s.* Toronto: Women's Educational Press, 1979.

Light, Beth, and Joy Parr, eds., *Canadian Women on the Move, 1867-1920.* Toronto: New Hogtown Press and OISE, 1983.

Parr, Joy, *The Gender of Breadwinners: Women, Men and Change in Two Industrial Towns 1880-1950.* Toronto: University of Toronto Press, 1990.

Prentice, Alison, and Susan Mann Trofimenkoff, eds., *The Neglected Majority.* Vol. 2. Toronto: McClelland and Stewart, 1985.

Strong-Boag, Veronica, and Anita Clair Fellman, eds., *Rethinking Canada: The Promise of Women's History.* Toronto: Copp Clark Pitman, 1986. 2nd ed., 1991.

Trofimenkoff, Susan Mann, and Alison Prentice, eds., *The Neglected Majority.* Vol. 1. Toronto: McClelland and Stewart, 1977.

Chapter Three

First Nations Women and Government Policy, 1970-92: Discrimination and Conflict

≈≈≈≈≈≈≈≈≈≈≈≈≈≈≈≈≈≈≈≈≈≈≈≈≈≈≈≈≈≈≈≈≈≈≈≈≈≈≈

In March 1992 a nationally televised forum on First Peoples and the Canadian Constitution highlighted a generation of conflict over the rights of First Nations women.[1] The conflict was primarily over equality of Indian rights for Indian women or, more specifically, the denial of those rights. In the early 1950s, Mary Two-Axe Early, a Mohawk woman from Kahnawake, near Montreal, had raised the issue of discriminatory treatment of Indian women in the Indian Act.[2] But the special problems facing Indian women did not become publicly visible until the early 1970s, when the women's movement for equal rights clashed forcefully with the Indian movement for special rights. During those years the demands of Indian women were supported not only by their own organizations, but also by non-Native women's groups and by the Native Council of Canada (NCC), the national body representing non-status Indians – persons not recognized as 'Indians' under the Indian Act – and nearly half the status Indian population that lives off reserves.

A generation later, however, as the March 1992 forum illustrated, First Nations women were still struggling to achieve equal rights as members of the First Nations. Although they had repeatedly rejected the claim that the male-dominated aboriginal political organizations spoke for them, the government had yet to recognize the right of Indian women to represent their own interests in policy matters. Just before the March forum opened, First Nations politicians had made a significant political gain by securing federal agreement that aboriginal leaders of the four major organizations (status Indian, non-status Indian, Inuit, Metis) could participate directly with premiers and territorial leaders in the upcoming talks to reform the Canadian constitution (March-August 1992). Gail Stacey Moore, the head of the Native Women's Association of Canada (NWAC), the national voice of aboriginal women,[3] had requested similar participation for her organization to ensure that aboriginal women's interests were protected. But the government did not concede to her request.[4]

The basic policy conflict at the March forum was not over First Nations self-government, for all Native groups agreed on entrenching self-government in the Canadian constitution as an inherent right of aboriginal peoples. Rather, the tension centred on whether the Charter of Rights and Freedoms should apply to Indian self-government.[5] The Assembly of First Nations (AFN), the political organ representing the five hundred thousand status Indians in Canada, opposed the application on the grounds that the Charter reflected alien cultural values and that it continued the colonial oppression of First Nations. The Native Women's Association insisted that all future Indian self-government regimes be subject to the Charter of Rights to ensure equal treatment of women and men. An alternative approach to secure equality for women under these regimes was to develop the oft-mooted Aboriginal Charter of Rights. If this were to materialize, the NWAC would consider it, but until then the NWAC would hold that the Canadian Charter was essential to enforce equality.[6] Although the relationship between the Charter and self-government remained a matter for future determination, the March forum ended with little doubt that many aboriginal women were relying on the Charter to guarantee them equality of rights and treatment under any new First Nations governments.

First Nations women had reason to distrust vague assurances that they would receive equal access to Indian rights and benefits. For over a century they had suffered legal discrimination in the Indian Act, the federal statute under which the federal government manages Indian Affairs in Canada. The Act's provisions on legal status and band membership contained section 12(1)(b), which caused an Indian woman who married a non-Indian to lose her legal status as Indian under the Act.[7] In contrast, an Indian man who married a non-Indian not only retained his legal status and band membership, but also transmitted status and membership to his white wife and their children under the Act through section 11(1)(f). The losses Indian women experienced on becoming 'non-status women' were wide-ranging, with legal, social, cultural, economic, and political consequences. In the broadest terms, as Native journalist Theresa Nahanee noted, these women lost their aboriginal "nationality."[8] The denigrating treatment accorded Indian women was graphically depicted by Cecilia Dore, from Kahnawake, Quebec, who pointedly observed that dogs owned by non-Indian people could be buried in a pet cemetery on her reserve, but Indian women born on that reserve were denied the same right because of 12(1)(b). Her point was simple but powerful: "Dead pets are better treated with more respect than the Indian woman who has married a non-Indian!"[9]

The losses Indian women suffered could be devastating, and the disabilities hurt not only them but also their children. Specifically, on marriage to a non-Indian the Indian woman became 'non-status' and lost:

- her legal status as 'Indian' under the Indian Act
- her band membership
- the right to transmit legal status and band membership to her children
- her right to reside on her reserve – her own community
- her right to own land on her reserve
- her right to inherit property on her reserve
- her freedom from land, inheritance, and income taxes as a band resident
- her right to vote for, and hold office in, her band council
- her right to vote in band referendums
- her right to collect band annuities
- her right to collect treaty payments
- the benefits of special government programs for reserve residents
- the benefits of special government programs for off-reserve Indians
- the ability to raise her children in her own cultural community
- the right to return home if her marriage broke down
- the right to be buried on her home reserve.

The exclusion of non-status women from their families and communities was felt as much psychologically as legally. And even when their band councils gave them permission to reside on their reserves, they were sometimes subjected to even more abuse, at times from 'married-in' white women. As Mavis Goeres, a Tobique woman from New Brunswick, recalled:

> Something I don't think other people are aware of, though, is the *hurt* that comes with it. No white woman actually came up and said anything to me personally, but there is one married to a man on this reserve that came up to my friend, Lilly Harris. Lilly had got up to say something at a band meeting, and this woman said, "Aw shut up! You non-status don't have nothing to say here." That hurt. [10]

This discrimination on the basis of sex and marital status had become law as part of the evolving Indian Act in 1869. [11] When the last major changes were made to the Indian Act, in 1951, these provisions remained intact. To understand them it is necessary to understand both the male bias of Victorian Euro-Canadian culture and the connection in government policy between Indian reserve lands and band membership.

Briefly, British colonial authorities had established the reserve system in Canada to provide a land base for the exclusive use and occupancy of Indian bands. The intent was to open Indian territory for white settlers while ensuring that sufficient land was set aside for Indian economic survival. Reserves also served the broader policy goal of protecting Indians by segregating them from the evils of white civilization until they could defend their own interests.[12] The ultimate policy goal was assimilation, and to achieve a "civilized" condition, Indian men were to abandon hunting and trapping and adopt farming as their livelihood. They would do so more effectively, the government reasoned, if white men were not allowed to control reserve lands. As some whites continued to purchase or occupy Indian lands, the government took measures to protect the lands by defining in law more precisely who it regarded as legally Indian under the Indian Act (that is, as having legal status), and who, therefore, was entitled to reside on reserve lands held by his or her band.

The first legal definitions of Indian persons appeared in the 1850 Indian Protection Acts of Upper and Lower Canada. These definitions were broadly framed and inclusive: the criteria of legal status were Indian descent and band membership as recognized by the Indian community. In addition, all persons married to band members, all persons adopted in infancy by band members, and all residents who had one Indian parent were regarded as 'Indian.'[13] As white depredations of Indian lands persisted, the government tightened the criteria on intermarriage to exclude the white husbands of Indian women. This was the government's intent in devising the 1869 provisions. Its precise objective, in the words of the Superintendent General of Indian Affairs at the time, was clearly one of "preventing men not of Indian Blood having by marrying Indian women either through their Wives or Children any pretext for Settling on Indian lands."[14]

In keeping with the colonial nature of nineteenth-century Indian administration in Canada, government policy on Indian status was decided within government and without including the views of Indian bands, whose opinions were neither seriously sought nor respected if offered.[15] Legal definitions of Indian status, like Indian policy in general, reflected Euro-Canadian values, in this instance those on gender, kin relations, and property. Thus in 1876 when the government consolidated all Indian legislation into one statute called the Indian Act, it kept the 1869 provisions [12(1)(b)], but it went further by adopting the patrilineal principle of descent to determine Indian status: legal status was now transmitted exclusively in the male line from one generation to the next.[16] Legal status and band membership were linked together, and residence became patrilocal: the woman resided with her husband and his band. As a result, the federal government's definition of legal status officially replaced traditional Indian customs for determining band membership. Aboriginally,

First Nations in Canada had determined the membership in their tribes by a variety of principles of descent, marriage, residence, and adoption. Traditionally, the predominant principle of descent among the tribes was bilateral in that descent was traced equally through *both* the mother's and the father's relatives. Next most common was matrilineal descent, the tracing of descent through the female line. Patrilineal descent was much less common. [17]

Through the Indian Act, Canada imposed on all bands a uniform system of criteria for band membership and legal status. This national law systematically discriminated against Indian women. At the official level it also denied bands the choice of retaining their aboriginal traditions of tribal membership. And it equally denied them any influence in determining the criteria for relinquishing Indian status, a process known as "enfranchisement" because when they lost Indian status Indians gained the franchise to vote federally. More accurately, this process disenfranchised Indians from their own aboriginal nations.

In the century after the 1869-76 amendments on Indian status, these provisions remained largely unchanged in the Indian Act. [18] During those generations, many bands became politically socialized to the Act's prescriptions. As NWAC noted: "By 1971, this patriarchal system was so ingrained within our communities, that 'patriarchy' was seen as a 'traditional trait.' Even the memory of our matriarchal forms of government, and our matrilineal forms of descent were forgotten or unacknowledged." [19]

With the emergence of the women's movement for equality in Canada in the late 1960s, enfranchised First Nations women were no longer willing to suffer unequal treatment in law and in practice. But their struggle to gain equality as First Nations persons was a long and at times discouraging experience both individually and collectively. The personal legal battles of Jeannette Lavell, an Ojibwa woman from Ontario, and Yvonne Bedard, a Six Nations Iroquois woman from southern Ontario, were widely publicized in the early 1970s, as was that of Sandra Lovelace, a Maliseet from New Brunswick in the early 1980s. All three women lost their Indian status and band membership under section 12(1)(b), and all three sought to regain status and remove the sexist provisions in the Act. The perseverance of these and other First Nations women to secure reforms was put into perspective by Gail Stacey Moore when she stated:

> These Aboriginal women of the 1970s never wavered in their battle for sexual equality. The Aboriginal women of the 1990s whom we represent, also, will never give up the struggle for sexual equality. What we are saying here today is that this struggle includes the right to represent ourselves in constitutional discussions. We want to

remind you that our women of the 1970s took their struggle to the international arena, to national meetings every year from 1971 to 1985, to feminist meetings, to Parliament and finally to the streets and highways.[20]

Pressures exerted by non-status women on the federal government persisted, and changes finally came in 1985 when that government was forced to amend the Act's contentious membership provisions by the imminent application of section 15 of the Charter of Rights to the Indian Act. Some of the changes brought about by Bill C-31, *An Act to Amend the Indian Act,*[21] addressed long-standing problems. But others introduced new and equally disturbing discriminatory provisions.

The First Pressures for Change:
The Judicial Arena, 1970-73

The first event to place the issue of discrimination against Indian women on the national stage was the 1970 report of the Royal Commission on the Status of Women. The Commission, appointed in 1967 to assess the status of women in the federal domain, was concerned about the high number of involuntary enfranchisements of Indian women resulting from 12(1)(b) compared to the much lower number of Indian male and female voluntary enfranchisements: between 1958 and 1968 there were 4,605 women who were involuntarily enfranchised under 12(1)(b) compared to only 891 adult Indians of both sexes who voluntarily enfranchised under other provisions of the Act.[22] The report recommended a more equal treatment of Indian women under circumstances of intermarriage by amending 12(1)(b) "to allow an Indian woman upon marriage to a non-Indian to (a) retain her Indian status and (b) transmit her Indian status to her children."[23] The government's failure to implement these recommendations clearly disappointed some non-status Indian women. Impatient with the lack of reform and motivated by certain local-level circumstances, two Indian women enfranchised under 12(1)(b) decided independently to take their case to the courts for redress.

The first woman, Jeannette Corbiere Lavell, is an Ojibwa born as a member of the Wikwemikong band on Manitoulin Island in southern Ontario. Lavell, living in Toronto where the women's rights movement was becoming active, had lost her Indian status in 1970 when she married a non-Indian. In 1971 her lawyer argued that section 12(1)(b) of the Indian Act was sexually discriminatory in violation of the equality clause in the 1960 Canadian Bill of Rights. The court, however, was not sympathetic to the issue, and the judge made it clear that he felt the matter rightly belonged in the political arena: "If Section 12(1)(b) is distasteful or undesirable to Indians, they themselves can arouse public conscience and thereby stimulate parliament by legislative amendment to correct any unfairness or injustice."[24] Lavell lost her case in the lower court, but succeeded on appeal,[25] by which time the second case was in progress.

Yvonne Bedard had been born on the Six Nations reserve near Brantford, in southern Ontario.[26] In 1964 she had married a non-Indian and moved away from the reserve until 1970 when she separated from her husband. She then returned to the reserve with her two children to live in the house that had been willed to her by her mother. The band council had given her permission to reside on the reserve for a year, during which time she was expected, according to the provisions in the Indian Act, to dispose of her property, which as a non-status Indian she was no longer entitled to inherit. She obtained an extension of her permit to reside from the band council, but when it expired and the band council decided she must vacate the reserve, she feared eviction and her lawyer took her case to the court. He argued, among other things, that 12(1)(b) violated the Bill of Rights. Bedard won her case on the recent precedent set by Lavell, but the federal Minister of Justice, John Turner, appealed both decisions to the Supreme Court of Canada, claiming that the consequences of the rulings were so far-reaching that greater clarification was required from the court.[27]

Both women had initiated court proceedings on their own, and they received no support from their communities, their band councils, or their regional and national Indian political organizations. The once matrilineal and matrilocal Iroquois, for example, had become so acculturated to the principle of male dominance in the Indian Act that their regional organization, the Association for Iroquois and Allied Indians (AIAI) based in southern Ontario, pressed the Minister of Indian Affairs to retain 12(1)(b): "It is the legal and moral duty of the husband to support his wife. Consequently by the Indian Act, the Indian woman lost her Indian status and took the status of the husband. This section in the Indian Act was merely a legislative embodiment of what had become Indian custom."[28]

Bedard had temporarily required social assistance, and Indian band councils had a valid concern about the financial drain on their already inadequate finances if many enfranchised women returned home in need of social aid. But some Chiefs went further and belittled the efforts of women to seek equality, claiming their actions were influenced by feminists or motivated by "do-gooders."[29] Status women were no more sympathetic to the plight of their enfranchised sisters than the men. The most vocal criticism came from status women in Saskatchewan and Alberta.[30] They firmly opposed Lavell's efforts and supported the Indian Act's patrilineal-patrilocal principles, arguing that these reflected traditional First Nations customs.[31] Often, the loss of status under 12(1)(b) was regarded by many First Nations people as a voluntary act whose consequences were well known and justified.[32] As one Six Nations woman said of Yvonne Bedard's circumstance: "You have made your bed – now lie in it."[33] In fact, many First Nations women were unaware of the legal consequences of intermarriage.

When the Lavell-Bedard cases were heard jointly before the Supreme Court of Canada in early 1973, the court was packed with supporters of women's rights and Indian rights. Protests occurred outside while the media gave national coverage to the cases. The issue was seen politically as women's rights versus Indian rights, but the public sentiment was clearly on the side of the Indian movement. The established male-dominated Indian political organizations, headed by the National Indian Brotherhood (NIB), the parent organization to the current AFN, opposed the women in court, showing unusual political unity on the issue. Although the NIB acknowledged that the membership provisions of the Act needed revision, it advocated a parliamentary and not a judicial route for change.[34]

The NIB concern over the case reflected not only the male bias in the contemporary political culture of First Nations, but also the recent political trauma of the 1969 White Paper. In June 1969 the Trudeau Liberal government had proposed a policy of legal equality for all Indians in Canada. This was to be achieved by abolishing the special Indian rights and their relationship with the federal government.[35] The reserves, the treaties, the federal government's jurisdiction over Indians under 91(24) of the BNA Act, the Indian Act, and the Department of Indian Affairs were all to be terminated, and responsibility for Indians was to be transferred to the historically distrusted provinces. The proposal came as a massive shock to First Nations political leaders, who had been led to expect a revision of the Indian Act, discussed in a year-long series of consultation meetings between Indian bands and the government. The duplicity of the government's actions fuelled the rapid mobilization of Indians to reject the White Paper. In their counterproposal called the 'Red Paper,' Indian leaders demanded that future policies be developed jointly between Indian leaders and government.[36] Pierre Trudeau suspended the policy in June 1970.[37] But the White Paper had already, unintentionally, focused Indian discontent and become the single major catalyst to the contemporary Indian movement for special rights and self-determination – the very outcome the government had sought to avoid. Although First Nations people had no desire to retain the Indian Act in its current form, they did value the rights and protections it embodied – rights that differed from those in treaties, land-claim settlements, and the Canadian constitution. The NIB's more immediate concern was that the Lavell case might lead to the abolition of the entire Indian Act on the grounds of previous case law saying it was racist legislation in violation of the Bill of Rights. This would bring about a major loss of Indian rights akin to that proposed by the infamous White Paper: in short, a judicial rather than a political abolition of Indian rights. This fear caused the NIB and almost all of the provincial Indian organizations to intervene against Lavell and Bedard at the Supreme Court level. The Indian Association of Alberta led the movement to oppose the Indian women, but the original decision to intervene, even at the lower court level, was not without political cost, as Harold Cardinal recalled: "We realized when we decided to intervene that we would, of course, alienate the feminist movement, and that we would also lose some of our traditional public support. It proved one hell of a mess to get into, because no matter what we did, everyone got mad at us, and it was difficult to maintain a sane and rational discussion on the issues involved."[38]

In contrast, those supporting the Indian women were fewer in number, less well funded, and less well organized politically. The supportive Indian Rights for Indian Women (IRIW), the activist organization formed in 1972 that would spearhead the 12(1)(b) issue in the 1970s, had yet to become legally incorporated and was consequently unable to intervene formally in the proceedings. But the Native Council of Canada fully supported the two women, just as it has generally supported non-status women since then.

The court's judgment, released in August 1973, was hailed as a victory for the Indian rights movement and a major loss for Indian women. The decision was regarded by lawyers and legal academics as "virtually unintelligible" and "baffling" in its conclusion that section 12(1)(b) was not discriminatory and therefore not in violation of the Bill of Rights.[39] The contentious 12(1)(b) provisions remained operative. The judgment's convoluted reasoning and "narrow notion of equality" led some lawyers to question the court's "intellectual soundness."[40] But this did not alter the fact that the judicial forum, initially sympathetic to the Indian women's cases, had failed to deliver legal reform and social justice.[41]

First Nations women had, however, made one incontestable victory in these early years. The discriminatory provisions of the Indian Act were now public knowledge, and no tangled jurisprudence could undo that accomplishment. But Indian women were not yet participants in the political process; indeed, as one journalist succinctly put it, this was "a time when the status of Indian women is being decided by everyone but Indian women – including the courts, the politicians, the lawyers and Indian men."[42]

Progress Stalls in the Political Forum, 1974-81

When the Supreme Court failed to offer redress, further attempts to eliminate sexual discrimination in the Indian Act were necessarily consigned to political channels. This was not a hopeful prospect, because Indian women in the mid-1970s were not politically organized on a national scale, and the two national organizations they had established (IRIW and NWAC) reflected the deep division among First Nations women over 12(1)(b). IRIW, originally composed mainly of enfranchised women, fought firmly for the removal of 12(1)(b), whereas the more politically conservative Native Women's Association focused on social and economic issues in those years. These bodies were also subject to internal conflicts over funding. [43] The financial tensions were partly due to the federal government's funding policy, which required both status and non-status membership in any woman's association it supported, thereby combining the protagonists in the discrimination issue. [44] Furthermore, in the three years following the Supreme Court judgment in Lavell, neither the federal government nor the NIB gave the matter serious attention.

In the aftermath of the 1969 White Paper, the NIB gave political priority to questions of treaty and aboriginal rights, education, and other matters. And in 1974 the federal government and the NIB created an unprecedented experiment in joint policy-making called the Joint Cabinet/NIB Committee. [45] This innovative structure linked together the executive of the NIB with several federal cabinet ministers for the purpose of developing mutually acceptable policies for Indians. But the government also intended the Joint Committee to be a conflict-management device to contain rising Indian militancy in mid-1974. Consequently, the federal government had little desire to antagonize the NIB by pressing forward with reforms on Indian women in the Joint Committee. The government had already promised the NIB that it would not change parts of the Act until the entire Act was revised. It had also promised the NIB not to introduce amendments to Parliament without clearing the changes first through the Joint Committee. [46]

In 1975 the Joint Committee had begun work on revisions to the Indian Act, using a working document prepared by the Indian Association of Alberta in 1974. These proposals were generally hard-line. For example, in a mixed marriage the non-Indian spouse was not to gain status, although the Indian spouse would retain status. Also, in a mixed marriage the non-Indian spouse was not to have residence rights, although the Indian spouse could return to the reserve if the marriage ended in death or divorce. Finally, children of mixed marriages were not to have status or membership. [47] Understandably, enfranchised Indian women were concerned about this approach. But the NIB denied requests by the IRIW and the NWAC to participate in the Joint Committee process. The NIB executive decided the issue of discrimination was a local one to be sorted out between the women and their band councils, [48] even though the NIB president, Noel Starblanket, publicly stated his personal belief that "12(1)(B) of the Indian Act is discriminatory and should be changed."[49] The NIB's exclusion of IRIW participation in the Joint Committee led to charges by MPs that the NIB was "unrepresentative" of Indian women[50] and to a more blunt conclusion by the new Human Rights Commissioner, Gordon Fairweather, who said, "The fact that they are not represented is itself discriminatory."[51]

By 1977 relations between the NIB and the government were becoming tense over several issues, but they were reaching the breaking point within the Joint Committee. The government had systematically evaded discussion of Indian *rights,* the central reason the NIB had proposed the Joint Committee process in the first place. Open confrontation finally occurred at a December 1977 meeting over Indian education rights. Ministers said they were unconvinced that Indians had the rights to education that the NIB had claimed. When the next agenda item, the status of Indian women, came forward, the NIB refused to discuss the matter, arguing that if Indian rights in general were uncertain, the rights of Indian women were even more tenuous.[52] When the Joint Committee collapsed in April 1978, due to the NIB's withdrawal, the issue of discrimination against Indian women remained unresolved. In fact, not a single policy agreement had been produced by the Joint Committee in its three and a half years of meeting.

By 1977 the government's failure to remove discrimination against Indian women was becoming increasingly difficult to defend in light of its own policy of equal rights for women and in the face of continuing pressure from various Native and non-Native groups for reform. With apparent government interest, Indian Rights for Indian Women spokespersons met informally with cabinet ministers in late 1977 to put forward a set of recommendations for change. The key ones were that:

1. all Indian women should keep their Indian status on marriage, and that no Indian woman should be evicted from a reserve until the Indian Act was amended.
2. Indian women who have lost status under 12(1)(b) should have their status and membership restored under a revised Indian Act.
3. all children of mixed marriages should be granted Indian status, and that the non-Indian spouse of any Indian should be allowed to live on the reserve.
4. Indians with one-quarter native ancestry should qualify for Indian status.[53]

The government agreed to fund the IRIW research program, but it made no concessions to the organization's proposals for change.

Additional criticism of the government's inaction arose during the passage of the federal Human Rights Act in 1977. Justice minister Ron Basford had been under increasing public pressure to amend the offensive sections of the Indian Act on women, but in 1977 the cabinet was still locked into the Joint Committee arrangement for discussing any changes to the Act. The government's solution to this dilemma, intended as a temporary one until the Act was amended – though it is still in effect today – was to exempt the Indian Act from the application of the Human Rights Act when it came into effect in 1978. This action fostered further criticism from the MPs in the Commons committee that reviewed the bill, but it served the government's purpose in pre-empting the possibility of Indian women using the new Human Rights Commission as a vehicle to secure reform. [54]

By 1977 frustrations were mounting among non-status women at the national level, but circumstances were no better at the local level, where individual Indian women who suffered from section 12(1)(b) continued to experience denial of their aboriginality, exclusion from their home communities, and hostility from many band councils as they sought support for change. In response to the unfair housing practices of the band council, several Maliseet women from the Tobique reserve in New Brunswick began to organize to press their case for adequate housing. [55] Against enormous odds of political inexperience, local resistance, and lack of funding, the 'Tobique women' became a force to be reckoned with. Their unfailing sense of humour and sheer grit kept them going in discouraging times. With mutual support and some funding from the United Church, as well as encouragement from non-status women leaders elsewhere in Canada, they carried their grievances to the national and international levels, where they mounted two highly publicized campaigns to renew public awareness and support for their case. The first was a hundred-mile protest march of Indian women from many parts of Canada. They gathered at Oka, near Montreal, and walked to Ottawa in July 1979 to demand better housing and reforms in the Indian Act. [56] Their encouraging reception by Joe Clark's Conservative government was heartening, but no reforms were instituted during his short tenure in office. [57]

The second initiative was undertaken by one of the Tobique women, Sandra Lovelace. Born on the Tobique reserve, Lovelace had married a non-Indian in 1970 and under section 12(1)(b) of the Indian Act had lost her legal status. When her marriage ended in divorce, she returned to live on the reserve with her children, but experienced difficulties in securing housing and other support services. With legal counsel from Professor Donald Fleming, an international rights lawyer, Lovelace took her case to the United Nations Committee on Human Rights in December 1977. She argued that Canada, because of section 12(1)(b), was in violation of certain family, minority, and sexual equality rights in the International Covenant on Political and Civil Rights. Specifically, she argued, "The major loss of a person ceasing to be an Indian is the loss of the cultural benefits of living in an Indian community, the emotional ties to home, family, friends and neighbours, and the loss of identity."[58] In July 1981 Sandra Lovelace won her case when the United Nations Committee used article 27 of the covenant to rule that Canada had contravened the international treaty because Lovelace was denied the right to live in her own cultural community.[59]

National media coverage of the Oka march in 1979 and the international exposure of the Lovelace case in 1981 stepped up pressure on the government to amend the Indian Act. So too did Jenny Margetts, the head of Indian Rights for Indian Women, when she asked the national Advisory Council on the Status of Women to help her organization document the discrimination suffered by Indian women for over a century. Her aim was to arouse public support for reforms, and the result was the publication of Kathleen Jamieson's book *Indian Women and the Law in Canada: Citizens Minus*, the first major study of the issue.[60] This account carefully substantiated the need for reform, while it provided politicians and the public with the first full record of discrimination against First Nations women. By 1978, as Jamieson noted, the issue of discrimination had reached an "impasse" between First Nations leaders and the government.[61]

When the Joint Cabinet/NIB Committee collapsed in early 1978, the Minister of Indian Affairs, Hugh Faulkner, remained firm in his commitment to revise the Indian Act. He especially wanted to introduce new powers for band governments in the Act. But other topics were to be included as well, among them the band membership provisions.[62] To focus the debate his officials released a "Discussion Paper" in June proposing changes in the Act, some of which originated in the discussions on the Indian Act in the Joint Committee. In June 1978 he discussed his plans with the NIB, hoping to secure its participation in the process,[63] and in the fall he published the proposals in the department's nationally distributed newsletter, *Indian News*, to precipitate public debate on the revisions.[64]

Faulkner's proposals for amending the membership sections of the Indian Act concentrated primarily on the sexually discriminatory provisions of 12(1)(b) and 11(1)(f). The proposals were general rather than detailed in scope, and they equalized the treatment of women and men. The key points were:

1. marriage would not alter legal status and band membership [Indian women would retain status and membership, and non-Indian spouses would not gain status and membership on marriage].

2. children of mixed marriages would have status and membership [all children of 50 per cent Indian ancestry would have status and membership].
3. enfranchisement would become "a free and personal choice" [compulsory enfranchisement of women would end].
4. a new category of persons called 'band beneficiaries' would be created. Band councils would define the criteria and benefits of this new category of persons in band by-laws, and this category might include:
   (a) grandchildren of mixed marriages (25 per cent Indian ancestry)
   (b) non-Indian spouses
   (c) non-Indian children adopted by Indian families.
5. no retroactive application of the amendments [no reinstatement of Indian women to legal status].[65]

The benefits to be granted the new category of "beneficiaries" might include residence on the reserve, inheritance of property on the reserve, participation in band government and band agencies (such as school boards), and government programs (such as housing, education). Faulkner's proposals introduced, in effect, a principle of 50 per cent Indian ancestry for legal status, applied in a bilateral descent system. The patrilineal-male bias of the historic legislation was replaced by a principle of treating women and men alike in respect to legal status, band membership, and enfranchisement provisions. To limit the size of the Indian status population, Faulkner's proposals excluded persons of one-quarter or less Indian ancestry. They also rejected the idea of the reinstatement of Indian women who had lost status and membership.[66] Retroactive amendments were seen to have many "practical" problems: increased financial cost to the government, increased pressure on Indian lands, the possibility of generating new inequities, setting a precedent for other groups discriminated against, and the expansion of Indian demands for redress in discriminatory provisions of the Act other than the 12(1)(b) and 11(1)(f) sections.[67] Under this scheme children of a quarter or less Indian ancestry had neither legal status nor band membership, but they might be classified as "band beneficiaries" if the bands desired. This new category was somewhat analogous to "landed immigrant status" in Canadian immigration policy in that beneficiaries would not be legal citizens but might have significant rights and benefits including those of residence, property, and certain government programs. Generally, the amendments were intended to prevent *future* inequities, not to correct historic ones. The rationale was: "It would be a difficult, if not impossible, task to right all the wrongs of past discrimination."[68]

Although Faulkner was personally committed to revising the Act, his proposals were essentially stillborn. The policy environment around the Indian women's issue in particular, and that around Indian affairs in general, shifted dramatically at the same time that Faulkner first made his proposals. That June Trudeau launched his initiative to reform the Canadian Constitution.[69] Almost immediately the NIB president, Noel Starblanket, made the constitution the NIB's top political priority. Whereas the NIB had refused in the past to negotiate Indian Act reforms until Indian rights were addressed in the Joint Committee, the NIB now rejected any government effort to promote Indian Act reform until Indian rights were entrenched, and possibly expanded, in a reformed Canadian constitution.

In 1980 and 1981 efforts by Faulkner's successor, John C. Munro (1980-84), similarly failed to secure NIB support for legislative reforms. Munro's proposals for optional self-government legislation were seen by the NIB as a diversionary tactic intended to deflect Indian attention and resources from their constitutional priority. In July 1980 Munro suspended 12(1)(b), and the recently controversial 12(1)(a)(iv) or "double-mother" clause, until legislative change occurred.[70] But cabinet, fearing that Munro's pursuit of the Indian Act reforms might endanger relations with First Nations in the constitutional arena, shelved Munro's Indian Act process in early 1981. In October 1981 a 'leaked' cabinet document proposing changes to eliminate sex discrimination was not simply a transparent effort to improve Canada's image in the wake of the United Nations ruling on Lovelace.[71] It tested the waters by proposing, for the first time, the reinstatement of enfranchised women. It also angered all Native political organizations in its secretive and unilateral preparation,[72] and it reflected growing concern within government over the financial costs of various options.[73] A commitment by the Minister Responsible for the Status of Women, Judy Erola, to remove the Indian Act's discriminatory provisions before the end of 1981 quickly evaporated in constitutional conflict. When the federal-provincial accord of November 5, 1981, removed aboriginal rights *and* women's rights from the Charter, powerful public protests were organized on Parliament Hill by advocates of both issues.[74] Both provisions were reinstated, on November 23, but not before major bitterness and distrust were created among aboriginal and women's groups. In the meantime, IRIW, the spearhead organization against 12(1)(b), virtually collapsed as a national body under the weight of internal political struggles and external funding conflict with the federal government.[75] In late December the government announced that changes to the Indian Act to remove sex discrimination would be pursued in the context of the new Charter of Rights – bringing on a new era of reform.

Generally, in the prepatriation phase of constitutional reform (1978-82), the NIB was preoccupied with reorganizing itself into the

Assembly of First Nations, a more representative national body for status Indians comprised of about six hundred band chiefs in Canada. And it was even more devoted to its lobbying efforts to entrench Indian rights in the Canadian Constitution.[76] By April 1982, when the new Canadian Constitution Act, 1982, came into force, the First Nations, indeed all aboriginal peoples, had made major advances. They had secured recognition of their treaty and aboriginal rights in section 35 of the Constitution, and in section 37 they secured the promise of a national First Ministers Conference (FMC) to be held within a year to identify and define the content of these rights.[77] In addition, section 15 of the Charter guaranteed equality before the law for all Canadians, prohibiting discrimination on the basis of sex and race, among other criteria.[78] The federal government had a three-year period after the enactment of the Charter on April 17, 1982, in which to remove all discriminatory legislation, including the membership provisions in the Indian Act.

The political arena of the late 1970s publicly recognized the blatant discrimination against Indian women. But the government was remarkably resistant to change, despite significant pressures from many sources including the government's own policy of sexual equality, the individual commitment of certain ministers and MPs to effect changes, the international concern about the Lovelace case, and the support of non-Indian organizations advocating human rights and women's rights. The government had defined the 'Indian women's problem' as 'an Indian problem' and locked its resolution into the politics and policy commitments of the Indian policy arena. That arena, at that time, was characterized by little forward action on any policy front, by the failure of consultation as a workable policy development instrument, and by the re-emergence of open conflict between First Nations leaders and the government over many policy issues, including budget cutbacks. Organizational changes on both sides – the federal elections of 1979 and 1980, and the NIB's restructuring into the AFN – absorbed further energies. In the end the Indian policy arena choked off any serious efforts to tackle the issue of discrimination against Indian women. Indian women's interests were seen as threatening to more general Indian interests, and to Indian-government relations, both of which took priority. But even then, Indian policy gains seemed brittle at times.

Liberal Government Efforts Under the Charter, 1982-84

In response to the Charter-imposed timetable, Munro moved ahead in August 1982 when his department published a booklet, *The Elimination of Sex Discrimination from the Indian Act*.[79] Intended to focus and inform discussion, it identified the "guiding principle" of reform: "Amendments will not discriminate on the basis of sex or marital status."[80] The federal government, it said, was determined to eliminate sex discrimination in the Act and similarly committed to consulting members of the First Nations because there was no consensus among them on the issue and because the consequences of change would be significant for them.[81] The booklet identified factors that would have to be resolved in removing discrimination against women, the now familiar (a) rights of the non-Indian spouse, (b) rights of the children and grandchildren, and (c) reinstatement. But the prime factor was one of agency: *who* would control the determination of status and membership, the government or the First Nations? For the first time in public debate, legal status was separated from band membership. On this basis, the booklet spelled out four possible options of control:

1. bands control status and membership
2. government controls status, and bands control membership
3. government controls status and membership unless bands opt for control
4. government controls status and membership.[82]

DIAND indicated no preference for any of these options, but the idea of distinguishing legal status from band membership was now in the policy arena for debate.

Also in early August, Munro mandated the House of Commons Standing Committee on Indian Affairs and Northern Development (SCIAND) to examine two issues: to recommend how *sex discrimination* could be eliminated from the Indian Act, and to recommend how Indian *self-government* could be developed in Canada.[83] Munro gave priority to Indian women and the Indian Act, stating that he wanted to receive the Standing Committee's report before Parliament resumed sitting in two months' time. But the Standing Committee under Liberal chairman Keith Penner bristled at the mandate. Although sympathetic to aboriginal peoples in general, the Committee was unhappy with the assignment because it had already recommended that its next task be an examination of "the Government of Canada's total financial and other relationships with Indian and Inuit people," including self-government, a goal partly reflecting the AFN's priorities.[84] Substantively, the Committee saw band membership as an integral part of the self-government issue and, like the AFN, felt the problem should be examined in that context.[85] The Native Women's Association of Canada, although supporting self-government, demanded action: "If band control of membership means Indian women must suffer under federal, discriminatory legislation for another five or twenty years while you hash out the meaning of Indian government, we will not accept this."[86] The Standing Committee appointed a Subcommittee to handle the sex-discrimination mandate, and after hurried consultations with major aboriginal organizations (such as AFN, NCC, NWAC), it reported on September 20, 1982, to the House of Commons.[87]

Despite affirmations of the importance of consultation, Munro's timetable excluded any meaningful participation by the First Nations. For the Subcommittee this was a highly reluctant exercise because the MPs clearly believed that membership should be under the control of the band "in accord with international standards."[88] However, the Subcommittee recognized the "urgency" for legislative changes as an interim measure until self-government was established.[89] Its recommendations for amending the Act accepted the distinction between legal status and band membership. Generally, the proposals were generous towards women and children. The major points in the report were:

1. marriage should not alter status;
2. 12(1)(b) women should be reinstated to status and membership;
3. children of 12(1)(b) women should be granted status and membership;
4. the matter of second-generation children (grandchildren) of mixed marriages should be studied further;
5. children of Indian males and females should be treated equally (legitimate and illegitimate);
6. bands should decide the rights of non-Indian spouses in future (for example, residency, legal, property, political);
7. the double-mother clause 12(1)(a)(iv) should be abolished;
8. the involuntary enfranchisement of the Indian wife and children when the husband enfranchises should be abolished;
9. Indian women should retain membership in their birth band when they marry an Indian of another band; the children should have the choice of either parent's band;
10. bands should be encouraged to develop their own membership codes in line with international standards;
11. parliament should provide adequate resources (funds, land, services) for all reinstated persons, for transitional programs, and for economic development programs;
12. research should be done on many issues, including the number of enfranchised women affected by the changes and the number of persons likely to be reinstated;
13. the Special Subcommittee (Penner) on Self-Government should examine further the issue of band control of membership and the status and membership of second-generation children of mixed marriages.[90]

This report departed from the previous approaches to reform in certain important ways. First, it proposed a more sizeable corrective measure by reinstating enfranchised women and their children to both status and membership, seemingly ignoring Faulkner's earlier concerns. Second, it served notice to the government that membership was a self-government matter in the opinion of both the AFN and the Subcommittee, and that amending the Indian Act was an inappropriate and unacceptable solution. Third, it endorsed the idea of distinguishing legal status from band membership, which was a significant step even though its ramifications were still unexplored. Fourth, it appeared to accede to the demands of the Native Women's Association that the Indian Act be amended to reinstate women *before* self-government was settled between aboriginal peoples and the government. Like Faulkner, the Subcommittee looked to the band council to determine the rights and benefits of non-Indian spouses. But unlike Faulkner's approach, the Subcommittee avoided the contentious issue of the status and membership of Indian persons with one-quarter or less Indian ancestry.

Munro was pleased with the "concrete" nature of the report's recommendations and the urgency it claimed for reform.[91] He expected the drafting of amendments to begin shortly. Meantime, the Standing Committee proceeded to its second task and established the Subcommittee on Self-Government, known as the Penner committee after its chairman, Liberal MP Keith Penner.

In Munro's presentation on self-government to the Penner committee, he proposed alternative legislation to the Indian Act to grant "band governments" greater delegated powers. The powers included those of determining band membership so long as the bands respected "acquired rights" (that is, rights granted under new legislation, and rights gained in the past by non-Indian women who married Indian men) and complied with the non-discriminatory provisions in the Canadian Constitution.[92] Munro did not use international standards to ensure compliance with acceptable principles as the Subcommittee recommended, presumably because these conventions applied unwanted criteria. Nor did he commit new government resources to bands in the form of funds, lands, or programs to support changes brought about by future amendments.

Munro's urgency to remove discriminatory provisions faltered once again when the Indian and government priority focused firmly on constitutional reform in the postpatriation series of First Ministers Conferences on Aboriginal Rights (1983-87). But the women's issue was not forgotten in this arena.[93] When the initial FMC was held in March 1983, the Canadian Constitution was amended by the addition of certain aboriginal provisions, among them section 35(4) of the Constitution, which stated: "Notwithstanding any other provision of this Act, the aboriginal and treaty rights referred to in subsection (I) are guaranteed equally to male and female persons."[94] Although Prime Minister Trudeau maintained, as did many in the federal government, that this amendment was unnecessary because section 15(I) already guaranteed equality rights for all Canadians,[95] it was at least a symbolic gain to ensure that Indian treaty and aboriginal rights were guaranteed to Indian women. The constitutional amendment, however, did not remove the sex discrimination from the Indian Act.

Following the spring 1983 FMC, little action occurred on the discrimination issue. When the Penner committee reported on self-government in October 1983, it placed band membership squarely in the jurisdiction of Indian governments. In moving from "band government" to "Indian government," the report suggested that First Nations should begin by defining "the true community identified with the band."[96] It said that "restrictive *Indian Act* definitions of membership would be inappropriate" for self-government: bands should determine their own membership by going beyond the band list if they wished and by incorporating persons who might be reinstated by legislative changes in the Act.[97] Bands should comply with international covenants on human rights and devise an appeal procedure. Band control over membership should be regarded not only as a right but also as "essential to ensure cultural, linguistic and ethnic survival" of First Nations peoples.[98] Like the Subcommittee on Indian Women and the Indian Act, the Penner committee found some merit in distinguishing legal status from band membership. Suggesting what would be referred to as "a two-tier system," the Penner report recommended that "the federal government consider using a general list as a means of providing special status to people who are Indian for purposes of Indian programs, but who are not included in the membership of an Indian First Nation."[99]

After the release of the Penner report, a flurry of political and bureaucratic activity occurred inside government as DIAND, Justice, and other central agencies responded to the Penner report (primarily negatively), prepared positions for the second FMC on aboriginal rights in March 1984, and drafted legislation on self-government.[100] To compound the confusion, in late February Trudeau announced his pending retirement (June), and John Munro launched an unsuccessful campaign for the Liberal leadership that inevitably diverted energies from his portfolio. Without consultation with First Nations, and amid the turmoil of the dying hours of the Trudeau government, on June 18, 1984, Munro introduced Bill C-47, the long-awaited amendments to remove sex discrimination from the Indian Act.

Munro's Bill C-47 proposed to abolish the discriminatory provisions in the Indian Act and to reinstate those who had lost status and membership under those sections.[101] "The challenge," he said, was to accomplish this "without worsening the social, cultural and economic condition of Indian communities."[102] The basic points in Bill C-47 were:

1. marriage should not alter status and membership;
2. all who lost rights under the discriminatory provisions will be reinstated to status and membership;
3. all first-generation children of reinstated persons will be granted status and membership;
4. second-generation children of reinstated persons will be granted status and membership if they had one status parent, or if they were born *after* these amendments take effect;
5. generally, all children of mixed marriages, "to one-quarter Indian blood," will have status and membership;
6. non-Indian spouses will have residency rights;
7. band councils will decide the other rights of non-Indian spouses or children in normal band council resolutions.[103]

Reinstatement was optional, and persons seeking it would go through a two-step procedure. When individuals applied, DIAND would assess their eligibility, and if they were successful DIAND officials would place their names on the "general list" kept by the department. In two years' time the names would automatically be transferred to the "band list" from which they had been removed at marriage. The two-year interval would give bands time to prepare for the effect of the amendments on their communities.[104] Funding, without specifying the amounts, would be available for programs for reinstated persons (the same programs then available to Indian individuals), the intent being "to avoid replacing one form of discrimination with another."[105] Funds would also be available "as practicable" to reserve communities for infrastructure, housing, and education, and for lands to be purchased to add to the reserve land-base.

Although Munro claimed that his Bill C-47 closely reflected the recommendations of the Subcommittee on Indian Women and the Indian Act, in fact it departed from that report in important ways. It used the old concept of the general list, but it did not separate legal status from band membership, other than in the transitional (two-year) reinstatement procedure. It also granted residency rights on the reserve to non-Indian spouses, whereas the Subcommittee had assigned residency rights to the determination of the band. It formally introduced the "one-quarter Indian blood" rule to determine status and membership in the future, its purpose being to avoid "infinite dilution of the Indian blood line."[106] It applied a less generous rule of 50 per cent Indian descent to the grandchildren of reinstated individuals. These "second-generation children" (grandchildren) of reinstated Indians could not have status unless one of their parents had legal status, or unless they were born after the proposed amendments came into force (July 1, 1984). This rule diminished the capacity of reinstated women to transmit status and band membership to their *already-born* descendants, in comparison with the capacity of existing status men and women to transmit status to their grandchildren. This more severe rule was rationalized as a way to reduce the financial cost of the changes, control the size of the reinstated population, and remove individuals who were distant from their Indian ancestry. [107] A final and significant feature of Bill C-47 was that it contained no provisions for bands to control their own membership or to influence reinstatement. The bill made no concessions whatsoever to the self-government that the Penner report and the Subcommittee on Indian Women and the Indian Act had recommended.

In the three days that Munro allotted for discussion of Bill C-47, it became quickly apparent that First Nations' reactions to it were largely negative, although for significantly different reasons. The re-emergent Indian Rights for Indian Women group criticized its use of a 'general list' to delay reinstatement of Indian women and children, demanding their immediate reinstatement to band membership and status. It was equally critical of the bill's differential and divisive impact on grandchildren. As Mary Two-Axe Early noted: "There are harmful provisions in the Bill. Those of us who are grandmothers will see our grandchildren divided. The little ones born to our daughters before June 30 will remain non-Indians; the little ones yet to come will be Indian. What a bitter legacy this government leaves the Indian people." [108] Jenny Margetts, spokeswoman for the Alberta IRIW, argued that the bill was still discriminatory in depriving Indian women of their rights, and thus responsible for creating a new form of injustice. But the IRIW still urged its passage, because the bill removed the long-contentious 12(1)(b) provision and, as Mary Two-Axe Early noted, once "the women get status they could do something and fight for their grandchildren." [109]

In an uncharacteristic move, the AFN and the NWAC had agreed to a joint position on removing discrimination against women in the Indian Act at a special meeting in Edmonton on May 17. David Ahenakew, then head of the AFN, described what became known as "the Edmonton consensus": "They propose the removal of all discrimination, including Section 12(1)(b), the reinstatement in the general band list of all generations who lost status or were never registered, the recognition of First Nations' control of and jurisdiction over citizenship. Bands will then determine who gets on active band lists. Bands only will determine the residency of non-Indians and non-members." [110]

The AFN's newly minted concept of "general band list" was not defined, and it clearly meant different things to different First Nations groups. Its meaning also differed from the government's "general list," which recognized status but not band membership.[111] The AFN strongly opposed both "mandatory reinstatement without community control" and residency rights automatically granted to non-band members.[112] The Native Women's Association now supported the AFN position, but it did argue that the bill would "continue to discriminate" in that it would "provide a split in the families in the second generation."[113]

MPs in the Standing Committee were equally concerned that the bill was substituting "one form of discrimination for another," but they generally favoured the AFN position that bands determine membership as an essential feature of self-government. One MP, the New Democratic Party's Jim Manly, even supported the right of bands to exclude the husband and children of a reinstated Indian woman from residence on the reserve with her, so long as the exclusion was non-discriminatory. Munro disagreed with Manly, saying, "If I put that in a Bill, it would be a pretty skeletal Bill about dealing with discrimination."[114] Munro also disagreed with the AFN's notion of a "general band list," as expressed in the Edmonton consensus, because it did not guarantee Indian women and their children reinstatement to both band membership and residency on a reserve.[115] Without these guarantees the situation that Sandra Lovelace faced – the denial of her right to live in her cultural community – would persist. Politically, Munro surmised that no minister could survive the attacks of women critics, inside and outside his party, if the amendments did not remove discrimination and reinstate Indian women and their children to status, membership, and residency.[116] But he was less forthcoming on the matter of 'dividing grandchildren' and of firmly guaranteeing funds to already impoverished bands to prevent further hardship because of the amendments. Financial practicalities had drawn the line at reinstating children, but not grandchildren. And a special fund, managed by a central agency of government separately from DIAND's regular accounts, was to ensure public scrutiny of the government's sincerity in putting its money where its principles were said to rest.[117] On the apparent contradiction between Bill C-47, which imposed government rules for membership on bands, and his newly drafted Bill C-52 on self-government, which gave bands certain powers to control membership, Munro was more direct. If bands controlled reinstatement now, they might deny membership and residence to reinstated women and thereby perpetuate discrimination. The government was responsible for removing discrimination and, he stressed, it had moved decisively to do so, purposely avoiding halfway measures.[118]

Although the government wanted Bill C-47 to pass,[119] it was delayed in the Senate and died that July with the end of the Trudeau era. The lines of argument in Bill C-47 and the notions underlying its proposed reforms were important in the evolution of policy thinking, because they revealed a stronger notion of equality than that which eventually informed Conservative government policy. Beyond the legacy of ideas, however, was the equally significant legacy of inaction: after nearly fifteen years in power and many rhetorical affirmations of the value of sexual equality, the Liberal government had failed to eliminate sex discrimination against Indian women in the Indian Act.

Conservative Government Policy, 1985-92

Following the September 1984 federal election, the Conservative government had six months in which to remove the discriminatory provisions in the Indian Act before section 15(1) of the Charter took effect in April 1985. Politically, the new government lacked a strong minister as spokesperson for women's rights in Canada. Similarly, within the Indian Affairs portfolio its minister, David Crombie, was not even a moderate proponent of Indian women's rights. Crombie soon became, however, a popular minister because, among other things, of his informal grassroots consultation with many Indian bands throughout Canada.

After taking office Crombie read extensively in the field of Indian policy, including the minutes of the Standing Committee on Bill C-47 and the resolutions of the AFN and NWAC on membership.[120] His starting point for most policy thinking was self-government. He personally endorsed the Penner report, which had recommended wide-ranging powers for First Nations governments, and he initially rejected the Indian Act as a route to self-government, believing that Indians regarded it "as a demeaning prison."[121] Aware of the conflict among First Nations on the issue of removing discrimination from the Act, and believing Bill C-47 was too flawed and unpopular to be redeemed, Crombie decided to prepare a new bill. It reflected his three policy objectives for legislative reform: "First of all, the removal of discrimination from the Indian Act; secondly, recognition of band control of membership; and thirdly, the restoration of rights to those who lost them."[122] These aims were compromises between women's interests with respect to equality and the bands' interests regarding self-government. He regarded compromise as essential, for the issue was not simply "a women's issue" as Munro had cast it; it was also "an Indian issue." Crombie believed that the failure of Bill C-47 lay in the fact that Munro had not understood this and had "lopped off" the band component.[123] The main points in Crombie's Bill C-31 (and in his final legislation) reflected his compromises:

1. remove discriminatory provisions in the Indian Act;
2. marriage and sex will not affect status in the future;
3. legal status and band membership are formally separated;

4. Indian status will be determined by the federal government;
5. band membership and reserve residency will be determined by bands;
6. Indian women who lost status under discriminatory provisions will have status and band membership restored;
7. first-generation children of restored persons will be granted first-time status, but not band membership;
8. second-generation children of restored persons will not be granted legal status or band membership;
9. in the future, generally, Indian status will be granted to those with at least one parent having status;
10. enfranchisement (loss of legal status) will be abolished;
11. all children (legitimate, illegitimate, adopted) will be treated equally;
12. a report to Parliament in two years by the minister on the implementation of Bill C-31.

For Crombie, Bill C-31 was a vehicle for advancing his central policy priority of self-government. He viewed the bill as "the beginning of a process aimed at full Indian self-government."[124] For him, the right of bands to control band membership was "an inherent right which should have been recognized before, [but] we are now through this bill indicating that the assumption of that right is available."[125] The right of bands to control residency was equally essential, and to have denied bands this right would have "made a mockery of band control."[126] Bill C-31 simply legalized the band's right to determine residency, a determination bands had been making de facto for many years.

Crombie spoke eloquently and with firm conviction of the right of First Nations to self-government. But he very rarely mentioned the rights of Indian women. Indeed, Crombie's Bill C-31 was a significantly weaker instrument for redressing sex discrimination than Munro's Bill C-47.

The innovative features of Bill C-31 (and the current legislation) had significant implications for First Nations women, as well as for bands. First, status and band membership were formally and legally separated. Henceforth, the federal government would determine legal status. And bands could determine band membership, if they wished, by devising their own membership codes.[127] These provisions allowed bands to grant membership to persons who did not have legal status. These persons would not be eligible for federal funding. Second, Bill C-31 granted legal status to the children of restored persons but, unlike Bill C-47, it did not grant them band membership. This meant that if a restored woman returned to live on the reserve, she could have her dependent children reside with her, but only until their maturity, when they would require band approval to remain in the community. Furthermore, because bands controlled residency a reinstated woman could not automatically have her husband reside with her on the reserve. More significantly, as a reinstated woman she, herself, might not be able to return to the reserve if the band council was unable or unwilling to grant her housing and other services. As Crombie admitted: "Residency will continue to be a matter to be determined by the bands. And naturally, this will be based on the availability of land, housing, and the essential services necessary to make residency possible."[128]

Like Munro and the AFN, Crombie had been concerned that amendments to the Act not increase the poverty already in place on reserves where housing backlogs existed and where services were acknowledged as substandard to those in surrounding non-Indian communities. Crombie promised adequate funding so reinstated persons would receive the normal on-reserve services to which they were now entitled,[129] and he repeatedly pledged that "the bands will be no worse off as a consequence of the legislation."[130] In the end, $295 million was actually spent on Bill C-31 implementation by 1989, a significant improvement over the $50 million briefly mentioned by Munro.[131] Neither minister, however, guaranteed to add new lands to the reserve land-base to accommodate the increased band population. Third, under Bill C-31, reinstated Indian women, unlike their status brothers, could not transmit band membership to their children. Fourth was the highly contentious distinction between 6(1) and 6(2) status Indians, a new provision that carried with it unequal abilities to transmit legal status (not band membership) to children. Under section 6(1) of the amended Indian Act, the government assigned legal status (a) to all persons who had status before April 17, 1985, (b) to all persons who are members of newly created bands, and (c) to all reinstated individuals who personally lost status through the discriminatory sections of the Indian Act: for example, 12(1)(b), 12(1)(a)(iv).[132] A 6(1) person can transmit legal status to her (his) children even if a partner has no status. Under 6(2) the government granted status to all persons with only *one* status parent. Most children of reinstated 12(1)(b) women were in the 6(2) category. A 6(2) person cannot transmit legal status to her (his) children unless the partner is a status Indian. A consequence of the 6(2) rule was the feature known as "the second-generation cut-off," which cuts off status to the grandchildren of the reinstated woman but not to the grandchildren of her status brother. All other factors being equal, this rule creates the situation in which "the sister's descendants have fewer Indian rights than have those of her brother, despite the fact that their degree of Indian ancestry is the same."[133] The second-generation cut-off provision, like the now abolished double-mother clause, was designed to reduce the future size of the status Indian population. Unlike the double-mother clause, however, it came into effect immediately, not two generations into the future. And its effects were significant in that DIAND estimated that about half of the grandchildren (that is, second-generation children) of reinstated persons were themselves adults in 1985.[134] Finally, there was the legal requirement in section 22 of the amended Act that the minister report to parliament in two years on the impact of Bill C-31 on the status and band populations, on band control of membership, and on the band lands and resources. Significantly, there was no requirement to study the impact of Bill C-31 on First Nations women.

In Crombie's opinion, Bill C-31 met all the provisions in the AFN-NWAC "Edmonton consensus" except NWAC's demand that "all generations" of First Nations persons deprived of, or denied, status be reinstated to status.[135] At the outset, Crombie had sought First Nations views on reform when he brought most groups together for an informal workshop in Toronto in mid-December 1984. But the chaotic session only revealed the volatility of the issue among the First Nations, and no common ground emerged.[136] When Crombie's "leaked" cabinet document on Bill C-31 tested the waters of First Nations opinion in February 1985, it found continued divisiveness. Furthermore, as time passed, the "Edmonton consensus" was assigned different meanings by different Indian groups and spokespersons, and subsequent agreements between the AFN and NWAC unravelled.[137] Initially, the AFN was generally more satisfied with the proposed policy than the women's groups. The AFN regarded the bill as having "fewer and less offensive provisions than C-47," and found Crombie's approach "to be largely in line with our position" in his recognition of the right of First Nations to determine their own citizenship.[138] In contrast, a new, more activist Aboriginal Women's Coalition, formed in November 1984, demanded that women and children be fully restored to all their rights, a position that the oil-rich bands from Alberta opposed, fearing it might diminish their wealth.[139]

Bill C-31 did not benefit from public scrutiny due to events in the wider political environment of Indian Affairs that emphasized the politics of Indian-government conflict rather than the politics of gender. These events began a week before Crombie introduced Bill C-31 to the Commons on February 28, 1985, when relations between Crombie and AFN National Chief Dave Ahenakew broke into public conflict over government funding of the AFN.[140] Internally, the AFN was in turmoil over Ahenakew's leadership style and management of funds, and it had already suffered a breakaway movement from the Alberta chiefs over the 12(1)(b) issue.[141] Within days attention shifted to the April 1985 First Ministers Conference on Aboriginal Rights in the Canadian Constitution. This conference ended in failure to entrench the right to self-government in the Constitution, as First Nations had sought. But the dramatic event that

Continued Discrimination Against Indian Women

a. Status of three generations of brother's descendants

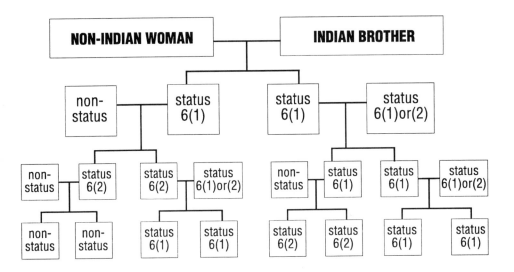

b. Status of three generations of sister's descendants

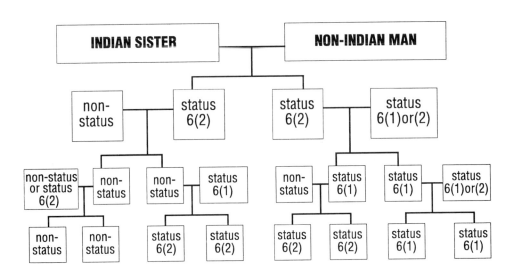

SOURCE: Joan Holmes, *Bill c-31: Equality or Disparity? The Effects of the New Indian Act on Native Women* (Ottawa: Canadian Advisory Council on the Status of Women, March 1987), 23.

absorbed media attention for the next few months came shortly after the FMC. A leaked cabinet document by Deputy Prime Minister Erik Nielsen revealed the government's desire to terminate its responsibility for Indians in Canada.[142] Like the 1969 White Paper, Nielsen proposed to abolish DIAND and transfer Indian Affairs to the provinces. The shock, and the knowledge, that the Mulroney cabinet had sought a "White Paper" solution to reduce government expenditures on First Nations almost instantly soured Indian-government relations. Bill C-31 was even further removed from public debate when Crombie's anger at Nielsen's proposal increased the turmoil to the point that the Prime Minister's Office intervened to shelve the Nielsen memorandum and calm the waters.[143]

This chaos in Indian Affairs overshadowed the fact that between March 7 and April 30, 1985, many Native groups made detailed submissions on Bill C-31 to the Commons' Standing Committee on Indian Affairs. To these were added several draft amendments proposed to Crombie by the joint legal team of the NCC and NWAC. Crombie accepted few changes, and Bill C-31 became law on June 28, 1985, retroactively taking effect as of April 17, 1985.[144]

As a compromise between two strong positions, the new policy (law) pleased few Native groups. While the AFN found it the most palatable, the NCC was the most critical.

Briefly, the NCC, which had long supported non-status Indian women, regarded the abolition of enfranchisement as a positive step but was angry because the government had undertaken no consultation on the bill "with the very people it presumes to legislate for."[145] It was particularly concerned that the bill would grant status to very few categories of people historically excluded by the old laws. The NCC's basic position was that all persons of Indian ancestry who identify as Indian should be granted status, including those who were never registered as status Indians, as well as those who were simply forgotten when the official lists were compiled and those who were unfairly enfranchised.[146] If the bill passed, the NCC feared that less than half the non-status Indians in Canada would be eligible for reinstatement. On the capacity of the bill to eliminate discrimination against women, NCC president Louis 'Smokey' Bruyere was blunt:

> The new bill will end only some of the more obvious forms of sexual discrimination. It will perpetuate others and will create some new ones, especially by passing on the current sexual discrimination imposed on Indian women to their children, thereby replacing overt sexual discrimination with a new blood quantum system based on distance from one or more parents who are registered.[147]

In response to Crombie's view that Bill C-31 was a compromise between competing interests, Bruyere was more accurate than cynical when he said, "There are only two interests that I see as being compromised by this bill; justice and money."[148] Indeed, some of the people working on Bill C-31 inside government would have agreed that Bruyere's assessment aptly described attitudes at the cabinet level.

The Native Women's Association liked the bill's reinstatement of 12(1)(b) women and the abolition of enfranchisement. It also supported the bill's explicit recognition of band control of band membership. Generally, however, NWAC's assessment was negative. It felt the bill failed to meet Crombie's three policy objectives and that it failed to meet NWAC's own goal that all persons of Native ancestry "must have their rights restored, in a full and equal manner."[149] In a careful analysis, NWAC President Marlyn Kane identified faults in the bill: these included its discriminatory treatment of women and children under the second-generation cut-off rule and other provisions, its divisiveness in creating new categories of First Nations people due to its separation of status and membership, its long-range effect of limiting the size of the status population through the "half-descent rule," and its failure to ensure a role for reinstated women in developing band membership codes.[150] NWAC regarded Bill C-31 as much weaker in protecting women's interests than Munro's Bill C-47 and much stronger on promoting band interests, even though it found Crombie's provisions for band control poorly conceived.[151]

The AFN welcomed the bill's recognition of band control, even though it was only a partial acceptance of the right of bands to determine their own citizenship.[152] But it remained hostile to the notion of automatic reinstatement of women to band membership. The official AFN explanation for this attitude was that compulsory reinstatement violated the self-determination of citizenship.[153] However, other motives for resistance were evident in the recent actions of bands in respect to section 12(1)(b). Between July 1980, when Munro instituted the suspensions of sections 12(1)(b) and 12(i)(a)(iv) on band request, and November 1984, when bands ended the requests in anticipation of new legislation, only 19 per cent of the bands in Canada had requested release from 12(1)(b). In sharp contrast, 53 per cent of the bands had requested suspension of 12(i)(a)(iv).[154] Joan Holmes saw this difference in request rates as suggesting "a general reluctance on the part of bands to support and protect the rights of Indian women."[155] Joyce Green was more direct in her conclusion:

> Bands have rarely protested the systematic loss of their women citizens who fell within the ambit of Section 12(1)(b), and the discrepancy of logic is apparent. If it is all right to separate Indian women from the reserve but not all right to return them, the issue seems to be the women rather than control of citizenship. If such is the case, at

least some First Nations are guilty of discrimination on the basis of sex and of a woman's choice of spouse.[156]

The AFN recognized the Liberal government's concern that bands might develop membership codes that discriminated against women, but it opposed the application of the Charter of Rights and Freedoms to the codes. The AFN's Vice-Chief from Ontario expressed the two positions on the issue:

> The Federal argument to date has been that unless band codes are obliged to be non-discriminatory on the basis of sex, some bands will discriminate against women. The First Nations argument has been, firstly, that it is none of Canada's business, and secondly that our value systems and traditions which have sustained us so far are different from Canada's non-Indian people and must be allowed to continue.[157]

The AFN also strongly opposed the government's separation of legal status from band membership and its refusal to change Bill C-31 so that persons granted membership by bands were automatically granted legal status by the government.[158] Like other First Nations groups, the AFN feared that the government would not fund programs and services for non-status Indians who became band members. Finally, the AFN disliked the failure of the government to commit more reserve lands to accommodate reinstated persons under the bill. The AFN criticized other aspects of the policy, but overall it was pleased that the bill "has moved dramatically toward the position that the Assembly of First Nations has put forward in the past."[159]

Generally, the Native organizations agreed with the abolition of 12(1)(b) and the removal of enfranchisement.[160] But they opposed the distinction between status and membership, demanding that the government grant status to band members. And they did not believe the government would provide resources to cushion the impact on bands of members taking up residence on reserves.

When the bill became law in June 1985, the media saw little gain for Indian women despite Crombie's assurance that it would "ensure equality between men and women."[161] Both Native and non-Native critics[162] anticipated difficulties with the new policy, but none predicted the serious problems that would arise with its implementation.

Although there were many unknowns with the new policy, the major surprise was its massive demographic impact: by December 1991 Bill C-31 had added nearly eighty thousand people to the status Indian population in Canada, increasing the population by nearly 16 per cent.[163] DIAND had seriously underestimated the number of persons and their children likely to seek reinstatement. Unprepared both administratively and financially for this scale of change, DIAND struggled unsuccessfully to implement the policy in an effective fashion.[164] The highly unsatisfactory implementation process only escalated the dissatisfaction of First Nations women and bands with the new policy.[165] First Nations women activists focused increasingly on the new forms of discrimination in the legislation and on the implementation difficulties.[166] For their part, bands found band control of band membership, as well as the development of membership codes, a more complex process than they had initially expected.[167] And most bands complained of the lack of resources from the government to finance the services and housing for the returning women and children, even though the government spent $295 million on the approximately 2 per cent of reinstated persons who actually returned to the reserves.[168]

Following the amendments to the Indian Act, the NCC[169] and the NWAC[170] published guidebooks to explain the complex and confusing legislation to aboriginal people and to identify the entitlements available under the new law. There soon followed a series of public reports, all intended to evaluate the nature and extent of change brought about by Bill C-31. The first was the March 1987 report by Joan Holmes,[171] commissioned by the Canadian Advisory Council on the Status of Women to study the impact of Bill C-31 on First Nations women. Holmes concluded that although the amendments had removed the most obvious forms of discrimination, Bill C-31 perpetuated the effects of the old discrimination while introducing new forms of inequality.[172] Next came DIAND's June 1987 report to Parliament,[173] required by section 22 of the amended Indian Act. Based on two years of implementation, DIAND was to assess the impact of Bill C-31 on the status and band population, on band control of band membership, and on band lands and resources. This perfunctory report noted that a very small percentage of reinstated persons were actually returning to the reserves, but it accomplished little other than to cite a few statistics and promise another report in three years' time (by June 1990). A more extensive assessment came in August 1988 from the Standing Committee on Aboriginal Affairs and Northern Development.[174] Between December 1987 and June 1988 it received detailed representations on Bill C-31 from many Native persons and organizations, including the AFN,[175] the NCC,[176] the NWAC,[177] and the PTNA.[178] On this basis it presented the government with a set of thirty-three recommendations, among them proposals for improving programs and the still problematic implementation process and for eliminating the new forms of discrimination in the Act.[179] Finally, in 1990 DIAND released five publications on the impacts of Bill C-31. These included its own impact studies on government programs and expenditures,[180] on bands and communities,[181] and on individual registrants.[182] DIAND summarized these findings in its own summary report. [183] The fifth publication, *Correcting Historic Wrongs?*, was the report of the National Aboriginal Inquiry on the Impacts of Bill C-31, organized jointly by the AFN, the NWAC, and the NCC. The Inquiry gathered the personal experiences of aboriginal people with Bill C-31 through a series of public hearings across Canada in late 1989. [184]

On the basis of these national reports, and other analyses, [185] some observations can be made about the major implications of the new policy for First Nations women.

Conclusion: *Implications of the Policy for First Nations Women*

First Nations women had fought for fifteen years to abolish discrimination against them and their children, in the Indian Act, on the basis of sex and marriage. The issue was so politically contentious among aboriginal groups and so damaging to government-Indian relations that successive ministers failed to take action until section 15 of the Charter of Rights imposed a deadline. When the government finally made reforms in 1985, the new policy and its implementation were a bitter disappointment to Indian women. Government proposals to eliminate discrimination had begun with Faulkner's limited notions for preventing future inequalities (not correcting past mistakes through reinstatement) and moved to the strongest proposals for equality by Munro. But neither approach resulted in action. The process ended when the weakest notions of equality, proposed by Crombie, were enacted into law. The two most contentious ideas in the new legislation – that of separating legal status from band membership as is practised in U.S. federal Indian policy, and that of "cutting off the second generation" from status – were introduced in Munro's time but expanded and implemented in Crombie's time. Munro had originally proposed the separation of status and membership for debate, [186] but he did not incorporate it in his Bill C-47, as Crombie did in his Bill C-31. And Munro's second-generation cut-off rule applied to the *already-born* grandchildren of reinstated persons, not to all the *future-born* grandchildren, like Crombie's rule. In addition, Munro's bill granted status and membership to the children of reinstated women, whereas Crombie's bill granted only status to these children. Finally, Munro's bill generally determined status by the "one-quarter Indian blood" rule, whereas Crombie used the more stringent "half-blood descent rule." [187] As the years passed, the trend of policy thinking to remove discrimination against Indian women became less sensitive to their interests and, at the same time, more divisive of Indian interests by implementing new forms of inequality that would affect all First Nations people. [188]

When the changes finally materialized in Crombie's bill, some of them addressed long-standing grievances. But others introduced new and equally disturbing discriminatory consequences. Still others provided ostensible benefits and rights that were so limited in practical realization they were virtually meaningless or indeterminate. In law, in policy, and in practice, discrimination against First Nations women and their children persists in the field of membership and status.

The starting point for examining the implications in law of discrimination against Indian women is the separation of legal status from band membership, because the total package of rights, benefits, and life conditions that flows from each legal category is significantly different. If a First Nations woman is reinstated to legal status and band membership, there is no guarantee that she can assume the benefits of membership because these are contingent upon reserve residence. Residence may be denied her, her children, and her husband not only on a *de jure* basis by exclusionary band by-laws, but also on a de facto basis by not providing them with the services or housing needed for their resettlement on the reserve. Without residence for her family, a reinstated woman is denied the ability to live in her cultural community and to gain access to the full range of rights for Indian women.

However, even without residence, a First Nations woman who regains status and membership has still made a significant advance over 12(1)(b) women before 1985 in that (1) she has regained Indian status in law,[189] and (2) she has access to the benefits (as at 1992) of two programs for off-reserve Indians: postsecondary education grants provided by DIAND, and uninsured health benefits (eye glasses, prescription drugs, ambulance) provided by the Department of National Health and Welfare (NH&W). She may also have access to certain (3) economic development programs offered federally by departments other than DIAND. Equally important, (4) she can transmit legal status to her children, and (5) she has finally received official legal recognition of her identity as a First Nations person in general. In legal and economic terms, these achievements constitute substantial gains over the pre-1985 condition of First Nations women who "married out" and consequently had none of these rights and benefits.

First Nations women placed the highest value on 'belonging' again to their community. They sought to re-establish their 'roots' by regaining membership in their band and securing official recognition of their cultural identity.[190] For most women, band membership without reserve residence satisfied their personal aims, because they had established their lives in cities and had no immediate desire to move back to the reserve.[191] Indeed, the vast majority of the Indian women reinstated since 1985 fell into this category.[192]

However, if a First Nations woman wanted the full benefits of membership, she must have residency on the reserve. If residency were granted her gains under Bill C-31 were of a much greater magnitude. She would have (1) all the benefits of the off-reserve status person, in addition to the benefits that flow from residence under the Indian Act, namely; (2) exemptions from certain taxes – from income tax on income earned on the reserve and from provincial sales tax, (3) a share in the band's assets and revenues, and in the band's decision-making processes regarding these assets, (4) the ability to inherit and own property on the reserve, (5) the right to vote and run for elected office in the band council, (6) the right to vote in band referendums, (7) access to on-reserve programs for primary and secondary education, welfare and health (similar, at least in principle, to those provided individual Canadians), (8) access to discretionary programs on housing and economic development, (9) the right to retire to the reserve or be buried on the reserve, and, finally, (10) official confirmation of her identity with, and "belonging" to, her home community and nation. These benefits are significant in cultural, social, and political terms to the First Nations woman and her family, not simply in economic terms.

This 'on-reserve package' is extremely costly to the government and to bands in comparison to the 'off-reserve package.'[193] The government's policy of assigning residency control to bands and, at the same time, of making financial support to the bands initially uncertain, significantly reduced the chances of reinstated First Nations women actually receiving these benefits and attaining the full measure of equality of life condition in their home communities. The policy also forced women into increasingly hostile political climates at the local reserve level where they have traditionally encountered the most explicit discrimination in access to services. The 'self-government' rationalization of the new policy served the government's interests in potentially reducing high expenditures, because bands were unlikely to admit women if they were already underfunded as local governments. This rationale also transferred the politically difficult decisions on residency from Ottawa to the First Nations communities.

Furthermore, the new law neither recognizes nor respects the integrity of the family unit. Indeed, through the residence factor the 1985 policy is highly destructive of family cohesion and stability. This damage is compounded by the 6(2) descent rule for status, because families are split legally in that most band membership codes exclude 6(2) persons from membership. The 'half-descent' rule, as the Meadow Lake Tribal Council study notes, divides families and the wider Indian population into what it calls "full" Indians registered under 6(1) of the Indian Act and "half" Indians registered under 6(2) of the Act.[194]

Legal discrimination is not only damaging to women and families, but its existence is also openly acknowledged. Aboriginal organizations such as the AFN, the NWAC, and the NCC recognized its existence in their

National Aboriginal Inquiry on Bill C-31: "Discrimination based on sex still exists within the *Indian Act,* although it now rests in section 6 rather than in section 12(1)(b)."[195] Aboriginal women's organizations have also recognized the existence of discrimination,[196] as have non-Native women's organizations,[197] and the Canadian Human Rights Commissioner.[198] Members of Parliament in the Standing Committee acknowledged its existence in their 1988 report on Bill C-31, where they recommended "that section 6(2) of *An Act to Amend the Indian Act,* 1985 be amended before the end of the current session of Parliament in order to eliminate discrimination between brothers and sisters." They also recommended the removal of another discriminatory section "to allow women to regain membership in their birth band."[199] Even the Minister of Indian Affairs who succeeded Crombie, Bill McKnight, admitted to the continuing existence of discrimination in the Act.[200] Despite widespread public acknowledgement of the persistence of sex discrimination in the Act, no amendments have been made to remove the offensive provisions.[201]

Discrimination exists not only in law and in policy but also in practice against First Nations women in reserve communities under Bill C-31 – a third level of reality. Attitudes towards returning women and their children vary regionally from the more liberal postures in parts of British Columbia and southern Ontario, to the more intolerant in the Prairies and in parts of the Atlantic region. As Pam Paul reported, however, the National Aboriginal Inquiry on Bill C-31 heard many complaints from women against bands: "Charges of blatant discrimination aimed at Indian bands is rampant throughout the country."[202] First Nations presenters at the hearings disclosed the emergence of a new category of persons with diminished social status in their communities, the returning "C-31s." The new policy led to "the creation of a status lowerclass," a "separate class of people" who are at times discriminated against and who become "scapegoats" for the wider ills that characterize many aboriginal communities.[203]

Discrimination against women in band membership codes and by-laws for residence is an integral aspect of the new policy. In Alberta, various combinations of traditional views, treaties, and royalty payments from oil revenues have produced some membership codes that are highly exclusionary of Indian women and their children.[204] In a few known instances, the provisions that severely disprivileged women and their children were introduced to the band's code *after* DIAND had officially approved it, an action permitted by the Indian Act.[205] Six bands in Alberta have gone even further by launching a constitutional challenge in court, claiming that certain amended provisions in the 1985 Indian Act violate their inherent right to self-government. More generally, prairie leaders often reject any changes under Bill C-31 on grounds that these ignore their treaty rights.[206]

Membership codes provide a vast new field of uncharted rules on membership and residence. First Nations women who appeared before the National Aboriginal Inquiry on Bill C-31 questioned "the contradictory actions of the government in removing sexual discrimination from federal legislation and condoning the continuance of such treatment under membership codes."[207] These codes are usually approved by the band's electors at the same time that they endorse the band taking control of membership. However, neither by law nor by common practice are the codes public documents. Indeed, beyond band council personnel and DIAND officials, the contents of the codes are rarely public knowledge, even to band members. In this respect the detailed study commissioned by the Meadow Lake Tribal Council on the impact of Bill-C31 on its membership confirms the very limited public awareness of the existence and content of the approved codes.[208] Nearly half of the bands in Canada have taken control of their band membership since Bill C-31 was passed in 1985.[209] Until information on the treatment of women and their children in these codes is publicly available, the extent to which the 'self-government' provision of band control in Bill C-31 respects Indian women's rights will remain unknown. However, in its very treatment of the membership codes, the new Indian Act, once again, legitimizes discrimination against Indian women.

Since 1985 the general circumstances of First Nations women in Canada have not changed substantially.[210] However, Indian women *are* survivors who continue to lobby for better living conditions.[211] While some women have played decisive political roles at the band level,[212] they still encounter resistance to their political participation not only at the local level but also at the national and international levels in the male-dominated political organizations.[213] In terms of socio-economic conditions, especially in respect to educational attainment, employment, and income, Indian women experience "multiple jeopardy" since they are disadvantaged on the bases of gender, culture, and class.[214] They are often single mothers without the benefit of culturally appropriate child care programs.[215] They and their children are often the subject of sexual abuse and "unconscionable levels of domestic violence."[216] They have a disproportionately high rate of incarceration in correctional institutions,[217] and they still have no matrimonial property rights on reserves if their marriages break down.[218] Clearly, the need for substantive equality and formal equality persists for Indian women.

First Nations women have continued to pursue socio-economic equality in Canadian society, while simultaneously seeking their primary targets of equality of Indian rights and human rights for Indian women.[219] Historically, the Indian women's movement began in the early 1970s primarily in the context of the women's movement for equal rights in Canada. To achieve their early victories, Indian women activists benefited from the support of non-Native women's groups. Soon, however, they received very tangible advocacy for their demands from the NCC, with the NWAC sitting on its board of directors until 1984. As Indian rights gained sharper focus for Indian women in the 1980s, the women sought a political coalition with the AFN rather than the NCC or women's organizations.[220] Bill C-31 facilitated this realignment, even though the political agreements it produced were highly unstable at times, as the 'Edmonton consensus' illustrated. By 1990 Native women's organizations were still associated more with the aboriginal movement than the women's movement[221] when they participated in the Aboriginal Inquiry on Bill C-31 with the NCC and the AFN. In early 1992, however, Indian women and their concerns returned to the national stage when NWAC clashed publicly with the AFN in the Canadian constitutional forum. The report of the AFN's own constitutional commission revealed very negative attitudes among the First Nations public towards their own women, indicating that First nations women face continued resistance to equality of treatment in their reserve communities.[222] At the same time, but more forcefully than in previous years, the Native Women's Association demanded equal political involvement in the constitutional process "at all stages so that we can participate in the definition of the structures and powers of our governments, and end the discrimination."[223] NWAC also insisted on the application of the Canadian Charter of Rights to all systems of Indian self-government to ensure that Indian women are treated equally and fairly.[224] But First Nations women lost on both counts when NWAC was shut out of the negotiations leading to the Charlottetown Accord of August 28, 1992, and when the Accord recognized the inherent right of aboriginal peoples to self-government but failed to ensure equality for Indian women under Indian government regimes.[225] Although NWAC's public criticism of the Accord's failure to protect women's rights under self-government led to improvements in the legal text of the agreement,[226] the possibility remained that First Nations women could be discriminated against by chiefs and councils under the Accord's provisions that allowed for the preservation of aboriginal cultures and traditions.[227]

The resolution of the discrimination issue is not yet apparent in suggestions for an Aboriginal Charter of Rights, the Canadian Charter, or some international standard of human rights.[228] What is apparent is the continuing need for First Nations women to be politically organized and to participate in policy negotiations at all political levels if they wish to secure reforms in Canadian society that reflect their interests. The agenda for action was set by Bill C-31. Legal discrimination against First Nations women on the basis of sex continues to exist in the current Indian Act. It was put there in 1985, not 1869. It is contemporary policy and law in Canada.

Sally Weaver

List of Abbreviations

AFN Assembly of First Nations
CCSD Canadian Council on Social Development
DIAND Department of Indian Affairs and Northern Development
FPRO Federal-Provincial Relations Office (Ottawa)
ICA Indian Chiefs of Alberta
IINC Indian and Inuit Nurses of Canada
IRIW Indian Rights for Indian Women
MLTC Meadow Lake Tribal Council
NAC National Action Committee on the Status of Women
NCC Native Council of Canada
NWAC Native Women's Association of Canada
PTNA Prairie Treaty Nations Alliance
RCSW Royal Commission on the Status of Women
SCAAND Standing Committee on Aboriginal Affairs and Northern Development, House of Commons
SCIAND Standing Committee on Indian Affairs and Northern Development, House of Commons
SOS Secretary of State (Ottawa)

NOTES

1. Research for this paper was funded by the Social Sciences and Humanities Research Council of Canada, whose support is gratefully acknowledged. I especially wish to thank staff of the Native Council of Canada, the Native Women's Association, the Assembly of First Nations, the Meadow Lake Tribal Council, Department of Indian Affairs, and the Canadian Human Rights Commission for their generous assistance and constructive comments on the first draft of this paper. Sandra Burt and Lorraine Code deserve special thanks for their patience and their valuable editing. My work definitely bene-fited from the assistance of all these people, but I retain full responsibility for all interpretations and errors.

2. SCIAND, *Minutes of Proceedings and Evidence*, No. 53 (May 25, 1956), 12.

3. The Native Women's Association is primarily an Indian women's organiza-tion, although it was founded in 1973 to represent the interests of all aborigi-nal women – Metis, Inuit, status, and non-status Indian women (Krosen-brink-Gelissen, 1991:86). Metis women do not have their own organization, whereas the Inuit women have their own body, the Inuit Women's Associa-tion. Also at the national level there are "the four major" political organiza-tions representing the basic cultural-legal categories of aboriginal peoples in Canada; the Assembly of First Nations (AFN) for status Indians, the Native Council of Canada (NCC) for non-status Indians and off-reserve status Indians (numbering an estimated 750,000 in 1992), the Metis National Council (MNC) for Metis, and the Inuit Tapirisat of Canada (ITC) for Inuit peoples. Of these "major" organizations, the NCC, formed initially in 1970, has been the major group to support the efforts of Indian women to end dis-crimination in the Indian Act. Since Confederation in 1867, Indians and Inuit have been a federal responsibility under section 91(24) of the BNA Act. Histor-ically, however, the federal government has denied responsibility for non-sta-tus Indians and Metis.

4. Immediately after the March 1992 televised forum ended, the Native Women's Association initiated litigation to stop the federal government from funding the four national organizations until the NWAC was granted similar funding. The NWAC lawyer argued that the federal government was discrim-inating against Native women by refusing to fund their organization and grant it a place at the constitutional table. The NWAC lost the case in the lower court when the judge, clearly unsympathetic to the issue, ruled against their demands on the grounds that it would open the gate to other groups and "par-alyze the process." (*See* "Native Women Want Unity Seat," *The Toronto Star,* March 19, 1992, and "Judge Rules Out Seat for Native Women at Unity Talks," *The Toronto Star,* April 1, 1992.) Joe Clark, the Minister for National Unity, had previously ruled out the NWAC demands on the grounds that their

presence would 'complicate' his job. (See "Women Try to Block Native Council Funds," *The Globe and Mail,* March 19, 1992.)

5. "Natives Divided over Charter," *The Globe and Mail,* March 14, 1992.
6. Stacey Moore, 1992a, 3.
7. Statutes, 1952.
8. *Indian News,* 1973a, 3.
9. *Indian News,* 1973, 1, 6.
10. Silman, 1987, 219.
11. Statutes, 1869, sec. 6.
12. Tobias, 1976.
13. DIAND, 1978, 24-25.
14. Letter from Hector Langevin, Superintendent General of Indian Affairs, to Anionkiu, Peter Karenho, and Other Iroquois Indians, Caughnawaga P.Q., August 20, 1869, in Public Archives of Canada, Record Group 10, Vol. 528. See also DIAND (1978:26). For a more expanded analysis of the government's intent behind the 1869 amendments on Indian women, *see* S. Weaver, "Report on Archival Research Regarding Indian Women's Status, 1868-1869," prepared for B. Kellock, legal counsel to the Six Nations Band Council, November 9, 1971.
15. For example, *see* DIAND, 1978, 54.
16. Statutes, 1876, clause 3[3].
17. See Driver (1961), especially chapters 15 and 16, maps 31 and 32, for a over-view of the descent, marriage, and residence patterns of aboriginal First Nations in North America. There is a growing literature on the traditional roles of First Nations women in their indigenous cultures. This literature often examines the effects of colonialism on their roles and on the ability of researchers to determine their roles. See, for example, the work of Brodribb (1984), Cruikshank (1969), Etienne and Leacock (1980), Matthiasson (1974), and Van Kirk (1980).
18. DIAND, 1978, 60.
19. NWAC, 1992, 14.
20. Stacey Moore, 1992, 4.
21. Statutes, 1985.
22. RCSW, 1970, 238.
23. RCSW, 1970, 238.
24. *Lavell v. Attorney General of Canada,* Ontario County Court, (Grossberg, J), 22 Dominion Law Record, (3rd), 1971, 182-186.
25. Cheda, 1977, 204.
26. Weaver, 1974.
27. Statements in the House of Commons by John Turner, Minister of Justice, House of Commons *Debates,* December 1, 1971, 10045.
28. AIAI, 1971, 63-64.
29. *Indian News,* 1977, 3.

30. *Indian News*, 1973.

31. Sanders, 1975, 666.

32. Cardinal, 1977, 111.

33. Letter to the Editor from "Forbidden Voice," *Brantford Expositor,* September 14, 1971.

34. National Indian Brotherhood, *Press Release*, "Resolution on the Lavell Case, Indian Status and the Indian Act," September 27, 1973, Ottawa.

35. DIAND, 1969.

36. ICA, 1970.

37. Trudeau, 1970.

38. Cardinal, 1977, 111.

39. Personal communication, Douglas Sanders, January 29, 1978; and Whyte, 1974, 41.

40. Whyte, 1974, 28, 41.

41. A third case of sex discrimination against the Indian Act also lost in the courts, but it did not have the political impact of Lavell and Bedard. Mrs. Canard, a First Nations woman from Manitoba, charged that the denial of her right to act as executor of her husband's estate constituted sex discrimination in the Indian Act. Her case failed before the Supreme Court of Canada in 1975 (Elliott, 1975). (Although Mr. Canard's first name is provided in the legal literature, Mrs. Canard's first name is not included.)

42. *Indian News*, 1973c, 5.

43. For example, *see Indian News*, 1973b, 1975.

44. Sanders, 1975, 667.

45. Weaver, 1982.

46. Cardinal, 1977, 115.

47. Ibid., 122-123.

48. *Indian News*, 1976a, 1977a.

49. *Indian News*, 1978c, 2.

50. House of Commons Standing Committee on Justice and Legal Affairs, *Minutes of Proceedings and Evidence*, No. 15, May 25, 1977, 44; "Interview with Gordon Fairweather," *Indian News*, 1978, 19(1):1-3; "Indian Brotherhood Attacked Over Rights," *Ottawa Citizen*, October 10, 1978.

51. *Indian News*, 1978b, 5.

52. Minutes of the Joint Cabinet/National Indian Brotherhood Meeting, Canadian Indian Rights Commission, Ottawa, December 12, 1977, 12-13.

53. *Indian News*, 1978a, 7.

54. House of Commons Standing Committee on Justice and Legal Affairs *Minutes of Proceedings and Evidence*, No. 15, May 25, 1977, 42-47.

55. Silman, 1987, 119-148.

56. Ibid., 149-172.

57. *Indian News*, 1980.

58. Davies, 1991, 771.

59. This UN ruling, officially released on September 2, 1981, was not made under the Covenant's sexual-equality article because of a technicality over the matter of retroactivity. Lovelace, having married in 1970, had suffered sexual discrimination *before* Canada had agreed to the convention in 1976. This raised the question of the retroactivity of the denial of her rights under the covenant, even though it was recognized that a case could be made for the continuing denial of her rights after 1976. Maureen Davies noted that the ruling, using article 27, was possibly even more significant for aboriginal peoples in general in that it affirmed the right of aboriginal peoples (and women) to live in their own cultural community (Davies, 1991:770). For a useful discussion of Article 27 and the Lovelace case *see* Davies, 1991:769-774; SCIAND 1982:16,24-26.
60. Jamieson, 1978.
61. Ibid., 2.
62. House of Commons *Debates*, June 15, 1978, 6453.
63. *Indian News*, 1978.
64. DIAND, 1978a.
65. Ibid., 7-9.
66. *Indian News*, 1979, 3.
67. DIAND, 1978a, 9.
68. Ibid.
69. Trudeau, 1978.
70. Munro would suspend both these sections of the Indian Act if formally requested to do so by band council resolutions (DIAND, 1980). The 'double-mother' clause automatically enfranchised all children at twenty-one years of age, whose parents had married after September 1951 and whose mother and father's mother were born non-Indian. This provision was created in the 1951 Indian Act for the explicit purpose of limiting the size of the status Indian population by excluding all persons with only one-quarter (or less) 'Indian blood' (*Indian News*, 1978d, 2). Most First Nations people in Canada were unaware of the existence of the double-mother provision (*Indian News*, 1980a, 3), but concern about its impact arose in Quebec bands where sons of influential band members or chiefs were affected by the section. Heavy pressure was put on Munro to alter the application of this provision, and he acted quickly to suspend it.
71. *Indian News*, 1981.
72. *Indian News*, 1981a.
73. *Indian News*, 1981b; Weaver, 1983, 74-75.
74. *Indian News*, 1981c.
75. *Indian News*, 1981d.
76. Sanders, 1985.
77. Statutes, 1982.

78. In December 1981 the Canadian government ratified the United Nations Convention on the Elimination of All Forms of Discrimination against Women ("Text of Joint Communique of Federal and Provincial Ministers Responsible for Human Rights concerning Ratification of the Convention on the Elimination of All Forms of Discrimination Against Women," Secretary of State, Ottawa, December 10, 1981; and "Canada Ratified Pact to Counter Discrimination Against Women," *News Release,* Secretary of State, Ottawa, December 10, 1981).

79. DIAND, 1982.

80. Ibid., 5.

81. Ibid., 4.

82. Ibid., 5-6.

83. DIAND, 1982a.

84. SCIAND, *Minutes of Proceedings and Evidence,* No. 56, May 27 and 31, 1982, 6.

85. SCIAND, 1982, 7.

86. SCIAND, 1982, 15.

87. SCIAND, 1982.

88. SCIAND, 1982, 40.

89. Ibid., 30.

90. SCIAND, 1982, 32-45.

91. DIAND, 1982b, 1.

92. DIAND, 1982c, 3-5.

93. Zlotkin, 1984, 10.

94. Statutes, 1982.

95. Trudeau, 1984, 151.

96. SCIAND, 1983, 54.

97. Ibid., 54-55.

98. Ibid., 54.

99. Ibid., 56.

100. Two bills on self-government were being drafted at that time: the bill negotiated by the Cree and Naskapi nations with the federal and Quebec governments following the self-government provisions in the 1975 James Bay land-claims settlement; and Bill C-52, a new legal framework for Indian bands across Canada who wished to opt for self-government outside the constraints of the present Indian Act. The Cree-Naskapi bill became law in June 1984, but Bill C-52 was intended only for discussion purposes.

101. House of Commons, Bill 1984.

102. Munro, 1984, 2.

103. Ibid., 4-6.

104. Ibid., 5.

105. Ibid., Appendix 1:4.

106. Ibid., Appendix 2, 3.

107. SCIAND, *Minutes of Proceedings and Evidence*, No. 17, June 26, 1984, 35.
108. SCIAND, *Minutes of Proceedings and Evidence*, No. 18, June 27, 1984, 45.
109. Ibid., p. 46.
110. Ibid., 5.
111. The vast majority of status Indians were also, at the same time, members of a particular band. In 1982, for example, there were about eighty Indian persons who were not members of a band, out of nearly three hundred thousand status Indians in Canada (DIAND, 1982:2).
112. SCIAND, *Minutes of Proceedings and Evidence*, No. 18, June 27, 1984, 5.
113. SCIAND, *Minutes of Proceedings and Evidence*, No. 19, June 28, 1984, 87.
114. SCIAND, *Minutes of Proceedings and Evidence*, No. 17, June 26, 1984, 56.
115. Ibid., 16, 55.
116. Ibid., 16-17.
117. Ibid., 17-18.
118. Ibid., 15.
119. Sanders, 1984, 34, 39.
120. SCIAND, *Minutes of Proceedings and Evidence*, No. 3, December 4, 1984, 11.
121. Ibid., 7.
122. SCIAND, *Minutes of Proceedings and Evidence*, No. 12, March 7, 1985, 7.
123. SCIAND, *Minutes of Proceedings and Evidence*, No. 3, December 4, 1984, 12.
124. SCIAND, *Minutes of Proceedings and Evidence*, No. 12, March 7, 1985, 7.
125. Ibid., 13-14.
126. Ibid., 8.
127. Band control of band membership is provided for in the Indian Act primarily in sections 10-14, 64, 81, and 83. Under section 10, bands wishing to assume control of membership must receive consent from a majority of the electors of the band and must devise a written membership code. The codes are expected to be "consistent" with the Indian Act and with the Charter of Rights (DIAND, 1985:24) although Crombie carefully avoided making explicit statements acknowledging the fact of Charter conformity. Indeed, the Indian Act's membership provisions were changed *because* they contradicted the provisions of the Charter. The Minister of Indian Affairs does not have the power of disallowance over the codes as he does over most band council decisions. Rather, the minister simply examines a code to ensure that it conforms with provisions in the Indian Act and then approves the transfer of responsibility for membership and for the maintenance of the Band List (a formal registry of band members) from the Department of Indian Affairs to the band. If the band changes the code the next day in a way that contravenes the Indian Act, the minister has no responsibility for that action. Also, when the minister considers the code in respect to the Indian Act he forwards a copy of the code to the Department of Justice for its legal opinion on whether the code conforms to the Charter of Rights. If the code is believed to be in conflict with the Charter, the minister merely notifies the band of this possibility in his covering

letter approving the band's control of membership. Under the 1985 legislation, if bands assumed control of membership during the first two years (up to June 28, 1987) they could exclude from membership certain categories of Bill C-31 registrants that they could not exclude after 1987; namely, 6(2) Bill C-31 registrants, which includes the first-generation offspring of reinstated women, many of whom were adults, and some 6(1) registrants. If bands decided not to assume control, DIAND remained in charge of membership, and all Bill C-31 registrants originally from those bands would be granted band membership. Bands may develop appeal procedures for band decisions, but they cannot remove "acquired rights" from First Nations persons (that is, people who acquired legal status and band membership rights under Bill C-31, or those who gained status in the past by marrying Indian men). Finally, under Bill C-31, bands were granted new by-law powers to make local laws (a) on reserve residency of band members, their spouses and children, (b) on the eligibility of band members (or electors) to vote on band control of membership, and (c) on payouts of band moneys to band members whose names are removed from the Band List.

128. SCIAND, *Minutes of Proceedings and Evidence*, No. 12, March 7, 1985, 9.
129. Ibid., 9-10.
130. SCIAND, *Minutes of Proceedings and Evidence*, No. 40, May 21, 1985, 25.
131. Munro at one time alluded to the sum of $50 million to implement his policy of reforms in Bill C-47 (SCIAND, *Minutes*, December 4, 1984, No. 3, 10; "Sex Discrimination Bill Discussed," *The Globe and Mail*, February 19, 1985).
132. This category also includes illegitimate children of an Indian mother and a non-Indian father [old section 12(2)], and persons, mainly wives and children, who were enfranchised when their husband/father was enfranchised [old section 109(l)]. See Holmes (1987:42-43) for a very clear description of the rules of eligibility for legal status.
133. Holmes, 1987, 22.
134. SCIAND, *Minutes of Proceedings and Evidence*, No. 12, March 7, 1985, p. 31.
135. Ibid., 14.
136. "Crombie Facing Conflict over Indian Issues," *The Globe and Mail*, December 17, 1984; "Non-status Native Women Fight for Reinstatement in Tribes," *The Globe and Mail*, December 20, 1984.
137. AFN, "Report to the Confederacy of Nations, January 29-30, 1985, Vancouver B.C., by Ontario Regional Vice-Chief Wally McKay, Re: Indian Act Amendments [12(1)(b)]," unpublished report, Ottawa, 9-11.
138. Ibid., 8, 6.
139. "Repealing Prejudicial Indian Act Clause Long Overdue," by Doris Anderson, *The Toronto Star*, January 26, 1985; "Indian Women Seek Compensation Fund Over Deprived Status," *The Globe and Mail*, January 29, 1985.
140. "Crombie Dictator, Ahenakew Says," *The Globe and Mail*, February 20, 1985.
141. Impeachment was raised and defeated at a special national assembly of the

AFN in Ottawa, February 18-20, 1985, held, among other things, to prepare the AFN's position for the forthcoming FMC on Aboriginal Rights (AFN *Bulletin*, 1985c).

142. "Drastic Cuts Proposed in Native Programs," *The Globe and Mail*, April 18, 1985; "Indians Outraged by Document," Saskatoon *Star-Phoenix*, April 18, 1985.

143. Weaver, 1986.

144. Bill C-31 amended the Indian Act by creating new sections on band membership, primarily sections 4-17, 22-23, 64, 81 and 83.

145. NCC, 1985, 7.

146. Ibid., 12.

147. Ibid., 9-10.

148. Ibid., 8.

149. NWAC, 1985, 56.

150. NWAC, 1985, 57-70.

151. Ibid., 62-64.

152. AFN, 1985, 7.

153. Ibid., 16.

154. Holmes, 1987, 6, 53.

155. Ibid., 6.

156. Green, 1985, 89.

157. AFN, "Report to the Confederacy of Nations, January 29-30, 1985, Vancouver B.C., by Ontario Regional Vice-Chief Wally McKay, Re: Indian Act Amendments [12(1)(b)]," Ottawa, 2-3.

158. AFN, 1985, 16; AFN *Bulletin*, 1985a, 1985b.

159. AFN, 1985, 16.

160. Enfranchisement was not entirely abolished. Although a First Nations person could no longer relinquish legal status, he/she could relinquish band membership and receive, if the band by-laws approved, his/her per capita share of the band's capital and revenue moneys.

161. *Maclean's*, 1985; Crombie, 1985, 1.

162. For example, *see* NAC, 1985.

163. In 1985, the "guesstimates" of DIAND officials were that 68,000 First Nations persons would seek reinstatement under Bill C-31. Of this number, 22,000 were estimated to be persons who personally lost status under the old Act (for example, 12[1][b] women), and the additional 46,000 were their (first-generation) children. DIAND then assumed that nearly all of the 68,000 would want to take up status, but that only 10 to 20 per cent of these would actually wish to move to reserves to live (SCIAND, *Minutes*, March 7, 1985, No. 12, 19). By June 30, 1990, five years after Bill C-31 became law, 69,593 persons had been granted legal status under its provisions (DIAND, 1990:13). By December 31, 1991, 79,639 persons had been granted status (since June 1985) under Bill C-31: 19,415 are reinstated persons and 60,224 are persons registered for the

first time, mostly the children of the reinstated persons. The total number of persons granted status under Bill C-31 by December 31, 1991, represented nearly 16 per cent of the total status Indian population in Canada. (These figures come from DIAND's Indian Registration System, Ottawa, June 3, 1992.)

164. DIAND's problems with Bill C-31 originated in its own implementation policy. These difficulties included inadequately hired and trained personnel to carry the workload, poor communication with applicants about reinstatement procedures, unrealistic demands for documentation from applicants, insensitivity to applicants' difficulties in complying with the rules, lack of communication to applicants about the rights and benefits under Bill C-31, and a heavy backlog of unprocessed applications (SCAAND, 1988:8-26; AFN et al., 1990:iii-iv, 8-17; Krosenbrink-Gelissen, 1991:195-209). The government provided $3.5 million to eighteen regional and national aboriginal organizations to assist applicants by providing them with information on the reinstatement process and on benefits and rights under Bill C-31 (for example, NWAC, 1986). As implementation problems persisted, the funding was renewed (SCAAND, 1988:89), but by 1990 applicants still found information on rights and benefits inadequate (AFN et al., 1990:34).

165. Paul, 1990, 2.

166. See, for instance, Joseph, 1991, 66, 71.

167. Opekokew, 1986; Manyfingers Jr., 1986.

168. The government eventually spent $295 million on implementing Bill C-31 between 1985 and 1988-89. In 1988 DIAND sought renewed funding from the cabinet and received approval for up to $2.3 billion for another five-year program for Bill C-31 costs, from 1989-90 to 1994.

169. NCC, 1985a, 1986.

170. NWAC, 1986.

171. Holmes, 1987.

172. Holmes, 1987, 40.

173. DIAND, 1987.

174. SCAAND, 1988.

175. AFN, 1987.

176. NCC, 1987, 1987a.

177. NWAC, 1988.

178. PTNA, 1988.

179. SCAAND, 1988, 83-87.

180. DIAND, 1990a.

181. DIAND, 1990b.

182. DIAND, 1990c.

183. DIAND, 1990.

184. AFN et al., 1990.

185. In recent years a few very useful undergraduate and graduate theses have been completed on the impacts of Bill C-31. For a very good overview of the gains

of the Indian women's movement, set in the context of social movement theory, see Stephanie Sanders, 1991, *The Gains of the Canadian Indian Women's Movement 1970-1990*, Senior Honours Essay, Department of Anthropology, University of Waterloo, Ontario. For an in-depth study of the affects of Bill C-31 on some First Nations women in Alberta see Vicki English-Currie's M.A. thesis (English-Currie, 1991). A more broad-scale analysis of the impact of Bill C-31 on First Nations individuals and bands is provided in Pam Paul's M.A. thesis (Paul, 1990). Finally, in her Ph.D. dissertation, Lilianne Krosenbrink-Gelissen has provided a comprehensive account of the Native Women's Association of Canada, including its relations with other Native and women's organizations and its position on Bill C-31 (Krosenbrink-Gelissen, 1991).

186. DIAND, 1982.
187. SCAAND, 1988, 28.
188. The impact of Bill C-31 on bands is a highly complex and continuing process. A few bands have undertaken research on the effects of the 6(2) rule on the future size of their status populations. Using their bands' out-marriage rate of 60 per cent, they have become alarmed at the major loss to the bands' status population (for example, SCAAND, 1988:28). This loss has led some First Nations people to refer to Bill C-31 as a "termination" and "assimilation" policy. The impact study undertaken by the Meadow Lake Tribal Council revealed an even more disturbing picture of a "shrinking" and "aging" membership population if bands adopted a membership code that excluded 6(2) registrants (MLTC, 1991:19). For a more general discussion of the impacts of Bill C-31 on bands see DIAND (1990b; 1990:26-50), SCAAND (1988:45-76), and AFN et al. (1990:52-60).
189. The matter of whether an Indian woman loses her treaty rights if she loses her legal status and Indian Act rights is no longer clear. Historically, once a treaty was signed and the Indian treaty group (population) was identified, it was DIAND's practice to determine the subsequent treaty members by applying the membership rules of the Indian Act. Under this practice, an Indian woman would lose her treaty rights when she lost her legal status under the Indian Act. (After 1951, she would receive her per capita share of band funds and, if appropriate, a sum amounting to a twenty-year payment of treaty annuities). Recently DIAND's practice has been called into question and litigation by First Nations on this matter may occur in the future.
190. DIAND, 1990, 15.
191. AFN et al., 1990, 35.
192. Some 90 per cent of the Bill C-31 registrants (persons restored to status under Bill C-31) live off the reserves (DIAND, 1990:iii). Most (58 per cent) of the Bill C-31 registrants are women who have higher levels of education, income, and home ownership than on-reserve women (DIAND, 1990:ii). Bill C-31 has not resulted in major migration of reinstated persons back to the reserves: in 1990,

80 per cent of the bands had less than 15 registrants living on-reserve. In small communities, however, even these low numbers can have a major impact on housing and other services.

193. The per capita cost per year for benefits for an off-reserve status person is $635, compared to a one-time cost of $12,108, and a subsequent annual per capita cost of $5,353 for an on-reserve status person in 1985 (Holmes, 1987, 24).

194. MLTC, 1991, 2, 7.

195. AFN et al., 1990, 1.

196. For example, *see* NWAC, 1988.

197. For example, *see* Holmes, 1987; NAC, 1988.

198. Yalden, 1992, 26. The Canadian Human Rights Act continues to exempt the Indian Act from its application (Statutes, 1985a, sec 67). The Native Women's Association has recently requested changes to the Human Rights Act (NWAC, 1992c), but there has been no government response to date.

199. SCAAND, 1988, 36.

200. SCAAND, *Minutes of Proceedings and Evidence*, No. 37, March 17, 1988, 13.

201. Other forms of sex discrimination under Bill C-31 amendments have also been identified by First Nations people. These include the discriminatory treatment between male and female illegitimate children (NWAC, 1986:21; SCAAND, 1988:34-35).

202. Paul, 1990, 89.

203. AFN et al., 1990, 27, 31.

204. English-Currie, 1991, 58-59.

205. Paul, 1990, 86-88.

206. AFN et al., 1990, ii.

207. Paul, 1990, 89.

208. MLTC, 1991, 7-8.

209. By September 4, 1992, 236 (39 per cent) of the 604 bands in Canada had been granted control of their own membership by DIAND. Requests for control from 53 bands had been rejected, and 9 requests were still pending. (Source: DIAND's membership division, Ottawa, September 4, 1992.)

210. SOS, 1985.

211. Brant Castellano, 1992, 39.

212. For example, *see* Fiske, 1990; Jeffries, 1991.

213. Turpel, 1990, 100-102.

214. Gerber, 1990, 80.

215. NCC, 1990.

216. Manitoba, 1991, 475. *See also* IINC, 1990, 1991, and CCSD and NWAC, 1991.

217. LaPrairie, 1987, 123, 1984.

218. Montour, 1987.

219. NWAC, 1992, 16.

220. Krosenbrink-Gelissen, 1991, 132-140.

221. Phillips, 1991, 775.
222. AFN, 1992, 61-65.
223. NWAC, 1992, 15; Stacey Moore, 1992a, 1.
224. NWAC, 1992, 16.
225. FPRO, 1992a.
226. FPRO, 1992b.
227. In the tentative Pearson accord on the Constitution of July 7, 1992, the decision was to leave the constitutional provision of 35(4) unchanged, and to deal with the Native gender-equality issue at a future FMC on the Constitution (FPRO, 1992, 17). NWAC legal spokesperson, Sharon McIvor, noted that this left the equality rights of First Nations women unprotected under self-government regimes ("Native Women Fear Loss of Rights: Gains 'Wiped Out' by Unity Proposal," *The Globe and Mail,* July 13, 1992, and "Premiers Blow it – Again," by Doris Anderson, *The Toronto Star,* July 13, 1992). The Charlottetown political accord on the Constitution of August 28, 1992, reached by the Prime Minister, the premiers, and the territorial and aboriginal leaders, simply repeated the provisions of the July 7th accord (FPRO, 1992a, sec. 52). In response to the Native Women's Association's demands, changes were made in the legal text of the Charlottetown Accord to strengthen women's rights (FPRO, 1992b). But NWAC spokespersons quickly noted that discrimination against aboriginal women would continue under the pretense of preserving aboriginal traditions ("Native Women's Fear Leads to Text Change," *The Globe and Mail,* October 7, 1992).

    Litigation by NWAC against the federal government and the major aboriginal associations initially to secure participation in the constitutional negotiations and later to block the referendum on the accord when the NWAC was denied participation has been unsuccessful to date. Despite a promising victory in an August 1992 ruling by Justice Mahoney of the Federal Court of Appeal, a subsequent Federal Court ruling went against the Native Women's Association ("Native Women Aim to Block National Referendum," *The Globe and Mail,* October 13, 1992; "Native Women Can't Bloc Vote," *The Toronto Star,* October 22, 1992). NWAC has indicated it will appeal the judgment to the Supreme Court of Canada.

228. For discussions of the relevance of the Canadian Charter and an Aboriginal Charter of Rights to Indian women's rights, *see* NWAC, 1991, 1992a, 1992b, and Turpel, 1989, 1990a.

REFERENCES

Analysis Bill C-31. AFN *Bulletin,* 1985, 3(3):7-8.

AFN (Assembly of First Nations), Presentation on Bill C-31. House of Commons Standing Committee on Indian Affairs and Northern Development, *Minutes of Proceedings and Evidence,* March 14, 1985, No. 16, 5-35.

AFN, Presentation on Bill C-31. House of Commons Standing Committee on Aboriginal Affairs and Northern Development, *Minutes of Proceedings and Evidence,* December 10, 1987, No. 26, 7-17.

AFN et al., *Correcting Historic Wrongs? Report of the National Aboriginal Inquiry on the Impacts of Bill C-31.* Prepared by AFN, NWAC, and NCC. Ottawa: DIAND.

AFN, *To the Source: First Nations Circle on the Constitution,* Commissioner's Report. April 13, 1992. Ottawa: AFN.

AIAI (Association of Iroquois and Allied Indians) *Position Paper,* Brantford, Ontario: Association of Iroquois and Allied Indians, November 27, 1971.

Bill C-31 Survey Results. AFN *Bulletin,* 1986, 4(1):6-7.

Brant Castellano, Marlene, "History and Tradition – Women in Huron and Ojibwa Societies," *The Canadian League,* 1992, 68(2):35-39.

Brodribb, Somer, "The Traditional Roles of Native Women in Canada and the Impact of Colonization," *Canadian Journal of Native Studies,* 1984, 4(1):85-103.

Cardinal, Harold, *Rebirth of Canada's Indians.* Edmonton: Hurtig, 1977.

CCSD and NWAC, *Voices of Aboriginal Women: Aboriginal Women Speak Out About Violence.* Ottawa: Canadian Council on Social Development, 1991.

Cheda, Sherrill, "Indian Women: An Historical Example and a Contemporary View," in Marylee Stephenson, ed., *Women in Canada.* Don Mills, Ont.: General Publishing Company, 1977, 195-208.

Crombie, David, "Legislation Introduced to Ensure Equality in the Indian Act." Ottawa: DIAND *Communique,* February 28, 1985.

Cruikshank, Julia M., *The Role of Northern Canadian Indian Women in Social Change,* M.A. thesis, University of British Columbia, Vancouver, 1969.

Davies, Maureen, "Aboriginal Rights in International Law: Human Rights," in Bradford Morse, ed., *Aboriginal Peoples and the Law,* revised first edition. Ottawa: Carleton University Press, 1991, 745-794.

DIAND, [The White Paper] *Statement of the Government of Canada on Indian Policy.* Ottawa: Queen's Printer, 1969.

DIAND, *The Historical Development of the Indian Act.* Ottawa: DIAND, Treaty and Historical Research Centre, August 1978.

DIAND, Discussion Paper for Indian Act Revision. *Indian News* (Special Edition), November 1978.

DIAND, Government Ready to Lift Discrimination. Ottawa: DIAND *Communique,* July 24, 1980.

DIAND, *The Elimination of Sex Discrimination from the Indian Act,* Ottawa: DIAND, August 1982.

DIAND, "Committee to Review Issues Affecting Indians." Ottawa: DIAND *Communique,* August 4, 1982.

DIAND, "Ending Discrimination Against Indian Women," *Minister's Letter,* Issue No. 2, November 1982, 1.

DIAND, "The Alternative of Optional Indian Band Government Legislation." [J. Munro's submission to the Penner Committee on Self-Government] Ottawa: DIAND, November 9, 1982.

DIAND, *Indian Band Membership: An Information Booklet Concerning New Indian Band Membership Laws and the Preparation of Indian Band Membership Codes.* Ottawa: DIAND, 1985.

DIAND, *Report to Parliament: Implementation of the 1985 Changes to the Indian Act.* Ottawa: DIAND, June 1987.

DIAND, *Summary Report: Impacts of the 1985 Amendments to the Indian Act* (Bill C-31). Ottawa: DIAND, 1990.

DIAND, *Survey of Registrants: Impacts of the 1985 Amendments to the Indian Act* (Bill C-31). Ottawa: DIAND, 1990a.

DIAND, *Bands and Communities Studies: Impacts of the 1985 Amendments to the Indian Act* (Bill C-31). Ottawa: DIAND, 1990b.

DIAND, *Government Programs: Impacts of the 1985 Amendments to the Indian Act* (Bill C-31). Ottawa: DIAND, 1990c.

Driver, Harold E., *Indians of North America.* Chicago: University of Chicago Press, 1961.

Elliott, David, "Canard: A Triad Returns," *University of Toronto Faculty of Law Review,* 1975, 25:317-332.

English-Currie, Vicki, *The Impact of Bill C-31 on Native Women in Alberta,* M.A. thesis, University of Calgary, 1991.

Etienne, Mona and Eleanor Leacock, *Women and Colonization: Anthropological Perspectives.* New York: Praeger, 1980.

Fiske, Jo-Anne, "Native Women in Reserve Politics: Strategies and Struggles," in *Community Organization and the Canadian State,* Roxana Ng, G. Walker and J. Muller, eds. Toronto: Garamond Press, 1990, 131-146.

FPRO (Federal-Provincial Relations Office), *Status Report: The Multilateral Meetings on the Constitution.* Ottawa: FPRO, July 7, 1992.

FPRO, *Consensus Report on the Constitution.* Ottawa: FPRO, August 28, 1992.

Gerber, Linda M., "Multiple Jeopardy: A Socio-Economic Comparison of Men and Women among the Indian, Metis and Inuit Peoples of Canada." *Canadian Ethnic Studies,* 1990, 22(3):69-84.

Green, Joyce, "Sexual Equality and Indian Government: An Analysis of Bill C-31 Amendments to the Indian Act," *Native Studies Review,* 1985, 1(2):81-95.

Holmes, Joan, *Bill C-31: Equality or Disparity? The Effects of the New Indian Act on*

Native Women. Ottawa: Canadian Advisory Council on the Status of Women, March 1987.

House of Commons, *Bill C-47: An Act to Amend the Indian Act.* Ottawa: House of Commons, 1984.

ICA (Indian Chiefs of Alberta), *Citizens Plus* [The Red Paper]. Edmonton: Indian Chiefs of Alberta, 1970.

IINC (Indian and Inuit Nurses of Canada), *Annual Assembly Report for 1990 on 'Child Sexual Abuse in Aboriginal Communities.'* Whitehorse, Yukon. Ottawa: Indian and Inuit Nurses of Canada, May 17-20, 1990.

IINC, *Phase I: National Family Violence Survey.* Prepared by Claudette Dumont-Smith and Pauline Sioui-Labelle. Ottawa: Indian and Inuit Nurses of Canada, August 1991.

Indian News, "Canadian Indian Women Demand Equal Rights: Support Committee Formed for Jeannette Lavell," 1973, 15(6):1,6-7.

Indian News, "Native Women's Steering Committee Meet in Winnipeg to Discuss Unity," 1973b, 16(5):10.

Indian News, "Indian Women Can Work Together Regardless of Their Status," 1973c, 16(7):5.

Indian News, "Fund Raising is Difficult for Indian Rights for Indian Women," 1975, 17(2):1,11.

Indian News, "N.I.B. General Assembly Held in Whitehorse," 1976, 17(9):l,4.

Indian News, "Margaret Thompson Makes a Plea for Native Women," 1976a, 17(9):5.

Indian News, "Chief States Problems," 1977, 18(6):2-3.

Indian News, "Relations Between the NIB and IRIW Have Improved But . . ." 1977a, 18(7):3.

Indian News, "Revision Process Planned," October 1978, p. 1.

Indian News, "Indian Rights for Indian Women Resolutions," 1978a, 19(3):7.

Indian News, "Starblanket Wins Election," 1978c, 19(6):l-2.

Indian News, "When is an Indian Not an Indian?" 1978d, 19(12):2.

Indian News, "Interview with Cam Mackie – ADM," 1979, 19(12):3-5.

Indian News, "NIB : No Equality for Women Just Yet," 1980, 20(9):7.

Indian News, "Double Mother Rule '. . . Great Injustice'," 1980a, 20(10):3,10.

Indian News, "Mohawks Scoff at Amendments," 1981, 22(9):3.

Indian News, "Natives Far From Pleased," 1981a, 22(7):3.

Indian News, "Changes Would be Expensive," 1981b, 22(7):1,4.

Indian News, "Rights Issue Reaches Boiling Point," 1981c, 22(9):3.

Indian News, "Bickering Will End," 1981d, 22(5):8.

IRIW (Indian Rights for Indian Women), Presentation on Bill C-31. House of Commons Standing Committee on Indian Affairs and Northern Development, *Minutes of Proceedings and Evidence,* March 26, 1985, No. 24, 31-56.

Jamieson, Kathleen, *Indian Women and the Law in Canada: Citizens Minus.* Ottawa: Ministry of Supplies and Services, 1978.

Jamieson, Kathleen, *Native Women in Canada: A Selected Bibliography.* Ottawa: Social Sciences and Humanities Research Council of Canada, 1982.

Jeffries, Theresa M., "Sechelt Women and Self-Government," in Doreen Jensen and Cheryl Brooks, eds., *In Celebration of Our Survival.* Vancouver: UBC Press, 1991, 81-86.

Joseph, Shirley, "Assimilation Tools: Then and Now," in Doreen Jensen and Cheryl Brooks, eds., *In Celebration of Our Survival.* Vancouver: UBC Press, 1991, 65-79.

Krosenbrink-Gelissen, Lilianne E., *Sexual Equality as an Aboriginal Right.* Saarbrucken, Germany: Verlag Brietenbach, 1991.

LaPrairie, C.P., "Select Socio-Economic and Criminal Justice Data on Native Women," *Canadian Journal of Criminology,* 1984, 26:161-169.

LaPrairie, C.P., "Native Women and Crime: A Theoretical Model," *Canadian Journal of Native Studies,* 1987, 7(1):121-137.

LaPrairie, C.P., "Redressing an Injustice," *Maclean's,* February 25, 1985.

Manitoba. Public Inquiry into the Administration of Justice and Aboriginal People, *Report of the Aboriginal Justice Inquiry of Manitoba,* Vol. 1, *The Justice System and Aboriginal People.* Winnipeg: Queen's Printer, August 12, 1991.

Manyfingers Jr., Morris, "Determination of Indian Band Membership: An Examination of Political Will," *Canadian Journal of Native Studies,* 1986, 6(1):63-75.

Matthiasson, Carolyn J., ed., *Many Sisters: Women in Cross-Cultural Perspective.* New York: The Free Press, 1974.

MLTC (Meadow Lake Tribal Council), *Bill C-31 Impact Study: Synopsis, Comments, Recommendations,* Vol. 1. Prepared by Anthony H. Smith, Living Dimensions Limited, Perth, Ontario. Meadow Lake, Sask.: Meadow Lake Tribal Council, August 22, 1991.

Montour, Martha, "Iroquois Women's Rights With Respect to Matrimonial Property on Indian Reserves," *Canadian Native Law Reporter,* 1987, No. 4, 1-10.

Munro, John, "Speaking Notes" on Amendments to Remove Sex Discrimination from the Indian Act. Ottawa: DIAND *Speech,* June 18, 1984.

Munro, John, "Bill C-47: Amendments to the Indian Act to End Discrimination," based on "Sex," Speech to the Standing Committee on Indian Affairs and Northern Development. Ottawa: DIAND *Speech,* June 26, 1984.

NAC (National Action Committee on the Status of Women), "Presentation" on Bill C-31. In House of Commons, Standing Committee on Aboriginal Affairs and Northern Development, *Minutes of Proceedings and Evidence,* March 1, 1988, No. 35, 4-12.

NCC (Native Council of Canada), "Presentation on Bill C-31," in House of Commons Standing Committee on Indian Affairs and Northern Development, *Minutes of Proceedings and Evidence,* March 19, 1985, No. 18, 6-27.

NCC, *Bill C-31 & The New Indian Act: Guidebook #1: Applying for Status.* Ottawa: NCC, 1985a.

NCC, *Bill C-31 & The New Indian Act: Guidebook #2: Protecting Your Rights.* Ottawa: NCC, 1986.

NCC, "Presentation on Bill C-31," in House of Commons Standing Committee on Aboriginal Affairs and Northern Development, *Minutes of Proceedings and Evidence,* March 10, 1987, No. 20, 5-18.

NCC, *Broken Promises: A Report to Parliament on Bill C-31 and the New Indian Act.* In House of Commons Standing Committee on Aboriginal Affairs and Northern Development, *Minutes of Proceedings and Evidence,* December 10, 1987, No. 26, 26A1-66.

NCC, *Native Child Care: 'The Circle of Care.'* Ottawa: NCC, 1990.

NWAC (Native Women's Association of Canada), "Presentation on Bill C-31," in House of Commons Standing Committee on Aboriginal Affairs and Northern Development, *Minutes of Proceedings and Evidence,* March 28, 1985, No. 28, 55-79.

NWAC, *Guide to Bill C-31: An Explanation of the 1985 Amendments to the Indian Act.* Ottawa: NWAC, 1986.

NWAC, "Presentation on Bill C-31," in House of Commons Standing Committee on Aboriginal Affairs and Northern Development, *Minutes of Proceedings and Evidence,* February 23, 1988, No. 33, 4-13.

NWAC, *On Aboriginal Charter of Rights and Freedoms: A Discussion Paper.* Ottawa: NWAC, 1991.

NWAC, "Aboriginal Women and the Constitutional Debates: Continuing Discrimination," *Canadian Woman Studies,* 1992, 12(3):14-17.

NWAC, *Native Women and the Charter: A Discussion Paper.* Ottawa: NWAC, 1992a.

NWAC, *Matriarchy and the Canadian Charter: A Discussion Paper.* Ottawa: NWAC, 1992b.

NWAC, *The Canadian Human Rights Act: Changes Requested on Behalf of the Native Women's Association of Canada.* Ottawa: NWAC, 1992c.

Nahanee, Theresa, "Who is an Indian in Canada!" *Indian News,* 1973a, 15(8):3.

Nahanee, Theresa, "Interview with Gordon Fairweather," *Indian News,* 1978b, 19(1):1,3,5.

Opekokew, Delia, "Self-Identification and Cultural Preservation: A Commentary on Recent Indian Act Amendments," *Canadian Native Law Reporter,* 1986, No. 2, 1-25.

Parliamentary Notes, AFN *Bulletin,* 1985a, 3(4):7, 10.

Parliamentary Notes, AFN *Bulletin,* 1985b, 3(5):5-6, 8.

Paul, Pamela, *Bill C-31: The Trojan Horse; An Analysis of the Social, Economic and Political Reaction of First Nations People as a Result of Bill C-31.* M.A. thesis, Department of Anthropology, University of New Brunswick, Fredericton, 1990.

Phillips, Susan D., "Meaning and Structure in Social Movements: Mapping the

Network of National Canadian Women's Organizations," *Canadian Journal of Political Science,* 1991, 24(4):755-782.

PTNA (Prairie Treaty Nations Alliance), "Presentation on Bill C-31" in House of Commons Standing Committee on Aboriginal Affairs and Northern Development, *Minutes of Proceedings and Evidence,* December 11, 1987.

RCSW (Royal Commission on the Status of Women), *Report.* Ottawa: Queen's Printer, 1971.

Sanders, Douglas, "Indian Women: A Brief History of Their Roles and Rights," *McGill Law Journal,* 1975, 21(4):656-672.

Sanders, Douglas, "Indian Status: A Women's Issue or an Indian Issue?" *Canadian Native Law Reporter,* 1984, 3:30-41.

Sanders, Douglas, "The Indian Lobby and the Canadian Constitution 1978-82," in Noel Dyck, ed., *Indigenous Peoples and the Nation-State.* St. John's: Institute of Social and Economic Research, Memorial University, 1985, 151-189.

Special Assembly – Ottawa. AFN *Bulletin,* 1985c, 3(3):2.

SCAAND (Standing Committee on Aboriginal Affairs and Northern Development), *C-31: Fifth Report,* House of Commons Standing Committee on Aboriginal Affairs and Northern Development, *Minutes of Proceedings and Evidence,* No. 46, June 28, 1988 (published August 1988).

SCIAND (Standing Committee on Indian Affairs and Northern Development) *Report of the Subcommittee on Indian Women and the Indian Act,* Minutes of Proceedings and Evidence, House of Commons, Standing Committee on Indian Affairs and Northern Development, No. 58, September 20, 1982.

SCIAND, "The Fifth Report to the House," *Minutes of Proceedings and Evidence,* No. 56, May 27 and 31, 1982.

SCIAND, *Indian Self-Government in Canada.* House of Commons, Standing Committee on Indian Affairs and Northern Development, *Minutes of Proceedings and Evidence,* No. 40, October 12 and 20, 1983.

SCIAND, *Minutes of Proceedings and Evidence,* No. 18, June 27, 1984.

SCIAND, *Minutes of Proceedings and Evidence,* No. 19, June 28, 1984.

SCIAND, *Minutes of Proceedings and Evidence,* No. 17, June 26, 1984.

Silman, Janet, *Enough is Enough: Aboriginal Women Speak Out.* Toronto: The Women's Press, 1987.

SOS (Secretary of State), *Native Women: A Statistical Overview.* Ottawa: Secretary of State, 1985.

Stacey Moore, Gail, *Statement on the 'Canada Package.'* February 5, 1992. Ottawa: NWAC, 1992.

Stacey Moore, Gail, *Opening Remarks by Gail Stacey Moore to the First Peoples Forum on the Constitution.* Ottawa, March 13, 1992. Ottawa: NWAC, 1992a.

Statutes, "An Act for the Gradual Enfranchisement of Indians," *Revised Statutes of Canada,* 32-33 Victoria, chapter 6, 1869.

Statutes, "An Act to Amend and Consolidate the Laws Respecting Indians," *Revised Statutes of Canada,* 39 Victoria, chapter 18, 1876.

Statutes, "The Indian Act," *Revised Statutes of Canada,* chapter 149, 1952.

Statutes, *The Constitution Act, 1982.* Ottawa, 1982.

Statutes, An Act to Amend the Indian Act. *Revised Statutes of Canada,* chapter 27, 1985.

Statutes, The Canadian Human Rights Act. *Revised Statutes of Canada,* chapter H-6, 1985a.

Statutes, *The Indian Act.* Ottawa: Office Consolidation, 1989.

Tobias, John L., "Protection, Civilization, Assimilation: An Outline History of Canada's Indian Policy," *The Western Canadian Journal of Anthropology,* 1976, 6(2):13-20.

Trudeau, Pierre, "Statement" by the Prime Minister at a Meeting with the Indian Association of Alberta and the National Indian Brotherhood, Ottawa, June 4, 1970. Toronto: Indian Eskimo Association of Canada, 1970.

Trudeau, Pierre, *A Time for Action: Toward the Renewal of the Canadian Federation.* Ottawa: Minister of Supply and Services, 1978.

Trudeau, Pierre, "Statement by the Prime Minister of Canada to the Conference of First Ministers on Aboriginal Constitutional Matters, 8-9 March 1984," reprinted in M. Boldt and J. Anthony Long, eds., *The Quest for Justice.* Toronto: University of Toronto Press, 1985, 148-156.

Turpel, Aki-Kwe/Mary Ellen, "Aboriginal Peoples and the Canadian Charter of Rights and Freedoms," *Canadian Woman Studies,* 1989, 10(2-3):149-157.

Turpel, Mary Ellen, "The Women of Many Nations in Canada," in *Indigenous Women on the Move.* Document No. 66. Copenhagen: International Work Group for Indigenous Affairs, 1990, 93-103.

Turpel, Mary Ellen, "Aboriginal Peoples and the Canadian Charter: Interpretive Monopolies, Cultural Differences," in *Canadian Human Rights Yearbook 1989-1990.* Ottawa: University of Ottawa Press, 1990a, 3-45.

Van Kirk, Sylvia, *Many Tender Ties: Women in Fur Trade Society in Western Canada 1670-1870.* Winnipeg: Watson and Dwyer, 1980.

Weaver, Sally M., Judicial Preservation of Ethnic Group Boundaries: The Iroquois Case. In *Proceedings of the First Congress, Canadian Ethnology Society.* Ottawa: National Museum of Man. Mercury Series, Canadian Ethnology Service, Paper No. 17, 1974, 48-66.

Weaver, Sally M., "The Joint Cabinet/National Indian Brotherhood Committee: A Unique Experiment in Pressure Group Relations." *Canadian Public Administration,* 1982, 25:211-239.

Weaver, Sally M., "The Status of Indian Women." in Jean L. Elliott, ed., *Two Nations, Many Cultures,* 2nd ed. Scarborough: Prentice-Hall, 1983, 56-79.

Weaver, Sally M., "Indian Policy in the New Conservative Government. Parts I and II." *Native Studies Review,* 1986, 2(1):1-43, and 2(2):1-45.

Whyte, John D., "The Lavell Case and Equality in Canada." *Queen's Quarterly,* 1974, 81:28-42.

Yalden, Maxwell, *A Submission to the Royal Commission on Aboriginal Peoples* by

Maxwell Yalden, Chief Commissioner, Canadian Human Rights Commission, Winnipeg, Manitoba. Ottawa: Canadian Human Rights Commission, April 22, 1992.

Zlotkin, Norman, "The 1983 and 1984 Constitutional Conferences: Only the Beginning." *Canadian Native Law Reporter,* 1983, No.3., 3-29.

Suggested Readings

By far the most sensitive and realistic portrayal of how Indian women were personally affected by the discriminatory laws and practices, and how they lobbied to change them, is provided by the Tobique women in *Enough is Enough: Aboriginal Women Speak Out* (Silman, 1987). A very useful single overview of discrimination against Indian women from the historical origin of the law in the 1860s up to the mid-1970s is provided in Kathleen Jamieson's book *Indian Women and the Law in Canada: Citizens Minus* (Jamieson, 1978). Her bibliography on Indian women is a valuable research tool (Jamieson, 1982). For the role of Indian women historically in the fur trade, Sylvia Van Kirk's *Many Tender Ties* (1980) is an excellent study. Article-length coverage of the discriminatory issue as it developed politically from the mid-1970s to the mid-1980s is available in Sanders (1975 and 1984) and Weaver (1983). A more lengthy treatment of the issue linked to an interesting history of the Native Women's Association of Canada is provided by Lilianne Krosenbrink-Gelissen (1991). Joyce Green (1985) and Joan Holmes (1987) published excellent early critiques of the new policy (Bill C-31), and the Native Council of Canada (NCC, 1985a, 1986), as well as the Native Women's Association of Canada (NWAC, 1986) produced guidebooks that describe clearly the rights and benefits Indian women have under the new law. The most current and most substantial body of literature on Bill C-31 and the status of First Nations women comes from Indian women authors. First Nations women lawyers led the field. Delia Opekokew identified the difficulties bands might encounter in developing band membership codes (Opekokew, 1986). Martha Montour published on the absence of matrimonial property rights for Indian women on reserves (Montour, 1987). And Mary Ellen Turpel wrote about the political development of aboriginal women's issues in Canada (Turpel, 1990) and about the relevance of the Charter of Rights to aboriginal peoples (Turpel, 1989, 1990a). These were followed by the most recent analyses of the impact of Bill C-31 on Indian women found in the work of Pam Paul (1990), Vicki English-Currie (1991), and Shirley Joseph (1991). The general reaction of aboriginal people to the new law is available in the report of the National Aboriginal Inquiry on the Impacts of Bill C-31 (AFN et al., 1990).

Chapter Four

The Canadian Women's Movement: The Second Wave

≈≈≈≈≈≈≈≈≈≈≈≈≈≈≈≈≈≈≈≈≈≈≈≈≈≈≈≈≈≈≈≈≈≈

In the 1960s no one expected the women's movement to re-emerge. In prosperous postwar Canada, women seemed to be doing well in both economic and political terms; their remaining problems looked like temporary disadvantages. Women were increasingly getting the education needed for better-paying work, and public opinion supported their right to work and to get equal pay (legally guaranteed since the 1950s). Even in Quebec women had been enfranchised for almost a generation. There were still few women in the federal Parliament, but the tradition of having one woman in the cabinet seemed secure, while local women politicians like Ottawa Mayor Charlotte Whitton were highly visible and vocal – often objecting to any specific concern for the status of women.

When something most often called the women's liberation movement gained media attention late in the decade, first in France and then in the United States, it was as part of a student movement radicalized by racism and imperialism: women were to be 'liberated,' like minorities and colonial dependencies. The newly visible feminism was initially interpreted as simply another, relatively unimportant part of an era of activism. In Canada the burning national issue was linguistic-cultural: a question of national unity played out in federal-provincial conferences and royal commissions. The Canadian student revolt was late and muted and, like it, the 'new' women's movement was seen as an American import. In Canada, as elsewhere, there was general astonishment when feminism proved able to tap massive discontent among even the most privileged women.

The renewed activism among women continued throughout the 1970s, and continued also to receive a real and increasingly favourable response. A significant minority of Canadian women were even willing to call themselves 'feminists' – 42 per cent in a poll taken for *Weekend* magazine in 1979, 5 per cent more in one taken for *Chatelaine* in 1986 – and by 1986 some three-quarters of Canadians agreed that 'the feminist movement' had had a positive rather than a negative effect on Canadian society. [1]

Looking back, we can see that feminist stirrings were unexpected for the same reason that they occurred: during the 1950s and 1960s, women's domestic obligations and their self-images had remained virtually unchanged, while their activities had altered drastically. Most importantly, women had retained responsibility for the household and family at the same time as their participation in the paid labour force had increased massively, reaching the previous wartime peak in 1967. Nevertheless, throughout their lives women continued to put success in marriage and childrearing high among their goals. They also continued to perform, and they expected to perform, the large majority of necessary domestic tasks. Even by the mid-1980s, there was general agreement in Canada only that husbands of women in the paid labour force should 'help' with the housework; the very wording showed whose task housework still was. [2] The result of all this was, unsurprisingly, growing strains and tensions for women.

More specifically, by the 1960s Canadian women had two sorts of grievances that fuelled the women's movement. An old set, identified as feminist in an earlier era, related to the areas where women were basically the same as men but were treated in a different, disadvantageous manner – in effect excluded from men's rights and privileges. There was still more outright discrimination than most people realized, including explicit or implicit refusals to allow women to hold family property or citizenship or Indian status on the same terms as men. Where the barriers were officially down and women shared in 'male' activities, they did it without the rewards men could expect. Feminists were to identify a 'glass ceiling' that stopped women at a certain level: they could vote, but few would become lawmakers and none would become premiers; they could graduate from university and even from professional schools, but they could not expect to be judges or surgeons; they could work for pay, but it would be for less pay than men received, and they were unlikely to become rich by their own achievements.

Furthermore, the few women who succeeded in public life found they had to do it the men's way, hiding their feminine qualities, neglecting or concealing their private lives, dressing for success, learning the conflictual 'games mother never taught us.' Respondents to a poll posed to 'successful' Canadian businesswomen complained that there was too much pressure on women to be good at everything. They agreed emphatically (72 per cent) that "to get ahead in this world a woman has to be twice as good at what she does as a man is," but 82 per cent of them wanted a daughter they might have to be "as interested in pursuing a career as getting married and raising a family." Men did not have to respond to such multiple, conflicting expectations.[3]

The second, new set of grievances was therefore related to women's specific qualities, characteristics that they valued and thought society appreciated insufficiently. Women wanted to stay different without being disadvantaged. More positively, they wanted credit for their valuable female qualities, as well as protection from their vulnerabilities in a male-dominated world. Women's situation in relation to the combination of paid labour and domestic responsibilities crystallized the old and the new demands: they were not compensated for their 'double shift' of paid and unpaid work, they were not protected against violence in or out of the home, and their socially valuable tasks of public and private nurturance were unrecognized.

These conditions produced individual dissatisfactions, felt by individual women even if largely unvoiced. In the aggregate, the resulting grievances implied an image of a more desirable society – one in which women were treated as well as men but also one in which public life had changed because women were actively in it. For most Canadian women, their continued commitment to home and family life was a value they cherished and which they thought society ought also to cherish. A society in which women were equally influential would be one that took women's preferences and experience seriously, and that was transformed by the result.

The basic situation of Canadian women was shared by women throughout the industrialized world. This goes a long way towards explaining why the revolt of the women students did not die down in the early 1970s like the activities of the male-dominated organizations from which they broke away. In addition, as the organizational history of contemporary women is gradually pieced together, the immediate causes of postwar feminism emerge as different in each location. Its successes and failures – and the form they took – were related to the history of women and of the women's movement in each specific place. Canada's newly visible feminist activism inherited the situation and the goals of its predecessor groups, which are described in Jane Errington's history of early Canadian women in this book. This continuity occurred in part because of the survival of these groups and their role in producing a 'second wave' of feminism. For that and other reasons, the long-held goals of the Canadian women's movement were reinvigorated to respond to the conditions of women's postwar lives.

It was not a 'rebirth of feminism.' Feminism and women's groups had not simply died off at the successful end of the suffrage campaigns. As we begin to uncover the history of women in the interwar and early postwar years, it becomes clear that, as might be expected, women like Nellie

McClung and Helen Gregory MacGill moved with their customary energy to make use of the new instruments of influence for which they had fought so hard. After enfranchisement, organized women were engaged in fewer concentrated campaigns, had less publicity and less success, but their activity never stopped. In the 1960s, with the appearance of new groups, the pace quickened and the visibility increased. The notion of a second wave catches what was happening, reminding us that in social change, as in oceans, calmer patches are followed by new and stronger peaks of activity. The second wave also implies the image of a tide pouring in, each wave going further up the beach, with a continuity of organizational and individual efforts over time and a hope of progress.

The Components of the Second Wave

It is now clear that women's liberation groups were not always the first to be active in feminism's second wave. Two different sorts of new women's organizations began independently at much the same time, towards the end of the 1960s: those which grew out of the student movement and also liberal-feminist groups organized specifically to pressure for government action in relation to the status of women. The latter groups were often similar in membership, structure, and beliefs to the women's organizations of the first wave; in Canada they were, initially, mainly coalitions of surviving first-wave groups. They were, nevertheless, something new, founded in response to the situation of women in the 1960s. Over time they developed new policy goals and, sometimes, new feminist analyses. Established women's movement policies, such as opposition to pornography and to violence against women, support of reproductive freedom and of peace, and the quest for equal pay, all acquired new importance in ways compatible with the analyses made by the members of women's liberation.

The groups which called themselves women's liberation brought into Canadian feminism for the first time a large infusion of younger women, students, or ex-students. These in turn brought with them, from the student movement, a significant commitment to a Marxist or at least an economic, class-oriented analysis of women's situation; they were to identify themselves as Marxist or socialist feminists. Distrust of government and a belief in revolutionary change were accompanied by organizational novelties: small non-hierarchical 'cells' and 'consciousness-raising' through small-group discussion. All these were new to the Canadian women's movement. But the women's liberation slogan "the personal is political" had close affinities to the views of nineteenth- and twentieth-century social feminists who thought politics should be cleaned up the way houses were.

In Canada the second wave of feminism made its first appearance, unrecognized, with the establishment in 1960 of the Voice of Women, followed by the 1966 reorganization of a large number of existing Quebec women's organizations into the Fédération des femmes du Québec and the Association féminine d'éducation et d'action sociale. In the same year, 1966, a Committee on Equality for Women was organized to obtain a government enquiry into the status of women. Its achievement, the establishment of the Royal Commission on the Status of Women (RCSW) in 1967, was the first success of the second wave of Canadian feminism. At that point in time the women's caucuses that were to become the Canadian women's liberation movement were in the process of forming.

The second wave of feminism also saw, in Canada as in all countries, numerous new women's groups, mostly small and local, that emerged to express the interests of specific categories of women. Women's caucuses and groups were revitalized within unions, religions, and political parties. Previously unaffiliated groups of women began to organize, including, in Canada, groups of Indian and non-status Indian women focusing on the issues related to women's right to Indian status; black women who formed a national congress; lesbian mothers co-ordinating the legal tactics for retaining custody of their children; farm women voicing their concern about the survival of the family farm and their own status in it; and wives of armed services members claiming the right to speak out politically in their own interest.[4] By the middle of the 1980s women from marginalized groups were forcefully voicing a broader demand: the white, heterosexual majority of Canadian feminists must take account of the perspectives of the minority groups with which so many women identified. Analyses based on gender and class had to be amplified to take account also of differences in race, religion, ethnicity, and sexual orientation as well as bodily conditions including disability and age. The movement's bruising but productive struggles with such issues were reported in gloating detail in the press, which took delight in proclaiming that feminism was self-destructing.

However, not even the recession of the 1980s stopped the continuing formation, beginning in the 1970s, of women-organized, more-or-less feminist service or cultural groups for women, often the successors to the women's liberation movement: rape crisis centres, health centres, and abortion referral services; transition houses for battered women, hostels for homeless women and for teenage mothers; women's centres and women's studies programs; women's magazines, journals, and presses; women's music and arts centres and companies. Such groups and institutions continue to appear and disappear, even if often with short life spans.

In the context of this book, our interest is in those parts of the second-wave movement that can be seen as influencing the treatment of women by Canadian society and, more specifically, by governments. These were the counterparts and often the causes of the government attitudes and activities detailed in the chapters by Sandra Burt and Beverley Baines; they are the better recorded parts of the movement. But it is important to remember that the vitality and importance of feminism were crucially dependent on the myriad small groups that influenced both individuals and the larger society simply because they existed.

In addition, any comprehensive account of the women's movement – which is not attempted here – will have to include some discussion of the resistance to the second wave of feminism by conservatives. In Canada this backlash has been slow to emerge, and in the 1990s it is only beginning to become significant. Groups like the anti-abortionist REAL Women and Alberta's AFWUF are related to the feminism they attack.[5] Furthermore, they, too, responded to the surviving inequities in the treatment of women; they, too, in their misinformed defence of a traditional family that no longer exists, attempted to obtain recognition and reward for the distinctive abilities and activities of women.

Royal Commission on the Status of Women

In general, it makes sense to date the second wave of feminism from the appearance of new women's organizations in the 1960s. Even though the first among these resembled their predecessors, they survived and changed into something unarguably part of a new era. In Canada the group that seems to have been the earliest, the Voice of Women, picked up in 1960 the feminist pacifism of the interwar period. Voice of Women was formed in response to a newspaper column by Lotta Dempsey asking desperately whether women couldn't do something to deal with international conflict and the threat of war. Hundreds of women wrote in and thousands eventually joined a grassroots organization whose activity over the next decades extended from anti-nuclear vigils to international conferences and protest marches. To their great pride, the Secretary of State for External Affairs, Howard Green, gave the group credit for Canada's delay in joining the missile alert at the time of the Cuban Missile Crisis. Guided by scientist Ursula Franklin, Voice members presented the government with thousands of baby teeth documenting how strontium-90 in fallout from nuclear testing had got into the food chain and into the bones of children; this demonstration played a role in producing the 1963 test-ban treaty. Other campaigns, ranging from knitting for the children of North Vietnam to boycotting war toys, mobilized a large number of women at the community level and helped to shape public opinion about Cold War and environmental issues.[6]

Voice of Women showed a familiar pattern of membership – married women with children – and motivation – concern for mainly well-being and therefore for a safe, peaceful, and non-nuclear world. Initially, this group did not look like anything new, but over the years it steadily became more political and more feminist. Many of its members went on to be active in other second-wave groups and in mainstream politics. Representatives of Voice of Women were important in the series of events, beginning in 1966, that produced the Royal Commission on the Status of Women and, later, the national women's organization formed in 1972 to pressure for implementation of the commission's recommendations. This was the National Action Committee on the Status of Women (NAC), an umbrella group, which by 1986 could claim to represent five million women in more than five hundred organizations.

After the founding of Voice of Women, the next important surge of feminist organization took place in Quebec. The Fédération des femmes du Québec, established in 1966 as a follow-up to the twenty-fifth anniversary celebrations of the enfranchisement of women in Quebec, drew together most of the existing women's groups, including some anglophone ones. At the same time, the Association féminine d'éducation et d'action sociale consolidated and reactivated two of the other, older, more Catholic women's groups, which focused on the interests of housewives and of women working in family businesses. By the mid-1960s a significant number of the existing francophone groups were realigned, and ready for action. The two large coalitions were in close and friendly contact, linked also with Voice of Women: suffragist Thérèse Casgrain was the chief organizer of the Fédération and of la Voix des femmes, the Quebec branch of Voice of Women, as well as the second national president of Voice of Women.[7]

It is a pattern of continuity and overlap, which makes it look as if there was no break between the first and second wave of the Canadian women's movement. Yet there was. To begin with, the push that produced the Royal Commission was itself something unprecedented.

The campaign for the Royal Commission on the Status of Women began publicly in 1966, when Doris Anderson wrote in a *Chatelaine* editorial: "Reluctant as I am to suggest one more be added to the groaning shelfful of past Royal Commissions, I believe it's time we had a study on the status of women in Canada today." Anderson justified the request by the level and nature of women's participation in education and the work force and concluded, reassuringly:

What we don't need in a commission is an all-woman witch-hunt. We do need a forward-looking commission composed equally of impartial men and women prepared to take a cool twentieth-century approach to our problems. Because these questions affect us all – men, women and children, and for our own collective good, we should set about getting some answers.[8]

Under Anderson's leadership, *Chatelaine,* the largest of Canada's popular women's magazines, had come to incorporate a fair amount of feminist content; she had rejected the offered serialization of Betty Friedan's *The Feminine Mystique* on the grounds that *Chatelaine* had already covered most of the same subjects.[9] In this editorial she was deliberately supporting an initiative spearheaded by Laura Sabia, who in 1966 was president of the Canadian Federation of University Women. A successful city councillor in St. Catharines, Ontario, unsuccessful provincial candidate, and popular radio talk-show host, Sabia was a charmer and a rabble-rouser, endlessly energetic as a campaigner and organizer, following in the line of women like Emily Murphy who had energized the first wave of Canadian feminism.

The thirty-two-member Committee on Equality for Women that Sabia drew together was made up of representatives of the large voluntary and professional women's organizations, including the most vocal and consistent campaigners for woman suffrage.[10] These groups had continued to be active, if relatively unnoticed; for instance, the National Council of Jewish Women had an early involvement with promoting birth control, and the Business and Professional Women's Clubs had been important in producing the equal-pay legislation of the 1950s. Their attitudes can be inferred from their ready response to Sabia's appeal; in the same year, their counterparts in the United States had explicitly refused suggestions that they become publicly involved in issues of women's equality.

The Committee on Equality for Women could reasonably claim to represent the organized women of Canada. Although the Fédération des femmes du Québec did not participate actively in drawing up a presentation to the prime minister, Thérèse Casgrain and Réjane Laberge-Colas (first president of the Fédération and later, first woman to be appointed judge in a Canadian Superior Court) joined the delegation to Ottawa. The women's groups of all three political parties also supported the brief, as did a considerable number of women's professional and service groups; there were some sixty observers accompanying the five women who made up the official delegation. That support of women meant support of national unity should have been obvious; that the second wave of feminism was going to be federalist was also clear.

The Pearson government nevertheless virtually ignored the group's first mildly posed request. Laura Sabia was provoked into what *The Globe and Mail* reported as an "ultimatum to the Government: establish a royal commission or face the consequences":

"We're tired of being nice about trying to get an official enquiry into women's rights in Canada," Mrs. Sabia said. "If we don't get a royal commission by the end of this month, we'll use every tactic we can. And if we have to use violence, damn it, we will."[11]

Sabia threatened to march two million women on Ottawa, which got her the headlines she needed. In terms of specific timing, her group was responsible for the establishment of the Royal Commission. But we may wonder whether Prime Minister Pearson (who, with his customary adroitness, had evaded any face-to-face meeting with the women's delegation) was more than embarrassed by such hollow threats.

Pearson's eventual action probably responded to the same interrelated patterns of women's education and work that explain the second wave of feminism. From the perspective of the government, women's lesser rewards and lesser opportunities to participate in the expanding economy translated into a lesser contribution to national growth. Doris Anderson made this point in her 1966 editorial: "Perhaps we should pause in our breast-beating about the brain drain to the United States," she wrote, "and consider whether we are using all of our own mental resources."

In addition, there were political reasons to placate women whom the 1966 approach to the government showed to be dissatisfied. In Cabinet, the Honourable Judy LaMarsh put up a lonely but highly visible fight on behalf of women and a commission of enquiry. In Parliament, the New Democratic Party, urged on by their only woman MP, Grace MacInnis, used the issue of a women's commission as yet another handy weapon against a government that lacked an absolute majority. By 1965 Canadian women were voting at approximately the same level as men and participating in campaign activities almost as frequently; women's votes might possibly be swayed.

The request for a royal commission was ideally suited to the double purposes of getting the necessary information about fully integrating women into the work force while appeasing and possibly defusing any feminist activism. This was a period of numerous royal commissions in Canada, most conspicuously the Royal Commission on Bilingualism and Biculturalism (1963-71). It is a truism of Canadian politics that one way to deal with insistent claims is to "royal-commission them to death." "There was a general consensus in editorials all across the country that the Commission would be pigeon-holed and forgotten," wrote Florence Bird, the U.S.-born Chairman of the Commission: "It was also often suggested that the Commission was a political gimmick to allow women to let off steam and appease Judy LaMarsh and Laura Sabia's cohorts."[12]

As occasionally happens, the Royal Commission on the Status of Women turned out to be far more dynamic, even more progressive, than might have been expected. For instance, Jeanne Lapointe, a Quebec academic selected for cultural (and political) reasons and for her experience with the Parent Commission on education in Quebec, was transformed by the experience into an active radical feminist. The unprecedentedly extensive public hearings held by the RCSW in fourteen cities over a period of ten months had a major impact on the media and on the public, and also on all the members of the group.

Most importantly, Elsie Gregory MacGill, past president of the Canadian Federation of Business and Professional Women, first Canadian woman to be an aeronautical engineer, was effectively the vice-president of the RCSW. Born in British Columbia, she could be seen to have a regional significance and to represent both women in business and women in science, a counterpart for the Quebec/education, prairies/farm, and Maritimes/law roles of commissioners Jeanne Lapointe, Lola Lange, and Judge Doris Ogilvie respectively.[13] MacGill was an ardent, committed, and highly effective third-generation feminist, and it was really she who educated the commissioners. Later she was to be active in NAC and other organizations founded in the 1970s to implement the RCSW's report. The Royal Commission thus inherited, from both founders and participants, the active tradition of the Canadian women's movement. It passed on that tradition through successor organizations and through the document they took as their agenda, the 1970 report of the Royal Commission on the Status of Women.

Canadian Women's Liberation

The key period for the second wave of the Canadian women's movement was the years 1967 to 1970. The activities of the Royal Commission in this period resulted in a significant increase in public awareness of women's situation. The same period produced women's liberation and radical feminism in Canada. These latter groups, which drew substantial public attention, can take much of the credit for directing attention to such crucial women's issues as equal pay, abortion, and violence against women. The groups themselves were crucial in the co-operative efforts that got such issues both onto the agenda for public policy and into the consciousness of individual women.

At the time of the Committee on Equality's project for a royal commission, the future members of women's liberation still identified with the student left. But they had become aware that, within their own movement, they were exploited as quasi-secretarial help and as sex objects, while the men who ran that movement failed to respond to a plea for liberation at home. In addition, they were unable to persuade the male students that the oppression of women was a valid political issue. Like their fore-

mothers, they were faced with the refusal to allow women a voice in politics – in their case, revolutionary politics. Finally, following earlier precedents, they organized autonomous, women-only groups that could work
for both women and society as a whole.

By 1967 Toronto housed one of the five women's liberation groups in
North America; in 1968 a Feminine Action League appeared at Simon
Fraser University, then a Women's Caucus in Vancouver. In 1969 similar
groups were established in Regina, Saskatoon, Winnipeg, Ottawa, Kingston, Guelph, Hamilton region, Halifax, Sudbury, Thunder Bay, and
Edmonton; Montreal Women's Liberation began in the fall of 1969
among students and faculty at McGill and Sir George Williams universities. In a student movement that was continental, the Canadian groups do
not seem anything special to U.S. historians. But their grievances were
articulated somewhat differently, and the Canadian segments of the
movement were indeed significantly different.

The 1967 document "Sisters, Brothers, Lovers, Listen . . ." shows just
how Canadian the members of women's liberation were. The piece's
authors, the women's caucus of the Toronto student organization, SUPA,
still hoped to persuade their comrades to recognize the significance of sexism. They continued to focus to some extent on the history that the Canadian student activists shared with the antecedents of women's liberation in
the United States: "male chauvinism" in the student movement was compared to "a civil rights organization with a leadership of southern racists."
But the women reluctantly went on to consider secession: "If we are really
serious about changing our role, then we better start doing it – no one is
going to do it for us." And they ended with an image drawn from Lord
Durham and used by Egerton Ryerson and Mackenzie King: "We are
going to be the typers of letters and distributors of leaflets (hewers of wood
and drawers of water) no longer."[14]

They also tapped Canadian traditions in other ways. Although "Sisters,
Brothers . . ." voiced the resentment felt by the student-activist women
who found they were expected to make coffee, not policy, women who
were part of the Canadian women's liberation groups agreed that they did
not leave with the same anger as their U.S. counterparts. In this they saw
an echo of the history of the Canadian reform movement. Groups such as
the Grain Growers of Alberta had supported women both in their suffrag-
ism and in their desire for separate, single-sex organizations. For the Canadian second wave, Manitoba suffragist Nellie McClung became a heroine once more. Later, Canadian feminists were to be more selective about
their history, so that the pacifist and socialist strands in Canadian suffrag-
ism were often preferred to the more patriotic and gender-oriented ones;
Nellie McClung was then criticized for ethnocentrism and for her support
of the Canadian entry into the First World War.[15] But feminist attention to

these individuals and issues in itself differentiated the Canadian movement from the U.S. one.

In Quebec the situation of feminists in the student movement was both similar to and different from that of those in the rest of Canada, with nationalism playing a crucial role. The anglophone sector of the movement was the first to make its appearance, and the student feminists at Sir George Williams and McGill universities then encouraged establishment of the first francophone group, le Front de libération des femmes du Québec. But the very name of the French group indicates its context: it was a response to the marginalization of women in the independentist Front de libération du Québec. The first public action of Toronto Women's Liberation had been, in 1968, an intervention in a winter bikini contest, protesting the marketing of women as sex objects. In contrast, the first public action of the feminist Front was a protest in 1969 against governmental repression of trade-union and other leftist-nationalist activity in Montreal. [16]

Many feminist issues were shared between Quebec and the rest of Canada; the priorities and the action were not. In 1970 women's liberation groups all across Canada joined in an Abortion Caravan that ended in Ottawa on Mother's Day with a demonstration that closed up Parliament, as women chained themselves to the Visitors' Gallery. The same day, the Front had its own pro-choice demonstration in Montreal; they had refused an invitation to join the caravaners on the grounds that they denied the legitimacy of the federal regulations. Challenging present and future governments of Quebec to serve women better, they placed their feminist efforts squarely in the context of independentism.

The effects of Quebec nationalism thus extended even to reproductive rights, the issue that most often transcended the differences within the women's movement. In 1968 the McGill Student Society had produced the widely distributed *Birth Control Handbook,* illegal until the 1969 reform of the Criminal Code that permitted advertising and sale of contraceptives. The Front helped to translate and distribute the handbook and, with Montreal Women's Liberation, staffed a follow-up abortion referral service. But in 1970 the francophones in women's liberation in Quebec expelled the anglophones, dividing up even the referral services. The struggle for independence, central among leftist issues in Quebec, meant that linguistic barriers were symbolic of Quebec identity: anglophone feminists were seen as representatives of the federalist 'colonizers.' Furthermore, autonomous, women-only feminist organizations faced practically insurmountable obstacles, for they seemed to deny the priority of the national struggle. The Front survived only into 1971, producing the first issue of its important newspaper, *Québécoises deboutte!* Its successor, the

Centre des femmes, struggled on for three years (1972-75), active mainly in abortion referral and in producing further issues of the newspaper.

Marxist and socialist feminism in Quebec, closely related to the strongly nationalist and well-organized union movement and to the independentist Parti Québécois, was effective only within those mainstream groups; from the early 1970s, all had status-of-women committees. Their major achievements were, under the Parti Québécois government, reforms in family and related law and a policy tolerating free-standing abortion clinics. The Front commun of public service unions also succeeded, in 1979, in obtaining generous paid maternity leave for its female members.

In anglophone Canada the pattern was different, in that women's liberation and its successors succeeded in co-operating with other feminist groups, including those of the first wave. In this case, Canadian issues and Canadian nationalism served to unify the different segments of the women's movement. Within the student movement – which shaped the founders of women's liberation – there was increasing hostility to the U.S. war resisters who came to Canada and expected to lead the left opposition. "The problem the Canadian left faces is not the draft," stated a 1969 pamphlet of the Toronto Women's Liberation Group; "It is American imperialism."[17] In the 1960s that issue included the cultural imperialism represented by the American intellectuals who came to fill the faculties and swell the student bodies of the expanding Canadian universities.

Such views made women's liberation converge somewhat with the Voice of Women. Socialist feminists shared from the start Voice's opposition to the Vietnam War; as both groups became more nationalist, they protested Canada's complicity in the process through arms sales and membership in NATO and NORAD. Both also came to share the general nationalist response to American cultural and economic as well as political influence. Possibly even more importantly, Voice of Women – as well as the surviving first-wave groups – had in common with women's liberation the Canadian feminist conviction that women were more able than men to protect Canadian values, including the equal treatment of women and active resistance to American influence.

In addition, the different women's groups became more similar as Voice of Women became more explicitly feminist and less concentrated on anti-nuclear issues. Peace and environmental concerns were close: both related to the world in which children were to live. Voice of Women found itself asking for a moratorium on exploration of the North until the environmental issues were investigated. It worried about dumping of radioactive substances and called for Canadian withdrawal from NATO and NORAD as well as refusal of nuclear weapons. Environmental issues included concerns for the social and political climate, and for the possible influence of women there. Halifax Voice made an investigation of the employment of blacks in Halifax and in 1971 Toronto Voice started a daughter group called Women for Political Action to assist women to become active in conventional politics. Women had commonalities across language and culture, and Voice had a Quebec branch, so Voice became a supporter of bilingualism, biculturalism, and Quebec's special identity. These are all leftist – and women's liberation – issues.

At the same time, liberation groups turned towards direct services for women. Class analysis of women's oppression made the middle-class liberationists set up organizations devoted to the needs of poor and needy women, much as their foremothers had. Their analysis of femininity as an ideology and their interest in reproduction as an analogue to production directed their attention to education, child care, and the family – 'women's issues.' Job-training and referral were obvious needs of working-class women. In addition, women's liberation groups became involved with health care and with referral services related to reproduction, as well as with hostels and counselling services for the predominantly female victims of public and family violence (battery, incest, rape). In spite of a primary goal of political education, they found themselves engaged in the long-established tradition of feminist philanthropy.

Radical Feminism

Meanwhile, Voice of Women continued to campaign against the sale of war toys. How more effectively could mothers make known their opposition to war? And how more effectively could they influence the social conditioning of sons as well as daughters? The concern with sexual stereotyping was, of course, shared by the liberal-feminist groups who critiqued textbooks and mass media for their image of women as dependent and inferior. But Voice of Women's commitment to notions of women's specificity aligned them less with liberal feminism than with the groups calling themselves 'radical feminist,' which grew out of women's liberation, beginning in 1969 in Toronto and much later in Quebec.

There were ironies here, for radical feminists were heterodox in their lifestyles and in their views of the family, explicitly theoretical in their analyses, and committed to the liberationist procedures of consciousness-raising. They were very different from the wives-and-mothers of Voice of Women. Indeed, it was from radical feminism that women often moved to feminist lesbianism. Yet radical feminists shared with Voice of Women the central assumptions that women were the crucial agents of social change, and that men and male values were responsible for much that was wrong with society.

In general, the Canadian women's liberation groups in their first years disliked and rejected the very term 'feminist,' associating it with an ideology "in which the critique of the family usually takes precedence over the critique of capitalism."[18] Proudly socialist and proudly nationalist, members of women's liberation initially felt that 'feminism' identified a U.S. movement that, unlike the Canadian, promoted a sort of sex war between men and women. Later they developed the notion of socialist feminism, and Canadian socialist-feminist academics did important work on the concept of 'reproductive' domestic labour. Here was a basis for more convergence among women's groups, for the household was always central to the analyses made by radical feminism. In fact, in 1969 Bonnie Kreps, who had been active in New York Radical Feminists, seems to have started the first radical-feminist group in Canada by walking out of a Toronto Women's Liberation meeting that refused to accept that "women were oppressed in the household."[19]

For the radical feminists, liberation was related to asserting the uniqueness of women's situation; their earliest goal tended to be obliteration of gender roles as a basis of oppression. In Canada a major target was the conditioning of children into (aggressive) men and (submissive) women; the logic produced campaigns to allow girl children to wear comfortable jeans instead of seemly skirts to school. Such concerns clearly have affinities to VOW's campaign against war toys as part of the process of socialization to male violence. Like Voice of Women and like much else in the Canadian women's movement, Toronto's New Feminists started from an insistence on the uniqueness and unique value of women's experience, and on the absolute right of women to define it for themselves and to reshape society accordingly. Voice and the first-wave survivors made such claims in the name of their own families and society; radical feminists spoke for women as a group; all called for a drastically reformed society responsive to women's values and priorities.

Toronto New Feminists seems to be the only radical-feminist group in English Canada to have left records, including a newspaper; they voluntarily dissolved in 1973. In Quebec an important radical-feminist paper, *Les Têtes de pioche,* was influential beginning in 1976. Certainly, radical-feminist groups or fragments must have existed elsewhere. They seem to have begun and continued in a pattern of political co-operation with other women's organizations. Like the Canadian women's liberation groups, they had connections with the National Action Committee on the Status of Women and, like them, they co-operated in lobbying campaigns such as those connected with the inclusion of 'sex' in human rights codes. More recently, groups such as Women Against Violence Against Women, most often associated with Take-Back-the-Night marches protesting street violence, were clearly radical feminist in orientation, as was the group that attempted to organize the Feminist Party of Canada beginning in 1979. The strong coalitions against pornography also seem to have had radical-feminist inspiration, as do many elements of women's studies in Canadian universities. The impact of radical feminism can be recognized by an insistence on the primacy of gender as a basis of women's oppression and usually also by the rule that no men can participate in the group.

But these last are, as we have noted, views shared by many elements of the Canadian women's movement over time, in both the first and second waves. In general a high degree of overlap and relatively amiable co-existence are major characteristics of the second wave of the Canadian women's movement. These characteristics produce (and are in part produced by) the overall umbrella of the National Action Committee on the Status of Women and the overlapping coalitions within it, as well as the relationship all groups share with the federal government. At a provincial level similar patterns of mutual toleration and co-operation exist, at least in public. For instance, in 1976 the British Columbia Federation of Women was able to organize a massive demonstration and lobbying effort at the provincial parliament to protest when the Social Credit government cut off funding to women's groups.

Quebec, of course, is always different. Even when co-operation within the province is possible, groups find it hard to work across linguistic boundaries and even harder to collaborate with the necessarily federalist national women's groups. It is remarkable that the Fédération des femmes du Québec and the Association féminine d'éducation et d'action sociale have been members of NAC during much of its existence.

After the Royal Commission

The Royal Commission on the Status of Women reported in 1970. The National Council of Women and the Fédération des femmes du Québec had been given advance access to the *Report* so that they could prepare summaries in English and French for wide distribution. Four underlying principles were stated in the introductory section; they encompassed the double set of demands of the second wave.

The first principle was "that women should be free to choose whether or not to take employment outside their homes." It recognized women's double role, noted the validity of both sectors of it, and gave women the right to autonomous decisions about their own choices. It also obligated society to make the considerable changes that would make such choices realistically possible. The same social obligation, as well as the desirability of major change in men's domestic responsibilities, was implied in principle two: "The care of children is a responsibility to be shared by the mother, the father and society." Principle three was that "Society has a responsibility for women because of pregnancy and child-birth, and special treatment related to maternity will always be necessary," a recognition of women's biological specificity and its value. Treatment of women exactly as if they were men was not acceptable. Finally, the *Report* specifically noted in principle four the existence of discrimination and the need for affirmative action to counteract its consequences: "In certain areas women will for an interim period require special treatment to overcome the adverse effects of discriminatory practices."[20]

Guided by these principles, the commissioners made 167 recommendations, whose implications were radical indeed. The majority of the recommendations dealt with direct or indirect discrimination against women. Some went further. For instance, they called for a national day care act committing the federal government to contribute to both operating expenses and capital costs. They also recommended adoption of the principle of equal pay for work of equal value (replacing the existing regulations, which provided only equal pay for equal work). And they recommended that abortion be permitted "by a qualified medical practitioner on the sole request of any woman who has been pregnant for twelve weeks or less."[21] None of these measures has yet been fully adopted, although there is limited federal and provincial legislation related to equal pay for work of equal value, and in January 1988 the Supreme Court ruled that the federal abortion law was unconstitutional.

Those who had been active in demanding the RCSW remained active in the follow-up period. Impatient when the government did not produce immediate responses to the Royal Commission Report, they turned the Committee on Equality for Women into a National Ad Hoc Committee on the Status of Women in Canada. It met during 1971, adding a number of new groups, including the liberal-feminist Manitoba Action Committee on the Status of Women, Toronto Women's Liberation, and Toronto's radical-feminist New Feminists.[22] This group presented a substantial brief to the government, and then early in 1972 it became the continuing organization, the National Action Committee on the Status of Women (NAC). As the continuation of the Committee on Equality for Women, it precedes the emergence of women's liberation in Canada.

NAC was inaugurated by a large, successful national conference held in the spring of 1972. Called "Strategy for Change," this conference set a pattern for feminist co-operation, with Voice of Women president Helen Tucker in the chair, Elsie Gregory MacGill as keynote speaker, Toronto New Feminists running the workshops, and over five hundred women from more than forty groups present. A group of militants protested what they viewed as excessive moderation. But although a radical caucus finally presented a minority report calling, among other things, for all-women media crews, the whole conference agreed to endorse all of the RCSW recommendations, except the proposal for status of women councils to be appointed by the government.

NAC quickly became and remained an almost all-encompassing umbrella group, which included through indirect affiliation a considerable number of organizations that did not belong directly. For the 1984 federal elections the group was able to pull off the considerable coup of sponsoring a public, nationally televised debate on women's issues between the leaders of the three major parties. The group had sufficient acceptability as the representative of Canadian women that, in the mid-1980s, anti-feminists began to challenge it.

The Impact of the Second Wave

Second-wave feminism in Canada is clearly distinctive. There seems to be no equivalent elsewhere to the way in which the National Action Committee on the Status of Women was able to incorporate into its membership – as it still does – first-wave survivor groups, representatives of women's liberation, the new pressure groups organized around the RCSW recommendations, and the many sectoral women's groups, as well as the cultural and service inheritors of women's liberation.

If we sort out the elements of NAC's membership in the ideological terms most commonly used to discuss feminism, we can say that the organization managed to accommodate groups whose ideologies ran the gamut of feminist belief from liberal through Marxist and socialist to radical, as discussed by Lorraine Code in the first chapter of this book. Putting it another way, we can say that NAC members ranged along almost all of the possibilities of equity feminism, which extends existing belief systems to include women. They were, by and large, groups that were separate from corresponding male or mixed groups because those organizations had failed or refused to incorporate into their agendas the demands made by women. NAC members also included, however, organizations that subscribed to social-feminist beliefs extending women's domestic values to public life.[23] These included the first-wave groups described in Jane Errington's chapter; they also included radical feminists, a second-wave category entirely novel in its analyses and actions.

This variety of feminists, however described and classified, can be found in every country. What is unique to Canada is their ability to co-operate in institutional terms, if only intermittently and incompletely. This account of the first years of the second wave suggests how the Canadian context – the situation of women, the history of women, and the convergence of feminist goals and beliefs – created clusters of compatible new and old organizations.

Analysis of their impact is another and even more difficult task. As Sandra Burt points out in her chapter on public policy, the commission contributed to a significant transformation in the federal government's treatment of women's rights. All assessments agree that the legal standing of women in Canada has been much improved since 1967, particularly in regard to citizenship and immigration and to family law and family property law, as well as the law concerning sexual assault (under which heading rape is now included). Legal regulation of workplace access and conditions is also much improved. However, equal-pay legislation has been disappointing in its impact, and government training schemes have made only minor adjustments to the necessity of retraining women, especially in relation to non-traditional trades for women (the ones that are expected to expand in the near future). In 1985, as Sally Weaver discusses in her chapter, the situation of Native women was finally equalized in law when those married to non-Indians were given back status for themselves and their children. The Canadian armed forces have lifted their bar against women in combat roles.

In addition the government cleaned up the sexist language it had previously used, began to increase the role and number of women in the public service, and put in place a fairly substantial bureaucracy directed towards status of women. Funds for the support of women's groups, including NAC, were made available through the Women's Program of the Ministry of the Secretary of State as well as, on a smaller scale, the Minister Responsible for the Status of Women. These funds decreased in the late 1980s, however, in response to economic and ideological pressures, and by the end of the decade were pretty much restricted to support of limited projects. The government has made something of an attempt to appoint women to federal boards and commissions: women even appeared on the governing body of Air Canada and at the head of the board of Canadian National Railway as well as, also for the first time, as head of the national granting agency for the arts, the Canada Council. The party in power during most of the 1970s, the Liberal Party, successfully ran a number of women in safe ridings, and appointed a more substantial number of women senators (including Thérèse Casgrain, Florence Bird, chairman of the RCSW, and the first black Senator, Anne Cools). It also appointed a woman governor general (former cabinet minister Jeanne Sauvé) as well as the first woman member of the Supreme Court of Canada (Bertha Wilson; the second, Claire L'Heureux-Dubé, was appointed by the Conservative government in 1987). In the federal Conservative government elected in 1988 women held the portfolios of finance and justice for the first time, and in 1990 the Ontario NDP government installed a cabinet that was 40 per cent women. Audrey McLaughlin of the NDP became the first woman to head a federal party and June Rowlands of Toronto became the first woman mayor of a major metropolitan centre. Still, by 1991 women MPs held only 13 per cent of the House of Common seats.

By 1987 most of the RCSW recommendations related to legal inequalities had been implemented on the federal level. In the meantime, discussions and disputes about the equality provisions of the Charter in the early 1980s had clarified feminists' perceptions of their goals in relation to government: equal administration of law, equal laws (no laws treating women in discriminatory fashion), and also no laws that indirectly had a discriminatory impact on women. After the 1984 *Report* of the Royal Commission on Equality in Employment, a one-person inquiry by Judge Rosalie Silberman Abella, the term "structural discrimination" was available to make it clear that even without intending it, existing policies and procedures could disadvantage women. The logical consequence was positive acts of remedy, an extension of the RCSW's notion of "special measures." In the mid-1980s, governments began affirmative action in a limited and gingerly fashion, mainly voluntary and slow to take effect.

As might have been predicted, the slowest area of change was in regards to abortion. It is significant that the RCSW disagreed internally on this matter, with three commissioners objecting to liberalization and Elsie Gregory MacGill asking for more radical measures. It is also significant, and probably an achievement of the second wave, that by 1988 over 70 per cent of the Canadian population agreed that abortion was a medical decision to be taken by a woman in consultation with her physician.[24] There was general support for that year's 5-2 Supreme Court decision declaring the federal legislation on abortion unconstitutional under the Charter of Rights. But right-to-life groups intensified their activities, picketing clinics and demanding new, restrictive legislation. The government prepared an attempt at compromise, a bill that would have recriminalized abortion under more liberal provisions than previously. It squeaked through the House but was defeated by the Senate on January 31, 1991, by the closest possible vote. Using their powers related to health care, some provincial governments continued nevertheless to block access to abortion.

By the 1990s it was still not easy to evaluate all this activity, difficult to see the causes, and more difficult still to make judgements about the outcome. Let us close with an example that illustrates the contradictions that feminists encounter: the integration of women into the Canadian armed forces.

In 1987 Sheila Hellstrom became Canada's first woman (Brigadier) General. "I am not a woman officer," she told reporters. "I am an officer first, who just happens to be a woman." Feminists were bound to realize that General Hellstrom had previously been disadvantaged as a woman in the military, whatever she believed. They also realized that she was promoted in part because of the insistence of the women's movement on not just equal treatment, but positive measures to advance women. At the same time many feminists are also pacifists who want equality for women in order to bring peaceful, domestic considerations to bear on public policy. "The main reason for the lack of women at senior levels in the Canadian Forces," commented Major (Res.) Doris Guyatt, "is the Canadian Forces policy that has denied women the opportunity to serve in combat roles and, consequently, the opportunity to gain the operational experience necessary to progress to the top."[25] It was also in 1987 that the Canadian forces began the steps necessary for integrating women into combat roles. This, like General Hellstrom's promotion, could count as a victory for the women's movement. In 1991 women were among the Canadian participants in the Gulf War. But if these changes removed discrimination, what did they do for women's hopes of changing society by their participation in public life?

The answer to that question, eventually, will be the answer to the question of the impact of the second wave of feminism on Canadian life.

Naomi Black

Brief Chronology of the Second Wave

1960
   Voice of Women; Quebec branch 1961

1961
   Planned Parenthood of Canada

1966
   La Fédération des femmes du Québec
   L'Association féminine d'éducation et d'action sociale
   The Committee on Equality for Women

1967
   The Royal Commission on the Status of Women
   Toronto Women's Liberation

1968
   Feminine Action League, Simon Fraser University; Women's Caucus, Vancouver
   1st edition of McGill *Birth Control Handbook*

Indian Rights for Indian Women
Birthright

1969

Montreal Women's Liberation starts at McGill and Sir George Williams universities

1969-1970

Women's Liberation groups in Regina, Saskatoon, Winnipeg, Ottawa, Kingston, Guelph, Hamilton region, Halifax, Sudbury, Thunder Bay, Edmonton

1969-1971

Le Front de libération des femmes du Québec; *Québécoises deboutte!* no. 1.

1969-1973

Toronto New Feminists

1970

Abortion Caravan organized by Vancouver Women's Liberation
Report of the Royal Commission on the Status of Women

1971

National Ad Hoc Committee on the Status of Women
Ontario Committee on the Status of Women
Women for Political Action

1972

"Strategy for Change" Conference (Toronto) and founding of National Action Committee on the Status of Women (NAC)
Le Centre des femmes (-1975) – remaining issues of *Québécoises deboutte!*

1973

Federal and Ontario Advisory Councils on the Status of Women
Le Réseau d'action et d'information pour les femmes (Montreal)
First national lesbian conference, YWCA, Toronto; first Canadian lesbian journal *Long Time Coming* (Montreal)
First national conference of black women

1974

Canadian Association for the Repeal of the Abortion Laws (CARAL – after 1980, Canadian Abortion Rights Action League)

Native Women's Association of Canada, l'Association des femmes autochtones du Québec

1975

Canadian Association of Women Executives

National Association of Women and the Law

1976-1979

Les Têtes de pioche published by radical feminists in Quebec

1976

L'Association des femmes collaboratrices

Lesbian Organization of Toronto

1977

Le Coop-femmes (Montreal)

Women Against Violence Against Women (WAVAW)

Pluri-elles; in 1978 becomes *Des luttes et des rires des femmes*

1979

Feminist Party of Canada

1981

Canadian Congress for Learning Opportunities for Women

AFWUF (Alberta Federation of Women United for the Family)

1983

Canadian Coalition Against Media Pornography

REAL Women (Realistic Equal Active for Life)

NOTES

1. *Weekend Magazine,* May 3, 1979; "Womanpoll: Women's Roles and Rights," *Chatelaine,* May 1986, 42; Christy McLaren, "Environment Tops Free Trade in Poll of Canadians," *The Globe and Mail,* January 15, 1987.

2. "Most Say Hubby Should Help at Home," *The Toronto Star,* March 10, 1986.

3. Betty Lehan Harragan, *Games Mother Never Taught You: Corporate Gamesmanship for Women* (New York: Warner Books, 1977); Isabel Bassett, *The Bassett Report: Career Success and Canadian Women* (Toronto: Collins Publishers, 1985), 282, 288.

4. Indian Rights for Indian Women, Canadian Congress of Black Women, Concerned Farm Women, and Society of Spouses of Military Personnel are a few examples of such groups, which represent most ethnic and occupational groupings of women.

5. The acronyms stand for Realistic, Equal, and Active for Life and Alberta Federation of Women United for the Family.

6. Kay Macpherson and Meg Sears, "The Voice of Women: A History," in Gwen Matheson, ed., *Women in the Canadian Mosaic* (Toronto: Peter Martin, 1976), 71-89; Peggy Hope-Smith and Muriel Duckworth, "Voice of Women Dialogue," *Atlantis* 6, no. 2 (1981): 168-177; Kay Macpherson, "Persistent Voices: Twenty-Five Years with Voice of Women," *Atlantis* 12, no. 2 (1987): 168-176; Candace Loewen, "Mike Hears Voices: Voice of Women and Lester Pearson, 1960-63," *Atlantis* 12, no. 2 (1987): 46-48.

7. Collectif Clio, *L'histoire des femmes au Québec depuis quatre siècles* (Montreal: Editions Quinze, 1982), 453-458; Azilda Marchand, "Les femmes au foyer: Hier et demain," *Canadian Woman Studies/Les cahiers de la femme* 2, no. 2 (1980): 15-16.

8. *Chatelaine,* July 1966.

9. Doris Anderson, "Women's Magazines in the 1970s," *Canadian Woman Studies/Les cahiers de la femme* 2, no. 2 (1980): 15-16.

10. Most important among these first-wave groups were the Canadian Federation of Business and Professional Women's Clubs; the Federation of Women Teachers' Associations of Ontario; the National Council of Jewish Women; the National Council of Women of Canada; the Imperial Order Daughters of the Empire; the WCTU; the YWCA; and the Federated Women's Institutes. *See*: Cerise Morris, "'Determination and Thoroughness': The Movement for a Royal Commission on the Status of Women in Canada," *Atlantis* 5, no. 2 (1980):1-21.

11. "Women's March May Back Call for Rights Probe," *The Globe and Mail,* January 5, 1967.

12. Florence Bird, *Anne Francis: An Autobiography* (Toronto: Clarke Irwin, 1974), 4.

13. There were also two men on the Commission, demographer Jacques Henripin and John Humphrey, a lawyer who had represented Canada at the United Nations' Human Rights Commission for twenty years. Humphrey replaced an initial appointee, Donald Gordon, who resigned after a few months and never played an active role on the Commission.

14. This document was prepared for the organizing meeting of the New Left Committee, which had just split away from the Students' Union for Peace Action. It is partly reprinted in Sara Evans, *Personal Politics: The Roots of Women's Liberation in the Civil Rights Movement and the New Left* (New York: Vintage Books, 1980) and more fully in *Women Unite!* (Toronto: Women's Educational Press, 1972). The citation about "hewers of wood and haulers of water" is from the latter, with changed emphasis (page 39).

15. Gloria Geller, "The Wartime Elections Act of 1917 and the Canadian Women's Movement," *Atlantis* 2, no. 1 (1976), 88-106.

16. On the Front de libération des femmes du Québec, *see*: Veronique O'Leary et Louise Toupin, *Québecoises deboutte!* (Montreal: Les éditions du remue-ménage, 1982).

17. The Toronto Women's Liberation Group, "Is Feminism Necessary for Women's Liberation?" (Canadian Union of Students, 1969), 3.

18. Charnie Guettel, *Marxism and Feminism* (Toronto: Women's Educational Press, 1974), 48.

19. Letter from Bonnie Kreps, November 1986.

20. Royal Commission on the Status of Women, *Report* (Ottawa: Information Canada, 1970), xii.

21. Ibid., Recommendation 127.

22. New volunteer status-of-women organizations developed in most provinces to pressure for implementation of the recommendations of the Royal Commission. These groups should not be confused with government-appointed Advisory Councils on the Status of Women, which were established at the federal level and in all but two provinces.

23. Naomi Black, *Social Feminism* (Ithaca, N.Y.: Cornell University Press, 1989).

24. Gallup poll conducted for the Canadian Abortion Rights Action League (CARAL) in October 1988.

25. Doris Guyatt, "Women in the Canadian Armed Forces: New Directions at Last," *The Business and Professional Woman*, Spring 1987, 1.

SUGGESTED READINGS

Clio Collective, *Quebec Women: A History*. Translated by Roger Gannon and Rosalind Gill. Toronto: Women's Educational Press, 1987. Especially chapters 14 and 15.

Demers, Jeanne, et Line McMurray, *Femme scandales, 1965-1985*. Montreal: La nouvelle barre du jour, 1987.

Fitzgerald, Maureen, et al., eds., *Still Ain't Satisfied! Canadian Feminism Today*. Toronto: Women's Educational Press, 1982.

O'Leary, Véronique, et Louise Toupin, *Québécoises deboutte! Une anthologie de textes du Front de libération des femmes (1969-1971) et du Centre des femmes (1972-1975)*. Montreal: Les éditions du remue-ménage, 1982.

Prentice, Alison, et al., *Canadian Women: A History*. Toronto: Harcourt Brace Jovanovich, 1988. Especially chapters 14 and 16.

Special issue, "The Decade," *Canadian Woman Studies/Les cahiers de la femme 2*, no. 2 (1980).

Women Unite! An Anthology of the Canadian Women's Movement. Toronto: Women's Educational Press, 1972.

Chapter Five

Changing the Picture: Women and the Media in Quebec

≈≈≈≈≈≈≈≈≈≈≈≈≈≈≈≈≈≈≈≈≈≈≈≈≈≈≈≈≈≈≈≈≈≈≈

This chapter is concerned with the relations of power underlying women's interventions in cultural practices in various media of communication in Quebec. It examines the mechanisms that shape the images of women in three different media: feminist magazines, women's writing, and television programs produced by and for women.

The period studied extends from the first participation of a woman in Québécois literature to the more radical feminist interventions in the 1970s and 1980s. This period includes two important political moments in Quebec society: the extremely conservative, even fascist, period of Duplessism, and the liberal and somewhat liberating period of the Quiet Revolution.

The Duplessis era was a long time of darkness in Quebec, especially for women. Maurice Duplessis's Union Nationale, a right-wing nationalist party, was in power from 1936 to 1939 and 1944 to 1959. Until Duplessis's death in 1959 the Catholic church, lavishly provided with subsidies and grants, strongly supported the government in its effort to keep the people under tight religious and political authority and in a condition of ignorance.

The church's position, called ultramontanism, advocated the prominence of the church over the state; religious criteria were to be applied to all aspects of public life. The Catholic church had developed a conservative nationalism that was readily adopted by Duplessis in the 1930s. Rigid ultramontanism was adopted by Duplessis as "a real monolithism"[1] that placed women in an entirely submissive role in families dominated by men. Man, the "head" of the family, was by extension head of the whole society. Thus, during Duplessism, the ultramontanist vision became "essentially defensive and repressive." It was translated into a fear of novelty, modernism, or progress and into a strong opposition to liberalism and freedom, for men as well as for women.[2]

The coming to power of a Liberal government in the early 1960s brought with it the period of the Quiet Revolution, which established a clear separation between the political and the religious. The political interventions of the Liberal government focused on the importance of education and to some degree encouraged women's emancipation. One consequence was a dramatic decrease in childbearing.[3]

Before the period of the Quiet Revolution, however, the oppressive conditions of ultramontanism did not encourage women to free themselves or to contribute significantly to social activities. The feminism of the time was conservative, and it encouraged women's contribution to society only in so far as their activities remained within the established social order. Women's participation in social and cultural activities seemed sometimes to be against their will, solely motivated by financial needs.

This feminism was followed by what Lorraine Code calls "early liberal feminism." According to this view, women's inferior status was due to their poor education; hence liberals encouraged mothers to send their daughters to school. "Contemporary liberal feminism" went further and claimed equal rights and opportunities for women, independent status, and the end of sexual discrimination. Finally, a small group of feminists in Quebec adhered to "radical feminism," convinced that women's oppression was at the root of all social oppression. The representation of women in the media during the whole period underwent changes reflecting these types of feminism. When we look at the changing representation of women in the media, it is important to consider who is speaking and under what conditions, and for this project the current debate on feminist issues offers useful insights.

Some Comments on the Study of Women, Culture, and Media

Current feminist debate emphasizes the importance of "experiences" and questions the notion of "women's analysis" used in earlier studies. Some poststructuralist feminists[4] argue that we should interpret the world according to women's experience. Experience, according to these feminists, should be understood in keeping with the notion developed by E.P. Thompson in his study of the English working class. Thompson argues that the experience of subordinate groups is formed both by their own actions and by the actions, ideology, and culture of dominant groups; it includes the idea of resistance. Women's experience should be understood not only through an analysis of the dominant culture, then, but also by focusing on popular culture and resistance.

In this context the question becomes: Are experiences the same for all members of a dominated group? For instance, can we talk about "women's experience" as a whole, without any differentiation by class, race, and so on? As Code stresses in chapter one, many feminist studies of patriarchy attempt to locate the "essence" of gender oppression, to identify some essential "characteristics" of women. They consider "male ideology"[5] as oppressive because it is based on material economic interests.

Feminists concerned with race and class oppose the notion of a uniform women's experience. Historians such as Joan Scott, for instance, argue that gender is not only a social construction based on one type of power/knowledge relation, but is also a field constituted by various forms of power relations.[6] These forms of power relations may vary according to the race or class to which women belong. Moreover, the way that these power relations are defined in different social spheres or situations can influence how other spheres are defined. For example, the dichotomy of female/male labour may entail other dichotomous factors of analysis, such as family/factory, moral values/economy, reproduction/production. It expresses dichotomous social and economic power relations.

Scott argues that it is important to investigate the historical struggles underlying the meanings that come to prevail in different social groups in terms of class, gender, and race, among other factors. This is no sterile intellectual exercise but a real, concrete problem for some social groups. Interests are not the same for all social groups and not necessarily the same for all members of a single social group. For example, ruling groups give different meanings to concepts than do subordinate groups. Scott mentions, for instance, that in the nineteenth century trade unionists, social investigators, and legislators, all of them men, fought to define the term "female worker," the only common ground being agreement that women workers were a social problem.

Poststructuralist feminists question the unity of the human subject or self (individual or collective) and consider such concepts as "women" more as "signifiers" than as "ready-made agents" of analysis. Because of this they see all political actions "in the name of women" as mystification. Yet Denise Riley asserts that although there may not be "women" in the sense of *to be*, as long as women's oppression occurs through the social belief that being a woman is an essential determining characteristic, we must act as if *there were.* So Riley maintains, "Maybe there are no women, but we must act politically as though there were."[7]

In media contents, women are presented as a group with essential characteristics. This procedure establishes a common ground for and justifies the use of the concept of "women" as an element of analysis. As human subjects in the mass media – television, magazines, popular literature – "women" are represented as members of a group with stereotypical characteristics. Historically, the media have stereotyped women as: "good" women, represented by mothers-and-housekeepers or by innocent and submissive "girls"; "bad" women represented by seductresses and kept women or by difficult-women. Whatever the variation in content, these stereotypes have been used repeatedly by both men and women.[8]

Mariana Valverde argues that a sociohistorical analysis of women should be "concerned with the process of social subjectivity: how it is formed, how it functions or undermines social domination, how it might be re-formed."[9] The process of social subjectivity entails the ways in which women are subjected to diverse roles and representations to fit into society. These may be suggested or imposed by social institutions such as the family, the church, or the media. Discourses (how women are talked about, represented, pictured, perceived) are the main channel through which social subjectivities are produced. In Valverde's view, discourses are not only the result but also the origin of social action. Different discourses carry divergent views of women as subjects, views that audiences may choose to accept or reject.

My analysis of women and the media in Quebec locates discourses about and by women in the media within the conditions under which they are produced. Women and the media will be examined in terms of economic, political, and temporal relations. But why choose the media to study the changing patterns of women in Quebec society?

Women and the Media in Quebec

Our knowledge of the world is mediated. This would not be a problem if the media simply reflected reality. Yet different media – books, magazines, and television programs, for example – codify reality in different ways. These media are means of communication that distribute cultural or informational contents of various types through a society. These contents are *mediated*: they are not directly transmitted by the person who creates them. They are influenced by the mechanical, economic, political, and social conditions in which they operate. The content of what is communicated is *constructed* in keeping with these conditions. We say then that media contents represent a *construction* of reality. The representation of women in the media is just such a construction. Although women's roles in society have changed noticeably over the last two decades, women are still under-represented and misrepresented in the media, often pictured in the stereotyped roles of good woman/housewife-mother or bad woman/sexpot.

Still different types of media (literature, magazines, newspapers) have been privileged by women for the expression of their ideas and their knowledge in certain domains, perhaps because they can contribute this expression from the privacy of their homes. These means of communication were especially useful during periods of great repression. As Maugin notes, to study women's activities and discourses during the period of Duplessism, it is often necessary "to proceed indirectly, to use the media: newspapers, literature" so great was women's oppression in terms of public activities. [10]

We can examine the relationship between women and the media from two main angles: from the angle of the production of media contents, and from the angle of the consumption of such contents. This chapter will be particularly concerned with the production process. Studies of the consumption of the media are rare. [11] However, where possible, I will examine the impact of women's media products on audiences. Still, the production of media contents is revealing in itself. Its investigation involves an examination of media producers (technicians, journalists, authors, administrators) and of media contents, elements that are in interactive relationship. We can say then that representations of women in the media are influenced by those who conceive and produce them, as well as by those who finance them. For instance in Quebec, Radio-Canada, [12] which is publicly owned radio and television, produces contents that differ from those of privately owned stations such as Télé-Métropole. The explanation may be that the two types of broadcasting have different sources of funding, aim at different audiences, and have different political agendas. Radio-Canada/CBC describes its broadcasting policy as follows:

> Recognizing that change is inevitable and that the instruments of mass communication are potent elements in the process of change, the CBC must remain open to all significant currents of change at work in Canadian society and the world as they now are. It must also give Canadians the opportunity to learn about the underlying issues they will be confronting, the forces for change at work among them and to examine the options that are open to them. It must bring them face to face with the inevitability of change and with its contemporary dynamics so that, as far as possible, they can be masters of the situation. [13]

CBC acknowledges that its role is to inform and to educate. Its information should then extend to all social groups, including minority voices. Yet its educational role obliges this network not simply to focus on the volume of testimony being heard, but to make judgements on "the actual or potential significance of the testimony being uttered." If the CBC did otherwise, it says, the result "would be to ignore some of the deeper, the less perceptible trends which are shaping society's future – trends which always tend to be perceived by the few, not the many." [14]

While Radio-Canada attempts to represent the cultural reality of the society within which it works and to take into account the marginal "less perceptible trends" that shape our society, the policy of privately owned

Télé-Métropole is guided by "emotions." "Television is the ideal medium for transmitting emotion," says its chairperson. "Even our information programs have to transmit their quota of emotions. . . . Our . . . television is more responsive to the expectations of Quebeckers." To keep its audiences, Télé-Métropole's policy is to "establish a special bond with viewers by appealing to their emotions. You don't have the urge to flick through the channels when you are emotionally involved in the program you're watching."[15] A similar differentiation in policies is true of book publishers. A large publisher like Gallimard operates under political and economic constraints that differ from those of a smaller publisher like Québec/Amérique.

The conditions of production have some impact on media contents, then. Policy differentiation, based as much on financial constraints as on social changes in the society within which the media are producing, influence how diverse social groups are represented in the contents. The changing picture of women in Quebec society will be examined through these interrelationships.

Feminist Magazines: *La bonne parole* and *Les têtes de pioche*

Feminist magazines aim at helping women develop the social and political knowledge necessary for their emancipation. They can be sites of women's resistance and opposition to the hegemonic ideology and culture. In Quebec such magazines have existed since 1913. I begin with an examination of two feminist magazines which, according to Monique Dumais, illustrate the evolution of the social conditions of women and their place in Quebec society. These two magazines represent two important periods in Quebec political conditions: Duplessism and the Quiet Revolution. The transition between these two periods was astonishingly rapid in Quebec society and had an important impact on women. The parallel between these two magazines helps explain this impact.

Dumais develops a comparative analysis of *La bonne parole,* published between 1913 and 1958, and *Les têtes de pioche,* published between 1976 and 1979.[16] Despite their different periods of publication, the magazines had many characteristics in common. Both involved a group of mainly petit-bourgeois women who had set themselves the mission of awakening women's social consciousness and of helping women to widen their sphere of activity. But the editors pursued these common aims under quite different political and social conditions for women and their writing in Quebec. Yet women's writing has also had some impact on society. It is this interrelationship that we will examine in this section.

La bonne parole ("The Wise Word") was published during what some historians call the period of survival and tradition in Quebec, and died at the end of Duplessism, only one year before the politician's death. By contrast, *Les têtes de pioche* was published during the period of the Quiet Revolution, a period of emancipation for Quebec people, particularly women. Although it was published only for a short period, it signalled the remarkable progress women had made between its first publication and the "death" of *La bonne parole*. What types of social subjectivities were offered to women by these magazines over the years?

La bonne parole was created by two well-known feminists in Quebec, Caroline Béique and Marie Gérin-Lajoie, as the organ of the Fédération nationale Saint-Jean-Baptiste, section Dames patronnesses.[17] This body was very close to the church. Some two thousand copies were published regularly, a relatively large number for the time. The magazine was created to encourage women to broaden their social interests and to play their patriotic roles in Quebec society. Béique's and Gérin-Lajoie's aim was to provide women with an intellectual publication in which they could express their moral qualities and their energies, satisfy their needs for initiative, and assert themselves. But the main purpose of the publication was to enlist women in the cause of Quebec nationalism, specifically by encouraging them to bear children and to raise them as French-Canadian patriots.

The first writers in *La bonne parole* were often priests and male doctors disseminating their "wise words." However, over the years these writers were almost entirely displaced by women. The ideology adopted by the magazine was what Dumais calls "reformist feminist," and Code "early liberal feminist": it attempted, step by step, to gain the same rights for women as those enjoyed by men, without fundamentally changing society.[18] Accordingly, the issues the magazine was concerned about had to be approved by the Catholic church. For instance, the writers could never dream of discussing birth control or abortion, although both were commonly practised by Quebec women. *La bonne parole* clearly identified itself as a feminist magazine "at the service of the Catholic church." As Dumais notes, the editors were submissive to the church, "a male institution if ever there was one."[19] To ensure the success and legitimacy of their magazine, these women had to keep the support of the Catholic authorities.

In fact, Dumais suggests that the main purpose of the publication was to encourage women to become saintly and to produce saints in their turn. She quotes Marie Gérin-Lajoie, who writes: "Woman, by her very nature, Pope Léon XIII tells us, is destined to domestic chores, chores that moreover admirably safeguard the honor of her sex, and are more agreeable to her natural role of giving her children good education and family prosperity."[20] But this kind of domestic "saintliness" was not woman's only option in life. She was also to be a domestic "politician." In *La bonne parole* the family was often compared to a government in which a woman was supposed to be sometimes "the queen of the home" ("*la reine du foyer*," a term we still hear nowadays) and at other times the "interior minister." This association of family and government made it the mission of *La bonne parole* to request women's help in building a nation. "The mothers, living cradles of a race, must take interest in the struggle for [national] survival," said the priest Brosseau in 1916.[21] Women's natural interest was to give birth to as many children as possible and to keep them healthy enough to fight for the nation if necessary.[22]

To meet this national interest, *La bonne parole* advised Quebec women to subject themselves to such values as "devotion," "charity" and "gentleness," "moral sense," "courage," and "submissiveness."[23] Prior to 1958 it was believed that these values were to be put to work in the home. The good wife-mother was to keep her husband at home, out of the taverns and brothels, and was to form and educate a family. Only in the home could women respond to God's plans for them. Among these plans figured women's duty to instill in their children the notions of faith *and* patriotism. *La bonne parole* encouraged women to communicate to their children a taste for formal culture as controlled by the church. This was not the only aspect of the editors' feminism. Although at the time it was literally unthinkable that these women should revolt against the church and the patriarchal ideology that it sustained, they had other ways of encouraging women's emancipation. Girls' education was one of the means used by *La bonne parole,* not to resist, but to circumvent religious and social oppression.[24]

Much emphasis was put on girls' education so that they would play a more important role in Quebec society. Although this role would mainly be limited to the family, it was meant eventually to shape the whole society through the children that the "girl" would have later to raise. "This century of progress and advancement," said Madame Lacroix, "does not allow us any more to think that woman has only a secondary role to play."[25] In the 1910s *La bonne parole,* and even the church, had to admit that a woman might be "compelled" to work outside the home, in which case it was suggested that she should choose to be a teacher. But female wage labourers formed 15.5 per cent of the work force in 1911 in Quebec,[26] and not all of them could afford to be teachers. Still, Marie Gérin-Lajoie reassured Pope Leon XIII that wage labour did not turn women away from their family duties. In 1943 *La bonne parole* considered Quebec women as essential assets to national prosperity and to social, economic, and political expansion. In spite of this fact, the magazine endorsed an opinion strongly held by the Fédération nationale Saint-Jean-Baptiste and advised women to go back to their homes after the war, and to take care of their families: this, at a time when 24 per cent of Québécois women were employed outside the home.[27] Dumais finds that this magazine, which was supposed to encourage the emancipation of women in Quebec, adopted an ambiguous position on female wage labour. Theoretically, women's domestic task is declared to be paramount; only when they are faced with economic necessity does the magazine accept that women might have to work outside the home.[28] This echoes the public policy themes explored by Sandra Burt in her chapter in this book.

We must remember, however, the social and political context in which these women were living. It was decades before the Quiet Revolution; the whole province was still under the yoke of a very strong and hierarchical church, seemingly omnipresent and omnipotent. Moreover, the moral order was entirely supported by the state. This religious patriarchal culture affected women at least as much as men. It is little wonder that even the most "radical" feminists would agree with the hegemonic social order and structures of the time. They made the most of the little they had.

For instance, in the political arena Marie Gérin-Lajoie was very actively involved in the struggle for women's suffrage, asserting that the public sphere was only an extension of the family. (Women's suffrage was granted in 1940 in Quebec.) Her struggle was at the provincial as well as the municipal levels of government, and the issues raised by her political intervention were often discussed in *La bonne parole*. Gérin-Lajoie defended the French civil code because she believed that it was better able than the common law to protect women's rights. She used *La bonne parole* to recommend changes to the Quebec civil code that would ensure women's rights to their own property and wages.[29]

Thus, *La bonne parole*, a Catholic feminist magazine, encouraged contradictory activities for women. At the same time that it advised women to stay home and do their domestic chores with love and submissiveness, it incited them to involve themselves in social action and strongly supported women's suffrage. It preached easy access to higher education for girls, while encouraging them to stay home and perform their domestic duties. In other words, the editors' writing reflected the contradictory conditions in which women found themselves in their everyday lives in Quebec, especially in the periods surrounding World War I and World War II. These contradictions created openings for later feminists to engage in more radical thinking, in such magazines as *Les têtes de pioche*.

Les têtes de pioche was the collective product of a group of Quebec radical feminists – radical, said one of its writers, Michèle Jean, in the sense that they believed that "patriarchy and the relations of power that it has created between men and women were at the root of all social oppression" in Quebec society.[30] The 1960s and 1970s were a period of general social change in Quebec, during which groups of women, especially young women, started to form a well-organized militant left. L.H. Forsyth reports that in

1967, when women united to "organize the first significant demonstration against the government's newly adopted anti-assembly law, 200 women were thrown in jail."[31] Women later formed a revolutionary feminist movement called the Front de libération des femmes du Québec,[32] which led to an increase in antagonism between feminist and nationalist groups.

The members of the collective *Les têtes de pioche*, like the editors of *La bonne parole*, were mainly from the petite bourgeoisie. However, their approach was radically different. *Les têtes de pioche* was created in 1975 by a group of five women,[33] both lesbian and heterosexual, who met weekly to exchange ideas and start a magazine based on the concept that "the personal is political."[34] "We say that it is political to think, to take account of life. It is political to demand the right not to be harassed, battered, raped by man the master."[35] These women were disgusted by the submissive and oppressive conditions in which Quebec women were living in the mid-1970s and by the slow pace of change. To overcome this they used the magazine to allow the most complete and disturbing expression of women's everyday experiences, to force "a change in the relations of oppression, in the stereotypes" and other mechanisms preventing the liberation of women. "They wished . . . to destroy all social structures which allow power to be concentrated in one dominant group, with one ideological perspective whatever the ideology might be."[36] The editors wrote: "Struggle against the system of secular domination named patriarchy." The texts were entirely written by women, and it was the first time in a Quebec magazine that women could use the pronoun "I" to write about their experience.[37]

This radical-feminist magazine opposed many of the positions taken by *La bonne parole.* The main purpose of the writers was to attack patriarchal society head-on, while *La bonne parole* encouraged women to submit to hegemonic rules and values. *Les têtes de pioche* denounced the myth of matriarchy, encouraged by expressions such as "the queen of the home," which implicitly suggested that women were actually ruling the world, although men believed that they were. Rather, the magazine asserted that women were so involved in domestic chores, which were becoming more demanding with higher standards of hygiene, that they did not have time to get involved in public issues. But the process of transforming women's ideology and cultural practices was long and hard. In 1976 Michèle Jean and France Théorêt wrote:

> It is only gradually that women have become aware of the weakness of their pedestal, of their poverty and of the emptiness of their power. They slowly began to talk, and to 'talk to each other'. They realised that, in fact, they did not possess anything within the familial institution, except the force to impose themselves as housewives untiringly

weaving a web of affective links in which many generations of québécois children got caught without being able to get out.[38]

For these women, the Quiet Revolution of the 1960s in Quebec had not noticeably changed women's position in Québécois society. Even the dramatic decrease in the birthrate, said the editors of *Les têtes de pioche*, did not bring the disappearance of women's "duty" at home; the myth had only been secularized, coming from political instead of religious power. *Les têtes de pioche* wanted to project a feminism that would disturb the existing social order. To do that the contributors ignored the issue of nationalism, as praised by *La bonne parole*, which they considered to be bourgeois.[39]

Hence, the values encouraged by this new magazine were either new or changed. They questioned the role of woman-mother-wife and strongly supported social equality between men and women. But since they were aware that these values were not easy for women to accept and adopt, they favoured the use of an "aggressive" style, where *La bonne parole* had favoured submissiveness. Consciousness-raising, denouncing abuse, and demanding one's rights could not be brought about without violence and anger, they reckoned, because there was so much violence against women. Michèle Jean identified two types of violence against women: male violence was that of hegemonic power imposing social norms; women's violence was violence that burst out when their oppression was too much for women. We can notice a different quality between these two forms of violence: while the former had been rationalized for centuries, the latter was spontaneous and unfortunately less efficient.[40]

Another value supported by *Les têtes de pioche* was women's autonomy. For Raymonde Lorrain, autonomy meant the "courage" to change the relations of power in Quebec society: "The question of autonomy is linked to the struggle led by women to abolish their specific exploitation, namely the exploitation that they have endured for millennia – well before the coming of capitalism and which could survive its abolition."[41] New values brought new activities. The home was demystified and presented as a place where a woman was the maid for the husband and the children rather than the queen of the home. Moreover, maternity was not a duty any more but a choice, and women's domestic chores should be paid for.

Among the norms privileged by *Les têtes de pioche* were the right to desired pregnancy and quality of life for women at home and at work. To meet these goals, *Les têtes de pioche* proposed that women should unite. The magazine was not fighting for women's domination over society, but for multiplicity, diversity, and freedom for each individual. Its approach encouraged a wide contribution from women and aimed at discussing women's common interests in Quebec. According to Forsyth, "It made a major contribution to feminist analysis and reflection at a time when a feminist movement was strongly aware of the need to articulate its reality." [42]

That the magazine's contribution was so short-lived can be explained by internal conflicts and external criticism. Forsyth identifies three distinct sources of conflict: 1) sexual – it appeared difficult to reconcile lesbian and heterosexual views on radical feminisms within the group; 2) socio-economic – it was not evident that women of all classes would agree on common problems to be discussed and common solutions to be sought; 3) political – it was not easy to determine what importance was to be given to the national question. [43] This third source of conflict was explosive in the Quebec of 1976-79 and brought the most external criticism. However, it was the internal sources of conflict that fragmented the original group, and frequent changes of collaborators meant that only three of the original members remained through the whole experience. Such conflicts were almost inevitable in this group, which refused to work within the hierarchical structures of traditional organizations.

At first glance, one is tempted to dismiss *La bonne parole* and to consider *Les têtes de pioche* as the only representative voice of Quebec feminists. However, we have to put ourselves in the historical context in which these two publications were distributed. The 1970s were years of strong social struggle in Quebec. Everything was magnified by the political and economic conditions that existed at that time. Economic abundance and liberal ideology, following the long period of Duplessism built on religious and conservative ideology, seemed to promise the universe to everyone, including women. The period of 1913-58 was quite different. Although the Quebec economy was relatively prosperous for long periods, people were suffocating under strict conservatism. In that context the openings for feminist politics and ideology were limited. However, Quebec feminists' activities were not limited to one medium; women were also active in the field of literature.

Feminine or Feminist Literature: *Laure Conan, Gabrielle Roy, France Théorêt*

Women have often expressed their experiences through literature. Writing was an activity that women could do even when they were confined in their home, and the use of a pen name allowed them to publish work that was more often biographical than fictional. In Quebec the first novel by a woman (*Un amour vrai*, the work of Laure Conan) appeared in 1879. [44] Although Conan was not prolific, she is seen by feminist scholars in Québécois literature as a pioneer who helped open the field to other writers.

Women have played an important part in Quebec literature not only because several of them have achieved wide recognition, but also because their works have reached a large portion of the Quebec audience, regardless of gender specificity. In her "Introduction" to *Traditionalism, Nationalism and Feminism: Women Writers in Quebec,* Paula G. Lewis asserts that there is "a long and well-established tradition of women writers" in Quebec.[45] She relates this tradition to the fact that Quebec patriarchal society, supported by the Catholic church, "traditionally imposed upon women the role of guardian of francophone culture, that is of religion and of French language, itself guardian of faith."[46] Indeed, *La bonne parole* had strongly advised mothers to educate their daughters. In that context, says Lewis, well-educated women, unable to use their education to work in a profession, wrote. What did women write? Was their work different from that of men?

Through the works of three female writers – Laure Conan's *Angéline de Montbrun* (1882), Gabrielle Roy's *Bonheur d'occasion* (1945), and France Théorêt's *Une voix pour Odile* (1978) – we will examine the evolution of the place of women in Quebec society. These three writers represent three important stages of evolution of female literature in Quebec. I will draw on Patricia Smart's *Ecrire dans la maison du père* to examine the different kinds of contribution each made to the evolution of the image of women in Quebec literature.[47] In her book Smart makes a historical and comparative analysis of men's and women's writing in Quebec. Following Smart's analysis, I will begin by looking at the differences between men's and women's writing in order to better understand the specific contribution of women writers.

According to Smart, women's and men's writing differs not only in content but also in what she calls the "texture" of writing. The "texture" involves the style, the form of writing, and the types of expression that the writers use to support the story. The first level of difference between men's and women's writing is in the content of the story. Men's writing presents women in oppressive roles, while women's writing, to the extent that the conditions in which it is written allow, unmasks the situation of women who have been "buried alive for centuries by a society built on the fear of power . . . and expresses all the feminine energy repressed by patriarchal culture."[48] Women's writing opens unexplored aspects of society, but this contribution is sometimes hidden in its texture. For that reason it is as important to *read* a novel from a feminist point of view as it is to write it as a woman. On the surface, the first works produced by women in Quebec did not appear much different from those of men. In most of them, female characters were effaced – either by death or by their positions in submissive roles. Daughters were subjected to fathers' and sons' authority. Mothers were often absent or situated in the background. Women were silenced.

The difference between men's and women's writing appears also at the level of the texture of the work. The texture of a literary work is related to patriarchal culture in society. This relationship confines men's writing as much as women's. This brings Smart to say, "Writing is really an activity which happens in the Father's House."[49] The Father's House (*La maison du père*) is a metaphor for patriarchal culture, with its ideological, artistic, and language structures projecting male subjectivity and authority. This house is erected on woman as an object built to reflect and to support male subjectivity, a reified *Other*.

Because men and women have different places in that house, it is not surprising that their writing would be different. In the Father's House, women who speak or write are seen as thieves stealing the Father's language. Writing in itself is thus a subversive act. Feminist writers in French also have to deal with the gender politics of the language. All nouns are gendered and the rules of grammar subordinate the feminine to the masculine. This grammatical code is in fact an "accessory element . . . in the silent embellishment of a significant structure axed on the masculine."[50] This creates grammatical asymmetry in literary production.

Within such a context, what would be the difference between women's and men's writing? Smart suggests that men's writing gives a greater place to linearity, to logic, and to a conception of social identities as fixed by legal codes (husband, father, wife). Women's writing by contrast is rich in texture: the gestures, rhythms, silences that underline the language are often sensual. The texture of women's work is close to the way women talk to one another; one can sense their pleasure in exchanging words. Quebec women's writing is also different from that of men in its tendency to break up the traditional masculine forms by using such literary forms as letter writing, personal diaries, or autobiography. It seems that women have used these forms not because they lack confidence, or experience, or authority to write like men, "but rather because their writing presents a way other than men's to re-present, to listen, and to feel the texture of the real. Between the sacred 'realism' of patriarchal culture and the 'real' as represented in women's writing, there is a world, a distinction worthy of exploration."[51]

In Quebec one of the most common myths in men's writing has been that of the French-Canadian mother with her numerous children clinging to her apron. The myth illustrates the ideology of 'national survival.' This ideological construction came from prerevolutionary France and was embedded in the hierarchy of a Catholic church founded on the belief that power was directly transmitted from God to the fathers and sons of that world.[52] Historically, in men's writing, man is represented as having the strength, intellect, and rationality to be the head of the family. But the perennial character of the role of the father depends on the acceptance by daughters and mothers of their roles, as constructed by patriarchal ideology. Thus the structure of early Quebec novels is that of the omnipotent father, and of the son and of women conniving to be objects in accepting the role they are given. For women's writing this meant there was no place for women. However, women's writing has changed in Quebec.

Smart asserts that women writers have been condemned to silence: either they have expressed their own style and perceptions and then have remained marginal forces in Quebec culture, or they have abstracted from their own gender to attempt to occupy the cultural space reserved for men. Moreover, at the beginning of their contribution, Quebec women writers were given so little recognition that they often needed a male mentor to give them confidence and to give their words legitimacy. It seems that Laure Conan experienced such a situation.

Conan was the first woman to publish a book in the province of Quebec, and the first to be honoured by the Académie Française. Born in 1845 at La Malbaie (Murray Bay), her real name was Félicité Angers; her father was a blacksmith and her mother died when she was young.[53] Although she used the pseudonym Laure Conan to publish, she continued to be terrified by the prospect of having her writing made public and read by a large audience. But she had to write because of financial difficulties. In 1882, just before the publication of *Angéline de Montbrun,* she wrote to her mentor, the priest Casgrain, "I am quite ashamed to find myself in print. . . . Necessity alone has given me the great courage to have my work published."[54] Why was Laure Conan so afraid? Smart suggests that women's writing is usually close to their personal experience, so that being published means having their feelings exposed. This situation makes them vulnerable.[55] Hence Conan's fears were understandable. Not only was her novel the first to be published by a woman in Quebec, but it was also largely autobiographical.

The novel is the traditional story of an orphan, an obedient young woman, Angéline, subjected to her father's authority. Her life is completely ruined when he dies accidentally. This constitutes the main thread of the novel and is underlined by a love story involving Angéline and Maurice, a man that her father had chosen for her. There have been different interpretations of the story. For instance, Roger Le Moine asserts that the object of the love story was to obscure the incest of the father/daughter relationship.[56] In "Reflections in the Pool: The Subtext of Laure Conan's Angéline de Montbrun," François Gallays supports Le Moine's assumption, saying, "It seems as if Laure Conan were going out of her way throughout the narrative to camouflage its [the novel's] true nature."[57] According to Gallays, a psychosociological analysis reveals that in Conan's novel, incest "conceal[s] itself behind the virtuous manifestation of filial devotion" and also behind the "love story" of Angéline with

Maurice, which finally ends in a drama in which the beloved father dies, Angéline is disfigured in an accident, and the love story ends.

Yet a feminist reading of the novel reveals a subversive potential, though of a different kind. Smart suggests that the opposition and resistance to patriarchal ideology are in the texture of the novel: in Conan's fully explored epistolary form that escapes the linearity so dear to male style and gives her writing a texture similar to "chatting." This form of writing allowed Conan, in some way, to represent characters who could escape the roles they were given in the story. For instance, it gave secondary characters such as Mina, Angéline's sister and her complement, the possibility of representing feminine resistance to the father's authority by being an urbane, fashionable woman. Those characters, and all Conan's work for that matter, "represented a long, guilty hesitancy between submissiveness and revolt."[58]

Gabrielle Roy's participation in Quebec women's 'resistance' to patriarchal culture took quite a different form from that of Conan's writing. Born in Manitoba, where she was a teacher from 1929 to 1937, Roy went to France and England for two years, where she took drama lessons. When she returned in 1939 she decided to live permanently in Quebec, working as a journalist for *Le bulletin des agriculteurs, Le jour,* and *Le Canada* until 1945.[59] Her first novel, *Bonheur d'occasion* (1945) (*The Tin Flute*) was written during World War II.[60] In this initial work Roy became the first Quebec writer to give the *leading* role in a novel to a woman.[61] Until that time women had played *submissive* roles, if they played any role at all. Roy, in introducing a mother as the main *subject* of a story taking place in French-Canadian working-class culture, gave to her book an explicitly political dimension. In fact, she "was seen as a social realist, and as a quasi-photographic writer."[62] In *Bonheur d'occasion* she presents a story about the difficult life of a poor family through the realism of a female character who does not resemble "the omniscient narrator of masculine realism."[63] Rather, working life is represented by a mother busy with her kids' demands and trying to lessen their misery. With the mother caught in the terrible conditions of working-class groups living in the cities during the war, the novel provided a new picture of women.

Roy's writing, in contrast to Conan's, differs from male writing not in its style, which remains the linear, rigid style used by male authors, but in the very fact that she gave a woman, even more a mother, full subjectivity as the main character of a novel full of political and social commitment. Her studies of society through the eyes of women "mercilessly unveil the power mechanisms which objectify human beings, especially women, and illustrate their cultural consequences."[64] Although women's, men's, and children's sufferings are described to readers, Roy's work is not just a novel of feelings, it is also a novel of ideas. She places the story in the context of contemporary class ideologies and national currents. Further, the characters often talk about politics, about their sufferings as French-Canadian, as educated members of a working class dispossessed of their traditional craft skills by technology and capital. Among them, women suffer the most because they cannot escape their situation, even temporarily. Their only way to lessen stress is to denounce the war and the totalitarian machine that annihilates the weak ones, women. Thus Roy's analysis included dimensions of class, nation, and gender at the same time as it went beyond the limits of these categories. The voices of resistance were political and formed "perhaps the only efficient opposition to the oppressive unity of the Father's House."[65] The voices of resistance became even more insistent with contemporary feminist writers.

France Théorêt is a contemporary author, coming from a different generation than Conan and Roy, from the generation of overt feminism. She was part of the group of writers and cultural activists at the origin of *Les têtes de pioche*. According to Forsyth, this group was "throwing out a serious challenge to the very foundations of the codes, symbols, and practices of dominant culture and its values . . . which led the way through the 1970s . . . to the emergence of a new modernity in literature."[66] Théorêt's work shows that difference. As Smart stresses: "All the writing projects of France Théorêt are concerned with the emergence of that [woman's] voice that never talked, that gropes around, breaks and comes back against itself."[67] In a novel like *Une voix pour Odile*, Théorêt makes women say what they had always kept to themselves. In contrast with women writers who came before her, as a feminist she is conscious that she is writing as a woman, in relation to other groups, and that she is limited by a language and a symbolic order in which there is no doubt about the reduction of women as the Other. In Théorêt's work, woman sees herself as herself, not through the father's eye, and defines herself as subject instead of object. The author attempts to open an aspect of women's lives that had been suppressed until then: her own voice.

However, in Théorêt's search for the origin of her voice through a consideration of the experience of her own mother, Smart sees a development identical to that of Gabrielle Roy, and perhaps the starting point for all women's voices. This situation would help women to remain close to reality while men's writing in Quebec after 1960 breaks with reality, that alienating reality of submissiveness that they want to forget. Even in the 1970s and 1980s, Quebec novels written by women remain close to autobiography, which is women's way of staying close to the reality, women's reality, so rarely expressed by them. Théorêt adheres to that situation in letting the body speak with gestures, laughs, smiles, glances, and silences, a whole part of life experience that was not part of the earlier novels written by women or men.[68] Yet Théorêt, like Conan, uses the epistolary form of writing in some parts of her work to express feelings such as friendship and pleasure in everyday life.

Through these forms of writing, and in keeping with Gabrielle Roy, Théorêt looks "for an engaged form of art that is not the domination of the real on ideas, but rather that listens to voices silenced by patriarchal culture."[69] This multiplicity of voices coming from silence and marginality is political, not only because of its content but because of the texture of the work as well – what Smart calls its embodiedness. Théorêt's writing, through nuances, succeeds in presenting a political analysis of women's most vital problems, such as rape and violence.

The examples of these novels may suggest that the representation of women in literature underwent a sudden and drastic change within a relatively short period of time. In reality, the change was much more gradual. To illustrate this point, I will now look at a television program "for women" produced by Radio-Canada and called *Femme d'aujourd'hui.*

Women's Representation in "Women's Programs": *The Case of Femme d'aujourd'hui*

Femme d'aujourd'hui ("Woman of Today") was the first "woman's" program to be broadcast on television. The broadcast began during the Quiet Revolution and ran for seventeen years (1965-82), a period that allows us to see a gradual change in the conditions of women in Quebec. This period is seen as having brought about profound changes in the economic, political, and social institutions in Quebec. The role of the media in the Quiet Revolution was crucial.

Femme d'aujourd'hui was produced by Michèlle Lasnier from its first year to its last; and Aline Desjardins conducted its interviews from 1965 to 1978. It was broadcast for one hour every weekday to an essentially female audience. According to Desjardins, the program was not intended to be feminist, but a shift in its message began with the nomination of Lasnier as associate producer in 1966. A reporter for the women's section of *La presse* for four years, Lasnier had also been associate director of the magazine *Châtelaine* at its beginning. According to Simone Monet-Chartrand, she was a "woman of culture and good judgement."[70]

Lasnier immediately began to invite women specialists in various fields and professions and to promote the discussion of women's issues in different social areas. A list of the issues discussed on the program in 1965, before Lasnier took charge, shows that *Femme d'aujourd'hui* was mainly concerned with knitting, cooking, dancing, or more serious themes such as marriage and health, and that priests or male doctors were invited to give counselling.[71] By 1975 the situation had changed drastically. Not only were women specialists invited to give their opinions about problems in marriage and health, but women were also called on to discuss birth control, vasectomy, divorce, wage labour, and leisure time: in other words, issues specific to Quebec women of the time. The program aimed to break the pattern of stereotypical and traditional values. The transformation in the content of the program both reflected and promoted social change in Quebec. As Aline Desjardins says, "We were addressing the most controversial women's issues in Quebec society, as well as cultural issues." The program's political stance had become that of contemporary liberal feminism, as it is defined in Lorraine Code's chapter here.

In a study of *Femme d'aujourd'hui*, Anne Légaré examines the program's conditions of production as well as the issues covered and its audiences. Légaré identifies thirteen mutually exclusive categories of issues: economy, politics, psychology, education, health, family, leisure, consumer affairs, household activities, light entertainment, social issues, arts and culture, and people's lives. She finds that a certain number of specific themes were addressed each year. For instance, 1972-73 was devoted to artistic and cultural issues, as well as to health and psychological problems; by 1973-74 the time spent on social issues related to women had tripled; while in 1974-75 the concern was mainly on family problems and the difficulties of couples. The focus on social issues came at the expense of attention to such domestic issues as sewing, cooking, and house decoration. Two themes were particularly popular: artistic and cultural events, and social issues. While few of the former were specifically for women (18 per cent), most interviews on the latter were concerned with women's issues. Few economic and political questions were discussed on *Femme d'aujourd'hui*, since, for male managers at Radio-Canada, these issues belonged to the domain of public affairs. What these men could not prevent, though, was the political undertone adopted in many discussions.[72]

Légaré identifies three important transformations during the 1971-78 period. The years 1972-73 saw "a marked increase in social preoccupations," averaging around 24 per cent of broadcast time. The percentage of time given to social issues increased notably again in 1974-75 and in 1977-78. This growing interest in social issues was linked to the general context of the program and to the changes affecting the province of Quebec at that time. Guided by their interest in providing contents that could help women obtain the rights to freedom and equality of opportunity, the team of *Femme d'aujourd'hui* was attempting to keep up with the exciting upheavals in Quebec. This increasing focus on social issues was not limited to *Femme d'aujourd'hui*, but could be noticed more generally in the relationship between media and society.[73]

In the 1970s there was a growing movement in Quebec towards collective solutions through group organization.[74] While it is usual for media productions to privilege individual solutions over group solutions, in the early 1970s *Femme d'aujourd'hui* was already beginning to place importance on group organization, and especially women's organizations. As Légaré comments, "When feminine issues are mediated by organized groups they obviously acquire a social influence that transcends individual examples."[75] Légaré asserts that the program did not attract a large popular audience, but that it was designed for family viewers and gradually shifted its content towards discussions of the collective solutions to social problems by social workers, government representatives, and other groups, especially women's groups. Although the program continued to privilege individual solutions, women's organizations were increasingly heard from during the 1970s – though, ironically, during International Women's Year the program continued to put more emphasis on individual solutions, particularly in discussions of problems concerning the couple and family life. The presentation of collective solutions coming from women's organizations did not increase during the following years. (See Table 1 below.) As Légaré notes:

> Feminism has gained ground in *Femme d'aujourd'hui*, but as a subject raised by individuals rather than as an attempt to highlight the solutions of organizations. The attention paid to popular organizations bears little relation to the rise of social movements among the people of Quebec during the seventies. *Femme d'aujourd'hui* turns out to be a selective programme.[76]

But, after all, *Femme d'aujourd'hui* was following the lines of liberal feminism.

A form of approach that became more popular with *Femme d'aujourd'hui* over the years was to present thematic programs that devoted the whole hour to discussing a particular issue, skill, personality, or event. The number of these programs increased after International Women's Year, when *Femme d'aujourd'hui* was allocated a bigger budget. Michèle Lasnier liked this format because it gave "the opportunity to explore a subject more deeply and with more resources, and this [made] for a treatment of even higher quality."[77]

Some of these thematic programs were:

- kindergartens
- teenagers and drugs
- women in their thirties studying full-time at university
- vasectomy
- a feminist film-director: Agnès Varda
- some female occupations and violence
- rape
- the nurse's role today
- interviews with Françoise Dolto.[78]

Table 1

Percentage of Collective and Individual Solutions to Social Issues
Discussed in *Femme d'aujourd'hui*

Year	Collective solutions (women's organizations)	Individual solutions
1971-72	145	289
1972-73	145	472
1973-74	153	297
1974-75	121	581
1975-76	38	817
1976-77	111	260
1977-78	139	729
Total	852 (19.8%)	3,445 (80.2%)

SOURCE: Adapted from Anne Légaré, "The Television Programme Femme d'Aujourd'hui (Canada)," in *The Influence of Audio-Visual Media on the Socio-Cultural Behaviour of Women* (Paris: Unesco, 1980), 60.

The number of these thematic programs increased from two in 1966-67 to twenty in 1970-71 to a peak of sixty-one in 1976-77. However, although the production of a large number of thematic programs was possible because of an increased budget during International Women's Year, the percentage of time given to women's issues with this format remained the same as that of regular broadcasts since the early 1970s (about 26 per cent). All the same, the shift in content reveals an important aspect of the change that Quebec women experienced during that period. The issues discussed in the program revealed the main preoccupations of the time, at least for women coming from classes interested in petit-bourgeois problems, namely those concerned with the place, role, and attitudes of the individual in the social structure – more so than with changes in the social structure itself.

Yet contents, as we asserted earlier, are constructions of reality. In this context, it is important to look at the people who were presented as specialists on issues. To have an idea of the magnitude of the change affecting *Femme d'aujourd'hui* and of its relation to the social change in Quebec society, we will now look at the guests invited to participate.

As noted above, most of the issues addressed in these programs were approached through discussions with individuals: businesspeople, professionals (doctors, lawyers, scholars), artists and craftworkers, as well as people engaged in household activities and those who agreed to talk about their personal experiences rather than their work. This last group included manual and office workers, housewives, students, volunteer workers, and people with "intriguing" leisure activities.[79] It is important to stress that these last guests were mainly invited to be "witnesses" – to listen to the experts, to ask questions, and to talk about their personal experiences.

Although most of the women came as witnesses, a significant percentage were also invited as specialists. For instance, 55 per cent of all artists and craftworkers and 53 per cent of all professionals invited between 1966 and 1978 were women (see Table 2 for details). In 1972-73 women outnumbered men as speakers. It may be assumed that this shift brought some changes in the messages. An indication of change occurring not only in the approach adopted by *Femme d'aujourd'hui* but also in Quebec society is the sharp increase in the number of women speakers between 1972 and 1978, especially in the category of the professions – an increase that "clearly" raises "the question of the relationship between ideology, social context and program."[80] Still, women were mainly represented in the category of witnesses (84 per cent). This is scarcely surprising, given that the program was labelled a women's program and targeted women's audiences. Nevertheless, for Légaré, this shows an important aspect of the production of the program. "Since so many women are chosen as 'witnesses' . . . it may be assumed that the women interviewed as professional people or artists are chosen more for their occupation than for their sex."[81] Michèlle Lasnier supports this assessment, saying that the choice of experts was based on the qualifications of the informants rather than on their sex. Since the percentage of women professionals was very low at that time in Quebec (and still is), it is a wonder that they succeeded at all in having a greater number of female speakers.

Organizations were poorly represented on the list of invited speakers in *Femme d'aujourd'hui*. Table 3 shows a proportional representation of three organizations on the show: state organizations, trade unions, and women's groups. Since *Femme d'aujourd'hui* was categorized as a women's program of light entertainment, it is little wonder that members of trade unions were not often invited. However, it seems surprising that so many state representatives would come as speakers. Légaré does not reveal which types of issues they discussed; but since political controversies were to be avoided, we can only assume that they were mainly speaking about social issues or giving information about state agencies. The proportion of women from women's organizations was low as well.

Yet one should not judge the importance of strictly feminine issues and the impact of the feminist movement itself in quantitative terms alone. As Légaré points out, many members of the production team were influenced by the feminist movement, including the program's leading interviewer.

Table 2
Number of Male and Female Guests from Professions, Arts, and Crafts
in *Femme d'aujourd'hui*

Year	Professions		Arts and crafts	
	Men	Women	Men	Women
1970-71	180	181	111	82
1971-72	255	121	132	101
1972-73	31	165	151	190
1973-74	143	96	61	144
1974-75	142	216	32	184
1975-76	99	214	32	65
1976-77	200	299	116	42
1977-78	95	207	28	192
Total	1,145	1,499	663	1,000

SOURCE: Adapted from Légaré, "Television Programme," 55.

Table 3
Proportional Representation by Gender of the Main Organizations
Invited to *Femme d'aujourd'hui*

	State organizations		Trade unions		Women's organizations
Year	Men	Women	Men	Women	Women
1970-71	32	32	–	15	15
1971-72	48	–	–	–	–
1972-73	9	–	–	–	–
1973-74	46	27	–	13	19
1974-75	18	47	–	–	52
1975-76	8	36	–	–	43
1976-77	9	23	10	–	–
1977-78	33	16	–	–	43
Total	232	277	18	46	190

SOURCE: Adapted from Légaré, 1980, 53-54.

"There is a correlation – impossible to measure here – between the participation of feminist movement representatives and the other interviews with women. In short, the changes in the social attitudes of the people concerned seem to us more decisive than certain figures and more indicative of new trends in relationships with society."[82]

Aline Desjardins proves Légaré right. She admits that there was a very close relationship between the transformation of the program and the evolution of her own feminist politics. "When I started as a hostess and interviewer at *Femme d'aujourd'hui*," she says, "it was only a regular job for me. Through the issues and the themes we addressed, I discovered that Quebec women had specific problems in terms of difficulties in organizing their lives and their work that men did not have. I gradually became a feminist."[83] As the program developed and Quebec society changed, Desjardins became more and more aware of women's issues and more willing to address them in her interviews. Because the hostess and interviewer have very important roles to play in orienting the discussion in this type of television program, Desjardins was certainly instrumental in determining the impact of the show on the audiences. Her relationship with the audience shows this. Throughout her work at *Femme d'aujourd'hui* she was stopped on the street or in public places by women expressing their gratitude for the information, support, and awareness that the program offered them.[84] Yet Desjardins had very little say in the production of the program. Who was behind these changes, then?

A description of *Femme d'aujourd'hui* published in a brochure advertising television programs at Radio-Canada for the year 1978-79 illustrates the transformation that the program experienced during its first thirteen years. It says: "At first devised and made for women, this series now takes an interest in so many subjects that form an integral part of daily life that men are as absorbed by each day's program as their wives. *Femme d'aujourd'hui* is much less concerned with fashion and cookery than with sociology, psychology, education, literature and even philosophy . . . with the constant aim of improving our quality of life."[85]

Still, the first objective of *Femme d'aujourd'hui* in 1965 was similar to that of *La bonne parole* in 1912: to "help women become better housewives." But when the responsibility of the program was given to Michèlle Lasnier in December 1965, it "changed direction and began to cover broader and more fundamentally human issues while at the same time following social changes in Quebec."[86] The program was broadcast in the afternoon, which limited the size and characteristics of the audience. Légaré asserts that its survival was due more to its momentum than to any planning by the management. As she puts it, the success was not granted, it was "won," especially through committed viewers who made sure that Radio-Canada's management knew they were unconditional supporters.

She gives much of the credit to the executive director, Michèlle Lasnier, and to the main interviewer, Aline Desjardins. Lasnier perceived the expectations of women of that period in providing them with the information that they required, and she aimed to make "women aware of themselves independently of their relations with other people, and to make them conscious of their rightful place in society."[87]

But the program was also oriented towards an attempt to make women talk about themselves: who they were, what they knew, and what they could do. This was Aline Desjardins's task. She helped women in their search for authenticity and truth. Her experience in interviewing and her growing interest in women's issues helped to make women who were not used to talking in public express themselves. These two women were supported by a team of researchers, most of them feminists interested in women's emancipation. With such a team directed by Lasnier, *Femme d'aujourd'hui* was able "to break out of the straitjacket of individualism and reflect much more than the sociological characteristics of its own audience."[88]

However, this team, and especially its executive director, had to fight continually to keep *Femme d'aujourd'hui* afloat. The fact is that this women's program was not taken very seriously by management, despite its popularity. For instance, *Femme d'aujourd'hui*, like all the other types of women's programs, was broadcast in the afternoon, although a large part of the female audience was working outside the home during the day and unable to watch it. In spite of the inconvenient broadcast time, the program was popular among women and even men (as the description in the brochure hinted). Still, Lasnier's request that it be broadcast during prime-time met with a categorical refusal from management. Women's programs were scheduled in the afternoon and were not to occupy the prime-time better employed by public affairs programs. In addition, Radio-Canada's management, which had exclusive power over the budget, gradually reduced the funding of the program.[89] Finally, the production team was in a precarious situation. Only the associate director and the main interviewer had permanent employment. Most producers, assistant producers, and some interviewers were hired by management on an annual contract basis, and the research assistants were paid by the episode and had no security at all.[90] In spite of the situation, some individuals remained on the team for years and seemed to be committed to women's issues. To Légaré's questions about their contribution to the program, they answered:

We try to encourage communication by fighting against the anonymous sets used in programs on public affairs; we try to give a more personal atmosphere to interviews; during the program we learn

more about women while encouraging them to talk; we feel committed to the women we question; the media professions are more difficult for women who are aware of their situation because they are
more sensitive to the constraints of the context within which they
work; women should not only 'make the news' but 'be ahead of the
news'.[91]

These women enjoyed their work because they said they found it easier to
pursue their own ideas with a female associate director than with a man.
They believed, however, that broadcasting the program in the afternoon
was a reflection of management's ideas of women: "Their place is in the
home." Thus, a program like *Femme d'aujourd'hui* seems to have had some
effect on the team that produced it. In response to a questionnaire distributed by Légaré, half of the thirty respondents answered that the program
had an impact on their personal lives; two-thirds said that it had helped to
change their attitudes towards the conditions of women, and many others
wrote that their views of male/female relationships had changed. Almost
half of them admitted that the word "feminism" had taken a more positive
connotation since their involvement in the program.[92] But did the ideas of
feminism have any impact on the audiences? What was the character of
that impact?

Although it took a few years before *Femme d'aujourd'hui* adopted a
"feminist" approach, in time its contents came to break with representations of women as housewives and pictured them rather as career-women,
creative artists, or witnesses telling their experiences. In Lorraine Code's
terminology, it was adopting a contemporary liberal-feminist approach.
Légaré stresses the difficulty of measuring the impact of the program on
individuals, and for that reason she limits herself to describing its impact
on specific cases.

Audience ratings during the broadcast period were a good indicator of
the program's popularity. In 1968-69 the average audience per season was
297,000, and this number declined gradually until 1978. There was a
major decline between 1975-76 and 1976-77, when the audience went
from 246,000 to 196,000.[93] However, there were peaks of popularity,
especially as a result of theme programs; some of those programs reached
as many as 500,000 and even 800,000 people, according to Desjardins.
These are very impressive numbers, if we remember that the program was
scheduled in the afternoon and that more than 40 per cent of women were
working outside the home. Pressures by the Fédération des Femmes du
Québec supported Lasnier's effort to have Radio-Canada reschedule the
program in a prime-time slot. The Fédération adopted a recommendation
to Radio-Canada management in 1971:

Considering that Femme d'aujourd'hui, besides being one of the best programs on State-owned television, *plays a leading role in the education and advancement of women,* and that many people are unable to benefit from it because of the time at which it is broadcast, FFQ is requested to recommend to CBC that the most important sequences of this program be repeated at least twice a week at a time when the whole family may watch. [94]

This request was met only five years later, in 1976, when the Réseau pour l'action et l'information des femmes (Action and Information Network for Women) succeeded, during ten days of the Salon de la Femme, in collecting 3,927 signatures for a petition requesting the management to reschedule the broadcasting of *Femme d'aujourd'hui* to the evening. The petition stated:

We have been able to ascertain that Femme d'aujourd'hui has a large following, so large in fact that all men and women are familiar with the program. Femme d'aujourd'hui is unique of its kind in that it has such a persuasive influence on public opinion that it paves the way for changes in attitudes and even in behaviour.

This has been amply proved by our work during the Salon de la Femme. Our theme was the identity of women and we were very surprised to find that most people had heard of this concept because they had already been introduced to it through the work of Femme d'aujourd'hui. This made it much easier for us to convince people who, owing to the program, were already well-informed and above all favourably disposed. [95]

These women based their argument on the facts that: a large proportion of householders were unable to watch the program because of household chores; working women were frustrated not to be able to watch it at all; female and male students who had watched it thought that it was a good source of information, but they were unable to watch regularly; many men were also interested in the issues discussed on the program and wanted to watch; couples were frustrated not to be able to talk over the subjects discussed in the program, since only women could watch it; and, finally, all women and many men wanted sports to be broadcast less often and to be replaced by *Femme d'aujourd'hui.* But the Radio-Canada management remained unmovable.

The popularity of the program could also be noted through the growing participation of the viewers, both in letters and telephone calls. Moreover, for the two thousandth edition of *Femme d'aujourd'hui,* a 145-minute program involving two hundred guests from seven television studios from across Canada, the theme was: "What, in 1976, are the values you think it vital to pass on to your children?"[96] The program was broadcast nation-wide using a satellite link.

According to Aline Desjardins, there were other big moments. One of them was the program team's tour of the province to discuss the 1970 Bird Report on the condition of women in Canada. They invited women to talk about various aspects of the report. "We went everywhere," says Desjardins. "We livened up the social scene in fact. The women were splendid." In 1973 *Femme d'aujourd'hui* produced its first large-scale program with public participation in which 230 women of all ages and from all parts of Quebec and French-speaking communities in Ontario and New Brunswick filled in a questionnaire on their personal lives. "It was during this program that the Femme d'aujourd'hui viewers club was founded."[97] Many more very topical theme programs, aiming, for instance, at increasing women's access to paid employment or at eliminating discrimination, were produced. Some women's groups were also pushing *Femme d'aujourd'hui* to rethink its approach and create closer links to women's organizations.

Conclusion

As feminists state, then, there is no uniform women's existence. Rather, as the study of Québécois women's cultural practices suggests, even when women are from the same class their activities and products propose diverse roles and representations as they attempt to fit into their society. The fact is that literature, magazines, and television programs are indeed influenced by social conditions. For instance, at the end of the nineteenth century, Laure Conan's writing, though based on a conservative approach, was almost provocative in a world of male writers. After all, she was the first woman writer to publish a novel in Quebec, and in addition the "texture" of her novel was different from that of a man's; she used letter writing and an autobiographical style. On the other hand, *La bonne parole*'s traditional liberal feminism was progressive in so far as it urged that women as individuals get more involved in social issues. Furthermore, it fought for women's suffrage, which was quite courageous on the part of these women writing in a magazine supervised by the Fédération nationale Saint-Jean-Baptiste, an organization upon which, at the time, the church had a strong hold. Women's suffrage was strongly opposed by the church.

Gabrielle Roy's liberal feminism may have been less risky. But her concern with social problems was innovative for a fiction writer of that time, especially in Quebec, even more so since her story figured a working-class mother as main character. Her realism unveiled not only the difficult social conditions in which Montrealers were living, but also women's strong character and capability to cope with that misery. She did not, however, contest the social order within which these conditions existed.

Although it is tempting to share Dumais's ironic reaction and to accuse the collaborators of magazines like *La bonne parole* of driving Quebec women even deeper into their oppression, it is important to put ourselves into the historical social context in order to understand their real contribution. These women proposed alternative examples of subjectivity that women could choose to emulate.

We had to wait until the 1970s and radical feminism to meet any form of conscious resistance to and contestation of patriarchal culture and ideology in the media. *Les têtes de pioche,* and the literary work of some of its contributors, such as France Théorêt and Nicole Brossard, sent the message that the present systems of culture and politics should be broken and replaced by a less violent and less exclusively male way of doing and thinking. These women's texts were radically feminist in the sense that they did not so much contest the capitalist system as argue that social problems were almost entirely due to gender discrimination in a patriarchal society.

We may assume that the different types of subjectivity suggested in feminist contributions to the media in Quebec generally corresponded to what was experienced by women in other parts of Canada. There were, however, some variations, especially attributable to the strong hold of the Catholic church on Quebec society in general and particularly on women, and to the national question. We have identified different social subjectivities according to the types of feminism (traditional, liberal, and radical) adopted by women in the media.

The contributions of Conan and *La bonne parole* proposed no dramatic changes in women's lives. They remained submissive to male authority and confined to the private sphere, in keeping with the rules of the Catholic church, which opposed any initiative by women outside the home and encouraged, with the support of the state, the development of a nation by enthusiastic maternity (called the "cradle revenge"). It was a grave sin to make love without the firm intention to procreate. Yet within this very rigid frame of activities, women in *La bonne parole* found ways to support and encourage sexual emancipation by encouraging a better education for their daughters and by promoting women's suffrage.

The liberal feminism that we find in Gabrielle Roy's work and the contents of *Femme d'aujourd'hui* is less preoccupied with the national question, although it is still under a certain religious authority. All the same, Roy, like *Femme d'aujourd'hui,* suggests models of women who are strong and capable of making decisions directly about their own lives. *Femme d'aujourd'hui* goes further and discusses controversial issues. This change in media content is closely related to social and political change in

Québécois society. *Femme d'aujourd'hui* defied the Catholic rules to propose new options in women's lives based on their personal needs and emphasizing such issues as abortion, divorce, or women's opportunities for a career. These options represented new social subjectivities that women could choose to live.

Finally, radical feminism suggested radical options for women. It more or less encouraged them to revolt against the present social order and to build a new order of their own. The church is definitely excluded from their interventions, and nationalism is not their priority. The types of subjectivity suggested were to result in a better and fairer world for women.

In short, Quebec women's contribution to social change through the media has taken diverse forms over the years. Rather timid in the late-nineteenth century, it has become more significant as Quebec society has liberated itself from the yoke of ultramontanism and as a larger number of feminists have participated in media production. Nevertheless, at the present time a regressive movement seems to be taking shape in some media activities and to be attempting to minimize, and sometimes discredit, feminists' contributions to social change. In the coming years, it will be interesting to look at the forms that these backlash movements and the feminist responses will take.

Michèle Martin

NOTES

1. Marcelle Maugin, "Du référendum de 1980 au duplessisme," in A. Yanacopoulo, ed., *Au nom du père, du fils et de Duplessis* (Montréal: Remue-ménage, 1984), 127.

2. Ibid., 131.

3. Until the Quiet Revolution, the childbirth rate in Quebec was the highest of all provinces in Canada, as the Catholic church very strongly opposed any means of contraception. During the 1960s and 1970s the rate decreased to the point where it became (and is still) the lowest in Canada.

4. Contributions to the poststructuralist debate in Canada came particularly from Denise Riley, *'Am I That Name?' Feminism and the Category of 'Woman' in History* (Minneapolis: University of Minnesota Press, 1988); Joan W. Scott, *Gender and the Politics of History* (New York: Columbia University Press, 1988); and Mariana Valverde, "Poststructuralist Gender Historians: Are We Those Names?" *Labour/Le Travail* 25, 1990: 227-236; and "As If Subjects Existed: Analysing Social Discourses," CRSA 28, no. 2, 1991: 173-187.

5. As if there were just one ideology, says Valverde, in "Poststructuralist Gender Historians."

6. Scott, *Gender and the Politics of History*.

7. Quoted in Valverde, "Poststructuralist Gender Historians."

8. While media production has used stereotypical contents, women producers have also nuanced and, at times, opposed such stereotypes.

9. Mariana Valverde, "As If Subjects Existed," 174.

10. Marcelle Maugin, "Je me souviens," in Yanacopoulo, *Au nom du père*, 67.

11. It is relatively easy to find the ratings for a program, but it takes huge and expensive surveys to find out the characteristics of the members of the audiences as well as the impact that media contents might have on them.

12. Radio-Canada is the French version of CBC.

13. CBC memorandum, May 1978, quoted in Anne Légaré, "The Television Programme Femme D'aujourd'hui (Canada)," in *The Influence of Audio-Visual Media on the Socio-Cultural Behaviour of Women* (Paris: Unesco, 1980), 53.

14. Ibid.

15. Daniel Latouche, "Television and the Harsh Reality of Audience Fragmentation," *Forces* 92 (hiver 1991): 54.

16. M. Dumais, *La mère dans la société québécoise. Etude éthique d'un modèle à partir de deux journaux féministes: La bonne parole (1913-1958) et Les têtes de pioche (1976-1979).* Ottawa: CRIAW Document 5, 1983.

17. For more information on the Fédération nationale Saint-Jean-Baptiste, see Jane Errington in chapter 2.

18. For more information on the "feminist" movement of that period, see Jane Errington's section "The Reform Movement" in chapter 2.

19. Dumais, *La mère*, 6.

20. "Entre nous," 1914, quoted in Dumais, *La mère*, 10.

21. Quoted in Dumais, *La mère*, 2.

22. For an interesting discussion of women's paradoxical contribution to the making of children/defenders of the nation, see Anna Davin's "Imperialism and Motherhood," *History Workshop Journal* 5 (1978): 9-65.

23. Dumais, *La mère*, 26-30.

24. We will see in the next section that girls' education might have been an element in the origin of the Québécois tradition of women's literary production.

25. "Préparation de l'enfant à la vie familiale," 1946, quoted in Dumais, *La mère*, 46.

26. Dumais, *La mere*, 49.

27. Ibid., 54.

28. Ibid.

29. Ibid., 57.

30. Michèle Jean, "Clio revisitée," in M. Zavalloni, ed., *L'émergence d'une culture au féminin* (Montreal: Les Editions Saint-Martin, 1987), 87.

31. L.H. Forsyth, "Beyond the Myth and Fictions of Traditionalism and Nationalism: The Political in the Work of Nicole Brossard," in P.G. Lewis, ed., *Traditionalism, Nationalism, and Feminism: Women Writers in Quebec* (London: Greenwood, 1985), 164.

32. The name was intended to create a parallel with the nationalist movement called Le front de libération du Québec (FLQ), well-known in diverse parts of Canada.

33. These were Nicole Brossard, France Théorêt, Michèle Jean, Eliette Rioux, Martine Ross, and Madeleine Howard-Egré. The magazine was funded by the members of the collective themselves and by the subscriptions.

34. Information gathered during an interview with Michèle Jean's daughter, Dominique Jean, who teaches at the Department of History at Carleton University.

35. *Les têtes de pioche* 2, no. 1 (1977), quoted in Forsyth, "Beyond the Myth," 165.

36. Forsyth, "Beyond the Myth," 166.

37. Dumais, *La mère*, iv.

38. *Les têtes de pioche*, March 1976, quoted in Dumais, *La mère*, 16-17.

39. Dumais, *La mère*, 20.

40. *Les têtes de pioche*, cited in Dumais, *La mère*, 34. This form of women's violence was often considered by men, and even by some women, as hysteria. As such it was easy to dismiss not only the angry response but also its cause.

41. *Les têtes de pioche*, December 1976, quoted in Dumais, *La mère*, 36.

42. Forsyth, "Beyond the Myth," 166.

43. Ibid., 166-167.

44. S. Monet-Chartrand, *Pionnières québécoise et regroupements de femmes d'hier à aujourd'hui.* Montréal: Remue-Ménage, 1990, 111.

45. Paula G. Lewis, "Introduction," in Lewis, *Traditionalism, Nationalism, and Feminism,* 3.

46. Ibid., 5.

47. P. Smart, *Ecrire dans la maison du père: L'émergence du féminin dans la tradition littéraire du Québec* (Montreal: Québec/Amérique, 1988).

48. Ibid., 19.

49. Ibid., 22.

50. Ibid., 27.

51. Ibid., 29.

52. The Catholic church still refuses to have women ordained as priests. They can help in different ways, even to distribute Christ in the host, but they cannot be given God's power.

53. Monet-Chartrand, *Pionnières québécoise,* 111.

54. "J'ai une assez belle honte de me faire imprimer . . . La nécessité seule m'a donné cet extrême courage de me faire publier." Quoted in Smart, *Ecrire dans la maison,* 43.

55. This is not limited to book writing or to nineteenth-century writing. When the Québécois singer Marjo received her Félix for being the best female composer/writer/singer in Quebec in 1991, she thanked the audience with these words: "Yes! This is true, I am a composer/writer. . . . Dear audience, if you only knew the number of times I undressed to make you happy."

56. Cited in François Gallays, "Reflections in the Pool: The Subtext of Laure Conan's *Angéline de Montbrun,*" in Lewis, *Traditionalism, Nationalism, and Feminism,* 10.

57. Ibid., 12.

58. Smart, *Ecrire dans la maison,* 54.

59. Monet-Chartrand, *Pionnières québécoise,* 308.

60. The English title represents neither the French title of the book nor its story. A correct translation of "bonheur d'occasion" would be "second-hand happiness," which more accurately reflects the spirit of the book.

61. In Conan's novel, the father had the leading role; Angéline's role was dictated by him, even after his death. She was his *object.*

62. P.G. Lewis, "Female Spirals and Male Cages: The Urban Sphere in the Novels of Gabrielle Roy," in Lewis, *Traditionalism, Nationalism, and Feminism,* 72.

63. Smart, *Ecrire dans la maison,* 201.

64. Ibid., 206.

65. Ibid., 208.

66. Forsyth, "Beyond the Myth," 157.

67. Smart, *Ecrire dans la maison,* 296.

68. Ibid., 306-307.

69. Ibid., 317.

70. Monet-Chartrand, *Pionnières québécoise,* 334.

71. Information provided by Aline Desjardins in an interview with the author.
72. Légaré, "Television Programme," 57-59.
73. Ibid., 59.
74. We saw in the discussion of *Les têtes de pioche* that women's movements were well-organized to contest government positions.
75. Légaré, "Television Programme," 60.
76. Ibid., 60.
77. Quoted in ibid., 61.
78. Légaré, "Television Programme," 63.
79. Ibid., 52.
80. Ibid., 54.
81. Ibid., 55.
82. Ibid., 56.
83. Interview with the author.
84. Desjardins says that in 1991 she still often receives such evidence.
85. Quoted in Légaré, "Television Programme," 43.
86. Légaré, "Television Programme," 44.
87. Ibid., 45.
88. Ibid.
89. There were no increases after 1973.
90. We may assume that although the hiring was done by the managers, the associate producer, Michèlle Lasnier, had some say in the process.
91. Légaré, "Television Programme," 51.
92. Ibid., 65-66.
93. This decline might be explained by the fact that the star interviewer, Aline Desjardins, quit in 1975.
94. Quoted in Légaré, "Television Programme," 67. My emphasis.
95. Quoted in Légaré, "Television Programme," 67.
96. Légaré, "Television Programme," 69.
97. Ibid., 69-70.

SUGGESTED READINGS

Collectif Clio, *L'histoire des femmes au Québec.* Montreal: Quinze, 1982.

Clio Collective, *Quebec Women: A History.* Toronto: Women's Press, 1987.

Cross D.S. "The Neglected Majority: The Changing Role of Women in 19th Century Montreal," in S. Mann Trofimenkoff and A. Prentice, eds., *The Neglected Majority.* Vol. 1. Toronto: McClelland and Stewart, 1977.

Cuthbert Brandt, G., "Weaving It Together: Life Cycle and the Industrial Experience of Female Cotton Workers in Quebec, 1910-1950," in A. Prentice and S. Mann Trofimenkoff, *The Neglected Majority.* Vol. 2. Toronto: McClelland and Stewart, 1985.

Danylewycz, M., "Changing Relationships: Nuns and Feminists in Montreal, 1890-1925," in Prentice and Trofimenkoff, *The Neglected Majority.* Vol. 2.

Fahmy-Eid, N. and M. Dumont, eds., *Maîtresses de maison, maîtresses d'école: Femmes, famille et éducation dans l'histoire du Québec.* Montreal: Boréal.

Forsyth L.H., "Beyond the Myth and Fictions of Traditionalism and Nationalism: The Political in the Work of Nicole Brossard," in Lewis, *Traditionalism, Nationalism, and Feminism.*

Foulché-Delbosc, I., "Women of Three Rivers: 1651-63," in Trofimenkoff and Prentice, *The Neglected Majority.* Vol. 1.

Gallays, F. "Reflections in the Pool: The Subtext of Laure Conan's *Angéline de Montbrun*," in Lewis, *Traditionalism, Nationalism, and Feminism.*

Jean, M., *Québécoises du 20e siècle: Les étapes de la libération féminine au Québec, 1900-1974.* Montreal: Quinze, 1977.

Lavigne, M. and Y. Pinard, eds., *Travailleuses et féministes: Aspects historiques.* Montreal: Boréal, 1983.

Légaré, M., "The Television Programme Femme D'aujourd'hui (Canada)," in *The Influence of Audio-Visual Media on the Socio-Cultural Behaviour of Women.* Paris: Unesco, 1980.

Lewis, P.G., ed., *Traditionalism, Nationalism, and Feminism: Women Writers in Quebec.* London: Greenwood, 1985.

Lewis, P.G., "Introduction," in Lewis, *Traditionalism, Nationalism, and Feminism,* pp. 1-11.

Lewis, P.G., "Female Spirals and Male Cages: The Urban Sphere in the Novels of Gabrielle Roy," in Lewis, *Traditionalism, Nationalism, and Feminism,* pp. 71-81.

Maugin, M., "Du référendum de 1980 au duplessisme," in Yanacopoulo, *Au nom du père.*

Noel, J., "New France: Les femmes favorisées," in Prentice and Trofimenkoff, *The Neglected Majority.* Vol. 2.

Smart, P., *Writing in the Father's House: The Emergence of the Feminine in the Quebec Literary Tradition.* Toronto: University of Toronto Press, 1991.

Vipond, M., "The Image of Women in Mass Circulation Magazines in the 1920s," in Trofimenkoff and Prentice, *The Neglected Majority.* Vol. 1.

Yanacopoulo, A., ed., *Au nom du père, du fils et de Duplessis.* Montreal: Remue-Ménage, 1984.

Chapter Six

The Changing Patterns
of Public Policy

≈≈≈≈≈≈≈≈≈≈≈≈≈≈≈≈≈≈≈≈≈≈≈≈≈≈≈≈≈≈≈≈≈≈≈≈≈

Public policy helps to shape the discourse of social interaction. The laws enacted by legislators in part reflect the values, or ideology, of the lawmakers. In turn these laws affect the fabric of society, imposing new limits on and possibilities for thought and action. The Canadian Charter of Rights and Freedoms, enacted in 1982, provides us with a good example of this process. For while that constitutional document reflects the tradition of human rights proceedings in Canada at least since the 1965 Bill of Rights, it also provides a new framework for thinking about rights and obligations. In Canada, as throughout the world, public policy has been made almost exclusively by men and has generally reflected men's assumptions about women's and men's needs and abilities. While over time some of these assumptions have changed, overall policy has been framed within the context of patriarchal patterns of authority. This chapter traces the transitions and considers the implications of the gap between the legislators' understanding of women's roles and the reality of Canadian women's lives.

Public Policy from 1867 to Women's Suffrage:
Preserving the Traditional Family

In 1867 most women and men accepted the view that there was a sharp distinction between family life and politics and business. Legislators believed that women by nature were suited to the private sphere and men to the public sphere. Women's roles were fairly inflexible and men's roles rather more flexible. Women were defined in terms of their relationships with men, and legislation was framed in the context of what Lisa Peattie and Martin Rein call a "discourse of social roles, interpersonal responsibility, and commitment," which focused on "family ties, home-making, masculinity and femininity in love and marriage."[1] It was a discourse of inequalities, which celebrated men as providers and leaders and women as caregivers and followers. To this end, marriage was viewed as the natural goal of all women. And in marriage, legally the husband ruled supreme. For example, the husband's citizenship determined the wife's status, according to the federal Act Respecting Naturalization and Aliens passed in 1881. Early legislation also designated the husband/father as the head of the household, with the power to decide the fortunes of all family members. [2]

Throughout Canada from 1867 until the turn of the century the husband was in charge of family finances and controlled any wages earned by his wife. He also held the exclusive right in the family to own and sell property or sign contracts. Guardianship rights were vested in the father by the terms of the 1867 British North America Act. Although after 1887 a mother living in Ontario could apply to the courts for guardianship of her children, the general practice was for the father to have absolute legal parental authority. Even a woman's citizenship was determined by her husband. According to the 1881 Act Respecting Naturalization and Aliens, married women took on the citizenship of their husbands upon marriage – and marriage was generally a lifelong proposition. Divorce was rare and available only to women who were able to prove adultery, extreme cruelty, or incest. [3]

In this early thinking about rights and responsibilities, legislators assumed that men would support their families financially in return for the right to rule as masters in what they referred to as the "pure Christian home." [4] But since men often failed to fulfill their responsibilities, as Jane Errington notes in her chapter in this book, legislators at both levels of government decided to take on some of them. Gradually at the beginning of the twentieth century some legislative initiatives reflected a growing commitment to transferring protective care from the husband/father to the state. This new protective legislation did not alter women's status, for legislators remained firmly committed to the principle that the wife owed allegiance to her husband. The new laws provided some financial relief to widows or deserted wives with small children still in the home, but divorced women were not eligible for funding; and if a deserted wife committed adultery, her payments were stopped. In some cases, such as in Newfoundland after 1872, the government itself paid the relief. In others, such as in British Columbia after 1901, the husband was ordered to make payments to his wife. In 1869 the federal government passed a law imposing a fine on a man who failed to provide for his wife, and in 1913 this was amended to include providing for his children.

The guardian principle also moved governments into pension policies for widows, long before pensions were placed on the agenda as a necessary social service. Beginning in 1868 the federal government awarded pensions to a small number of widows of men who had performed great services for Canada. In 1914, with the granting of $100 to the widows of volunteers who had defended the government in the Fenian Raids, the federal government began the practice of providing for the widows of servicemen. All pensions ceased if the widow married again. These relief payments never matched living expenses, but alleviated the worst cases of poverty.

In their concern for the continued strength of the family, legislators also began to pass laws that gave women slightly more power over family finances. These laws were not intended to make women independent or equal, but to provide them with some economic security in case of their husbands' death or desertion. Between 1872 and 1922 in English Canada, although not until 1940 in Quebec, property laws were changed to permit the purchaser to become the owner, regardless of sex. By 1897 in English Canada and 1931 in Quebec, a wife employed outside the home was allowed to retain her wages. The Homestead Act of 1878 provided limited property rights to married women in what was then known as the Northwest Territories. Legislators who favoured this act underlined the importance of the family for the growth of Canada. They argued that this property provision would recognize "the fact, although the law generally treated the head of the family as the absolute proprietor of the property which he controlled, that this property was also the product of the industry of his wife and children, that they had some interest in it which the law ought to recognize and, in some measure, to protect."[5]

These early legislative initiatives were intended to strengthen the family as a building block of the new social order. In an ongoing attempt to preserve the roles of wife and mother, governments took some action to safeguard the purity of young girls before they married. Chastity laws were passed in an attempt to eradicate prostitution. The separate incarceration of female convicts became the practice in the 1870s, and female reformatories were the scene of crusading attempts to purify the inmates. The morality crusade also led the federal government in 1910 to prohibit any contact between female immigrants (many of whom were brought to Canada for marriage to frontier men) and the ship's crew during passage. But while the state was prepared to defend the interests of innocent young women, it was also concerned with protecting men from what it considered to be the mercenary schemes of evil women. Women were viewed as both victims and seductresses, and the 1886 amendments to the Criminal Code provide a good example of this double image. The amendments punished seducers of young women between the ages of twelve and sixteen, but placed the onus of proof on the accuser. They also decreed that one witness to the act of seduction was insufficient, and that the defendant was a competent witness for the defence. Men were protected from unscrupulous women, but women found it nearly impossible to win convictions against unscrupulous men.

In this early vision of women's proper roles there was some allowance for women to participate in the labour force, but this participation was seen to be class specific and temporary. Working-class girls were actively recruited for domestic service, for they were needed to keep the middle-class family alive and well. It was assumed that these young girls were merely putting in time as domestic workers before marriage. The federal government went so far as to advertise for female domestics both in Canada and abroad, and in 1881 there were 800,410 households in Canada employing 49,345 servants.[6] But the thought of women taking part in industrial labour was unpalatable to the early lawmakers. In the *Report* of the Royal Commission on the Relations between Capital and Labour, women's presence in the economy was described as an unfortunate corollary of industrial expansion.[7] There were even some formal attempts to limit the extent of women's work. Nova Scotia and Ontario passed laws restricting women from mining underground in the late nineteenth century. Quebec and Ontario established minimum wages and maximum hour restrictions in the 1880s for women in some industrial occupations. All provinces excluded women from hazardous jobs. These regulations may have afforded some protection to women, but they also demonstrated women's lack of control over the manner of their participation in the labour force and kept them out of some of the better-paid jobs. They reinforced the paternalistic treatment of women by governments and did nothing to break down the principle that women were both different from and unequal to men.

There were some exceptions to the prevailing notion of separate spheres. In the Western regions in particular, women who had taken risks side by side with men were less willing than their Central-Canadian sisters to sit back and be controlled by these same men. On the whole, however, until the twentieth century there were few challenges by women to legislators' judgments about the patterns of their lives.

Public Policy from the Franchise to the 1940s:
Growing Recognition of Equality Rights

There were two new developments in the pattern of policies enacted during the first half of the twentieth century, in the context of new challenges to the stereotypes of women's appropriate roles. Increasingly, legislators came to accept the principle that women ought to share in decision-making within the family. And slowly they adopted the notion that women could be members of the paid labour force, as a prelude to marriage and family responsibilities. Undoubtedly the suffrage issue was one catalyst for change. Suffragists "demanded for women a kind of power and a connection with the social order not based on the institution of the family and their subordination within it."[8] While it is true that most suffragists saw the vote as a means of safeguarding peace in the home, there was a small group of working women who sought equality rights in the labour force. Manitoba, Saskatchewan, and Alberta were the first provinces to grant women voting rights in 1916, with British Columbia and Ontario following in 1917. The federal government also enfranchised some women in 1917 with the Wartime Elections Act, which gave the vote to close relatives of members of the armed services. In the same year the Military Voters Act gave the vote to women who were themselves in active service. By 1918 the federal government had granted women full suffrage in federal elections. In the same year Nova Scotia enfranchised women, followed by New Brunswick in 1919 and Prince Edward Island in 1922. Quebec women did not gain the right to vote in provincial elections until 1940. The extension of suffrage to women was based on the premise that women would use the vote only to improve the quality of life in the home. One member's speech in the federal House of Commons in 1918 during the debate on women's suffrage captures this attitude well: "Here I approve, but with the understanding that the exercise of these rights will not go to lengths where woman will be diverted from her function, from her natural and sacred duty."[9] But nonetheless the vote offered women "a relationship to the larger society that was entirely and explicitly outside the boundaries of women's familial relations."[10]

Indeed, suffrage did improve women's lot in the home. Between 1917 and 1923 most provinces enacted equal guardianship laws, which gave mothers equal rights with fathers to the custody, control, and education of children. Divorce laws were made less discriminatory. Adultery alone was accepted as grounds for divorce for either the husband or wife, although property settlements still did not recognize the housewife's contribution to family assets. Citizenship laws were amended in 1931 to allow a woman who was a British subject before marriage to retain her British citizenship after marriage to a person classified as "alien."

Even the participation of women in the labour force became more acceptable to legislators in this post-suffrage period. The change in thinking was partly due to the need for labour in the rapidly expanding Canadian industrial economy. Legislators expected that women workers would be single, segregated from male workers, and paid less than men. These expectations were most apparent during the labour policy instituted during World War II. Then, in the face of labour shortages resulting from men's involvement in the war effort, the federal government reluctantly recruited women into the labour force. It was a case of single women first. "Government officials publicly expressed a reluctance to draw upon those people in the female labour reserve whose mobilization would disrupt the traditional family system."[11] Nevertheless, by 1944 the need for female labour in the war industries was so great that even married women with children were called out. To facilitate their participation in the war effort, day nurseries were set up in some industries, and tax concessions were offered to make women's earnings more attractive. As soon as the war was over, however, married women with children were expected to return home. The nurseries were closed and the tax concessions cancelled. It was obvious that the "large-scale employment of women was not supposed to last."[12]

During the first half of this century, these and other changes in the working patterns of Canadian women led to another series of protective laws, for governments felt responsible for safeguarding the reproductive capabilities of single women who, they now conceded, could play a limited role in the developing industrial economy. To develop guidelines for this new policy, most provinces set up commissions to investigate women's work. The Nova Scotia Commission of Inquiry into the hours of labour, wages, and working conditions of women employed in industrial occupations was typical. The commission was made up of three men and one woman, and its report, presented to the provincial government in 1920, was based on open hearings and a survey of employment practices. In its deliberations the commission was guided by the principle that "If we are to have a healthy virile race, it is of primary importance to preserve the homes and conserve the health, morals and efficiency" of women.[13] The commission recognized that there was "a striking disparity between wages paid to men and their hours of labour," but did not try to remove this inequality.[14]

At the time there was generally little concern among legislators for gender inequalities in wages. Even J.S. Woodsworth, leader of the Co-operative Commonwealth Federation – a party committed publicly to the principle of social justice – rose in the House of Commons in 1926 to complain about the wages paid to married men, but not about the even lower wages paid to single women. Ten years after the Nova Scotia Commission's *Report* was tabled, women still were earning on average only 39 per cent of men's earnings. But the commissioners' concern for women's childbearing potential did lead to a proposal for minimum wages and maximum hours of work for women, together with the adoption of standards essential "to the health and morals of these women."[15]

Most provinces acted on these proposals, and minimum-wage laws for women were passed in the early part of the century, considerably in advance of minimum-wage laws for men. In 1918 British Columbia became the first province to pass a Women's Minimum Age Act. The act stipulated that experienced women would not be paid less than the living wage. Between 1918 and 1922 all provinces except Prince Edward Island and New Brunswick passed minimum-wage legislation for women.

Alberta was the only province that had a minimum wage for both women and men. In each case the legislation established a minimum-wage board, which was to determine the amount needed to sustain a single woman. Farm labourers or domestics were not covered, which meant that only about one-half of the women in the labour force were protected. In most cases the acts gave the cabinet the power to decide if the wage board's recommendations should be followed. As a study of the Ontario board shows, "Co-operation with employers was made a goal in itself, as important as the goal of ensuring that women's wages would meet the cost of living."[16] At best these laws alleviated only the worst instances of exploitation. They did nothing to advance the principle of equal pay for equal work – and working women were beginning to make this demand, as Jane Errington notes earlier in this book. Telephone operators in Toronto had already brought public attention to their plight in 1907 by striking for better wages and shorter hours of work. This and other calls for justice were ignored.

In the same spirit of protecting women's reproductive capabilities, there was legislation restricting the lifting of heavy objects. Then in 1920 the federal government amended the Criminal Code to provide penalties for male employers who tried to take sexual advantage of female employees under twenty-one who were "previously chaste."[17] These protective laws were a mixed blessing for women. While they undoubtedly moderated some of the harsh conditions in the labour force, they did not guarantee healthy working conditions or a decent living wage. At the same time they further reduced women's access to employment. They were enacted by a paternalistic government that gave little thought to the ambitions or proposals of working women themselves, but was concerned, as in earlier times, with protecting women's reproductive functions and with keeping young working girls pure for marriage.

Throughout this period, most legislators remained convinced that marriage was a woman's calling. To make it easier for some mothers to stay at home with children, the provinces gradually introduced the notion of a mothers' allowance, then called mothers' pensions. In 1916 Manitoba was the first province to enter "into inadequate homes as the active agent of middle-class values."[18] The program provided a small subsidy to permit working mothers to stay at home for at least part of each day. The first mothers' pensions were not distributed to all mothers. While there were some provincial variations in requirements, generally the applicants had to be needy widows with two or more children. Some provinces allowed wives of insane men to apply. Most provinces disallowed divorcées or unmarried mothers, for the move was not meant to sanction marital breakdown. These mothers' pensions were designed to reduce infant mortality rates and the incidence of juvenile delinquency. They were instigated in the belief that "If the present and next generation of widows' children are to be conserved for the nation, a mothers' allowance is the present practical solution."[19]

Women in the Developing Welfare State

The welfare state took a firm hold in Canada in the period following the end of World War II. It brought governments into areas of legislation such as employment and income security, which formerly had been regarded as outside the scope of public policy. But governments seemed ignorant of the impact these changes would have on women's lives. They passed a series of measures to encourage women to continue to stay at home and raise healthy future workers for the rapidly expanding economy.

Some of the earlier relief measures that had been developed to assist needy single mothers became part of a universal program of benefits. The mothers' pensions provide a good example. By 1940 all provinces but New Brunswick and Prince Edward Island provided mothers' pensions, although the amounts paid to women varied widely from province to province. In 1942, for example, average monthly benefits were $39.19 in British Columbia but only $13.77 in Saskatchewan, one of the provinces hardest hit by the postwar depression.[20] In 1944 the federal government stepped in and took over the program. The means test was dropped and the family allowance, as it was called, was sent to all mothers with children aged sixteen or younger.

This family-allowance program was one of the first in the federal government's growing package of income-security measures. It helped to set the tone of the welfare state, underscoring the fact that "The Welfare State is not just a set of services, it is also a set of ideas about society, about the family, and – not least important – about women, who have a centrally important role within the family, as its linchpin."[21] The federal government's motives in making family allowance a universal program were linked to the needs of the expanding economy. Canada needed healthy workers to fill the increasing number of available jobs, and women were urged to stay at home, have babies, and raise them to become strong and productive workers.

In his speech to the House of Commons justifying the introduction of family-allowance payments, Mackenzie King, the Liberal prime minister, noted: "This measure proceeds upon the assumption that children are an asset to the state." He went on to argue: "Properly nourished children become active, productive members of society, and there is no doubt that this is the only way in which a strong and healthy citizenry can be built up."[22] Family-allowance cheques, payable to the mother, would make it easier for women to stay at home and raise these citizens. Clearly, the value of women's labour in the home had changed from the time of Confederation. Whereas the nineteenth-century mother was viewed as the moral guardian of the nation, the twentieth-century mother was viewed as the producer of workers for an expanding economy. The language of social purity and morality, which dominated legislative discussions about women's roles in the early 1900s, had been replaced by the language of healthy babies, strong soldiers, and better workers.

At the same time the need for more workers also led to greater acceptance of the possibility that women without children might work outside the home. In the egalitarian spirit of the postwar years, governments slowly adopted some equal-rights legislation for women with paid jobs. For, once governments with liberal principles had accepted the possibility that women could be members of the paid labour force, it was difficult to deny them the rights being extended to male workers. Most employees were under provincial jurisdiction, and there was a series of provincial legislative initiatives in the 1950s to improve equal opportunity for women at work. Slowly, beginning in 1951 in Ontario and ending in Newfoundland in 1970, the provincial governments passed equal-pay legislation, which was generally worded to guarantee women and men in both the public and private sectors the same pay for similar or essentially similar jobs. Unfortunately, these initiatives were too weak to have much effect because then, as now, the labour force was highly segregated by gender and relatively few women actually worked in the same jobs as men.

In 1954 the federal government finally decided that it should know more about women's labour-force participation and established a Women's Bureau in the federal Department of Labour. According to the 1951 census, 24 per cent of Canadian women were then members of the paid labour force. Governments knew very little about these women, and the Women's Bureau was designed to "promote a wider understanding of problems peculiar to women workers and the employment of women." The bureau, in keeping with the spirit of labour legislation for women in that period, was to help women "make a more effective contribution to the development of Canada."[23] The bureau struggled to carry out its mandate with one director and only two staff members. Even with this small staff, the bureau played a vital role in informing governments, civil servants, and the public about the nature of women's work outside the home, and in its first year it undertook a survey of married women working for pay in Canada.

The bureau also played a role in preparing the federal equal-pay legislation, introduced in 1956. This legislation had most of the flaws of the provincial laws and did not go very far in guaranteeing true equality for women workers. It applied only to federal works or businesses, or corporations performing work on behalf of the government, and limited equal pay to "identical or substantially identical work." The aggrieved employee was required to complain in writing to the minister of labour, who might then ask a fair-wage officer to make an inquiry. This proved to be a cumbersome procedure that was rarely used. In spite of these limitations, the federal and the earlier provincial equal-pay laws were significant landmarks in the legislative history of women's rights. First, they recognized the possibility that women and men might hold similar jobs in the public world. Second, they established the principle that when women and men were performing similar work they should receive the same rewards. The earlier presumption that women and men were different and, therefore, always unequal was being replaced by the notion that they might, in some cases, be the same and therefore equal. The boundaries of policy-making for women had begun to shift. But the movement was gradual, and it was marked by important setbacks. The Canadian Bill of Rights, which became law in 1960, guaranteed women and men equal treatment before the law, in cases where they were in equal situations. As Beverley Baines demonstrates in her chapter, litigation based on the Bill of Rights demonstrated quickly how few instances there might be in which such equal situations would be judged to exist.

The principle of equal treatment was applied unevenly and primarily in the public sphere. The 1969 amendments to the Criminal Code illustrate how far governments were from legislating in the spirit of equal rights in the home. These amendments permitted the sale of contraceptives and made it legal for doctors to perform abortions in hospitals in cases when a therapeutic abortion committee had given its approval. The committee was instructed to make its decision on the basis of the medical need of each case. Women seemed to be on the brink of winning control away from men over reproductive rights. However, the abortion amendments had two consequences, neither of which protected the rights of individual women. First, they moved the issue of abortion to the local level, thereby institutionalizing unequal access to abortions and at the same time removing some pressure from federal politicians to change abortion laws. Second, they failed to remove men's control over women's reproductive rights, because the therapeutic abortion committees were made up primarily of male doctors. The federal government had not yet come to terms with the growing conflict between its laws for women in the public sphere, where individual rights were becoming more important, and its laws for women in the home, where the preservation of the family was still the dominant theme.

On other measures, particularly those requiring new thinking about women's and men's roles, government performance remained poor. Native women by law were still unequal to Native men; rape laws still favoured the accused at the expense of the accuser; property distribution on dissolution of marriage rewarded men and penalized women; day care provisions were woefully inadequate; government-run pension programs discriminated against housewives; and there was unequal pay for women and men working in different but equivalent jobs.

1970 to the 1980s: *Growing Adherence to the Equal Opportunity Principle*

Two events in 1970 signalled a transition in legislators' thinking about women's roles: maternity-leave provisions became part of the Canada Labour (Standards) Code, and the *Report* of the Royal Commission on the Status of Women was published. While the *Report* was not implemented in its entirety, it nevertheless unleashed forces that contributed to the development of a new view of women by legislators. In the legislation of the 1970s and 1980s, the concept of the working mother was recognized; there were improvements in women's equality rights in the public sphere; and there was better protection for women from sexual harassment and wife assault.

With the introduction of maternity-leave provisions, the traditional view that women must be mothers first and workers in the labour force second began to disintegrate. The 1970 legislation provided pregnant women with eleven weeks of paid leave and automatic job reinstatement at the same level of pay and seniority at the end of the leave period. The legislation was far from perfect. The payments made by the unemployment insurance program were lower than the wages earned before the leave. If pregnancy and unemployment coincided, the applicant was refused benefits. Because the benefits were part of the unemployment package, the cost of maternity was borne by taxpayers rather than employers. Nevertheless, the legislation was significant because it was national, and across all of Canada the message was clear that the employment cost of childbearing, although not child care, was a community responsibility rather than an individual woman's burden.

In keeping with this new philosophy of welcoming women more fully into the public sphere, both levels of government enacted a series of equal-opportunity laws for women. As a first step, governments tried to remove discriminatory practices from existing laws. At the same time they progressed rapidly to establish women's formal legal equality. In 1981 the federal government ratified the United Nations Convention on the Elimination of All Forms of Discrimination Against Women. In 1984 a federal parliamentary task force was set up to identify discriminatory laws. In 1985 the task force issued its report with eighty-five recommendations, and in 1986 the government tabled *Toward Equality,* its response to the report. *Toward Equality* affirmed the federal government's commitment to legal equality rights for women. Finally, in April 1985, the equality rights provisions of the Charter of Rights and Freedoms came into effect. Section 15 of the Charter guarantees the equality of women and men before and under the law and their right to the equal protection and benefit of the law. Provincially, the pattern was similar. In 1969 British Columbia became the first province to make discrimination in the employment of women illegal under its Human Rights Act. By 1975 all provinces except Prince Edward Island and Newfoundland had similar legislation.

The early equal-opportunity laws were based on the philosophy that discrimination against women in the labour force was a human relations problem, a consequence of "evilly motivated conduct."[24] Individuals who felt that they had suffered discrimination had to take their case to either a provincial or a federal human rights commission, and the onus was on the individual to demonstrate her case. But by the late 1970s it was recognized that women's access to jobs was limited also by systemic barriers such as height and weight restrictions in job descriptions. Governments started to put in place affirmative action programs, which would remove these factors and increase women's access to jobs formerly held primarily by men. For the most part, these programs have been voluntary and limited to government employees. They have had only minimal impact on employment practices.[25] In 1979 the federal government set up the Affirmative Action Directorate of the Canada Employment and Immigration Division. It contacted over 1,400 employers "to encourage them to participate in a voluntary affirmative action program. As of July 1984, only seventy-one companies had agreed to do so."[26] In addition, a national training program was established to try to prepare more women for non-traditional jobs. The Treasury Board was put in charge of an affirmative action program in the public service, but it has been slow to implement this program.

Today the principle of affirmative action has been accepted by both major levels of government because it merely affirms that women and men should be treated equally when they are the same. It improves women's access to the public sphere but requires them to behave like men and compete equally on men's terms for jobs that men have created and defined. Most provinces now have a version of affirmative action in place. In 1986 the federal government took affirmative action one step further and passed Bill C-62, which requires federally regulated and Crown companies with over one hundred employees to report to the government on their adherence to the principle of fair competition. But only the reporting is mandatory. There are no provisions to enforce compliance with fair-competition practices. In addition, the success of this program is dependent on the watchdog talents of the Canadian Human Rights Commission. With its backlog of roughly 1,500 cases, the Commission is not able to act quickly on complaints.

Equal pay for work of equal value laws have been less common. In 1977 the federal government passed the Canadian Human Rights Act, which established the principle of equal pay for work of equal value in the federal public service. On the face of it, this was a great leap forward for women. However, the federal guidelines for equal value were poorly written, and the program has had only limited effectiveness. In 1984 the federal government also implemented a national Equal Pay Program to ensure that employers under federal jurisdiction adopt the principle of equal pay for work of equal value. The success of this program has not yet been determined. In 1975 Quebec affirmed the equal-value principle, and in 1986 Manitoba imposed it on all public-sector employees. Ontario introduced a bill covering both public and private employees in 1986, and this became law in 1988. The Ontario legislation applies to all firms with more than one hundred employees, and wage adjustments came into effect between two to four years from the date of proclamation of the act.

Pat and Hugh Armstrong note the positive aspects of pay equity, which requires that jobs be compared on the basis of skill, effort, responsibilities, and working conditions. But they note as well that it negates the impact of gender, by enforcing comparisons on the basis of value. And "This requirement ignores the fact that value is primarily determined by power, not by job content."[27] There are indications that early feminist optimism about the promise of equal-pay laws may not be realized. For as long as job evaluation criteria are established by employers rather than by the workers themselves, pay equity falls short of the promise of allowing women to be equitably (rather than equally) rewarded for their labours.

In general, the programs to redress imbalances in the labour force have not been very effective to date. The authors of the 1987 *Report* of the federal government's Nielsen Task Force made this observation about the program of equal opportunities for women:

> In spite of the existence of several government programs directed at the achievement of equal pay/value and employment equity/affirmative action goals, the significant wage gap between men and women employed on the same full-time, full-year basis has remained virtually unchanged since 1978, according to a variety of detailed and comprehensive studies as recent as the Abella and MacDonald Commissions.[28]

As the Abella Commission on Equality in Employment recognized, one of the keys to labour-force equality for women is improved access to affordable, reliable day care.[29] In 1984, 52 per cent of mothers with children under age three were working outside of the home, and 80 per cent of those mothers were forced to use unlicensed day care. The Canadian Commission for the International Year of the Child estimated that in 1979 over one million Canadian children were left at home alone or with siblings while their parents were at work.[30] The lack of day care has hurt women in different ways. Low-income women, who must work to survive, have responded either by working part-time or by making do with less than adequate child care. Middle-class women have been "made to feel guilty by the idea that they might be damaging their children if they went out to work."[31] At the same time the scarcity of reliable, affordable day care has reinforced class differences.

By far the greatest amount of political action undertaken in the 1970s and 1980s to improve women's status was bureaucratic, and it facilitated a process of government redefinition of "women's issues." The members of the Royal Commission on the Status of Women recommended in 1970 that the federal government establish offices charged with status of women concerns. Gradually an extensive bureaucratic group was assembled at the federal level, with less elaborate mechanisms in most provinces. The commissioners also recommended that the federal government provide financial support to women's groups. In 1973 the federal cabinet approved the creation of the Women's Program within the Secretary of State. Before 1988 its budget, which reached $12.7 million in 1987, was used primarily to support women's groups.

In the 1970s the federal government also rediscovered its earlier mandate of legislating for morality. In 1979, when the government adopted a Plan of Action as part of its strategy for the United Nations Decade of Action, three of the five areas selected for consideration were morality issues. The plan included action on rape, sexual harassment, wife-battering, women in the media, and pensions. The concern for protecting women had been transmitted to governments by women's groups, and it continues to be a central issue in women's struggle to control their lives. Yet one cannot help but be somewhat suspicious of the government's motives. The switch in focus from equal pay for work of equal value and affordable, accessible day care to rape and wife-beating has reduced the pressure on federal finances and on federal-provincial renegotiation of social service funding.

Women and the Neoconservative Agenda

The election of a Conservative government at the federal level in 1984 signalled a renewed tension between the equal-opportunity principle, which had gained some ground during the Trudeau years, and the traditional view of separate spheres. The new Conservative government was committed to privatization and free-market values. It superimposed on this neoconservative economic agenda a renewed reverence for women's familial responsibilities, which has often led to the distortion of the debate on issues affecting women into a pro-family, anti-family perspective. In 1992, newspaper reports revealed the existence of a Conservative "family compact," thirty-five MPs and two Senators committed to incorporating traditional family values based on a vision of the male wage-earner nuclear family.[32]

The Conservative agenda ended the restriction of federal support funds to groups committed to moving towards greater equality rights for women and opened new financial doors for groups committed to the traditional view of a nuclear, exclusively male, wage-earner family. In 1989 the Women's Program provided funding for the first time in its history to Realistic Equal Active for Life (REAL), a group committed to the preservation of traditional family values and opposed to feminist goals.[33] In the same year the budget of the Women's Program in the Secretary of State was reduced by 15 per cent. In 1990 another 15 per cent was removed. Groups like the National Action Committee on the Status of Women (NAC), working for greater economic equality for women, have seen their budgets cut dramatically.

The impact of the federal Conservative government's agenda has been most apparent in the area of child care. In the period following the 1984 election the recommendations of the Cook Task Force on Child Care were put aside in favour of more study by a Parliamentary Task Force on Child Care. In December 1987 the government announced its National Strategy on Child Care, which called for an increase of two hundred thousand spaces in non-profit and commercial facilities and an increase to $4,000 per child in the child care tax deduction. In 1988 the government introduced Bill C-144, which would have replaced the existing child care programs funded under the Canada Assistance Plan with a separate child care shared-cost program. The new proposal provided no guarantees that low-income earners would have access to spaces. It treated non-profit and for-profit child care facilities equally. And the two hundred thousand new spaces would have been added over a seven-year period. Bill C-144 died on the order paper in the Senate when a federal election was called in late 1988. It was followed in 1992 by a White Paper on child benefits.[34] In it the government declared that it had abandoned the proposal for a separate national child care shared-cost program. It announced an increase in the child care tax deduction to $5,000 per child and the establishment of a new benefit to replace family allowance and child tax credits. Effective January 1, 1993, the principle of a universal family-allowance payment was removed. The new benefit includes a payment of up to $500 per year for low-income families where both parents are working for pay. The 1992 proposals reflect a shift away from providing support for services towards income relief for families. But critics of the plan note that the average increase in benefits for families with combined incomes of less than $50,000 a year will be only $250.

Other issues such as pensions for housewives and employment equity have also seen little progress. The decentralizing thrust of Meech Lake and subsequent constitutional proposals raises the possibility of a freeze on new national social programs (such as child care) and the disintegration of the principle of universality in those programs already in place. In the negotiations that led to the development of the Meech Lake Accord, women's concerns about possible conflict between the Accord and equality rights provisions in the Charter were ignored. In subsequent constitutional negotiations women's voices have been heard only briefly, and from afar. These concerns led the National Action Committee on the Status of Women to reject the Charlottetown Agreement, offered to voters as a package for constitutional renewal in a referendum on October 26, 1992.

Explaining the Pattern

In the years following Confederation legislators viewed the family as they viewed society – as a hierarchical structure, with men at the top. But while women were legally inferior to men, by custom and later by law men had certain obligations to fulfill towards women. It was a feudal arrangement, based on man's presumed natural superiority. This patriarchal view was slowly modified over the years, and there is convincing evidence that women themselves have contributed to the transformation. The work done by the few women who have been elected to public office, the activity of women's groups, working both independently and inside institutions, and the pressures exerted by women working in government bureaucracies have had an impact on the increasing acceptance of equality rights. There is evidence, too, that the pattern of laws would have been very different if women had been more actively involved in writing and implementing them.

Women are relatively new to the world of politics and are still quite far removed from political and economic power.[35] In the governing side of politics, women's experience in Canada, as throughout the world, "ranges from total exclusion to selective inclusion, from discrimination to paternalism, from rejection to condescension."[36] While the participation rates of women and men in mass-based political activities are becoming similar, a gap has remained at the higher levels of politics where power is concentrated.

Women have been active in politics in the sense of working for political parties or for specific candidates for a very long time. When Canadian survey data on political participation were first collected in the 1960s, it was found that about the same proportion of women as men were helping out the parties at election time. In addition, about the same proportion of women as men turned out at the polls on election day. However, the similarity in the political behaviour of women and men breaks down as we move from activities such as voting or political campaigning to activities such as seeking elected office or the leadership of party organizations. In 1919 it became legal for women to be federal candidates, but between 1919 and 1972 women never held more than 5 per cent of the seats in the House of Commons.[37] After 1972 the percentage of women seeking election increased, and more women ran in their own right rather than as a replacement for a husband (legislator) who had died. In the 1984 election the percentage of women in the federal House increased dramatically, to 10 per cent. In 1988 the figure rose to 13 per cent. It is not clear how much of this increase can be attributed to unexpected Conservative victories in ridings that had not traditionally returned Conservative members; women are more likely to be nominated in such 'lost cause' ridings.[38] Provincially the record is somewhat better. For example, in 1983, 12 per cent of the members in the legislatures of both British Columbia and Manitoba were women, although the figure was only 2 per cent in Nova Scotia.[39]

In other words, while Canadian women have been active politically, particularly since the end of World War II their activity has been concentrated in the support positions that keep the political system running smoothly. This has meant that women have not been making the important decisions in either the political parties or government. From the time that women won the right to seek elected office, they have had a voice in the legislatures, but it has been muted by their minority status and their distance from powerful cabinet posts. This may be significant for policy decisions. In Finland, for example, it has been noted that women in the legislature, regardless of their views on feminism, are more likely than men to introduce feminist or humanitarian reforms directed to solving the problems of deprived groups.[40] In Canada a review of the debates in both the federal and provincial legislatures reveals how frequently female legislators have brought the needs and perspectives of women to the attention of their male colleagues. A forceful reminder of the significance of the female presence came in 1980 when the Ad Hoc Committee on the Constitution was working to ensure that women's equality rights remain in the Constitution. The members of the committee were supported almost exclusively by the female members of Parliament. Reflecting on her Charter experience, one committee member observed: "Parliament, with 282 men, all of them concerned and all of them trying to put our views forward, will not do it like 141 women and 141 men. So that there's a combination of they do not and they cannot. Forget about will not!"[41]

The first women elected to public office found themselves surrounded by men, and they struggled to bring women's points of view into the legislatures. Many of these early female legislators were members of reform parties committed to social change and improved welfare policies. Irene Parlby is a good example. She was first elected in the 1919 provincial election of Alberta, as a member of the United Farmers of Alberta. She was named minister without portfolio in the cabinet and used her position to press for legislation on child welfare, support for deserted wives, and the joint guardianship of children.[42]

At about the same time (in 1921) one of Canada's best-known feminists, Nellie McClung, was elected to the opposition bench in Alberta as a Liberal. She often broke party lines to vote with the government on issues that she felt would benefit women. She tried, unsuccessfully, to liberalize the divorce laws in the province, and to change the naturalization laws so that a woman marrying an alien would not be disenfranchised. She also tried to alter the Married Women's Property Act. When she was defeated in the 1925 provincial election she left political life to work in women's organizations.[43] In British Columbia, Mary Ellen Smith, a Liberal elected provincially in 1916, became a minister without portfolio. She was active in promoting concern for public health and education and is best known for working for mothers' pensions and minimum wages for women.[44]

The history of Quebec female legislators did not begin until 1940, when women in that province were first given access to elected office. It was twenty-two years after that, in 1962, when the first woman, Claire Kirkland-Casgrain, was elected to represent the Liberals in the provincial legislature. Her record in office for advancing the cause of women's rights is impressive. One of her most significant victories was a civil-rights bill in 1964 that changed Quebec women's legal status. It gave Quebec women the right to be legal guardians of their children, a reform the other provinces had adopted in the early part of the century. It also provided that women could sign leases or enter into business transactions without their husbands' consent. Quebec women were experiencing their own Quiet Revolution.

At the federal level, the first woman MP was Agnes Macphail (elected in 1921), who represented the United Farmers of Ontario. She operated outside the boundaries of the established parties, and her impact was limited to the role of critic. She was an untiring champion of women in the labour force and regularly reminded her male colleagues that not all women were provided for by men. Grace MacInnis (also in opposition as a member of the NDP) stands out for her work as an advocate of women's rights in the labour force. Among other things, she worked diligently for maternity leave provisions, pointing out in 1970 that the International Labour Organization had supported maternity leave as early as 1919. She stressed that pregnancy is not women's "burden alone, but the burden of society,"[45] and was one of several women who brought a new perspective on women's roles to the legislative arena.

These are only a few examples of the early work done by women in the legislatures to advance the cause of other women. Some of these early female legislators have supported the notion of separate spheres. In the House of Commons, Martha Black made a strong defence of women's special place in the home in 1936 when she noted: "By the nature of our being we must be home-makers, we have to bring up our children in the service of the world, otherwise where would the world be, where would all the smart men in the House be?"[46] But even this defence of women's separate roles led Black to request that one member of the newly established National Employment Commission be a woman. On the whole, however, women's contributions to legislative deliberations have contributed to the recognition of the legitimacy of women's claims.

The granting of votes to women may have had some impact on the pattern of policy as well. This was the view of Helen Gregory MacGill in 1939, when she reviewed the laws affecting women and children in British Columbia. She explained the passage of the Equal Guardianship Act of 1917, which gave mothers equal custody rights with their husbands over children, in the following way: "As naturally as daylight follows darkness, with the recognition of the rights of women as citizens came justice to the married mother in regard to her children."[47] However, after 1918, the political parties generally ignored the 'women's vote' when it became obvious that women were not voting in a block. It was not until 1984 that indications of a possible gender gap led to a national debate on women's issues in the federal election campaign of that year. This debate was precipitated by Gallup polls of 1983 that indicated women were more likely to support the Liberal party by about 10 per cent.[48] A more recent example of the new-found strength of women voters came in 1987, when the federal Conservative government declared its intention to concentrate on women's issues in an attempt to improve its standing in the polls. While it is true that much of the interest in women's issues was mere posturing, the concern for women's political allegiance has at least forced the parties at various times to take note of women's concerns.

Women's voices have been raised to governments through their voluntary group memberships as well, and both Jane Errington and Naomi Black discuss the political action of these groups in their chapters. The lobbying efforts of Canadian women's groups have been a significant force affecting policy. Until recently little was known about the political work of early groups like the National Council of Women or the Women's Christian Temperance Union. Early accounts of these and other groups classified them as charitable and social organizations. The work of feminist historians has shown that they were also very active politically, pressing governments for welfare, labour, and equal-rights legislation.[49]

Most of the newer groups, such as the National Action Committee on the Status of Women, support political action. A national survey of women's groups conducted in 1984 revealed that 76 per cent of the 144 groups participating in the survey had tried to influence government policy at least once in the preceding ten years. Among their successes, these groups can include fairer asset splitting at divorce and improved sexual assault laws. However, women's groups have also met with many failures. In the 1984 survey, only 19 per cent of the groups that had tried to influence governments reported success, and a surprising 25 per cent of them described public officials as hostile.[50] Women's groups have been restricted in their effectiveness by several factors. For one thing, many of them rely heavily on government funding, which puts them at the mercy of government programs, places them under government control, and has restricted their freedom to act as lobbyists. The role of critic is compromised by this financial tie. Another factor is that many groups, such as the Canadian Congress of Learning Opportunities for Women (CCLOW), are committed to democratic practices within their organizations, which means that membership agreement is sought on important issues. In the high-powered world of pressure politics this consensus approach is often a disadvantage because it is time-consuming and expensive.

In addition, women's groups are not all agreed on what should be done for women, or how reforms should be accomplished. The most publicized disagreement has been on the abortion issue, where anti-abortion and pro-choice groups compete for government approval. Less well publicized has been debate on issues such as pensions, censorship, affirmative action, and child care. There is no consensus, even among groups committed to equality rights for women in the public sphere, on how these issues should be resolved. The spectrum of opinions has been altered dramatically, as well, by the recent emergence of groups that argue for a return to the traditional family values and lifestyle of the nineteenth century. In the face of these differences of opinion, governments have been content to proclaim, as they did at the turn of the century, that they need more information about what women really want. At the same time, evidence of public support for feminist goals, particularly among younger (18-29) women and men, may be responsible for moderating the policy impact of the Conservatives' agenda. A Gallup poll conducted in the summer of 1992 indicated that 71 per cent of this age group supported the goals of the feminist movement. Overall, support was 60 per cent.[51]

It has been suggested that this record of limited successes was finally broken in 1980 with the emergence of the Ad Hoc Committee on the

Constitution. [52] This was a new, single-issue group that emerged when it became clear to a small number of feminists in Toronto and Ottawa that the existing women's groups might not succeed in ensuring that sex-equality rights would be written into the new Charter, which was to become part of the Constitution. The Ad Hoc Committee ultimately adopted hard-sell pressure tactics to convince the federal and provincial justice ministers to support a sex-equality clause in the Charter. At the same time the Committee was prepared to combine the consensus style of decision-making with the less democratic practices of most successful interest groups. In addition Committee members learned how to use personal contacts to bring pressure to bear on politicians. They phoned friends working in government and solicited their help. The use of non-governmental funding also gave the Committee independence from government. One of the most significant lessons learned during the Charter negotiations was that political decisions in Canada are made within the framework of federal-provincial relations. The members of the Ad Hoc Committee mobilized supporters in all of the provinces and forged an alliance with the federal government when it looked as if the provinces would destroy the federal bargain on equality rights for women. Finally, there was a willingness to compromise. Women on the Ad Hoc Committee later admitted that they presented two sets of demands to the federal government. Publicly they pressed for the resolutions that had been adopted by the conference they organized in February 1981. Privately some of their members pressed the justice minister to agree to a shorter list of what they felt were attainable demands.

One can only be cautiously optimistic about the future potential of groups adopting the Ad Hoc Committee's model. While it is true that the women on the Committee learned how to work in the federal-provincial framework of policy-making, the Charter success may not be replicated easily. The Ad Hoc Committee was working with a government already committed to the issue in question – equality rights for women. There was no disagreement in principle. In addition, the support from Canadian women was almost unanimous – a rare occurrence in political life. On issues involving transformations in the distribution of power between women and men in both the public and the private spheres, even well-orchestrated tactics such as those used by the Ad Hoc Committee will probably fail. There is already some evidence that governments are not prepared to act on women's demands when these demands conflict with their own agenda. Just as significant is the impact of Charter negotiations on the development, among women's groups, of strategies for change. Among these groups – in particular, the National Action Committee on the Status of Women – there has been enthusiastic support for Charter litigation as a vehicle for improving equality rights for women. This enthusiasm may be misplaced. Some reviews of Charter litigation suggest that men have achieved more victories than women in this process of court challenges.[53]

Women's voices have been heard as well within the bureaucracies of government since 1956, when the Women's Bureau in the Department of Labour was established federally. Given the resources devoted to these offices, women might have expected a significant change in their fortunes. In the 1970s the number of voices increased dramatically with the establishment of a network of status of women officers. But the voices of these officers have been muted by several factors. They lack financial resources, are constrained by their role as advisers to government, and are frequently invisible within large departments.

At the federal level, since 1971 there has been a minister responsible for the status of women. The minister is assisted by Status of Women Canada, which began as part of the Privy Council Office and became a separate central agency in 1976. The funding of women's groups is controlled by the Women's Program in the Secretary of State. In addition, advisers on women's issues were appointed in the departments of justice, employment and immigration, and health and welfare. In 1973 the government also appointed an Advisory Council on the Status of Women to give advice on women's concerns. An overview of the government's record following the establishment of these offices generates a mixed review of their success.

The power of the minister responsible for the status of women has been constrained by a set of variables. There has been strong cabinet resistance to any change in women's status. Bryce Mackasey encountered this resistance when he tried to introduce government support for day care in the early 1970s. Judy Erola found it on the issue of equal pay for work of equal value.[54] Without the support of Prime Minister Pierre Trudeau who, while he was not a feminist, was committed to justice for all, their achievements would have been even less impressive. They were constrained as well by the lack of support staff. The problem of funding first became publicly apparent when, in 1968, the Women's Bureau in the Department of Labour was the subject of parliamentary debate focusing on the director's lack of authority and funds. Size has also been a problem. The Office of the Co-ordinator, first established as part of an interdepartmental committee assigned the task of considering the recommendations of the Royal Commission on the Status of Women, was too small in the beginning, although it has now expanded to what the bureaucrats call forty-three person-years. Conflicts between the minister and her/his status of women advisers have also served to weaken the significance of the portfolio. Such conflicts were common during the early days of the ministry, and they sapped the energy of those involved.[55]

In addition, ministers have tended to view their responsibilities for women through the perspective of other portfolios. This has had the effect of limiting the scope of reforms. For example, Bryce Mackasey was minister of labour while he held the women portfolio. Most of his contacts with women's issues were through the Women's Bureau in the Department of Labour rather than the Office of the Co-ordinator on status of women.[56] When Marc Lalonde held the post he even proposed to reorganize the Office of the Co-ordinator and make it part of his other portfolio, the Department of Health and Welfare.[57] This move would have weakened the co-ordinator's position as a ministry adviser and as a co-ordinating officer. This points to the potentially negative consequences of linking two portfolios. On the positive side, ministers who have another powerful portfolio in addition to their status of women responsibilities sit on important cabinet committees where they can, if they wish, advance the cause of women's rights.

In addition, status of women officers have played an important part in presenting the reality of women's lives to the government. They have also served as a liaison between government and the growing number of women's groups. However, they too have been constrained by a set of factors. There is a history of weakness vis-à-vis other government departments. There has also been friction between status of women departments and the ministries within which they operate.[58] In addition there has been too little co-ordination either among the various status of women departments or between these departments and the other ministries. There is a formal mechanism for co-operation. The co-ordinator was to "be responsible for the interdepartmental examination of the report and drafting of the necessary Cabinet documentation."[59] According to Freda Paltiel, the first woman appointed co-ordinator, that early attempt at co-operation was a success.[60] But over time the pattern of interdepartmental consultation and co-operation has broken down.

There is good evidence that status of women concerns are not taken seriously by all civil servants. This problem must have been obvious to government officials as well, for in 1976 an interdepartmental committee, chaired by the assistant secretary to the cabinet's Social Policy Committee, met to consider mechanisms to integrate status of women concerns in government policy. This was the preliminary to the cabinet's ruling that it would consider each of its decisions in light of the impact on the status of women. The committee recommended that a standing interdepartmental committee chaired by the co-ordinator, Status of Women, should monitor the implementation of this policy. It also recommended that in "each department and agency of the federal government a structure shall be established or designated which will be responsible for implementing the integration of status of women policy concerns."[61] It stressed that the people in these status of women structures should be knowledgeable in the workings of their department overall, and not just in the status of women. This was a clear call for the integration of status of women concerns into the regular operations of government.

In spite of the efforts of women's groups and female legislators and bureaucrats, male domination of the legislatures has persisted, and women continue to press for reforms from positions that are, on the whole, outside the centres of power. This has meant that women still lack control over the decisions that so obviously affect their daily lives. However, even within the framework of a gender-based explanation of policy it must be recognized that other factors interacting with gender have set the limits for policy debate and action. The most significant of these other factors is the nature of the economic system within which the dialogue between government and groups takes place. It is clear from the preceding review of legislation that men's ideas about women's roles have changed as the needs of the economy have changed. Throughout the period in which women took note of their political system and sought policy decisions that would favour them, our economic system has been capitalist. Marxist-feminist scholars in particular have noted the link between capitalist thinking and the pattern of laws affecting women. They stress the impact of industrial capitalism in its changing forms in the nineteenth and twentieth centuries on the decisions reached by legislators. [62]

There are several reasons why capitalism contributes to the perpetuation of segregated gender roles. At the very least, the willingness of governments to adopt equality measures is related to their faith in free-market forces. The more a government is committed to the law of supply and demand, the less willing it is to intervene in the economy and enact pay-equity measures or government-funded day care. Since mid-century the Liberal party federally has been prepared to legislate for equal opportunity. The Conservative party has been more reluctant to interfere with market forces. Neither party has been prepared to work outside the boundaries of the competitive market economy. The impact of capitalism can be seen in other ways. First, women in the home reproduce the workers needed for economic development. Second, women provide a reserve pool of cheap labour, which can be pulled from the home at little cost to the employer in times of economic necessity and sent back home when unemployment levels rise. Third, women in the home are consumers of the goods the capitalist state produces. Finally, women perform, unpaid, the job of domestic servants, sustaining the work force and getting it ready for work.

Another factor interacting with gender and capitalism is the set of priorities established by the party in power. Each political party in Canada operates according to a different set of principles, and women's rights fit more comfortably in some party platforms than in others. There are several examples of this in Canadian history. Provincially, suffrage for women was a Liberal Party policy in British Columbia and Quebec. In Alberta, minimum-wage legislation, resisted by the Conservatives, was brought in by the United Farmers of Alberta. Status of women officers were appointed by the Parti Québécois in Quebec.

At the federal level a concern for individual rights dominated the government agenda during the Trudeau era. Under Trudeau's leadership, while there was little movement from the notion that women are the natural guardians of the home, there was a dramatic shift from the language of political obligation to the language of individual rights. Within that government's new rights package, women's claims were given some space – as made clear in policy directives circulating within government in the 1970s. In 1971, for instance, in a situation report prepared by the Privy Council Office Briefing Team for the Priorities and Planning Committee, there were indications that the government was at least concerned about changes in attitudes on gender roles. That 1971 report listed for consideration: the increasing socio-economic power of women; change in women's images of marriage, work, and the family; increased resistance to women in the male work world; and increased diversity in sexual expression. [63] This was followed in 1972 by a memorandum to the cabinet from Trudeau, in which he included the equalization of opportunities for women in his list of government goals. However, there were clear limits on how far this notion of the just society was to go. It did not include rewriting the rules for relations in the private sphere, but concentrated on equal opportunities in the public world of paid labour. Women were to be integrated "into the development process as equal partners with men." [64]

Perceptions of gender roles, the nature of the economic system, and the government's priorities all influence legislators' perceptions of what should be done. In addition there are more immediate structural constraints that limit their discourse. In Canada the most significant structural characteristic of the political system is the division of powers between the federal and provincial levels. Federal-provincial relations have had a profound impact on the pace of reform in areas such as child care, divorce, and even the definition of women's rights. Because the two levels of government, for either financial or constitutional reasons, share responsibility for most of the social-service package in Canada, co-operation between them is essential. That co-operation is often hard to obtain. Constitutional changes that offer a decentralized vision of Canada with reduced central control over national programs have serious implications for women. They will limit new federal initiatives and fragment existing social programs.

Canada is a country of great regional diversity. The special status of Quebec, with its separate language and culture, is best known, but the other provinces also differ significantly from one another in economic development, patterns of settlement, and culture. In his review of the Canadian welfare state Keith Banting concludes, "The evolution of federalism is the institutional feature that has had the greatest impact on income security in Canada." He argues that in "comparative terms federalism is clearly a conservative force in welfare politics."[62] In the area of policies for women, the impact of federalism has been mixed. In the early twentieth century the Western provinces were innovators in the area of women's rights, establishing a pattern that the other provinces generally followed. In the 1980s, with complicated funding arrangements in place, the provinces were often unwilling to reopen discussions of social security to include, for example, child care, out of the fear that other programs might be cancelled.

Conclusion

This overview demonstrates the frameworks within which successive governments have made laws with particular significance for women. These frameworks have shifted gradually over time (and the policies reflect this gradual transition) from an exclusively patriarchal to a partially liberal-feminist world view, and recently back to a more patriarchal vision. In the early days of Canada, legislators saw women primarily as wives and mothers. They were prepared to make laws that would help women carry out these functions. Slowly, with the development of the welfare state, equal opportunity for women in the public sphere began to infiltrate the discourse in the legislatures. In the 1970s, women's groups gave new strength to the equal rights agenda, pressing governments for improved access to politics and work. In the 1990s new challenges from the neoconservative political right, from anti-feminist women's groups, and from the pressures of economic recession have slowed the pace of change and underlined the limits of the equal-rights agenda. In addition, women's new reliance on the Charter of Rights and Freedoms has resulted in less pressure on legislatures to make gender-sensitive policies. The "52 per cent solution" – a legislature with a majority of female members – continues to be a distant goal – which only diminishes the prospect of obtaining policies in Canada that take gender into account.

Sandra Burt

NOTES

1. Lisa Peattie and Martin Rein, *Women's Claims: A Study in Political Economy* (Scarborough: Prentice-Hall, 1986), 37.
2. This was a complete reversal of the practice that developed in New France, described by Jane Errington in her chapter. Errington points out that many women who settled in New France in the eighteenth century participated in the economic activities of the colony and enjoyed liberal property and guardianship rights.
3. Divorce was somewhat easier for men to obtain, for they had to prove only adultery, without additional cause.
4. Canada, House of Commons, *Debates*, April 1, 1886, 442.
5. Canada, House of Commons, *Debates*, March 29, 1878, 1512.
6. Genevieve Leslie, "Domestic Service in Canada, 1880-1920," in Janice Acton et al., eds., *Women at Work* (Toronto: Women's Educational Press, 1974), 75.
7. Veronica Strong-Boag, "Working Women and the State: The Case of Canada, 1889-1945," *Atlantis* 6, no. 2 (1981), 7.
8. Ellen DuBois, "The Radicalism of the Woman Suffrage Movement: Notes Toward the Reconstruction of Nineteenth Century Feminism," *Feminist Studies* 3 (1975), 64.
9. Canada, House of Commons, *Debates*, April 11, 1918, 646.
10. Ibid., 66.
11. Ruth Pierson, "Women's Emancipation and the Recruitment of Women into the Labour Force in World War II," in Susan Mann Trofimenkoff and Alison Prentice, eds., *The Neglected Majority*, Vol. 1 (Toronto: McClelland and Stewart, 1977), 125.
12. Ibid., 145.
13. Nova Scotia, Commission on Hours of Labour, Wages, and Working Conditions of Women Employed in Industrial Occupations, *Report*, December 2, 1918, 7.
14. Ibid., 6.
15. Ibid., 19.
16. Margaret E. McCallum, "Keeping Women in Their Place: The Minimum Wage in Canada, 1910-1925," *Labour/Le Travail* 17 (1986), 53. For an earlier perspective on this legislation *see*: Kathleen Derry and Paul H. Douglas, "The Minimum Wage in Canada," *Journal of Political Economy* 30 (1922): 155-188.
17. There were some indications of changing attitudes in the deliberations about the wording of the amendment. The House of Commons resisted using the phrase "previously chaste," on the grounds that young girls "have not reached that stage of mentality and maturity of character that enables them to come to resolution for their own protection, and to resist importunity not physically

but mentally." *Debates,* July 5, 1919, 4635. The Senate insisted that the words be included in the legislation.

18. Veronica Strong-Boag, "Wages for Housework: Mothers' Allowances and the Beginnings of Social Security in Canada," *Journal of Canadian Studies* 14, no. 1 (1979), 25.

19. Ibid., 33.

20. Keith G. Banting, *The Welfare State and Canadian Federalism* (Montreal: McGill-Queen's University Press, 1982), 91.

21. Elizabeth Wilson, *Women and the Welfare State* (London: Tavistock Publications, 1977), 9.

22. Canada, House of Commons, *Debates,* July 25, 1944, 5331, 5336.

23. Canada, Department of Labour, Women's Bureau, Draft of Material for Women's Bureau Section of the Minister's Current Information Book, May 6, 1958.

24. Peter C. Robertson, "Some Thoughts on Affirmative Action in the 1980's," paper prepared for the Affirmative Action Division, Canada Employment and Immigration Commission, March 1980, 9.

25. For a study of the effectiveness of these programs, *see*: Sandra Burt, "Voluntary Affirmative Action: Does it Work?" *Relations industrielles* 41, no. 3 (1986), 541-50. This systemic interpretation of discrimination has now been written into the federal government's definition of affirmative action. Some of the provinces have followed this practice as well.

26. Canada, Royal Commission on Equality in Employment, *Report* (Ottawa: Ministry of Supply and Services Canada, 1984), 197.

27. Pat and Hugh Armstrong, *Theorizing Women's Work* (Toronto: Garamond Press, 1990), 124.

28. Canada, House of Commons, Nielsen Task Force, *Report* (1987), 109.

29. Canada, Royal Commission on Equality in Employment, *Report.*

30. Canada, Task Force on Child Care, *Report* (1986), 45, 47.

31. Wilson, *Women,* 165.

32. Geoffrey York, "Tory Politicians Form Family Compact," *The Globe and Mail,* June 3, 1992, 1, 4.

33. Canada, House of Commons, *Debates,* September 26, 1989, 3948-3949.

34. Department of Health and Welfare, *The Child Benefit: A White Paper on Canada's New Integrated Child Tax Benefit* (Ottawa, 1992).

35. There is an excellent summary of the history of women's participation in Canadian political life in Jill McCalla Vickers and Janine Brodie, "Canada," in Joni Lovenduski and Jill Hills, eds., *The Politics of the Second Electorate* (London: Routledge & Kegan Paul, 1981).

36. Thelma McCormack, "Toward a Nonsexist Perspective on Social and Political Change," in Marcia Millman and Rosabeth Moss Kanter, eds., *Another Voice* (Garden City, N.J.: Anchor Press, 1975), 25.

37. For a review of women's participation in party politics at all levels, *see*: Sylvia Bashevkin, *Toeing the Lines: Women and Party Politics in English Canada* (Toronto: University of Toronto Press, 1985). *See also*: Janine Brodie, *Women and Politics in Canada* (Toronto: McGraw-Hill Ryerson, 1985).

38. Brodie, *Women and Politics,* 109.

39. Ibid., 3.

40. Sirkka Sirkkhonen and Elina Haavio-Manilla, "The Impact of the Women's Movement and Legislative Activity of Women M.P.s in Social Development," in M. Rendel, ed., *Women, Power and Political Systems* (London: Croom Helm, 1981), 210-214.

41. Interview with Ad Hoc Committee member, March 1983.

42. Una Maclean, "The Honourable Irene Parlby," *Alberta Historical Review* 7, no. 2 (1959): 1-6.

43. Veronica Strong-Boag, "Canadian Feminism in the 1920's: The Case of Nellie L. McClung," *Journal of Canadian Studies* 12, no. 4 (1977): 58-68.

44. Diane Crossley, "The British Columbia Liberal Party and Women's Reforms, 1916-1928," in Barbara Latham and Cathy Kess, eds., *In Her Own Right* (Victoria: Camosun College, 1980).

45. Canada, House of Commons, *Debates,* November 3, 1970, 842.

46. Canada, House of Commons, *Debates,* April 6, 1936, 1855.

47. Helen Gregory MacGill, *Laws for Women and Children in British Columbia* (B.C.: Women's Institutes and Local Councils, 1939), 17.

48. John Terry, "The Gender Gap: Women's Political Power," paper prepared for the current issues series, Political and Social Affairs Division, Research Branch of the Library of Parliament, Ottawa, 1984.

49. For a review of this work, *see*: Margaret Conrad, "The Re-Birth of Canada's Past: A Decade of Women's History," *Acadiensis* 12, No. 2 (1983): 140-163.

50. This study was carried out by the author in the spring of 1984, with support from the Social Sciences and Humanities Research Council.

51. "60% in Favour of Feminism," *The Toronto Star,* June 25, 1992, A17.

52. Penney Kome, *The Taking of Twenty-Eight: Women Challenge the Constitution* (Toronto: Women's Educational Press, 1983).

53. See, for example, Gwen Brodsky and Shelagh Day, *Canadian Charter Equality Rights for Women: One Step Forward or Two Steps Back?* (Ottawa: Canadian Advisory Council on the Status of Women, 1989).

54. Interviews with Bryce Mackasey and Judy Erola, April 1986.

55. The communications between one minister, John Munro, and his Co-ordinator, Martha Hynna, suggest that there was some serious disagreement between them. In one conflict Hynna objected to the attempt by Munro to downgrade the position of the Director of the Women's Bureau, Department of Labour. Letter dated April 16, 1974.

56. Interview with Bryce Mackasey, March 1986.

57. Interview with Marc Lalonde, March 1986.

58. This problem appears in correspondence between Sylva Gelber, when she was in charge of the Women's Bureau, Department of Labour, and the Staffing Branch of the Public Service Commission of Canada, July 1969.

59. These are the functions that were set out in the Record of the Cabinet Committee on Social Policy of February 23, 1971. From a letter to Marshall Crowe, Chairman of the Interdepartmental Committee.

60. Interview with Freda Paltiel, Women's Adviser, Health and Welfare Canada, March 1986.

61. This was taken from a briefing document for deputy ministers on status of women policy. There is no date on this document, but it was probably prepared in 1976.

62. For a discussion of this perspective, *see*: Jane Jenson, "Gender and Reproduction," *Studies in Political Economy* 20 (1986).

63. Privy Council Office, Planning Division, "Situation Report on Canada," for planning of cabinet priorities, September 1971-1972, 11.

64. Memorandum to Cabinet from Pierre Trudeau, 1972.

65. Banting, *The Welfare State*, 172.

SUGGESTED READINGS

Bashevkin, Sylvia, *Toeing the Lines: Women and Party Politics in English Canada.* Toronto: University of Toronto Press, 1993, 2nd ed.

Brodie, Janine, Shelley A.M. Gavigan, and Jane Jenson, *The Politics of Abortion.* Toronto: Oxford University Press, 1992.

Brodsky, Gwen, and Shelagh Day, *Canadian Charter Equality Rights for Women: One Step Forward or Two Steps Back?* Ottawa: Canadian Advisory Council on the Status of Women, 1989.

Burt, Sandra, "Canadian Women's Groups in the 1980's: Organizational Development and Policy Influence," *Canadian Public Policy* 16, no. 1 (1990), 17-28.

Currie, Dawn H., "Battered Women and the State: From the Failure of Theory to a Theory of Failure," *The Journal of Human Justice* 1, no. 2 (1990), 77-96.

Findlay, Sue, "Facing the State: The Politics of the Women's Movement Reconsidered," in Heather Jon Maroney and Meg Luxton, eds., *Feminism and Political Economy.* Toronto: Methuen, 1987.

Chapter Seven

Law, Gender, Equality

≈≈≈≈≈≈≈≈≈≈≈≈≈≈≈≈≈≈≈≈≈≈≈≈≈≈≈≈≈≈≈≈≈≈

Many people do not realize that the Canadian courts were asked to recognize women's equality rights long before the Canadian Charter of Rights and Freedoms was passed. During the first three decades of this century, for example, there were legal cases involving the admission of women to the legal profession, the capacity of women to be police magistrates, and the eligibility of women for appointment to the Senate. Since men were already entitled to participate in these various activities, women sought the same (or equal) rights. More recently, in the decade immediately preceding the adoption of the Charter, women's rights were raised in cases about Indian status, matrimonial property, pregnancy benefits, employment, sports teams, prostitution, rape, abortion, and pornography.[1] Although some of these later cases raised issues that seemed to differentiate between women and men (for instance, pregnancy), all were nevertheless considered to be "equality" cases.

These equality cases were litigated at all of the levels of the court system from the trial courts, where the decisions are usually made by a single judge, to the Supreme Court of Canada, where as many as nine judges may decide a case. One case – the Persons case – was appealed to the Judicial Committee of the British Privy Council when it was still the final court of appeal for Canadian cases. Not every case was heard at every level of court; litigation is costly, and appellate litigation even more so. Nor were these cases always initiated by women, the great majority of whom cannot afford to defend, let alone pursue, a lawsuit. Even when they were not litigants, however, Canadian women relied on these equality cases to challenge the boundary between the private and public spheres.

Unfortunately, their expectations were seldom met. To the contrary, in most of the early cases the Canadian courts relegated women to the private sphere; and even in the cases decided in the 1970s the judges continued to deny women full equality in the public realm. In effect, the courts rendered decisions that lagged well behind the changing patterns of women's lives. Thus it is important to understand why this happened, not only for reasons of historical accuracy but also for more immediate reasons. Such explanations have contemporary relevance because they provide a basis for evaluating the process of judicial decision-making that has begun to take place under the auspices of the new Canadian Charter of Rights and Freedoms.

Some people, including some judges, offer a structural analysis of the juridical lag in the pre-Charter women's rights cases. Their contention is that it is not the function of the courts to make the law. This is a pointless, semantic argument based on the questionable assumption that there is a distinction between making and applying (or, as it is usually referred to in legal parlance, "interpreting") the law. In fact, this distinction fails to reflect the reality of judicial decision-making in the pre-Charter sex-equality cases. When these cases are examined, it becomes apparent that the judges were never asked simply to apply a self-evident law to a particular set of facts. Instead they always were asked to decide between competing versions of the existing law. Not surprisingly, they responded by resolving these controversies, thus performing the function expected of them irrespective of whether it is labelled making or "interpreting" the law.

Underlying the dubious contention that these labels represent different functions is the conviction that courts should perform different tasks from legislatures. Frequently it is said that because legislatures are elected and courts are appointed, only the legislatures are democratic institutions while the courts are counter-majoritarian. Women, who have never been elected to legislatures in significant numbers and whose presence in courtrooms still yields outcomes that are more debilitating than affirming, have no reason to subscribe to the dichotomy between democratic legislatures and counter-majoritarian courts. Nor is this surprising, because this theory originated in the traditionally malestream disciplines of philosophy, political science, and law. Indeed, women would be well advised to rely on strategies that relate legislatures and courts dialogically (or, alternatively, to reject both institutions), because they have nothing to gain from an approach that dichotomizes these institutions.

A more compelling explanation for the failure of the courts to keep pace with the changes in women's lives lies behind the actual outcomes in the cases, in the written reasons that the judges must always give to support their decisions. Since these reasons were expressed quite differently according to whether they were contained in the early "persons" cases or in the later Canadian Bill of Rights cases, it is somewhat surprising to find that they all are consistent with the same theory of equality. According to this theory, alikes must be treated alike or equally, while unalikes must be treated unalike or differently. This view has also informed legislators in their formulation of public policy, as Sandra Burt shows in her chapter in this book. Less surprisingly, perhaps because it can be traced at least as far back as Aristotle, the validity of this theory remained unchallenged in these pre-Charter cases.

Instead, the Aristotelian theory of equality, discussed more fully by Lorraine Code in her chapter on feminist theory, was regarded as controversial only in its application to women and men, when the question of whether women and men are alike or unalike was posed. Aristotle himself answered this question by arguing, "The male is by nature superior, and the female inferior; and the one rules, and the other is ruled; this principle, of necessity, extends to all mankind." Few Canadian judges hesitated to follow where he led; in other words, most subscribed to the Aristotelian principle of male supremacy.

Under these circumstances, equality-seekers confronted not just one but two major legal hurdles in the pre-Charter cases. First they had to convince the judges, virtually all of them men, to disavow Aristotle's male supremacy principle. If that succeeded, then it was still necessary to persuade these selfsame male judges to treat women like men. Since there are a myriad of ways in which women and men appear to be different, this second argument often failed. In the process, however, no one seemed to notice that this second contention was at least as gender-biased as the first because it meant that women's experiences did not count unless they met the male standard. Thus male gender-bias, not judicial function, explains why Canadian courts have rendered decisions lagging behind the changing patterns of women's lives.

Not unreasonably, some women turned to the legislatures for redress. Indeed, Canada recently opted for a generalized type of remedial legislation in the form of the Canadian Charter of Rights and Freedoms. The Charter contains two sex-equality provisions. One is section 15, which provides that:

> Section 15(1). Every individual is equal before and under the law and has the right to the equal protection and equal benefit of the law without discrimination and, in particular, without discrimination based on race, national or ethnic origin, colour, religion, sex, age or mental or physical disability.
>
> Section 15(2). Subsection (1) does not preclude any law, program or activity that has as its object the amelioration of conditions of disadvantaged individuals or groups including those that are disadvantaged because of race, national or ethnic origin, colour, religion, sex, age or mental or physical disability.

The other is section 28, which provides that:

Section 28. Notwithstanding anything in this Charter, the rights and freedoms referred to in it are guaranteed to male and female persons.

These two sections make the right to sex equality mandatory by entrenching it in the Canadian Constitution for the first time in Canadian legal history.

However, there are two significant limitations on this mandate. In the first place, it applies only to legislation and not to everyday relationships, many – but not all – of which are governed by the non-discrimination provisions in federal and provincial human rights codes. Secondly, the Charter nowhere defines "equality," which leaves the task of resolving any disagreements that may arise about the meaning and practical application of these two new Charter sex-equality provisions with the courts. Since this responsibility is consigned to the very institution that has historically rendered such problematic equality decisions, it behooves us all (including judges) to understand not only that historical record but also how the contemporary context, including the new Charter, changes it.

The Early "Persons" Cases

The "persons" cases were aptly named because they were about whether women were included in the legal interpretation of the word "persons." There were five such cases, and all five had already been decided by 1930.

Not surprisingly perhaps, the three earliest of the "Persons" cases were initiated by two women who wanted to become lawyers; Mabel Penery French initiated the first case in 1905 in New Brunswick and the second in 1911 in British Columbia, and Annie Macdonald Langstaff initiated the third case in 1915 in Quebec.[2]

These women were obliged to launch three cases because it was, and is, the provinces that have the jurisdiction to regulate who is entitled to practise law. The New Brunswick, British Columbia, and Quebec regulations about admission to the practice of law were surprisingly similar. None of these regulations explicitly denied women admission, nor did they explicitly restrict admission only to men. Rather, in New Brunswick and British Columbia the regulations referred to the admission of "persons" and, in Quebec, to "candidates." However, when women first applied for admission to the practice of law, their applications were refused initially by the professional lawyers' organizations that administered these regulations in each province and then by the judges before whom they subsequently argued their cases.

By the time that Mabel Penery French and Annie Macdonald Langstaff applied for admission in their respective provinces, they had already completed the required courses of study to become lawyers. Mabel Penery

French had also "fully satisfied" the Barrister's Society of New Brunswick of her "moral character, habits and conduct," and, by 1914, Annie Macdonald Langstaff had become the first woman to graduate from the Faculty of Law at McGill University. But despite their evident qualifications, both were denied the right to practise law solely because they were women.

This denial was more suspect than surprising. By 1905, several women had already been admitted to the practice of law in Ontario.[3] The first woman lawyer in Ontario – indeed, in the whole British empire – was Clara Brett Martin, who was admitted eight years before Mabel Penery French initiated her first case. Clara Brett Martin, too, had to fight for admission. Although she never went to court, she fought the Law Society of Upper Canada for six years. Ultimately she won, but only after the Ontario legislature passed two statutes: one, in 1892, admitting women as solicitors; and the other, in 1895, admitting women as barristers.

While Clara Brett Martin was the first woman lawyer in Canada, she was by no means the first in North America. That record apparently belongs to Margaret Brent, who arrived in the American colonies in 1638. The first woman admitted to a state bar in the United States – Arabella Mansfield – began to practise law in 1869 in Iowa. And in 1879 the U.S. Congress passed legislation allowing women to practise in the federal courts, including the United States Supreme Court.[4]

Given these precedents, the applications of Mabel Penery French and Annie Macdonald Langstaff were neither novel nor radical. Yet when their cases got to the courts, they lost; and they lost resoundingly: fourteen of the fifteen men who sat as judges in their cases refused to admit women to the practice of law. Of these fourteen judges, ten put their reasons, such as they were, in writing, and although those reasons varied somewhat, all were completely consistent with Aristotle's defence of male supremacy.

Mabel Penery French's first case began with representations from three lawyers. First, the president of the Barrister's Society presented all of the previously decided British and U.S. legal cases and other pertinent information, without arguing either for or against her admission. Then two other lawyers presented arguments clearly supporting her admission. Both argued that the previously decided British cases excluding women were not decisive precedents; and one of the two, the recorder for the City of Saint John, also argued that since the previously decided U.S. cases went both ways, they too should be ignored.

According to him, what really mattered was the contemporary context in which this case was being decided, particularly the contemporary trend to increase the number of vocations open to women. At this point, the Chief Justice simply could not contain himself; he intervened and argued that admitting "this young lady" as an attorney would, in a few years, make her "eligible to be appointed to the bench." In response, the recorder was not prepared to agree that admission to the practice of law necessarily led, in turn, to a judicial appointment; and even if it were so he was ready to contend that "worse things might happen."

This case is particularly striking because none of the lawyers argued against Mabel Penery French's admission. That did not stop the five-man New Brunswick Supreme Court from unanimously refusing to admit her, however. Nor did it stop the Chief Justice from exceeding the conventional limits of judicial reasoning when he wrote: "If I dare to express my own views I would say that I have no sympathy with the opinion that women should in all branches of life come in competition with men. Better let them attend to their own legitimate business."

Traditionally, judges do not express their own personal views. So the Chief Justice's statement was, if nothing else, a forthright admission of male bias. Indeed, his statement was the most forthright admission of male bias offered by any judge, not only in this case but also in all of the 'persons' cases to follow.

Lacking the Chief Justice's gall, the four remaining judges relied on more traditional legal reasoning, concentrating on interpreting the word "persons" as used in the New Brunswick lawyers' statute. Their task was not easy because, as they themselves acknowledged, the word was "sufficiently comprehensive to include both sexes." Moreover, as one of them also acknowledged, Mabel Penery French "undoubtedly would be included in that word as used in many statutes." Nevertheless, they decided that the same was not true of the New Brunswick lawyers' statute, apparently because the context demanded otherwise.

By context, they did not mean the recent trend to increasing the vocations open to women. To the contrary, one of the two judges who provided written reasons characterized the admission of women as a "radical change," one that the court was in no way bound to make. The other emphasized that "the remedy in this case is with the legislature and not with this court." With these words, he – and the many other judges who have echoed him in subsequent cases – was warning women not to rely on the courts to implement the changing patterns of their lives.

Instead, what these judges meant was the historical legal context. Specifically they meant the previously decided British and U.S. legal cases, or what is usually referred to as the "common law." Although they both agreed that the common law excluded women from the practice of law, they differed over which of the common law cases were actually decisive. While one judge relied on "the British authorities, and also some of the authorities in the United States," the other characterized the British authorities as "useless" and relied only on two of the U.S. cases. In one such case, the U.S. Supreme Court had refused to admit Myra Bradwell to the practice of law in Illinois because:

> the civil law, as well as nature itself, has always recognized a wide difference in the respective spheres and destinies of man and woman. Man is, or should be, woman's protector and defender. The natural and proper timidity and delicacy which belongs to the female sex evidently unfits it for many of the occupations of civil life. The constitution of the family organization, which is founded in the divine ordinance as well as in the nature of things, indicates the domestic sphere as that which properly belongs to the domain and functions of womanhood.

Simply by quoting this passage with approval, one of the New Brunswick judges added the constraints of nature and divine ordinance to those of history and outright male bias as the bases for treating women as inferior to men.

Since the judiciary had, to a man, adhered to Aristotle's defence of male supremacy, Mabel Penery French wisely refrained from appealing to another court. She turned instead to the provincial legislature, where her argument did prevail. In 1906, after the legislature had passed a law admitting women to the practice of law, she became a lawyer in New Brunswick. Although it might appear from these facts that the legislatures are more willing than the courts to move forward on the question of women's rights, such is not always the case.

When Mabel Penery French applied to transfer her practice of law to British Columbia six years later, it was as if time had stood still. Although the British Columbia judges knew that she had already been admitted in New Brunswick, they were unanimous in denying her the right to become a lawyer in their province. Again, it was because she was a woman, and again it was because the judges relied on arguments based on the historical context. One judge even harkened back to "the Mirror of Justice, a work issued at the time of William the Conqueror" for the quotation that "femmes ne poient estre attorneys." Not surprisingly, therefore, this judge concluded, "The context of our Act refers to a profession for men, and men alone." French appealed the first judgment she received in British Columbia, but at the Court of Appeal, where her case was heard by three judges, she was again denied admission.

In these British Columbia cases a new argument was raised about the use of the pronoun "he" in the Legal Professions Act. This pronoun had also appeared in the New Brunswick lawyers' statute, but the lawyers there had simply argued that a mere pronoun was not enough to exclude women. In British Columbia, however, French's lawyer offered a more constructive pronominal argument. First he pointed out that a provision in another British Columbia statute – the Interpretation Act – extended words importing the masculine gender to women. Then he applied this provision to the Legal Professions Act, arguing that these two acts, when read together, expressly gave women the right to be lawyers, even if they had no such right under common law. None of the British Columbia judges agreed with this argument. As one put it, echoing the words of one of the New Brunswick judges, the Interpretation Act should "not be used to bring about so radical a change." Therefore the British Columbia judges also subscribed to Aristotle's defence of male supremacy. Again Mabel Penery French turned to a provincial legislature for legislation admitting women to the practice of law. She was admitted in the same year.

Three years later, Annie Macdonald Langstaff was not so fortunate. Although she worked for a law firm until she retired in 1965 at the age of seventy-eight, she was never admitted to the practice of law.[5] Not only was she denied admission by two Quebec courts, but also the Quebec legislature refused to amend the Bar Act to admit women to the practice of law until 1941. By 1941, however, admission to the Bar required an undergraduate degree as well as a law degree, and while Langstaff had a law degree she did not have an undergraduate degree. So although she could work for a law firm, she could never appear in court or, technically speaking, call herself a lawyer.

Annie Macdonald Langstaff's case differed from that of Mabel Penery French in only three respects. First, unlike either French or the Ontario lawyer Clara Brett Martin, Langstaff was not only married but also separated from her husband. As one historian argues, "In a Province that did not grant divorce and that 'protected' its women to such an extent that husbands' authorizations in writing were required before they could contract any obligations, the fact that Annie Langstaff was separated from her husband set the seal on her lost cause."[6] But her cause was lost as much because she was a woman as because she was married or separated. In the words of the trial judge, "To admit a woman, and more particularly a married woman, as a *barrister,* that is to say, as a *person who pleads cases at the bar before judges or juries in open court and in the presence of the public,* would be nothing short of a direct infringement upon public order and a manifest violation of the law of good morals and public decency."

He belaboured this point by picturing a woman lawyer questioning a complainant in a rape case: "No woman possessing the least sense of decency could possibly do so without throwing a blur upon her own dignity and without bringing into utter contempt the honour and respect due her sex." Given his example, it was most peculiar that he singled out married women. Their sense of dignity, decency, honour, and respect was surely less vulnerable than that of unmarried women, at least when it came to questioning the complainant in a rape case.

Second, Annie Macdonald Langstaff's case differed insofar as the Quebec judges relied not only on the previously decided British and U.S. cases but also on the civil law tradition in France. They did so because, as one of the appeal judges put it, "La loi française, comme la loi anglaise, était alors à l'effet que la profession d'avocat était interdite aux personnes du sexe féminin." Nor did it seem to trouble the Quebec judges that their information about the French legal profession was no longer current because France, unlike Britain, had just recently passed a special law admitting women to the practice of law.

Her case differed in a third and final way because, on appeal, one of the five judges dissented. In doing so he did not rely on the argument that vocational opportunities for women were increasing. Nor did he rely on the Interpretation Act argument about applying masculine pronouns to women. Instead, the dissenting judge offered a completely new argument in which he focused on the Bar Act.

Specifically, he focused on the fact that the Bar Act did not expressly exclude women. But the significance of that omission was not clear until he contrasted it with another fact, that: "Dans beaucoup de nos lois, quand on a voulu exclure la femme de certaines situations, de certaines charges, on l'a mentionné formellement." Once it was clear that there were laws that explicitly excluded women and some laws – for example, the Bar Act – that did not, it also followed that, "Si le législateur avait voulu dire qu'une femme ne pourrait être avocat, il l'aurait dit." With these words, the dissenting judge signified that unless there was an express provision to the contrary, women and men should be treated alike. In other words, unlike the other fourteen judges in these three cases, he did not subscribe to Aristotle's defence of male supremacy.

Nor did four of the five judges who considered the next persons case. This case, decided two years later in 1917, did not involve the admission of women to the practice of law. Rather, it involved a prostitute named Lizzie Cyr, alias Lizzie Waters, who was convicted of the crime of vagrancy and sentenced to six months' hard labour. Not surprisingly given her sentence, Lizzie Cyr appealed her conviction on various grounds, two of which raised sex-equality issues. But to say that Lizzy Cyr raised two sex-equality issues is not to say that she argued for sex equality. On the contrary, she defended sex inequality.

She argued that only men could be convicted of vagrancy because the provision that made vagrancy a crime used only masculine pronouns. Now, given that Mabel Penery French and Annie Macdonald Langstaff had already made the opposite argument and lost, Lizzie Cyr should have won this argument. But she lost, too, simply because the five judges who heard both of her appeals invoked the Interpretation Act argument that words importing the masculine gender included women. The message was clear: the Interpretation Act worked against women, applying only when burdens (such as vagrancy convictions) but not benefits (such as lawyering) were at issue.[7]

Lizzie Cyr raised a second sex-inequality issue involving Alice Jamieson, the police magistrate who initially convicted her. Alice Jamieson was one of the two women – the other being Emily Murphy – who had been appointed as police magistrate in Alberta. Indeed, when Emily Murphy was appointed as police magistrate for the City of Edmonton on June 13, 1916, she may have been the first woman in the British empire to receive such an appointment. However, although defence counsel objected to Emily Murphy's appointment from time to time, it was Alice Jamieson's appointment as police magistrate for the City of Calgary in December 1916 that was actually challenged.[8] Most likely this was because Alice Jamieson almost convicted Lizzie Cyr without giving her lawyer the opportunity to present his defence argument.

On appeal, Lizzie Cyr's lawyer argued that Alice Jamieson was "incompetent and incapable of holding the position of police magistrate" because she was a woman. While the first judge to hear this appeal entertained "serious doubt whether a woman is qualified to be appointed to that office," he refused to act on his doubt. Surprisingly, the Alberta Court of Appeal also refused to uphold Lizzie Cyr's appeal on this issue, and did so without relying on the Interpretation Act. Instead the Court offered two other arguments, both of which merit consideration. One was a new argument about the recently passed Alberta equal-suffrage statute. The other was a more novel and detailed version of the argument advanced by the dissenting judge in Annie Macdonald Langstaff's case.

When Lizzie Cyr's lawyer interpreted Alberta's equal-suffrage statute as excluding women from being police magistrates, he completely ignored the intention behind the legislation. In 1916 Alberta had become the second province, after Manitoba and almost simultaneously with Saskatchewan, to pass women's suffrage legislation. The Alberta legislation was the most comprehensive. It provided that, in some twenty-four statutes, "Women shall be upon an absolute equality with and have the same rights and privileges and be subject to the same penalties and disabilities as men." But as Lizzie Cyr's lawyer pointed out, the police magistrate's statute was not among the twenty-four. This, he argued, meant that women could not be police magistrates.

Fortunately, this argument was completely rejected by the Alberta Court of Appeal. According to the Court, Lizzie Cyr's lawyer had totally misunderstood the purpose of the equal-suffrage statute. Instead of excluding women from the statutes that were not mentioned, as he had argued, the Court held that the purpose of the equal-suffrage statute was one of "wiping out the expressly enacted disqualification of women" in the statutes that were mentioned.

The other argument the Alberta Court of Appeal offered was even more novel. In this argument, the Court canvassed the historical context in considerable detail and came to a number of conclusions. First, there were "well-established facts" showing "that women had on many occasions held high and important public offices in England, some of a judicial character." Second, where their capacity to do so was questioned, it was answered with "a decision favourable to the existence of the capacity." Third, no British legal case had disqualified women from holding public office until the middle of the nineteenth century. Fourth, the British cases decided after that time were not "strictly" binding because of the "different conditions" in Alberta. Fifth, "at a very early stage" in Alberta law, "it was recognized that women should be put in a new position" such that "it was considered necessary if women were not to vote or hold public office that it should be so expressly stated." Finally, since the relevant Alberta statute did not expressly exclude women, therefore women could be police magistrates.

This argument was significant for four reasons. It meant that Alice Jamieson, who was neither plaintiff nor defendant nor even represented in this case, and Emily Murphy, who later initiated the Persons case, could continue to sit as police magistrates. It also meant that women were henceforth entitled to be treated like men, whose capacity to sit as police magistrates was never in question, and in this respect it was one of only a few cases in which this outcome occurred. Further, it meant that this outcome could be achieved without challenging the historical perspective so favoured and yet so perversely interpreted by other Canadian judges in sex-equality cases. Finally, this argument was significant because it was totally ignored only eleven years later when the Supreme Court of Canada decided the Persons case.

The Persons Case

The Persons case was initiated in 1927 by five women from Alberta: Emily Murphy, Nellie McClung, Louise McKinney, Irene Parlby, and Henrietta Muir Edwards.[9] Their case raised the question of whether women were eligible for appointment to the Senate. The answer depended on how section 24 of the Constitution Act, 1867 (formerly known as the British North America Act, 1867), was interpreted. Section 24 provided that "qualified persons" were eligible for appointment to the Senate. However, the federal government refused to interpret section 24 as making women eligible. According to the federal government, women were not persons.

This was a strange position for the federal government to take in 1927, particularly because between 1916 and 1922 (or 1925, if Newfoundland is included) women had become eligible to vote in elections for the federal House of Commons and all of the provincial legislatures, except Quebec. Indeed, for some time before 1916 women had been eligible to vote in various school and municipal elections. For example, women with property, whether married or single, were eligible to vote for school trustees in Ontario as early as 1850 and in municipal elections in British Columbia as early as 1873.

Moreover, between 1916 and 1925 women had become eligible to sit as members in the federal House of Commons and in all of the provincial legislatures except New Brunswick and Quebec. In Alberta the first two women legislators, Louise McKinney and Roberta MacAdams, had been elected in 1917, followed by Nellie McClung in 1921. In British Columbia Mary Ellen Smith had been elected in 1918; in Saskatchewan Mrs. M.O. Ramsland had been elected in 1919; and in Manitoba Edith Rogers had been elected in 1920. As well, in March 1921 Mary Ellen Smith had been appointed to the cabinet in British Columbia – the first woman cabinet member in the British empire – and in August 1921 Irene Parlby had been appointed to the cabinet in Alberta.

Unlike the processes for electing members of the federal House of Commons and the provincial legislatures, which could be changed by ordinary statutes, the process for appointing Senators was governed solely by the Constitution Act, 1867. Since that Act had been enacted by the British Parliament, only that Parliament could amend it. In the case of the Senate appointment process, such an amendment would have required the prior unanimous consent of all of the Canadian legislatures. We will never know whether such a political agreement might have been forthcoming, because the five women from Alberta opted instead for a litigation strategy. They petitioned the federal government to initiate a reference case in which the Supreme Court of Canada would be asked to rule on the meaning of the word "persons" in section 24 of the Constitution Act, 1867.

Although the federal government agreed to obtain the opinion of the Court, its position remained unchanged: women were not "persons" for the purposes of eligibility for appointment to the Senate. According to the lawyer who argued for the federal government in court, the word "persons" had to be defined by the meaning that it had in 1867 when the Constitution Act was passed, not the meaning that it might have acquired by 1927 when the case was being litigated. He argued that in 1867 women did not hold public offices of any kind in the provinces that were then joining the Canadian federation. Nor could they hold any public offices under

British common law. Of course, his argument totally ignored the Alberta Court of Appeal's considered decision to the contrary eleven years earlier.

So did the five Supreme Court of Canada judges who first decided the Persons case. Indeed, all five simply agreed with the arguments offered by the lawyer for the federal government. It has since been said by a biographer of one of these five judges that he "rejected the common law rule excluding women from government."[10] However, what he rejected was not the common law rule itself but rather the contention that the judiciary could change it. Nor was his rejection significant. Not only did it merely echo the position of the judges in the earlier cases involving Mabel Penery French and Annie Macdonald Langstaff; but also all four of the other Supreme Court of Canada judges in the Persons case took exactly the same position, maintaining that it was the function of legislatures, and not judges, to change the law.

Fortunately, the Supreme Court of Canada did not have the last word in the Persons case. The decision was appealed to the Judicial Committee of the British Privy Council. There was no special reason to assume that the British judges would be any less conservative in their outlook than their Canadian counterparts, except perhaps for the fact that the British judges were being asked to interpret a law that had been passed by their own parliament. Nevertheless, while waiting for the Judicial Committee's decision, one of the five women who had initiated the case – Emily Murphy – wrote a friend: "Going to win, Dear? You bet!"[11] And Emily Murphy was right. On October 18, 1929, the five-man Judicial Committee decided that women were eligible for appointment to the Senate under section 24 of the B.N.A. Act. It decided, in other words, that women were "persons."

The Judicial Committee's decision was certainly surprising by British standards. In effect the decision meant that "Six decades of precedent stating that women could not be included in the term 'persons' were swept aside."[12]

Indeed there had been a British case on this point just seven years earlier, in 1922. In that case, Margaret Haig, Viscountess Rhondda, had sought a seat in the House of Lords. Even though she was a peeress in her own right, the House of Lords had denied her a seat simply because she was a woman. Surprisingly, just two years before Viscountess Rhondda was denied the right to sit in the House of Lords, the British Parliament had passed a law providing that "A person shall not be disqualified by sex or marriage from the exercise of any public function."

Notwithstanding this law, it was a further forty years after Viscountess Rhondda's case was decided that British women were admitted to the British House of Lords. By contrast, the first woman – Cairine Wilson –

was appointed to the Senate of Canada in 1930, just one year after the Judicial Committee's decision in the Persons case.

What is most surprising, however, is that the significance of the Judicial Committee's decision is still somewhat controversial. On the one hand, at least two scholars have gone so far as to argue that this decision "changed . . . the conception of women and women's position in public life held by judges."[13] On the other hand, some legal commentators have been more restrained.[14] Among the latter, one of the more cautious simply maintained that the Judicial Committee's decision "opened a very small door for women to creep through."[15] This controversy cannot be resolved without examining what the Judicial Committee actually said.

In the first place, unlike the Alberta Court of Appeal, the Judicial Committee never denied that the common law excluded women from holding public office. On the contrary, the Judicial Committee acknowledged the common law exclusion by referring to it as a "relic of days more barbarous than ours," which excluded women "probably due to the fact that the deliberative assemblies of the early tribes were attended by men under arms, and women did not bear arms." Then, having exposed this rationale for the anachronistic and irrelevant notion that it was, the Judicial Committee simply said that "The appeal to history . . . in this particular matter is not conclusive." With these words, the Judicial Committee discredited the common law exclusion.

The members of the Judicial Committee also did what none of the previous judges had been prepared to do. They changed the law. Even the Alberta Court of Appeal judges had stopped short of changing the law and insisted that they were just following in the tradition of the early ordinances. By contrast, therefore, it could be said of the members of the Judicial Committee, and only of the Judicial Committee, that "in practice, if not in theory, they accepted the view so emphatically denied by their predecessors . . . that the law was the instrument of the judges rather than the judges the instrument of the law."[16]

The Judicial Committee's view made complete sense because the law it changed – the common law exclusion of women from holding public office – originated as judge-made law when earlier cases about women's rights were heard and decided by various British courts. So, as judges had been the ones who initially made this exclusionary law, why should subsequent judges not be the ones to change it?

Although the Judicial Committee had changed the law, it had not changed the "conception of women and women's position in public life held by the judges." This distinction was initially acknowledged by the Supreme Court of Canada when one of the judges stated, "We are, of course, in no wise concerned with the desirability or the undesirability of the presence of women in the Senate, nor with any political aspects of the question submitted." But the Judicial Committee members also acknowledged the same distinction when they said that they were not "deciding any question as to the rights of women but only a question as to their eligibility for a particular position."

There is even more explicit evidence that the Judicial Committee did not change "the conception of women and women's position in public life held by the Judges." This evidence derives from what the Judicial Committee said and did not say about the interpretation of the word "persons." The word, according to the Judicial Committee, "may include members of both sexes." But it did not say that it must include members of both sexes. Instead it said, "The burden is upon those who deny that the word includes women to make out their case." Were such a case to be made out, however, then it could not be said that the Judicial Committee had changed "the conception of women and women's position in public life held by the judges."

Nor could the Judicial Committee resist making out just such a case. Indeed, it made out two such cases from two other sections of the B.N.A. Act, albeit not from the Senate sections. While none of the Senate sections explicitly excluded women, sections 41 and 84 referred specifically to men. Accordingly, the Judicial Committee concluded that such references were "expressly used when it is desired to confine the matter in issue to males."

Furthermore, the members of the Judicial Committee used sections 41 and 84 as the basis of comparison with section 24. In their words, "If Parliament had intended to limit the word 'persons' in section 24 to male persons it would surely have manifested such intention by an express limitation, as it has done in sections 42 and 84."

In the end, the Judicial Committee offered the same qualified interpretation of the word "persons" as had the Alberta Court of Appeal judges in the case of Lizzie Cyr and Alice Jamieson and as had the dissenting judge in Annie Macdonald Langstaff's case. According to all of these judges, the word "persons" only included women if they were not expressly excluded.

Nevertheless, even this qualified interpretation was an improvement over the interpretation it had displaced. It was better that the word "persons" be interpreted as including women unless they were expressly excluded than to interpret it as excluding women unless they were expressly included. As Mary Eberts wrote, "These opposite attitudes . . . have a significant bearing on whether women will have to seek legislative permission to do something or just do it and put the burden on their opponents to stop them." [17] But the more inclusive interpretation was not all that the Judicial Committee might have decided. It should have decided that the word "persons" always includes both sexes.

In the sixty years since the Persons case was decided, there are no further "persons" cases whose stories are known. However, we can draw some conclusions from the five stories we do know. We know that nineteen of the thirty judges who decided these five cases were not prepared to include women in the word "persons." As none of these judges ever suggested that the word did not include men, it is clear they subscribed to Aristotle's defence of male supremacy. The remaining eleven judges were prepared to include women in the word "persons" only under some circumstances. For them, sometimes – but only sometimes – women and men were to be treated alike, or equally. Not one of the thirty men who decided these five cases was prepared to argue that the word "persons" must always include both sexes.

This argument is not merely of historical interest. For example, until recently the Canadian Armed Forces excluded women from service in combat and combat-related positions even though the National Defence Act clearly refers to all military service personnel as "persons," not "men." This policy had more than economic and employment consequences; it affected women's rights and responsibilities as citizens. For, as one commentator has noted, "Risking one's life in battle is the most extreme act the state can ask or demand of its citizens."[18] However, a federal human rights tribunal was finally required to address this issue in 1989. Concluding that the policy was discriminatory, this tribunal gave the forces ten years to integrate women into all remaining military occupations, with the singular exception of service on submarines. For reasons of privacy, the tribunal decided that only men could serve on submarines. What the tribunal failed to recognize is that privacy is gender-neutral; either sex could serve, albeit separately, on submarines. In effect, the real justification for excluding women and not men from service on submarines is not privacy, but history – our history of equating maleness with personhood. Thus the Judicial Committee's ruling in the Persons case has not mandated a change in "the conception of women and women's position in public life held by the judges." Women are not yet perceived as persons, always and everywhere.

The Canadian Bill of Rights Cases

Although we have as yet no comprehensive study of the cases litigated by women in the years since 1930, during the 1970s a new cluster of sex-equality cases arose in the context of the Canadian Bill of Rights.[19] In theory, the Canadian Bill of Rights guaranteed sex equality. This guarantee was enshrined in section 1(b), which provided that:

Section 1. It is hereby recognized and declared that in Canada there have existed and shall continue to exist without discrimination by

reason of race, national origin, colour, religion or sex, the following
human rights and fundamental freedoms, namely . . .
(b) the right of the individual to equality before the law and the protection of the law.

Despite the wording of section 1(b), there are several good reasons for
arguing that the Canadian Bill of Rights never guaranteed sex equality to
women.

One reason is historical and dates back to the time the Canadian Bill of
Rights was passed by the federal Parliament in 1960. At the committee
hearings that preceded passage, the Minister of Justice, who was supposedly defending the legislation, in fact did precisely the opposite. At one
point he offered to withdraw section 1(b) completely. Then he changed his
mind, saying, "I do feel that the expression . . . would not be interpreted by
the courts so as to say we are making men and women equal, because men
and women are not equal: they are different."[20] Although his words were
only part of the legislative history and, by tradition, should not have been
taken into account when the judges were deciding the sex-equality cases,
they nevertheless indicate the framework in which this legislation was formulated.

Another reason to doubt the guarantee of equality is coverage. As a
federal law, the Canadian Bill of Rights could only cover claims involving other federal laws and not claims involving provincial laws. For
example, many employment laws are within the area of provincial legislative responsibility and, as such, are not covered by the Canadian Bill of
Rights. Under these circumstances, therefore, the Canadian Bill of
Rights was unable to cover all of the possible claims for sex equality that
women might make.

But the most important reason is the judiciary. In effect, the judiciary
denied every claim in which women relied on the guarantee of sex equality
in the Canadian Bill of Rights. Although there were at least five lower-
court decisions that were favourable to women, every one of these cases
was reversed – either on appeal or in a later case on the same issue – by a
higher court. Thus, from the perspective of women, the judiciary effectively emptied the guarantee of sex-equality in the Canadian Bill of Rights
of any meaning.

This happened even though women did not launch any sex-equality
cases until after the Canadian Bill of Rights had proved effective in a race-
equality case. In 1970 a male Indian named Drybones used the race-equal-
ity provision in the Canadian Bill of Rights to challenge a federal law, the
Indian Act, which made it an offence for an Indian to be intoxicated off a
reserve.[21] Drybones ultimately litigated his case in the Supreme Court of

Canada and won, meaning that the law he had challenged was no longer enforceable.

By contrast, the laws upholding female inequality always remained enforceable whenever women challenged them, even though they used the same argument as Drybones. Drybones had argued that the law he had challenged treated Indians more harshly than non-Indians. Similarly, when women used the Canadian Bill of Rights to challenge various laws, it was always on the grounds that those laws treated women more harshly than men. Even so, in the sex-equality cases the judges always found reasons for upholding the laws even though the laws treated women more harshly than men.

In the earliest of these cases, brought in 1970 and 1971, several women challenged the prostitution provision, or what was then known as the vagrancy provision, in the criminal law because it was being applied only to women and not to men.[22] At least one trial judge agreed that the prostitution law violated the sex-equality provision in the Canadian Bill of Rights, but he was overruled in a subsequent case by a higher court judge. According to the higher court judge, prostitution referred to "activities which can only be engaged in by females." It followed, therefore, that the law could treat women more harshly than men, at least in the context of prostitution.

None of these prostitution cases was ever appealed to a provincial court of appeal, possibly because the federal government changed the law in 1972. This change was supposed to make the prostitution – or soliciting, as it is now known – law applicable to men as well as women. But at least one Ontario judge refused to do so, albeit without making any reference to the Canadian Bill of Rights. Fortunately, in a subsequent case, the Ontario Court of Appeal indicated its displeasure with the view that men could not be prostitutes. Thus this particular issue, at least, is unlikely to be troublesome in the future.

The prostitution cases were followed by three cases that were ultimately decided by the Supreme Court of Canada. Two of these cases were brought by Indian women – Jeannette Lavell and Yvonne Bedard – and the remaining case was brought by Stella Bliss.[23] Not surprisingly, all three of these women used the same argument as Drybones. After all, Drybones had won in the Supreme Court of Canada, and although his argument had not worked in the earlier prostitution cases, those cases had not gone to the Supreme Court.

Jeannette Lavell and Yvonne Bedard even challenged the same statute as Drybones had, namely, the Indian Act. Specifically, they challenged the section that deprived them of their Indian status when they married non-Indian men. In Bedard's case, this section had also stopped her from returning to her reserve when she subsequently separated from her husband. But as Sally Weaver points out in her chapter here, the Indian Act denied Indian status only to Indian women who married non-Indian men; it did not deny Indian status to Indian men who married non-Indian women. Lavell and Bedard both argued that the Indian Act violated the sex-equality provision in the Canadian Bill of Rights because it treated women more harshly than men.

Similarly, Stella Bliss challenged a section of the Unemployment Insurance Act on the grounds that it treated women more harshly than men. That section denied unemployment insurance benefits to otherwise qualified women simply because they were about to give birth or had just given birth. Although some women qualified for pregnancy benefits during that time, others – including Bliss – could not qualify because they had not worked long enough. However, Stella Bliss had worked long enough to qualify for unemployment insurance benefits and so, shortly after giving birth, she applied for those benefits. No one at the Unemployment Insurance Commission disputed her evidence that she was capable of and available for work. Nevertheless, she was denied the benefits – solely because she had been pregnant. In other words, Stella Bliss was treated more harshly than any man who might apply for unemployment insurance benefits.

All three women should have won their cases on the basis of their arguments. However, the Supreme Court of Canada issued a single decision ruling against both Jeannette Lavell and Yvonne Bedard by a five to four majority in 1973. Then, in 1978, a unanimous seven-man Court also ruled against Stella Bliss. Of the three men who sat on both cases, one wrote the majority judgment both times and the other two agreed with him both times. In the Lavell and Bedard case, the Court ruled that it was permissible to deny Indian status to Indian women who married non-Indians because that had been happening "for at least one hundred years." In the Bliss case, the Court ruled that it was all right to deny unemployment insurance benefits to pregnant women because "any inequality between the sexes in this area is not created by legislation but by nature." In these two cases the judges relied on history and on nature, respectively, to justify the harsher treatment of women, just as they had done more than forty years before in the "persons" cases.

But just as history and nature were spurious rationales in the "persons" cases, so were they in the Canadian Bill of Rights sex-equality cases. In the case of Jeannette Lavell and Yvonne Bedard, the historical justification was spurious for two reasons. First, there is evidence that it was not Indians who originated the idea of denying Indian status to Indian women who married non-Indian men.[24] Second, what the historical justification protected was simply the sex-based stereotype of powerful men (whether Indian or white) and subordinate women (whether white or Indian). In Stella Bliss's case, nature was a spurious justification because it could only dictate that a pregnant women would give birth and not that certain social arrangements, such as the denial of unemployment insurance benefits, must necessarily follow.

Moreover, it is worth noting that neither history nor nature had played any role in the Drybones decision. This contrast with the women's cases suggests that the judges, some of whom participated in all three decisions, may well have subscribed covertly, if not overtly, to Aristotle's defence of male supremacy. Fortunately, the federal Parliament did not continue to do so. In 1983 Parliament repealed the offending section of the Unemployment Insurance Act, and in 1985 it repealed the offending section of the Indian Act. But the situation was still not finally resolved, at least with respect to the 1985 changes to the Indian Act, because legal Indian status was still denied to the grandchildren, and succeeding generations, of Indian women who marry non-Indian men.

Some men also brought sex-equality cases to court under the Canadian Bill of Rights.[25] However, they did not argue that women were more harshly treated than men. Had they done so, they would have lost before they had begun. Instead these men argued that women were given special benefits not available to men, and that doing so violated the sex-equality provision in the Canadian Bill of Rights. The judges did not agree. In each case the judges were able to rationalize women's special need for that benefit and ruled that this special treatment did not violate the guarantee of sex equality in the Canadian Bill of Rights.

Several unpalatable conclusions followed from the judicial decision-making process as manifested in the Canadian Bill of Rights sex-equality cases. First, the Bill was ineffective in protecting the equal rights of women. However limited the arguments had been in the Cyr and Persons cases, at least the outcomes of those cases were acceptable. The Canadian Bill of Rights sex-equality cases were, by contrast, unleavened by a single favourable judgment. Second, in the Canadian Bill of Rights cases the judges seemed unconstrained by the tenets of consistency. In the cases brought by women, the judges rationalized and upheld laws that treated women more harshly than men; while in the cases brought by men, they rationalized and upheld laws that ostensibly benefited women. Third, a clear majority (nine out of thirteen) of the Supreme Court of Canada judges who decided these cases subscribed to Aristotle's defence of male supremacy. Consequently, it seemed obvious that the judiciary did not believe that the Canadian Bill of Rights guaranteed sex equality to women.

The Canadian Charter of Rights and Freedoms

When the federal government finally decided to patriate the Canadian constitution and to add to it a Charter of Rights and Freedoms, it was important for women to ensure that it was drafted properly, because it was to contain a sex-equality provision. Yet women's choices were limited. On the one hand it was clearly necessary to avoid replicating the unpalatable outcomes of the Canadian Bill of Rights sex-equality cases. On the other hand, while the outcomes of the Cyr and Persons cases were clearly acceptable, their underlying arguments were much less reliable. In Aristotelian terms, it seemed as if the choice was between perpetuating the defence of male supremacy or subscribing to the theory that women were like men.

Fortunately, the Canadian Advisory Council on the Status of Women became one of the first organizations to lobby actively for changes to the proposed Charter. Early in the summer of 1980, its president, Doris Anderson, commissioned a series of studies on the impact of the proposed Charter on women. The results of these studies were to be made public at an Advisory Council Conference on Women and the Constitution scheduled to take place immediately before the First Ministers meeting in September 1980. The conference was subsequently rescheduled because of a translators' strike. When it was finally held in May 1981, the purpose of the conference had been eclipsed by the intervening events.

The first event occurred when the Advisory Council presented its brief to the Special Joint Committee of the Senate and the House of Commons on the Constitution of Canada on November 20, 1980. Immediately preceding the Advisory Council's presentation, the National Action Committee on the Status of Women made its presentation. When the National Action Committee's president, Lynn McDonald, finished speaking, one of the co-chairmen of the Special Joint Committee, Senator Harry Hayes, made the following unsolicited comment: "We want to thank the National Action Committee on the Status of Women for being present today and for your brief. We appreciate your coming and as a matter of fact we are honoured. However, your time is up and I was wondering why we do not have a section in here for babies and children. All you girls are going to be working and we are not going to have anybody to look after them."[26]

Although the "stark chauvinism" of his words may have helped "sensitize the committee to the concerns of the women appearing before it,"[27] what really mattered were the briefs presented by such women's groups as the Canadian Advisory Council on the Status of Women, the Canadian Committee on Learning Opportunities for Women, the National Action Committee on the Status of Women, the National Association of Women and the Law, and the Native Women's Association of Canada. The influence of these presentations was specifically acknowledged by the Minister of Justice, Jean Chrétien, in February 1981.

By then the second event was under way. It had begun on January 5, 1981, with yet another postponement of the Advisory Council's conference, which prompted Doris Anderson's resignation as president. She said that she was resigning because Lloyd Axworthy, the federal minister responsible for the status of women, had pressured the other members of the Advisory Council into cancelling the conference. Doris Anderson's resignation hit the press. As Chaviva Hosek wrote, "The political costs of cancelling the conference turned out to be high. The women's movement suddenly had a heroine, a villain and an event, all of which symbolized its exclusion from the constitutional process. The media had a field day. The complex issues involved were reduced to a dramatic fight between a woman and a man."[28]

The day after Doris Anderson resigned, a small group of women met and decided that the conference should go forward on February 14-15 as scheduled, despite the Advisory Council's cancellation. These women formed what became known as the Ad Hoc Committee of Canadian Women on the Constitution. Within three weeks they had organized a two-day National Conference on Women and the Constitution in Ottawa, attended by thirteen hundred women from across Canada.

After the conference the Ad Hoc Committee continued to lobby for changes to the proposed new Charter. Initially, it concentrated on strengthening the proposed sex-equality provision, section 15, as did the National Action Committee and the National Association of Women and the Law. These lobbying activities resulted in the creation of a new sex-equality provision, section 28. On April 23, 1981, the House of Commons approved the inclusion of section 28 in the Charter. According to one commentator, Penney Kome, section 28 "became the law of the land only because of one of the most impressive lobbies in recent history."[29] Kome attributed the success of this lobby to three factors:

> One is solidarity: organized women, from women's Institutes to the Feminist Party, agreed on what they wanted and got it. Another is the grass-roots nature of their support: they were able to demonstrate that they had vast, non-partisan backing among the women in Canada. The third and perhaps most important reason was surprise. Their movement was spontaneous and therefore swift, thrown together at more or less the last moment. It caught opponents off-guard.[30]

The massive lobby for section 28 worked because section 15 did not offer a strong enough guarantee of sex equality. Section 15 was, and is, still subject to the limitations clause in section 1. In other words, whatever protection section 15 might guarantee, section 1 could remove it if a government were to persuade the courts that there was a reason for doing so. But section 28 is different; it prevails "notwithstanding anything in this Charter." So section 28 should prevail over the limitations clause in section 1. Thus section 28 has more potential to guarantee sex equality than has section 15.

The third and last event occurred in November 1981 when the prime minister and nine of the ten provincial premiers finally agreed to patriate the constitution. In doing so they also agreed to add a new provision to the Charter. This provision, section 33, became known as the override provision. When invoked, the override provision protects the continued existence of laws that would otherwise violate one or more of the rights and freedoms contained in the Charter; and it does so for up to ten years. When the override provision was announced on November 5, it clearly applied to most of the rights and freedoms in the Charter. But no reference was made to whether it applied to section 28. It turned out that all ten first ministers had forgotten about the existence of section 28. By November 9, however, the prime minister had decided that the override provision should apply to section 28.

The women's lobby was devastated by this decision, but not deterred. First, they lobbied the federal government to exempt section 28 from the override provision. The federal government agreed to do so, but only on condition that the nine provincial premiers involved also agreed. The women's lobby then set out to persuade those provincial premiers through a combination of telephone calls, telegrams, and letters, as well as through personal contact. The Saskatchewan premier was the last holdout. Finally, on November 23, 1981, the Minister of Justice, Jean Chrétien, announced in the House of Commons that he(!) had obtained the agreement of all nine provinces to exempt section 28 from the override provision.

Together, these events reveal how some politicians – both federal and provincial – actively resisted women's claims for sex equality. In that respect, very little seemed to have changed since the passage of the Canadian Bill of Rights in 1960. Without the intervention of a large women's lobby, women's constitutional rights would have been much weaker than they currently are. In other words, it would have been folly for women to rely too heavily on the legislative process to protect, never mind promote, their equality rights.

The intervention of the women's lobby did secure two sex-equality provisions in the Charter. One of the members of the Ad Hoc Committee best captured the value of both of these sections when she said that section 28 "would have been a helluva lot to lose, but it's not a helluva lot to gain."[31]

These sections were not "a helluva lot to gain" because they do not explain the meaning of sex equality. That meaning is no more self-evident in the Charter provisions than it was in the Canadian Bill of Rights sex-equality provision. The Charter does not preclude the gender-bias that permeated most of the "persons" cases and all of the Canadian Bill of Rights cases. This puts an enormous burden on women before they even begin to litigate the Charter sex-equality cases.

The Charter Cases

Although the Charter came into effect in April 1982, the Supreme Court of Canada has not yet issued any decision that is based on either of the sex-equality provisions. This is partly because the implementation of section 15 was delayed for three years to give the federal and provincial legislatures time to bring their laws into conformity with it. Section 15 was the only section to be treated this way. Because very few legislative changes were made by April 1985, the delay mainly served to stave off section 15 litigation. However, when sex-equality cases reached the Supreme Court, either leave to appeal was refused (the single-sex sports team case) or the Court relied on other grounds, including other provisions of the Charter, to decide them (the abortion, rape, and pornography cases).[32] On occasion the Crown failed to invoke the sex-equality provisions (the prostitution reference case) or ceded them (the maternity/paternity benefits case).[33] Therefore, there have mostly been no sex-equality decisions because the Canadian Supreme Court found, or was given, ways to avoid rendering them.

Under these circumstances, it is difficult to predict with any certainty how (and when) the Supreme Court will interpret the sex-equality provisions. Although the lower courts have made various pronouncements about them, the Supreme Court is not compelled to adopt any of their decisions. However, it may be instructive to examine one of the Supreme Court's section 15 decisions, even though it does not involve sex equality. As well, the Court's abortive sex-equality cases may shed some light. Similarly, the Court has recently decided some non-Charter cases that raise sex-equality issues in the areas of human rights, criminal, and tort law. While even the best of these cases is vulnerable to being distinguished, they may offer some indication of how the Court will decide Charter-based sex-equality cases in the future.

In the lower courts the earliest experiences with Charter-based sex-equality litigation were relatively positive. In May 1985 a woman successfully challenged the Yukon change-of-name law because it denied married women the right to change their names; in December 1985 a married woman successfully challenged the Ontario vital-statistics law because it denied her the right to give her child her surname; and in 1986 a twelve-year-old girl (Justine Blaney) who wanted to play hockey on an all-boys team successfully challenged the Ontario law that protected single-sex sports teams. These victories were not without cost. In the case of the sports teams, the legal victory did not extend to changing the social behaviour of some male team members when the decision to allow girls to join has been made. Moreover, there is ample evidence that integrated teams continue to disadvantage women.[34] Thus, some commentators have suggested that the better remedy would involve redefining what we think of as 'sports.'[35]

Gwen Brodsky and Shelagh Day raised a different order of concerns in a recent study of 591 equality decisions handed down by the lower courts during the first three years that section 15 was in effect.[36] First, they noted that only 52, or less than 10 per cent, of these 591 decisions involved sex-equality claims. Second, only 9 of the 52 sex-equality challenges were brought by or on behalf of women, mainly in the context of civil litigation. Third, the remaining sex-equality challenges were made by or on behalf of men, with a strong concentration in the area of criminal litigation. Fourth, although women won five of their nine cases, men won almost three times as many of the remainder. Fifth, of the 591 decisions studied, only 17 were initiated by a member or members of an historically disadvantaged group – women, aboriginal peoples, disabled persons, and members of national, ethnic, or racial minorities.

Given what these figures reveal about the disadvantages women and other marginalized groups confront in the context of equality litigation, it was not surprising that Brodsky and Day reported: "There is no serious discourse in these decisions about inequality in Canada, its dimensions, its patterns, its cures. There is no developing discussion, no public conversation about the pervasive disadvantage of certain groups. Instead, most discussion turns on comparisons – the superficial comparisons that formal equality requires."[37] "Formal equality" is simply another name for the Aristotelian theory of equality, the theory that assumes equality is achieved when the law treats alikes alike.[38]

Sometimes it is appropriate for the law to treat women and men as alike or formally equal – the right to vote being a prime example. However, since women and men are not identically situated much of the time, mostly "the formal equality model breaks down; in fact, it is inherently discriminatory."[39] Formal equality is inadequate because it fails to encompass or even to acknowledge that "Women's conditions are worse than men's; they are disadvantaged, exploited, degraded, and brutalized."[40] Formal equality is, in short, "meaningless to those whose equality interests are most in need of protection and advancement."[41] Worse, as Brodsky and Day observed, "A judicial policy of formal equality for all will not meet the needs of disadvantaged groups. Instead, it will perpetuate and further entrench their inequality."[42]

Not surprisingly, Brodsky and Day ended their study of the first three years of section 15 equality jurisprudence on a pessimistic note. Since their review of almost six hundred equality cases had established that the lower courts were continuing to apply the formal equality model that had already failed women and other disadvantaged groups in the Canadian Bill of Rights cases, the only possibility for change rested with the Supreme Court of Canada. Thus they argued that the Supreme Court must endorse a new model of equality, one that they referred to as the substantive equality model. According to Brodsky and Day, this new model "is concerned with equality of results for women as a group. . . . It means that governments and courts must do whatever is necessary to allow women to enjoy all of society's resources, benefits, and protection with equal dignity, respect, and opportunity."[43] More succinctly, the substantive equality model "is about group disadvantage and subordination."[44] Brodsky and Day concluded, "The entrenchment of equality rights may go down in history not as one step forward for women, but as two steps back."[45]

Before leaving the lower courts, it is worth noting one very recent case that offers limited grounds for optimism.[46] In it the Native Women's Association of Canada argued that they were entitled to be funded and to participate on the same terms as the other four aboriginal groups (the Assembly of First Nations, the Native Council of Canada, the Metis National Council, and the Inuit Tapirisat of Canada) who were already involved in the most recent round of constitutional negotiations. The trial court denied their equality claim on the ground that the government did not recognize it; but the Federal Court of Appeal disagreed, holding that "by . . . excluding the equal participation of NWAC, the Canadian government has accorded the advocates of male dominated aboriginal self-governments a preferred position in the exercise of an expressive activity, the freedom of which is guaranteed to everyone by section 2(b) and which is, by section 28, guaranteed equally to men and women." Unfortunately, the Court undermined the strength of this holding by failing to guarantee NWAC either equal funding or participation in the final constitutional negotiations.

By 1992 the Supreme Court of Canada had decided fourteen cases under the general section 15 equality provision.[47] The earliest of these involved religious equality; five raised the issue of age discrimination; another focused on discrimination on the basis of mental ability; and the remaining seven raised non-enumerated grounds. Since the legislation was upheld in all but two of these cases, the outcomes resemble our earlier experience with the Canadian Bill of Rights. However, one case that was decided in 1989 is frequently cited by judges, lawyers, and academics as the new paradigm for equality jurisprudence under the Charter.[48] The Andrews case involved a challenge to the Canadian citizenship requirement imposed by legislation on anyone who wanted to become a lawyer in British Columbia. Although section 15 makes no reference to citizenship, the Court decided that non-citizens as a group lack political power and are vulnerable to having their rights violated; they fall, in other words, into a category analogous to the groups specifically protected in section 15. Since the Court then struck down the Canadian citizenship requirement for lawyers, this decision has been more celebrated than not.

Aside from suggesting that the Court might be inclined to support the claims of equality-seekers, there are three reasons why this decision really tells us very little about likely outcomes of future sex-equality cases. First, the Andrews judges did not jettison the Aristotelian principle of formal equality (the treat alikes alike test); all they did was to hold that it "cannot be accepted as a fixed rule or formula." Second, their discussion of disadvantage – the concept that is central to the development of a substantive equality model – was very cursory; for example, there was "no recognition in the judgments that the term 'sex' in section 15 covers both an advantaged and a disadvantaged group, and that courts will have to distinguish between men's sex equality claims and women's sex equality claims."[49] Finally and perhaps most significantly, the Andrews judges found neither the meaning nor the application of the section 15 equality guarantee controversial; but they split 3-3 over the test that the government had to meet in order to justify the constitutionality of a law that would otherwise infringe that equality guarantee.

Any government can justify infringing a Charter guarantee by successfully invoking the section 1 limitations clause. Section 1 provides that the rights and freedoms set out in the Charter are subject "to such reasonable limits prescribed by law as can be demonstrably justified in a free and democratic society." Three years before Andrews was decided, in a case called Oakes, the Supreme Court decided that a government would have to meet a high standard – its legislative objective must be "pressing and substantial" – to justify limiting a Charter right or freedom under section 1.[50]

In Andrews, three judges challenged the Oakes test, arguing that it was too stringent. More specifically, they contended that a government objective need only be "reasonable" to justify infringing the section 15 equality guarantee. Although this interpretation of the section 1 limitations clause did not prevail in Andrews, neither has it disappeared. With changes in the composition of the Court it might prevail, thereby making it relatively easy to deny women the protection of the section 15 equality guarantee in the future. What is even more significant is that this could happen irrespective of whether the Court subscribes to the formal, or to the substantive, model of sex equality.

The indeterminacies of Andrews were not resolved in the abortive sex-equality cases. In fact, women were not even parties to eight of these ten cases (the two exceptions being Blaney and Daigle), even though they focused on issues of great concern to women: abortion, rape, prostitution, maternity/paternity benefits, and pornography. The Legal Education and Action Fund (LEAF), a legal defence fund set up in 1985 to litigate sex-equality cases on behalf of women, was granted intervenor status in seven of these cases; while the Canadian Organization for the Rights of Prostitutes intervened in an eighth. Thus, no one represented the interests of women in one of the abortion cases (Morgentaler) and in one of the rape cases (Hess), unless it was the one woman judge (Wilson) who heard Morgentaler, or the three (Wilson, L'Heureux-Dubé, and McLachlin) who decided Hess.

Since the Supreme Court of Canada disposed of three cases on procedural or remedial grounds (Blaney, Borowski, and Schachter), and one without relying on the Charter (Daigle), this leaves six cases in which the Court relied, not on sex equality, but on other provisions in the Charter. When the Court held that the abortion (Morgentaler), statutory rape (Hess), and rape shield (Seaboyer) laws violated section 7 of the Charter, the section that guarantees the right not to be deprived of "life, liberty and security of the person . . . except in accordance with the principles of fundamental justice," they were struck down. In contrast, although the rape publication ban (Canadian Newspapers), soliciting (Prostitution Reference), and anti-pornography (Butler) laws infringed the section 2(b) guarantees of "freedom of thought, belief, opinion and expression, including freedom of the press and other media of communication," the Supreme Court nevertheless upheld these laws as reasonable limits that were justified by section 1 of the Charter. Stated thus, it is not always self-evident whether these decisions were good or bad for women, although many approved of the outcomes in Morgentaler, Canadian Newspapers, and Butler while questioning or disagreeing with those in the Prostitution Reference, Hess, and Seaboyer cases.

From the perspective of sex equality, what really matters is whether these six cases signalled any changes in the Supreme Court's understanding of, and willingness to remedy, the systemic disadvantages that women experience in Canadian society. Because the Charter was invoked by men who were accused of criminal offences in four of these cases, much of the reasoning in these decisions focused not on women's, but on men's, disadvantages. Even when arguments based on the disadvantages experienced by women did prevail, as they did in Morgentaler, Canadian Newspapers, and Butler, they were never without qualification. In Morgentaler the

Court left open the possibility that some form of abortion legislation might be consistent with the section 7 guarantee of liberty and security of the person; and since the Canadian Newspapers and Butler decisions depended not on substantive rights, but on section 1 arguments, it is possible that another Court, differently composed, might find these section 1 arguments less persuasive in the future. In sum, while women's experiences did not go unrecognized, neither were they more than contingent features of the Supreme Court's decision-making in the abortive sex-equality cases.

Fortunately, when it comes to predicting the outcomes of future Charter-based sex-equality cases, there is more cause for optimism to be derived from several recent non-Charter cases. For example, it makes sense to speculate about the possible spillover effects of two successful human rights sex discrimination decisions released by the Supreme Court shortly after the Andrews case.[51] In the Brooks case the Court held that discriminating on the basis of pregnancy could constitute sex discrimination, hence overturning its own decision to the contrary a decade earlier in the Canadian Bill of Rights Bliss case. Brooks is particularly significant because it focused on one of the major differences between women and men ("only women . . . bear children; no man can become pregnant") and acknowledged that this difference could wrongfully disadvantage women ("It is unfair to impose all of the costs of pregnancy upon one half of the population"). In the Janzen case, the Court defined sexual harassment as "practices or attitudes which have the effect of limiting the conditions of employment of, or the employment opportunities available to, employees on the basis of a characteristic related to gender," and then unanimously concluded that it constituted sex discrimination.

Since Brooks and Janzen, three more non-Charter cases have affirmed the Supreme Court's ability and willingness to take women's experiences into account.[52] In 1990, in Lavallee, the Court held that the mental state of a woman who had been repeatedly and brutally battered (the battered woman syndrome) justified her action of shooting her partner in the back after he threatened to kill her. Before this decision a battered woman had to wait until her assailant instigated another battering episode before she could act to defend herself, a requirement the Lavallee Court discredited as tantamount to "murder by installment." More recently, in Norberg, the Court held a male medical doctor civilly liable for sexual assault when he instigated a sex-for-drugs arrangement with a female patient who was addicted to prescription drugs. Five of the six judges based their judgment on the unequal power relationship existing between the doctor and his patient. Lastly, in Miersma, the Court recognized that a post-incest syndrome of denial, memory repression, and self-guilt could block adult survivors of childhood incestuous abuse from connecting their injuries with the wrong done to them. Accordingly, the Court held that, unlike other litigants, an incest survivor might not be able to initiate a lawsuit against the perpetrator of the incest until long after the abuse had ended.

If these five non-Charter cases were the only recent decisions of the Court involving issues of concern and interest to women, there would be every reason to be optimistic about the possibility of achieving substantive equality for women in future sex-equality cases. However, in the context of the Charter it is impossible to ignore the Supreme Court's record of avoidance when the sex-equality provisions are invoked. Moreover, on the only occasion when the Court did advert to a section 15 sex-equality argument, the judges split 4-3, with a majority (including two of the three women) concluding that the statutory rape law did not infringe section 15. Because all seven judges in the Hess case had already found that this law violated section 7 of the Charter, their opinions about section 15 were essentially irrelevant; which is fortunate, given that the majority appeared to base their argument on biological rather than social differences. If such an argument were to prevail, it would mean disregarding the realities of women's subordinate lives. Indeed, it would be difficult to avoid concluding that the old Aristotelian notion of equality as sameness still lurked untrammelled in the minds of many members of the contemporary judiciary.

Although Aristotelian theory fails to explain treating unalikes equally, others have. There are feminists whose theories about the meaning of sex equality have the potential to elucidate the meaning, purpose, and effect of treating unalikes equally. In particular, the theories of feminists such as Carol Gilligan, Catharine MacKinnon, and Mary O'Brien draw on the realities of women's experience to explain the meaning of sex equality.[53] Accordingly, their theories have the potential to explain how sex equality might involve treating unalikes equally. An understanding of these theories should be required of Canadian judges who are seeking to explain the meaning of sex equality under the Charter.

This is especially important in view of the fact that so few of our judges are women. Despite recent efforts to increase the appointment of women, less than 10 per cent of federally appointed court judges were women as of January 1990; and the figures for the judges appointed by the provincial governments across Canada were not significantly different.[54] The first woman to sit on the Supreme Court of Canada was Madame Justice Bertha Wilson, appointed in 1982 just before the Charter came into effect; she remained on the Court for nine years. In the intervening period, Madame Justice Claire L'Heureux-Dubé was appointed in 1987, and in 1989 Madame Justice Beverley McLachlin was also appointed to the Supreme Court of Canada. Nevertheless, the Canadian judiciary remains overwhelming male.

Until more women are appointed as judges, it really matters that male judges begin to listen to what feminists are saying about sex equality. Unless they do, there is every reason to assume that the bias of past sex-equality decisions – that is, the gender-bias of the Aristotelian theory of equality – will continue to prevail. Unless they do, in other words, the likelihood that future judicial decisions will really accomplish sex-equality objectives under the Charter remains bleak.

Beverley Baines

NOTES

1. For accounts of twenty-two of these landmark cases, see: M. Elizabeth Atcheson, Mary Eberts, and Beth Symes with Jennifer Stoddart, *Women and Legal Action: Precedents, Resources and Strategies for the Future* (Ottawa: Canadian Advisory Council on the Status of Women, 1984).

2. Unless otherwise noted, quotations cited in the discussion of these early "persons" cases are from the pertinent court reports. See: *In Re Mabel P. French* (1905), 37 New Brunswick Reports, 359; *In Re Mabel Penery French* (1912), 17 British Columbia Reports, 1; *Dame Langstaff* v. *The Bar of Quebec* (1915), 47 cour supérieure 131, affirmed (1915), 25 cour du banc du roi 11; *Rex* v. *Cyr (Alias Waters)* (1917), 2 Western Weekly Reports, 1185, affirmed 3 Western Weekly Reports, 849.

3. Constance B. Backhouse, "'To Open the Way for Others of My Sex': Clara Brett Martin's Career as Canada's First Woman Lawyer," *Canadian Journal of Women and the Law* 1 (1985), 37.

4. Karen Berger Morello, *The Invisible Bar: The Women Lawyer in America: 1638 to the Present* (New York: Random House, 1986).

5. Margaret Gillet, *We Walked Very Warily: A History of Women at McGill* (Montreal: Black Rose Books, 1981), 309.

6. Ibid., 305.

7. Marguerite E. Ritchie, "Alice Through the Statutes," *McGill Law Journal* 21 (1975), 702.

8. Eleanor Harmon, "Five Persons from Alberta," in Mary Quayle Innes, ed., *The Clear Spirit* (Toronto: University of Toronto Press, 1966), 162.

9. Catherine L. Cleverdon, *The Woman Suffrage Movement in Canada* (Toronto: University of Toronto Press, 1966), 162-163.

10. Sources used in this discussion on the Persons case include: David Ricardo Williams, *Duff: A Life in the Law* (Vancouver: University of British Columbia Press, 1984); James G. Snell and Frederick Vaughan, *The Supreme Court of Canada: History of the Institution* (Toronto: The Osgoode Society and University of Toronto Press, 1985). Unless otherwise noted, quotations used are from pertinent court records; see: *In the Matter of a Reference as to the Meaning of the Word "Person" in Section 24 of the British North America Act, 1867* (1928), Supreme Court Reports 276; reversed sub nom *Henrietta Muir Edwards et al.* v. *Attorney-General for Canada* (1930), Appeal Cases 124.

11. Byrne Hope Sanders, *Emily Murphy: Crusader* (Toronto: Macmillan, 1945), 243.

12. Albie Sachs and Joan Hoff Wilson, *Sexism and the Law* (New York: The Free Press, 1978), 41.

13. Ibid., 42.

14. *See*: Mary Eberts, "Sex-based Discrimination and the Charter" and Katherine J. De Jong, "Sexual Equality: Interpreting Section 28" in Anne Bayefsky

and Mary Eberts, *Equality Rights and the Canadian Charter of Rights and Freedoms* (Toronto: Carswell, 1985).

15. Ritchie, "Alice Through the Statutes," 702.

16. Sachs and Wilson, *Sexism and the Law*, 42.

17. Mary Eberts, "The Persons Case," *National Action Committee on the Status of Women, News* 5, (March 1979).

18. Jill Laurie Goodman, "Women, War, and Equality: An Examination of Sex Discrimination in the Military," *Women's Rights Law Reporter* 5 (1979), 246.

19. Unless otherwise noted, quotations used in this discussion of the Canadian Bill of Rights cases are from the pertinent court record.

20. *See*: Special Committee on Human Rights and Fundamental Freedoms, *Minutes of Proceedings and Evidence*, 1-12, (July 12-29, 1960), 641.

21. *R. v. Drybones* (1970), Supreme Court Reports, 282.

22. *R. v. Viens* (1970), 10 Criminal Reports (new series), 363, *R. v. Lavoie* (1970), 16 Dominion Law Reports (3d), 647, affirmed (1972), 23 Dominion Law Reports (3d), 364; *R. v. Beaulne*, ex parte Latreille (1971), 16 Dominion Law Reports (3d), 657. See also: *R. v. Patterson* (1972), 19 Criminal Reports (new series), 289; *R. v. Obey* (1973), 21 Criminal Reports (new series), 121; *R. v. DiPaola and Palatics* (1978), 43 Canadian Criminal Cases (2d), 199; *Hutt v. The Queen* (1978), 38 Canadian Criminal Cases (2d), 418; *Westendorp v. The Queen* (1983), 32 Criminal Reports (3d), 97.

23. *Attorney-General of Canada v. Lavell, Isaac et al. v. Bedard* (1973), 38 Dominion Law Reports (3d), 481; *Bliss v. Attorney-General of Canada*, (1979), 1 Supreme Court Reports, 183.

24. Kathleen Jamieson, *Indian Women and the Law in Canada: Citizens Minus* (Ottawa: Advisory Council on the Status of Women, 1978). See also Sally Weaver's chapter in this book.

25. *See*: *Joseph v. Joseph* (1969), 4 Dominion Law Reports, 646; *Re Schmitz* (1972), 31 Dominion Law Reports (3d), 117; *Rose v. the Queen* (1972), 19 Criminal Reports (2d), 66; *R. v. Halliday* (1973), 23 Criminal Reports (new series), 332; *R. v. Mackay* (1976), 30 Canadian Criminal Cases (2d), 349, reversed (1977), 36 Canadian Criminal Cases (2d), 349.

26. Special Joint Committee of the Senate and House of Commons on the Constitution of Canada, *Minutes and Proceedings of Evidence*, 32nd Parliament, 1980, 1st session, Issue no. 9, 75.

27. De Jong, "Sexual Equality," 506.

28. Chaviva Hosek, "Women and the Constitutional Process," in Keith Banting and Richard Simeon, eds., *And No One Cheered: Federalism, Democracy, and the Constitution Act* (Toronto: Methuen, 1983), 289.

29. Penney Kome, "Anatomy of a Lobby," *Saturday Night*, January 1983; *see also*: Penney Kome, *The Taking of Twenty-Eight: Women Challenge the Constitution* (Toronto: Women's Educational Press, 1983).

30. Kome, "Anatomy of a Lobby."

ma
ma

31. Linda Ryan Nye as quoted in Kome, "Anatomy of a Lobby."

32. *Re Blaney and Ontario Hockey Association et al.* (1985), 52 Ontario Reports (2d), 225, appeal allowed (1986), 54 Ontario Reports (2d), 513, leave to appeal to Supreme Court of Canada refused (1986), 58 Ontario Reports (2d), 274 (single-sex sports teams); *R.* v. *Morgentaler*, [1988] 1 Supreme Court Reports 30 (abortion); *Canadian Newspapers Company Limited* v. *Canada*, [1988] 2 Supreme Court Reports 122 (rape); *Borowski* v. *Canada*, [1989] 1 Supreme Court Reports 342 (abortion); *Tremblay* v. *Daigle*, [1989] 2 Supreme Court Reports 530 (abortion); *R.* v. *Hess*, [1990] 2 Supreme Court Reports 906 (statutory rape); *R.* v. *Seaboyer*, [1991] 2 Supreme Court Reports 577 (rape shield); *R.* v. *Butler*, [1992] 1 Supreme Court Reports 452 (pornography).

33. *Reference re sections 193 and 195.1 of the Criminal Code*, [1990] 1 Supreme Court Reports 1123; *R.* v. *Schachter*, [1992] Supreme Court Judgments No. 68.

34. See: John Sopinka, *Can I Play? The Report of the Task Force on Equal Opportunity in Athletics* (Government of Ontario).

35. Helen Lensky, *Out of Bounds: Women, Sport and Sexuality* (Toronto: Women's Educational Press, 1986).

36. Gwen Brodsky and Shelagh Day, *Canadian Charter Equality Rights For Women: One Step Forward or Two Steps Back?* (Ottawa: Canadian Advisory Council on the Status of Women, 1989).

37. Ibid., 119.

38. Ibid., 148.

39. Ibid.

40. Ibid., 150.

41. Ibid.

42. Ibid., 197.

43. Ibid., 192.

44. Ibid., 198.

45. Ibid.

46. *Native Women's Association of Canada* v. *Canada*, [1992] Federal Court Judgments No. 715.

47. Peter W. Hogg, *Constitutional Law of Canada* (Toronto: Carswell, 1992), 3rd ed., 1147-1195, omitting *R.* v. *Hess* (see text accompanying note 32) and adding *Canadian Council of Churches* v. *Canada*, [1992] 1 Supreme Court Reports 236.

48. *Andrews* v. *Law Society of British Columbia*, [1989] 1 Supreme Court Reports 143.

49. Brodsky and Day, *Canadian Charter Equality Rights For Women*, 207-208.

50. *R.* v. *Oakes*, [1986] 1 Supreme Court Reports 103.

51. *Brooks* v. *Canada Safeway*, [1989] 1 Supreme Court Reports 1219; and *Janzen and Govereau* v. *Platy Enterprises*, [1989] 1 Supreme Court Reports 1252.

52. *R.* v. *Lavallee*, [1990] 1 Supreme Court Reports 852; *Norberg* v. *Wynrib*,

[1992] Supreme Court Judgments No. 60; *K. M.* v. *H. M.,* [1992] Supreme Court Judgments No. 85.

53. Carol Gilligan, *In a Different Voice: Psychological Theory and Women's Development* (Cambridge, Mass.: Harvard University Press, 1982); Catharine A. MacKinnon, *Feminism Unmodified: Discourses on Life and Law* (Cambridge, Mass.: Harvard University Press, 1987); Mary O'Brien, *The Politics of Reproduction* (Boston: Routledge & Kegan Paul, 1981).

54. Chantal Maille, *Primed For Power: Women in Canadian Politics* (Ottawa: Canadian Advisory Council on the Status of Women, 1990).

SUGGESTED READINGS

Atcheson, M. Elizabeth, Mary Eberts, and Beth Symes, with Jennifer Stoddart, *Women and Legal Action: Precedents, Resources and Strategies for the Future.* Ottawa: Canadian Advisory Council on the Status of Women, 1984.

Backhouse, Constance, *Petticoats and Prejudice: Women and Law in Nineteenth-Century Canada.* Toronto: Women's Press, 1991.

Bayefsky, Anne, and Mary Eberts, *Equality Rights and the Canadian Charter of Rights and Freedoms.* Toronto: Carswell, 1986.

Brodie, Janine, Shelley A.M. Gavigan, and Jane Jenson, *The Politics of Abortion.* Toronto: Oxford University Press, 1992.

Brodsky, Gwen, and Shelagh Day, *Canadian Charter Equality Rights for Women: One Step Forward or Two Steps Back?* Ottawa: Canadian Advisory Council on the Status of Women, 1989.

Canadian Journal of Women and the Law.

Dawson, T. Brettel, ed., *Relating to Law: A Chronology of Women and Law in Canada.* North York, Ont.: Captus Press, 1990.

Dawson, T. Brettel, ed., *Women, Law and Social Change: Core Readings and Current Issues.* North York, Ont.: Captus Press, 1990.

Doerr, Audrey, and Micheline Carrier, *Women and the Constitution in Canada.* Ottawa: Canadian Advisory Council on the Status of Women, 1981.

Dranoff, Linda Silver, *Women in Canadian Law.* Toronto: Doubleday Canada, 1987.

Dymond, M.J., *The Canadian Women's Legal Guide.* Toronto: Doubleday Canada, 1987.

Kome, Penney, *The Taking of Twenty-Eight: Women Challenge the Constitution.* Toronto: Women's Educational Press, 1983.

Martin, Sheilah L., and Kathleen E. Mahoney, eds., *Equality and Judicial Neutrality.* Toronto: Carswell, 1987.

Razack, Sherene, *Canadian Feminism and the Law: The Women's Legal Education and Action Fund and the Pursuit of Equality.* Toronto: Second Story Press, 1991.

Smith, Lynn, and Eleanor Wachtel, *A Feminist Guide to the Canadian Constitution.* Ottawa: Canadian Advisory Council on the Status of Women, 1992.

Chapter Eight

Racism, Sexism, and Immigrant Women

≈≈≈≈≈≈≈≈≈≈≈≈≈≈≈≈≈≈≈≈≈≈≈≈≈≈≈≈≈≈

Immigrant women have always been part of the Canadian historical landscape. The contributions of pioneer gentlewomen such as Catharine Parr Traill and Susanna Moodie are well known. Less visible is the fact that, in order to develop Canada as a colony and preserve white supremacy, working-class women from Britain were recruited into Canada in the early days of settlement as wives and domestic workers.[1] For the most part their contribution to nation-building has been erased from recorded history. Later, as a result of the postwar boom and the relaxation of immigration policy, many non-white immigrants came to Canada. While immigrant men integrate relatively quickly into Canadian society through their paid work, many immigrant women, especially if they do not speak English, become marginal members of society. Together with Native women they became the most disadvantaged and invisible group in our society.

This chapter focuses on two groups of women: those who are permanent residents (landed immigrants) in Canada and those who are here on temporary work permits under the Foreign Domestic Worker program. Due to the lack of reliable information, the situation of undocumented migrant women (that is, women who are in the country illegally) will not be addressed here. Frequently, the difficulties of immigrant women and domestic workers are attributed to cultural differences and problems of adjustment. On closer examination it becomes apparent that while these women may come from different social and cultural backgrounds, they face similar situations – especially if they are non-white and non-English-speaking. This commonality has to do with how their experiences are shaped by the legal, economic, and social processes in Canadian society regardless of their ethnic, racial, and sometimes class backgrounds.

This is not to say that their cultural heritages and origins are unimportant. Certainly culture, ethnicity, political orientation, religion, language, customs, and social class are among the things that mark the internal differences within this group of women. But the immigration process has a homogenizing effect: the legal and institutional processes of Canada create certain common, shared conditions. It is these processes which I seek to explicate here. I will examine how, due to the racism and sexism that are deeply embedded in Canadian society, notably in our institutions and in the labour market, immigrant women are held "captive" to their husbands, their families and communities, and their employers. Domestic workers, especially, are subject to the whims of their employers. This kind of physical and psychological dependence has implications for these women's physical and mental well-being, which the term "adjustment" does not fully capture.

In adopting a "structural" approach to understanding immigrant women's experiences, I deliberately avoid looking at women's "traditional" roles and the issue of assimilation. By describing women's work as their "role," there is an assumption that this is what they are supposed to do "naturally." I want to draw attention to the fact that their experiences are created by certain institutional arrangements, and I suggest that if these conditions persist, immigrant women will not assimilate into Canadian society. While the issue of assimilation is an important one, my focus here is on the institutional and structural barriers that prevent their integration into Canadian society.

Specifically, I argue that sexism and racism are relations that underpin many immigrant women's and domestic workers' experiences in Canada. The terms "sexism" and "racism" are usually used to point to people's prejudicial attitudes towards individuals of a certain gender (for example, women) and/or a certain racial background (for example, Afro-Caribbean). They are also used to indicate certain discriminatory practices (in employment, for instance) directed at these individuals. While these attitudes and practices are important elements of sexism and racism, when I use the terms I am referring to the system of oppression and inequality based on the ideology of the superiority of one gender and/or race over the other gender and races. Thus, white European men, especially those of British and French descent, see themselves as superior to women and to people from other ethnic and racial origins. Accordingly, they have developed systems of ideas and practices over time to justify and support this notion of superiority. These ideas have become the premise on which societal norms are based, and the practices have become the "normal" ways of doing things. In the lives of immigrant women we see how this system of oppression produces the specific experiences they have in Canada.

In using the terms "sexism" and "racism" in this way, I go beyond the notion of prejudice among groups of people and underscore the unequal access to power of members of society, whether they are women or people from ethnic and racial groups. In particular, I draw attention to the institutional relations that work together to produce systemic inequality among groups of people, in this case immigrant women and domestic workers. In examining the experiences of these two groups of women, we gain insights into how race, gender, and class converge to shape these women's lives.

In this chapter I will analyse the institutional and labour-market relations that shape immigrant women's experiences in the labour force and in the home. I will then examine the experiences of domestic workers on temporary work permits. Although technically they are not landed immigrants, their working conditions are shaped by processes similar to the ones faced by immigrant women in Canadian society. Finally, I will end by describing some of the struggles immigrant women, including domestic workers, wage to better the conditions of their lives in Canada.

Institutional Determinants of Immigrant Women's Experiences

Technically the term "immigrant women" refers to women who have a certain legal status in Canada; that is, women who are landed immigrants, rather than citizens. This technical definition is deceptive, however. In everyday life, only certain groups of women are seen to be "immigrant women" by other members of society. They are women of colour, including women from Southern Europe and the "Third World"; women who do not speak English or who speak English with an accent other than British or American; and women who have certain jobs – for instance, a cleaning lady or a sewing-machine operator. In other words, the common usage of the term presupposes class and racist biases.

My purpose here is not to redefine the term "immigrant women" to include all women who are landed immigrants. I will preserve this common-sense usage. My aim is to understand how this common-sense notion arises. In so doing I will show that this understanding is rooted in the legal and economic processes of our society, which contain certain sexist and racist assumptions. To begin this exploration, the first thing to take into account is immigration law and policy. Canada's immigration program has always been designed with the express purposes of directing demographic growth on the one hand and meeting economic needs and labour-market demands on the other.[2] We see this very clearly in our immigration history: people from Northern and Eastern Europe (for example, Scandinavia and the Ukraine) were encouraged to immigrate to populate and open up the agricultural west; Chinese men were brought in as indentured labourers to build the railway; British and other white European immigrants entered to fill the bureaucratic, professional, and technical strata of the labour market; more recently, South Asians were brought in as farm labourers, and West Indian and Filipino women as domestic workers.[3] While Canada's immigration policy has always been racist, in that white English-speaking immigrants are preferred, non-white immigrants have been allowed to enter the country when there were demands for particular kinds of skills, and as Canada established trading relations with non-European nations.[4] Thus the Canadian mosaic[5] is a direct result of Canada's history as a land of colonization and immigration. In addition to using immigration as a means of filling gaps in the economy, from time to time Canada relaxes its immigration policy to make room for refugees to enter the country (for example, the Jews during the war periods, and more recently Southeast Asians).[6] But this is a relatively small part of the immigration program.

As immigration policy developed historically, the federal government made efforts to tie immigration more closely to economic and labour-market needs.[7] Thus it introduced a "points system" in 1967 as a labour-recruitment strategy. Since that time, immigrants have been selected on the basis of points they earn in nine areas such as education, language, and occupation. The points given to occupation, in particular, are constantly revised to reflect Canada's occupational demands. Immigrants are admitted into Canada according to different classes: independent class, family class, and so on.[8]

There are three categories of "independent" immigrants: self-selected workers, assisted relatives, and business immigrants. Their eligibility is measured by the points system. The "self-selected" group is granted landed-immigrant status on the basis of accumulated points for education, work experience, occupation, and economic resources. Those in the "assisted relatives" category are granted landed-immigrant status through the nomination of a relative other than an immediate family member (if they cannot obtain enough points on their own), as well as the application of the points system. "Business" immigrants include entrepreneurs, the self-employed, and investors, and are assessed by different criteria. Applicants qualify as business-class immigrants if they have money to invest in business and industries in Canada. The amount of capital necessary for an individual to qualify as a business-class immigrant changes from year to year.

A "family-class" immigrant is someone who cannot qualify to enter Canada under the points system; people are granted this status through the sponsorship of immediate family members who are either independent landed immigrants or Canadian citizens. The family-class category usually includes the spouse, children under twenty-one, or parents over sixty-five, of the independent immigrant. Here I will confine my discussion to "independent" and "family-class" immigrants, because it is the

Table 1
Immigration by Sex, 1988

	Male	Female	Total
Family class	21,019	30,006	51,025
	41%	59%	100%
Refugees and designated classes	15,729	10,846	26,575
	59%	41%	100%
Independent	42,042	41,126	83,168
	51%	49%	100%
Total	78,790	81,978	160,768
	49%	51%	100%

SOURCE: Immigration Canada, *Immigration to Canada: A Statistical Overview* (Ottawa, 1989), 15.

relationship between these two groups that contributes to immigrant women's experiences in Canada.

Usually, in an immigrant family, only one member is granted the independent status. In most cases it is the husband who is so designated, because he is perceived to be the head of the household, and the wife is categorized as a family-class immigrant along with the children. Table 1 gives the breakdown of numbers and percentages of immigrants by class of immigrants and by sex for 1988. The majority of the family-class immigrants were female (59 per cent).[9] Although this table does not specify the age breakdown of the male and female immigrants, it is likely that most male immigrants in the family-class category are children and retired parents of the independent-class immigrant.

This classification system ignores the fact that wives may have comparable education and work experience to their husbands and may have made essential contributions to family income before immigration. For example, among the industrial workers in Hong Kong and the Southeast Asian urban centres, a family of two income-earners is the norm.[10] Moreover, once immigration takes place, the financial security of many immigrant families often depends initially on the labour-force participation of the wife, and later that of both spouses. This has to do with the structure of the Canadian labour market, where there are more demands for cheap labour in the marginal sectors of the economy. There is also an increasing need for Canadian families to survive on at least two incomes; this reality means that most immigrant wives have to join the paid labour force as wage-earners.[11] Yet the assignment of family members according to the classification of "independent" and "family class" negates this reality. The official view of the immigrant family, according to immigration procedures, is that of one "independent" member upon whom others depend for their sponsorship, livelihood, and welfare. Thus the immigration process systematically structures sexual inequality within the family by rendering one spouse (usually the wife) legally dependent on the other.

Although this system does not distinguish between white and non-white women as such, immigration officers have a great deal of discretionary power that they exercise according to their assumption of certain gender and racial stereotypes. These stereotypes, together with the accreditation process, which gives more weight to education and training obtained in the Western, English-speaking world, can mean that non-white women from the Third World are more disadvantaged in the immigration selection and assessment process.

The sponsorship system places many immigrant women in a totally dependent and subordinate position vis-à-vis the sponsors, who are legally responsible for their financial welfare for a period of five to ten years. First, an immigrant woman's entry into Canada is conditional upon the financial support of her sponsor. If, for some reason, the sponsor should be deported, it is likely that she will also be deported. Thus, prior to an immigrant woman's entry into the country, her legal status as a dependant is already established. This dependence is rooted in the institutionalized (sexist) practices of our legal apparatus, which have tremendous implications for immigrant women's status and self-concept in Canadian society.

Once she is classified as a dependent immigrant, a whole series of consequences follow, placing a woman in a progressively disadvantaged position. Despite its responsibility for immigration, the Canadian government is minimally involved in the provision of direct services to immigrants. Traditionally, it has relied on the voluntary sector (for example, family networks and ethnic communities) to provide the assistance and services needed by newcomers. Even today, state responsibility for services to immigrants is largely interpreted by federal departments to mean support for voluntary organizations through funding to community groups and ethnic organizations. Apart from a few statutory services, social assistance is the responsibility of provincial governments; eligibility criteria for various programs thus differ from province to province. In general, family-class immigrants are ineligible for most forms of state assistance during the five- to ten-year sponsorship period.[12] They cannot obtain family benefits, welfare, and other benefits unless there is a break in the sponsorship.

For an immigrant woman, this may involve proving that she and her husband are legally separated; or, in the case of a relative, that the sponsor is unwilling or no longer able to support her and her children. In any event, the procedure of legally terminating this relationship is degrading and painful for both the woman and her family. [13]

The major statutory service to immigrants is full-time training in one official language and employment training for the household head. These kinds of educational programs are available free of charge. The household head obtains an allowance from the federal Department of Employment and Immigration while taking a program. Since the husband is usually designated as the "household head," most immigrant women are denied one important resource that could potentially open the door for them to better employment and educational opportunities. According to a study conducted in Saskatchewan, many women were told by immigration officials that they did not need to learn English because they were housewives. In fact, these women work in garment factories, food-processing plants, janitorial work, and other low-paying, menial jobs while their husbands go to school. [14] Thus, institutional discrimination of immigrant women is built into the statutory services for immigrants.

As "dependants," if women wish to take language and job-training programs, they or their sponsor have to pay. Frequently, the high costs of these programs render them inaccessible to immigrant women. In terms of job-training programs, a minimum of Grade 8 English, or the equivalent, is required. Most immigrant women from the non-English-speaking world are automatically excluded by this admission criterion. [15] Thus, in many cases, educational programs are more of a hindrance than a help to non-English-speaking, non-white immigrant women. This is how sexist and racist assumptions are manifested in the institutional processes of our society.

Since 1986, as a result of agitation by ethnic communities and immigrant women's and other human rights groups, the federal government has set aside special funding for English-language training for immigrant housewives. Child care is provided as part of this special grant program. English classes operating under this special funding are run by community organizations. And although they come a little way in meeting the needs of non-English-speaking immigrant women, many women complain that these classes provide elementary lessons only and do not facilitate their entry into the labour market. Moreover, they still do not have access to the regular programs subsidized by Employment and Immigration, unlike their male counterparts. [16] Hence, a two-tier system of privilege based on gender hierarchy is perpetuated.

Finally, the lack of recognition by Canadian institutions and employers

Table 2
Occupation by Sex and Place of Birth, 1981 Census of Canada

Occupational Classification	Males		Females	
	Born in Canada	Foreign Born	Born in Canada	Foreign Born
Total number	5,708,765	1,371,320	3,888,100	908,825
Total per cent	100.0	100.0	100.0	100.0
Managerial & Administrative	11.1	11.8	5.4	5.5
Social & Physical Sciences, Teaching	8.7	12.1	10.1	8.2
Medicine, Health, Artistic, Literary	3.0	3.8	10.2	9.7
Clerical	7.3	5.9	37.8	30.2
Sales	9.0	7.2	9.6	8.3
Service	9.2	11.2	15.3	17.6
Farming, Forestry, & Mining	9.0	4.1	2.5	2.1
Processing, Fabricating & Assembly	29.4	35.0	6.3	14.7
Transport, Equipment & Other	13.3	8.9	2.8	3.7

of women's previous education and training is an effective barrier to their participation as equal members in society. Since immigrant women lack the Canadian work experience often required by employers, gaining recognition for educational levels and professional qualifications acquired in their country of origin is an important step in (a) seeking jobs in the primary labour market, and (b) upgrading their training and skills in Canada. The Saskatchewan study indicates that, while it is relatively easy for women to obtain recognition for lower levels of education, such as elementary or secondary education, gaining recognition for university, postgraduate, vocational, and professional training is much more difficult. Women wishing to take graduate classes are expected to take some, or all, of their undergraduate classes again. Women with professional degrees and considerable expertise in their fields were denied the opportunities to

Table 2 continued

Occupational Classification	USA	UK	Southern Europe	Other Europe	Asia	Other
Total number	65,195	200,675	179,245	200,810	137,740	125,165
Total per cent	100.0	100†	100†	100.0	100.0	100.0
Managerial & Administrative	7.7	7.5	2.7	6.9	4.6	4.3
Social & Physical Sciences, Teaching	18.7	9.7	3.2	9.5	6.6	7.0
Medicine, Health, Artistic, Literary	11.5	10.4	2.9	9.9	12.3	13.9
Clerical	30.4	40.4	18.7	28.5	28.3	34.9
Sales	9.3	11.0	6.0	10.8	5.8	5.7
Service	12.9	13.1	24.2	18.3	18.7	15.6
Farming, Forestry & Mining	3.2	1.2	1.7	4.1	1.7	0.7
Processing, Fabricating & Assembly	4.0	4.4	34.6	8.9	18.3	13.8
Transport, Equipment & Other	2.3	2.4	6.1	3.1	3.7	4.1

SOURCE: Adapted from M. Boyd, "Immigrant Women in Canada" in *International Migration: The Female Experience,* ed. R.J. Simon and C.B. Brettell (Totowa, N.J.: Rowman and Allanheld, 1986), 55.
† Figures rounded.

work until they passed expensive examinations that were designed to limit the intake of foreign graduates into Canadian professions. [17]

According to the study, recognition of their upper-level education was reported by only four out of the ninety-five women interviewed. The four women credited this to the fact that their previous education had been in British or U.S. universities. The fact that women who received their educational credentials from Britain and the United States were given preferential treatment suggests racist assumptions in the accreditation process as well as in Canada's dominant relation to less developed parts of the world. The findings of this study are corroborated by other research. [18] As we will see in the next section, these procedures help to keep immigrant women in marginal positions in the paid labour force, and they contribute to their sense of dependence, isolation, and powerlessness.

Immigrant Women's Labour-Force Participation

The legal barriers in our institutions have a negative impact on immigrant women's participation in the paid labour force. In addition, the fact that the Canadian labour market is segregated by gender and ethnicity serves to exacerbate their experiences. This is not the place to provide a detailed account of the structure of the labour market. Simply put, a segregated labour market refers to the fact that some jobs are "reserved" for women and ethnic/racial minorities, and some for white, English-speaking men.[19] In examining the organization of the labour force, we see how racism and sexism as systems of inequality come into play to keep immigrant women captive in a supposedly free society.

Immigrant women in Canada appear to be concentrated in the upper and lower echelons of the occupational hierarchy, either in highly skilled professional jobs or in job ghettos.[20] (See Table 2.) This characterization is deceptive, however, because it glosses over differences among women who immigrate to Canada. Taking a closer look at these statistics, we see that women holding managerial, administrative, and professional positions (for example, in medicine, the social and physical sciences, the arts) are from Britain and the United States. In everyday life they are not seen as "immigrant women." By contrast, women from Southern Europe, Asia, and other parts of the globe tend to concentrate in the service, processing, fabricating, and assembly sectors of Canadian industry.[21]

Non-white immigrants in general are disadvantaged in a competitive labour market in which "Canadian" (that is, English-speaking) training and work experience are major determinants for entry into occupational classifications. Many non-white immigrants, even those who were in professional and highly skilled technical occupations in their home countries, have to take lower positions because of the lack of recognition of their qualifications and credentials by Canadian governments and employers.[22] Women's experience is exacerbated due to sex segregation in the Canadian labour market. In her research on the Portuguese community, Alison Boulter found that a female immigrant's first job in Canada, usually a low-skilled menial job, is treated as her Canadian experience, and she is subsequently locked into similar kinds of jobs.[23] Independent immigrants are at least eligible for state-subsidized educational programs that may provide them with an avenue of upward mobility. For immigrant women who are family-class immigrants, even this alternative is barred to them. This fact, coupled with their family responsibilities and obligations, means that their choice of jobs and opportunities are severely limited. They are forced to find paid employment in what economists refer to as the "marginal" or "secondary" labour market and are restricted to a separate and captive labour pool.[24]

Non-English-speaking and non-white immigrant women are commonly recruited into three kinds of services and industries. First, they are recruited into private domestic and janitorial services by doctors, lawyers, managers, and the like. Although this kind of employment is usually low-paid and without labour-standards protection, it suits the requirements of immigrant women because it can be fitted into their schedule of housework and child care more easily than jobs with more rigid schedules.[25] As well, they do not have to use English as part of their work. Increasingly, women from Asian and Southern European countries are recruited to industrial home-sewing, doing piece work in similarly isolated conditions within their own homes.[26] Second, immigrant women are found in the lower strata of the service industries, including restaurants, janitorial and cleaning services, and the food industry. Third, they are found in the lower echelons of the manufacturing industries, such as light manufacturing in textiles and garments, in plastic factories, and in the retail trade. Frequently they are hired either by small operations owned by ethnic entrepreneurs (such as small retail stores, supermarkets, delicatessens) in ethnic neighbourhoods or by large institutions (factories and hotels) employing over a hundred workers. In the case of large institutions, the size of the industry or business seems to be important in determining whether immigrant women will be hired, because it is essential that other employees in the workplace speak the same language as the new employees. Apart from businesses run by ethnic entrepreneurs, smaller companies are less likely to hire non-English-speaking immigrants because there is less likelihood that other employees can speak their language.[27]

The jobs open to immigrant women have been described as "unskilled and dead-end." But in our study of the organization of job ghettos of immigrant women, Tania Das Gupta and I found that to procure these jobs, immigrant women must have a variety of general, interchangeable skills that they have developed from housekeeping and childrearing. These jobs are available on a short-term, temporary, or even on an emergency basis. Working hours are also extremely irregular, ranging from a temporary, on-call basis in domestic and kitchen work to shift work in factories and hotels. Very few of these women, with the exception of those in the garment and textile industries, are protected by labour standards legislation and union contracts. Fringe benefits, such as medical and pension plans, are not provided.[28]

The story of Maria, a fifty-nine-year-old semi-retired worker, epitomizes the experience of many non-English-speaking immigrant women in the "captive labour force."[29] Maria came to Canada in 1955 with her husband and five children. They were tenant farmers in southern Italy and had gone bankrupt. They were sponsored as immigrants to Canada by Maria's brother, and Maria held a variety of jobs after arriving. Two days after the family arrived in Toronto, she got a job in a restaurant washing dishes. For ten years, Maria's daily routine went something like this:

She started her day cleaning people's houses at eight a.m. and worked until four p.m. At four she went to work at the restaurant until one a.m. From her domestic service Maria acquired cast-off clothing for her children; from the restaurant she brought home left-over food to feed her family. On the weekend she did housework with the help of her eldest daughter, who was responsible for looking after the younger children. She also did the shopping and banking on weekends.

Maria did stay home for a couple of years after the birth of her sixth child. Then she went back to work because the family needed the money. At one time she got a job cleaning in a bank, and she would go to work between four and eight in the morning, before the bank employees arrived. She got home just in time for her oldest daughter to leave for school. She stayed home during the day looking after the baby and went around cleaning houses and offices again at night. Maria is proud that she now has a nice house and that her children all had a good education. At the time of the interview she was still working as a cleaner in a textile factory. "Now," said Maria contentedly, "I go to work because I enjoy it. When I am tired, I go home."

Maria's experience reveals that the "benefits" non-English-speaking immigrant women receive from their jobs are dependent upon good personal relationships with employers or supervisors. As individual workers, they have few rights. The wages they earn are inadequate to maintain themselves and their families. As workers they are completely unprotected and vulnerable to exploitation.

Occasionally in the garment industry, if a woman shows initiative, works hard, and learns a bit of English quickly, she may become an assistant to the supervisor. But most often women are confined to operating sewing machines. The more prestigious positions, such as garment-cutting and supervisory positions, are usually occupied by men, and women are rarely promoted to them. Thus, although more research on the hiring and promotion policies of businesses and industries is necessary, the effects of the policies are clear: immigrant women are confined to the bottom layers of the labour force, with the worst working conditions and wages. The jobs they occupy are those that other workers are in a position not to take.[31]

When we consider how immigrant women are locked into job ghettos, we cannot overlook the role of labour unions in maintaining a segregated labour force. Most of the jobs occupied by immigrant women, with the exception of about 40 per cent of those in the textile and garment industry, are non-unionized. In her study on immigrant women in the labour force, Sheila Arnopoulos found that most of the unions that have organized the textile and garment trade are weak. Some of them have a long history of collusion with management.[31] Apart from the problems of organizing the sectors of business and industry where immigrant women are concentrated, until recently most labour unions have not made a concerted effort to organize women workers in general, and immigrant women workers in particular.[32]

To understand the historical animosity between the labour movement and immigrants, we must refer back to immigration policies. The goals of those policies and of organized labour have always been antagonistic. Immigration policies are designed to meet the demands of industries by allowing workers with specialized and general skills to enter Canada, thereby helping to depress wages by increasing the competition for jobs. To protect themselves from excessive exploitation, Canadian workers band together to form labour unions, thereby replacing competition with co-operation. With sufficient numerical strength, organized labour can demand higher wages and better working conditions. In the past male workers organized by excluding or selectively organizing women, ethnic minorities, and children, thus contributing to the formation of a segregated labour force.[33]

Although there are still gaps in our knowledge in this area, recently published materials have shed light on the relationship between the labour movement and women workers.[34] In her study on women in trade unions in British Columbia during the first two decades of the twentieth century, Marie Campbell found that in attempting to protect themselves against competition and employers' exploitation, white Canadian male workers used racist and sexist tactics in organizing to exclude other workers, namely immigrants, women, Native peoples, and children, from their occupations. They organized these groups into a relatively cheap labour pool that did not pose a threat to the male labour force. When women were organized into unions, it was done to exclude Chinese and Japanese workers, thus promoting racism within the union movement. Union practices were sexist in the sense that women's problems were not reflected in union demands. Women workers were consistently paid lower wages than men. The leadership was more concerned about women's morality and health than about bargaining for an adequate living wage on their behalf.[35] As a result of this tradition in our union history, many jobs in the lower echelons of the labour market remain unorganized to this day.

In sectors where organizing efforts have taken place or are still taking place, union organizers are frequently unaware of the critical needs of immigrant women, whose hesitation and reluctance to participate in union activities are interpreted as apathy or a manifestation of traditionalism and backwardness.[36] The point is not to negate the important contribution of the union movement in bringing about higher wages and better working conditions for immigrant women, but to draw attention to the fact that these women have been systematically disadvantaged both in the labour market and other institutions. There are concrete barriers that curtail the options available to them.

We cannot understand immigrant women's experiences today without considering the effects of the free-trade agreement between Canada and the United States. According to Marjorie Cohen, a leading feminist economist, the sectors most likely to be harmed by the deal are manufacturing (especially the garment industry) and the service sector. [37] These are sectors in which women, including immigrant women, are concentrated. Although it is impossible yet to assess the direct impact of free trade on these industries, we know that in the textile and garment industries there have been bankruptcies and plant closures that are disrupting the livelihood of immigrant women. In the unionized sector of the garment industry in Toronto alone, there were at least seven plant closures in 1991, affecting a great number of workers. [38]

To soften the impact of massive plant closures and layoffs, the federal government, in co-operation with provincial governments, is allocating funding for "industrial adjustments" and job search programs. [39] However, while some of these programs may solve short-term employment problems for workers, they do not address the structural reorganization of the labour market. Meanwhile, organized labour, together with immigrant groups and educational institutions, is developing strategies (such as retraining of workers) to counter progressive job loss experienced in certain sectors of the labour market. [40] These are positive steps, but they confirm the vulnerability of immigrant women workers in these industrial sectors.

The Organization of Domestic Labour

Women's work in the home – their domestic labour – is often seen to belong to the "private" domain and as unconnected to the "public" work world. It has been undervalued because it doesn't directly bring in money. Moreover, domestic labour, popularly known as "housework," is seen to entail the same tasks for all women. In this section, we will discuss how women's domestic work is *transformed* as a result of the immigration process; it cannot be understood without reference to the social organization of Canadian society and immigrant families' economic circumstances, notably the husband's paid labour outside the home.

For the purpose of this discussion I am assuming the household to be the so-called "nuclear family" because this is a common family form among immigrant families in Canada regardless of people's household patterns prior to immigration. The nuclear family form is partly a product of Canadian immigration policy, which only recognizes certain members of an extended household as "family-class" immigrants (for example, the spouse and children under age eighteen).

While the home may be a place to rest, eat, and relax for the male worker, it is not merely a refuge for the woman. This is not to say that the home is not a source of support for her, but to suggest that it also presupposes a work process that has to be continuously managed and organized. The work of holding a family together is essentially the work of the woman. It is her labour that produces the material basis for the other family members' enjoyment: the planning and preparation of meals as well as the emotional and material support she gives to other members of the household. The labour involved in sustaining a family is, in many ways, common to all women across class and ethnic groups. What is special about the work of immigrant women is that when immigrant families come to Canada, the woman's work in the home is *intensified*. In our study of immigrant housewives in Toronto, women complained about the difficulties of doing housework properly in Canada.[41] For some reason, housework seemed more difficult; life seemed more hectic; there were more worries, from the husband's paid employment to the kinds of troubles that children could get themselves into. Together with this work intensification is a concomitant increase in, and indeed enforcement of, the woman's dependence on her husband.

How does this occur? Our study discovered that when immigrant families come to Canada they become totally immersed in a money economy. This does not mean that families were untouched by industrialization and a monetary economy before immigration. Indeed, industrialization has long disrupted traditional peasant economies. It is precisely the penetration of a wage economy into the farm economy that forces many immigrants to leave their home countries in the first place.[42] The pattern of the worker who goes from industrial centre to industrial centre in search of wage work, leaving his (and sometimes her) spouse and children in the village or home town, is a common phenomenon in less developed parts of the world. However, in this kind of situation, women's work in the home is not fully incorporated into a money economy and appropriated by modern industries. To a larger extent, the woman remains in control of the *pace* of work within the family unit. Her labour is directly visible in the products consumed in the home, such as the bread and noodles that she makes. In many instances she may also produce a variety of products for home consumption, such as food from a garden or the children's clothes. In a rural or semi-rural setting, the woman's work is indispensable in sustaining the economy of the household unit.

In Canada the production of family goods has been largely taken out of the home and appropriated by business enterprises. The immigrant housewife finds herself becoming increasingly reliant on consumer goods, not only because they reduce her workload and make her work easier, but also, and more importantly, because the material conditions in Canada do not lend themselves to the production of subsistence goods within a single-family unit. Practically everything that a housewife produces or needs for her work, from dinners to laundry service, can be purchased with money outside the home. There is a preponderance of services available in the city, from dry-cleaning facilities to fast-food outlets, which replace the services that used to be obtained only in the home. This is a process Margrit Eichler identifies as the "industrialization of housework."[43] Virtually overnight, then, immigrants are forced to become consumers. At the same time, because many working-class immigrant men work in the lower echelons of the male occupational hierarchy, their wages are not always enough to sustain the family economy. Thus many immigrant women have to produce some of the basic foodstuffs, such as canned foods, themselves. These efforts are sometimes interpreted simply as an exhibition of traditionalism by other Canadians. As a matter of fact, it is a way of cutting down costs when family income does not permit the indiscriminate purchasing of processed foodstuffs.[44]

Together with this increasing commercialization of household products is the need for what were previously luxury goods, such as colour televisions, automobiles, and a paraphernalia of electrical appliances from dishwashers to electric razors. In Canada these items are not luxuries; they are considered by many to be basic to a normal standard of living. Thus, whereas previously only the wage-earner was directly tied to a money economy, when the immigrant family comes to Canada the entire family is immersed in it. Everything now requires money. In addition immigrants also find themselves absorbed into an elaborate formal credit system, either through buying a house or a car, or simply through the use of credit cards.[45]

To acquire the goods and services necessary for maintaining a minimum living standard in Canada, immigrants have to work doubly hard in the paid labour force. Thus there is a much greater need for money in the household. Since women's work in the home does not directly bring in a wage, it does not have the same importance socially or in the family. The family's reliance on a wage puts an immigrant woman in a dependent position vis-à-vis her husband, because she and the children rely on his wage for their livelihood. This dependency is a product of the immigration process, in addition to the institutional practices (in our immigration law, for instance) that create and enforce her dependency. Because the wage is paid to the husband, it obscures the fact that it is not just for him; it is for him to maintain his wife and children. He considers it his money because it is paid to him as an individual, and in this process the woman's work in the home is seen merely as her private service to a man. At the same time, because of the work location of working-class immigrant men (namely, in the bottom rungs of the male job hierarchy), their wages are inadequate to meet all the family expenses, and they have to depend heavily on their wives' services to sustain the family. Clearly, the woman's unpaid labour is an essential component in the maintenance of the immigrant worker and the immigrant family. [46]

Women's work in Canada, then, is determined *industrially* by the husband's paid work outside the home. Because the husband is seen as the major wage-earner in the family (because it is he who is recruited into the Canadian labour force), his needs and demands come to dictate and organize the schedule of immigrant women's work in the home. The woman's major responsibility is to ensure his earning power, so that each day he can return to the paid work force. Her work in the home must be oriented to this consideration. If there are other wage-earners in the household, then she must cater to their needs and demands as well. In this connection, children's activities in schools also impinge on housework, because the mother in Canada is seen to be responsible for how her children present themselves and perform in school. [47] Furthermore, changes of a material kind shape and determine the woman's work. Housework in Canada is privatized in the sense that it is conducted within the confines of the single-family unit. The layout of houses and apartments does not permit the co-operation of neighbours and friends in doing housework. While the privatization of basic utilities, such as running hot and cold water and electricity, is meant to and does cut down on the amount of labour that individual housewives expend on housework, it also prevents and makes irrelevant the co-operative network that women have traditionally established in industrially less advanced settings. An account by an immigrant woman illustrates this vividly:

> The structure of housework for the women in the peasant neighbourhood, whose husbands have already migrated away to earn a family wage, was far more communal than it could ever be here, if only because of the physical feature of the neighbourhood. When I was growing up, we all lived on a block. And inside the block it was hollow. There was a yard. So there was a yard culture. And everyday, you would do certain things, wash or iron, whatever. Ways were devised for things to be shared. It also had a built-in daycare system. The children had to play in the yard, not on the street. The women would kind of look after the children, informally, you know. You didn't appoint anyone. It just happened. It was a matter of course

because that was the place where they would go to do their laundry.[48]

In this regard, the organization of shopping and other facilities also serve to shape women's domestic labour and isolate them from each other. While the centralization of marketplaces, in the form of supermarkets, cuts down on work for middle-class and professional Canadian women, and cuts down costs for businesses, it only serves to create more work for immigrant women. This kind of shopping pattern assumes the ownership of automobiles and adequate storage facilities, such as large refrigerators and freezers. Large-scale shopping expeditions are certainly not attractive ventures for immigrant women, who do not know the language or the geography of the city and who have to subject themselves to the whims of the public transportation system, sometimes under intolerable climatic conditions.[49]

Finally, we can also come to appreciate how the possession of modern household appliances such as vacuum cleaners and washers/dryers also organizes the pace of women's work in determinate ways. All in all, immigrant women's work comes to be organized by the physical set-up of houses, distances to the market and laundry facilities, as well as, and most importantly, their husband's paid work outside the home. The autonomy they might have enjoyed previously is seriously undermined. In this new setting they have to become more dependent on the husband, both economically and practically.

While the studies cited above concern the situation of working-class immigrant women, a recent study conducted on middle-class women from Hong Kong shows that they, too, experience similar problems of isolation and alienation due to the severance of previous support networks. The same is true also for wives of business-class immigrants. Many men of this class of immigrants still have business interests back home and spend a good portion of their time away from Canada, leaving their wives to manage family affairs. This pattern exacerbates feelings of loneliness for this group of women, because many of them do not speak English and initially have little knowledge of the organization of Canadian society. Furthermore, the high cost of living in Canada prevents all but the most affluent women from purchasing services (such as domestic help) that they previously enjoyed. In this way, they share similar experiences with their working-class counterparts.[50]

All of these institutional practices, notably as they relate to immigration policy, the structure of the labour market, and the social organization of domestic labour, contribute to immigrant women's dependency and isolation in Canada. Ironically, their isolation also renders them invisible to other members of society.

Domestic Workers

While many women who work as live-in domestics are not strictly speaking landed immigrants, we cannot end this chapter without drawing attention to their situation in Canada. Like immigrant women who are non-English-speaking and of colour, they are among the most neglected and exploited groups in society.

Domestic workers, many of them women from so-called "Third World" countries such as the Caribbean islands and the Philippines, enter Canada under the Foreign Domestic Worker (FDW) program. They are here as temporary workers, issued with temporary employment authorizations for a specific period of time. Before 1981 women who came to Canada under this program had to return home when their work permits expired, unless they could secure further employment as domestic workers. Since 1981, as a result of agitation by civil rights groups and immigrant women's and domestic workers' organizations (such as INTERCEDE), they have been able to apply for landed-immigrant (permanent resident) status from within Canada after living here for two years.[51] The main criterion governing the admissibility of domestic workers as landed immigrants is self-sufficiency.[52]

It is difficult to calculate the actual number of women entering Canada under the FDW program. Employment visas are issued on a short-term basis, and workers can apply to have their visas renewed at the end of the specified period. Thus the number of visas issued does not necessarily correspond to the number of workers granted this status. According to one estimate, however, the number of women in Canada under this program is sizeable. Together with women residing in the country with student authorizations, their numbers equal those of women who are permanent residents.[53] In the early 1990s the majority of domestic workers entering Canada came from the Caribbean, the Philippines, and Europe, including Britain.[54]

Legally the working conditions of live-in domestic workers, similar to those of other workers, are governed by provincial labour legislation. That is, they have to be paid at least minimum wage and are entitled to a certain number of days off in a week and all statutory holidays. As for other workers, CPP, UIC, and income tax are deducted from their wages by the employer. In addition the employer can deduct a certain amount for room and board. At the point of employment, a contract is made between the worker and the employer through the Canada Employment Centre.[55]

In actual fact, because domestic workers work within the privacy of an employer's home, it is extremely hard to monitor and enforce labour standards. Their isolation makes this group of workers difficult to organize. There are many areas where abuse of the legislation and of the individual workers can take place. For example, since they reside on the same prem-ise as their workplace they can be called upon to perform duties beyond their regular work-hours. Like all female workers, they can be victims of sexual harassment and assault. Their situation is exacerbated because they live in the homes of their employers and are without the protection of labour unions; therefore the abuses can persist over the duration of their employment, with few avenues of recourse for the workers.[56] As well, the FDW program contains certain assumptions that disadvantage selected groups of women. We will look at some of these assumptions and explore their sexist and racist implications for domestic workers.

We cannot understand the exploitation experienced by domestic work-ers without acknowledging the lack of value attached to domestic work in general. In the first place, as we've seen, housework is undervalued for a number of reasons: because it is done in the home and does not bring in a wage; because it is done by women; and because it is not considered skilled work. The assumption that domestic work is unskilled and of little value is carried over to the status of those individuals doing the work.

This assumption is implicit in the FDW program, which treats domestic workers as a dispensable work force that does not deserve equal treatment under immigration policy. The employers of domestic workers are upper-middle-class professionals (such as doctors and lawyers) and members of the elite. Many of them require domestic help to free both spouses for par-ticipation in the paid labour force.[57] Furthermore, due to the low status, low pay, and poor conditions of domestic work, most Canadians tend to choose other jobs over domestic work, thereby creating a demand for the work. In fact upper-class households have always lamented the difficulty of securing "reliable" domestic help. It was upper-middle-class women who organized the emigration of working-class girls from Britain to Can-ada to serve as domestic workers at the end of the nineteenth century.[58] The need for these workers has always been part of the Canadian reality. Indeed, the incorporation of domestic workers as temporary workers within Canada's immigration program is the result of lobbying efforts by elite and upper-middle-class families, especially women.[59] In this instance we see how women are by no means a homogeneous group. They are divided by class and race.

When we examine the criteria according to which women can apply for domestic work and landed-immigrant status, many sexist and racist assumptions come into view. Workers are assessed based on their educa-tion, experience, skills, financial security, and social adaptation.[60] Whereas many women from Europe have formal training, including "nanny" training, this kind of formal education is unavailable in the Caribbean and the Philippines, two of the major sources of domestic workers. Thus, white European women are favoured under one of the admissibility criteria. This fact, coupled with the general lack of recognition of training from Third World countries, means that women of colour are disadvantaged in the assessment procedures. This is one way in which racism operates in a supposedly neutral and objective process. A quotation from the findings of an investigation conducted by INTERCEDE illustrates the effects of certain biases in the assessment process:

> In the London area, where all applicants are expected to be landed, the domestic workers are all single and all but one are from Europe. In the Windsor area, only one refusal is currently anticipated and the domestic worker concerned is an older woman from the Caribbean with five children. In British Columbia, there has been a decision to refuse one domestic worker to date, an older woman from the Caribbean with six dependents who has been in Canada approximately seven years.[61]

There is a recent legislative proposal (1992) that nannies entering the country should have a minimum of Grade 12 education. This legislation, if passed, would prohibit many women from the Third World from coming to Canada as domestic workers. This kind of legislative proposal would render the FDW racist in the terms in which I described systemic racism above.

Another major principle for assessing domestic workers for landed-immigrant status is proof of self-sufficiency. Implicit in this criterion is the notion that domestic work is not self-sufficient, and that domestic workers should be able to be employed outside of domestic work, in other sectors of the labour market. In the INTERCEDE investigation, one immigration official was quoted as stating: "The idea is to get people out of being domestics because the labour market demand for domestic work is unstable."[62] To facilitate self-sufficiency, domestic workers are encouraged to attend skill upgrading and training courses that would enable them to secure other employment.[63] Again, this strategy tends to favour younger women from European countries who have formal recognized education and to disadvantage older women, many of whom came from Caribbean countries and lack formal education.[64]

While the FDW program was designed, originally, to ameliorate the exploitation of temporary domestic workers (who were never granted landed-immigrant status before 1981), the situation of domestic workers nowadays has not improved significantly. The exploitative conditions under which they work are constantly contested by groups working for and with domestic workers. Unless there are structural changes to the present organization of the labour market, we can expect that the struggles of domestic workers for equal rights with other workers will continue.

Conclusion

Immigrant women and domestic workers are by no means passive victims of the legal, economic, and social processes at play in Canada. Riding on the momentum developed by the feminist movement, especially since International Women's Year in 1975, immigrant women and domestic workers have come together and organized. They are demanding their rights to equal treatment in Canadian society. Today there are immigrant women's organizations in most major centres across Canada, from lobbying groups (such as Immigrant Women of Saskatchewan), to service organizations (Toronto's Immigrant Women's Centre), to coalitions (the Ontario Immigrant Women's Association). After November 1986, out of the second National Conference on Immigrant and Visible Minority Women, a national umbrella organization, the National Organization of Immigrant and Visible Minority Women of Canada (NOIVMWC) was established to co-ordinate the organizing efforts of immigrant women's groups across the country and act as a national lobbying body. Similarly, in major cities there are organizations acting as advocates for domestic workers. INTERCEDE, for example, has gained a high profile as a national lobbying group while serving domestic workers in the Toronto area. These organizing and lobbying efforts have led to policy and programmatic changes within Canadian institutions (the FDW program is an example).

Within the feminist movement, immigrant women, together with women of colour, have begun to challenge traditional assumptions of a movement that has developed with strong middle-class and racial biases.[65] They draw attention to the fact that the demands of the feminist movement are defined according to white middle-class women's perspectives and priorities. Quoting Angela Davis, Noga Gayle points out that the emphasis on women working outside the home, one of the major efforts of the feminist movement in the 1960s and 1970s, stemmed largely from the concerns of middle-class women who had the privilege to be full-time homemakers. Immigrant and black women have always worked outside the home.[66] Similarly, feminist theories about women's oppression, based mainly on the experiences and perspectives of white women, are being challenged by immigrant women, women of colour, and Third World women.[67] They point out the Eurocentric nature of these theories and draw attention to the diversity of women on the basis of race, class, religion, and other attributes.

These debates, while ridden with tension and occasionally leading to divisions within the feminist movement, have also contributed to the development of new theories and creative alliances. Many white women's organizations, such as the National Action Committee on the Status of Women (NAC) and the Canadian Research Institute for the Advancement of Women (CRIAW), have been forced to examine their own practices and develop more inclusive approaches to organizing.

As the immigrant women's movement develops, new contradictions, tensions, and alliances are generated, both within the movement itself and in relation to the larger society. While the challenges posed by immigrant women and other minority groups (such as the aboriginal peoples) create discomfort among members of the dominant groups, we should remember that it is these challenges and struggles, and societal responses to them, that sustain the ideal of Canadian democracy as a reality.

Roxana Ng

NOTES

Thanks are due to the editors for their comments on the original chapter; to Felicita Villasin and Columbia Tarope Diaz of INTERCEDE for sharing with me information and materials on domestic workers; and to B.J. Cook for assisting with manuscript preparation.

1. *See*: Jackie Lay, "To Columbia on the Tynemouth: The Emigration of Single Women and Girls in 1862," in Cathy Less and Beth Latham, eds., *In Her Own Right: Selected Essays on Women's History in B.C.* (Victoria: Camosun College, 1980), 19-42; Barbara Roberts, "Sex, Politics and Religion: Controversies in Female Immigration Reform Work in Montreal, 1881-1919," *Atlantis* 6, no. 1 (1980), 26-38.
2. *See*: Warren Kalbach, *The Effect of Immigration on Population* (Ottawa: Department of Manpower and Immigration, 1974), and Freda Hawkins, *Canada and Immigration: Public Policy and Public Concern* (Montreal: McGill-Queen's University Press, 1972).
3. *See*: Alma Estable, "Immigrant Women in Canada: Current Issues," in original background paper prepared for the Canadian Advisory Council on the Status of Women, March 1986; Jean Leonard Elliott and Augie Fleras, "Immigration and the Canadian Ethnic Mosaic," in Peter S. Li, ed., *Race and Ethnic Relations in Canada* (Toronto: Oxford University Press, 1990), 51-76.
4. Anthony H. Richmond, "Immigration and Racial Prejudice in Britain and Canada," in Jean L. Elliott, ed., *Two Nations, Many Cultures: Ethnic Groups in Canada* (Scarborough, Ont.: Prentice-Hall, 1979), 290-310; and Doreen M. Indra, "Canada's Immigration: A Retrospective Look at the Past Ten Years," *RIKKA* 4, nos. 3&4 (1977), 3-10.
5. John Porter, *The Vertical Mosaic: An Analysis of Social Class and Power in Canada* (Toronto: University of Toronto Press, 1965).
6. *See, for example*: Irving Abella and Harold Troper, *None Is Too Many* (Toronto: Lester & Orpen Dennys, 1982); and Doreen M. Indra, *Southeast Asian Refugee Settlement in Canada: A Research Bibliography* (Ottawa: Asian Studies Association, Carleton University, 1984).
7. See Elliott and Fleras, "Immigration and the Canadian Ethnic Mosaic."
8. There are two additional categories of newcomers: the conventional refugees and the designated class of immigrants. The latter group refers to those persons displaced from their homeland, such as the "boat people" from Indo-China and exiles from some Latin American countries. They are either government-sponsored or privately sponsored (for example, by the churches or ethnic organizations). Furthermore, people who enter Canada to work on work permits are also governed by provisions in the Immigration Act. Their stay in Canada is tied strictly to a specific job (such as domestic work for a particular employer), and they are not considered landed immigrants. In the fall of 1990, the Minister of Employment and Immigration announced a five-year

immigration plan. Although it is too early to assess the impact of this plan, it is clear that its purpose is to make use of immigration to recruit a larger proportion of skilled workers as Canada undergoes yet another round of economic restructuring. *See*: *Annual Report to Parliament: Immigration Plan for 1991-1995* (Ottawa: Immigration Canada, October 1990).

9. *Immigration to Canada: A Statistical Overview* (Ottawa: Immigration Canada, 1989).

10. *See, for instance*: Janet Salaff, *Working Daughters of Hong Kong: Filial Piety or Power in the Family* (Cambridge: Cambridge University Press, 1981) and Guida Man, "Dispelling the Media Image: Women in Recent Middle-Class Chinese Immigrant Families from Hong Kong," paper presented at the 33rd International Congress of Asian and North African Studies, University of Toronto, August 1990.

11. For a discussion of changing household patterns, *see*: Nancy Jackson, *Stress on School + Stress on Family = Distress for Children* (Ottawa: Canadian Teachers' Federation, 1983). For the situation of immigrant families, *see*: Roxana Ng and Judith Ramirez, *Immigrant Housewives in Canada* (Toronto: Immigrant Women's Centre, 1981). For a discussion on the segregated labour market, *see*: Pat Armstrong and Hugh Armstrong, *The Double Ghetto: Canadian Women and Their Segregated Work* (Toronto: McClelland and Stewart, 1978, 2nd edition, 1984).

12. The guidelines for social assistance in relation to landed immigrants vary from province to province.

13. *See*: Ng and Ramirez, *Immigrant Housewives in Canada*, 49-55.

14. Immigrant Women of Saskatchewan, *Doubly Disadvantaged: The Women Who Immigrate to Canada* (Regina, 1985).

15. Brenda Janke and Ronnie Yaron, *A Report on Conditions in the Labour Market and Training Opportunities for Non-English Speaking Immigrant Women in Metro Toronto* (Toronto: Working Women Community Centre, 1979); and Roxana Ng and Tania Das Gupta, "The Organization of the Non-English Speaking Immigrant Women Labour Force," a preliminary report to the Wollstonecraft Research Group, Ontario Institute for Studies in Education, March, 1980.

16. Immigrant Women of Saskatchewan, *Doubly Disadvantaged*.

17. Ibid.

18. Angela W. Djao and Roxana Ng, "Structured Isolation: Immigrant Women in Saskatchewan," in Kathleen Storrie, ed., *Women: Isolation and Bonding: Readings in the Ecology of Gender* (Toronto: Methuen, 1987); Estable, *Immigrant Women in Canada*.

19. *See*: Ng and Ramirez, *Immigrant Housewives in Canada*, 55-60. For a discussion of the development of a segregated labour force, *see*: Armstrong and Armstrong, *The Double Ghetto*; and Paul Phillips and E. Phillips, *Women and Work: Inequality in the Labour Market* (Toronto: James Lorimer, 1983).

20. Sheila Arnopoulos, *Problems of Immigrant Women in the Canadian Labour Force*

(Ottawa: Advisory Council on the Status of Women, 1979); and Monica Boyd, "Immigrant Women in Canada," in R.J. Simon and C.B. Brettell, eds., *International Migration: The Female Experience* (Totawa, N.J.: Rowman & Allanheld, 1986), 45-61.

21. Boyd, "Immigrant Women in Canada," 56.
22. Rachael Epstein, Maggi Trebble and Roxana Ng, "The Social Organization of Family Violence: An Ethnography of Immigrant Experience in Canada," a report to the Non-medical Use of Drugs Directorate, Health and Welfare Canada, 1979; Djao and Ng, "Structured Isolation."
23. Alison I. Boulter, "Constituting Ethnic Difference: An Ethnography of the Portuguese Immigrant Experience in Vancouver," M.A. thesis, Dept. of Anthropology and Sociology, University of British Columbia, 1978.
24. Phillips and Phillips, *Women and Work*; Roxana Ng and Tania Das Gupta, "Nation Builders? The Captive Labour Force of Non-English Speaking Immigrant Women," *Canadian Woman Studies* 3, no. 1 (1981), 83-85.
25. Ng and Ramirez, *Immigrant Housewives in Canada*; Ng and Das Gupta, "The Organization of the Non-English Speaking Immigrant Women Labour Force."
26. *See*: Laura C. Johnson, *The Seam Allowance* (Toronto: Women's Educational Press, 1982).
27. Arnopoulos, *Problems of Immigrant Women*; Janke and Yaron, *A Report on Conditions in the Labour Market*; Ng and Ramirez, *Immigrant Housewives in Canada*, 55-56; Ng and Das Gupta, "The Organization of the Non-English Speaking Immigrant Women Labour Force"; Boyd, "Immigrant Women in Canada."
28. Ng and Das Gupta, "Nation Builders?"
29. The interview on which this story is based was conducted in connection with the study by Ng and Ramirez, *Immigrant Housewives in Canada*, 47.
30. Arnopoulos, *The Problems of Immigrant Women*; Ng and Ramirez, *Immigrant Housewives in Canada*, 57-58. For an excellent case study of a garment factory, *see*: Charlene Gannage, *Double Day, Double Bind: Women Garment Workers* (Toronto: The Women's Press, 1986).
31. Arnopoulos, *Problems of Immigrant Women*.
32. *See*: Julie White, *Women and Unions* (Ottawa: Advisory Council on the Status of Women, 1980); and Winnie Ng, "Organizing Workers in the Garment Industry" in *By and About Immigrant Women*, information package (Toronto: Women Working with Immigrant Women and Cross-Cultural Communication Centre, October 1979).
33. Ng and Ramirez, *Immigrant Housewives in Canada*, 58.
34. *See, for example*: White, *Women and Unions*; Cynthia Cockburn, *Brothers: Male Dominance and Technological Change* (London: Pluto Press, 1983); Marie L. Campbell, "Sexism in British Columbia Trade Unions, 1900-1920," in Kess and Latham, *In Her Own Right*, 167-186.

35. *See*: Marie Campbell, "Sexism in British Columbia Trade Unions."

36. Ng, "Organizing Women in the Garment Industry." These stereotypes of immigrant women are also prevalent in the women's movement; *see*: Winnie Ng, "Immigrant Women: The Silent Partners of the Women's Movement," in Maureen Fitzgerald, C. Guberman and M. Wolfe, eds., *Still Ain't Satisfied! Canadian Feminism Today* (Toronto: Women's Educational Press, 1982), 249-256.

37. Marjorie Griffin Cohen, *Free Trade and the Future of Women's Work: Manufacturing and Service Industries* (Toronto: Garamond Press, 1987).

38. I am indebted to Tariq Kidwai, Co-ordinator of the Apparel and Textile Action Centre, and Alex Dagg of the International Ladies Garment Workers' Union (ILGWU) for this information. The number quoted here is conservative. It is impossible to obtain statistics about the actual number of plant closures and job losses because smaller shops may not be recorded in official statistics when they close. The ILGWU only keeps statistics on its own shops.

39. An example of this is the South Etobicoke Centre for Experienced Workers, which organizes a job-search program for unemployed workers who are on UIC benefits and over the age of forty (Etobicoke *Guardian*, Sunday, January 19, 1992, 1).

40. For example, the Apparel and Textile Action Committee (ATAC) was set up in August 1991 to develop strategies for the training needs of workers in the garment and textile sector. This committee, funded by the Industrial Adjustment Program, was initiated by the ILGWU and the Amalgamated Clothing and Textile Workers Union (ACTWU). I am thankful to the Committee for permission to use this as an example.

41. Ng and Ramirez, *Immigrant Housewives in Canada*. This discussion appeared in an article by Roxana Ng, "Immigrant Housewives in Canada: A Methodological Note," *Atlantis* 8, no.1 (1982), 113.

42. For a theorization of this relation, *see*: Saskia Sassen-Koob, "Toward a Conceptualization of Immigrant Labour," *Social Problems* 29, no. 1 (1981), 65-85; Folker Frobel, Jurgen Heinrichs and Otto Kreye, *The New International Division of Labour* (Cambridge: Cambridge University Press, 1977, translated into English in 1980).

43. Margrit Eichler, "The Industrialization of Housework," GROW Paper no. 3 (Toronto: OISE, 1976).

44. Ng and Ramirez, *Immigrant Housewives in Canada*, 28-29.

45. I am not suggesting that this is true only in Canada. Certainly, as capitalist development penetrates Third World countries, this pattern of commercialization of the home becomes globalized. I am using this description here to draw attention to the changing material requirements brought about by this process.

46. Ng and Ramirez, *Immigrant Housewives in Canada*, 29-30.

47. *See*: Jackson, "Stress on School + Stress on Family"; A. Marguerite Cassin

and Alison I. Griffith, "Class and Ethnicity: Producing the Difference that Counts," *Canadian Ethnic Studies* 8, no. 1 (1981), 109-129.

48. Quoted in Ng and Ramirez, *Immigrant Housewives in Canada*, 32.

49. Ibid., 39. *See also*: Djao and Ng, "Structured Isolation."

50. Man, "Dispelling the Media Image"; Guida Man, "The Experience of Women in Recent Middle-Class Chinese Immigrant Families from Hong Kong," paper presented at the Canadian Women's Studies Association Annual Meeting, Kingston, Ontario, May 1991.

51. *See*: Makeda Silvera, *Silenced* (Toronto: Williams-Wallace Publishers, 1983), 17; Monica Boyd, "Migrant Women in Canada: Profiles and Policies," an immigration research working paper prepared for the Policy Analysis Directorate, Immigration Policy Branch, Employment and Immigration Canada, March 1987, 4.

52. Boyd, "Migrant Women," 5.

53. Ibid., 3.

54. Ibid.

55. INTERCEDE (Toronto Organization for Domestic Workers' Rights), Orientation Kit for Newly-Arrived Foreign Domestic Workers, A-1.

56. The moving accounts of Caribbean domestic workers' experiences are compiled in the collection by Makeda, *Silenced*. *See also*: Abigail B. Bakan, "The International Market for Female Labour and Individual Deskilling: West Indian Women Workers in Toronto," *Canadian Journal of Latin American and Caribbean Studies* 12, no. 24 (1987), 69-85; Sedef Arat-Koc, "'In the Privacy of Our Own Home': Foreign Domestic Workers as Solution to the Crisis in the Domestic Sphere in Canada," *Studies in Political Economy* 28 (Spring 1989), 33-58.

57. Rachel Epstein, "Domestic Workers: The Experience in B.C.," in Linda Briskin and Lynda Yanz, eds., *Union Sisters: Women in the Labour Movement* (Toronto: The Women's Press, 1983), 225; Noga Gayle, "Black Women's Reality and Feminism: An Exploration of Race and Gender," in Dawn Currie and Valerie Raoul, eds., *Anatomy of Gender: Women's Struggle for the Body* (Ottawa: Carleton University Press, 1991). Thanks are due to Noga Gayle for early access to this article.

58. *See*: Jackie Lay, "To Columbia on the Tynemouth."

59. *See*: Agnes Calliste, "Canada's Immigration Policy and Domestics from the Caribbean: The Second Domestic Scheme," in Jesse Vorst et al., eds., *Race, Class, Gender: Bonds and Barriers* (Toronto: Between the Lines with the Society for Socialist Studies, 1989), 133-165; Epstein, "Domestic Workers"; Silvera, *Silenced*.

60. Boyd, "Migrant Women," 5.

61. INTERCEDE, "Implementation of the Special Policy on Foreign Domestic Workers: Findings and Recommendations for Change," a brief to the Minister of Employment and Immigration Canada, March 1983, 6.

62. INTERCEDE, "Implementation of the Special Policy," 6; *see also*: Boyd, *Migrant Women in Canada*, 5.

63. Boyd, *Migrant Women in Canada*, 5.

64. INTERCEDE, "Implementation of the Special Policy," 3.

65. *See, for example*: Kathleen Jamieson, "Sisters under the Skin: An Exploration of the Implications of Feminist-Materialist Perspective on Research," *Canadian Ethnic Studies* 13, no. 1 (1981), 130-143; various 1986 issues of the *International Women's Day Committee Newsletter* and *Cayenne: A Socialist Feminist Bulletin*, both from Toronto.

66. Gayle, "Black Women's Reality and Feminism."

67. See the critiques in various articles in Vorst, *Race, Class, Gender* and in Gayle, "Black Women's Reality and Feminism."

SUGGESTED READINGS

Arnopoulos, Sheila McLeod, *Problems of Immigrant Women in the Canadian Labour Force*. Ottawa: Canadian Advisory Council on the Status of Women, 1979.

Barndt, Deborah, Ferne Cristall, and dian marino, *Getting There: Producing Photostories with Immigrant Women*. Toronto: Between The Lines, 1982.

Boyd, Monica, "Immigrant Women in Canada," in R.J. Simon and C.B. Brettell, eds., *International Migration: The Female Experience*. Totowa, N.J.: Rowan & Allanheld, 1986.

Cohen, Marjorie Griffin, *Free Trade and the Future of Women's Work: Manufacturing and Service Industries*. Toronto: Garamond Press, 1987.

Estable, Alma, *Immigrant Women in Canada: Current Issues*. A background paper prepared for the Canadian Advisory Council on the Status of Women, March 1986.

Ng, Roxana, "Immigrant Housewives in Canada: A Methodological Note," *Atlantis* 8, no. 1 (1982).

Ng, Roxana, and Judith Ramirez, *Immigrant Housewives in Canada*. Toronto: Immigrant Women's Centre, 1981.

Silvera, Makeda, *Silenced*. Toronto: Williams-Wallace Publishers Inc., 1983.

Special Issue on "Ethnicity and Femininity," Danielle Juteau-Lee and Barbara Roberts, *Canadian Ethnic Studies*, 13, 1 (1981).

Special Issue, "Immigrant Women," ed. Marguerite Cassin and Jennifer Newton, *Multiculturalism*, 2, 4 (1979).

Special Issue, "Immigrant Women," ed. Roxana Ng, Himani Bannerji, Joyce Scane, Didi Khayatt, Makeda Silvera, *Resources for Feminist Research* (RFR), 16, no. 1 (1987).

Vorst, Jesse, et al., eds., *Race, Class, Gender: Bonds and Barriers*. Toronto: Society for Socialist Studies and Garamond Press, second revised edition, 1991.

Chapter Nine

Women and Traditional Culture

≈≈≈≈≈≈≈≈≈≈≈≈≈≈≈≈≈≈≈≈≈≈≈≈≈≈≈≈≈≈≈≈≈≈

Early in life many Canadians learn that little girls wear pink and are made of "sugar and spice and everything nice" and little boys wear blue and are made of "snips (or snakes) and snails and puppy dog tails." Such forms of folklore contribute to the symbolic process of forming a gender identity. Women and men are born with anatomical differences that determine their biological sex, but folklore contributes to the elaborate development of their feminine and masculine personalities and traits. Folkloric aspects of that gendered construction are informally passed on from one generation to another and take expressive or aesthetic forms in stories, songs, jokes, quilts, family celebrations, and much more. Traditional culture – a term we use interchangeably with folklore to indicate that we include material as well as oral forms – and women are sometimes intertwined, as in the well-known expression "old wives' tales." In that phrase are the usual negative associations and connotations of both traditional and women's culture;[1] both tend to be relegated to the insubstantial, the trivial, and the objectively false. But that is not the only possible interpretation of "old wives' tales," or of women, or of folklore.

In this chapter we offer alternative views. We are convinced that "old wives' tales" and other forms of women's folklore are accurate and significant interpretations of women's experiences and are central to an understanding of women's culture, as well as to a demystification of women's place in the world. Women's everyday lives and their creative expressions are linked in traditional culture. Women's own traditions, and the depiction of women in traditional genres, are our subjects.[2]

Before we go on to detail women's traditional culture in Canada, we want to turn to the role of women in collecting and documenting folklore in this country and to how traditional culture has served to display and re-create images, notions, and positionings of women in society. We also discuss how women's culture contests stereotypical perspectives, and we reflect upon what folklore has to say about the question of women's place in public and private sociocultural spheres.

The Recovery Process of Identifying, Collecting, and Interpreting Women's Folklore

The idea that women possess and perform folklore is not new. In fact, if asked to describe women's folklore, many people first think of older, even archaic forms like quilting, traditional recipes, or home remedies. But everyone, even now, has some folklore they share with others in their particular sociocultural groups. Folklore has been described as "the ways in which we are creative, clever, and artistic in our everyday lives."[3] Such a broad notion does not really specify what folklore is, but it gives a good general idea of the range of material in traditional culture. Folklore could also be described as whatever folklorists study, which tends to be:

> the *communal* (a group or collective), the *common* (the everyday rather than the extraordinary), the *informal* (in relation to the formal and institutional), the *marginal* (in relation to the centres of power and privilege), the *personal* (communication face-to-face), the *traditional* (stable over time), the *aesthetic* (artistic expressions), and the *ideological* (expressions of belief and systems of knowledge).[4]

Thus, the kinds of traditional culture that many of us know and participate in include such rituals, skills, and creative expressions as holiday observance practices (having a cake on someone's birthday, or turkey "with all the trimmings" for Christmas or Thanksgiving); family stories or sayings; school playground chants and games ("Apples, peaches, pears and plums/Tell me when your birthday comes"); jokes; recipes (for regional foods like bakeapple jam, ethnic specialities like perogies, or your mother's special meatloaf); and quilting or woodworking.

Throughout history, women have contributed to what literary historian Raymond Williams describes as the "dominant," central aspects of culture – to gain power within patriarchal systems – as several of the chapters in *Changing Patterns* clearly show. However, much of women's experience remains within the informal levels of culture. As such women's experience offers alternatives or counterpoints to patriarchal ideas, particularly by attesting to women's power and value. We will present examples of this process.

The traditional texts – songs, stories, beliefs, and objects – that women create and re-create, and the rituals and performances they participate in, are of three related types. The "archaic" – "that which is wholly recognized as an element of the past, to be observed, to be examined, or even on occasion to be consciously 'revived'"[5] – fits conventional notions of folklore. The "residual," which has been "effectively formed in the past, but . . . is still active in the cultural process, not only and often not at all as an element of the past, but as an effective element of the present," and the "emergent," where "new meanings and values, new practices, new relationships and kinds of relationship are continually being created . . . which are substantively alternative or oppositional to it,"[6] are less readily associated with everyday ideas of tradition than the archaic, but are much more significant for our purposes here. Through the residual and emergent, we see that women's folklore is not just a passive reflection of sociocultural norms; it can be an active instrument of and for social change. However, folklorists' attention to collecting and understanding women's folklore in Canada from the archaic to the emergent is just beginning.

One reason for the past neglect of women's traditional culture stems from early collecting priorities and practices. Until quite recently – beginning in the 1960s – most folklorists wanted only to record texts. They went into "the field," usually a remote or "isolated" location, in search of stories, songs, and beliefs they could publish in collections, compare with other versions, and trace to historic and geographic sources. The fastest and easiest method of obtaining the numbers and range of texts they needed was to seek out public performers; individuals who were well-known within their communities as singers and tale-tellers at dances, concerts, weddings, and other public events. Early collectors[7] usually overlooked women primarily because, unlike men, women did not perform publicly, but instead told their stories, sang their songs, and practised their beliefs within the more private world of their families.

Another reason why we know relatively little about women's folklore is because, as an academic discipline in Canada, folklore studies have remained an almost exclusively male enterprise.[8] Hence, as Marta Weigle notes, the discipline has focused on high-performance, public, male genres.[9] It has been biased against the more communal, collaborative forms associated with the domestic sphere.[10] Because male academic folklorists and men from whom they collect data do not know about, have access to, or value women's expressive culture, it has until recently been relegated in the discipline to the secondary status of "minor genres."

The near exclusion in Canada of women from academic folklore studies and the neglect of women's folklore are also ironic because women, both nationally and internationally, have been our best-known collectors. From the turn of the century Canadian women such as Helen Creighton (1899-1990) and Edith Fowke, who is still active, have gathered the repertoire of Canadian folkloric texts and added significantly to our knowledge about traditional culture, despite sometimes facing daunting odds. Almost all were guided by male models and canons for collecting. They were hindered by meagre or precarious funding and many of them lacked permanent affiliation to any institution. Part of our recovery and understanding of the intersection of women's culture with traditional culture must begin with an analysis of their work.

Some women who collected folklore did so with their male partners. W. Roy Mackenzie (1883-1957) initially encountered folksongs during his studies at Harvard University, and for several summers thereafter he and his wife Ethel Mackenzie (1884-1972) spent their vacations visiting traditional singers in their home community of River John, Nova Scotia. Ethel Mackenzie accompanied her husband on collecting expeditions and helped to take down the songs by hand as they were being performed – a task Roy Mackenzie found very difficult. According to Helen Creighton, it was Ethel Mackenzie who first drew Roy Mackenzie's attention to the folksong repertoire in River John, and Roy himself acknowledged that Ethel's enthusiasm ensured his completion of the project.[11]

Similarly, in Western Canada, James Teit (1864-1922), who collaborated with the famous anthropologist Franz Boas in studies of (Native) interior Salish culture, had a unique perspective on and entrée into local women's culture through his Salish wife, Lucy Antko (c.1865-1899).[12] As a result his portrayal of Native women as "strong, independent, and fully-participating members of their community," as well as his attention to aspects of the culture which concerned women, from pictography to ethnobotany to basketry, are unique for his time.[13]

Like so much of women's work, however, the involvement of women like Ethel Mackenzie and Lucy Antko in their husbands' documentation of traditional culture usually goes unrecognized. Instead, it is invisibly absorbed into the men's projects. For W. Roy Mackenzie, fieldwork resulted in publications and a reputation as a pioneer.[16] Today James Teit is praised for his extensive knowledge of the Salish and his significant contributions to our understanding of Native cultures. The rich results netted by couples like the Mackenzies and Teit and Antko led Kenneth S. Goldstein to refer frequently in his *Guide for Fieldworkers in Folklore* to the value of the folklorist's wife and children to a collecting team.[15] His near-pervasive assumption that the folklorist will be male, and that his wife must be willing and able to assist her husband's work at all times, is now dated. But Goldstein was unusual in claiming that, for example, "There are certain areas of superstition and custom of which it would be more difficult for any male to obtain knowledge, but which a woman, because of her sex, would have no difficulty whatsoever in obtaining."[16]

But there were also women like Helen Creighton who usually worked alone in the field and became known as collectors in their own right. Creighton's focus was on Nova Scotia, and she did the majority of her collecting within easy driving distance of her home in Dartmouth.[17] Like many other women, Creighton fit this work around her domestic responsibilities, which for much of her adult life included caring for her elderly parents. Her autobiography, *A Life in Folklore,* is a highly individualistic social history, in her own unique terms, of her involvement with traditional culture – gathering, recording, and documenting it – as well as of her other life experiences. Her motivations for collecting were partly personal – she was looking for things to write about – and partly regionalist/nationalist – as a Nova Scotian she wanted to celebrate the distinctiveness of Maritime culture. In contrast to Roy Mackenzie, who was interested in folksongs as reflections of international patterns, Creighton wanted to show the specific historic value, ability, and creativity of people in the Maritimes.

As an upper-middle-class Nova Scotia woman who stepped outside the private sphere, Creighton was unusual for her time. She comments:

> In the days when I grew up, it was assumed a girl would marry and set up her own home, probably with a maid to wait on her. If not, she would live with her parents and do volunteer work or enjoy the social round. The former hadn't happened, and the latter had never appealed to me as a way of life, so I looked . . . for a place where I could be useful. [18]

Collecting folklore meant entering into rural, Native, and working-class spheres, none of which was seen as appropriate for a woman of her class at that time. Her ability to move easily in these unaccustomed and sometimes problematic contexts necessitated circumspect behaviour. She commented that on visiting strange farms alone, "You can't take your safety for granted." [19] Her disinclination to collect by plying performers with liquor is one example of the kind of control she had to assert. She suggests that "A male collector might use liquor effectively; a woman, particularly a young one, would forfeit respect." [20] Similarly, her unequivocal rejection of bawdy songs not only was necessary to her personal comfort and safety while doing fieldwork – a woman alone could be vulnerable to unwanted sexual attention – but also made it possible for her to continue her research on other topics. She writes of one experience:

> At Little Harbour on the eastern shore I was once recording Ned MacKay in a fishing shack with some half dozen of his friends sitting around listening. A young Lunenburgher came in and contributed a number that not only had no merit as a song, but was definitely vulgar. I let the machine run and when it was over the young men went out laughing while the local fishermen fidgeted in embarrassment. I put the machine in reverse and remarked that I had erased it from the tape. You wouldn't believe how those few words eased the situation. [21]

Developing a reputation for interest in "vulgar" material and liquor would quickly have ended Creighton's collecting career.

Helen Creighton is not the only woman who contributed to our repertoire and knowledge of Canadian folklore.[22] Many of those women who collected folklore are known only within their home communities. For example, Albertan Frances Fraser (1920-89) made a lifelong commitment to collecting and translating southern Albertan Blackfoot narratives, which were printed in her columns for the *High River Times* and the *Calgary Herald*. Her work has recently been republished as *The Bear Who Stole the Chinook*.[23] On the east coast, Jean Heffernan (c. 1900-80) documented aspects of folk culture in her home town of Springhill, Nova Scotia. Like Fraser, her collecting results were published in the local newspaper.[24] We do not want to suggest that these women's work provides flawless sources, or that their research would fit modern standards; rarely did they include information now considered vital – names, dates, places, and contexts of performance, among others. But these part-time researchers made a significant contribution to the documentation of traditional Canadian culture. As their names are being discovered, appreciation for their work is growing.

Recently, some folklorists (usually female) trained in contemporary techniques and with modern theoretical orientations have begun the task of uncovering women's folklore, although few make it a specialty. They follow the field's current interest in the texture and context of folklore.[25] Not content merely to record and analyse texts, they want to understand how people use their traditional culture, where and why it is performed, and what it means as well as the forms it takes. Some women have taken advantage of the unique opportunities they have to enter and observe the often private domain of female work and play contexts normally closed to male fieldworkers.[26]

Full-time or part-time, formally trained or self-educated, resident or outsider, women have pioneered the research of folklore in Canada and have contributed abundantly to – and sometimes even foreshadowed – academic work in the field. But it is not wholly coincidental that the gendered marginal position of Helen Creighton and other female collectors in their own social milieux is paralleled by their marginality to the academic enterprise, by the marginality of the scholarly field they chose, and often by the social and economic marginality of the regions and peoples they investigated.[27] To some extent, collecting as opposed to analysing and theorizing is a "female" enterprise, involving such tasks stereotypically relegated to women as gathering, annotating, archiving, and popularizing. Yet women folklore collectors have left an important legacy of documented folk traditions, and as we try to discover more about women's culture, their work will be invaluable.[28]

As women's folklore becomes a more central field of study, we will surely learn more about genres and cultural groups not conventionally considered by folklorists. But we should not expect a unified vision of women's folklore in Canada to emerge. Women's folklore does not exist in isolation from other cultural groupings to which women belong – ethnic, racial, class, linguistic, religious, familial, and so on. The idea of one women's folklore shared by all members of the sex – heterosexual or lesbian, in the north or south of Canada, working in or outside the home, middle or upper class – is problematic. Even the goal of an ideal universal women's culture may be unrealistic. However, as the following sections show, common themes and ideas in the folklore about and by women unfold in widely varying sociocultural groups.

Although the pluralism of women's folklore is central to our understanding of it – there is no unified body of women's traditional culture – we will draw on our own experience and collecting, almost exclusively with anglophone women in Eastern Canada. We do not want to suggest that women in Native, francophone, non-white, or other cultures lack vibrant and fascinating traditions that could exemplify female folklore; instead, we are drawing from the materials we know best. We hope that coming generations of Canadian women will realize how much remains to be gathered and analysed. If we are to better understand ourselves, our cultures, and our creativity, Canadian folklore research must be extended into previously unexplored areas.

Images of Women in Canadian Traditional Culture

The few collections of folklore in Canada demonstrate definite bias. They are geographically centred in Atlantic Canada and Quebec, linguistically focused on English and French cultures, and primarily concerned with oral genres.[29] As well, it is difficult to know if the material that has been gathered is broadly representative or merely serendipitous. However, it shows that whether traditional cultural forms – songs, stories, beliefs, rituals, material culture – represent individuals or women in general, their symbolism and imagery construct and reinforce ideas about female gender identity.

Sometimes female characters are depicted as bold and forceful, which suggests that women are strong, resourceful, and positive; at other times they are portrayed as conniving, malicious, and evil. The latter are perhaps the most familiar, powerful images to come to mind – the wicked stepmother in "Cinderella" and other folktales, or the figure of the witch – and not all are archaic or associated with childhood culture. Recent misogynist jokes stereotype women as stupid, dirty, or oversexed, just as ethnic jokes do for the groups they refer to. Women are presented as the slaves and manipulators of their bodies: "What's the difference between a pitbull and a woman with PMS? Lipstick." Such jokes assert that the veneer separating women from their essentially animal nature is all too thin, and covers very little. Women are linked with nature, with danger, and with evil.

Many jokes also associate women with the private domain or assert that they are out of place in public, non-traditional jobs. The cycle about blondes popular in 1991 in the Maritimes, Ontario, and Manitoba – and probably elsewhere – is indicative. It includes texts like, "How do you know a blonde has been using the word processor? There's white-out on the screen." The underlying message of all such jokes is suggested in "What's the difference between an intelligent blonde and a sasquatch? There have been sightings of sasquatches." This mirrors a joke predating the blonde cycle, in which sasquatches were differentiated from all intelligent women, not only blondes. Every blonde joke, like the sasquatch text, is implicitly and by extension about every woman. Students at the University of Waterloo reported observing that blonde jokes were used to refer to someone who was neither female nor blonde, but who fit the "airhead" image. Such usage does not mitigate the misogyny of blonde jokes, of course; it may even be amplified, because it reaffirms that the image of stupid women is so clear that the joke's signifier need not resemble or be closely identifiable with what it signifies.

Other jokes and folklore forms are yet more overtly ominous, mirroring or applauding the violence women experience on an everyday basis. They may even advocate or support it, as did the item of graffiti that appeared at the University of Waterloo a month after the Montreal massacre: "What do you call 14 dead feminists in Montreal? – A good start." This text was signed "The M. Lepine fan club" and was certainly interpreted as a threat by most of the women who saw it.

While we cannot ignore the misogynist images of women found in much traditional culture, it would be misleading to suggest that all representations of women are as disturbing. Although they are not always positive, they are by no means univocally negative, either. For example, the traditional song "The Farmer's Curst Wife," well-known across Eastern Canada, concerns a woman taken to hell by the devil. Her aggressive actions on arrival so terrify its inhabitants that they beg the devil to bring her back, and he does. The song concludes: "Now this proves that the women are worse than the men/When they go down to hell they're sent back again."[30] The meaning here is ambiguous, for as bad as women are asserted to be, it is clearly better to be "worse" if this gets one out of hell.

Similarly, in "John and Joan Blount" a couple who forget to bar their door before going to bed make "a bargain firm and sure, O'/The very first one that should speak the first word/Should go down and bar the door, O."[31] When travellers come by and make themselves quite thoroughly at home in the house, and the man has finally had enough, he says:

'You've eat of my victuals, you drank of my drink,
You've kissed my wife on the floor, O'

His wife's reply is immediate:

'John Blount," she said, 'you've spoke the first word!
Go down and bar the door, O.'[32]

The woman gets the final word and, superficially anyway, she wins the contest. But it is up to the singer and the audience to decide if the woman, the man, or both are being made to seem ridiculous.

The representations in traditional folksongs are of a plurality of women's personalities and experiences. Many characters are powerful, if not necessarily positive: "Barbara Allan" slights her lover and is the cause of both his death and her own; one of "The Twa Sisters" kills the other because of jealousy over a lover; "The Cruel Mother" murders her children; and there are the victims like "Sally Munroe," murdered by her lover.[33] Or there are deserted women who simply die of grief. But there are also positive images: women who remain true to their lovers and are rewarded by fidelity in return, or, more enjoyable to a modern sensibility, women who turn the tables on a man who is trying to rob or murder them. "The Highway Robber" is by no means the only such example:

'Tis of a rich merchant of London,
Who had lots of land that he sold,
Who sent out his daughter to market
To receive every penny in gold.

She sewed the gold up in the saddle,
And that with good leathers well-lined;
She sewed up the gold in her saddle,
For fear any danger would find.

She sewed up the gold in her saddle
And starts out for home on the highway;
She chanced for to meet a bold robber,
He bid this fair damsel for to stay.

Three blows of his whistle he gave her,
And the pistole he popped to her breast,
Saying, 'Now deliver your money,
Or else you'll die a cruel death.'

This pretty fair maiden got frightened,
And so did Dobbin her steed;
Down off his saddle she lightened,
And Dobbin trots home with good speed.

He stripped this fair damsel stark naked
And gives her his horse for to hold;
She stood there a shivering and a-shaking
Like one who was dying with cold.

This fair pretty maiden got courage
While he was in search of his prey;
Saying 'Young man, it's no time to be idle;
I'll show you a trick on the highway.'

From the stirrup to saddle she mounted,
She threw her legs 'cross like a man,
She drove the thief's horse off on a stretch gallup:
'Now catch me bold thief, if you can.'

He runned and he bawled and he shouted,
He runned and he puffed and he blowed,
He runned and he bawled and he shouted,
'Come back, and I'll give you your clothes.'

'My clothes ain't of very much value,
You can keep them kind sir, if you please.'
He runned and he bawled and he shouted,
Till his boots they hackered his heels.

She rode over hills and through valleys,
And arrived at her home twelve o'clock;
Her father was very much frightened
To see her ride home in her smock.

She shoved the thief's horse in the stable,
And in his portmantel she found
Some hundred of bright sparkling diamonds
To the value of ten thousand pounds.

'Here's five thousand pound for you, pa,
and I will keep five thousand more.
Don't you think it a suitable trifle
To keep the wolf from the door?'[34]

The highway robber's female adversary is obviously a fictional character, but there are also realistic ones. Mythic and legendary Canadian women include several who perform heroic acts: Laura Secord, who walked some thirty kilometres to warn the British of an impending American attack, with the legendary embellishments that she took her cow to divert suspicion as she went through American-held territory; or Madeleine de Vercheres, Madame LaTour, and women of the south shore of Nova Scotia who without the aid of adult men defended forts or communities against attack. Two quite different women appear in the Icelandic sagas of the first Europeans to land in North America; the loyal wife Gudrid contrasts with the powerful virago Freydis, who is clearly more than a match for her male companions. In Native tradition there are figures like the powerful D'Sonoqua who individually embody multiple characteristics. She is ambivalent: sometimes ugly and terrifying, sometimes beautiful and gracious.[35] The sea goddess Sedna is a central figure in Inuit mythology. Myths describe her as a woman who originally refused to marry. Eventually she does marry, and narratives offer various descriptions of how her fingers are severed by either her father or her own children and turn into the animals of the sea. After this takes place, she sinks to the bottom of the sea, where she becomes a powerful goddess who not only rules over the sea but also presides over the earth as well. Sedna participates in the act of creation and exercises control over the people.[36]

Much traditional material examines women's roles in Canadian society and explores their access to power. Ella Lauchner Smith was the first female acting department head on the faculty of Mount Allison University in New Brunswick.[37] She came to the position during World War II when it was vacated by a professor who entered military service. For others on the predominantly male faculty and for her male students, Smith was an anomaly. Her unique position and colourful personality ensured that she soon entered campus and community tradition as the subject of narratives. While some stories focused on the same kinds of "flaws" that form the basis for local-character anecdotes elsewhere – extreme thrift and lack of flexibility in social situations – others explored her position within the university and town. One anecdote that is still well-known became an identifying image for Smith. It relates to an interaction she had with university president George J. Trueman. As a former neighbour remembered:

> Dr. George J. used to have a lot of visitors to Sackville during the summer and this was when they had a chapel in the old centennial, I think it's called the old centennial hall, and it was on the third floor and it was a lovely little chapel. It really was. . . . And he had a visitor this particular day and of course they used to go on a visitation of the campus and Dr. George J. told this man, he said, 'Now,' he said, 'this is our centennial building here, our administration offices. But,' he

said 'there's something on the third floor that we're really quite proud of, Mount Allison never had it before.' And he took him up to show the chapel and when he went through the door and into the chapel, here was these ladies' clothes and undies and everything all hung on a line drying. And Dr. George J. Trueman knew who they belonged to because there was no one else on the campus that would do a thing like this, you know. . . . Just like army banners, you know, they were all drying. And of course he spoke to her about it and he said how embarrassing it was because he had this friend from Toronto or Montreal who was being conducted on this visitation of the Mount A. campus. And she said, 'Well,' she said, 'I don't think God would mind me trying to be clean and having my clothes in the chapel drying.'[38]

While the anecdote is consistent with local-character narratives elsewhere in that it shows Smith embarrassing the powerful university president, it does not allow her to leave the encounter entirely victorious. Smith, like the president, is made to look foolish. The underwear hanging "just like army banners" becomes an image identifying her to those of her students and colleagues for whom she was as out of place in an authoritative position as was the public display of her underwear in the chapel. Stories like this, and others that focus more particularly on Smith's vulnerability as a woman, challenge as well as affirm her power.

Another example of folklore that encounters and constructs the sociocultural place of women in everyday life is the contemporary rural Ontario shivaree.[39] Described by both male and female participants as a way of "welcoming a new bride into the community," these events involve activities that appear decidedly unwelcoming: the disruption, rearrangement, or even destruction of the bride's possessions and of her domestic domain.[40] We can better understand how shivarees are a "welcome," as well as a way of asserting control over women and their fertility, by looking at how the shivaree unfolds and at its relation to its nineteenth-century historic predecessors.

Charivari (shivaree), as described by Susanna Moodie in *Roughing it in the Bush,* allowed young, rowdy men in pioneer Ontario to express their disapproval of inappropriate marriages – matches between two older people, an older and a younger person, or two people of different races.[41] In these early charivaris, young men from the community disguised themselves with blackened faces, went to the newlyweds' house on the wedding night, and made loud discordant noise with whatever implements were at hand, such as pots and pans. The intention was to extract a sum of money, or liquor, from the couple. If the bride or groom refused to comply, the groom could be roughed up, or even murdered. The social concern was not with the relationship between the two individuals – which is no one else's business – but with the couple's fertility, which enables the continuation of the community. An older person in a marriage could reduce the chances of children being conceived; an interracial couple could be fruitful, but the mixed-race children could not be community members in a racist white society.

Shivarees in contemporary Ontario are much more benign, yet they too are concerned with fertility. There is considerable variation from community to community in how shivarees are organized, but they have a common pattern in that a couple can be shivareed any number of times until their first child arrives. The shivaree usually does not take place on the wedding night, but instead can be held any time after the couple returns from their honeymoon. Again, the shivareers – young married and unmarried men and women and the couple's relatives – arrive late at night with noisemakers – the preferred choices being car horns and chainsaws – and awaken the newlyweds. The couple must then let them into the house and stand by to watch the visitors cover the property with toilet paper, move the furniture from one room to another, tie socks together, and generally disrupt the household and farm area. Refusal or protest is unwise; it would occasion further and sometimes more serious trickery.

While damage outside the house, particularly of any building or equipment related to agricultural production – considered to be the domain of the groom – is always rectified, and the man can call upon his neighbours in returning "his" part of the farm to normal, the bride gets no similar assistance the next day. She is expected to work alone in returning everything inside to its proper location, cleaning up, and repairing damages. Yet many women do in fact consider the shivaree a "welcome," because it acknowledges their female-identified power as outsiders coming into the community. It is a general rule that men who will farm stay on or near their family's property, whereas their wives are usually from elsewhere. The shivaree demonstrates the bride's stoic ability to put up with the worst the shivareers can give her. It also serves as a potent reminder that the community considers the woman's fertility its own concern, implicitly suggesting the value of women as reproducers of the community.

Clearly, the kinds of attitudes or belief structures implied by shivarees – that women and their fertility must be controlled and that a woman's primary meaning and use come from her ability to have children – circumscribe and limit female social roles. However, unlike some other forms of cultural expression, folklore rarely ignores women. Their power is clearly recognized, even if through an attempt to control it.

Another traditional enactment documented in Ontario and Western

Canada, the mock wedding, also comments on women's place in society.[42] Mock weddings are usually incorporated as the entertainment in a wedding shower or milestone anniversary celebration – a twenty-fifth or fortieth anniversary, for example. In these events a group of community members, usually the close friends and relatives of the honoured couple, perform a travesty of the traditional wedding ceremony, in which the male roles – groom, father of the bride, and so on – are played by women, and the female roles – like the bride and maid of honour – are played by men. While it is usually women who organize these events – composing or recomposing the text, finding players for the parts, gathering costumes, and so on – the men have the "starring" roles. It is considered laughable when a man dresses as a woman, but much less so in the opposite situation. Folklorist Michael Taft argues that this is because in the primarily rural areas where mock weddings are popular, women regularly do take on "men's work" and sometimes their role behaviour, from dealing with financial institutions to driving a tractor. Much less common, more deviant, and thus humorous in the mock wedding, is the man who does "women's work" – taking care of children, doing laundry, cooking, and so on. The mock wedding displays this paradoxical – even unfair – situation in public to members of the community, who acknowledge it by laughing at the men who dress as women. Again, the mock wedding does not aim to change social conventions – it may even celebrate them – but it certainly recognizes them in a clear and understandable fashion. Women's power is displayed in their control over the mock wedding and in what the event says about the significance and necessity of women's roles: only women can do them.

The representation of women in folklore is as varied as the available texts and contexts, and the images are diverse. In addition, recent contextual approaches to folklore show that meaning cannot be understood from the text alone, but must be interpreted and clarified by the performer and audience. But perhaps in part because of our past reliance on public space, and on largely male performances, we have no trouble identifying numerous negative images of women in Canadian traditional culture. Yet there are many positive, active women who, like the cunning protagonist of "The Highway Robber," exercise and profit from their own intelligence and courage. More generally, women are not depicted in folklore in a simplistic light, positively or negatively. Rather, like the Ella Smith stories, shivarees, and mock weddings, most traditional culture reveals a complex understanding of sex roles and stereotypes, as well as of women's power. It is important that we consider all these representations and revisions, for collectively they instruct about how women's gender identity is fashioned and how their power is periodically negotiated.

Women (Re)Create Their Own Image in Traditional Culture

Women are not simply the subjects of traditional culture; they also create and re-create culture in their own right, representing themselves and their own voices. Here we caution against the essentializing of women or of culture; individual women's participation in traditional culture may radically differ from person to person. In any case, women's culture is pluralistic; most also relates to some other cultural group that the women belong to.

Women's traditional expression must be placed in a sociocultural context. Some female performers have been restricted to such "private" venues as the kitchen and nursery by their community's and society's expectations; their access to public stages is minimal. Though they may have abilities equal to those of the men in their families, they often perform only in the home or in all-female contexts. Thus, for example, in his study of Calvert, Newfoundland, folklorist Gerald Pocius discovered during fieldwork in 1974 that while he was told by his hosts that he would "get some good songs from Mr. Vince Ledwell," he found instead that Mr. Vince's wife Mrs. Mon possessed a wider repertoire, had a more complete memory for songs, and was a better performer than her husband.[43] Since the community designated Mr. Vince as a singer, more because of his parents' roles as singers than because of his own talents, Mrs. Mon as an outsider "forfeited any possibility of achieving status as a singer because of community pressure. She decided not to challenge the community social system and hazard partial social ostracism."[44] She could, however, support, collaborate, or even try to correct Mr. Vince when he sang in public, as she did when he sang for Pocius.

This secondary role is shared by many women, including the ones in Nova Scotia visited by the Mackenzies and Creighton. These collectors mention women who knew all the words to the songs performed by male family members but who in performance took a role secondary to the men. In English Canada a few women singers, like LaRena Clark of Ontario and Marie Hare of New Brunswick, who frequently appears at the Miramichi Folksong Festival, could traverse the boundaries to public performance and come to be known in their communities, and even beyond, as singers.[45] But they remain a minority.

The whole issue of defining the male world as public and the female world as private, too, often comes from the perspective of male folklorists who have not often had entrée into women's – all female – public interactions. Folklorist Debora Kodish's work in Newfoundland suggests that women may exchange songs differently from the way men do, often by way of notebooks or written collections.[46] Thus women's interest in songs is communicated in forms not usually thought of as performative, and hence their work is ignored by male folklorists. Differences between men's, women's, and mixed contexts for performance and presentation influence the recognition and perception of gendered activity.

All-female contexts are a rich source of women's folklore and suggest that women have sometimes turned to traditional folklore genres not generally embraced by males to express their creativity and to communicate their feelings. For example, textile traditions such as quilting and rug-hooking allow women to demonstrate their individual artistry in choice of colour, material, and pattern, as well as a skilful mastery over the actual processes, often involving such exacting community standards as the idea that a quilt should have ten stitches to the inch. Frequently, a communal aspect is essential to these activities. Not only do women often gather to help one another quilt or to hook a mat – a social outlet for women and an opportunity to exchange news and reinforce personal links – but they also express and reinforce their female network of family and friends through the circulation of common materials and patterns.[47] Or community recognition of individual skills and communal effort can be joined when one woman is asked to design a quilt, another to piece it, another to mark it, and another to set it up in her home for the expert quilters. Looking at the material in a finished quilt or rug, a woman may be reminded of others in the family or neighbourhood who once owned the garment from which the pieced scraps were taken. Additionally, she may think of other quilts or rugs that have provided models, and their makers. Thus these objects – and other forms of women's traditional culture like the sharing and making of recipes – come to symbolize the ties between members of a woman's family and her friendship networks, as well as to provide opportunities for them to gather as groups.

Much of women's folklore similarly functions to integrate women within their communities, families, and friendship groups. Characteristically, women's narrative exchange has taken place within conversation. Women's anecdotes, their narratives of personal or community experience, and their knowledge centring on local people and events are commonly and derogatively termed "gossip."[48] Anthropologist James Faris observed that in Newfoundland, "Gossip is news transmitted privately rather than publicly."[49] When the same information is later presented in the public contexts frequented by men, it instead becomes "news." However, an earlier meaning of "gossip" referred to that special circle of women present at a lying-in and thus bound together by mutual participation in an event then closed to men. While gossip has lost its specific link with childbirth – and has acquired negative connotations – it has retained an association with close groups composed of women.

While we think of gossip generally – as with other forms of women's folklore – as negative, idle, or destructive – and some gossip certainly can be hurtful – the integrative and healing qualities of women's talk are often overlooked. Through gossip, women explore others' personalities and motivations and offer emotional support. Gossiping is most often a collaborative process whereby participants negotiate a mutual understanding of an event or individual's behaviour. They establish a shared mutual outlook as members of a family or friendship group. The exchange of narratives may help members to better understand one another and more clearly articulate the expectations and boundaries of the group they belong to. It is in part through women's narratives that many of us develop an individual, family, and community identity.

Some of women's folklore originally set in all-female contexts, such as the lying-in to which gossip originally referred, has been removed to other locations. Traditional practices of midwifery give an example of how the movement of a practice away from the female domain corresponds with its move from traditional to professional learning and into arenas of male power. As women are excluded from traditional cultural forms, these not only tend to be considered non-folkloric, but they also tend to be appropriated as venues for the expression of male rather than female power.

Within genres that are shared by performers of both sexes, such as folksongs, men and women may choose to perform or circulate different types or versions of songs. Edward D. Ives's folksong collecting in the Maritimes leads him to suggest that women, at least in the past, were more likely to know the older, British traditional ballads while many of his male informants preferred the less poetic, more sensationalist broadside ballads.[50] While this pattern may not always hold, even in Atlantic Canada, it seems clear that women frequently express interest in or choose to present different texts than do men.[51] Take, for instance, the several folksongs in the total repertoire of Eastern Canada about women who dress in men's clothing or otherwise appropriate some object belonging to a man. In "The Highway Robber," for example, the woman takes the man's horse, equipment, and stolen property. These songs may be women's more than they are men's. While some male performers do sing them, these men most often have large total repertoires, indicating an unusually great interest in any traditional song. Men who sing only a few songs – not every song they can get their hands on – rarely sing ones with strong, forceful female heroes. Yet a glance at some of the standard folksong collections indicates that such figures appear to be overrepresented in the song repertoires of women.

In these songs the motivation for women to dress in men's clothing or to appropriate men's possessions is usually to test the lover's fidelity or to travel safely in search of him. The most common outcome is a marriage between the reunited lovers, a clear partnership of equals who share a bold, adventurous nature. But marriage is not always the result; often the woman finds her lover to be untrue or simply discovers that she enjoys the life she has assumed. Interestingly, it is very rare for a woman in one of these songs to meet outright disaster, quite unlike the outcomes for female characters in other traditional songs. Like the mock weddings, these songs celebrate the distinctiveness of female culture and women's opportunities to move into other symbolic and cultural domains, including men's.

Similarly, women sometimes use a genre that has been performed by men to make comments on women's culture and to assert how women's culture differs from men's. For example, in a number of different cultures the verse or prose monologue or recitation is a male-dominated expressive form. In Newfoundland it is a popular informal entertainment. Many recitations from that province are overtly misogynist: "St. Peter at the Gate," for example, describes how a loud, obnoxious, shrewish woman is barred from heaven and indirectly makes it possible for her husband to enter because, having had to put up with his wife, "he's had about all of the hell that he needs."[52] Significantly, this text is popularly requested at wedding receptions. Women's recitations reverse the negative evaluations of women and their speech and celebrate their relationships with others as co-operative and good-humoured. When female characters in women's recitations speak critically, it is most often only to poke very gentle fun at men's proclivities.[53]

Women show themselves able to retaliate and often capitalize on their negative representations in folklore. There are examples from any number of genres, but a few relate to earlier illustrations. Some make outright substitutions, such as the female singers who when performing "The Farmer's Curst Wife" reverse its chorus's evaluation that women are worse than men, so that "It's true that women are *better* than men." And perhaps in counterpoint to the blonde-joke cycle that demeans and objectifies women, texts are circulated that do the same thing to men, like "What's the insensitive skin around a penis? A man" or "Why are all blonde jokes one-liners? So men can understand them."

One of the most complex manipulations of folk tradition is in women's use of witchcraft belief. The practice's long history in the Maritimes – it was prevalent in some communities until the 1960s – helped to crystallize many people's fear of women who lived on the social and economic margins.[54] Often these women were old, alone, and represented an ethnic or racial minority. They were rumoured to have all kinds of evil powers, and the stories that circulated about them furthered their isolation. While to be named a witch was undoubtedly an awful and alienating experience for rural Maritime women, some were aware of the power it afforded them.

Capitalizing on community belief, they would ensure that their physical needs were met; that they and their dependents had food in the house and wood to burn. To refuse a witch's request was considered very bad luck, and some marginal women exploited this, and their "witch" designation, to survive or even to improve their standard of living.

Finally, not all examples of women transforming tradition for their benefit are oral or date from earlier times. Rather, some women use their comfort with modern technology to produce computer, fax, or photocopy lore – cartoons or written texts circulated with the aid of mechanical or electronic devices – that gives voice to the frustration of marginal individuals. Workers who are underpaid, overworked, and alienated may periodically rely on this form to express their frustration with powerlessness or to assert a power they normally hide or choose not to exercise. Often incorporating bawdy humour, they turn the tables on sexist jokes directed at them by their bosses or fellow workers, or artistically put their male supervisor down. One item of photocopy lore has the caption "Grow your own dope. Plant a man" and shows a male head surrounded by grass and plant life. Not only does this reverse the assertions of misogynist jokes that women are stupid and men are intelligent, it also associates men with fertility, growth, and nature. This is contrary to the near-universal cultural stereotype, discussed by anthropologist Sherry Ortner, which equates women with nature and men with culture.[55] The mode of communication – technological – and the implicit content of the joking statement link women with culture, which is powerful and valued, and relegate men to an inferior place: on the ground and controlled by women who may or may not choose to plant them and thus give them life.

These examples demonstrate that women are not always passive victims in traditional lore but can shape it to create their own images. In the area of emergent culture, research has shown that Inuit women's written autobiographies – a newer genre of expression for a people whose precontact literature was oral – comprise inventive circumventions of the cultural "taboo against drawing attention to themselves as mature adults [either by confining] their autobiographical writings to memories of pre-adolescence, or [by not writing] about themselves until they are approaching old age," or through fictionalizing their lives, using "autobiographical elements to structure stories rather than the other way around."[56] Robin McGrath points out that the autobiographies of Inuit women such as Kenojuak and Marion Tuu'luk (with Susan Tagoona) frequently include the theme of the woman's miraculous recovery or escape from death, often through the intervention of her dead father whose spirit or disembodied voice "had, in effect, given his permission for her to put herself forward."[57] Leah Idlout (D'Argencourt), another Inuit woman, described her life with white foster parents in a beast fable patterned on the Dr. Seuss story, *Horton Hatches an Egg. The Little Arctic Tern, The Big Polar Bear* is . . . about a bird who allows her egg to be hatched by a polar bear; the result is a bear-bird who does not know who its mother is and who is eventually exhibited as a freak in a Florida circus. [Similarly] Idlout's foster parents wished to adopt her, but she eventually returned to Pond Inlet where she found re-entry into the culture difficult. She felt that she had lost touch with her own people and was neither white nor Inuit.[58]

Evidently, women find methods and opportunities to compose and tell their own stories even in the face of cultural proscriptions, and the results not only circumvent the taboos but also critique their existence by showing that despite a taboo, women can tell their stories in a compelling and truthful yet poetic fashion.

The Public, The Private

The orientations of folklore imply the relegation of traditional culture – and of women – to the private domain. Our recognition of the fact that folklore and women have been seen as irrelevant to public culture does not, however, require us to accept this evaluation uncritically. The idea of separate spheres for men and women should be a useful critical starting point, not a simple method of categorization. We've argued this throughout by looking at the influence of men and women as collectors and analysts, at images of women in folklore, and at women as creators and presenters of traditional culture.

Sometimes the public-male/private-female association seems to have merit. Clearly, both men and women are present when some male singers or storytellers are performing, while circulating written song collections, quilting, and telling "gossip" are restricted to women, and to limited groups of them. Yet we must question the assumption that any venue a male folklorist has access to must be both public and significant, and that any place where he is denied access or unwelcome is not only private but also of lesser significance. Because the analysis and theory of folklore have been male-dominated, folklore studies have only recently come to recognize the biases involved in such assumptions.

Further, sometimes folklore confines women to being "barefoot, pregnant, and in the kitchen." But much traditional culture recognizes that women rarely fit this stereotype; they are shown as active agents in their own lives. And for every joke that says that women should keep to their traditional place, there are others that assert, like a popular item of photocopy lore, that "a woman's place is in the boardroom," or "a woman's place is wherever she wants to be."

It is an overstatement to equate the linkages between women's culture and folklore as simplistically as we connect "old wives' tales" and "gossip" simultaneously with the female and with tradition. Relegating folklore to the simple and frivolous is like suggesting that all women's activities occur in the private sphere; it obfuscates central issues. As we rethink women's culture, we also challenge existing notions of tradition. As we rethink our notions of who women are and what their culture is, we correspondingly rethink our ideas of folklore.

As in the other areas addressed by *Changing Patterns,* in folklore the process of recovery, reconstruction, and analysis continues. As woman-centred research comes to characterize more folkloristic collecting and evaluation, and as case studies of women from all parts of Canada and from a greater variety of sociocultural groups expand the literature, we will develop a better understanding of how women are represented in traditional culture as well as of how women shape and reshape folklore. New insights promise to aid our appreciation of folklore genres, such as personal-experience narrative, which have been relatively neglected. More importantly, further study will not only develop our understanding of women's conventional roles and the kinds of power they can entail, but also show how women contest, rework, and manipulate convention.

Traditional knowledge can assist in social change, in affording women a stronger voice in developing our own destinies, as we come to better understand how we have always sought this power, and how we have sometimes achieved it. Like other traditional figures, the song character whose quick thinking and ingenuity allowed her both to escape the highwayman and to enrich herself and her family can be a symbol for women who need to overcome adversity in their own lives. We can value the strength of women who, in working on a quilt, simultaneously express their creativity, draw ties with their community, and make a bed-covering to warm their family. And although our struggles are very serious, we can also use folklore to find humour in oppression, to mark the structures of a society that constrains us, and even to laugh at ourselves.

Pauline Greenhill & Diane Tye

NOTES

1. We are using "culture" in its ethnographic or anthropological sense, referring to all learned as opposed to instinctive behaviour shared by groups of people.
2. "Genre" is a term used to categorize folklore expressions. Each genre – that is, each type of tale, song, joke, or quilt – is characterized by specific themes, vocabularies, structures, styles, and contexts.
3. Michael Taft, *Discovering Saskatchewan Folklore* (Edmonton: NeWest Publishers, 1983), 12.
4. Elliott Oring, ed., *Folk Groups and Folklore Genres: An Introduction* (Logan: Utah University Press, 1986), 17-18.
5. Raymond Williams, *Marxism and Literature* (Oxford: Oxford University Press, 1977), 122.
6. Ibid., 122, 123.
7. We distinguish between "collectors" – those who record folklore, often for posterity – and folklorists – who may collect as well, but who analyse folklore's meaning according to theoretical perspectives.
8. Elli-Kaija Kongas-Maranda (1932-82), the first woman to be given a regular faculty position in a Canadian folklore program, began teaching at Laval in 1976. It took ten more years for the folklore department at Memorial University of Newfoundland to get its first and so far only female tenure-track member of a faculty of around ten. This male domination is particularly ironic since, like many other disciplines in the humanities and social sciences, folklore programs tend primarily to attract female students.

    For an overview of folklore studies in Canada, *see*: Carole Henderson Carpenter, *Many Voices: A Study of Folklore Activities in Canada and their Role in Canadian Culture,* National Museum of Man Mercury Series (Ottawa: National Museums of Canada, 1979).
9. William Hugh Jansen proposed the idea of classifying "performance" in verbal folklore in 1957. He wrote: "The very existence of a piece of verbal folklore, however insignificant, implies an auditor, frequently a group of auditors, and, of course, some person or occasionally persons to 'do' that piece of folklore for that audience. . . . The speaker, or the reciter of the bit of folklore steps outside himself (sic)as an individual and assumes a pose toward his audience, however small, that differs from his everyday, every-hour-in-the-day relationship to that same audience." William Hugh Jansen, "Classifying Performance in the Study of Verbal Folklore," in *Studies in Folklore in Honour of Stith Thompson,* ed. W. Edson Richmond (Bloomington: Indiana University Press, 1957), 112-13.

    The level of performance depends on many factors, including the skill of the performer – how well she tells the joke, for example, and audience expectation. When someone begins a narrative, "Let me tell you a story . . .", takes the floor, and tells the story, incorporating gestures and acting out various parts, there is a high level of performance. Certain genres – like folksong – usually exhibit this quality. Other genres are characterized by a lower performance level: for example, personal experience narratives pieced together by more than one person during conversation.

10. Marta Weigle, "Women as Verbal Artists: Reclaiming the Daughters of Enheduanna," *Frontiers* 3 (1976), 1-9.

11. Helen Creighton, "W. Roy Mackenzie, Pioneer," *Canadian Folk Music Society Newsletter* 2 (1967), 15; W. Roy Mackenzie, *The Quest of the Ballad* (New Jersey: Princeton University Press, 1919), xi.

12. For examples of Teit's work, *see*: James Teit, "The Thompson Indians of British Columbia," ed. Franz Boas, *American Museum of Natural History Memoir* 2 (New York, 1900), 167-396; James A. Teit, "The Salishan Tribes of the Western Prairies," ed. Franz Boas, *45th Annual Report of the Bureau of American Ethnology* (Washington, 1930), 23-396.

13. Wendy Wickwire, "Women in Ethnography: The Research of James A. Teit," *Ethnohistory* (forthcoming).

14. Mackenzie, *Quest of the Ballad*, and *Ballads and Sea Songs from Nova Scotia* (Cambridge, Mass.: Harvard University Press, 1928).

15. Kenneth S. Goldstein, *A Guide for Fieldworkers in Folklore* (Hatboro, Pa.: Folklore Associates, 1964), 11, 55-56, 66-68.

16. Ibid., 56.

17. For example, *see*: Helen Creighton, *Songs and Ballads from Nova Scotia* (Toronto: Dent, 1933); *Bluenose Magic* (Toronto: McGraw-Hill Ryerson, 1968); and *Bluenose Ghosts* (1957; Toronto: McGraw-Hill Ryerson, 1976).

18. Helen Creighton, *A Life in Folklore* (Toronto: McGraw-Hill Ryerson, 1975), 39.

19. Ibid., 68.

20. Ibid., 102-103.

21. Ibid., 162.

22. Women have contributed extensively to the recording of Newfoundland's vast song tradition, for example. Americans Elisabeth Bristol Greenleaf and Grace Yarrow Mansfield did fieldwork there in 1929 and published *Ballads and Sea Songs of Newfoundland* (1933; Hatboro, Pa.: Folklore Associates, 1968) while the contemporaneous folksong expeditions of English woman Maud Karpeles resulted in *Folk Songs of Newfoundland* (London: Faber, 1971). More recently, Newfoundlanders Anita Best and Genevieve Lehr collected folksongs from 1975 to 1983 to produce *Come and I Will Sing You* (Toronto: University of Toronto Press, 1985). In New Brunswick, Louise Manny was not only responsible for publishing (with James R. Wilson) *Songs of Miramichi* (Fredericton: Brunswick, 1968), but also for founding in 1958 and directing the Miramichi Folksong Festival. This event, Canada's longest running folk festival, continues to provide a forum for traditional singing of the region.

Francophone women have also made unique and significant contributions to Canadian traditional culture studies. Carmen Roy worked from the 1950s with Marius Barbeau at the National Museum (now the Canadian Museum of Civilization). As first Chief of the Canadian Centre for Folk Culture Studies, she not only built up a large staff of researchers and collections managers, but also set the direction of the Centre. She felt strongly that it should examine multiculturalism, contrary to earlier notions of folklore as pertaining only to Native people and French Canadians, and that all folk culture, rather than folk*lore* – oral tradition exclusively – should come under its purview. Her own research, from St. Pierre and Miquelon to Vancouver, covers not only the songs and tales that were the focus of the (mainly male) researchers at Laval, but also life histories, foodways, and fishing culture. Female collectors, some trained at Laval, did focus on song and tale legend traditions, but as often as not they worked outside Quebec – Charlotte Cormier and Catherine Jolicoeur in Acadia, for example. Madeleine Doyon studying costume, and Simonne Voyer, examining traditional dance, indicate that women researchers looked beyond the narrow boundaries of the field and worked on folklore as culture – again a modern view.

Edith Fowke's work on Ontario is well known and includes numerous recordings as well as such publications as *Traditional Singers and Songs from Ontario* (Hatboro, Pa.: Folklore Associates, 1965) and *Lumbering Songs from the Northern Woods* (1970; Toronto: NCP, 1985). More recently, ethnomusicologist Anne Lederman collected and published a two-volume set of recordings of *Old Native and Metis Fiddling in Manitoba* (Toronto: Falcon Productions, 1987).

Ethnomusicologist Laura Boulton collected English, French, Gaelic and Inuit musical traditions to produce *The Music Hunter: The Autobiography of a Career* (Garden City, N.Y.: Doubleday, 1969), and Ida Halpern's work on Native traditions in British Columbia resulted in publications including "On the Interpretation of Meaningless Nonsense-Syllables in the Music of the Pacific Northwest Indians," *Ethnomusicology* 20 (1976), 253-271. In Saskatoon, Barbara Cass-Beggs collected both Metis (*Seven Metis Songs of Saskatchewan* [Toronto: BMI Canada, 1967]) and non-Native (*Eight Songs of Saskatchewan* [Toronto: Canadian Music Sales, 1963]) traditional songs. In British Columbia Wendy Wickwire's collaboration with Native storyteller Harry Robinson resulted in *Write it on Your Heart: The Epic World of an Okanagan Storyteller* (Vancouver: Theytus Talon Books, 1989).

23. Frances Fraser, *The Bear Who Stole the Chinook* (Vancouver: Douglas & McIntyre, 1990).

24. For information on Jean Heffernan and her work, *see*: Springhill Heritage Group, Bertha J. Campbell et al., *Springhill: Our Goodly Heritage* (n.p.: privately published, 1989).

25. Since the 1960s folklorists believe that a folklore item can only be understood in relation to its context. "Context" refers to: textual context – how the item

relates to other folklore expressions; situational context – the scenario of the folklore event; social context – its wider social setting; and societal context – the whole society to which the piece of folklore belongs.

26. For example, *see*: Geraldine Barter, "The Folktale and Children in the Tradition of French Newfoundlanders," *Canadian Folklore Canadien* 1 (1979), 5-12; Carole Carpenter, "Tales Women Tell: The Function of Birth Experiences Narratives," *Canadian Folklore Canadien* 7 (1985), 21-34; Barbara Kirshenblatt-Gimblett, "A Parable in Context: A Social Interactional Analysis of a Storytelling Performance," in *Folklore: Performance and Communication*, ed. Kenneth Goldstein and Dan Ben-Amos (The Hague: Mouton, 1975), 105-130; Barbara Rieti, *Strange Terrain: The Fairy World in Newfoundland* (St. John's, Nfld.: Institute for Social and Economic Research, Memorial University, 1991) and Kay Stone, "Things Walt Disney Never Told Us," *Journal of American Folklore* 88 (1975), 42-50.

27. Helen Creighton's work is sometimes dismissed as inaccurate, as Robert Arlidge suggested in a 1986 paper to the Folklore Studies Association of Canada. Arlidge questioned tune variations among Creighton's collections, which he credited to errors on Creighton's part. On the other hand, discussant and audience response to Arlidge's work named other possible reasons, including changes the singers made in versions of their songs or differences in tune between verses. Some critics of Creighton claim she missed valuable aspects of repertoire, such as bawdy narrative, song, and belief. This criticism comes from the perspective of male folklorists whose collecting parameters are not similarly limited. Significantly, this critique has not been matched by any balancing attention to those of Creighton's techniques that pioneered modern collecting. For example, unlike many academic folklorists working at the same time, she collected materials not then thought worthy of scholarly attention, but which are now central to our studies – personal experience stories, popular songs, and so on. She collected these partly out of a wish to gather anything that might be important, and partly because she did not want to offend singers and storytellers by implying that something they thought interesting wasn't valuable. Thus, her collections are uncommonly useful for current folklorists because they reflect personal and regional repertoires. *See*: Pauline Greenhill, *Lots of Stories: Maritime Narratives from the Creighton Collection*, Canadian Centre for Folk Culture Studies MS 57 (Ottawa: National Museum, 1985).

28. Creighton's fieldnotes concerning her female informants have yet to be fully examined, and an analysis of their repertoires remains to be done. Edith Fowke's forthcoming book on LaRena Clark, a singer with whom she has worked since 1961, promises to offer valuable insights into the world of a female traditional performer and will perhaps also explore the relationship of performer with fieldworker.

29. Anthropologists at the turn of the century were interested in gathering Native

ethnohistorical traditions, but most of their work now focuses upon different issues; Native people are now recording their own traditional culture. For example, Freda Ahenakew's *Stories of the House People* (Winnipeg: University of Manitoba Press, 1987), is based on Cree narratives while her *Preliminary Check-List of Plains Cree Medical Terms* (Saskatoon: Saskatchewan Indian Languages Institute, 1987) is a study of Native medical terminology. This latter work is clearly of a collaborative nature: the seven elders whose knowledge provided the basis of the work are listed as co-authors. The preface includes a request for further information with the comments, "PLEASE pay close attention – and keep pencil and paper handy – when the elders talk about health and illness. PLEASE watch when animals are being cut up, and ask the elders for the Cree names of many different parts of the body." This research is clearly in its early stages.

30. Kenneth Peacock, *Songs of the Newfoundland Outports* (Ottawa: National Museum), Bulletin No. 197, Vol 1 (1965), 268.
31. Greenleaf and Mansfield, *Ballads and Sea Songs,* 41.
32. Ibid., 42.
33. Ibid., 26, 9, 15, 120.
34. Ibid., 47-48.
35. *See*: Emily Carr, *Klee Wyck* (Toronto: Oxford, 1941).
36. *See*: Nelda Swinton and Michel Forest, *The Inuit Sea Goddess* (Montreal: Musée des beaux-arts de Montreal, 1980).
37. For more information on Smith and the oral narrative corpus surrounding her, *see*: Diane Tye, "Narrative Gender, and Marginality: The Case Study of Ella Laucher Smith," *Canadian Folklore Canadien* 13, no. 2 (1991), 25-36.
38. This item is from Diane Tye's collection. The interview was held on 28 May 1990 in Amherst, Nova Scotia.
39. "Shivaree" – also "chivaree" – is a corruption of the French "charivari," which the *Oxford English Dictionary* describes as "a serenade of 'rough music,' with kettles, pans, tea-trays and the like, used in France in mockery and derision of incongruous or unpopular persons generally; hence a confused, discordant medley of sounds; a babel of noise."
40. *See*: Pauline Greenhill, "Welcome and Unwelcome Visitors: Shivarees and the Political Economy of Rural-Urban Interactions in Southern Ontario," *Journal of Ritual Studies* 3 (1989), 45-65.
41. Susanna Moodie, *Roughing It in the Bush* (1852; Toronto: McClelland & Stewart, 1962).
42. For a full discussion, *see*: Michael Taft, "Folk Drama on the Great Plains: The Mock Wedding in Canada and the United States," *North Dakota History* 56, no. 4 (1989), 16-23; and Pauline Greenhill, "Folk Drama in Anglo Canada and the Mock Weddings: Transaction, Performance and Meaning," *Canadian Drama* 14 (1988), 109-205.
43. Gerald Pocius, "'The First Day that I Thought of It Since I Got Wed': Role

Expectations and Singer Status in a Newfoundland Outport," *Western Folk-lore* 35 (1976), 110.

44. Ibid., 112.

45. Georges Arsenault has challenged the applicability of this public-private dichotomy for female folksingers within the Acadian tradition. See his "C'est pas pour en insulter, c'est juste pour en ajouter, les chansons de Léah Maddix," *Canadian Folklore Canadien* 13, no. 2 (1991), 71-84.

46. Debora Kodish, "Fair Young Ladies and Bonny Irish Boys: Pattern in Vernacular Poetics," *Journal of American Folklore* 96 (1983), 131-150.

47. For a related discussion, *see*: Gerald Pocius, "Hooked Mats in Newfoundland: The Representation of Social Structure in Design," *Journal of American Folklore* 92 (1979), 273-284.

48. For explorations of gossip, *see*: James Faris, "The Dynamics of Verbal Exchange: A Newfoundland Example," *Anthropologica* 8 (1966): 235-248; Debora Kodish, "Moving Towards the Everyday: Some Thoughts on Gossip and Visiting as Secular Procession," *Folklore Papers of the University Folklore Association Centre for Intercultural Studies in Folklore and Ethnomusicology*, No. 9 (Austin, Tex.: U. of Texas, 1980): 93-104; and Robert Paine, "What is Gossip About? An Alternative Hypothesis," *Man* (NS) 2 (1967), 278-285.

49. James Faris, *Cat Harbour: A Newfoundland Fishing Settlement* (St. John's, Nfld.: Institute of Social and Economic Research, Memorial University, 1972), 144.

50. Edward D. Ives, "Lumbercamp Singing and the Two Traditions," *Canadian Folk Music Journal* 5 (1977), 17-23.

   British traditional and broadside ballads are forms of traditional ballads – songs that tell a story. The British traditional ballads, known as "Child" ballads (because they were gathered from hundreds of manuscript and published sources by Professor Francis James Child of Harvard in the late nineteenth century), begin abruptly *in medias res* (in the middle of the story), and their action unfolds through dialogue and action, leaping and lingering on crucial scenes in much the same way a film does. The tone is impersonal; there is no narrator explaining the action or moralizing. Child ballads are characterized by various kinds of repetition, reflecting the fact that they are a part of oral tradition.

   Broadside ballads are more recent than Child ballads, many originating as broadside sheets sold on the streets of Britain and North America. Often likened to modern-day tabloid newspapers, their plots are more sensational, dealing with subjects such as murders, robberies, scandals, and love-triangles. Their attitude is subjective – they often include a narrator's voice – and their language is less poetic.

51. Colin Quigley and Laurel Doucette, "The Child Ballad in Canada: A Survey," *Canadian Folk Music Journal* 9 (1981), 3-19.

52. Wilfred Wareham, "The Monologue in Newfoundland," in *The Blasty Bough,* ed. Clyde Rose (St. John's, Nfld.: Breakwater, 1975), 210.

53. *See*: Pauline Greenhill, "'The Family Album': A Newfoundland Woman's Recitation," *Canadian Folklore Canadien* 6 (1984), 39-62.

54. For examples of witchcraft belief, *see*: Creighton, *Bluenose Magic.*

55. Sherry Ortner, "Is Female to Male as Nature is to Culture?" in *Women, Culture and Society,* ed. M. Z. Rosaldo and C. Captere (Stanford: Stanford University Press, 1974).

56. Robin McGrath, "Circumventing the Taboos: Inuit Women's Autobiographies," unpublished ms, 1991, 3.

57. McGrath, "Circumventing the Taboos," 15. *See also*: Jean Blodgett, *Kenojuak* (Toronto: Firefly Books, 1985); and Marion Tuu'luk, with Susan Tagoona, "A Story of Staruahon," *Inuit Today* 6, no.9 (1977), 26-31.

58. McGrath, "Circumventing the Taboos," 17.

SUGGESTED READINGS

Farrer, Claire R., *Women and Folklore*. Austin: University of Texas Press, 1975.

Jordon, Rosan A., and Susan J. Kalcik, *Women's Folklore, Women's Culture*. Philadelphia: University of Pennsylvania Press, 1985.

Jordan, Rosan A., and F. A. DeCaro, "Women and the Study of Folklore," *Signs: Journal of Women in Culture and Society* 11 (1986), 500-518.

Special Issue, "Folklore and Feminism," *Journal of American Folklore* 100 (1987), 387-588.

Stoeltje, Beverly, ed., Special Issue, "Feminist Revisions in Folklore Studies," *Journal of Folklore Research* 25 (1988), 141-241.

Weigle, Marta, *Spiders and Spinsters: Women and Mythology*. Albuquerque: University of New Mexico Press, 1982.

Chapter Ten

By and About Women

≈≈≈≈≈≈≈≈≈≈≈≈≈≈≈≈≈≈≈≈≈≈≈≈≈≈≈≈≈≈≈≈≈

Some of us are here
because we were visited
at dawn
were given a third
ear . . .

Some of us are here
as messages
because in the small womb
lies all the lightning. [1]
– Dorothy Livesay

Since 1965 there has been an explosion in the number of novels and books of poetry written by women and published in Canada – so much so that now it is impossible to derive a sense of the true texture of Canadian literature without looking at the writing by women. Yet this was not always the case; before the 1960s, Canadian-published literature was dominated by male writers. This male tradition was a natural manifestation of the patriarchal culture in which we all live. Although in the past many fine women writers were ignored, the female tradition in writing is today getting the recognition it deserves. In fact, the amount of material available is such that no single chapter can include all of the writers who should be represented. So I have instead chosen to concentrate on a few broad themes that run through the writing of English-Canadian writers and discuss only briefly the work of contemporary playwrights and some of the experimental writing that is developing in Quebec.

These authors are writing ourselves and our lives into being, and in the process they bring into focus subjects such as our sexuality, our experience of aging, the politics of mothering – subjects previously ignored. The portrayal of women by women is not new, but the contemporaneity of the exchange – fact for fiction, fiction for fact – *is*. Similarly, a question not always raised when we discuss literature centres on access. Some women writers in our society have voices we rarely hear, so this chapter will open up the question of women's silencing. Because writing never develops in a vacuum, and because the earlier women writers had little or no recognition, it is important to consider briefly the female tradition in Canadian English literature.

Establishing the Tradition

Writing is something women have always done. In fact, "In the development of modern Western civilization, writing was the first of the arts . . . which it was possible for women to practice."[2] Women write because writing is done in private, usually in the home, and requires little outlay for materials – just a pad of paper, a pen, much courage, and talent. So it should come as no surprise to find that Canadian fiction begins with a woman, indeed with two women.

While visiting Quebec in the 1760s, Frances Brooke wrote the first Canadian English-language novel, *The History of Emily Montague,* published in London, England, in 1769. Then, in 1824, H.C. Thomson of Kingston, Upper Canada, published the first indigenous Canadian novel, *St. Ursula's Convent; or, The Nun of Canada,* by Julia (Beckwith) Hart. The long and complex story had begun. The diaries of Elizabeth Simcoe (1791-96) give us detailed information about the lives of the upper class in York (Toronto). This form of writing was used by many of the women who were early settlers in Canada. Diaries and letters, such as the correspondence of Anne Langton (1835-46), later published as *A Gentlewoman in Upper Canada,* are now being recovered and collected by feminist historians, who are also writing the oral histories of older women whose lives span much of this century.[3] In this way we are now establishing the place of women in the literature and in the history of Canada. As Elizabeth Thompson suggests, the composite picture that emerges from the early writing by women "is of a self-assured, confident woman, one who adapts cheerfully to adverse circumstances, one who is capable and active in an emergency."[4] Thompson traces the emergence of a fictional character that is Canadian – female, autonomous, heroic – across the early literature and on into the work of Laurence, Wilson, Beresford-Howe, and others. Sylvia Hamilton, in her article "Our Mothers Grand and Great: Black Women of Nova Scotia," reminds us of an oral tradition stretching back to the eighteenth century. In 1945 Carrie Best established *The Clarion,* the first Nova Scotia newspaper for black people. In doing so, she was following the example set by Mary Shadd Cary, the first black woman in North America to become publisher and editor of a newspaper, *The Freeman* (1853), printed in Windsor, Ontario.[5]

One writer whose work needs no re-establishing is Susanna Moodie (1803-85). She was a prolific writer and her Canadian classic, *Roughing It in the Bush* (1852), has been reissued many times. Moodie's work has taken on a new dimension because of Margaret Atwood's epic poem *Susanna Moodie*. Moodie's sister, Catharine Parr Traill, was neither as graphic (nor as honest) as Susanna when describing the grim life they both experienced in their new country. But then she was less fortunate than her sister; her writing provided the only economic support for her seven surviving children and for her husband, who was never able to adapt to Canada's backwoods. The idealism and optimism in her work are often condemned, but these seem to have been effective strategies for survival – Traill lived to be ninety-seven and wrote her final book at the age of ninety-two. Anna Jameson, by contrast, did not have to provide for her family with her writing. An early visitor to Canada, she wrote for and about 'the gentry.' In *Winter Studies and Summer Rambles in Canada* (1838) she sets the lives of the civilized colonial garrison against the immense and overpowering wilderness of the Canadian North.[6] Wayne Fraser, in *The Dominion of Women,* suggests that the "distaff view of colonization" was extremely political. These early women writers were conscious of the complex pattern of their own colonization with its code of gentility and subservience – a code that was difficult to reconcile with their own heroic behaviour as they settled a savage and hostile land.[7]

Although Isabella Valancy Crawford (1850-87) was a professional fiction writer (many of her short stories and novellas were published in U.S. magazines), it is as a poet that she is important in the history of Canadian literature. She is a central figure in the male-dominated, popular nineteenth-century tradition of narrative poetry, but her poems were largely ignored, uncollected, and only published at her own expense. In the 1970s, Dorothy Livesay, working on the Crawford manuscripts at Queen's University, discovered an incomplete but powerful narrative poem, which has subsequently been published. This act of reclamation brings into focus the continuing need of revisionist work not only to establish the early writing of women in Canada, but also to reassess women's writing that has previously been analysed according to a masculinist tradition.[8] Sandra Djwa, speaking of the new feminine consciousness that was influencing Canadian literature in the late 1950s and early 1960s, tells this anecdote concerning Crawford's status: "Roy Daniels in 1964, when he came to write on Isabella Valancy Crawford for the *Literary History of Canada,* hovered over the adjective 'lady' as descriptive of a female poet and then abandoned it. Crawford was far too good a poet, he judged, to be called a 'lady poet.' No Canadian critic before this time would have shown this distinction."[9]

Two decades after Crawford, we find Sara Jeannette Duncan (1861-1922) tackling her work as a freelance journalist with audacity and courage. She was a prolific and astute fiction writer, some of whose work has now been reissued in answer to the demands of feminist studies. One of her most important novels, *Cousin Cinderella; or, a Canadian Girl in London* (1908, reprinted in 1971), gives a perceptive analysis of the colonialism directed at an expatriate woman who is extremely conscious of the need for a national identity.[10]

An analogous search for a sense of belonging in a new and vast land is central to the work of Laura Goodman Salverson (*The Viking Heart*, 1923) and Martha Ostenso (*Wild Geese*, 1925). Both of these writers explore the early immigrant experience of women in the prairie settlements – a region currently producing many fine women writers (Sharon Butala, Lois Braun, Bonnie Burnard, to mention just a few). Ostenso's novel, while providing us with a somewhat dated experience of female sexuality, is shockingly current in its exposé of the brutality inherent in many marriages. Addressing a somewhat different issue, but one of equal brutality, is Gwethalyn Graham (*Earth and High Heaven*, 1944). She exposes the anti-Semitism of Canadian society, and although her novel is male-centred the narrative provides an early example of current feminist concerns with issues of race and class.

Elizabeth Smart's novel *By Grand Central Station I Sat Down and Wept* (1945) is the story of a passionate love affair that began three years prior to the narrative. Smart chooses the object of her passion (a young poet) from a photograph she found in a book of his poems. She pursues him and courts him passionately and shamelessly – subsequently bearing his children, even though he is married. Structurally and linguistically the book is a forerunner of postmodernism, fracturing chronological time and recording experience in free association with myth and symbol. Biblical phraseology and liturgical ritual are juxtaposed with the raucous demands of police goons. The work mocks the social pretensions of the diplomatic circle in Ottawa that included the Smart family. The publication caused outrage, the book was banned in Canada, and it was forgotten until it was reprinted in 1966. Recent interest in her work[11] includes a brilliant and comprehensive biography by Rosemary Sullivan, who notes that when Smart is speaking about her vision of life, as recorded in the novel, she is not referring to romantic love – which many have identified as her theme. The book speaks to "the law of pain . . . she always insisted on disavowing safety; life was high risk and must be lived to its sharpest edges."[12] Elizabeth Smart's life, as well as her stories, provides us with an experience that encodes the autonomy and the empowerment of a woman living her life, making choices, as a man might. And in doing so she records the pains and the joys of womanhood lived to its fullest.

A decade later Sheila Watson wrote *The Double Hook* (1959). The mythical language and the symbolic configurations of this book, spanning cultures as diverse as Japan and Spain, have recently been analysed by Angela Bowering. Her comments on the figure of the old woman who dominates the 'narrative' refer the reader back to the empowering female deity: "The forms of female divinity and the forms of the female *figurae* in this novel are the many faces of one female form. It dies and is reborn as the old lady." Watson makes of this old woman "the sign for all the dispersed and occulted fractions of the divine female that are multiplied in the diverse and dying cultures of the world. She is the glyph of origin, cut into origin itself; the earth, searching for origin."[13] Constance Rooke finds that "Both collectively and as individuals, these women (or figures, if you like) have been under-valued, under-read." Her perceptive analysis of *The Double Hook* as portraying an intensely sexist society allows the reader to enter the text in a dynamically new way.[14] 'Malestream' criticism has been so pervasive that this book, misinterpreted consistently, has been blocked for women students. Sheila Watson was prefiguring the poets and novelists now writing about the association of woman's physicality and spirituality as it colludes with the forms of nature across the cultural histories of the world.

The list of earlier women writers could continue, for as Atwood says in the Introduction to *Roughing It in the Bush* (1986):

> When you place the early literature of the Canadas beside that of the United States, a curious thing emerges. It's possible to cover American literature from, say, 1625 to 1900, without spending much time at all on women writers, with the exception of Ann Bradstreet and Emily Dickinson. Attention focuses on the 'great' and overwhelmingly male American writers of the period: Melville, Poe, Hawthorne . . . English Canada produced no such classics at this time – it was settled later – but if you study the literature at all, you can't ignore the women.[15]

Atwood suggests that it may be the difference in the dates of settlement (seventeenth century versus nineteenth century) that accounts for the larger proportion of women writers in Canada, but significantly, "It's a situation that has persisted until today: the percentage of prominent and admittedly accomplished women writers, in both prose and poetry, is higher in Canada than it is in any of the other English-speaking countries."

But in spite of this, women writers were not acknowledged as part of mainstream writing. This omission was due, in part, to a national hesitancy in recognizing any Canadian literary canon. Sandra Djwa suggests that although "the tide had begun to turn about 1943" with the recognition that we did indeed have a literature that must be acknowledged, this literature was largely ignored by the universities and "up to the middle fifties the tradition was the English (and male) tradition of Milton, Wordsworth" et al.[16] So even after Canadian Literature became a recognized field of study, it took special effort on the part of (mainly women) scholars to unearth the early works of women writers and get them reissued.

One writer whose work spans much of the century, and continues as vigorously as ever, is Dorothy Livesay. Her work was ignored for years, but she is in many senses one of the most important foremothers of our writing. Actively engaged in left-wing politics since the 1920s, Livesay has written poetry that is both political and lyrical. She was an early feminist and an ardent advocate of trade unionism, becoming a social worker in order to practise the social justice she believed in. Livesay has acknowledged the strong and solitary figure of Emily Carr as central in the female tradition. As a visual artist, Carr was totally marginalized and, although she was a contemporary of the Group of Seven, she remained excluded from the Group. Her magnificent West Coast paintings remained relatively unknown until after her death. Her journals, not published until 1966, provide a graphic description of what it means to be a woman and artist. Her struggle is confirmed in *The House of All Sorts* (1967), a series of anecdotes about her life as a landlady – a project undertaken in a vain attempt at economic security. Towards the end of her life, Carr wrote *Klee Wyck* (1941), an immediate success that won a Governor General's Award. At least as a writer, Carr was 'acceptable' – writing was something women could do, painting was not. Despite the award, Carr's writing has received the readership it so clearly deserves only since the advent of Women's Studies courses in the 1970s.

In *Klee Wyck* Carr not only captures the essence of the natural landscape, but she also provides portraits of many Native women. Until Native women themselves broke their silence, as Maria Campbell does in *Halfbreed* (1973), Emily Carr's voice was one of the strongest on their behalf. Carr's stories depend on the oral tradition, a tradition absorbed by the contemporary West Coast poet Daphne Marlatt. Like Carr's writing, Marlatt's poetry relies heavily on the Canadian landscape and on the affinity of human and natural cycles.

The 1950s marked a watershed in Canadian writing for both prose and poetry. There was now a growing number of women who were writing innovative and dynamic poetry. Miriam Waddington and P.K. Page were both members of the Montreal group who published in *Preview* during the 1940s. P.K. Page was a scriptwriter at the National Film Board, and her poems in *The Meal and the Flower* (a winner of the 1954 Governor General's Award) take both their style and their theme from the kinetic cinematography of her film work. Waddington has an ease and civility in her use of language and metaphor, often turning the mundane into the extraordinary, achieving much the same effect as Alice Munro does in her short stories. Listen to what Waddington says about "The Secret Life":

> There is a man who calls me wife
> who knows me but does not know my life,
> and my two sons who call me mother
> see me not as any other
> yet if the fabric of my day
> should be unwound and fall away
> what coloured skeins would carelessly
> unwind where I live secretly?[17]

The poet speaks to each one of us who has experienced this hidden – yet shared – experience, and she does so in a language of utter simplicity and compassion.

Jay Macpherson, as both teacher and poet, is noted as an early influence on the work of Margaret Atwood, and both women were students of Northrop Frye. Atwood's critical work *Survival* (1972) depends heavily on Frye's interpretation of the Canadian wilderness as motif and construct in Canadian fiction. The writing in Margaret Avison's *Winter Sun* (1960) has a precision of form and language also evident in Pat Lowther's poetry in the representation of various states and levels of consciousness. Phyllis Webb was also writing in the 1950s, but it is her later work, especially *Selected Poems* (1971), that has influenced many of today's young poets. Her recent poem about Bronwen Wallace, "Bronwen's Earrings," gives us a glimpse of the esteem and joy that women poets share in their work and in their lives. The whole poem is a tribute to Wallace's short life and to her glorious poetry:

> long, or large and circular
> the only decoration on her
> tall frame, her plain façade
> the better to hear the high
> vibrations of your health, your
> sorrows. A touch of fantastic
> as she moved her head
> to follow the plot
> silver or gold flashing
> hilarious light on the lure
> of the pierced ear.
> Spangles. Trapezoids, fluttery
> things. Wild bird.

The pair I gave her
turquoise, oval, Chinese
I think and very long
with a history of survival.

As I drink this tea
on an ordinary day
someone crosses
a street in Kingston
picking up flute notes
soprano complaints
her earlobes tugged
by a small weight
of chimes
the need to be heard, desire.[18]

Even though we have an extensive tradition of writing by and about women, it would be wrong to assume that women authors have enjoyed a privileged or equitable environment and an audience eager for their writing. There was a new wave of the women's movement in the late 1960s which focused almost entirely (in its early stages) on the individual experiences of women and derived strength from the consciousness-raising groups, which Naomi Black discusses in her chapter on the women's movement. It was during the 1960s that Canadian Literature came of age, emerging as a *bona fide* field of study.

Writing the Self into Being

If in general there was a new audience for Canadian Literature in the 1960s, then in the 1970s the women novelists enjoyed a rapidly expanding readership. The obvious spin-off to this is an increasing body of criticism (sometimes feminist) to which the authors themselves contribute. Margaret Atwood's critical prose is almost as important as her creative writing, and she warns us:

Writers, as writers, are not propagandists or examples of social trends or preachers or politicians. They are makers of books, and unless they can make books well they will be bad writers, no matter what the social validity of the views . . . . Writing tends to concentrate more on life, not as it ought to be, but as it is, as the writer feels it, experiences it. . . . [A writer's] work may include the Movement, since it is so palpably among the things that exist. The picture that she gives of it is altogether another thing, and will depend, at least partly, on the course of the Movement itself.[19]

The body of work women writers are producing does indeed record the hopes, dilemmas, failures, and successes of the women's movement, providing the creative counterpart to the political and social changes taking place. But Adele Wiseman reminds us that when many of the current women writers began their novels they were ahead of the feminist movement: "We took the creative leap into the issues of our age which others had not defined clearly as issues, and which they have since begun to use our fiction to help them understand."[20]

The search for individual selfhood, the motivating force of the consciousness-raising groups of the late 1960s, finds its analogue in the writing of the past three decades. A surprisingly large number of these writers choose to explore the emerging self through a writer/protagonist: the woman who writes herself, her story, her life, into being. Miriam Waddington, in an essay on "Women and Writing," describes how "Women artists can make known what has been – and still is – unknown, and they can claim, out of the anonymity that Virginia Woolf so eloquently describes, a new awareness and new identities." In an analysis of Elaine Showalter's article on "Feminist Criticism in the Wilderness," Waddington discusses a critical approach to women's writing that takes the form of historical and cultural analysis.

> There is a lot of truth in the statement that women's culture forms a collective experience, and I want to emphasize that the experience is a historical one. The feminist movement didn't spring up full-grown in 1970, but long before that, and this needs to be remembered. Every woman who was an artist and who wrote out of herself, her life, and her values was a feminist whether she knew it or not. She may or may not have been part of the political feminist movement – which was true in my case. But I was certainly writing out of and about my body – pregnancy and childbirth, mothering, aging, and death – and since I was shaping my language to suit what I had to say, it must have been a woman's language. Theory always comes after the experience – and it is only when we experience the theory through our own living that we can really know it.

In agreement with Showalter's cultural critique, Waddington believes that "A cultural theory acknowledges that there are important differences between women as writers; class, race, nationality and history are literary determinants as significant as gender."[21] This aspect of feminist criticism, RE-MEMBERING the cultural histories of all women, is the vital issue that feminist scholarship must begin to address.

Many of the writers discussed here fall under the general heading of realists, though the cultural realities they explore are totally different from those usually portrayed in 'malestream' writing.[22] Women, especially women in the home, live in a subculture in which the norms are closer to abnormal when assessed by external criteria. To portray this reality women writers use different techniques in their writing. They fracture time, as it is constantly fractured in their own lives by countless demands. The narrative voice will vary to include a character talking to herself, or God, or anyone else who will listen. The closures of the novel will alter and break. Whereas the traditional ending of a story often shows the woman protagonist as happily married (or dying of unrequited love), contemporary women writers may alter the closure, leaving the protagonist with ever-increasing options. [23]

Believing in the validity of their own culture, their own experience, sufficiently to write it into being has not been an easy task for women writers. Alice Munro expresses this unease when she describes the mornings she spent, during the 1950s, with a group of house-bound friends. How could she, as writer, transform what she perceived as 'trivia' into the stuff of serious literature? Her experience is told in an 'Appreciation' of Marian Engel's two novels *Honeymoon Festival* and *Sarah Bastard's Notebook*:

> And here was a woman writing about the lives of women at their most muddled, about a woman who can't quite believe in the world of careers, academic strivings, faith in work, and another who is just managing to keep afloat in the woozy world of maternity, with its shocks and confusions and fearful love and secret brutality. You have to remember how shunned, despised, misused, this material was at that time . . . most of us thought there was no way to deal with it except to turn it into the layer-cake fiction of the women's magazines, or hype it up to the manic level of the humor of the professional harried housewives who write newspaper columns. [24]

Munro goes on to explain that it was Engel's bravery and skill in transforming such experience into literature that gave her "that clear glimpse of possibilities which is one of the things a writer is always looking for, and must be most lastingly grateful for, in another writer." [25] It is significant that Margaret Laurence, when interviewed in a 1978 video about *The Fire-Dwellers* (1969), felt impelled to defend what had been discounted by critics as "trivial content." [26] But the world of Stacey MacAindra, which Laurence presents in this novel, is one experienced by many women in Canada. Stacey's secret drinking, her fight to achieve a "perfect body," her fear of aging, her constant guilt over mothering, her longing for a man who will communicate with her, and her fantasy of a lover who is gentle, caring, passionate, and strong are (in large part) the 'trivia' of our lives.

The new thematic material that Munro finds in Engel's work overthrows the established concept of 'universality' and posits a new set of criteria. For instance, much has been written about death and how the heroic male faces it. Death is, of course, universal, and 'great' literature concerns itself with such things. But birth is as universal as death, and until very recently little has been written about the process of birth or about the cultural and political relevance of birthing.[27] Although everyone experiences birth, women are the only people who can record the reality of giving birth. Women writers are now creating protagonists who choose to remain childless, who accept motherhood with reluctance, or who disengage themselves from the mothering role even after they have become biological mothers. In the process, they are recording the radical shift that women's lives will take when the androcentric family institution is challenged and declared invalid. The problem of universality, which takes the masculine norm as its point of reference, annuls the specificity of women's experience, as Lorraine Code observes in chapter one of this book. Women writers give voice to that specificity while recognizing a commonality in the diversity, in the particulars, and in the 'trivialities' of women's lives. As Margaret Atwood reminds us: "Feminism has done many good things for women writers, but surely the most important has been the permission to say the unsaid, to encourage women to claim their full humanity, which means acknowledging the shadows as well as the lights."[28]

Audrey Thomas deconstructs the concept of motherhood and mothering when she deconstructs language: *Birthday.* "Birth Day. The child is told that it's his birthday, but it's the mother who knows." *(M)other.* "Who can see the 'other' in mother?" *Mummy.* "Body of human being or animal embalmed for burial; dried up body . . . 'This is Anne's mummy.' Mummy . . . All wrapped up in her family."[29] The technique alone releases a new set of truths about the shadowy, bleak side of motherhood.

In *ANA Historic* Daphne Marlatt creates a 'history' for an ordinary woman, a Mrs. Richards, who (like many other women) never made it into any of the traditional histories of Canada. But in this 'history' the prose reads like poetry; the traditional, verbose, historical novel form has been deconstructed – in fact, demolished. In this postmodern novel Marlatt uses snatches of verse, songs girls skip to, entries from a dictionary, the titles of popular songs, to strip away the accumulated cultural interpretations of a word as simple (and as complex) as "f/act." The structure of the book satirizes 'malestream' history, its form and its content. It is ahistoric in its construction. The dictionary entry for the prefix "ana" is significant: "a collection of a person's memorable sayings . . . gossip about a person . . . back, again, anew." The title of the book alone spins off incredible sparks for reinvention and in the process Marlatt gives us a new perspective on ourselves, inviting us – not to anger – but to laughter. Her irreverence is contagious, but it is her talent for focusing on the political truth that drives this 'novel' along:

a book of interruptions is not a novel

what is her first name? she must have one –
so far she has only the name of a dead man,
someone somewhere else[30]

The process of creating 'an ahistoric' persona in *ANA Historic* depends heavily on linguistic and structural patterns that seem to deny a 'story-line'; nevertheless a story is produced. And in it, Annie – the researcher – gives the reader access to new interpretations of cultural history and new insights on autonomy (on both the loss of it and on the methods by which we might regain it).

Bronwen Wallace, writing "A Simple Poem for Virginia Woolf," is paying tribute to the tradition of women writers and to the gift of autonomy that is intrinsic to the act of writing. But in doing so she is also describing for us the paralysing frustrations a mother experiences responding to the needs of small children:

This started out as a simple poem
for Virginia Woolf   you know the kind
we women writers write these days
in our own rooms
on our own time . . .
I wanted it simple
and perfectly round
hard as an
egg   I thought
only once I'd said egg
I thought of the smell
of bacon grease and dirty frying pans
and whether there were enough for breakfast . . .

And Wallace includes our friendships as an integral part of our lives – more as a motivating force for our writing: "and I certainly wasn't going/ to tell you about the time/ my best friend was sick in intensive care . . . but they wouldn't let me in . . . I wasn't family/ I was just her friend/ and the friendship of women/ wasn't mentioned/ in hospital policy . . . but that's what got me/ started I suppose   wanting to write / a gesture of friendship/ for a woman for a woman writer/ for Virginia Woolf."[31] The whole poem is a testimony to the transformative power of relationships without denying the pain and the cost of living inclusively. And the first experience of bonding/bondage often occurs for women with pregnancy and birth.

In a posthumously published book of brilliant short stories, *People You'd Trust Your Life To*, Bronwen Wallace moves from poetry to fiction.[32]

This collection, written shortly before her death, is a rare gift. She writes with honesty and grace about the many stages of our womanhood. We see ourselves growing up and getting hooked on vivid purple lipsticks and scarves from Zeller's. We recognize ourselves as the mother who is guilty, resentful, joyous – and all at the same time. Or we are fat and old and tired and rightfully lazy. Wallace has the exceptional ability to turn the everyday tedium of our lives into high art, much as Alice Munro does. But Wallace's stories record the 1990s and are shockingly current.

In the ironically titled "Christmas Carols," Margaret Atwood describes yet another aspect of pregnancy that is rarely articulated but is experienced by thousands of women who are caught and controlled in wars fought by men:

Children do not always mean
hope. To some they mean despair.
This woman with her hair cut off
so she could not hang herself
threw herself from a rooftop, thirty
times raped & pregnant by the enemy
who did this to her. [33]

The final section of the poem refers us back to the well-known virgin/whore double standard incorporated into the myths of Mary, mother of God, and Eve, mother of Man.

. . . If mother-
hood is sacred, put
your money where your mouth is. Only
then can you expect the coming
down to the wrecked & shimmering earth
of that miracle you sing
about, the day
when every child is a holy birth [34]

The title "Christmas Carols" underscores Atwood's comment about the ritualization of society's hypocrisy – a cost demanded of women with sickening regularity.

Sharon Butala (*Luna* [1988] and *Country of the Heart* [1990]) is a prairie writer concerned about recording the daily lives of women in a circumscribed region. She is not writing about the urban or the international experiences that are Atwood's interest. She does not deal with the shocking. Instead she explores, in great detail, the lives of farm women. We experience the costs to these women – the isolation, the loneliness, the back-breaking work – that the Western landscape imposes on its settlers. But simultaneously we experience the richness of extended families – of mothering – and the satisfaction women feel in close relationships with each other.

In *Lives of Girls and Women,* Alice Munro questions the concept of conventional marriage as the defining role for women.[35] Alongside this theme, she gives us insight into the unique bond/bondage between a mother and daughter; she illustrates the fearful and comic struggle of each to become her own person – growing to potential and yet attempting to retain the links that are life-giving and self-affirming. The narrative of the sexual evolution of Del Jordan is the portrait of the writer as a young girl and, more importantly, it is Munro's realignment of certain social conventions.

Munro uses the writer/protagonist to question the old dispensations. She simplifies the proposition for the reader by making Del Jordan the 'photographer of life' (the apprentice), who knows by the end of her story "that the only thing to do with my life was to write a novel," which is, of course, the one Munro has written.[36] All of the action is filtered through the narrative "I": in this way Munro explores the changing patterns of women's lives.

Later, in a brilliant short story, "The Office," Munro directs the reader to what might constrain an older Del, and in the process she politicizes the concept of space; in particular, the space that the creating mind requires.[37] The writer/narrator, a wife/mother, demonstrates tenacity and determination to get and hold on to "a room of her own," namely an office. The invasion – almost a rape – of the psychological and creative space transforms the story: the protagonist is forced into a power struggle with a disturbed and disturbing landlord. She must fight for her creative life. She has to move out of her office, and the story we read is the only evidence that she survives. Munro writes a different survival story in "Friend of My Youth."[38] Remembering her mother as the heroic woman she really was helps the writer survive now. Mothers, seen from the vantage point of our own maturity, demand new respect and offer an unexpected, shared understanding and compassion. But Munro remains irreverent, we piece together the lives of our mothers (and, by association, explore our own) through the wacky eccentric friendships and escapades of this mother in her youth. What Munro noticed in Marian Engel's work, the desperate honesty, the bravado, the subversive wit, and above all the vindication of our experiences and of our lives as women, are all characteristics of her own work. A similar honesty is obvious in the work of Susan Swan. In *The Last of the Golden Girls* (1989), Swan writes about the sexuality of teenage girls and what has been traditionally taboo – female sexual fantasy, orgasm, masturbation – as a natural part of our experimentation and our experience of growing into womanhood.[39]

Writing the self into being is also the main narrative of Laurence's novel

The Diviners (1974). Laurence uses the snapshot and memory-bank movie sequences as a structure through which Morag 'divines' herself as a girl, as woman, and as writer. These images are kept "not for what they show but for what is hidden in them,"[40] and it is the slow, painful, solitary craft of weaving them together, writing them, that Laurence/Morag explores throughout the novel. An anonymous phone call to Morag offers insight into the fear and doubt that accompany every act of writing:

> The woman only wanted to find out. . . . Wanting the golden key from someone who had had five books published and who fre-quently wondered how to keep the mini-fortress here going and what would happen to her when she could no longer write. Golden key indeed. . . . A daft profession. Wordsmith. Liar, more likely. Weaving fabrications. Yet, with typical ambiguity, convinced that fiction was more true than fact. Or that fact was in fact fiction.[41]

Laurence has created a unique community of women in her five Manawaka books. It is Morag's final movement into the role of novelist that gives added meaning to the struggles (in Laurence's previous books) of each protagonist searching for herself. The many acts of divination are realigned in the final novel, which closes with Morag returning "to the house, to write the remaining private and fictional words, and to set down her title."[42] The dictionary defines 'divining' as the "act of predicting or foretelling events, or of discovering hidden or secret things by real or by alleged supernatural means; also to find out by inspiration, magic or intui-tion." This definition of Laurence's title applies as well to all of the authors who frame their novels around a writer/protagonist.

Atwood also addresses the problem of divining the self and the process of autonomy (as it is related to gender) in the competitive and ruthless world of journalism. The female protagonist in "Hack Wednesday" seems to have the heightened consciousness of a feminist who is committed to issues of social justice.[43] But this woman has difficulty maintaining her political integrity in newsrooms that depend on sex, violence, power (over women) – the daily 'headliners' that make sales. In this story, and in "Uncles," Atwood explores the complex issues facing women who are 'successful' in professions that are masculine preserves of power. Political allegiances break along gender lines and a raised consciousness becomes a liability. Atwood demonstrates that autonomy is difficult to maintain in these working conditions.

Marian Engel in *The Glassy Sea* (1978) uses the epistolary form as a pro-cess of self-discovery. Rita Heber, the protagonist, moves from her life as a single woman into a religious order, out to a marriage, and back again into the communal life. In compiling the novel/letter, Rita is writing herself (and some of her revolutionary ideas) into being. Hers is a story unique in women's writing: Engel/Rita finds practical ways of transforming the comfort and privilege of 'Mother Church' into a communal comfort for all women of all classes. The social and political changes initiated by women in some religious orders are among the most radical of the past decades. Engel, writing in 1976 and 1977, was recording these reforms, which have the potential to change the church irrevocably. Engel's dedication to her craft, to getting the form and structure absolutely right as the 'container' for such thematic material, is obvious throughout the novel. A letter comprising some 120 pages is a daunting technical challenge, but it is the ideal structure for the necessarily long resolution of the spiritual with the secular.

Intertidal Life (1984) by Audrey Thomas is an intensely secular work, recording the complex, convoluted experiences of women who are searching for new patterns in their lives. While the book attempts no answers, it is specific in its questioning. Alice Hoyle is Thomas's woman writer, who must not only write her experience, but must also extricate herself from it in order to write it, a problem faced by many women writers. Privacy (space and free time away from domesticity) is essential if Alice is to write, yet her insistence on privacy makes her suspect to her women friends. She is a woman *voyageur*:

> But one went on a true quest alone and, except for magical or divine intervention, one fought the terror of the dark wood alone. One didn't bring along three kids, a lame dog and a spiteful cat. . . . How many of the men who explored these fog-shrouded coasts and uncharted inlets were actually married? Only Vancouver's gunner on his ship and he didn't bring his family along. Questers have to Pay Attention or they miss the sacred signs.[44]

Alice is a woman obsessed with writing. She does not choose the art: it chooses her. She is a language junkie collecting words, dissecting meaning, spinning connections that in turn create new ideas and act as commentary on the story-line. We have already seen how she deconstructs the word "mother," and she uses this technique throughout the novel. "*Deliver* . . . Rescue, save and free *from*; disburden (woman in parturition) . . . hand on *to* another" as in marriage; "*deliberare* . . . *liber* free Let no man put ass under."[45]

Here Thomas is deconstructing and reconstructing our concept of womanhood. In fracturing the continuity of the narrative through language, through the shifts from the third- to first-person narrator, through the inclusion of diary entries and children's games, Thomas releases the truth about the fractured life of 'woman as writer,' mother, friend, wife, divorcée. Alice Hoyle is also portrayed as Alice in Wonderland, forever falling through the gaps in her life made by her trendy husband and discovering an upside-down world in which truth is usually the opposite of reality. She explains: "What's happening to men and women today is just as exciting and terrifying as the discovery that the earth was round, not flat. . . . But we all need new maps, new instruments to try and fix our new positions. . . . Women have let men define them, taken their names even, with marriage, just like a conquered or newly settled region."[46] She concludes that mothers and wives must always be available and "artists are never 'always there.'"[47] So Alice Hoyle 'housewife' is crossed out on her divorce papers and Alice Hoyle 'writer' inserted instead. "The woman artist has an even harder time . . . if she is to move forward at all she has to develop a layer of selfishness-self-is-ness-that has been traditionally reserved for men."[48] In a short story, "Mothering Sunday," Thomas writes about the hypocrisy and the media hype that has evolved around this special day that 'honours' mothers, and she adds a wacky account of a woman gathering sperm in order to impregnate herself with a turkey baster. "It was the turkey baster that made me laugh. Birds still involved in immaculate conception."[49]

Thomas's writing records the shift in relationships that takes place as women find autonomy, and the transition is complex, difficult, and unresolved. Thomas, in an interview, says, "I want to write a really positive novel of women who live without men. I want to do a real quest story."[50] It is interesting that another West Coast novelist, Ethel Wilson, wrote such a story – *Swamp Angel* – in 1954. Dorothy Livesay pointed out that Wilson's work inexplicably went unnoticed. (Livesay's protest did not go unnoticed: six of Wilson's titles were reissued by McClelland & Stewart in 1990.)[51]

In *The Handmaid's Tale* (1985) Margaret Atwood depicts her protagonist, Offred, as a writer even though we know that writing is an impossible luxury (and an act of anarchy) in the monolithic Republic of Gilead. Offred not only records her experience as a 'surrogate womb,' she is also recording history for future generations of women. All writing is an act of hope; in this story it is the sole indication of survival. The text we read is evidence of Offred's life beyond the regime: "By telling you anything at all, I'm at least believing in you, I believe you're there, I believe you into existence. I tell, therefore you are."[52] Offred's words suggest the power of the creative act and are applicable to other women protagonists/novelists who are writing our lives into being.

Constance Rooke, in *Fear of the Open Heart,* suggests that in Canadian literature our national psyche is most often portrayed as a 'garrison mentality.' But this gender-specific "militaristic . . . and male term" must be reworked if it is to be applied to women writers. Rooke describes it as a "fear of the open heart . . . a female wording of a basic Canadian mindset."[53] Rooke's thesis explores the degrees to which current women writers portray, openly and courageously, or subtextually, issues of concern to women, and in the process she asks to what degree are these writers generating a new 'awareness, a new openness?' (a characteristic that Rooke finds lacking in much of the traditional, malestream, writing). There is a new community of women writing and reading that is generating its own dynamic. And because we have a literature that is newly inclusive, we are encouraged to explore dimensions of ourselves, such as our sexual needs and our experiences of aging, which were largely ignored in writing before the 1960s.

Helen Potrebenko is one of the few writers who continually writes the world of the working-class woman into being. Her stories centre on the women in the service industries, the women with the triple load of house, children, and paid work – the women with very little security and enormous stress. Since her first book *Taxi* (1975) – about a protagonist who drives a cab to earn a living – to the latest anthology of short stories, *Hey Waitress and Other Stories* (1989), Potrebenko has explored the lives of those working-class women who are usually ignored in creative writing and often neglected in feminist analysis.

Sexuality and Selfhood

In an important book, *Sex, Power and Pleasure* (1985), Mariana Valverde reminds us of the distinction the English language makes between the words 'sex' and 'sexuality.' Sex is "what we do in bed (or wherever)"; sexuality is "an ever-present social issue."[54] She goes on to make two other points, which are relevant to the writing under discussion: first, that "for the women's movement as a whole, 'sexuality' brings to mind sexual politics: our struggles to equalize relations between men and women, to open up social space for bisexuality and lesbianism." Second, what Valverde calls "sexual pessimism" – caused by the shadows of violence, guilt, and repression – has, she says, become "a powerful force in the women's movement. . . . However, in most women this pessimism is checked and balanced by glimpses of a world in which women explore their sexual desires without fear . . . and by the recognition that if male sexual violence is a serious problem, so is female sexual unhappiness and guilt."[55] Literary works, in this context, both complement and learn from psychology's new efforts to take women's experiences seriously, which Joanna Boehnert discusses in her chapter of this book.

The guilt and repression that are basic to female sexual unhappiness are subjects that very few writers, men or women, have tackled. And until very recently women have rarely written their sexual fantasies, which are the core of the sexual self. Such fantasies locked in the subconscious become blocking or controlling agents, and only by bringing such inhibitions into consciousness and speaking them, or writing them, do we control them instead of allowing them to control us. So we find that the erotic in literature is a catalyst for the imagination: we envision ourselves in new ways, with empowerment, with a larger sense of self, and with a sense of new possibilities that heightens our pleasures and adds to our self-knowledge.

In Marian Engel's *Bear* (1976), the erotic and the sexual are dimensions of the psychological and physical self that propel the protagonist, Lou, into change and growth. She is an archivist, a pre-writer, a woman who works in solitude, gathering and documenting facts that do not give her the knowledge she is seeking. Lou has a routine, mechanical occupation that parallels the sex she submits to automatically during her lunch hour, on top of a library table. Moving north to catalogue more archival material, Lou escapes into the primitive world of earth and water, which is the habitat of the bear. While Engel has fun describing this exotic affair of woman and animal, she makes clear that the erotic begins in Lou's mind, in her sexual fantasies. It is emphatically the woman who controls and guides; her needs are gratified, her pleasures fulfilled. This exploration of change and growth through woman's sensuality completely explodes the myth of our sexual passivity. (And on another level it revisions the simple fairy tale of beauty and the beast. Engel transforms beauty, the beast remains just that.) Engel breaks new ground with this novel. Just as Munro saw Engel's early work as revolutionary in legitimizing the mundane aspects of women's experience, here, too, she is daring.

Whereas Engel's novel releases women into new dimensions of self, Atwood's *The Handmaid's Tale* is about the ultimate control of women's sexuality. The novel is a dystopian view of womanhood, which, although futuristic, is grounded in current sociopolitical trends.[56] Atwood, always aware of the fragility of Canadian identity, warns of a future that is possible for Canadian women as she observes the political swing to the right in the United States. This book looks forward into an Old Testament world in which patriarchal religion determines that biology is destiny. Here, Atwood analyses the politics of sexuality as dispassionately as she does in her poetry.

The appended "Historical Notes" form a brilliant synopsis, which redefines Atwood's novel according to patriarchal ideology. The notes form a critique, which is a re-enactment of traditional masculinist criticism. The history of Offred (specifically) and of the handmaidens (generally) is trivialized as Professor James Darcy Pieixoto warns against accepting this text as authentic. The appendix is Atwood's statement about the delegitimization and devaluation of women's history and women's writing. The tale/tail of the handmaid are the two sides of the same coin; her profession and her gender are inseparable, and each one marginalizes the other. Pieixoto's call for questions at the end of his lecture is rhetorical: the academic jury has been out and the verdict declared: this handmaid's tale is invalid.

Atwood's poetry returns again and again to these power relationships between men and women, back to the deadly game of sexual politics. The terse and brilliant opening poem in *Power Politics* (1971) encapsulates in four lines the warning sounded in *The Edible Woman* (1969) and fully articulated in *The Handmaid's Tale*:

> You fit into me
> like a hook into an eye
>
> a fish hook
> an open eye[57]

The poem moves from the domestic realm to the savage; the hook in the eye of corset or boot is containing, constricting, but the hook of the hunt is deadly. The images that spin off these lines are all of closure. The eye is filled up, space is obliterated, a living organism dies, the linear invades the circular and destroys it; the I/eye becomes silent/blind. The sardonic, brief four lines effectively leave the page blank, and we realize that here Atwood's poetry is informed by a sexual pessimism that approaches that of Valverde.

In *Cat's Eye* (1988) Atwood introduces us to the cruel, taunting – sometimes dangerous – games played by adolescent girls who know, and do not know, the sexual gridlock that they are approaching. And Sylvia Fraser in *My Father's House: A Memoir of Incest and of Healing* (1987) recounts with brutal honesty (and much compassionate understanding) her long years of victimization. The courage that it takes to write a childhood and an adolescence such as Fraser's onto the page cannot be underestimated, nor can the empowerment that it gives to women readers – especially when read collectively by women students who are also exploring the political issues involved in the control of women's bodies.

While Engel's *Bear* is an exploration of the sensual self, Atwood's writing is driven by an incisive analysis of women's place in the power games of sexuality, which are themselves a deadly reflection of social and cultural realities. *Bodily Harm* (1981) and *Surfacing* (1972) are both novels in which Atwood's protagonists face the traumatic consequences of physical and psychological violation set within the context of sexual politics. In both cases the woman must extricate herself from a relationship with a man before her healing process is possible. Engel's *The Honeyman Festival* (1970) provides another dimension. While the story can be read on one level as that of any harassed housewife barely coping with having too many children too close in age, it is the particular characterization of Minn that carries the narrative line. This complex, wacky individual provides Engel with sufficient scope to link the maternal and the sexual in a set of hilarious, yet compelling circumstances.

Margaret Laurence in *A Jest of God* (1966) depicts Rachel Cameron as a profoundly repressed woman who plays out the stereotypical role of spinster; the sexual fears and hypocrisies that cripple her psychologically are manifested in her phantom pregnancy. The double standard of male-female sex roles and the damage accruing to the female psyche form a sub-theme throughout the novel. In Laurence's *The Fire-Dwellers* (1969) we watch Stacey discovering herself as she responds to her own sexual needs. Luke, her lover, is the only male character in the novel who is not locked into the stereotypical masculine role. Luke as symbolic (and actual) healer releases Stacey into a new dimension of self.

Such writing challenges the 'comfortable' roles and traditions that have shored up patriarchal family structures. Because of this, Margaret Laurence came under attack when *The Diviners* was put on school reading lists. Obviously this woman novelist had gone too far. In writing a protagonist who rejects traditional marriage, controls her own sexuality, opts for single motherhood (by selecting a Métis man to father her child), Laurence became the target of a bigoted right-wing censorship group. Through the characterization of Morag, Laurence challenges the traditional, patriarchal concept of womanhood. In doing so, as Engel says, she creates "one of the few heroines who achieves the apocalypse of knowing what her life has been about, not through the agency of a man, but through her own experience."[58]

The concept of woman as 'generous whore' has been a popular depiction (or caricature) of woman in 'malestream' literature, and during certain historical periods this concept has assumed the proportions of an archetype. In British Restoration comedy no play was complete without such a character, and the trend has continued to thrive in the pulp industry across cultures and centuries. Adele Wiseman's *Crackpot* (1978) is a Canadian classic that subverts this myth. The protagonist, Hoda, is a survivor, and despite her promiscuity she remains an innocent throughout a large portion of the novel. This is the story of a girl/woman who lives on the very edge of society. Marginalized by poverty, ethnicity, and gender, she slips into prostitution very naturally as a means of survival for herself and her father, but she remains ignorant of her own physiology. Wiseman builds her story so convincingly that we believe in Hoda's innocence, just as we know that in accepting her son as a client Hoda finally confronts her innocence and moves beyond it. Hoda's moment of knowing resembles the reversal point in Greek tragedy, when the hero steps into the boundary situation – from which there is no return – and the chorus of commoners (we, as readers) draws back to watch in horror. Hoda steps over the boundary and breaks the taboo of incest. She enters her own knowledge but preserves the innocence of her son, David. Wiseman's novel is not merely about sexuality; it is the story of woman as redemptive agent. The Kabbalistic legend of creation, which prefaces the novel, suggests Hoda's agency: "He stored the Divine Light in a Vessel, but the Vessel, unable to contain the Holy Radiance, burst and its shards, permeated with sparks of the Divine, scattered through the Universe."[59] In the tradition of female writing, Wiseman deflates the grandiosity of divinity by turning her hero into a mere 'crackpot.'

Although many contemporary novelists deal with women's sexuality, and Dorothy Livesay, Betsy Warland, and Gail Scott, among others, are writing erotic poetry, English-speaking novelists are not deconstructing language in the way that Quebec writers are. To write the experience of woman's physicality onto the page not only demands a celebration of the physical, but also requires techniques that subvert 'rational' discourse.[60] The need for such subversive methods is easily understood: the language and stylistics we have appropriated are those of a dominant masculine ideology that has never interested itself in female-centred eroticism.

Speaking of women's relationship to language, Gail Scott explains:

> [This] relationship is first formed in our mother's womb as we listen to the rhythms and sounds of her body, and, as women, we continue to develop this largely oral tongue in our continuing relationship and identification with the mother. But at the same time we are developing another relationship to language, that of the 'fathertongue' of education, the media, the law, all of them patriarchal institutions. Consequently we end up with a split relationship to language.[61]

These and Scott's following remarks serve as preface to the methodology and theory of the postmodernist writing in Quebec: "Our texts differ as much from those of men as the shape of our sex and its movement towards pleasure differs from theirs." Women's writing, if it is to speak for us, will "reflect the rhythms of our bodies, our minds, more circular, more holistic."[62] This, by Nicole Brossard, is the theory in poetry:

Aroused

emotion is a sign
an attentive rejoinder to meaning

aroused her face and the relays
of complicity fullness of the images
leaning over the lure, her mouth
whereas lips normally hold words
on the edge of emotions a sentence bound
crouched and ignored caressed

while running along her arms in excitement
concentrating, the idea clung fast
for linking[63]

While Brossard writes 'holistically' – weaving together theory and poetics, celebrating and affirming "the link with the maternal body" – she is also "refusing its enveloping contours, which speak to her of the millennial silence of women. The Venus of Willendorf with her sightless, mouthless face is not an object of worship, but one to be destroyed in order for women to write themselves into history . . . production, not reproduction, becomes women's role. The production of ideology occurs within linguistic systems so these become the feminist focus."[64] Gail Scott, an anglophone living in Quebec, says that for her the "very notion of fiction has been transformed by the fact that [she] happened to start writing seriously in a lieu culturally distanced from the realist tradition of strong English-Canadian women writers, a lieu where women were more concerned with syntax and language than with 'story.'"[65]

It is the Quebec feminists – Nicole Brossard, Madeline Gagnon, Helene Ouvrard, Louky Bersianik (to mention just a few) – who are paralleling the revolutionary work of the French feminist theorists and writers in claiming the physicality of the female body as the starting point for their creative work. It is in the power of their sexual affirmation as much as in their craft that these postmodernist writers are exciting. They are writing sexual liberation into being. The use of the female body as a "creative force capable of generating new linguistic structures"[66] will, they believe, provide Canadian women with a 'tactile' body of work, which will give new dimensions to selfhood.

But this new writing has been hampered by its poor dissemination. To be useful politically, feminists know that both creative and theoretical work must have a large readership and that the primary problem of translation must be addressed. For instance, Nicole Brossard's long poem "Amantes" was written in 1980 but translated into English by Barbara Godard as "Love(h)ers" only in 1986. The lapse of six years between the two publications points to one of the problems faced by Canadian women readers. Our national literature is at times not available to us because of this barrier of language. As well, this new writing demands that a translator be extremely flexible in her feminist theory and linguistic skills. Godard has written a key essay on this subject, "The Translator as She."[67]

But there are other, earlier, modern writers in Quebec whose work is essential to our understanding of the revolutionary writing of the postmodernists. Women such as Gabrielle Roy, Anne Hébert, Marie-Claire Blais, and Claire Martin have written a literature not of sensuality but of sexual politics. They have catalogued the sexual repression of generations of women, demonstrating how we experience our sexuality when it is a socio-religious construct built upon a schizophrenic ideology of the virgin/ mother. These francophone writers have given us the darkest vision of womanhood in Canada, and some of them did so even before the social and political liberation movements of the 1960s. And they wrote in the face of extreme social censure. The sexual pessimism that Valverde speaks of as a spin-off from the women's movement was an early, desperate cry in Quebec literature. In her chapter here, Michèle Martin analyses the current feminist debate in Quebec more specifically.

Although the francophone postmodernist work is not as well-known as it should be, even by feminists in the rest of Canada, this is not so with the work of Jovette Marchessault. And it is because Marchessault is a dramatist and has had plays translated and performed outside of Quebec that her work is becoming familiar to English-speaking women. Her writing is also more accessible to a larger audience because it does not rely on deconstruction as a basic mode of expression. The ritualistic "Night Cows" (1979) is a celebration of female physicality, and although it is Utopian in vision, it is also gutsy, irreverent, satiric, and comic, as the opening line demonstrates:

MY MOTHER IS A COW! That makes two of us.
Two beautiful milk cows, butter cows; creators of sweet oceans of magnetic milk which surge through the human body. . . . All cows, regardless of race, weight, or colour, are castrated young. [68]

In poetry, prose, and drama, the Quebec writers have introduced a new female tradition, experimental in its technique and revolutionary in its politics.

Jane Rule has not experienced the sociopolitical and cultural restrictions of the French-Canadian tradition, yet in an article entitled "Lesbian and Writer" she tells us that she decided to be a writer "because I wanted to speak the truth as I saw it. To understand and share that understanding." [69] Her critical and creative writing is not wholly concerned with lesbian experience because neither is the world she lives in. Most of Rule's writing falls within the category of social realism, portraying fully developed characters of various sexual persuasions. Anne and Eve, the lovers in *Desert of the Heart*, experience the traditional problems that result from living as women in a patriarchal society, but the fact that they are sexual partners gives them no added power as the story unfolds, nor does it give them any edge on human suffering. This story concerns a search for identity and selfhood:

If there is no face in the mirror, marry. If there is no shadow on the ground, have a child. These are the conventions the will consents to.

But there is a face. There is a shadow. They are simply unsuitable.
I'm a case of mistaken identity. . . . So are we all?[70]

Our response is solicited and obtained: so are we all. Catherine Brett has
written a story for young readers, *S.P. likes A.D.* (1989), that enables us to
appreciate the complex relationships of girls growing into womanhood in
their own, specific ways – about Stephanie who has a crush on Anne, about
sexual experimentation and budding lesbian relationships. And Jovette
Marchessault, in an autobiographical trilogy, rejoices in her Métis heritage
and celebrates her lesbian sexuality. This is a rare narrative that opens up
to us the experiences of a woman across her life, from childhood to
womanhood, sharing with us the intimate bonds between women – across
generations – but at the same time exposing the brutal suppression of a
race and a gender. The third volume is a reconciliation that celebrates a
new understanding of women with men, of humans with the earth. Marchessault is unique in her ability to weave together political ideology, the
great goddess myths and the stories and oral tradition of the First Nations
– and she accentuates the power of each with her fabulistic storytelling.[71]

It is important to note that because Rule depicts both heterosexual and
lesbian protagonists, she is warned by critics from both groups that she
risks alienating her readership.[72] Rule is acutely aware of the political
aspect of women's lives, not only as it pertains to our sexuality, but also
with respect to our writing and our publications, too (as her analysis of and
support for the feminist presses demonstrates). She is also outspoken on
the power that will accrue to us if we listen to our women writers: "They
will be our voices if we live up to their intent, severe, humane visions, if we
learn to grow with rather than cut down those who have so much to offer
us and in our name."[73] Just as sexuality and sexual difference are part of
the new writing, so too are the voices of older women. In *Memory Board*
(1987) Jane Rule writes the story of a lesbian relationship into extreme old
age. She shares with us the support and love that extend into caring for a
disabled lover, and in doing this she also explores the complexities of a sib-
ling relationship in a non-traditional family. This is a rare book – not only
thematically: Rule fractures sequential time and the logistics of place to
give the reader a composite portrait of two heroic women who live an
'ordinary' existence with flair and great joy across many years.

Equally rare, and extraordinary, is the title story of Ingrid MacDonald's
recently published collection of lesbian short stories. "Catherine, Catherine" is based on a historical account of a lover who testified against her
partner and then was burned as a witch.[74]

In *The Medusa Head* (1983) Mary Meigs is recalling (in a lucid and
transparent prose) the dilemma of one partner in a long-standing lesbian
love affair that has suddenly turned into a love triangle. *The Box Closet*

(1987) gives us entry into her family and the world of childhood and adolescence through a closet full of old diaries and letters that Meigs finds after her mother's death. And again it is the lucidity – the verbal eloquence, which is stunning – even though she is describing emotional complexities (barely understood by the protagonists themselves) within a world of privilege and security. But it is surely Meigs's screen performance in *The Company of Strangers* that demolishes all barriers between us, the reader, the viewer, and her – the strong, passionate old woman, sure of her sexuality, happy and comfortable, and able to express the pain and the fears of her old age as well as the empowerment. She writes: "As women, I believe we have to recognize that our power does not lie in hope (we can learn to live without it), but in our invincible power to remember and to warn. . . . Memory is the secret power of old women. . . . Memory is an ecosystem. It is much like the ecosystem of the rain forests and the oceans on which the lives of all species depend."[75] And Meigs calls on women of all ages to help in saving the planet before it is too late, because she believes women are uniquely conscious of the problems of survival. In her article "Memories of Age" Meigs recalls the making of the film, in which a group of old women create a survival plan when a bus breaks down in the Canadian wilderness. In the film we learn that each woman has survived war, poverty, and racial/sexual harassment. Meigs talks about coming out again – "on camera this time" – to Cissy, who is old, and tolerant, and "lets [her] live."[76] It is this tolerance (and complete acceptance) of each other and by extension of the eccentricities of age, sexual difference, ethnicity, race, and class that invites us to celebrate with the women in this film – a rare celebration on the screen – of age instead of youth, of understanding instead of confrontation, of compassion instead of violence.

Old Women at Play

The cult of youth and its sexist bias have roots deeply embedded in Western society. In Canada the media ignore demographic facts about the increasingly aging population and portray the world as if it consisted only of the young. However, we are now witnessing the first wave of postmenopausal women who, as a generation, have choices to make and fruitful lives to live. As feminist research shows, these women "are often endowed with new energy and vitality, but society perceives them as declining and almost obsolete."[77] Old women have rarely been portrayed in literature as the resourceful and productive people many of us are. As Barbara Horn notes: "We need fiction that counteracts ageism. We want stories that present older women as individuals, not as stereotypes . . . to read about spirited, capable, resilient aging females . . . and we should not deny . . . the angers, frustrations, and fears of older females – these are as important to capture as are their courageous acts and hard won pleasures."[78]

In giving us Hagar Shipley, over ninety years old and "rampant with memory," Margaret Laurence created one of the best-known Canadian fictional characters and pioneered the charting of an old woman's psyche. In *The Stone Angel* (1964), we hear the story of the last two days in Hagar Shipley's life. Because the structure of the book is one of recall, we listen as Hagar pulls into the present the events of her life that have made her the strong, angry, stubborn, bitter, and glorious woman she is. Hagar's vision of her life is intensified and clarified in her final hours; such clarity is part of that ironic gift of 'dying well.' *The Stone Angel* is a rare book that explores the subtle and complex relationship between the culturally dictated process of social integration and the responses it elicits from a woman who remains strong and rebellious through her life. Here, Laurence is exploring those aspects of age and womanhood that, traditionally, are not expressed: the destructive and manipulative power often inherent in motherhood; the sexuality of women and the repressive intent of cultural norms; the sexual needs of women into old age; and the isolation and despair that fuel so many 'happy' marriages. Hagar is one of the few tragic heroes in Canadian literature. She is like Lear both in her blindness to her own follies and in her final movement into grace and redemption.

Another astonishing venture into women's old age is *The Book of Eve* (1975) by Constance Beresford-Howe. In it Beresford-Howe touches a previously unrecognized nerve in society. Eva, her comic hero, escapes the "Eden of marriage" the day her old-age-pension cheque arrives: she puts on her sneakers and is gone! Naturally, as an old woman without spousal support, what she escapes into is a life of extreme poverty in which sustenance often comes from grubbing in garbage cans. But emotionally and psychologically, the quality of Eva's life improves dramatically. As the victim of marital rape, her own sexuality has been nullified; after her escape she indulges her fantasies and begins to respond to her own sexual needs. By imagining this Eve into life, Beresford-Howe gives to older women truths about the sexual politics governing their own lives. Although the narrative suggests possibilities that may seem bizarre, they are also seductive. The enormous quantity of mail that Beresford-Howe received from Canadian women in response to this novel suggests the power of art to articulate life.[79]

There is a double standard in the chronicle of aging. For a man, the facial signs of aging, the wrinkles and lines, suggest character. They indicate maturity and celebrate his engagement with life. For a woman they signify obsolescence. We are all aware that as old women we should be invisible, ashamed that we no longer fit the mold of perfection required by Western society. Miriam Waddington does not flinch in telling us:

Old women
should live like worms
under the earth,
they should come out
only after a good rain . . .

Or be a wood-worm
that patiently winds
its journey through
history's finest
furniture like those
old women we see
in the corridors of
nursing homes. [80]

Gretel Miles lets her poetry comment on how the media prey on the self-image of women as we age. In "November 1983: Riding the Bus," she asks:

Would I like to be known
for my beautiful skin at eighty-nine?
I think rather
than gazing down on bus interiors
in black and white photographs,
with plunging neckline,
I would rather be known
for my poems.
Or pickled eggs,
oral sex technique or
even ancient drunken
performances, or
as a fine dancer. [81]

Dorothy Livesay has been writing poetry since the 1930s, but is only now enjoying the popularity and celebration her work deserves. And this is largely due to the women's movement, whose members recognize her commitment to feminism and respond with joy to her writing. Livesay, as an old woman, is unafraid to face her own aging and celebrates her sensuality still. She writes with humour (in anger and in frustration) about this stage of her life, her poetry growing in strength and vitality. Her writing has the wisdom and compassion that we need to hear as we grow old:

But I had yet to discover
    how even in old age
    a woman moves
    with freshness

is a leaf   perhaps
or a breath of wind
in a man's nostrils. [82]

Livesay remains acutely aware of the politics of sexuality; she knows the power that accrues to men through their appropriation of women's bodies and the self-doubt that is endemic to womanhood.

Men have never been
subjected to physical scrutiny
as have women
What is private? . . .

For a woman
nothing is private!
she is invaded
night after night
has only the soul's essence
through which to believe herself
human, and right [83]

A very different example of a woman's self-creation into old age is outlined in Adele Wiseman's book celebrating the life of her mother, Chaika Wiseman. *Old Woman at Play* (1978), written when Chaika was eighty-two, traces her life and work as a maker of fantastical dolls – thousands of doll couples, who generate their own myths and stories. Wiseman proposes that "what the artist creates is consciousness . . . [an] awareness of our situation, which enlarges creation and ourselves. This sense of enlargement, of augmented power, helps us, even briefly, to imagine that we may somehow become 'better.'" [84] Although Chaika created her dolls over a lifetime, using perishable and throw-away stuff like old buttons, tin, plastic, and bone, her urge to impose whatever form she found available onto the chaotic experiences of her life gives it a new and vital meaning.

Contemplating Chaika Wiseman's art, most aptly through her daughter's reconstruction of her mother as artist, we realize that the joy of this old woman's play could so easily have been lost. So much of women's history and creativity has been expressed in unpublished material, in letters and diaries, or in lace, embroidery, tapestry, quilts, dolls, and other 'trivia.' In *Old Woman at Play*, Wiseman demystifies and democratizes the creative process. She dislodges art from the concept of fine art, disrupting the male-defined categories. While Canadian women novelists are bringing the total female experience into fiction as a legitimate theme, Wiseman parallels the process by demonstrating that a 'disposable craft,' an 'old woman's play,' is a creative response to life and, as such, is an important artistic statement. Adele Wiseman's suggestion about the sense of empowerment that art brings to life is contained in the figure of the old woman as sage, as soothsayer, as crone – a central and powerful image in ancient female lore. [85]

At one level, Atwood's epic poem *The Journals of Susanna Moodie* (1970) can be read as a reclamation of this figure. While the story of Susanna Moodie is told with some historical accuracy, Atwood transforms Moodie in old age into a strong, defiant, eccentric sage. After her death her spirit dominates the poem, and this is the aspect of Susanna Moodie that we remember as we close the book. As old woman, she appropriates the land, interpreting it as her element in which we are the neophytes.

> I am the old woman
> sitting across from you on the bus,
> her shoulders drawn up like a shawl;
> out of her eyes comes secret
> hatpins, destroying
> the walls, ceiling. [86]

In modern Toronto, in midtown, her power transforms the city into her own domain. She defies the concrete and the "unexplored/wilderness of wires."

> Turn, look down:
> there is no city;
> this is the centre of a forest
>
> your place is empty. [87]

Susanna Moodie, as pioneer and as writer, is central to woman's history in Canada, and Atwood's reworking of the story assures her this place. The poem is a clear instance of the female tradition in writing. Marya Fiamengo, within that same tradition, but from her own Slavic background, writes:

> Yes, Tadeusz Rozewicz, I too
> prefer old women . . .
> they give advice
> or tell fortunes,
> they endure . . .
>
> But Tadeusz,
> have you been to America?
> Where we have no old women . . .
>
> Everyone, Tadeusz, is young in America.
> Especially the women

with coiled blue hair
which gleams like steel . . .

and I will liberate all women
to be old in America
because the highest manifestation of wisdom,
Hagia Sophia,
is old and a woman.[88]

This realignment of the wisdom of older women from many cultures is heard increasingly in creative writing. And it is also heard – amazingly – in film, the medium that craves young female, 'sexy' bodies. *The Company of Strangers* is cause for celebration, so too is *Older, Wiser, Stronger* (NFB, Studio D), a film by Dionne Brand:

> I am working on a film. Another Black woman is working with me. We're making a film about women. Old women. All have lived for more than sixty years and there are five minutes in which to speak, feel those years. In a film, in a Black dream, will it be all right if five old women speak for five minutes? Black women are so familiar with erasure, it is so much the cloth against the skin, that this is a real question.[89]

Silencing – "so much the cloth against the skin" – especially when the skin is not white; Brand's work reminds us that an *integrated* analysis of gender, age, race, class, and sexuality remains the central issue that needs addressing in feminist theory and practice. Analysing the process of this filmmaking, Brand says: "As the cutting ends, I feel the full rain of lesbian hate. It hits the ground, its natural place. . . . For me, it pushes up a hoary blossom sheltered in race. I will smell this blossom I know for many years to come."[90] Such an experience, recorded, forces us to acknowledge the urgency for comprehensive and integrated feminist research, which we are still far from attaining.

In Our Own Voice

Although we celebrate the growing number of books written by women each year in Canada, it is a celebration tempered by Brand's words about erasure. For some women, getting their work published is a minor miracle. While there are no formal structures in society to keep women from writing, there are still countless cultural and political barriers that effectively silence some of us. If we add the triple bind of race, class, and sexual preference to the restraints already imposed by gender, we realize that for certain groups of women the sense of communion, which results from having ourselves 'written into being,' and which empowers us, is not available to all women. As Ravida Din says in an interview on racism and homophobia: "I can deal with the anger and fear that arises from hearing homophobic comments but when I hear racist remarks from women/lesbians, the feeling of pain and powerlessness is incomparable. . . . I have constantly to remind white women that there are no degrees . . . racism is racism is racism."[91] The words that remain for some women are:

jap, bitch, chink, dyke

and silence
the other lies[92]

In an article about overcoming silencing, "The Absence of Writing or How I Almost Became A Spy," Marlene Nourbese Philip (lawyer, poet, political activist) analyses the inheritance of colonization and the subversion of language that has ensued for the victims:

> At the risk of being reductionist, I see the issue as being one of power and so one of control. Writing entails control in many areas: control of the word, control of the image . . . control of information, and . . . control in the production of the final product. As a female and a Black living in a colonial society, control was absent in each of these areas, hence the absence of writing, especially creative writing, and hence the lack of recognition of writing as a possible vocation or profession.
>
> For the many like me, Black and female, it is imperative that our writing begin to recreate our histories and our myths, as well as integrate the most painful of experiences – loss of our history and our word. The reacquisition of power to create in one's own image and to create one's own image is vital to this process, which can only serve to reassure us that we belong most certainly to the race of humans.[93]

In *Looking for Livingstone: An Odyssey of Silence* (1991), Philip dislocates both language and silence. In a narrative that has the scope of an epic, the poet journeys through time and across space. She fractures form – juxtaposing lyric poetry, letters, journal entries, dreams, ritual, and incantation – insisting that we listen to silence while simultaneously she is reclaiming the voices of people silenced for centuries. This is an exploration similar to Daphne Marlatt's *ANA Historic*. Both poets revision cultural history using a feminist lens, and both dislocate form and language in order to legitimize and democratize their reclamation.

Lillian Allen says that concepts such as race and ethnicity are problematic when applied to women and their writing: "The uniformity they presume glides over the intrinsically significant differences that exist within any group."[94] As a black woman, she is immediately seen as speaking for all black women, and this simplistic assumption denies the specificity of the individual. But, as she goes on to say, there is a "common sisterhood, a common destiny" that black writers share. Allen identifies the problem of publishing: "When a black/minority/ethnic writer submits work to publishers, they don't have the tools or frame of reference to make a proper analysis."[95] But gradually, largely through their own initiatives, and with the help of small presses and journals, this writing is being added to the national literature, giving it a diversity and complexity that reflects the cultural reality of this country.

All writing is a political act, but it is women from the minority groups who have the sharpest political consciousness informing their work. Dionne Brand, in her epic poem "Chronicles of the Hostile Sun," records her return to Grenada, which coincided with the U.S. air attack and invasion in October 1983. Her description is vivid and riveting: the language in this section of the poem has the kinetic effect of docu-drama – one understands how Brand turned to film. But it is Brand's explicit stance as a black Canadian woman (the outsider to the event) that politicizes the experience and binds us into it. In the same book, the poem celebrating the author's grandmother evokes joy, intimacy, and compassion and binds us again, but in a very different way. Brand's writing runs the gamut from epic to epigram, and her fiction has the same complexity and force as her poetry. Her short story, "Sans Souci," is lacerating in its portrayal of a woman alienated, silenced, and destroyed, yet the tone is never harsh and the imagery is lush, almost seductive. In a book of poems, *No Language is Neutral* (1990), Brand implodes historical/cultural memory with current feminist political issues. She draws on ancestral/mythological voices to sharpen her analysis and to develop a tension that runs through the poetry, constantly testing the power of language to resist cultural suicide. Complex ideologies are explored in a language that only seems 'neutral':

> Old woman, that was the fragment that I caught in
> your eye, that was the look I fell in love with, the piece
> of you that you kept, the piece of you left, the lesbian,
> the inviolable, sitting on a beach in a time that did not
> hear your name or else it would have thrown you into the sea . . .[96]

In the "Women of Colour" issue of *Fireweed*, Himani Bannerji echoes the thoughts of Lillian Allen concerning the difficulty of getting into print. Editors, even of feminist journals, have fixed ideas about language. "They have a particular way of deciding what they'll count as 'saying' and that 'saying' is not how we speak. . . . In that sense they are forcing all the most middle class, the most male bourgeois ways of speaking, on to us."[97]

Bannerji's poetry is uncompromising and diverse, ranging from lyric to polemic. In "Paki Go Home," her voice is raw, angry, honest, and desperate. It has an immediacy that aligns the reader with the pain, humiliation, and urgency of the poet:

3 pm
sunless
winter sleeping in the womb of the afternoon
wondering how to say this
to reason or scream or cry or whisper
or write on the walls
reduced again
cut at the knees, hands chopped, eyes blinded
mouth stopped, voices lost . . .

Now, then and again
we must organize.
The woman wiping the slur spit
from her face, the child standing
at the edge of the playground silent, stopped.
The man twisted in despair,
disabled at the city gates.
Even the child in the womb
must find a voice
sound in unison
organize.
Like a song, like a roar
like a prophecy that changes the world. [98]

Behind the poem is what Bannerji has described elsewhere as "the long train of history" of non-white people – kept suppressed. Many women are now bringing this history to their writing, where it restructures reality and our experience of it.

Claire Harris, speaking about her work, says: "I am a black woman. Any poetry I write is black poetry. I am not prepared to surrender the truths of my particular personal history. Neither am I prepared to lose the great advantage of those who have historically been denied mainstream participation; those who have been enslaved or savaged by others: the necessary clarity that ensures survival." [99] Her collection of poetry, *Fables From the Women's Quarters* (1984), speaks about the experience of displacement and of the communities of poor people, worldwide. But, above all, she is speaking for communities of black women everywhere:

Now female I stand in this silence where somebody's black girl child
jaywalking to school is stripped spread searched by a woman who

finds that black names are not tattooed on the anus pale hands soiling the black flesh through the open door the voices of the men in corridors and in spite of this yea in spite of this black and female to stand here and say I am she is I say to stand here knowing this is a poem black in its most secret self.[100]

Harris makes sure that we understand that the woman spread-eagling this black child is white. She is the modern colonizer, perpetuating the assumptions and the violations of the patriarchs. In another poem, Harris interprets the village experience of elderly Italian women "who crunch their old faith who trail their faint air of the women's quarters past the small shops."[101] By revisioning the fables of women, Harris speaks on behalf of many who do not have a voice and who are still locked into the old customs and practices.

There are two anthologies of writing by Caribbean women (and the first text includes the work of Canadian poets): *Creation Fire: A Cafra Anthology of Caribbean Women's Poetry* (1990) and *Blaze a Fire: Significant Contributions of Caribbean Women* (1988).[102] Both are produced in Canada by Sister Vision, Black Women and Women of Colour Press. The importance of this publishing house to those of us who teach in Women's Studies cannot be overemphasized. The second book, while not about women and writing, provides information that is vital if we are to teach Caribbean writing. It is impossible to find out about the lives of women from traditional texts; the women are missing, their cultural histories and their achievements in their own countries have never been recorded. One of the main barriers against women getting into print has been the homophobia of traditional publishing houses: Sister Vision has broken the monopoly.

Some immigrant women have to break free of confining cultural traditions before they can establish themselves as writers, but the barrier of language remains the most difficult. The creative voice is born in the unconscious, and to write in a new language requires enormous confidence and faith. Many women continue to publish in their own language in ethnic magazines, but increasingly they are writing in English or their work is being translated. For instance, *Frictions: Stories by Women* (1989) is an anthology of short stories with twenty-nine contributors from a multiplicity of cultural backgrounds. All are Canadian writers and many are voices we have rarely heard before – and again it is a small press (Second Story Press) that accounts for the breaking of their silence.

Maria Adizzi is an Italian-Canadian whose novel *Made in Italy* (1982) analyses the experiences of a traditional protagonist. Adizzi uses the symbol of the cage to reveal the constrictions of a hostile culture and a dwindling community as these affect an aging woman. Similarly, Mary Melfi and Mary di Michele use images of mutilation and paralysis to portray the experiences of silencing and isolation particular to women.

These poets and novelists are writing the history of immigrant people, as Joseph Pivato explains in his article, "Italian-Canadian Writers Recall History."[103] But they are doing much more than rewriting history. Mary di Michele writes with a feminist consciousness, as do Eleni Albani and Caterina Edwards. Di Michele's poem "Hunger" demonstrates the politics of power and the vulnerability of women as sex objects. By juxtaposing images of the high-gloss mannequin disguised as a child with the actual child who is raped and murdered, she underlines the destructive potential of the media as initial seducer and betrayer of women from girlhood to womanhood.[104]

In *Shakti's Words,* a collection of poetry by South Asian Canadian women, the editors explain: "After reading these poems we understand again why Canadian literature has eulogized the immigrant. She is us, but a little newer and fresher, and her poems are a little more honest and passionate than ours."[105] And this is what we gain from these voices that have been silenced for too long – an honesty that forces us to turn our eyes upon ourselves and confront the racism that is basic, even in our feminist ideologies. In *Other Solitudes: Canadian Multicultural Fictions* (1990), Linda Hutcheon and Marion Richards have gathered together short stories written by both men and women from diverse cultural backgrounds. Himani Bannerji's story "The Other Family" is about "the terrible cost of assimilation, of wiping out one's racial identity." The discussion that follows the story is between Arun Mukherjee and Himani Bannerji – used together this material provides a unique departure point for exploring the issues of racism and ethnocentricity.

Representing a different community is Marrilu Mallet, a Chilean writer and filmmaker living in Canada. In *The Voyage to the Other Extreme: Five Stories* (1985), Mallet uses the first-person narrative throughout the book, but the voice switches from male to female in specific tales. This is an unusual technique for a woman writer, but it gives an immediacy and a validity to Mallet's stories, which record the abuse and torture of Chileans under a fascist regime. Such punishment is not gender-specific, and neither are the effects it produces in its victims after their escape to Canada. There is a grim, Kafkaesque humour in some of these stories, such as "Blind Alley," but nothing relieves the horror that Mallet's characters experience. These stories form part of a new perspective, which is growing steadily in Canadian literature with the influx of political refugees.

In a very different voice, and with a different intent, Greek-born Smaro Kamboureli's *In the Second Person* (1985) takes the reader on a journey. The poet seeks to reconcile 'the other' in herself – the woman split between two languages and two cultures. The poetry takes its form from the writing of Anais Nin – Kamboureli is reading Nin's earlier journals while writing her own. And the journal form, used by so many women throughout history, is precisely right for the process the poetry records. This is a complex text, which weaves together philosophical and emotional responses to an ancient culture that is discarded even as a new one is explored. Kamboureli's poetry is not about the loneliness and isolation that many ethnic women experience. Instead it is a celebration of the richness and complexity that "a second cultural skin" affords. More, it reflects a sense of empowerment, which comes from the communion the poet shares with such writers as Anais Nin and Virginia Woolf, Nicole Brossard, Phyllis Webb, and Daphne Marlatt.

Joy Kogawa's work displays no such affinity with other authors. Instead, she writes about the effects of silencing, especially of Japanese-Canadian women. Her novel *Obasan* (1982) is an act of exorcism. During the writing Kogawa finds the voice that was doubly repressed by cultural expectation and by political oppression. The diaspora of her people, enforced by the Canadian government during the Second World War, ensured that all communication among them was lost. Kogawa is finally able to ask: "If I could follow the stream down and down to the hidden voice, would I come at last to the freeing word?"[106] The act of writing *Obasan* releases not only the voice of the poet, but also a political self. Since publishing the novel, Kogawa has become the Aunt Emily of her story and is now an insistent voice on behalf of her people and a political activist for the Issei, the first-generation Japanese Canadians

After the publication of *Obasan*, Kogawa wrote of the paralysis she was overcoming: "I knew that by silence I would be bowing to the tyranny of fear itself. By silence, I could be a collaborator in chaos, guilty before conscience of inaction where action was required. So I am speaking publicly now about these matters for the first time and with no small terror."[107] Kogawa's reluctance to break her silence is understandable when it is framed by her poetry and prose. Further evidence that Kogawa continues to overcome that paralysing fear is the recent publication of a new novel, *Itsuka*, based on the Japanese-Canadian struggle for redress.[108]

In a similar way, Native women writers are finally breaking their silence. These women come from an oral tradition in which the rituals of their culture and a sense of communality are basic and essential to the creative act. But they have been denied their culture for almost a century, and in many cases their communion with each other has been disrupted. Jeanette Armstrong of the Penticton Indian Band started writing by accident: "I started answering back."[109] She began by refusing to be told how her people experienced life and soon realized that the aboriginal people had much to teach the rest of Canada before it was too late for ecological survival. Armstrong lists the things that have been lost to large parts of the world "through years and years" of colonization: languages, cultures, religions – and most importantly a sense of self that has been denied the individual. [110] Beth Brant, a Native Canadian lesbian, echoes Armstrong, but she chooses a line by Nicole Brossard to explain her own experience: "In order to write one must know that one exists." [111] And because she has found autonomy, Beth Brant is now able to write "A Long Story" – using the memories of her great-grandmothers – about the abduction of Native children, about the loss, the dreadful vacuum produced in homes from which the children are missing. "The agent said . . . It is good for them It will make them civilized . . . I do not know civilized." [112] Brant, and other First Nation writers, are now in the process of creating what she hopes will be a female tradition in Native writing. These women express their experiences in their own words using prose/poetic structures suited to their own thematic material. In the process they are eradicating the old asexual stereotype of "woman as squaw." Beth Cuthand reminds us of the racist "assumption that Indian people don't have the skills to write and that therefore none of us exist." She calls on Native women to write in English for greater ease of communication and to write collectively for the strength this imparts. [113]

In *Life Lived Like a Story* three Yukon elders – who are multilingual – tell the stories of their lives. This is one of the richest texts we have from Native women, combining as it does anecdotes from daily life and interweaving these with the legends of the tribe: "The recurring theme is one of connection – to other people and to nature. Connections with people are explored through kinship; connections with land emphasize sense of place. But kinship and landscape provide more than just a setting for an account, for they actually frame and shape the story." [114] The text is interspersed with poetry, chants, historical facts, rituals of womanhood, but the voice is always that of the elder weaving her life into the tale that unfolds before us. The worth, the total morality, of such an act is emphasized in the words of Angela Sidney: "Well I've tried to live my life right. Just like a story." [115]

Maria Campbell and Jane Willis are Native women who, in the same year (1973), published their autobiographies. When a writer uses this genre, she is attempting to understand and order the chaotic life experiences, bringing the self into being deliberately and consciously. Campbell's *Halfbreed* reveals the isolation suffered by a Native woman who has lost contact with her people and whose loss of community finds its apotheosis in the figure of her Cree great-grandmother. This figure is Campbell's Cheechum, the traditional old woman/storyteller, who is both prophet and guide. Through her, historic and cultural truths are transmitted and, more importantly, a sense of self is created. This tradition of empowerment through the grandmother is basic in the writing of Native women, and it is this matrilineal voice that Barbara Godard analyses in a comprehensive article about the oral tradition in literature by Native women.[116] Godard concludes with some interesting speculations on how we might use the oral model to understand the more traditional text (written by women) as a collective, and communal, event.

The Book of Jessica (1989), a collaborative drama by Maria Campbell and Linda Griffiths, is a unique document. It includes the process that these women of different races had to negotiate in order to bring their work to the stage. *Jessica* is a drama about Jessica – "Métis. Female, Stubborn, fiesty, a survivor" – and, while it includes myth and legend, it also depicts the political activism and the brutal survival tactics that are basic to this woman's life. The total *Book* includes the 'script' of how this collaboration lurched along. It is angry, compassionate, and totally transformative; it is an extremely rare document for anyone to write – especially two women of different race. Griffiths dares to explore her own racism and Campbell is relentless in calling her on it. This text, read alongside "Native Women,"[117] provides us with an experience of Native women as the empowered group they are when controlling their own lives and their own stories. Another work that provides us with this experience is *A Gathering of Spirit* (1988). This is a collection of verse, short stories, letters, and articles by North American aboriginal women that should be read in conjunction with two other books: *The Spirit Weeps* (1988) and *Enough is Enough: Aboriginal Women Speak Out* (1988). The last two titles tell the factual history of women who have been sexually abused and rendered invisible and mute. *A Gathering* transforms the shocking reality into a process of hard-won autonomy and healing that sometimes crosses into celebration and even laughter.

While there are many fine Native poets now in print, it is the strength of the oral tradition that we hear constantly behind the most successful written text. In a similar way, the dramatic monologue by Antonine Maillet in *La Sagouine* (translated 1986) derives its power from an oral culture. This Acadian monologue celebrates the old woman as storyteller – the scrubwoman who "brings from her bucket of water" her culture and her history. In the collective experience of the drama we share most intimately the experience of the woman speaking to us.

Women Playwrights

Margaret Atwood reminds us that the novelist wills into existence a reader for her work: "I tell, therefore you are." But to a much greater degree, the dramatist creates a collaborative text. The ritual of the theatre demands the participation of an audience/listeners who believe in the transforming power of the actor/word/symbol. Each time we are part of successful theatre, we are reminded that theatre and religious ceremony have common roots; the audience/congregation is involved in similar rituals and experiences, and similar emotional and psychological effects are solicited. It is the participatory nature of the Mass/drama and the inclusivity of the 'masses' that make these events memorable, compared with the solitary stance of reader to text. Although there are fewer women playwrights than poets and novelists, their output has been augmented by a significant number of adaptations of novels into dramas. Because of this, the total impact of theatrical events by and about women since the late 1960s has been impressive.

The crossover from one artistic form to another has always been popular. Mazo de la Roche's famous *Jalna* saga was one of the longest running theatrical events in London, England, after she adapted her work for the theatre in the 1930s. More recently, and using the medium of television, *Anne of Green Gables* (adapted from the novels of Lucy Maud Montgomery) has been performed and acclaimed internationally, particularly in Japan, where it has achieved cult status. Many current women novelists have had their work transferred to screen and stage.[118] Among the most successful adaptations are Constance Beresford-Howe's novel *The Book of Eve*, mounted at the Stratford Festival; her *The Marriage Bed*, reproduced for television; and Margaret Laurence's Manawaka protagonists, who were played brilliantly by Norma Edwards in *The Women of Margaret Laurence*. Maria Campbell's *Halfbreed* serves as a partial subtext for the drama *Jessica* discussed above. And of course some writers – among them Atwood, Laurence, Rule, and Munro – have had their books adapted for film.

Carol Bolt is an important dramatist, and the production of *Red Emma* (1974) established her as a writer who brings a sharp political analysis to the stage. In this production Bolt brings into the spotlight the life of a woman too often neglected by political historians. Bolt depicts Emma Goldman with compassion and humour, allowing the romantic and idealistic dimensions of the character to develop alongside the anarchic and rebellious. Sharon Pollock has chosen to retell the Lizzie Borden history/myth in *Blood Relations* (1980), proving that a well-worn tale can have many new perspectives. Lizzie Borden's sexuality had never been considered before, but Pollock's drama reveals a lesbian relationship, altering many preconceived ideas. The play also explores the darker side of human nature and suggests that most women and men have the potential to be murderers, given the appropriate circumstance. Commenting on how critics review plays, Pollock points out the gender-bias of some male reviewers who went "to some trouble to state that this play [*Lizzie Borden*] has nothing to do with feminism. . . . It's only women who see it making a statement about women today. Of course it says something . . . about me

... today." She notes that reviewers who refuse to acknowledge the feminist perspective in her work are lacking in sensitivity or imagination. She has also been accused of preaching to the converted and replies, "Well, it's the converted who make changes. And if the converted come to see the play and are moved to action, or it endorses them and gives them strength to continue their fight, I don't see anything wrong with that."[119]

In the mid-1970s a group of women who were committed to social and cultural change banded together and formed the Redlight Theatre group. Inspired by the women's movement, the company was determined to write and produce drama by and about women. Diane Grant, an early member of the collective, wrote a series of vignettes that evolved into a fast-paced, hilarious satire, *What Glorious Times They Had* (1974), a devastating critique of the men in Parliament who opposed Nellie McClung and her supporters. In the process Grant underscores the similarities of current and historic gender inequities. The company doubled up in playing certain roles; they researched the characters they performed, helped write and score the music in the play, and encouraged each other as singers. The collective went on to develop other plays, such as *Broom Hilda* based on the comic strip character, and their collaborative effort continues to give energy and zest to their productions. Other dramatists and companies working with overtly feminist material have been successful commercially, proving that there is a viable audience for such plays.[120]

Margaret Hollingsworth is writing some of the most explicitly political drama in Canada, and in doing so she is analysing and exploding some of the repressive ideologies of the late 1980s, which are threatening to block the small inroads that the feminist movement has made for women in public (and private) life. Her writing is ironic and sceptical, with a black edge of humour that sometimes spills over into the hilarious:

> Winifred . . . The family is the cog that keeps the wheel turning. . . . It didn't matter how hot it was, the fire had to be lit and Herr Hitler spent hours poking it. He would come to Wahnfried whenever he could – he was part of the family, my children called him Uncle Wolfi. . . . Oh it's easy to be against Hitler when there is no Hitler. Not accepting the darker side of man means not loving him enough.[121]

Using Hitler, Picasso, and Ezra Pound as the characters who use Wagnerian ideology to nurture their manic egos, Hollingsworth is able to transform world politics into the *minutiae* of domestic ritual centring around Winifred Wagner. In the process she displaces and deflates the masculine paradigm. Hollingsworth uses the technique of clowning and masking to help her generate the text. She tells us: "Much of my work explores the power politics between men and women, and clowning provided me with an excellent tool with which to mine this territory. . . . Clowning deals in extremes, so I chose to go with three of the most powerful men in the century and look at them in relationship with one woman who had featured in each of their lives."[122]

In closing, I want to concentrate on Gwendolyn MacEwen's *Trojan Women* (an adaptation of Euripides' text). MacEwen is one of Canada's foremost poets, and this drama is a formidable showcase for her skills. While MacEwen did not claim to be a feminist it is impossible to ignore this political aspect of the play. Again and again the reader is directed to some of the most basic concerns of contemporary feminism. MacEwen transforms myth into life by ruthlessly paring down the original text.[123] The writing is irreverent, pithy, even colloquial, stripping away the heroic and religious trappings of classical drama. Poseidon is the only god on stage, and his early speech frames the action:

Family life in Troy was flawless.
Everyone slept with whomever
They were supposed to sleep with.
It was a perfect society.
Women learned to sew; men learned to kill.
Honour and glory shone everywhere.[124]

The irony and scepticism of the speech not only set the tone for the play as a whole, but they also mock traditional family roles, suggesting that the gender-bias of 'honour' requires some analysis. Hecuba's opening speech, while picking up Poseidon's observations, introduces the more nebulous concept of piety, the nurturance and preservation of which have always depended on women: "everything is gone . . . /Piety and honesty and honour and glory./Especially piety."[125] As the drama progresses, each woman begins to explore the demands of piety as she questions the loss of selfhood that results from the traditional role she has played.

MacEwen achieves an important dramatic effect by cutting out the rhetoric of the glory (or the glory of the rhetoric), which allows her to focus instead on a gender-based concept of honour. This shift in focus in turn dramatizes the specificity of the women's reality, which becomes the true centre of the play. We witness each woman's personal confrontation with 'self' as she faces her own loss, shapes her own response, and articulates how she will survive even in defeat. Running parallel to the testing of the self along the line of female 'virtue' and masculine 'honour' is MacEwen's debunking of the glory of war. As the women compare their experiences and question the traditional roles that have trapped them, MacEwen is able to show the empowerment that comes through self-knowledge. The drama becomes a political statement about the use and abuse of power, and it suggests that until women analyse the process we will remain its victims. After the conflagration of the 1991 Gulf war, this play becomes achingly current. We are able to enter this text and appropriate the action because it is written by a woman: 'war games' are usually depicted by men with women as their victims.

In this play MacEwen is working with many of the themes we have traced in both fiction and poetry. Helen is the archetypal 'woman as sex object.' She is "a woman abducted by violent men!/And all because of this cursed beauty/which should have been my glory!"[126] MacEwen shows Helen as a manipulative woman; she remains the quintessential winner of every beauty parade ever held. But what prizes do the 'winners' get? They become just another 'royal possession.' The whole myth of Helen – her birth as a result of the divine rape of Leda by Zeus, her 'face that launched a thousand ships,' her self as prize in a game devised by the gods – lies behind MacEwen's drama; this is a series of events that, taken together, give us the archetype of objectified beauty. Significantly, it is Helen who expresses the loss of selfhood which is essential if we are to be manipulated: "We women live beneath the shadows of men . . . /we have no shapes, we have no souls./We fight among ourselves because we can't locate the enemy./Is that not so sisters?"[127]

This lack of selfhood reaches its complete expression in the characterization of Andromache. MacEwen portrays her as the quintessential 'virtuous' woman, a woman who could have stepped out of the pages of Helen Adelin's *Fascinating Womanhood*: in fact, a woman of the current far right. These lines describe her role in family life:

> I was a *perfect wife!* I was perfect
>   for Hector's sake.
> There is nothing wrong with being perfect.
> In fact there is everything right with
>   being *perfect.*
> I curbed myself, I never gave in
>   to the least of my whims.
> I stayed at home; I had few friends.
> I knew when to guide my man
>   and when to obey.[128]

Hecuba's response to this catalogue of feminine traits is totally in keeping with her characterization throughout the play. She sees through the manipulations and control necessary in a gender-based hierarchy and speaks as a feminist might:

> Oh, your virtues begin to sicken me!
> Did you ever possess your self, Andromache?
> Did you live with Hector, or through Hector?

I wonder, I really wonder . . .
You 'perfect' wife, you 'suffocating' mother. [129]

MacEwen portrays a Hecuba who not only guides/goads the other women
into self-consciousness, but also monitors and comments on the cultural
realities that have contributed to their victimization. Hecuba is the crone
figure who locates the reasons why: 'malestream' history is "all a web of
lies/Where all the gore becomes glory/In the telling and re-telling/Of the
lies." [130]

In *Trojan Women*, MacEwen shows that an unquestioning loyalty to a
bankrupt culture, especially one built around the paradigm of stereotypic
gender roles, is deadly. Through the development of the Hecuba figure
MacEwen reveals the process of women's subordination. Through the
rage and despair of Hecuba's poetry we make discoveries about the roles of
men and women:

Men are Beautiful, predictable, utter fools.
They believe, because they must believe
That a single night in their blessed bed
Will turn a normal healthy woman
        into their eternal slave! [131]

But without men, women are invisible:

When my lord and my sons were killed
I too was nothing
It was as though I had never been. [135]

Hecuba learns that war brings into sharp focus the gender-role paradigm
she has been exploring:

I will tell you something I've only recently
        learned –
    war is blood and blood and blood,
    war is babies falling
    from the cradles of the sky.
War is the final nightmare.
The last sick page in a long sick story.
War is something that we do –
All of us, all of us . . . [133]

Finally the drama comes full circle, back to the opening statement by
the god Poseidon: "Family life in Troy was flawless. . . . /Women learned to
sew; men learned to kill./Honour and glory shone everywhere."

Gwendolyn MacEwen's *Trojan Women* demands a more detailed analysis than is possible here, but what I have tried to show is how a great poet

transforms a classical myth. Current social and political issues are picked up and incorporated into the mythic material, the old story remains but it has ourselves written into it. And this process of transformation gives an authenticity to the experience of these Trojan women that readers often find lacking in the original poetry. There is an added bonus: when this play is read by a group of women the political analysis that develops focuses on many of the themes we have been discussing in this chapter.

This is what the women writers do for us. They make available collective truths that we have rarely shared before, and they speak at the same time of our individual experiences as women. They place before us the fictions that are my life and yours. We are fortunate to be living in an age when we are questioning our traditional roles as women, and we have an incredible resource to help us in our exploration of autonomy. But there are reactionary forces lining up against feminism, and writers are beginning to recognize this. Margaret Atwood (whose satire is shockingly prophetic) is speaking about feminism:

> Writing and *isms* are two different things. Those who pledge their first loyalties to *isms* often hate and fear artists. . . . Modern dictators shoot them. And as the germination stage of any *ism* ends and it divides into cliques and solidifies into orthodoxies, writers – seized upon initially for their ability to upset apple carts – become suspect to the guardians of the *ism* for that very reason. Prescription becomes the order of the day. . . . I have supported women's efforts to improve their shoddy lot in this world which is, globally, dangerous for women, biased against them, and at the moment, in a state of reaction against their efforts. [134]

But, she reminds us, women are not devoid of faults merely because of their gender. And women who are "guardians of feminism" must speak out about problems they are experiencing within their own *ism*. Atwood warns of the danger she sees, and she sees it as coming from women themselves: "The fear that dares not speak its name, for some women these days, is a fear of other women. But you aren't supposed to talk about that: if you can't say something nice, don't say anything at all." [135]

Just as women writers dared to 'upset the apple cart' by telling the realities of our lives – about our rage, our frustrations, our guilt fostered within the formal, traditional, structure of the family – so too they empower us to rejoice in our friendships, our love affairs, and our bodies – even into old age. And they do more. The act of writing holds a promise; the woman who claims the time, the space, the freedom to work – to write – for herself, of herself, gains autonomy. Such a woman is finished with being 'nice.' Dionne Brand speaks for us all:

She looks like a boy in a dress, my big sister say,
a lyric and feminine correction from a watchful aunt,
don't say that, she look nice and pretty.
Nice and pretty, laid out to splinter you, so that never,
until it is almost so late as not to matter do you grasp
some part, something missing like a wing, some
fragment of your real self. [136]

Shelagh Wilkinson

NOTES

1. Dorothy Livesay, "Why We Are Here," in *The Woman I Am* (Erin, Ont.: Press Porcepic, 1977), 65.

2. Margaret Atwood, *Second Words: Selected Critical Prose* (Toronto: House of Anansi, 1982), 193.

3. *See* Beth Light and Veronica Strong-Boag, *True Daughters of the North: Canadian Women's History: An Annotated Bibliography* (Toronto: OISE Press, 1980). *See also*: Beth Light, "Recent Publications in Canadian Women's History," *Canadian Woman Studies/Les cahiers de la femme* 3, no. 1 (1981).

4. Elizabeth Thompson, "Introduction," *The Pioneer Woman: A Canadian Character Type* (Montreal and Kingston: McGill-Queen's University Press, 1991), 4.

5. Sylvia Hamilton, "Our Mothers Grand and Great: Black Women of Nova Scotia," *Canadian Woman Studies/Les cahiers de la femme* 4, no. 2 (1982).

6. *See*: Clara Thomas, *Love and Work Enough: The Life of Anna Jameson* (Toronto: University of Toronto Press, 1968 and 1978). *See also*: Clara Thomas, "Heroinism, Feminism and Humanism: Anna Jameson to Margaret Laurence," *Atlantis* 4, no. 1 (1978), 19-20.

7. Wayne Fraser, *The Dominion of Women: The Personal and the Political in Canadian Women's Literature* (New York: Greenwood Press, 1991).

8. See Lorraine McMullen, ed., *Re(dis)covering Our Foremothers: Nineteenth Century Canadian Women Writers* (Ottawa: Ottawa University Press, 1990).

9. Sandra Djwa, "The Where of Here: Margaret Atwood and a Canadian Tradition," in Arnold E. Davidson and Cathy M. Davidson, eds., *The Art of Margaret Atwood: Essays in Criticism* (Toronto: House of Anansi, 1981), 19-20.

10. *See*: Marion Fowler, *Redney: A Life of Jeanette Duncan* (Toronto: House of Anansi, 1980).

11. See also: *In the Meantime* (Ottawa: Deneau, 1984), a collection of poetry and previously unpublished prose; Alice Van Wart, ed., *Necessary Secrets: The Journals of Elizabeth Smart* (Toronto: Deneau, 1986); and *Elizabeth's Garden: Elizabeth Smart on the Art of Gardening* (Toronto: Coach House Press, 1989).

12. Rosemary Sullivan, *By Heart: Elizabeth Smart: A Life* (Toronto: Viking/Penguin Group, 1991), x.

13. Angela Bowering, *Figures Cut in Sacred Ground: Illuminati in the Double Hook* (Edmonton: NeWest Press, 1988), 105.

14. Constance Rooke, *Fear of the Open Heart* (Toronto: Coach House Press, 1989), Ch. 6.

15. Margaret Atwood, "Introduction," in Susanna Moodie, *Roughing It in the Bush* (London: Virago Press, 1986), xiv.

16. Djwa, "The Where of Here," 19, 16.

17. See p.143 in Greta Hofmann Nemiroff, ed., *Celebrating Canadian Women:*

Prose and Poetry By and About Women (Toronto: Fitzhenry & Whiteside, 1989).

18. Phyllis Webb, *Hanging Fire* (Toronto: Coach House Press, 1990).

19. Margaret Atwood, *Second Words*, 203-204.

20. Adele Wiseman, *Memoirs of a Book Molesting Childhood and Other Essays* (Toronto: Oxford University Press, 1987), 88.

21. Miriam Waddington, *Apartment Seven: Essays Selected and New* (Toronto: Oxford University Press, 1989), 201-202.

22. For an interesting analysis of "Authentic Realism," *see*: Sara Mills, Sue Spaull, Lynne Pearce and Elaine Millard, eds., *Feminist Readings, Feminists Reading* (Charlottesville: University Press of Virginia, 1989), Ch. 2.

23. *See* Rachel Blau Du Plessis, *Writing Beyond the Ending: Narrative Strategies of Twentieth Century Women Writers* (Bloomington: Indiana University Press, 1985) for a comprehensive and perceptive approach to this subject. Relevant material is in Ch. 1, "Endings and Contradictions."

24. Alice Munro, "An Appreciation," *A Room of One's Own* 9, no. 2, 32.

25. Ibid., 33.

26. This comment is made on a video-taped interview, "Our Kinda Talk: An Introduction to Margaret Laurence," National Film Board, 1978. *See also*: Margaret Laurence, "Ivory Tower or Grassroots? The Novelist as Socio-Political Being," in Douglas Daymond and Leslie Monkman, eds., *Canadian Novelists and the Novel* (Ottawa: Borealis Press, 1981), 251-259. Of particular interest, *see* pp. 257-258 on the 'colonial mentality' of women and the responses of Laurence's female protagonists to the dilemma of powerlessness.

27. For a definitive analysis of birthing as a social construct (and the economic and political power that has accrued to patriarchy in its control over birth), see: Mary O'Brien, *The Politics of Reproduction* (Boston: Routledge & Kegan Paul, 1981). *See also*: Meg Luxton, *More Than a Labour of Love: Three Generations of Women's Work in the Home* (Toronto: Women's Educational Press, 1980). This is a brilliant study of three generations of women's work in the Canadian home. Luxton demonstrates, in a sociological analysis, what women are imagining into life. "The Poet Mother," a special issue of *Cross Canada Writers' Quarterly* 8, no. 2, provides an interesting perspective on creativity and birthing.

28. Margaret Atwood, "If you Can't Say Something Nice, Don't Say Anything At All," in Libby Scheier, Sarah Sheard, and Eleanor Wachtel, eds., *Language in Her Eye: Views on Writing and Gender by Canadian Women Writing in English* (Toronto: Coach House Press, 1990), 24.

29. Audrey Thomas, *Intertidal Life* (Toronto: General Publishing, 1984), 51, 136. *See also*: Audrey Thomas, "The More Little Mummy in the World," in *Two in The Bush and Other Stories* (Toronto: General Publishing, 1981).

30. Daphne Marlatt, *ANA Historic: A Novel* (Toronto: Coach House Press, 1988), 37.

31. Bronwen Wallace, "A Simple Poem for Virginia Woolf," in Nemiroff, ed., *Celebrating Canadian Women,* 348-349.

32. Bronwen Wallace, *People You'd Trust Your Life To* (Toronto: McClelland & Stewart, 1990).

33. Margaret Atwood, "Christmas Carols," in *True Stories* (Toronto: Oxford University Press, 1981), 56.

34. Ibid., 57.

35. *See* "Princess Ida," in Alice Munro, *Lives of Girls and Women* (Toronto: McGraw-Hill Ryerson, 1971) for the history of Del's mother, as she rebels against the traditional role of woman.

36. Ibid., 203.

37. Alice Munro, "The Office," in *Dance of the Happy Shades* (Toronto: McGraw-Hill Ryerson, 1968).

38. Alice Munro, *Friend Of My Youth* (New York: Alfred A. Knopf, 1990). Title story, 3.

39. Susan Swan, *The Last of the Golden Girls* (Toronto: Lester & Orpen Dennys, 1989).

40. Margaret Laurence, *The Diviners* (Toronto: McClelland and Stewart, 1974), 6.

41. Ibid., 25.

42. Ibid., 453.

43. Margaret Atwood, *Wilderness Tips* (Toronto: McClelland & Stewart, 1991).

44. Thomas, *Intertidal Life,* 141.

45. Ibid., 157-158.

46. Ibid., 171.

47. Ibid., 161.

48. Ibid., 173.

49. Audrey Thomas, *Goodbye Harold, Good Luck* (Toronto: Viking, 1986), 155.

50. Audrey Thomas, interview with Ron Graham, *The Gazette* (Montreal), March 29, 1980.

51. Dorothy Livesay, interview, in Bruce Meyer and Brian O'Riordan, eds., *In Their Own Words* (Toronto: House of Anansi, 1984), 81. The reissued books are *Hetty Dorval, The Innocent Traveller, The Equations of Love, Swamp Angel, Love and Salt Water,* and *Mrs. Golightly and Other Stories* (Toronto: McClelland & Stewart, 1990).

52. Margaret Atwood, *The Handmaid's Tale* (Toronto: McClelland and Stewart, 1985), 279.

53. Constance Rooke, *Fear of the Open Heart* (Toronto: Coach House Press, 1989), 9.

54. Mariana Valverde, *Sex, Power and Pleasure* (Toronto: Women's Educational Press, 1985), 10.

55. Ibid., 11-15.

56. Margaret Atwood, interview, *Herizons* 4, no. 1, 20-22.

57. Margaret Atwood, *Power Politics* (Toronto: Oxford University Press, 1974), 1.

58. Marian Engel, quoted in Patricia Morley, *Margaret Laurence* (Boston: Twayne Publishers, 1986), 133.

59. Adele Wiseman, *Crackpot* (Toronto: McClelland and Stewart, 1974), 9.

60. *See*: Shirley Neuman and Smaro Kamboureli, eds. *Amazing Space: Writing Canadian Women Writing.* (Edmonton: Longspoon Press, 1986). Articles by both anglophone and francophone feminists on feminist theory and technical strategies of 'subverting' the text.

61. Gail Scott, "Shaping a Vehicle For Her Use: Woman and the Short Story," in Ann Dybikowski et al., *In The Feminine* (Edmonton: Longspoon Press, 1985), 184.

62. Ibid., 185.

63. Nicole Brossard, *Exile* 12, no.1, 105.

64. Barbara Godard, ed., *Gynocritics/La Gynocritique: Feminist Approaches to Writing by Canadian and Québécoise Women. Démarches féministes à l'écriture des Canadiennes et Québécoise* (Toronto: ECW Press, 1987), 21-22.

65. Gail Scott, *Spaces Like Stairs* (Toronto: The Women's Press, 1989), 30.

66. Ibid., 135.

67. Barbara Godard, "The Translator as She: The Relationship Between Writer and Translator," in *In The Feminine*, 193.

68. Jovette Marchessault, "Night Cows," in *Lesbian Triptych* (Toronto: Women's Educational Press, 1985), 73.

69. Jane Rule, *A Hot-Eyed Moderate* (Toronto: Lester & Orpen Dennys, 1986), 43.

70. Jane Rule, *Desert of the Heart* (Vancouver: Talon Books, 1977), 134.

71. Jovette Marchessault, *Like a Child of the Earth, Mother of the Grass, White Pebbles in the Dark Forest* (Vancouver: Talon Books, 1988, 1989, 1990).

72. Rule, *Hot-Eyed Moderate*, 42-46.

73. Ibid., 24.

74. Ingrid MacDonald, *Catherine, Catherine* (Toronto: Women's Press, 1991).

75. Mary Meigs, "Memories of Age," *Trivia: A Journal of Ideas* (Fall 1988), 57-65.

76. Ibid.

77. Leah Cohen, *Small Expectations: Society's Betrayal of Older Women* (Toronto: McClelland & Stewart, 1984), 10.

78. Barbara Horn, "Beyond Hags and Old Maids: Women Writers Imagine Aging Women," in *Women and Aging: An Anthology by Women* (Corvallis, Oreg.: Clayx Books, 1986), 63-67.

79. In a lecture at Sheridan College, Oakville (October 1976), Beresford-Howe told the audience that the mail she received in response to the novel was overwhelming and totally unexpected. She insisted she was "not writing a blueprint for marital breakdown – just a story."

80. Miriam Waddington, "How Old Women Should Live," in *Collected Poems* (Toronto: Oxford University Press, 1986), 324.

81. Gretel Miles, "November 1983: Riding the Bus," *Canadian Woman Studies/Les cahiers de la femme* 5, no. 3, 31.
82. Dorothy Livesay, "Breathing," in *The Woman I Am*, 81.
83. Dorothy Livesay, "Nothing is Private," *A Room of One's Own* 5, nos. 1 and 2, 67.
84. Adele Wiseman, *Old Woman at Play* (Toronto: Clarke Irwin, 1978), 59.
85. *See*: Barbara Walker, *The Crone: Woman of Age, Wisdom and Power* (New York: Harper & Row, 1985).
86. Margaret Atwood, *The Journals of Susanna Moodie* (Toronto: Oxford University Press, 1970), 61.
87. Ibid., 61.
88. Marya Fiamengo, "In Praise of Old Women," in *North of the Cold Star* (Ottawa: Mosaic Press, 1978), 90-91.
89. Dionne Brand, "Bread Out of Stone," in Scheier, Sheard, and Wachtel, eds., *Language in Her Eye*, 49.
90. Ibid., 51.
91. Mutriba Din and Ravida Din in "Sisters in the Movement," *Fireweed*, "Awakening Thunder: Asian Canadian Women" issue, no. 30 (Spring 1990).
92. Tamai Kobayashi, "Untitled," *Fireweed*, no. 30 (Spring 1990).
93. Marlene N. Philip, "The Absence of Writing or How I Almost Became a Spy," *Fireweed* (Summer/Fall 1983), 20-26.
94. Lillian Allen, "A Writing of Resistance: Black Women's Writing in Canada," in *In The Feminine*, 63.
95. Ibid., 64.
96. Dionne Brand, *No Language Is Neutral* (Toronto: Coach House Press, 1990), 50.
97. Himani Bannerji, "We Appear Silent to People Who Are Deaf to What We Say," *Fireweed* 16 (1983), 11. *See also*: the first issue of *Tiger Lily*, a magazine dedicated to publishing works of minority women.
98. Himani Bannerji, "Paki Go Home," *Fireweed* 23 (1986), 17.
99. Claire Harris, *Fireweed* 23 (1986).
100. Claire Harris, *Fables From the Women's Quarters* (Toronto: Williams-Wallace, 1984), 40.
101. Ibid., 10.
102. For the intersection of creative writing and critical work and the political analysis produced, *see*: Rhonda Cobham, "A Caribbean Feast," *The Women's Review of Books* VIII, no. 12 (September 1991).
103. Joseph Pivato, "Italian Canadian Women Writers Recall History," *Canadian Ethic Studies* 18, no. 1 (1986).
104. Mary di Michele, "Hunger," in Mary di Michele, ed., *Anything is Possible* (Oakville, Ont.: Mosaic Press, 1984), 80-82.
105. Diane McGifford, Judith Kearns, eds., *Shakti's Words* (Toronto: TSAR Publications, 1990), xii.

106. Joy Kogawa, *Obasan* (Toronto: Lester & Orpen Dennys, 1981), Preface.

107. Joy Kogawa, "Is There a Just Cause?" *Canadian Forum* (March 1984), 24, paper presented originally to the Canadian Caucus on Human Rights, December 1983. Dorothy Livesay spoke out on this subject in a documentary poem, "Call My People Home," written for radio (1950).

108. Joy Kogawa, *Itsuka* (Toronto: Penguin, 1992). See also Maryka Omatsu, *Bittersweet Passage: Redress and the Japanese-Canadian Experience* (Toronto: Between the Lines, 1992).

109. Jeanette Armstrong, "Writing from a Native Woman's Perspective," in *In the Feminine*, 55. See also: Dolores T. Poelzer and Irene A. Poelzer, *In Our Own Words: Northern Saskatchewan Metis Women Speak Out* (Saskatoon: Lindeblatt and Hamonic, 1986).

110. Armstrong, "Writing," 55-57.

111. Beth Brant, "Coming Out as an Indian Lesbian Writer," in *In the Feminine*, 58.

112. Beth Brant, "A Long Story," in Rhea Tregebov, ed., *Frictions: Stories by Women* (Toronto: Second Story Press, 1989), 26-33.

113. Beth Cuthand, "Transmitting Our Identity as Indian Writers," in *In the Feminine*, 53-54.

114. Julie Cruikshank, Angela Sidney, Kitty Smith, Annie Ned, eds., *Life Lived Like a Story* (Nebraska: University of Nebraska Press, 1990), 3.

115. Ibid., 146.

116. Barbara Godard, "Talking About Ourselves: The Literary Productions of the Native Women of Canada," *CRIAW Papers* 11, (1985). The article contains useful resources and is one of the very few in-depth studies of the oral tradition in Native women's writing.

117. *Canadian Woman Studies/les cahiers de la femme* 10, nos.2 & 3 (Summer/Fall, 1989).

118. Some of these include: Atwood, Barfoot, Carr, Gibson, Laurence, Munro, and Rule.

119. Sharon Pollock interview, in Robert Wallace and Cynthia Zimmerman, eds., *The Work: Conversations with English-Canadian Playwrights* (Toronto: Coach House Press, 1982), 122, 123.

120. See: Joan Mason Hurley, *Canadian One Act Plays For Women* (Victoria: A Room of One's Own Press, 1975); Joan Mason Hurley, *Women's Women* (Victoria: A Room of One's Own Press, 1979); Liberty Jane Carter, *Satin Thigh* (Toronto: Playwrights' Co-op, 1976).

121. Margaret Hollingsworth, *Endangered Species: Four Plays* (Toronto: Act One Press, 1989), "Poppycock," Sc.1, 54.

122. Ibid., 49.

123. Margaret Atwood has written perceptively about this aspect of MacEwen's work. *See:* "MacEwen's Muse," in Atwood, *Second Words*, 67-68.

124. Gwendolyn MacEwen, *Trojan Women* (Toronto: Exile Editions, 1981), 34-35.

125. Ibid., 38.
126. Ibid., 73.
127. Ibid., 72.
128. Ibid., 59. (MacEwen's emphasis throughout.)
129. Ibid., 61.
130. Ibid., 94.
131. Ibid., 60.
132. Ibid., 66.
133. Ibid., 77.
134. Atwood, "If You Can't Say Something Nice," 21.
135. Ibid., 25.
136. Brand, *No Language Is Neutral,* 49.

Chapter Eleven

The Medical Treatment of Women

≈≈≈≈≈≈≈≈≈≈≈≈≈≈≈≈≈≈≈≈≈≈≈≈≈≈≈≈≈≈≈≈≈≈≈≈≈≈

In recent years the popular press has directed a good deal of attention to the medical 'problems' and treatment of women. Headlines have warned about the side-effects of various forms of birth control; articles have detailed the ongoing debate over home versus hospital birth. Caesarian section, mastectomy, and hysterectomy have become household words, as have puberty and menopause. However, the press has not shown an equivalent interest in the medical care meted out to men or to their various physiological processes. This reflects the assumption that man's body is the norm or the given against which woman's is judged. Woman's body is seen as different from man's, more complex in its design and, consequently, more mysterious and challenging in its workings. It is, in Simone de Beauvoir's words, "the Other" and as such it intrigues, repels, and in general fascinates. [1] But the physical distinctions between the two sexes go beyond the physiological; for many Canadians they also account for perceived psychological differences. As a result, physicians, who for centuries have claimed to be and have been accepted as experts on the body, are given enormous credence when they expound on the potential limitations of the female body and psyche.

This chapter attempts to place the medical treatment of women in Canada in historical perspective, focusing on conventional medical practices from the mid-nineteenth century to the present day. It stresses the historical continuities of issues such as birth control, childbirth, and gynaecological surgery rather than the emergence since the late 1970s of new ones such as toxic shock syndrome, premenstrual tension, *in-vitro* fertilization (discussed in Rona Achilles' chapter), or the new medical 'treatment' of women's aging process. The study emphasizes the role of women as patients and not as health providers, although the two cannot be separated completely. It also only looks at the medical profession as represented by physicians rather than other health care participants. From such a historical overview, three interrelated themes become evident: the relationship between medicine and culture, the medicalization of society, and the interventionist nature of medicine.

Physicians are a product of their particular culture just as any one of us is. They reflect their society's values, and their treatment of women is a concrete representation of those values. A study of the medical perception and treatment of women can tell us much about how the wider society perceives women. However, the repercussions of those perceptions can be very great when held by physicians, since their opinions and views can, and do, have physical and psychic consequences for their patients. Also, because doctors' views do reflect those in the wider society, until recently doctors have not met serious opposition to their attempts to increase their status and expand their influence in society. This expansion has led to the second theme of this chapter, what one might call 'the medicalization of society.'

Physicians are members of a profession and, like other professionals, they have made concerted efforts to become experts in a particular field and to enlarge that field. In the twentieth century, they have been very successful as Canadians have increasingly turned to experts for advice on almost every aspect of their lives. People have always looked to experts for guidance, but in the past the experts tended to be religious representatives. With the advent of the scientific revolution, new experts came to the fore, doctors among them. As a result, doctors were able to expand their area of expertise into spheres traditionally deemed non-medical and private, and in that way they intruded into what had once been the preserve of the family. They have become spokespersons on the health not only of the body but also of the psyche. They define what it is to be 'normal' in our society and what it is to be 'deviant.' They are present at our births and increasingly at our deaths. They advise us on what to eat and how much, what we should weigh, and how much exercise we should have. This is a far cry from the mid-nineteenth century, when Canadians seldom saw a physician and women generally ministered to themselves.

The medicalization of our society would not be so significant if physicians limited themselves either to giving advice or preventing illness. However, they do not. They want to intervene and cure our ills. Indeed, this is their main concern. As one physician has commented, "If we measure interest by activities rather than protestations, physicians have been and are, for the most part, as little interested in health as soldiers [are] in peace."[2] This means that physicians wait until illness strikes and then intervene in a visible and active way by advocating specific therapy, be it medicinal, surgical, or psychological. The teaching methods used in medical schools reinforce this interventionist stance since they focus on the weaknesses of the body, which result in ill health, rather than on the strengths of the body, which maintain health. Because the medical paradigm views the patient as a passive agent and the physician as the active one, physicians seldom receive opposition to their intervention. The physician defines the best interests of the patient and treats her/him accordingly. But best interests are determined within the context of a particular culture and set of moral and ideological as well as scientific beliefs.

The impact of culture on medicine, the medicalization of society, and the interventionist nature of medical practice affect both women and men. Nevertheless, it is the contention of this chapter that women patients have been and continue to be more vulnerable than men patients to that intervention. This is a result of several factors. The disproportionate number of male physicians means that most physicians have never experienced the normal physiological processes of the female body. When coupled with the tendency to view the male body as the norm, this has often led to the perception that deviation from it is illness. For example, it was quite common in the nineteenth and early twentieth centuries to refer to menstruating women as 'unwell.' The 1884 *Practical Home Physician*, a popular health manual read by Canadians, even went so far as to blame menstruation for gonorrhoea.[3] Yet viewing the male body as the norm is not the only perspective. As one critic of medicine has pointed out, there are two others. "If the standard of health had been female rather than male, menstruation would have been the norm and men's failure to menstruate the 'physiological peculiarity.' If the health standard had been a human one, neither menstruation in women nor the lack of it in men would have been peculiarities."[4] But neither the female nor the human perspective dominates; the male perspective does. More significant, however, than using the male body as the norm is that physicians, both female and male, share the biases and views of their own society. If that society perceives women to be other than equal to men, it is not surprising that the medical profession reflects that perception in its treatment of its women patients. This is not an indictment of the medical profession as much as it is a commentary on the values of that society.

Two caveats, however, are necessary. First, the medical profession has never been and is not now a monolith; indeed, some of the best critiques of the medical treatment of women over the last one hundred years have come from within the profession itself. Second, contrary to the standard medical view, patients are not passive and should not be treated as such. They often place pressure on physicians to provide them with the latest treatment, believing that the newest and most technologically intricate must be the best.[5] But if patients are not passive, neither are they equal in their relationships with doctors. In the case of women, that inequality has been particularly apparent.[6]

History of the Medical Profession in Canada

In Canada, physicians have not always been held in high esteem, have not always been well educated, and have not always had a monopoly over the health care system. Traditionally, women in the home dominated health care, and religious women established and ran hospitals; only as the professionalization of medicine occurred did this responsibility lessen. In the mid-nineteenth century, few medical schools existed in Canada. Consequently, many young men apprenticed themselves to a licensed physician for a number of years and then sat a licensing examination. At that point, the newly licensed physician had to face an array of competitors. In addition to regular practitioners like himself, there were the Thomsonians who believed in herbal remedies, the Homoeopaths who believed the more diluted a medicine was the more effective it became, and the Eclectics who practised a mixture of all systems depending on what they felt would be more suitable for the case at hand. Specific groups, such as the Amerindians, preferred their own traditional healers. Canadians could also seek help from midwives, patent medicine people, or anyone who seemed to have a natural skill for healing. Or they could try to heal themselves, using family nostrums handed down from one generation to another. In an effort to restrict this competition the regular practitioners pressured authorities to increase the educational requirements for a medical licence. They were particularly concerned about the Homoeopaths and Thomsonians, both of whom called themselves doctors and had their own medical schools. By the end of the century 'orthodox' physicians triumphed when a medical degree from a university became a requirement for licensing. This process, however, occurred not without opposition from within the profession itself. Increased educational requirements ensured that only the more affluent would be able to practise medicine, and it also meant that young men in rural areas with little access to universities would be forced to go to the major urban areas to study, thus increasing the cost of their training substantially.

One reason for the success of the 'orthodox' physicians in both homogenizing and increasing the training required for medical licensing was that they saw themselves and convinced other Canadians to see them as participants in the great discoveries occurring in scientific medicine in the late nineteenth century, the most important of which was the germ propagation theory of disease. This led to the acceptance of the need for cleanliness on the part of patient and doctor alike when medical care was being provided. It introduced the concept of antisepsis and did much to improve the conditions of health care facilities through the recognition and elimination of germs. The advances made in scientific medicine did not necessarily translate into better care of the patient, but at least the medical profession could explain more of what was wrong than it could before. As a result of the alignment between medicine and science, the profession gained in prestige, which, together with its association with the elite class in society, aided its efforts to acquire a monopoly over health care.[7]

At the same time that the regular practitioners were succeeding in their efforts to monopolize medical practice, the nature of that practice began to alter. Specialties developed that subdivided the profession. In the late nineteenth century, specialists such as psychiatrists, public health doctors, and gynaecologists emerged. This specialization has only accelerated in the twentieth century. The reasons for this are complex, but they were partly linked to the absolute increase in knowledge available about the human body and the inability of any one physician to comprehend all there was to know. They also reflected the objectification of illness and the division of the body into its component parts. Once physicians accepted that germs caused disease, it became understood that certain germs could cause specific diseases. This resulted in a move away from holistic medicine – that is, from medicine that saw all aspects of a person as interrelated and in need of care in order to treat the diseased part – to medicine that concentrates on the apparent diseased parts only. Once this occurred, physicians could specialize more easily. One result of this specialization was the elaborate creation within the profession of a hierarchy, with status usually linked to the degree of technical intervention required in the specialty. For example, surgeons have more prestige and make more money than general practitioners and, among surgeons, neuro-surgeons have higher status than gynaecological surgeons.

Status within the profession is not only linked to the area of specialization. It is also linked to gender. Indeed, the fact that most physicians have been and are men maintained the status of the profession in general. Medicine has not been particularly accepting of women, and when it has accepted them it has placed restrictions on them. In the mid-nineteenth century, nursing in Canada was not a field attractive to respectable women. The only exceptions to this were the religious nursing orders of the Roman Catholic church, which were predominantly, although not solely, located in the province of Quebec. Because lay or non-religious nurses worked long hours for low pay and often in squalid conditions, nursing attracted only the poorest of women, who were unable to obtain other employment. However, as a result of Florence Nightingale's efforts to establish a training school for nurses in Britain, the situation of nurses entered a new era. In 1874 the Mack Training School for Nurses, one of the first training schools for nurses in North America, opened in St. Catharines, Ontario, and the image of nurses began to improve. Nevertheless, nursing still remained drudgery. Student nurses were a source of cheap labour in the hospital, and when they finished their training they became private-duty nurses with no job security. Needless to say, nurses were trained to be assistants to doctors, subordinate to them in every way. When attempts were made to equalize this situation, doctors tended to respond in a negative fashion. For example, the Victorian Order of Nurses was founded by the National Council of Women in 1897 to aid women in rural communities who had limited access to physicians. Originally the scope of their work was to include midwifery. However, the opposition of the medical establishment in Canada was so great to what it saw as an infringement of its prerogatives that the idea was allowed to die.[8] Doctors had been hostile to women for most of the nineteenth century, and partially because of their oppositions midwifery had been severely weakened.[9]

Similar opposition occurred when some women indicated a desire to practise medicine. At first it was easy to prevent them. To qualify for a licence one had to have apprenticed with a doctor or to have taken a medical course at a university. No self-respecting male physician would take on a female apprentice, and until late in the nineteenth century no university in Canada would accept women students. When pressure increased on the universities to open their doors to women, university administrators and faculty argued that women were not strong enough, physically or mentally, to complete a medical course of instruction and that the morality of co-education in a field that dealt so intimately with the human body was, to say the least, most questionable. When it became clear that the women were going to insist on being allowed into the profession, rather than giving in with good grace, both the University of Toronto and Queen's University set up separate medical colleges for women in 1883. McGill University was not so generous. It refused to allow women a McGill degree in medicine until 1922.[10]

Although women had gained entry to the profession, the battle was far from over. Internships for women were few and far between, and the normal problems of setting up a practice were compounded when the newly licensed doctor was a woman. It was so difficult for many women to get started that instead of practising medicine in Canada they chose to practise as medical missionaries outside the country.[11] Those who remained still had to face the antagonism of some of their male colleagues, who argued that women doctors should limit themselves to the easier aspects of medical practice.[12] The *Canada Medical Record* in 1890 opportunistically suggested that women physicians could take over midwifery, particularly among the poor, since there was not enough money in it to interest most male physicians.[13] They could also help wean expectant women patients away from the use of untrained midwives in childbirth. Eliminating these women had long been an ambition of regular physicians, since the

midwives provided competition for them and also undermined the prestige of the profession by offering a medical service without formal training
and for a low fee. The women doctors, themselves, would not be in competition with each other or with male doctors, because medical schools
only admitted a handful of women each year.

One last change in the nature of medicine must be mentioned before an
examination of its treatment of women can begin, and that is where
patients were treated. In the mid-nineteenth century, most Canadians
remained at home when ill. Hospitals existed, but they were for the poor
who had nowhere else to go or no one to care for them. Canadians viewed
hospitals, quite correctly, as places of death. Conditions in them were
squalid and the care provided was minimal. Only slowly did they change,
aided partly by the improvements in nursing begun as a result of Florence
Nightingale's work and partly because acceptance of the germ theory of
medicine necessitated an antiseptic environment. As medicine developed
technologically, hospitals became the logical repositories of new medical
equipment and of the people trained to use it. Home treatment was ineffi-
cient for the kind of medicine practised. Hospitals thus proliferated in the
twentieth century and increasingly catered to paying patients. They represented a further success on the part of orthodox medicine for, unlike
patients' homes, hospitals were environments doctors could and did control. As a result, health care became less private, less intimate, and less
controlled by the family.

Culture and Medicine

For most Canadians, biology is destiny. This concept has its roots in the
Aristotelian heritage of Western civilization and focuses on the differences
between women and men rather than on their similarities. The persistent
effects of this focus are described in other chapters in this book. Lorraine
Code discusses its influence in shaping concepts of biological determinism, Joanna Boehnert shows how these concepts affected accounts of the
psychology of women, and Beverley Baines discusses the influence of Aristotle's linkage of difference and inequality on legal decisions. For Aristotle, the obvious differences were the physical. The differences were there
for a reason, and the reason was to indicate the proper role of women and
men in society. Because women were capable of bearing children, the
assumption was that they *should* bear children and that the maternal role
was primary for them.

Physicians, too, have seen maternity as the main function of women.
The result for women has been a concentration on obstetrics and reproduction to the neglect of other areas of health care that would promote

their general well-being. The concentration on obstetrics, however, did not reflect a concern for women as whole human beings, but for women as childbearers. For that reason, in Protestant Canada the survival of the woman has always had priority over the survival of the child during childbirth. Nevertheless, physicians and other Canadians only became concerned about high rates of maternal mortality in the mid-1920s, at least two decades after similar concerns had been expressed regarding infant mortality.

If maternity was woman's natural role, then any interference with that role had to be resisted. In a critique of the rising number of ovariotomies (removal of one or both ovaries from a woman) performed at the end of the nineteenth century, Dr. Hingston of Montreal made it clear that his primary concern was that such surgery interfered with a woman's ability to conceive. This he viewed as "a crime against society" and "the interests of the state."[14] He did not view it as a crime against the woman. Physicians believed that marriage and maternity were ultimate goals for women because of the dictates of their bodies and that if any woman rejected them, the health of her body would suffer as a result. In 1884 a text used in several Canadian medical schools made this clear – spinsters and married women without children were at risk:

> Especially is the liability to the formation of fibromas of the uterus greater in unmarried and nulliparous women than in those who have born children, as if the uterus, deprived of the function of building up a new being, were more liable to use the material for the formation of a tumour.[15]

So convinced were some physicians that the maternal role was natural to women that they advocated marriage and motherhood as cures for uterine disease.[16]

In a culture that for so long had viewed marriage and motherhood as the proper goals for women, it was difficult to imagine that both might be a burden. Consequently, women who experienced problems with their pregnancies or marriage were blamed for rejecting their natural role. In the 1950s, one physician connected miscarriages to "difficulty in the feminine role," that is, among women who miscarried were those who with "a possessive mother and their underrelatedness to a paternal offset, find femininity, particularly as it relates to motherhood, difficult, if not hazardous."[17] In the same decade, premenstrual tension and even amenorrhoea (absence of menstruation) were attributed to women's unhealthy attitudes towards femininity.[18] In the early 1970s a young woman whose husband objected to her desire to work was told by her therapist that her husband was correct and that she was at fault for not being satisfied with her wifely and maternal roles.[19] In a manner consistent with the prevailing views of the psychology of women, which Joanna Boehnert discusses in her chapter, women who were uncomfortable with their marital or maternal roles were viewed as deviant, as ill, for their minds were not following the dictates of their bodies. What such women were rejecting, however, was not their bodies but specific social roles that their bodies provided the potential to perform.

The close alliance between social perceptions of women and their health is strikingly evidenced in the medical view of hysteria. Women have long been encouraged to show their emotions. Yet this places them at risk of being labelled irrational and hysterical. In the late nineteenth century, physicians viewed hysteria as an affliction "to which every woman is liable."[20] It was exhibited in a lack of control of the emotions, and because women were traditionally viewed as more emotional than men, it seemed logical for physicians in the nineteenth century to assume that the hysteria was simply a natural female characteristic run wild. This would also account for the reluctance to admit hysteria in men. Hysteria in men would be more than pathological; it would be the exhibition of deviant attributes.

The primary cause of hysteria was the physical or biological makeup of women. This was a long-held view dating back to the Greeks, who saw hysteria as an affliction of the womb and named it accordingly (*husterikos*: of the womb). It was rooted in the very nature of being female. *The Canada Lancet* in 1880 deemed the advice of Dr. Goodell, a noted U.S. gynaecologist, worthy enough to reprint:

> When you are called to treat a young girl with a hysterical attack, there are three things which you had better do. (1) Institute at once firm pressure in the neighbourhood of both ovaries. This is very apt to quiet the patient at once. (2) Administer an emetic. I have found that a woman who is well under the action of an emetic has not the opportunity to do anything else than be thoroughly nauseated. . . . (3) And this method of controlling the spasm will often act charmingly – take a good size lump of ice and press it right down upon the nape of the neck. This produces quiet by its powerful impression upon the nervous system.[21]

Fortunately for their patients, Canadian physicians, unlike some U.S. practitioners, seldom prescribed excision of the clitoris for the treatment of hysteria. They were much more conservative about sexual matters and thus were reluctant to propose such surgery to patients who were equally reticent. Nevertheless, cauterization of the clitoris was advised, and one textbook used in Canadian medical schools suggested Battey's or Tait's operation, both of which consisted of removal of the ovaries.[22]

The concentration on controlling women's emotions has only increased over the years. Physicians still tend to view their female patients as suffering more from emotional problems than their male patients. They give almost twice as many prescriptions for minor tranquillizers and, in particular, anti-depressants to women than to men.[23] A 1984 report by the Toronto Public Health Department revealed that electroconvulsive therapy (shock treatment) was used twice as often on women as on men, and that this ratio was even higher in other provinces.[24]

Social attitudes not only influence medicine's perception of women's emotional or psychological nature, but also influence its attitudes towards the physical capabilities of women. It has been commonplace in society for years to focus on women's physical weakness compared to men's strength. This is reflected in medicine in the perception that a woman's body is prone to disease. Such a belief is not surprising. Gynaecology, the specialty that pays most attention to women, emerged in the latter part of the nineteenth century, when the concept of true womanhood was at its peak. This ideology usually characterized women as different from men mentally, emotionally, morally, and psychologically. In the final analysis these differences were based on and assumed to be caused by physical differences, the most significant of which was the reproductive system. Gynaecology was, and is, predicated on the assumption that woman, that is, her reproductive system, is prone to disease. This view of woman as being somehow weaker than man dominated the nineteenth century and is still present in Canadian society. It is an interesting perspective given the pain of childbirth that women endure and the work that they have historically done either at home or in the work force. To see women as weaker than men contradicts what biologists have long known: that females are more mature than males at birth, and that from conception to old age males have a greater incidence of disability and death than females.

Nevertheless, society persists in viewing women as the weaker sex, and physicians reflect this in their perception of women's health. They assume women to be at risk at almost every stage of their lives, beginning with puberty. In the nineteenth century, physicians and Canadians in general believed there were very few biological differences between boys and girls until they reached the age of puberty. At that point, the two sexes separated physically, emotionally, and intellectually. Young girls were urged to cut down on their activities during this time and to rest so as not to over-exert themselves. Doctors believed that the body had only a finite amount of energy, and that during puberty much of a young woman's energy was directed towards the development of her reproductive system. Particularly threatening in their view was education:

Education has great influence in the development of gynecological diseases. Too great assiduity in study in early youth concentrates the nerve-energy on the brain, and deprives the uterus and ovaries of their share at a time when these organs are undergoing an enormous development, and preparing for the important functions of woman-hood and motherhood.[25]

Opponents of higher education for women used such arguments to good effect.[26] Even today, the perception that puberty is a time when young women are at risk has not disappeared.

The danger to women does not decrease as they pass puberty. Adult-hood brings with it the likelihood of marriage and with that the dangers of childbirth. Physicians over the decades have argued that women, espe-cially the middle-class women who could afford their services, needed help in giving birth, and the increase in technological apparatus surround-ing birth in the present day attests to that view. Even the end of her repro-ductive life brings no relief to woman in the medical model. Menopause is simply another ordeal that women experience. In the late nineteenth cen-tury, menopausal women were viewed as irrational and subject to person-ality defects. They were liable to "every form of neurasthenia, neuralgia, hysteria, convulsive disease, melancholia," and even insanity.[27] Meno-pausal women are still ridiculed in contemporary medical literature. In a study of pharmaceutical advertisements between 1966 and 1983, Anne Rochon Ford discovered that menopausal women were depicted as help-less people who could not cope. They were a bother to their families, a nui-sance to others, or, as one advertisement phrased it, "beside themselves." The ads viewed menopause as a time "when women outlive their ovaries," as if this was not a normal physiological process.[28] But while the act may be physiologically normal, it signifies the end of the perceived social usefulness of women: childbearing. Medicine and culture cannot be separated.

The Canadian medical profession has consistently reflected society's attitudes towards women. This has influenced how physicians have per-ceived the physical well-being of women and the advice and treatment given to them. Woman's role was to be a mother, and doctors condemned surgical procedures that interfered with or prevented women from bearing children. Canadians saw women as more emotional than men, which con-firmed physicians in their historic predisposition to see hysteria as a female disorder. The apparent muscular differences between the two sexes translated into women being perceived as weaker at every stage of their life cycle. Society viewed the higher education of women as unnecessary, and medical practitioners concluded that education undermined the health of young women. Medical practitioners did not create the stereotypical view of women as maternal, emotional, and weak, but provided a medical rationale or support for it. That support has been effective. As one medical historian has explained it:

> When the belief structure of the physician is threatened, even in fields outside of medicine, he often uses his medical expertise to justify his prejudices and in the process strikes back with value laden responses which have nothing to do with scientific medicine. Unfortunately, since he is assumed to speak with authority, his response, perhaps as he intended, has influence far beyond that of the ordinary man. [29]

Medicine is not an objective science (if indeed one even exists). It and its practitioners are caught up with the prejudices and biases of their milieu as much as any one of us is.

Medicalization

Since the mid-nineteenth century we have seen the increasing medicalization of our society and our lives. This results partly from the esteem placed on learned or formal knowledge compared to experiential wisdom and from the power we give to holders of such knowledge. Doctors have been able to take advantage of this to extend their influence in society by speaking out on traditionally non-medical subjects and linking them to health, that is, medicalizing them. In their efforts to determine the cause of disease in women and in their belief that they have a right and a duty to speak out about those causes and their origins, physicians have expanded their area of expertise. Although they have focused on the physical manifestations of illness, over the years they have pushed their inquiries to expose what they perceive to be the social and moral origins of those manifestations as well. In effect, they have expanded the definition of 'legitimate medical concern,' and in so doing have increased the prestige of the medical profession. This medicalization has affected almost every aspect of women's lives.

One early example was the exercise women should engage in. Physicians argued in the late nineteenth century that exercise was necessary "to secure normal development of the reproductive organs." [30] Of course, they also believed the amount of exercise should be dictated by the needs of the female body and that doctors should be the ones to advise women on what those needs really were: 'appropriate' exercise was consequently defined by doctors' perceptions of the needs of women. Of particular concern was the new craze of bicycle riding. Some feared that it led to ill health. As stated in the *Dominion Medical Monthly and Ontario Medical Journal* in 1892:

> The best saddle does not meet the comforts or requirements of the female pelvis, that aside from the pedal motion that ever tends to provoke erethism the jolt of the machine is not without evil effect upon the uterus and other generative organs, and is especially apt . . . to induce laxity, version, prolapse, with all the concomitants of endometritis, menorrhagia, etc.[31]

Not all agreed. Some physicians believed cycling was good for women because it took them outdoors and made them use their muscles. They believed it would bring about dress reform and, by providing exercise, would aid in the cure of female complaints such as anaemia, constipation, amenorrhoea, and dysmenorrhoea.[32] Cycling was a challenge to the Victorian image of woman. It represented a change that some physicians could accept and some could not. What is significant is not whether they supported bicycling, but that they felt compelled to voice an opinion at all. Whether they disapproved or approved, they were exerting their influence in society to the point that one physician argued, "No woman should ride a bicycle without first consulting her medical man."[33] Even today, in the discussion of whether girls should participate on boys' sports teams, as evidenced in the Justine Blaney case (mentioned by Beverley Baines in her chapter), physicians have given testimony about the degree of exercise healthy for girls.

Another area over which the medical profession has extended its competency is the definition of healthy sexuality. For the late nineteenth century and much of the twentieth century, sexual intercourse has been deemed healthy only within the limits of a heterosexual, marriage relationship. Certainly masturbation, until fairly recently, has been censured. Some nineteenth-century physicians argued that masturbation in women led to a dullness in the sensibility of the genitalia and thus weakened the enjoyment of sex. This was a problem, not for the woman, but for her husband, who would find his wife cold and indifferent to him.[34] Other commentators maintained that it could result in flaccid breasts, deafness, decreasing strength, loss of memory, leucorrhoea, melancholy, nervousness, paralysis, imbecility, and insanity.[35] Central to most discussions on the topic was the role played by motivation. Masturbation was dangerous to health, not because it was a sexual act but because it was a solitary sexual act. The motivation was self-gratification, and the result was individual enjoyment. Marital sex was not dangerous because it was regarded as a moral act, focusing on another human being who was a loved one and engaged in for procreation. It was an altruistic act. The idea that the body could distinguish between types of sexual acts and their motivations suggests that "sexuality [began] to be defined in terms of the mind as well as the body."[36]

By acknowledging that women masturbated (even though they disapproved of it), doctors recognized an active female sexuality. Physicians have always asserted the strength of the male sex drive but have been more ambivalent in their attitudes towards female sexuality. Women were the childbearers and childcarers, and so it was very important for them to remain virtuous in both mind and body. Nineteenth-century popular wisdom insisted, and some physicians agreed, that a pregnant woman's thoughts and feelings could affect the future moral outlook of her child. Although it was difficult to deny women's sexuality, this sexuality became less threatening for the well-being of the race when physicians linked it to the maternal instinct. The Victorians and many of their descendants believed in a balanced society. The strengths and weaknesses of each sex were offset by the other, that is, each sex complemented the other. Thus if men were rational, women were intuitive, if men had a strong sex drive, women's by logical necessity must be weaker. For women to transgress sexually has been and still is seen to be more reprehensible than for men. Sexually active women are believed to be acting against their very nature. It is one of the reasons that being a prostitute has long been a crime in this country but, until recently, going to a prostitute has not. The men who sought out prostitutes were simply succumbing to their 'natural' drives, whereas the prostitutes were acting in an 'unnatural' fashion. They were the deviants. In the early part of the twentieth century the medical profession gave support to the idea that most prostitutes were feebleminded – how else could you explain what they did?

Such ideas about female sexuality were slow to change. In World War II, when women joined the armed forces, they were not given either information or prophylactic protection to arm themselves against venereal disease, as men were. Again the assumption was that good women did not need that protection because they would not engage in illicit intercourse. In the early years of the war, when a woman did contract VD, she was forced to leave the service, whereas an infected man was not. Authorities believed that a woman who had VD was at fault, but that male service personnel who had VD were the victims of 'loose' women in the civilian sector.[37]

The tendency of the medical profession to speak out on sexual morality was also evidenced in the 1950s. When the Kinsey Report was made public, some physicians became concerned because its recognition of a strong female sexuality went against the moral standards of society. Most physicians acknowledged the benefits of sex for women, but only if it remained within the marital relationship. Not only was the sex act to remain within marriage, but so also was discussion of it. Doctors advised wives not to talk about their sexual lives with other women. As Deborah Findlay states in her study of medical attitudes towards women in the 1950s, "This assertion was quite consistent with the doctors' approach to sex as a means of combating the rising divorce rate and bonding a marriage – pro-familial concerns. Not only that, but a good sex life on the part of a married couple was deemed to keep the husband competing successfully at work!"[38]

What is particularly curious about physicians becoming sex counsellors and Canadians accepting it is that most physicians had no knowledge in this field beyond conventional wisdom. Human sexuality was not part of the medical curriculum for most of this period, and even if it were, medical knowledge about it was not necessarily accurate. Indeed, for parts of the twentieth century medical knowledge about sexuality was less accurate than in the nineteenth century. Despite the view of Victorian physicians that female sexuality was not as strong as male sexuality, they never denied that it existed. What is more, they knew that female sexuality was centred in the clitoris. As Joanna Boehnert describes in her chapter, once the Freudian revolution occurred, this vital piece of information was neglected and concentration focused on the vaginal orgasm as the epitome of the mature woman's sexual response. This meant that those women experiencing clitoral orgasm, both heterosexual and lesbian, were considered "infantile."[39] It needed the studies by Kinsey and by Masters and Johnson to centre the female sexual response on where physiologically it provided most pleasure to women.

Another major area that has become medicalized over the years is contraception. At one time doctors did not involve themselves with this issue. However, by the mid-nineteenth century practitioners had become antagonistic to the use of birth control and insisted that it was immoral, unnatural, and, therefore, unhealthy. Physicians stated that the use of birth control could lead to nervous disease, insomnia, insanity, and impotence.[40] The practical consequences of these beliefs and attitudes could be cruel. In his text *Lessons in Gynecology,* William Goodell related that he had refused to treat a woman with uterine troubles until she and her husband stopped practising birth control.[41] Yet there was little medical evidence for the medical stance physicians took, because the most popular type of birth control used well into the 1930s was coitus interruptus, which has no medical side-effects despite nineteenth-century arguments to the contrary.

The reasons for the medical profession's hostility to birth control was not medical but social. Birth control negated woman's proper role. Goodell mentioned that husbands and wives were constantly beseeching physicians for means to prevent pregnancy, but he argued that physicians must refuse on moral grounds.[42] Others agreed, arguing that contraception made marriage a form of prostitution. It cheapened sex and dulled sexual enjoyment and so led to unfaithfulness. Doctors were also concerned that contraception was being practised by the 'better classes.'[43] These were, of course, the women whom the physicians were treating and the ones on whom they depended for their livelihood. Doctors accused women of limiting their families for selfish reasons, to maintain their figures, for instance, or so they could go out in society.[44] The main indicator, however, that the disapproval of contraception was social and not medical was the profession's knowledge of safe ways to prevent conception.

This hostility to birth control gained added support in the early decades of the twentieth century from concerns about racial suicide, as immigration from non-English-speaking countries increased and altered the ethnic balance of Canada. This was a particular concern of English Canadians, who correctly perceived that native-born middle-class English Canadians were limiting their families more than the new immigrants and native-born French Canadians. They feared that, as a result, Canada would no longer be an English nation but become a polyglot. Their solution was to encourage a higher birth rate by discouraging birth control. Physicians were at the forefront of this movement, for in it they perceived a way of extending their own sphere of influence. They would become moral arbiters as well as medical arbiters. As one physician explained it, the success of the Roman Catholic church, especially in Quebec, in dissuading its adherents from limiting family size would then be balanced in Protestant Canada by using the weight of scientific arguments through the medical profession. This could only enhance the position of the profession.[45]

Although the medical profession opposed the use of birth control, many Canadians did not, as demonstrated by the plummeting birth rate since the late nineteenth century. However, birth control had few public adherents in Canada except for some feminists and activists on the left. This changed in the early 1930s, when the economic plight of large families became a public concern during the Great Depression. Various groups such as the clergy, business people, and society women were willing to endorse birth control as a solution to economic problems, whereas they had never been willing to endorse it as a recognition of woman's right to control her own body, as feminists had and still maintained. The result of this concern was the opening of the Hamilton (Ontario) Birth Control Clinic in 1932 and the establishment of the Parents' Information Bureau in Kitchener, Ontario, in 1933. The latter was begun by A.R. Kaufman, owner of the Kaufman Rubber Company. In 1936, one of Kaufman's nurses, Dorothea Palmer, was arrested for canvassing in favour of birth control in a poor, working-class, predominantly Catholic, French-Canadian suburb in Ottawa. The trial pitched a French-Canadian, Catholic prosecutor supported by French-Canadian Catholic obstetricians against supporters of a more liberalized approach to birth control. The defence witnesses were able to show that birth control, contrary to the prosecution's testimony, did not impair the health of women. Indeed it was an aid in preserving health and thus was deemed to be in the 'public good.' The court found in favour of Dorothea Palmer. This did not change the law against selling and advertising birth control, but it did signal to the police that they would have to step very warily before they prosecuted anyone who did so. Not until 1969 were the selling and advertising of contraceptives legalized.[46] In that same year, doctors were allowed to perform abortions in hospitals if the abortion was approved by a committee of physicians who deemed it was in the interest of preserving the life or health of the woman.

Abortion had been medicalized in the same way as birth control. Up until the mid-nineteenth century, residents of British North America did not perceive abortion as an issue of public concern. Popular convention accepted that there was nothing morally reprehensible with abortion, at least before quickening, the first perceptible movement of the foetus at about the sixteenth to eighteenth week of pregnancy. However, at that point there was some concern, although women who aborted their foetuses were seldom prosecuted.[47] The real hostility to abortion came from the medical profession, who were the first group to understand the continuous nature of the spectrum from conception to birth and, as a consequence, no longer viewed quickening as a significant biological signpost of a foetus's viability. They were also very much concerned that abortionists were in competition with them, as were midwives and other irregular practitioners. Certainly the fact that abortionists were prosecuted, rather than the women who had requested the abortions, suggested that more than the morality of the act was at issue. As with birth control, physicians originally argued that abortion was a dangerous procedure, even though the risks had decreased dramatically by the 1890s.[48] Today there is more medical danger for many women in pregnancy than in abortion in the first trimester. This 'medical fact' indicates that the control of and opposition to abortion by many physicians continues to be non-medical in nature.

In the 1986 doctors' strike in Ontario, many physicians used women wanting abortions as pawns in their confrontation with the provincial government. Before the strike, some withdrew their services from hospital abortion committees, even though the longer an abortion is delayed the more harmful it is to the woman. After the strike, doctors made it known they would levy certain administrative charges. In the case of abortion, some of those charges totalled $400.[49] The medical profession did not use procedures such as prostate surgery, which affected male patients, as bargaining tools in the same way. These and other actions resulted in the abortion law in Canada being implemented unevenly across the country. One physician pointed out that decisions taken by some therapeutic abortion committees were quite irrational. "Consider, for instance, that a healthy woman with one child was granted an abortion but a 43-year-old Roman Catholic woman with four children and a sick husband was refused. Why was one woman with three girls turned down because her next child might be a boy?"[50] By the end of 1986 no abortions could be performed in Prince Edward Island or Newfoundland, because no hospitals there had therapeutic abortion committees. This forced women to travel either to the United States or Quebec, to self-induce abortion, or to have an illegal abortion. The minimum estimate in 1984 was that 3,484 Canadian women obtained abortions in the United States.[51] This violated one of the four principles of the Consumers Association of Canada Statement on Consumer Rights in Health Care, the right of equal access to health care.[52] The 1988 Supreme Court decision striking down the abortion law acknowledged this very lack of access as a major problem with the law.

Underlying the actions of the physicians opposed to abortion is hostility to women who are rejecting, for whatever reason, the maternal role. Reasons for accepting or rejecting a woman for an abortion are clearly not based on medical grounds. The reasons are linked more to the perceived nature of woman's proper role and morality, in which physicians have no more expertise than other Canadians. Yet they are the ones who make the decisions, because the law has medicalized abortion with the support of both the medical profession and the public.

The major area of medicalization for women, however, is not abortion but birth. Doctors indicated their desire to exert influence in this field very early on. When anaesthesia in labour was introduced in 1848, most doctors and their patients welcomed it. However, some physicians were uneasy about the effect it would have, not on a woman's health, but on her moral well-being. The American specialist Meigs opposed it, considering the pain of childbirth to be "a desirable, salutary, and conservative manifestation of life force."[53] Tyler Smith in his major text, *Parturition and the Principles and Practice of Obstetrics*, argued that pain was a natural part of childbirth and referred to the morality of that pain. Without it, he feared, woman would descend to the level of the lower animals:

> Provident nature has, moreover, specially exempted women from the dominion of all passion save that of maternity at the time of childbirth. I believe this exemption and moral superiority arises, in a

very great degree, from the physical suffering of parturition. The natural throes deliver woman-kind from those emotions natural to the inferior animals. Here it is that we see more clearly than under any other circumstances, the *morality of pain* . . . The pains of natural labour are hard to bear . . . but they ennoble the sufferer morally.[54]

What is intriguing about this quote is the association of pain with higher development. This would not be so striking except that many physicians believed that the experience of pain was class related, that is, working-class women did not feel pain in childbirth to the same extent as middle-class women. While most physicians did not share the concern about the "morality of pain," for which many of their patients were thankful, the opinions expressed by Meigs and Smith do underline the concern of doctors for more than medical well-being and show how willing some were to make judgements in areas outside their expertise. Such judgements were clearly influenced by society's attitude towards women at that time and the desire of physicians to become spokespersons for their society and to extend their influence to non-medical areas.

Doctors were only partially successful in the late nineteenth century in extending their influence over childbirth. At mid-century, most women were still attended by other women and gave birth in their homes. Traditionally, the only women who gave birth in a hospital were the very poor or unmarried women, the latter usually in lying-in hospitals. Gradually, however, physicians began to take over, partially encouraged by the middle-class women who could afford them and demanded the most up-to-date treatment. Physicians rationalized the emergence of the male doctor-midwife in the same way men rationalized their control over other areas of economic endeavour. They had the expertise and, according to physicians, this medical expertise was increasingly needed in the management of childbirth. The term 'management' itself suggests an attempt to widen their sphere. They announced widely and clearly that women were no longer fit to have babies without aid. By the turn of the century, increasing numbers of women were attended by a physician during childbirth, although most still had their children at home. As late as 1939 only 41.7 per cent of births in Canada occurred in a hospital. Today it is 99 per cent.[55]

As a result of the increased belief in and use of medical technology, women have seen their control over childbirth decline. It has become an event dominated by strangers in an equally strange environment; an act between patient and doctor, not between woman and woman. Increasing numbers of women have felt alienated from the birth experience. In recent years childbirth has even gone beyond being primarily an act between patient and doctor to being an act between the doctor and the foetus, particularly when new technologies are employed. The mother is treated as merely the foetus's container, upon which the doctor can act at her or his discretion in her or his interest or in the interest of the foetus, not of the mother. The common statement "Dr. So-and-so delivered the baby" indicates how incidental the mother (who actually delivers the baby) has become.

When women tried to regain some control over the process by demanding more natural childbirth in the 1950s and 1960s, the profession did make some concessions. The introduction of a hospital birthing-room was deemed acceptable by many physicians because they interpreted it as a way of helping the mother respond to parenting and accept her role in society.[56] However, in recent years, when the women's movement lobbied for reform of birthing practices and some women opted for home births, various medical societies across the country placed pressure on doctors to cease attending home births. They also brought criminal charges against midwives in Halifax.[57] This despite that, historically, home births have been the norm and that many studies have indicated that they are as safe as or safer than hospital births.

Medicalization does not stop with the act of birth. In the twentieth century it has also encompassed the childrearing years. Medical practitioners, psychiatrists, and psychologists have been deluging women with advice on the best way to raise children. The most blatant example of how experts have interfered in childrearing was in the 1930s with the birth of the Dionne quintuplets. So miraculous an event was this that some within the medical profession advised the government of Ontario that the natural parents were unsuitable to raise these children. Instead of helping the family to cope financially and emotionally with the birth of the five little girls, the government removed the children from their parents' custody. Leading child experts, such as Dr. Blatz and Dr. Brown from Toronto, oversaw the quintuplets' development, using the most up-to-date psychological and medical knowledge. The sad results of the experts' advice, in the adjustment problems experienced by the five girls and their later unhappy lives, are only too well known.[58] Yet the advice continues to come. Women are told it is their responsibility to raise a well-adjusted child, and if this does not occur the mother is blamed. A recent study of U.S. and Canadian journals of psychiatry from 1970, 1976, and 1982 revealed that two-thirds of the articles faulted mothers for the problems of their children.[59]

The result of the medicalization of women's lives and society in general is that physicians have become moral arbiters. This is a responsibility for which they have no training and which many physicians themselves do not want. But by medicalizing so much of our lives, they have extended their influence. This perhaps would not be so worrisome except, as we have seen, medical treatment of women is not unbiased.

Intervention

Medical advances and technology have made it easier for physicians to intervene more drastically in their patients' bodies. All sorts of instruments were invented to 'aid' physicians in examining and treating their patients. The vagina and uterus were particularly prone to being prodded and examined. In the late nineteenth century, physicians had a regular arsenal to choose from: vaginal speculums, dilators, sounds, tents, curettes, and pessaries. In addition, favoured treatments of gynaecological disorders consisted of the use of cauterization, electricity, leeches, vaginal injections consisting of ice, belladonna, laudanum, bromine of potassium, sulphuric and gallic acids, acetate of lead, port wine, carbolic acid, nitric acid, and nitrate of silver. By the end of the nineteenth century, surgical intervention had captured the imagination of the profession. Earlier it had not been resorted to that frequently because infection too often occurred, resulting in an extremely high mortality rate. However, with the acceptance of the need for a clean and antiseptic environment, mortality rates declined. When coupled with the introduction of anaesthesia in Canada, surgery became less of a trauma for both patient and surgeon. However, along with the advantages that accrued, there were disadvantages. Operations became more common, to the point that many within the profession argued that too much surgery was being performed. This was certainly the concern of an article in the *Canadian Practitioner* of October 1898, which traced the change the treatment of women had undergone.

> Prior to the dawn of aseptic surgery, the uterus was mercilessly treated to all sorts of applications. . . . Since the introduction of asepsis the abdominal cavity had become the happy hunting ground of the surgeon, and the very impunity with which it may be eviscerated or mutilated is a strong incentive to the specialist in search of surgical glorification to play his art. The danger of all specialism is to warp the judgment and contract the mental horizon within the range of its own narrow field of operations.[60]

When the ability to operate safely was linked with the popular belief that gynaecological disorders caused mental instability in women, the result was often unnecessary surgery. A good example of this was the treatment of insane women at the London (Ontario) Asylum at the turn of the century. Believing that gynaecological disorders could cause insanity, the superintendent, Richard Maurice Bucke, introduced gynaecological surgery (varying from simple curettage to complete hysterectomy) into the asylum. When some women seemed to recover their sanity after such surgery, the operation proceeded apace, with the result that as many as 75 per cent of newly admitted women were operated on. As a result, Bucke claimed an increased recovery rate on the female ward of 14 per cent. Critics of the operations pointed out, however, that factors other than the surgery could explain the recovery of the women, for example, the individual care received after the operation. In addition, operations were performed only on those women who had been recently admitted to the asylum, namely those patients who all agreed had a better chance of recovery even if nothing was done to them. Critics also pointed out that some women died from the operations, while others pointed out that if Bucke was going to operate on his female patients, he should perform similar surgery on his male patients, since masturbation in men was considered a cause for insanity. After Bucke's death in 1902 the operations essentially ceased, although Dr. Ernest Hall in British Columbia continued to support them for many years.[61]

Not only was surgery used on insane women and not on insane men, in the 1930s it was used on women with mental disabilities and women from racial minorities. In the 1920s and 1930s, doctors and others advocated sterilization as a way of controlling the propagation of the feeble-minded, and two provinces, British Columbia and Alberta, passed sterilization acts for that purpose. Medical supporters of this legislation made it clear that medicine had a particular responsibility, because doctors' intervention had caused part of the problem. Left on their own, many of the 'unfit' would not have survived, but medical science had intervened and saved them. Now, "Medical intervention in the form of sterilization was needed to counter the surge of mental deficiency created by earlier forms of intervention."[62] In the sixty-four cases of persons sterilized in the Essondale Provincial Hospital in British Columbia from 1935 to 1945, fifty-seven were women.[63] In a study of surgery on the Native population in Canada in the early 1970s, Dr. Clarence Ekstrand discovered "a surgery rate five times *higher* than the general population, particularly for women and particularly for tubal ligations."[64] Both in the case of the retarded and in the case of the Native people a double standard prevailed. The women of both groups bore the brunt of surgical intervention. Despite the emphasis that Canadian society has placed on the reproductive capabilities of women and the reluctance to intervene with those capabilities, it has been even more hostile to intervention with the sexual/reproductive system of men.

Not surprisingly, the real arena of increasing medical intervention in women's lives is in childbirth. This was a logical step once medicalization of childbirth occurred. At the end of the nineteenth century forceps were popular, so much so that some physicians argued there was too much intervention with them. In the early part of this century, Caesarians were performed more and more until today almost one-third of all births are through Caesarian section, a much higher rate than in Great Britain and

Europe, where midwives are used. The practice of inducing births has become more common as well: a phenomenon once viewed as natural is now viewed as a medical problem and in need of assistance. Over the years, the percentage of births considered normal by the medical profession has been declining, resulting in more intervention. Abnormal births are emphasized in medical literature. Physicians write about their unusual cases; no one wants to hear about the normal delivery. As a result, young medical students graduate with the expectation of seeing problems in the delivery room.

Critics of interventionist childbirth techniques have asked, who benefits from it? Caesarians and induction are a medical necessity for a small minority of women. They are also convenient for the scheduling needs of the hospital and physicians, and the numbers of women undergoing such procedures suggest that it is this convenience that is often of most concern. In addition, making the woman less of a participant places the attending physician at centre stage. It is difficult to assume that patient welfare and comfort were uppermost in the minds of those obstetricians who, after the Ontario doctors' strike, asserted that they would no longer be present at normal deliveries (this may actually decrease the amount of intervention and benefit women) and would no longer guarantee that a woman's doctor would be the one to attend her if she was to deliver after hours and the doctor was not on call. Because we have come to accept childbirth intervention, doctors gain power through the willingness to provide it and through the threat of withdrawing it.

In the late 1920s and 1930s, several studies were made to determine the reason for the high rate of maternal mortality in Canada. The studies pointed to two major causes: the weak health of the women because of socio-economic factors; and the medical care the women received. The medical profession understandably focused on the second, which eventually led to better prenatal care and supervision.[65] However, the best care over nine months of pregnancy cannot offset years of poor health. The focus on the maternal role of women led the medical profession and Canadian society to overlook the health needs of women when they were not acting as childbearers. Instead of encouraging preventive medicine, we depend on doctors' ability to intervene.

Conclusion

The focus of medical treatment of women over the years has been on their reproductive/sexual system. To some degree this makes sense, considering that it is one of the factors that distinguishes women from men. However, the male sexual-reproductive system has never exerted the same fascination. This is partly because woman's is more prone to disorder because of its greater complexity, but it is also this complexity that offers the challenge to the medical profession. This perspective is not new. In 1898, one critic of gynaecological operations to cure insanity made it very clear why he believed surgery was more prevalent among women than men: "Happy, thrice happy, should man be because of the simplicity of his genital outfit and its meagre attraction for the operation of surgical science. Had nature decreed him to wear his genitals within the abdominal cavity, he, too, might have been compelled to suffer surgical martyrdom for the sake of restoring his reason." [66]

The medical treatment of women has closely reflected the attitudes of Canadians towards women. It reveals how fundamental the differences between the two sexes were and are believed to be. They were rooted in the deepest core of sexual identity and as such exerted a tremendous power over personal identity. Canadians believed that the individual was an organic whole. All parts of the personality – sexual, intellectual, spiritual, biological, moral, and mental – were interrelated. Any biological differences between individuals resulted in differences in every sphere.

Has the medical attention focused on women benefited them? There is no doubt that women are outliving men and have done so since the late nineteenth century. Fewer women now die in childbirth than ever before. However, most studies of mortality suggest that environmental factors, such as better nutrition and sanitation, have been more significant in increasing life expectancy than any medical therapeutic.

In recent years there has been a backlash against the medical care provided women. Women are making themselves more knowledgeable about their own bodies so they can understand what is happening to them when they are ill. The physical fitness movement attests to the growing awareness among both sexes that good health is based on preventive measures. The increase in the number of women doctors will make some difference to the care given to women. As women, these doctors will at least not view the female body as something divorced from their own. However, it is not only the sex of the physician that stands in the way of sensitive medical care for women. It is medical education itself. Female doctors are trained in the same way as male doctors, and historically there is indication of only slight differences in their treatment of patients. For medical treatment of women to change, medical education will have to focus increasingly on the whole person and not on one aspect of that person. In addition, our society will have to place as much emphasis on preventive medicine as it does on interventionist medicine. More significantly, doctors will have to stop using the male body as a norm by which to measure woman's health.

There is still so much we do not know about the medical care of women. For example, we do not have very much information on how the treatment of women varies by class and ethnicity. We are not even sure how much access to health care Canadian women have. We certainly do not have very much knowledge about how nursing care differs from male doctoring. This is unfortunate, for nurses tend to be in closer touch with patients and base much of their actual activity on their knowledge of the needs of the individual patient rather than on the more theoretical demands of any specific illness. We also need to appreciate the preventive health care provided by mothers within their own families. After all, it is they who, more often than not, determine whether they or their children even need medical assistance.

Wendy Mitchinson

Glossary

Mastectomy surgical removal of breast tissue; radical mastectomy consists of the amputation of the breast with wide excision of the pectoral muscles.

Hysterectomy surgical removal of the uterus.

Hysteria in the nineteenth century it referred to a state of excitement in which there is loss of control over the emotions.

Antisepsis prevention of contamination by bacteria by destruction of the infective matter.

Fibroma a tumour.

Nulliparous a term to describe a woman who has not given birth to a live child.

Emetic causing vomiting.

Erethism excessive irritability or sensitivity to stimulation.

Version the act of turning, in this case a uterus that has turned.

Prolapse downward displacement of the uterus.

Endometritis inflammation of mucous membrane of the uterus.

Menorrhagia excessive menstruation.

Dysmenorrhea painful menstruation.

Leucorrhoea a whitish or yellowish discharge from the vagina or uterine cavity.

Coitus interruptus when a man removes his penis from a woman's vagina and ejaculates outside her body.

Prostate an accessory reproductive organ in the male located next to and under the bladder.

Speculum an instrument for opening or distending a body opening, e.g., the vagina, for visual inspection.

Sound a slender instrument to be introduced into body passages.

Curette a spoon-shaped instrument for cleansing a diseased surface.

Pessary an instrument placed in the vagina to support the uterus or rectum.

NOTES

1. See Lorraine Code's discussion of de Beauvoir's view of women's Otherness, judged according to a male norm, in chapter one.

2. Andrew Weil, *Health and Healing: A New Look at Medical Practices – From Folk Remedies to Chemotherapy – and What They Tell Us About* (Boston: Houghton Mifflin, 1983), 114.

3. Henry Lyman, *The Practical Home Physician and Encyclopedia of Medicine* (Guelph, 1884), 515.

4. Gena Corea, *The Hidden Malpractice: How American Medicine Mistreats Women* (New York: Harper Colophon, 1985), 24.

5. An excellent example of this is the introduction of Twilight Sleep as a childbirth treatment in the early twentieth century. It put the birthing mother in a "state of semi-consciousness induced by morphine and scopolamine." This allowed the woman to be conscious during birth, but to forget the pain of birthing. It was a complex procedure and one that women, not doctors, insisted upon. Margarete Sandelowski, *Pain, Pleasure, and American Childbirth: From the Twilight Sleep to the Read Method, 1914-1960* (Westport, Conn.: Greenwood Press, 1984), 3-26. Of course, one reason that women may have insisted upon the newest techniques, such as Twilight Sleep, is that they have accepted the scientific model, based on the supposed rationality and objectivity of scientific investigation.

6. The primary sources used in this chapter are the medical journals published in Canada and the textbooks used in Canadian medical schools, including those published outside Canada. The paucity of Canadian textbooks remained until well into the twentieth century.

7. For further information on the early history of medicine in Canada *see*: Ronald Hamowy, *Canadian Medicine: A Study in Restricted Entry* (Vancouver: The Fraser Institute, 1984); William Canniff, *The Medical Profession in Upper Canada, 1783-1850* (Toronto: William Briggs, 1894); John J. Heagerty, *Four Centuries of Medical History in Canada* (Toronto: Macmillan, 1928); C. David Naylor, "Rural Protest and Medical Professionalism in Turn-of-the-Century Ontario," *Journal of Canadian Studies* 21 (1986), 5-20.

8. For further readings on women in the medical profession, *see*: G.W.L. Nicholson, *Canada's Nursing Sisters* (Ottawa: National Museum of Man, 1975); Suzann Buckley, "Ladies or Midwives? Efforts to Reduce Infant and Maternal Mortality," in Linda Kealey, ed., *A Not Unreasonable Claim: Women and Reform in Canada 1880-1920* (Toronto: Women's Educational Press, 1979); Margaret Street, *Watchfires on the Mountain: The Life and Writings of Ethel Johns* (Toronto: University of Toronto Press, 1973); Leslie Briggs, "The Case of the Missing Midwives: A History of Midwifery in Ontario from 1795-1900," *Ontario History* LXXV (1983), 21-36.

9. For a further description of the decline in midwifery, *see* Wendy Mitchinson,

The Nature of Their Bodies: Women and Their Doctors in Victorian Canada (Toronto: University of Toronto Press, 1991), 162-175.

10. For detailed descriptions of women's attempts to receive a medical degree, *see*: Carlotta Hacker, *The Indomitable Lady Doctors* (Toronto: Clarke, Irwin, 1974); Peter Dembski, "Jenny Kidd Trout and the Founding of the Women's Medical Colleges at Kingston and Toronto," *Ontario History* LXXVII (1985), 183-206; Veronica Strong-Boag, ed., *A Woman with a Purpose: The Diaries of Elizabeth Smith 1872-1884* (Toronto: University of Toronto Press, 1980); Hugh MacDermott, *Maude Abbott: A Memoir* (Toronto: Macmillan, 1941); Mary Beacock Fryer, *Emily Stowe: Doctor and Suffragist* (Toronto and Oxford: Hannah Institute and Dundurn Press, 1990).

11. Veronica Strong-Boag, "Canada's Women Doctors: Feminism Constrained," in Kealey, ed., *A Not Unreasonable Claim.*

12. *The Canadian Medical Record* 16 (1888), 239.

13. *The Canadian Medical Record* 8 (1890), 215.

14. *Canadian Practitioner* 9 (1884), 272. There was a great deal of discussion in the nineteenth century about when to perform ovariotomies. Physicians recognized that removing a woman's ovaries was a serious step and stated that it should only be done when a woman was suffering from debilitating problems, which only a premature menopause could cure. *See*: Wendy Mitchinson, "A Medical Debate in Nineteenth Century English Canada: Ovariotomies," *Histoire Sociale/Social History* XVII (1984), 133-147.

15. Henry Garrigues, *A Text-book of the Diseases of Women* (Philadelphia, 1894), 127.

16. Paul Mundé, ed., *A Practical Treatise on the Diseases of Women* (Philadelphia, 1891), 511.

17. Deborah Findlay, "Professional Interests in Medicine's Construction of Women's Reproductive Health," paper given at the Canadian Sociology and Anthropology Association Meeting, Winnipeg, 1986, 8.

18. Ibid., 10.

19. Interview by the author with the woman (who wishes to remain anonymous), Summer 1977.

20. *The Canadian Medical Record* 8 (1890), 237. See also: Wendy Mitchinson, "Hysteria and Insanity in Women: A Nineteenth-Century Canadian Perspective," *Journal of Canadian Studies* 21 (1986), 87-105.

21. *The Canada Lancet* 12 (1880), 244.

22. *Canada Medical Journal and Monthly Record of Medical and Surgical Science* 4 (1867), 207; *The Canadian Medical Record* 7 (1879), 319; *The Canada Lancet* 15 (1883), 310; *Canadian Practitioner* 14 (1889), 338.

23. Kathleen McDonnell and Mariana Valverde, eds., *The Healthsharing Book: Resources for Canadian Women* (Toronto: Women's Educational Press, 1985), 19, 112.

24. Ibid., 113.

25. Garrigues, *A Text-book,* 125.

26. *Dominion Medical Monthly and Ontario Medical Journal* I (1893), 68; *The Sanitary Journal* 6 (1894), 56; *Canadian Practitioner* 16 (1891), 261; *The Canada Lancet* 6 (1874), 233; *The Canada Medical Record* 8 (1879), 319; *The Montreal Medical Journal* 25 (1897), 682; Mundé, *A Practical Treatise,* 37.

27. J. Thorburn, *A Practical Treatise of the Diseases of Women* (London, 1885), 192-193. *See also*: Wendy Mitchinson, "Causes of Diseases in Women: The Case of Late 19th Century English Canada," in Charles G. Roland, ed., *Health, Disease, and Medicine: Essays in Canadian History* (Toronto: Hannah Institute for the History of Medicine, 1984), 381-395.

28. *Healthsharing* 7 (1986), 16.

29. Vern Bullough and Martha Voight, "Women, Menstruation, and Nineteenth Century Medicine," *Bulletin of the History of Medicine* 48 (1973), 66.

30. Garrigues, *A Text-book,* 126; Mundé, *A Practical Treatise,* 36; Alexander Skene, *Medical Gynecology* (New York, 1895), 23; *The Canada Lancet* 12 (1880), 186-187; William Goodell, *Lessons in Gynecology* (Philadelphia, 1890), 551.

31. *Dominion Medical Monthly and Ontario Medical Journal* 8 (1897), 134-135.

32. *Canadian Practitioner* 21 (1896), 331; *The Canada Medical Record* 24 (1896), 555; *Dominion Medical Monthly and Ontario Medical Journal* 11 (1898), 29.

33. *Dominion Medical Monthly and Ontario Medical Journal* 7 (1896), 501; and 11 (1898), 28, 30.

34. R. Pierce, *The People's Common Sense Medical Adviser in Plain English* (Buffalo, 1882), 751.

35. Ibid., 749-50; *The Canada Medical Record* 11 (1883), 255; George Napheys, *The Physical Life of Woman* (Toronto, 1890), 35.

36. Mark Poster, *Foucault, Marxism and History: Mode of Production versus Mode of Information* (Cambridge: Cambridge University Press), 132. For a more detailed examination of medical perceptions of female sexuality, *see*: Wendy Mitchinson, "Medical Perceptions of Female Sexuality: A Late Nineteenth Century Case," *Scientia Canadensis* 9 (1985), 67-81.

37. Ruth Roach Pierson, *"They're Still Women After All": The Second World War and Canadian Womanhood* (Toronto: McClelland and Stewart, 1986), 169-214.

38. Findlay, "Professional Interests," 9.

39. Anonymous, "Self-Love in Women," *Popular Sex Science* II (August 1, 1940), 18.

40. *Kingston Medical Quarterly* 3 (1898), 165; Goodell, *Lessons,* 570, 573; *Canada Medical Journal and Monthly Record* 3 (1867), 226; *Canadian Practitioner* 18 (1883), 296.

41. Goodell, *Lessons,* 566.

42. Ibid., 562.

43. Mundé, *A Practical Treatise,* 43; *Canada Health Journal* 1 (1870), 66.

44. *The Canada Lancet* 4 (1871), 185-186; *Canada Health Journal* 1 (1876), 67.

45. *The Canada Lancet* 7 (1875), 291.

46. For a history of birth control in Canada *see*: Angus McLaren and Arlene Tigar McLaren, *The Bedroom and the State: The Changing Practices and Politics of Contraception and Abortion in Canada, 1880-1980* (Toronto: McClelland and Stewart, 1986).

47. Constance Backhouse, "Involuntary Motherhood: Abortion, Birth Control and the Law in Nineteenth Century Canada," *The Windsor Yearbook of Access to Justice* 3 (1983), 61-130.

48. McLaren and McLaren, *The Bedroom*, 36.

49. *Kitchener-Waterloo Record*, July 25, 1986, 1.

50. *Pro-Choice News*, Summer 1986, 8.

51. Ibid., 1.

52. J. Storch, *Patient's Rights: Ethical and Legal Issues in Health Care and Nursing* (Toronto: McGraw-Hill Ryerson, 1982), preface.

53. Walter Radcliffe, *Milestones in Midwifery* (Bristol: John Wright and Sons, 1967), 81.

54. William Tyler Smith, *The Modern Practice of Midwifery: A Course of Lectures on Obstetrics* (New York, 1858), 128.

55. McDonnell and Valverde, *Healthsharing Book*, 62.

56. Findlay, "Professional Interests," 13.

57. McDonnell and Valverde, *Healthsharing Book*, 66.

58. For a fuller description of the Dionne quintuplets' lives, *see*: Pierre Berton, *The Dionne Years: A Thirties Melodrama* (Toronto: McClelland and Stewart, 1977).

59. *Healthsharing* 7 (1986), 18.

60. *Canadian Practitioner* 23 (1898), 579.

61. *See*: Wendy Mitchinson, "Gynecological Operations on Insane Women: London Ontario, 1895-1902," *Journal of Social History* 15 (1982), 467-484.

62. Angus McLaren, "The Creation of a Haven for Humane Thoroughbreds: The Sterilization of the Feeble Minded and the Mentally Ill in British Columbia," *Canadian Historical Review* LXVII (1986), 128; for a fuller description of the eugenics movement *see*: Angus McLaren, *Our Own Master Race: Eugenics in Canada, 1885-1945* (Toronto: McClelland and Stewart, 1990).

63. Ibid., 146.

64. Robert Morgan, ed., *The Introgenics Handbook: A Critical Look at Research and Practice in the Helping Professions* (Toronto: IPI Publishing, 1983), v-vi.

65. Suzann Buckley, "Hospital Records and Historians: The Case of Maternal Morality," in W. Mitchinson and J. Dickin McGinnis, eds., *Essays in the History of Canadian Medicine* (Toronto: McClelland and Stewart, 1988).

66. *Canadian Practitioner and Review* 23 (1898), 580.

SUGGESTED READINGS

Bliss, Michael, "Pure Books on Avoided Subjects: Pre-Freudian Sexual Ideas in Canada," *Historical Papers* (Canadian Historical Association, 1970), 89-108.

Buckley, Suzann, "Ladies or Midwives? Efforts to Reduce Infant and Maternal Mortality," in Linda Kealey, ed., *A Not Unreasonable Claim: Women and Reform in Canada, 1880-1920*. Toronto: Women's Educational Press, 1979.

Buckley, Suzann, "Efforts to Reduce Infant and Maternity Mortality in Canada Between the Two World Wars," *Atlantis* 2 (Spring 1979), 76-84.

Buckley, Suzann, "The Search for the Decline of Maternal Mortality: The Place of Hospital Records," in Wendy Mitchinson and Janice Dickin McGinnis, eds., *Essays in Canadian Medical History*. Toronto: McClelland and Stewart, 1988.

Dodd, Diane, "The Canadian Birth Control Movement on Trial, 1936-1937," *Histoire sociale* 16 (November 1983), 411-428.

Dodd Diane, "The Canadian Birth Control Movement: Two Approaches to the Dissemination of Contraceptive Technology," *Scientia Canadensis* 19, no. 1 (1985), 53-66.

Lewis, Nora, "Reducing Maternal Mortality in British Columbia," in Barbara Latham and Roberta Pazdro, eds., *Not Just Pin Money*. Victoria: Camosun College, 1984.

McLaren, Angus, and Arlene Tigar McLaren, *The Bedroom and the State: The Changing Practices and Politics of Contraception and Abortion in Canada, 1880-1980*. Toronto: McClelland and Stewart, 1986.

Mitchinson, Wendy, *The Nature of Their Bodies: Women and Their Doctors in Victorian Canada*. Toronto: University of Toronto Press, 1991.

Nicholson, G.W.L., *Canada's Nursing Sisters*. Toronto: Samuel Stevens Hakkert, 1975.

Raymond, Jocelyn Motyer, *The Nursery World of Dr. Blatz*. Toronto: University of Toronto Press, 1991.

Special issue, "Women and Medicine," *Ontario History* 75, no. 1 (1983).

Strong-Boag, Veronica, ed., *A Woman with a Purpose: The Diaries of Elizabeth Smith, 1872-1884*. Toronto: University of Toronto Press, 1980.

Strong-Boag, Veronica, and Kathryn McPherson, "The Confinement of Women: Childbirth and Hospitalization in Vancouver, 1919-1939," *B.C. Studies* 69-70 (Spring-Summer 1986), 142-174.

Valverde, Mariana, *The Age of Light, Soap and Water: Moral Reform in English Canada, 1885-1925*. Toronto: McClelland and Stewart, 1991.

Ward, Peter, ed., *The Mysteries of Montreal: Memories of a Midwife*. Vancouver: University of British Columbia Press, 1984.

Chapter Twelve

The Changing Canadian Family: Women's Roles and the Impact of Feminism

≈≈≈≈≈≈≈≈≈≈≈≈≈≈≈≈≈≈≈≈≈≈≈≈≈≈≈≈≈≈≈≈≈≈≈≈

Understanding the family as a social institution and recent changes in families is fundamental to understanding the position of women in Canada in the present, in the past, and in the future. Women's situations are inextricably intertwined with family because of the social roles women play, because of how we are both constrained and provided with opportunities through these roles, and because of the prevalent images of both family and of women held by Canadians. Sorting out these complexities is not an easy task, but it is essential to understanding the changing patterns of Canadian women's lives.

In Canadian society, family, whatever form it takes, is expected to meet our needs for affection, understanding, emotional support, and solace in an increasingly harsh world. Considerable flexibility is necessary in defining family in Canada in the 1990s, because the institution takes many and varied forms. For the purposes of this chapter, family is whatever people living in caring, long-term relationships commonly think of as family. In many parts of the world, an individual's emotional needs may be met through friends, religious commitments, civic duties, or from a more extended family group than generally exists in Canada. The range and intensity of needs that people expect to be met by the family may explain why family is a place of conflict. Conflict can result, for example, from the dual function of family as an agent of society and as a source of emotional support to the individuals within it. Although these conflicts are experienced by most members of families at some time, they tend to be particularly pronounced and poignant for women, who are often caught between their own and societal expectations of the family.

Most people consider the family to be the basic social institution: the family may give birth to new members, teach them how to behave appropriately, inculcate ethical and moral principles shared by society, produce and/or distribute goods and services, as well as maintain social order.

Family membership is a dominant fact of life for most of us and an important vehicle for becoming a person – developing an identity, belonging to a group, acquiring a sense of values, caring for others as well as oneself, and passing on traditions as well as wealth. These needs often conflict with each other. Further conflict arises when what is needed by society differs from what is needed by individuals within a family.

The family is both idealized and ideologized. Images abound of the ideal family, ranging from the extended family of days gone by; the 'Father Knows Best' family; the family we think we remember from childhood; or the family as sanctioned by the Bible, the Koran, or the Torah. It is seldom, if ever, the family in which we actually live. These idealized images can lead to a longing for what is lost, even if what we long for may never have actually existed. Some have referred to this as the "world we have lost syndrome."[1] The power of idealized images is such that we can long for Mom's apple pie and times gone by, even if Mom never made apple pie and our adult lives are far better than our childhoods ever were. It is as if we mourn for something that few people actually experience, but we feel somehow as if it is only we who missed out. The mass media, and advertisers in particular, are adept at selling nostalgic images of family life.

Given the conflicts built into the modern family, the expectations of society and of individual family members, the interconnections of families with other social institutions, the ideologies and the images of the family, both true and fictionalized, it is hardly surprising that considerable confusion exists about the changing roles of women in the family. Explanations of women's social roles tend to be surrounded by considerable vested interest, muddled thinking, and out-and-out misrepresentation. So it is understandable that women's roles in the family are not seen clearly. In this confusion, it becomes tempting to simplify everything by attributing all contemporary change in the family, whether bad or good, to feminism and to what are seen by some as women's 'selfish' needs – and in Canada in the 1990s, this temptation is not always resisted.

Few people living in Canada in the late twentieth century can be unaware that there have been changes in the family, if only because those changes are regularly discussed and analysed by the mass media. Unfortunately, many of these discussions generate as much misinformation as information. To get the 'hook' necessary to sell their programs or articles, the media often exaggerate the extent of these changes. Alarm is raised about what is happening to the family, laments are offered about what we have lost, or women's growing self-awareness is blamed for the 'demise' of the family, meaning typically the 1950s-style family.

It is not possible in a single chapter to discuss all aspects of the changing Canadian family. Several recent books analyse aspects of family change more completely than can be done here.[2] In this chapter, only the more salient changes will be highlighted. The discussion will focus on the impli-cations of these changes for women and on the roles played by women in bringing them about. Issues such as socialization of children or of women at various stages of the life cycle are beyond our scope.

Three of the most basic changes that have occurred in the Canadian family since the mid-1960s are a decrease in family size, an increased labour-force participation of married women and mothers, and an increase in marital dissolution through divorce and separation. These trends are not independent of one another, but intertwined, and they have been accompanied by large-scale socio-economic changes.

In this chapter some of the confusion about women and the family is stripped away to show how feminism can have positive effects on the fam-ily and to explore the implications for women of the changes occurring in Canadian families.

Declining Family Size

We moved from the baby boom of the mid-1940s to early 1960s to a period of baby bust in the 1970s and 1980s. The number of births per woman, on average, fell from a high of 3.9 in 1959, the peak of the baby boom, to 1.6 in the early 1990s.[3] The Canadian birthrate is now at an all-time low (although the Quebec birthrate has recently increased modestly) and is expected to remain at a very low level for some time. The fertility decline has been sufficiently pervasive in Canada that it includes a precipitous decline in family size also among Native people, whose traditionally high birthrates have been replaced by a pattern more similar to that of other Canadians. This trend towards smaller families parallels a similar trend in most Western industrialized countries.

An exclusive focus on the recent drop in the Canadian birthrate obscures the longer-term historical trend. When long-term trends are analysed, it is not the current low levels of birth that are striking, but the exceedingly high birthrates of the baby boom era. The Canadian birthrate has been declining since 1851.[4] The average number of births per woman in 1937, for example, was 2.6. The baby boom period produced the largest generation known in history. It may be that the long-term downward trend in fertility is simply resuming as the conditions that fostered the baby boom alter.

To understand how women's family roles and reproduction are bound to the needs of society, some of the factors behind the baby boom must be considered. Contrary to popular belief, the baby boom was not solely the result of lonely soldiers returning to hearth and home from World War II. Rather, a convergence of late and early childbearing with an overall increase in family size produced increased fertility. Women's roles were redefined as more family-centred than in the 1920s and 1930s. In the post-war period, women returned to housework and motherhood, leaving the jobs in the labour force they held during the war. S.J. Wilson cites the efforts of the Parliamentary Subcommittee on Postwar Problems of Women as having an important role in working to elevate the status of housework and family life for women in postwar Canada.[5] Paralleling this concerted and deliberate effort, which may not have succeeded impressively, was the appearance of women's magazines singing the praises of motherhood, of family, and of the joys of making meatloaf. The propaganda of the day pictured women at home and strong families as hedges against another war or as ballast in the Cold War. Economic expansion in the postwar period enabled male workers to be paid a family wage, meant to support a family. It is not surprising, then, that women married in record numbers and focused their attention on building families.

Competition among baby boomers was fierce in the 1960s and 1970s for teachers' attention, for university places, for jobs, even for mates. According to Susan McDaniel and Ben Agger, "This generation has experienced high unemployment, high dissatisfaction with the existing system and high educational and societal drop-out rates."[6] The postwar years also produced a group of dissatisfied and frustrated full-time mothers, who followed social expectations but felt unrewarded and depressed. Betty Friedan expressed these feelings in her 1963 book *The Feminine Mystique*, the implications of which Lorraine Code discusses in her chapter. Friedan focused on "the problem that has no name," that is, that women's work at home is not considered work by society, so its accompanying frustrations, as well as its rewards, go unrecognized.

The convergence of economic problems and women's growing dissatisfaction with their socially prescribed familial roles may explain, in large part, the current low levels of childbearing. It is not that women do not want children (most do), but that they find it difficult to be mothers of large families given the constraints of working outside the home to support families, inadequate day care options, limited extended families, and the escalating costs of raising children. The pattern of change in childbearing suggests that economic factors are as important as social factors in explaining smaller family sizes. The proportion of large families (in which there are six or more children) has dropped from 40 per cent in 1876 to less than 5 per cent in the mid-1980s.[7] This decline was particularly pronounced in Quebec, where the traditionally high birthrate was known as 'cradle revenge,' taken against the English-speaking majority in Canada. The decline is also dramatic among Native people. The decline in fertility among younger women suggests that couples may be postponing childbearing until they feel they can afford it.

Two recent trends suggest that women's changing self-images also play a role in reducing family size. One is that voluntary childlessness is increasing among Canadians. Women may appear to be voluntarily childless as they postpone births for longer periods. However, the long-term postponement of births can result in inadvertent voluntary childlessness, as women become accustomed to a child-free lifestyle or subsequently find that they are unable to have a child. Nonetheless, Statistics Canada projects that as many as 16 per cent of all young Canadian women at present may ultimately forgo maternity.[8] The previous record of childlessness, 21 per cent, occurred among women who were in their prime reproductive years during the Depression. The rewards of motherhood for women may not be as large as they once were, or were perceived to be. Alternatively, of course, the causes could be economic. Both partners in a two-parent family now often have to work full-time to make ends meet; babies are very costly in both money and time; and day care opportunities are limited.

A second social factor important in the decline in family size has to do with the satisfaction derived from having children. It used to be thought, and still is by some, that fulfillment in life, particularly for women, was not possible without children. In her chapter here, Wendy Mitchinson discusses the extent to which the medical profession subscribed to this belief. However, new evidence suggests that children may not be essential to life satisfaction. Researchers B.K. Singh and J.S. Williams, for example, have discovered that having children has little effect on life satisfaction, while N.D. Glenn and S. McLanahan and G.B. Spanier and R.A. Lewis have found that having children has a negative effect on marital happiness, especially for women.[9] Canadian women may no longer see themselves as life-long mothers and wives, with childbearing and childrearing the core of their lives.

The trend towards postponing births and having fewer babies means that a much smaller proportion of women's lives is devoted to childrearing. Ellen Gee and Meredith Kimball have calculated that women born 1951-60 spend an average of 23.6 years married with no children at home.[10] This compares with no years spent in this life stage by Canadian women born 1841-50, 12.2 years for women born 1901-10, and 18.1 years for women born 1931-40. Clearly, the life patterns of women in Canada have been transformed.

Research by Carl Grindstaff challenges the conventional belief that women limit their education and labour-force participation to have babies and find fulfillment in the domestic realm.[11] His findings reveal that childbearing, particularly early childbearing, substantially diminishes women's future economic and social options and opportunities. Women's lost opportunities, both to themselves and to society, may be the price that society pays for reproducing itself, according to Grindstaff. Canadian women, in postponing childbearing, forgoing it altogether, or having smaller numbers of children, may be voting with their wombs. They may have concluded that the price society asks of them for having children is simply too high to pay. Women may not want to forgo childbearing or larger families at all, but find that the social-support system for having children is inadequate.

The declining birthrate and the emergence of smaller families are not simply a consequence of women's enhanced reproductive choice. While some women have had the choice to postpone or opt for or opt out of childbearing, many continue to face unwanted pregnancies, most notably poor, young, immigrant, differently abled, and physically and mentally abused women. Any assumption that childbearing has become a choice for all Canadian women overlooks women's continuing quest for reproductive control. The abortion debate in Canada and the way policy-makers have dealt with it highlight many of the issues involved in women's campaign for choice in reproduction. The media, in focusing on well-to-do couples agonizing over the decision about whether or not to have a child, have lent support to the misconception that childbearing is now a clear choice for all women.

The new reproductive technologies, discussed in greater detail in Rona Achilles' chapter, highlight the reproductive-control challenges that women face in new ways. Women's reproduction is now segmented, so that we can be genetic mothers (egg donors), gestation mothers (who may or may not be genetic mothers or legal mothers), and socio-legal mothers who raise children. None of this is governed by *any* existing law in Canada. This is why a group of feminists, including this author, lobbied for the setting up of the Royal Commission on Reproductive Technologies, which began deliberations in 1989.

Women's Increased Labour-Force Participation

Shifts in childbearing patterns and family size in Canada have been accompanied by the dramatically increased participation of married women and mothers in the labour force. Prior to the Second World War, married women generally did not work outside their homes, except in family businesses or farms. Family was women's central vocation, as Jane Errington discusses in her chapter. Until recently, marriage alone was sufficient reason for an employer to fire a women employee. This past half-century has seen a dramatic change in women's work-force participation, as shown in Table 1. In 1931 there was a wide discrepancy in the labour-force participation of single and married women. By the late 1980s most women in Canada worked, whether married or not. Most dramatic has

Table 1

Shifts in Labour-Force Participation of Women in Canada:
Women Who Work Outside the Home, 1931-1986

	% of all women	% of married women	% of mothers with children under 6
1931	19.4	3.5	–
1951	24.4	11.2	–
1961	29.3	22.0	–
1971	38.3	37.0	27.7
1981	51.6	50.5	47.2
1986	58.0	57.7	58.2

SOURCE: Adapted from Statistics Canada Census data.

been the change in the labour-force participation of women with young children. Margrit Eichler notes that women now more often work throughout their lives, whether they are married or mothers or not. [12]

A combination of demographic, economic, and ideological changes explains the massive increase in female work-force participation. A decline in real wages forced women to contribute economically to their families, at the same time as families grew smaller and attitudes towards women's rights to work became more liberalized. [13] In her classic study of families in Flin Flon, Manitoba, Meg Luxton found that wives work for the same reasons that husbands do – to support themselves and their families. [14] The dual-earner family is the most common family form in Canada in the 1990s.

The majority of married women in Canada now work. But this reality has not been fully assimilated into the thinking of employers or even of women themselves. A surprising number of studies have focused on whether women with young children *should* work, whether they feel guilty about working, and whether their marital situation is compromised by their work. That these questions are raised *at all* points to the assumption that working husbands or fathers do not feel any such divided loyalty. Nonetheless, most Canadians still seem to feel that, ideally, mothers with small children should *not* work outside the home. While work-force participation for married women living with their husbands rose from 34 to 62 per cent between 1971 and 1986, the participation rate of women with preschool-age children rose even faster, from 27 per cent in 1971 to 58 per cent in 1986.[15] Clearly, public attitudes are lagging behind the realities of women's lives.

Working mothers with young children face dilemmas both at home and at work. They continue to hold chief responsibility for child care and housework, even if they also work outside the home. Hence, there emerges a 1990s pattern of work outside the home combined with a modified 1950s division of labour at home. Inadequate child care options, inflexible school hours, and the unsympathetic attitudes of most employers all add further problems for the working mother. At work a woman with children, particularly young children, is often perceived as having divided loyalties.[16] While marriage and children are more often seen as assets for a man in motivating hard work, for a woman they still tend to be seen as liabilities or distractions. A woman with children is seen as a risk for permanent employment, for a job with responsibility, and for promotions. She may be made to feel guilty about 'leaving' her children to work, even if she is working to support them.

The increased participation of married women in the work force parallels changes in housework. Tasks that used to be done at home (baking bread, making clothes, and so on) have been largely taken over by industries. The time spent by women in housework, however, has not necessarily decreased, because expectations have also increased. Breadmaking and washing, for example, used to be done by groups of women who enjoyed each other's company while working. Housewives now seldom work with other women in performing these tasks. Bread is bought and clothes are washed by machines in the home or laundromat by women at every socioeconomic level, with the result that the services provided by housewives are even less valued by society than before and women at home are increasingly isolated. Women at home might seek paid work, in part, to be with other people and to reduce their alienation. Evidence, however, questions this motivation, since so many women work in boring, isolating, and low-paying jobs.

It is not surprising that there is a minor rift between women at home and women who work outside their homes over what should be on the political agenda for women. Even though the extent of this rift may be exaggerated by politicians eager to splinter the potential political power women could have if we acted *en bloc*, there is some truth in the claim that housewives and women working in paid employment have different interests. In the late 1980s in Canada, the group REAL (Realistic, Equal, and Active for Life) Women formed to lobby for the interests of traditional homemakers.

Women's changing work-force patterns have brought about, and have been accompanied by, changes in family structure and in the way the family is seen. Some of these changes are paradoxical. The increased work-force participation of married women has both reinforced and undermined the idea that marriage may be women's best economic option. Reinforcement results from the realization that women's labour is worth less than men's, even when both do comparable work. Women seeking paid employment are often channelled into women's job ghettos, sometimes called pink-collar ghettos, characterized by poor pay, low status, and minimal opportunity for promotion. Such poor conditions are especially evident in the ghettoized labour of immigrant women, described by Roxana Ng in her chapter. Graphic evidence is thus provided for what women have been told for decades: the answer for women facing exploitation and low pay at work or on welfare is to find a man and settle down. When women still earn, on average, sixty to seventy cents for every dollar earned by a man, marriage to a man whose earnings are higher might be seen as women's best option for economic security. Economic inequality between women and men may force women's silent acceptance of their need to marry. Charles Westoff, a leading U.S. demographer, puts it succinctly: "Women have traditionally offered child-bearing and domestic services in exchange for the protection, security and status deriving from men's economic position."[17] This trade-off may continue to appeal to women faced with the alternative of low pay, long hours, and poor conditions in the workplace.

At the same time, increased labour-force participation undermines the idea that marriage is women's best economic bargain. Until recently in Canada, married women were, by law, under the control of their husbands and families. Their options and rights were limited, and any money they earned was considered to belong to their husbands. With more married women working outside the home, even for low pay and few benefits, the consideration of women and women's earnings as family 'property' is called into question. Men are no longer the sole breadwinners for most families today in Canada. In sectors of the economy and regions where unemployment is chronic, women frequently assume the breadwinner role. Some credibility is gained from this shift, although too often at the price of abuse from a resentful husband and/or the poverty of supporting a family on one inadequate, woman's income. Women with jobs and incomes of their own, of course, also have more of an option to leave a marriage if they so choose.

The increased participation of married women in the work force calls into question the 'separate but equal' doctrine. This is a traditional view of the family that holds that men and women do different tasks but are held in equal regard in society. Women who work for pay find that their jobs are often extensions of the work they do at home: child care, food preparation, cleaning, and so on. Women do this work for considerably less pay and less prestige than men receive for their work. The message to women is clear –

their work, relative to men's, both at home and outside the home, is undervalued by society. Both the Wages for Housework movement of the 1970s and the pay-equity discussion of the late 1980s and 1990s make it clear that women's work subsidizes the economy. Wages for housework could, according to economic analysts, bankrupt the country by paying women fairly for the work they already do.[18] Similar statements have been made about pay equity. Fairness aside, argue the pundits, Canada cannot afford to pay women what they are worth. The message is clear: the Canadian economy runs on women's work, which is systematically underrewarded, undervalued, and performed out of good will.

Women's increased participation in the work force highlights the inequitable division of labour at home as well. Despite all the hype about shared work at home, it is women who continue to do most of the housework, whether or not they hold a job outside the home. This is even more the case in single-parent (typically mother-led) families, where mothers must do everything. Women now often do a double day of work, or even a triple day if they have children. When domestic work is shared in two-parent families, it is seldom shared equally. In 1975 Martin Meissner found that husbands of wives who go out to work increase their share of work at home by an average of one hour per week.[19] Recent studies provide little evidence that this has changed.[20]

Also highlighted by the changed work-force patterns of married women is the fact that child care is considered predominantly the private responsibility of individual families. The family in Canada is perceived as virtually self-contained, responsible for itself and its children. This privatized view of the family takes its toll on its members and on society in terms of overlooked violence, assumed economic responsibility of family members for each other, and work/family conflicts that are never discussed. Inadequate facilities for child care result from the assumption that is the parents' responsibility to care completely for their own children. If the mother works in order to feed her children, she is made to feel guilty and selfish. If she chooses to seek welfare so she can stay home with the children, she is considered lazy and dependent. Some of the issues involved in child care options are discussed later on in this chapter.

Women who work and also have families are regarded with some suspicion in the workplace, as mentioned earlier. Recognizing this, many women are forced into the untenable position of 'choosing' a family or a career, but not both. The choice is actually an empty one, since the rewards of each are separate and cannot be compared. Yet the notion of choice conveys to women the idea that they must decide one way or the other and, as a result, must 'pay the price' for this choice. Thus, women's poorer wages in comparison to men are 'justified' by our 'choosing' work, knowing its problems, instead of following our more 'natural' vocation of motherhood. Employers see themselves as justified in paying women less than men because women made the 'choice' to accept less pay when we 'decided' to work. If we choose motherhood, we are assumed to have made this choice knowingly, and we cannot expect equal consideration in the workplace.

Marital Dissolution

Many Canadians see increasing rates of marital dissolution as a fundamental change in the Canadian family, even signalling the death of the family, and one that largely accounts for the dramatic increase in single-parent families. Levels of public awareness of this trend are impressive, although the level of public knowledge about it is less so. Statistics Canada estimates that the divorce rate among Canadians rose by 82 per cent in the ten-year period between 1972 and 1982, declined somewhat from 1983-85, and rose again after 1986. [21]

Divorce-trend analysis poses a number of challenges, which have implications for how divorce trends are interpreted. One problem in analysing divorce trends is a conceptual one. The point of legal divorce seldom coincides with the point of actual separation. Thus, divorce rates can rise and fall with changes in the legal grounds on which divorce is possible, since divorce can be postponed almost indefinitely. Between 1968 and 1969, for example, the number of divorces granted to Canadians nearly doubled. [22] The liberalization of the legal grounds for divorce in the amendments to the Divorce Act of 1968 explains this increase better than any substantive change in the popularity of marriage. Couples who had been long separated decided to legalize their marital situation by applying for divorce. A smaller surge in divorce rates in Canada occurred between 1972 and 1975. This, too, seems attributable to changes in the legal code, which, in effect, gave legal sanctions for divorce to those who had been separated. The 1986 changes in the divorce law reduced the minimum time allowed between separation and application for divorce, and another small increase in the divorce rate occurred. Reliance on divorce rates as an indicator of marital dissatisfaction, therefore, can be misleading. Changes in the divorce law, however, do not *cause* divorce; they merely enable those whose marriages have dissolved to legalize their situations. People do not take on lightly the formal dissolution of their marriages, as the process involves considerable personal pain and anguish.

The divorce rate in Canada is high, yet Canada's rate of divorce is far from being the highest in the world. Canada's divorce rate parallels rates in most countries of the industrialized world, so conditions unique to Canada are most likely not responsible for the change. Divorce is more common among couples in which one partner was previously divorced. Thus, as second or third marriages increase, the divorce rate could increase. Divorce statistics may be 'inflated' by the same people reappearing.

Too often, an increase in divorce rates is equated with an escalation of marital unhappiness, for which women's changing roles are sometimes cited as contributing factors. S.J. Wilson argues: "It is erroneous to conclude that the rising divorce rate is indicative of the disintegration of family life in Canada. Two-thirds of divorced women and three-quarters of divorced men remarry."[23] Eichler adds, "There is a fair amount of research which suggests that unhappy marriages are not necessarily unstable, and that happy marriages are not necessarily unstable, and that happy marriages are not necessarily stable."[24] The reasons for divorce are extensive and varied, ranging from an increasingly secularized view of marriage to overly hasty marriages made under pressure due to premarital pregnancy. Rather than necessarily indicating a decline in family values or of interest in marriage, divorce rates might be an indicator only of the poor first matches people make – and many of these people then reaffirm their faith in family and marriage by trying again.

Women who are divorced are less likely to remarry than divorced men. This may be because divorced men seek younger single women to marry, while divorced women, because of social norms, have a more limited selection of potential mates. Divorced women more often have responsibility for the children of the dissolved marriage, which can affect their prospects for remarriage. The most profound difference between the divorce experience of men and of women is their altered financial circumstances, however. Contrary to public belief, fewer than 5 per cent of women receive alimony after divorce.[25] With child care responsibilities (and limited day care facilities), limited job opportunities, and, all too often, inadequate or non-existent child support, divorced women often find themselves among the ranks of the poor. A 1988 report of the National Council on Welfare of Canada found that families headed by women (most single-parent families) still run over four times the risk of poverty as families headed by men.[26]

One result of the high divorce rate is that the ranks of the poor are becoming filled by women, often mothers with dependent children. Although men may sometimes lose close contact with their children as a result of divorce, the economic implications of divorce for men are far less severe. Margrit Eichler and Phyllis Chesler both find that men's real incomes actually rise after divorce, while women's incomes decline substantially.[27] Many divorced women, even middle-class women, find themselves facing welfare. In part, and somewhat paradoxically, this results from society's changing views of marriage. It used to be that wives were legally regarded as their husband's property. Despite the drawbacks to this, wives then had something to bargain with in court. If their husbands' adultery led to the divorce, women could often win alimony and child-support payments as the 'wronged wife.'

Divorce 'reform,' intended to make divorce more equitable and fair, and changes in family law have led to a different perception. Women are no longer seen by judges as 'wronged' dependent wives, but as equal partners who, because of the presumed strides women have made in the workplace, are now able to support themselves and their children. Alimony payments are now less likely to be awarded by the courts, and child-support payments are generally smaller. Judges now assume that even women with limited job skills and no work experience are as capable of self-support as heads of single-parent families. Eichler finds, "The courts are therefore moving towards an assumption that self-support after divorce is the expected course of action for the wives as well as the husbands."[28] Although this seems egalitarian, it overlooks women's lesser real wage and job prospects, as well as the demands and expenses of child care.

In situations where courts award child-support payments, "Apparently up to 75 per cent of support payments are at some point defaulted on, while average child support payments are very low."[29] Canadian courts have made little attempt to enforce court-ordered child-support payments. In a society that claims to value women as mothers and to put a high premium on reproduction and children, one cannot help but wonder what the poverty of divorced mothers suggests. Possibly it is as Letty Cottin Pogrebin has argued, that women who are not under male control are viewed with suspicion and punished economically for their 'unwillingness' to conform.[30] Needless to say, the anguish of divorce is made worse by the poverty that divorced women so often experience. This, without doubt, has fundamental consequences on divorced women's ability to parent.

A new trend in child custody is evident in Canada as part of an attempt to make family laws more equitable. Courts increasingly are granting fathers custody of their children. This may seem fair at first glance, but closer inspection reveals a bias in these court decisions. Chesler's study of mothers' challenges for custody in the United States between 1960 and 1981 found that 87 per cent of the fathers awarded custody were not involved in child care at all prior to the divorce, and 67 per cent paid no child support.[31] Fathers' rights groups in Canada have been increasingly successful in winning custody battles.[32] Janice Drakich, in a study of the consequences of the new ideology of fathers equally involved in parenting, concludes that courts and social policy ignore the inequities of parenting, giving the father undue credit for *any* participation while undervaluing the mother's contribution. A particularly insidious aspect of the new trends in child-custody cases is that mothers contesting custody are often in a no-win situation, according to Chesler. If they were stay-at-home mothers, they often lost custody because they had limited incomes; if they were working, they lost custody because they were away from home too much. Mothers, most amazingly, even lost custody for 'deserting' abusive marriages, for 'interfering' with incestuous relationships of the fathers with their children, and for having other relationships, even after their divorces had become final.[33] This is a case of how seemingly egalitarian reforms in law and policy lead to inequality.

A second trend has been towards mandatory joint custody. While this, too, seems egalitarian, it, too, may not be. Implementing court-ordered joint custody for parents who have not equally shared parenting, cannot get along, or do not wish to live in physical proximity to each other poses challenges. Mandatory joint custody is now viewed by many women's groups as retrogressive. The different economic resources of women and men may relegate women to permanent subservience to their ex-husbands, who can make the major decisions about the children because of their greater economic resources and their continued legal control. Eichler cites studies that indicate that mandatory joint custody can work well in cases where the couples might have worked out voluntary joint custody anyway.[34] The relative merits of joint custody versus sole custody are obvious to many women. Women who are offered the Solomon's choice of the demands of their own sole custody, joint custody, or father custody, seem to prefer to have sole custody, no matter how difficult the financial burdens. The other alternatives, they argue compellingly, are so weighted in favour of the father (despite the public image of the poor, hard-done-by divorced father) that women's and children's interests are overlooked.[35]

The number of marriages in Canada that involve at least one previously married spouse is increasing. In 1986, 32.8 per cent of all marriages involved a previously married partner.[36] The phenomenon of remarried families with children – the so-called 'blended' family – is so new that terms have not yet been developed for the possible relationships. Eichler has estimated that 120 different family types are possible, assuming that husband and wife have only one previous marriage.[37] Clearly, research on these new family types is needed; research that does not assume that the only 'proper' family is a traditional nuclear family. One striking aspect of the blended family, whatever future research shows, is that biological roles and social roles in the family are becoming increasingly divergent. This, without doubt, has profound significance for women, about whom it has been incorrectly assumed that biology is destiny.

Challenges on the Family Front

In the 1990s, many challenges to the family and women's roles have emerged that have brought about a new appreciation of the family in society. Only a few of these can be discussed here. There was a time, not too long ago, when what went on in the family was considered private: nobody's business but one's own, and perhaps God's or the parish priest's. This, of course, was not really true – particularly when it is understood that the family is doing work on behalf of society – but this is the way it was seen. The distinction between the public world and the private world was 'discovered,' established, and maintained by men and the patriarchal system. Sheila Rowbotham sums it up:

> This difference in the sexual division of labour in society means that the relationship of men as a group to production is different than that of women. For a man, the social relations and values of commodity production predominate and home is a retreat into intimacy. For women, the public world belongs to and is owned by men. She is dependent upon what the man earns but is responsible for the private sphere, the family.[38]

This split between the private and the public, artificial as it is, is maintained by the 'separate but equal' doctrine – the idea that women and men are equals who exist in separate spheres doing functionally interdependent tasks. Yet numerous feminists have noted that there is much that is separate about the realms of women and of men, but little that is equal. Nonetheless, the notion that women and men exist in separate spheres, one private and one public, tends to preserve the traditional division of labour within the family and the labour force, which is rationalized as biologically based. Further, and this is emphasized by most of the dominant sociological theories of the family, a functional fit is maintained between the family as a social institution and the requirements of an industrial, capitalist economy. Women who work in the home are both secondary sources of labour and consumers, with this latter role becoming vastly expanded in recent times. Men, then, are freed through women's domestic and emotional labour, to be hard-working and productive. As Rowbotham suggests, "The family under capitalism carries all the rags and bones and bits of old iron not used by the commodity system."[39]

It is not surprising, given this patriarchal view of the family, that men view family as a retreat from stress, from work, a "haven in a heartless world" as Christopher Lasch has viewed it.[40] There may be some truth in Dorothy Smith's statement that the family is a place where: "People are stored when they are not at work, where they are maintained, serviced, fed and cleaned, where they are psychologically repaired and the injuries of daily routine and tensions generated on the job made good, and where the next generation of employees is produced and trained for their future occupational roles."[41]

Given this view of the family, and the tightness of fit between the economic system and the family, women's work at home can be seen as essential to the smooth running of the capitalist system. This work is so essential that it is done by women whether they work outside the home or not. Should women's performance of this work be impeded by pressures of paid work, marital dissolution, or other factors, the family is thought to be in disarray. What this may mean is that women's unpaid, unrecognized, and unrewarded labour on the home front is no longer as fully devoted to the service of the economy and of men as it once was. Women increasingly are questioning, sometimes without knowing it fully, why we are asked to provide these services on the homefront for the 'compensation' of vulnerable dependency on a man who might leave us at any time and on a system that provides little reward.

The separation and isolation of the family work against women in hiding the widespread violence it is now known we face on the intimate frontier. Although some progress has been made by the women's movement in bringing family violence into public awareness, violence against women at home is still viewed by police, judges, doctors, lawyers, and, indeed, large segments of society either as resulting from a domestic dispute, in which societal agents have little right to intervene, or as precipitated by the woman herself, in which case she is thought to be 'getting what she deserves.'[42] Abused women who seek help from the police, hospitals, and courts are still often disbelieved, because the experience of the women facing domestic violence does not fit the idealized image of the family. The private nature of the Canadian family permits women's pain to go unheard, unseen, and unheeded by the public authorities. Campaigns to improve public recognition, such as those undertaken recently by several provincial governments, help, but do not solve the problem.

Sexual abuse and assault within marriage also go largely unacknowledged, despite the growing number of women and girls who have brought their painful experiences to the attention of those they thought would help, and despite the greater availability of shelters and assistance. All too often the woman's or girl's experience is reconstructed, under the influence of a police officer, court official, therapist, or member of the helping professions, to become more consistent with the prevailing societal images of family and of women. This doubly victimizes women, first by the violence itself, which often has life-long effects, and second by the denial of their version of the experience. This can be crazy-making to the woman who knows what she experienced yet is obliged to accept a reconstructed version of that experience. The privacy accorded the nuclear family prevents investigation of the women's experience and ends up denying the harshness of it, even to the woman herself. Fortunately, as Joanna

Boehnert shows in her chapter, some feminist therapists are beginning to move away from such prejudicial methods of reconstructing women's experience.

The view that the Canadian family is in crisis often holds feminism accountable for the changes occurring in the modern family. The right-wing political agenda, of which the family-in-crisis view is a fundamental component, holds that women's familial and reproductive roles are political. The intent is to bring women's sexuality and reproduction back firmly under the control of men and patriarchy. The irony is that this agenda is carried out under movements that call themselves pro-family.

Perhaps the most striking example of this is the contemporary abortion debate in Canada, but issues of day care and the new reproductive technologies are also significant in this regard. The abortion debate is particularly salient to the agenda of the New Right because the issues involved are not discussed openly in Canada by politicians. Abortion and women's roles have become politically contentious issues, covered in the cloak of morality and privacy. Years of legislative inaction and the repackaging of abortion as an essentially moral issue have obscured the overt political dimensions of abortion and the ways in which the New Right would like to redefine women's roles.

The latest abortion bill, defeated by the Senate after it passed in the House of Commons, would have put abortion back into the Criminal Code and made women seeking abortions and their doctors liable to criminal prosecution. The handling of this bill epitomizes the centrality of abortion in politics. Admittedly, as compromise, the bill nonetheless made doctors fearful of criminal prosecution, frivolous or otherwise, despite repeated assurances by the federal government that this would not happen. Women's reproductive control became lost in the flurry of debate involving high-minded ethics experts, usually male.

Encroachments on women's legal access to abortion continue to escalate in Canada. Several provinces now have no legal abortion facilities at all. In those that do, there has been a substantial reduction in the number of hospitals with functioning therapeutic-abortion committees and a reduction in the numbers of doctors willing to perform therapeutic abortions.[43] This has resulted from local pressure on doctors and hospitals in their own communities by groups calling themselves 'pro-life' and/or 'pro-family.' These groups, sometimes without being fully aware of what they are doing, cite their opposition to any regulation or interference with the family, yet by their actions they are making motherhood compulsory, thereby also making state control over reproduction and women's roles complete.

Eichler argues, given the agenda of the "pro-family movement, that it must be seen as detrimental to the well-being of the majority of Canadian families."[44] Its agenda includes denial of equal opportunities for women, compulsory heterosexuality, banning of contraception and abortion, eradication of day care, and denial of the existence of wife abuse, sexual assault within marriage, and child sexual abuse. In short, the movement might be more appropriately called, as Eichler suggests, a "Movement for the Restoration of the Patriarchal Family."[45]

Paralleling the 'pro-family' movement in Canada and working in conjunction with it are groups that claim to represent the interests of women at home, such as REAL Women. The position of REAL Women is anti-abortion, anti-pay equity, anti-day care, anti-no-fault divorce. Their agenda includes restoration of the traditional patriarchal family in which women have few choices and few rights. The concern and the challenge to feminists posed by groups like REAL Women is that these groups seem (or claim) to have the ear of numbers of politicians who think that groups like this represent Canadian women, or who for their own reasons simply like the idea of the restoration of patriarchy. There is growing concern among Canadian social scientists and feminists who do research on women and the family that feminist research funding, which was never large, may be cut further as a result of the lobbying of groups such as these.

The new reproductive technologies represent another challenge to the small gains women have made in changing the traditional patriarchal family and its confining familial roles. Rona Achilles' chapter addresses these matters specifically. These technologies are still being developed, and legislation does not exist to govern their use. However, some things are clear.[46] First, the new technologies are being developed or controlled by the same medical and scientific elite that gave us the Dalkon shield, the drug DES, and the high-estrogen birth control pill whose damaging side-effects on women have been amply documented and publicized. Second, infertile women are being used to develop the technologies, as experiments essentially, without sufficient knowledge of long-term or even short-term consequences. Third, the availability of reproductive technologies may force some women into a painful and absorbing quest for motherhood, rather than a search for fulfillment in other realms. The degree to which societal coercion may be evident in the new reproductive technology is also being addressed by critics and concerned observers. The advent of new reproductive technologies, like the advent of the birth control pill, not only has the potential for freeing women to choose reproduction, but also the potential, as we know all too well from past experiences, to place our reproduction and our social roles under further control by patriarchy.

An area of challenge for women in families of the 1990s and beyond is the aging of Canadian society. As families have fewer children and more older relatives to look after, the burden and responsibility (as well as joys) of care-giving fall on women's shoulders. It has been clearly revealed by research that women tend to do the "looking after" of young, old, sick, and frail family members whether or not we also work outside the home.[47] This means that women are caught in a further family/work conflict; and that could involve a "tree" of older relatives, including parents, grandparents, in-laws, and assorted cousins and aunts. Most of these older relatives will be women, given the greater life expectancy of women compared to men.

Compounding the challenges of care-giving by women to women is the lesser economic circumstance in which women live. Older women with limited pensions and mothers who head families alone are the poorest of people in Canada. Many of those women called on to care for aging relatives may have been single parents and have few resources to work with. Old women are more often poor as a result of the presumption by the women themselves, as well as by governments, that women are family members first and workers only secondly. This leads to two false assumptions: 1) women who are married are less in need of pensions, because their husbands, it is thought, can support them; and 2) women who work do not need pensions, because they are either wives first or not 'real' work-force participants.

Biases in Research on the Family

It has been recognized for several decades that theory, research, and data collection in the social sciences are biased against women, against discovering the truth about our lives and our patterns. Not surprisingly, the time (1960s and 1970s) when the sexist biases became an issue coincided with the increased involvement of women in intellectual work and in higher education. Spurred on by real social problems, an increasingly critical feminist social science emerged. By 1985 the Social Sciences and Humanities Research Council of Canada had adopted guidelines as routine policy for developing sound non-sexist research.[48] This is an example of lobby and educational efforts by feminists resulting in a change of policy.[49]

Sexist bias, or the unintentional or deliberate misrepresentation or distortion of women's and men's behaviour in theory and research, can take many forms and is both pervasive and invisible. Androcentrism – the assumption that men's experiences are more representative of human experience than are women's – is one example. Until recently, social scientists have not provided useful tools to women to better understand ourselves and the society we live in. Work is typically defined as what men do: exchange labour for a wage. Unpaid work, most often done by women at home, on the farm, or in the family business, is not seen as work and therefore is often not included in the concept of Gross National Product.

In analyses of women in families, sexist biases become particularly strong. We may wish to think that biases about women being primarily wives and mothers have become outdated, but recent research provides compelling evidence to suggest that not only have things *not* improved much in family research, but that new ways of being sexist have been discovered.[50] Examples include the new anti-feminist backlash on many university campuses and the emerging views that being non-sexist and non-racist is a kind of politically correct tyranny. Another example would be the many studies that focus on women's family/work role conflicts as opposed to the few that ask men whether they experience such conflicts – with the Conference Board of Canada survey, mentioned earlier, being a notable exception. Yet another example would be the common practice of asking only one member of a family, usually the wife/mother, how the family operates and how various members behave, feel, and think. The assumption here is that family life is the domain of women, so women can speak authoritatively about family experience, not only for themselves but for *all* members of their families.

Sexist biases work against a clear understanding of women's roles in families in many ways, including the assumption of a natural differentiation by sex in families, the assumption of one reality within families, the androcentric view of society, and the power of labels. One prevalent sexist bias is the assumption that there is a biologically based, functional differentiation within families that accounts for the differences in opportunities and talents of women and men. This assumption can be self-fulfilling. If a woman believes herself to be limited by her biology, she may act within those limits, thereby curtailing her opportunity. Alternatively, if it is believed that women, because of biology, are capable of less than men, society can expect, ask, and provide less to us. Those in power tend to attribute aspects of a situation they wish to maintain to 'nature' (an observation made by Roland Barthes),[53] thus rendering the structural power imbalance apparently unchangeable. This tendency is accelerating in the latter part of the twentieth century in North America with the propagation of sociobiology, an attempt to explain all human social behaviour as biologically determined.

The assumption of natural differentiation within the family works to dichotomize human experience into male/female and thus emphasizes and exaggerates the differences between men and women rather than the similarities. The view that women are the natural reproducers and child-carers and men are producers of goods and services keeps women from being producers and keeps us out of high-paying jobs, professional work, and other kinds of work that might give us power. Women are seen as suited to work that is an extension of our 'natural' function, such as child care, nursing, or typing. Research tends to focus on male issues and away from female issues except when they are seen to be consistent with the bias, such as women's role conflict. As Ann Oakley has suggested, "A way of seeing is also a way of not seeing."[52] The sexist interpretation that argues that because women give birth and men do not there is a biological basis for the economic and social limitations under which women struggle is particularly insidious. This is one aspect of biological determinism, the effects of which Lorraine Code discusses in her chapter on feminist theory. The danger, of course, is that in accepting the belief that this division of labour is natural, we may be blinded to changes that are occurring and, importantly, to the possibility of innovative changes that may benefit both women and men in the future.

The assumption of one reality within the family may seem to be in contradiction with the assumption of natural differentiation. Eichler states, however, that these obviously contradictory assumptions "happily co-existed for many decades." Eichler goes on to argue, compellingly, that these two biases are actually mutually supportive:

> *Because* we have assumed that there is a natural functional differentiation between spouses we have not bothered to ask individuals to what extent these assumptions are true. . . .
>
> *Because* we assume that family members share one reality we often find it sufficient to ask only one family member about family circumstances. . . . Because we ask, in general, one-sided questions of only one member of an entire family unit, we can maintain both fictions.[53]

Jessie Bernard's 1973 analysis of 'his' and 'her' marriages was among the first to reveal the one-family bias. In contrast to prevailing myth, Bernard discovered that married men benefit impressively from marriage: they live longer and are happier and healthier than men who remain unmarried. Married women, on the other hand, despite recurrent images of marriage as women's ultimate fulfillment, suffer more often from depression, unhappiness, and general ill health than do unmarried women.[54] Clearly, popular beliefs about a single reality in the family require reassessment, as do contemporary myths about the happy, care-free bachelor who tries to avoid marriage, and the miserable 'spinster' who pines away looking for a husband.

Since Bernard's pathbreaking research, evidence has accumulated about both subjective and objective differences in the family experience for women and for men. For example, for many married men, marriage and family tend to be assets as well as incentives to work hard. For married women, on the other hand, marriage and family tend to be liabilities and a justification for lower-paid jobs or lack of promotion, as we have seen. Divorce, as well, is a radically different experience for men and for women.

Divorced men are much less likely to have money problems than divorced women, and much more likely to remarry.[55] A U.S. study has found that men's average incomes increase by some 73 per cent after divorce while women, who more often have custody of the children, experience a decline of some 25 per cent in their living standard.[56] Eichler cites numerous examples of widely discrepant subjective responses from husbands and wives on who makes the decisions, on marital happiness, on marital expectations, and even on numbers of children they have.[57] An androcentric bias runs through most research and theory on the family. The behaviour of women is either analysed in male terms, compared to a male standard, or rendered invisible or meaningless.

An example of androcentric bias is the use of tools and theories developed by men, which are then applied to women without women ever actually being studied. Studies of male-only samples that are generalized to all people are one example. Two well-publicized examples of this include Lawrence Kohlberg's study of the stages of moral development, which was based entirely on males, and David McClelland's study of need-achievement, which also included only males in the sample.[58] When compared to the male standard, women may appear to be lacking in both moral development and achievement motivation. Similarly, women have more often been chosen as the subjects of studies of family dynamics, childbearing, and child care.[59] It is concluded that men are not particularly good in these areas, when, in fact, questions have seldom been put to men about family and childbearing. Both Joanna Boehnert and Lorraine Code discuss in their chapters how Carol Gilligan's recent work has challenged these entrenched views. This kind of research might be what the distinguished British biologist C.H. Waddington referred to as the 'Conventional Wisdom of the Dominant Group,' or the evocative acronym 'COWDUNG.'[60]

Quantitative analysis of data, even when not appropriate to the data, is another example of androcentric bias. While S.J. Wilson calls this 'the machismo factor in social research,' it has also been termed 'physics envy' by male social scientists who feel emasculated when their methods are compared to those used in the (significantly termed) harder natural sciences.[61] Quantitative methods allow for control of data (in this case people) from which the researcher remains distant, a distinctly masculine approach. Demographic analyses of family change, including marriage and divorce rates, family composition, and birth rates, provide an extreme example of how quantitative analysis removes the problem from its context. Jill McCalla Vickers suggests that the use of quantitative methods tends to remove human behaviour from its context: "Mathematics as a language for the expression of feminist reality is often the most context-stripped of all."[62] What is needed is a feminist methodology that involves respondents in the process of understanding what is happening to them, rather than equating them with atoms. Steps taken to develop such a methodology include action-oriented research strategies and an interactive interviewing technique, which gives credence to respondents as people rather than as only data. [63]

One further example of how androcentric bias prevents us from understanding our family patterns as women is the inappropriate use of cultural relativism, a kind of laissez-faire approach to practices of other cultures. Examples of this include the widespread overlooking or acceptance of violence against women in our homes (as well as on the streets and at work) as a private and even subcultural phenomenon. Institutionalized sexism, in this case, goes so far as to enlist the legal and medical professions to justify and excuse patriarchal violence against women by arguing that the source of the problem lies with the woman who 'asked for it,' either by her behaviour or by her mental or emotional 'problems.'

The power to label gives those in a dominant position in society the capacity to categorize and discuss the experiences of those who have less power. This bias, like the others discussed here, distorts what we know about women in families and about women generally. The very name by which adult human females are known, 'women,' had to be reclaimed by us, in defiance of the dominant group's preferred usage of the term 'girls.' The term 'lady' can still control women who were taught to take special care in how to behave and be seen by others. Most distorting, perhaps, are the images held by society of the family as caring, loving, sharing, of family as the bedrock of society, of family as a 'haven in a heartless world,' of family as women's place where women 'build nests' for the happiness of men, children, and ourselves. Supported by religion, art, literature, and the media, as well as by professionals such as social scientists, counsellors, lawyers, and doctors, these images are sufficiently powerful to overwhelm women's reality. Some families may be all this, but familism tends to deny that family can have negative aspects, too.

The mass appeal of familism and the widespread propagation of nostalgic family images rest on the assumption that there is no better alternative to the family. This creates the impression that people in families, particularly women, should not be unhappy or try to change the family because there is no real alternative to the family as we know it. Feminist analysts of the family have argued that family images, combined with the legitimacy and privacy of the family in our society, can mask the oppressive relations engendered by the economic dependency of women and children in the patriarchal family. [64] Michele Barrett takes this one step further with her insight that "The family sucks the juice out of everything around it, leaving other institutions stunted and distorted." [65] According to Barrett, sharing and loving might be more widespread if the family did not claim them for its own.[66] Socialist and Marxist feminists, among others, have taught us that caring and sharing among people in a non-familial situation can be preferable to living with false images in the patriarchal nuclear family.

Taking Stock:
Women's Family Patterns in the Future

We have seen, in this chapter, how the family in contemporary Canada is central to the lives of women, yet that it is not all it can be. The patriarchal family as a social institution may be imbued with too many expectations, too many false images, to enable us to thrive within it. Yet, as women, it is often important to us, whether we are feminists or not, to have a good family life.

Changes have occurred in the Canadian family over the past few decades and will, no doubt, continue to occur in the future. The family cannot be a static institution. But change, as we have seen, may not be unwelcome. The decline in family size among Canadians appears to be a part of a worldwide trend, yet we have seen that women seldom opt out of childbearing altogether. Although families are no longer as large as they once were, for a variety of reasons, having children is still important to the vast majority of women. Motherhood is an option now as never before, yet it is an option most women want. While some alarmists may worry that women are forsaking their traditional roles as mothers, it seems more likely that motherhood continues to be an important, if not always dominant, feature of women's lives, but in an altered form. Smaller families and the decreased portion of women's lifetimes spent in childrearing both result from and provide greater opportunities for women to be people as well as mothers. It seems clear that small families are here to stay.

The dramatic increase of married women and mothers in the paid work force is another salient change in Canadian society. Out of economic necessity, the dual-earner family is becoming the norm among Canadian families today. Although the tasks are often difficult to balance, given the division of domestic chores within the patriarchal family, mothers who work are saying that both activities matter. Women work to support their families and themselves. An unfortunate aspect is that working mothers, like most women, are paid so little, on average, and offered so few benefits and opportunities in the work force because of the widespread, mistaken belief they are not working out of necessity. One change that the future must hold is a more equitable sharing of child care and domestic responsibilities among spouses. Enhanced recognition of the value of women's work to the economy is another. A third would be *real* acknowledgement of different family forms. It is untenable to think that women can continue

forever carrying a double or triple work load without calling out for substantial change.

Divorce, although an increasingly important factor recently for the
Canadian family, may not be a sign of disenchantment with family. Prohibition of divorce does not guarantee marital happiness or even that a marriage will stay together. Increases in the divorce rate might instead indicate
a dissatisfaction with traditional family expectations and constraints. It
can be a vote for a new kind of family: one that is more egalitarian, flexible,
caring, and giving. Because most divorced people do remarry, there is
strong evidence that they are searching for something marriage and family
provide. There is no hint that marriage in Canada will go out of style, yet
the variety in types of marriage is likely to widen, allowing couples a flexibility to be and become more themselves, regardless of rigid social expectations.

Only some of the challenges to the Canadian family of the 1990s have
been explored here. The family has emerged on the political agenda of the
New Right as well as on the feminist agenda. On the right, the decline of
the patriarchal family is lamented. The challenge for the right is to restore
that family by stemming the tides of change in women's work-force participation, in availability of contraception, abortion, and divorce, and in
shifting patterns of domestic division of labour. On the feminist front,
these changes are welcomed and encouraged as signs that the family is
alive, well, and capable of adapting as the world around it changes. These
new twists further allow for human mistakes and different human needs,
but they do not suggest that the family is being abandoned.

Many other changes have occurred in the Canadian family. Some social
psychologists, for example, have suggested that socialization of children in
the family in less gender-specific ways is one such change. Every book on
gender roles, of which there are many, focuses on socialization, as do many
contemporary magazine and newspaper articles and TV programs.
Whether, in fact, changes are evident in socialization patterns is not clear.
Other analysts focus more on socialization by the schools, the media, and
the work force. They suggest that family roles might change as a consequence of changes occurring outside the family. This, too, is being studied
and debated among experts. The roles of older women in families as
grandmothers, of women as widows and as caretakers for the elderly members of their families are now being explored as Canada's population ages.
The effects of family changes on people's self-images and expectations are
being examined. All these are important issues, but they are beyond the
scope of this chapter. Our hope is that readers will seek further information on these and related family issues that could not be discussed here.

Susan A. McDaniel

NOTES

1. Peter Laslett, *The World We Have Lost,* 3rd ed. (New York: Scribner, 1973).

2. *See* Margrit Eichler, *Families in Canada Today,* 2nd ed. (Toronto: Gage, 1988); Nancy Mandell and Ann Duffy, eds., *Reconstructing the Canadian Family: Feminist Perspectives* (Toronto: Butterworths, 1988); Statistics Canada, *Current Demographic Analysis: New Trends in the Family* (Ottawa: Ministry of Supply and Services, 1990); S.J. Wilson, *Women, Families and Work,* 3rd ed. (Toronto: McGraw-Hill Ryerson, 1991).

3. Statistics Canada, *Current Demographic Analysis: Report on the Demographic Situation in Canada, 1990* (Ottawa: Ministry of Supply and Services, 1990), 16.

4. Statistics Canada, *Current Demographic Analysis: Fertility in Canada, From Baby Boom to Baby Bust* (Ottawa: Ministry of Supply and Services, 1990), 130-131.

5. Wilson, S.J., *Women, the Family and the Economy,* 2nd ed. (Toronto: McGraw-Hill Ryerson, 1986), 93-94.

6. Susan A. McDaniel and Ben Agger, *Social Problems Through Conflict and Order* (Don Mills, Ont.: Addison-Wesley, 1982), 231.

7. Statistics Canada, *Fertility.*

8. Ibid., 33.

9. B.K. Singh and J.S. Williams, "Childlessness and Family Satisfaction," *Research on Aging* 3 (1981), 218-227; N.D. Glenn and S. McLanahan, "Children and Marital Happiness: A Further Specification of the Relationship," *Journal of Marriage and the Family* 44 (1982), 63-72; G.B. Spanier and R.A. Lewis, "Marital Quality: A Review of the Seventies," *Journal of Marriage and the Family* 42 (1980), 825-839.

10. Ellen Gee and Meredith Kimball, *Women and Aging* (Toronto: Butterworths, 1987).

11. Carl Grindstaff, "Adolescent Marriage and Childbearing: The Long-Term Economic Outcome in Canada in the 1980s, " *Adolescence, 1987.*

12. Eichler, Margrit, *Families in Canada Today: Recent Changes and Their Policy Implications,* 1st ed. (Toronto: Gage, 1983), 170-172.

13. Cited by Wilson, *Women,* 2nd ed., 88.

14. Meg Luxton, *More than a Labour of Love: Three Generations of Women's Work in the Home* (Toronto: Women's Educational Press, 1980).

15. Statistics Canada, *New Trends in the Family,* 88.

16. A 1988/89 Conference Board of Canada Survey of 7,000 employees found that work/family conflicts are a problem for the majority of workers, but more so for women with young children. See Conference Board of Canada, *Work and Family: The Employment Challenge of the '90s* (1991).

17. Charles Westoff, "Fertility Decline in the West: Causes and Prospects," *Population and Development Review* 9, no. 1 (1983), 99-104.

18. Evidence cited by Wilson, *Women,* 1st ed., 67-69.

19. Martin Meissner, Elisabeth W. Humphreys, Scott M. Meis, and William J. Scheu, "No Exits for Wives: Sexual Division of Labour and the Cumulation of Household Demands," *Canadian Review of Sociology and Anthropology* 12, no. 4 (1975), 424-439.

20. Eichler, *Families*; Luxton, *Labour of Love*; Wilson, *Women.*

21. Statistics Canada, *Current Demographic Analysis: Report on the Demographic Situation in Canada, 1983* (Ottawa: Ministry of Supply and Services, 1984), 22; Statistics Canada, *New Trends in the Family,* 20.

22. Statistics Canada, *New Trends in the Family,* 20.

23. Wilson, *Women,* 1st ed., 22.

24. Eichler, *Families,* 1st ed., 188.

25. Anne Marie Ambert, *Divorce in Canada* (Don Mills, Ont.: Academic Press, 1980).

26. National Council on Welfare, *Poverty Profile 1988* (Ottawa: National Council on Welfare, 1988), 19.

27. Eichler, *Families,* 219; Phyllis Chesler, *Mothers on Trial: The Battle for Children and Custody* (New York: McGraw Hill, 1986).

28. Eichler, *Families,* 297.

29. Ibid.

30. Letty Cottin Pogrebin, *Family Politics: Love and Power on an Intimate Frontier* (New York: McGraw Hill, 1983).

31. Chesler, *Mothers on Trial.*

32. Janice Drakich, "In Search of the Better Parent: The Social Construction of Ideologies of Fatherhood," *Canadian Journal of Women and the Law* 3 (1989), 69-87.

33. Chesler, *Mothers on Trial.*

34. Eichler, *Families,* 236.

35. Drakich, "In Search of the Better Parent," 85-86.

36. Statistics Canada, *Report on the Demographic Situation in Canada, 1990,* 8.

37. Eichler, *Families,* 1st ed., 236.

38. Sheila Rowbotham, *Women's Consciousness, Men's World* (Harmondsworth: Penguin, 1973), 211.

39. Ibid., 212.

40. Christopher Lasch, *Haven in a Heartless World: The Family Besieged* (New York: Basic Books, 1977).

41. Dorothy E. Smith, "Women, the Family and Corporate Capitalism," in Marylee Stephenson, ed., *Women in Canada* (Don Mills, Ont.: General Publishing, 1973), 22.

42. Linda MacLeod, *Wife Battering in Canada: The Vicious Circle* (Ottawa: Canadian Advisory Council on the Status of Women, 1980).

43. Susan A. McDaniel, "Abortion, Reproductive Technology and Women's

Roles as the Barter of the New Right," paper presented at the Ontario Association of Sociology and Anthropology, Waterloo, Ontario, 1985.

44. Margrit Eichler, "The Pro-Family Movement: Are They For or Against Families?" in *Feminist Frameworks* (Ottawa: Canadian Research Institute for the Advancement of Women, 1985).

45. Ibid.

46. Susan A. McDaniel, "Women's Roles, Reproduction and New Reproductive Technologies," in Duffy and Mandell, eds., *Reconstructing The Canadian Family.*

47. *See* Gee and Kimball, *Women and Aging*; Susan McDaniel, "Women and Aging: A Sociological Perspective," *Journal of Women and Aging* 1, no. 13 (1989), 47-67; and Joan Kaden and Susan McDaniel, "Caregiving and Care-Receiving: A Double Bind for Women in Canada's Aging Society," *Journal of Women and Aging* 2, no. 3 (1990), 3-26.

48. Margrit Eichler and Jeanne Lapointe, *On the Treatment of the Sexes in Research* (Ottawa: Social Sciences and Research Council, 1985).

49. Linda Christiansen-Ruffman, Alleyne Morphy, Cannie Stark-Adamec, and Robert Davidson, *Sex Bias in Research: Current Awareness and Strategies to Eliminate Bias Within Canadian Social Science,* Report of the Task Force on the Elimination of Sexist Bias (Ottawa, 1986).

50. Eichler and Lapointe, *Treatment of the Sexes*; Christiansen-Ruffman et al., *Sex Bias in Research*; Jill McCalla Vickers, ed., *Taking Sex Into Account* (Ottawa: Carleton University Press, 1984).

51. Roland Barthes, *Mythologies* (Paris: Editions du Sevile, 1957), cited by Eichler and Lapointe, *Treatment of the Sexes,* 13.

52. Ann Oakley, *The Sociology of Housework* (New York: Pantheon Books, 1974), 27.

53. Eichler, *Families,* 66, 87.

54. Jessie Bernard, *The Future of Marriage* (New York: Bantam Books, 1973).

55. Maureen Baker, *Support Networks and Marital Dissolution,* Final Report of Connaught Foundation Project (Toronto, 1980).

56. Chesler, *Mothers on Trial.*

57. Eichler, *Families,* 93-97.

58. Cited in Eichler and Lapointe, *Treatment of the Sexes,* 10; cited in Rhoda K. Unger, *Female and Male: Psychological Perspectives* (New York: Harper & Row, 1979).

59. James A. Doyle, *Sex and Gender: The Human Experience* (Dubuque, Iowa: Wm. C. Brown, 1985); Susan A. McDaniel, "Explaining Canadian Fertility: Some Remaining Challenges," *Canadian Studies in Population* 11, no. 1 (1984), 1-16.

60. Cited in John Archer and Barbara Lloyd, *Sex and Gender,* (Cambridge: Cambridge University Press, 1985).

61. Wilson, *Women*, 5.

62. Jill McCalla Vickers, "Memoirs of an Ontological Exile: The Methodological Rebellions of Feminist Research," in Angela Miles and Geraldine Finns, eds., *Feminism in Canada: From Pressure to Politics* (Montreal: Black Rose Books, 1982).

63. Ann Oakley, "Interviewing Women: A Contradiction in Terms," in Helen Roberts, ed., *Doing Feminist Research* (London: Routledge & Kegan Paul, 1981); Michelène de Sève, "Prospects for Feminist Research: Towards a New Paradigm," *Feminist Perspectives* 3 (1985), 47-60.

64. Evan Star, Ann Flitcraft, and William Frazier, "Medicine and Patriarchal Violence: The Social Construction of a 'Private' Event," *International Journal of Health Services* 9, no. 3 (1979), 461-493; Chris Huntley Hutchinson and Susan A. McDaniel, "The Social Reconstruction of Sexual Assault by Women Victims: A Comparison of Therapeutic Experiences," *The Canadian Journal of Community Mental Health* 5, no. 2 (1986), 17-36; D. Herman and L. Hirschman, "Father-Daughter Incest," *Signs: A Journal of Women in Culture and Society* 2, no. 4 (1977).

65. Michele Barrett and Mary McIntosh, *The Anti-Social Family* (London: Verso, 1982); James Dickinson and Bob Russell, eds., *Family, Economy and the State: The Social Reproduction Process Under Capitalism* (Toronto: Garamond Press, 1986); Bonnie Fox, ed., *Family Bonds and Gender Divisions: Readings in the Sociology of the Family* (Toronto: Canadian Scholars Press, 1988); Pogrebin, *Family Politics*; Smith, "Women, the Family and Corporate Capitalism"; Dorothy E. Smith, "Women's Equality and the Family," in A. Moscovitch and G. Drover, eds., *Inequality: Essays on the Political Economy of Social Welfare* (Toronto: University of Toronto Press, 1981).

66. Michele Barrett, *Woman's Oppression Today* (London: Verso, 1980), 78.

SUGGESTED READINGS

Barnhorst, Richard and Laura C. Johnson, eds., *The State of the Child in Ontario*. Toronto: Oxford University Press, 1991.

Jones, Charles, Lorna Marsden, and Lorne Tepperman, *Lives of Their Own: The Individualization of Women's Lives*. Toronto: Oxford University Press, 1990.

Kaden, Joan, and Susan A. McDaniel, "Caregiving and Care-Receiving: A Double Bind for Women in Canada's Aging Society," *Journal of Women and Aging* 2, no. 3 (1990), 3-26.

Mandell, Nancy, and Ann Duffy, *Reconstructing the Canadian Family: Feminist Perspectives*. Toronto: Butterworths, 1988.

McDaniel, Susan A., "Towards Family Policy in Canada with Women in Mind," *Feminist Perspectives*, no. 17 (1990).

Statistics Canada, *Current Demographic Analysis: New Trends in the Family*, by Bali Ram. Ottawa: Ministry of Supply and Services, 1990.

Statistics Canada, *Current Demographic Analysis, Report on the Demographic Situation in Canada, 1990*, by Jean Dumas. Ottawa: Ministry of Supply and Services, 1990.

Statistics Canada, *General Social Survey, Preliminary Data Cycle 5: Family and Friends*. Ottawa: Ministry of Supply and Services, 1991.

Vanier Institute of the Family, *Canadian Families*. Ottawa: Vanier Institute of the Family, 1991.

Chapter Thirteen

The Psychology of Women

≈≈≈≈≈≈≈≈≈≈≈≈≈≈≈≈≈≈≈≈≈≈≈≈≈≈≈≈≈≈≈≈≈≈≈

Psychology has nothing to say about what women are really like, what they need and what they want, for the simple reason that psychology does not know. Yet psychologists will hold forth endlessly on the true nature of women with dismaying enthusiasm and disquieting certitude. [1]

At the time these words were written by Naomi Weisstein in the late 1960s, the psychoanalytic view of female personality development provided the basis of what was accepted to be the psychology of women. Psychoanalytic theory's relatively comprehensive description and interpretation of the psychological evolution of a girl into a woman was created primarily by Sigmund Freud (1856-1939). [2] Because of the central importance it gave to biological rather than cultural factors in determining personality, Freudian theory was assumed to provide a broad basis for a general understanding of human personality development. In the case of the psychology of women it provided an explanation (in terms of anatomy) for the fact that the majority of women were wives and mothers with a clearly inferior social status to men. This particular theory, then, not only supported the societal norms for female behaviour, but also clearly grounded this behaviour in nature rather than in culture.

Since Weisstein wrote these words, many changes have occurred in our conceptions of the psychology of women. Instead of providing an all-encompassing description of how personality development proceeds and a prescription for how a normal woman *should* feel and behave, the psychology of women today is an active, evolving area of scholarship, teaching, and practice. Its focus is upon a wide variety of psychological issues that were previously either ignored by psychology or presented almost entirely from a male point of view. Now, however, it is possible to find psychologists who are interested in studying varying aspects of events that occur exclusively in the lives of women, such as menstruation, pregnancy, childbirth, and menopause. Others are doing research in areas traditionally assigned to women, such as caring for others or maintaining relationships. It is also possible to find psychologists who are seeking to understand the psychological implications of events that almost exclusively victimize girls and women in our society, such as childhood sexual abuse, rape, sexual harassment, or battery. Others attempt to help the victims deal with the often long-lasting consequences of such criminal activities. Some psychologists are providing a new perspective by focusing upon women's experiences in areas that are usually approached from a male point of view, such as achievement, work, leadership, power, and sexuality. Still others are seeking to rediscover the pioneering women psychologists whose names and accomplishments have been hidden from view. And others are exposing the myths and biases that permeate so much of psychology's knowledge of women. In the search for and construction of new knowledge about the psychology of women, there is the potentiality for personal, disciplinary, and societal change. Thus, the work in this area has political implications and is not simply knowledge for knowledge's sake.

Our understanding of the psychology of women has undergone tremendous changes in the past twenty-five years. Instead of describing what women are and/or should be like as a result of their 'true nature,' psychologists today are attempting to describe, analyse, and understand the diversity as well as the commonality of the experiences of women that affect their development. Women share the experience of being female in male-dominated societies, but their experiences are also determined by interactions between their personal attributes such as their race, class, ethnicity, and/or sexual orientation and the complex environments within which they live. Thus, even though many women are mothers, their experiences of motherhood are influenced by factors such as their own health as well as that of the child, the practical child care support they receive from others, the financial resources they have available, and the expectations they have for themselves and their child – whether they are lesbian or heterosexual parents, whether they are single parents, and whether they are the parents of several children. As well, their experiences of motherhood change along with other changes within their lives.

No chapter or book on the psychology of women can say what it means to be a woman, but it can explain why women are still plagued by some of the common beliefs on women's nature, and it can provide another perspective for understanding personal experiences. This chapter includes a discussion of, first, the historical treatment of women by psychology, focusing on psychoanalytic influences; second, the impact of the feminist movement in evaluating psychology and contributing to changes within the discipline; and finally, some of the innovative interpretations and studies that are contributing to the development and practice of a women-centred psychology of women.

There are, however, some terms that should be explained before we look at the history of the psychology of women. Throughout, the chapter refers to psychologists, psychiatrists, psychoanalysts, and psychotherapists. Individuals who identify themselves by any one of these titles can all be involved in providing some kind of psychotherapy (help that involves achieving insight into problems through talking) to people who are experiencing difficulties in dealing with their everyday lives. However, different psychotherapists hearing the same person describe her or his problems may see quite different causes for those problems; and consequently they may approach the treatment in very different ways. How the problems are understood and treated by the therapist depends very much upon which approach to personality development the therapist embraces.[3]

The specific kinds of professional training that psychotherapists receive also influences the kind of therapy they administer. For example, *psychiatrists* receive medical degrees before embarking upon a residency program in psychiatry. Because of their medical training, they may view psychological problems as illness and use drugs or other medical treatments in addition to or instead of psychotherapy. (Psychotherapists who are medical doctors are the only ones who can prescribe drugs at present.) *Psychoanalysts* (who may or may not be psychiatrists) have been trained at a psychoanalytic institute to analyse others using techniques to make conscious those unconscious memories, feelings, or desires that are assumed to be the cause of the problems. Some, but not all, *psychologists* provide counselling or psychotherapy. Clinical/counselling psychologists have generally earned a Ph.D. degree, taking a program that includes supervised clinical work. (Many of the psychologists whose work will be referred to in this chapter are not primarily psychotherapists, but are university teachers and researchers.)

All of these professionals as well as others (such as social workers or M.A. psychologists with appropriate training) may be considered to be psychotherapists. Psychotherapy provides the point at which many women encounter psychological beliefs and theories. What the therapist believes to constitute the psychology of women can have extremely important consequences for individual women.

Psychoanalytic Theory

The psychology of women was, until very recently, assumed to be explained by psychoanalytic theory, developed by Freud and added to by several of his colleagues. The impact of Freud's ideas and work upon psychology generally and psychotherapy specifically has been and continues to be very significant. His ideas have served as a stimulus both for further development within psychoanalysis and for the creation of opposing interpretations of what it is to be human. Freudian ideas, although controversial, have also been influential in areas such as literature, art, and history and have been integrated into popular thought. Freud's work on the psychology of women grew directly out of his conceptualization of the stages of sexual development, which he thought represented a universal pattern for all men and women. Before considering what Freud had to say about women specifically, it is important to look at his general psychosexual stage theory. [4]

Freud postulated that the infant is born with undifferentiated sexual energy, called libido, which becomes organized around different areas of the body as the child matures. What happens at each stage of psychosexual development is seen to have crucial implications for personality development, as well as for the observable differences between the sexes in puberty and adulthood. The stages are identified by the area of the body that was seen by Freud to be the primary locus of sexual pleasure at that time. During the first year of life, sexual pleasure is derived from activities focused on the mouth. This period is designated as the *oral stage*. In the second or third year, as the child gains control over its bodily functions, the area of pleasure moves. This second phase is known as the *anal stage* of psychosexual development. When the child has achieved mastery over the anal functions in the third or fourth year, the pleasure potential of the genitals is discovered through infantile masturbation of the penis for boys and of the clitoris for girls. This phase of development is referred to as the *phallic stage* and is seen to be especially important for personality development. It is in this stage that the Oedipal complex (the child's sexual desire for the opposite-sex parent) is aroused and, later, successfully repressed through identification with the same-sex parent. The resolution of the Oedipal complex is believed to be more difficult for girls than for boys. According to Freud, the child ceases to display overt sexuality around the age of six and enters the *latency stage* during which sexual impulses remain dormant until their re-emergence at puberty. During the *genital stage*, which appears at puberty, the libido may be directed towards a member of the other sex, indicating that the individual has reached psychosexual maturity.

Boys and girls pass through the early stages of psychosexual development in much the same manner, with both, according to Freud, engaging in masturbatory acts and then connecting these acts with the ideas of sexual intercourse in the phallic phase. Both are also attached to the mother as the first love-object. Freud believed that girls were destined to notice the visible and large penis of a brother or playmate early in the phallic stage, which would lead to them falling victim to envy for the penis and "leave ineradicable traces on their development and the formation of their character."[5] The little girl comes to believe that she was castrated. This belief, according to Freud, is a wound to her self-esteem, which leads to a permanent sense of inferiority. The discovery by the girl that all women lack a penis becomes the basis of her life-long devaluation of other women.

In predictable fashion, Freud claims that the girl blames her mother for her castration and consequently turns away from her mother, ending the attachment to her "in hate." The turning away from the mother paves the way for the attachment to the father, to whom she turns with "the wish for the penis which her mother has refused her and which she now expects from her father." The wish for the penis is then transformed in normal femininity to a wish for "a baby from the girl's father, and thereafter is the aim of the most powerful feminine wish."[6] With the transfer of her libido from her mother to her father and the equation of the penis with a child, she resolves her penis envy and is on the course towards what Freud considers to be normal femininity.[7]

To achieve sexual maturity, however, she must also renounce phallic clitoral orgasm in favour of orgasm from vaginal penetration. Freud saw other consequences of penis envy in female personality development. In addition to her sense of inferiority, the woman is also left with a residue of penis envy in the form of jealousy, which Freud argued was much more prevalent in the mental life of women than men, resulting in their having little sense of justice.[8] Other traits that Freud thought characterized adult women were narcissism (a preoccupation with the self), which was exhibited in a strong need to be loved; vanity (value placed on physical charms), which was compensation for their original sexual inferiority; and shame, the purpose of which was to conceal genital deficiency.[9]

Although it may be difficult to understand today why Freud's views on the psychology of women were taken seriously, it must be remembered that they were indeed taken very seriously. They did have, and continue to have, consequences for the lives of individual women. In large part this was because Freudian theory provided the first "scientific" explanation based on female anatomy for much of what was believed (and continues to be believed by some) to be generally true of women in Western society. For example, both men and women in Freud's era believed that women were inferior beings; their main goal in life (no matter what else they did) was to marry and have children; they did not get along with other women or with their mothers; they were emotional and thus could not make rational decisions; and they were vain creatures who concentrated on their physical appearances. The influence of such beliefs extended well beyond the domain of psychology. It is apparent, for example, in the medical treatment of women, as Wendy Mitchinson shows in her chapter; and the 'complementarity' thesis, which Lorraine Code discusses in her chapter, gained increased credibility from Freud's views. Because Freudian theory pointed to a natural cause for these effects, there was no need to consider how women were controlled or restricted by the various institutions of society, from the state through the church to the family. It was a theory that reinforced many of the beliefs about and practices towards women, and it did this in a way that was accepted at the time as intellectually and scientifically respectable.

With the growing realization that knowledge is constructed, it becomes ever more obvious that "All psychological theories, including those that claim universal applicability, are grounded in the experiences of particular people."[10] Freud's theory is no exception, and a good many books, articles, and conference sessions focus on aspects of his life and work. It has long been known that Freud's theorizing reflected his own personal experiences as well as insights gained from his work with patients. However, it was not until the publication in the late 1980s of the biography of his daughter, Anna, that it became more generally known that Freud actually psychoanalysed her for four years.[11] It is most interesting to discover that it was after the completion of the final phase of the analysis, which went from 1924 to 1925, that Freud wrote his first major paper on female development, "Some Psychological Consequences of the Anatomical Distinction Between the Sexes."[12] Elisabeth Young-Bruehl, in the biography, documents the attachment between Freud and his youngest daughter as well as her competition with her mother and aunt for his affections. She indicates that there is good reason to believe that Anna's psychoanalysis provided much of the material for Freud's theory of feminine development.[13]

Freud was not the only psychoanalyst who supported an "anatomy is destiny" theory of women's personality development. His position was (and is) supported by other analysts, at least two of whom (Helene Deutsch and Erik Erikson) achieved popular recognition and made their own contributions to the psychology of women. Helene Deutsch (1884-1982) underwent analysis with Freud, worked closely with him in Vienna before immigrating to the United States, and has been referred to as one of Freud's "dutiful daughters."[14]

Although she did not accept Freud's views on penis envy, Deutsch did believe that narcissism, along with passivity and masochism, were the essential core-personality characteristics of the normal feminine woman. All three terms tend to have negative connotations for us today, but Deutsch did not see them as pejorative. For instance, she saw passivity as an attitude of receptive waiting and expectancy. In trying to give it a positive connotation, Deutsch referred to feminine passivity as "activity directed inward."[15] Healthy narcissism, for her, was a loving and valuing of the self, which supports the instinct for self-preservation. And maso-chism, in Deutsch's sense, is a normal condition for women, who are more attracted to suffering than men and who, in the normal course of life, expe-rience pain with pleasure in such events as childbirth and defloration. Nar-cissism and masochism are in balance in normal femininity. The healthy woman is seen to accept discomfort, even pain, associated with her normal functions because of the pleasure that accompanies them, but her healthy narcissism will not allow her to accept too much.[16]

It is ironic that Deutsch, an independent, active, woman who com-bined marriage, motherhood, and a successful career, embraced and expanded the Freudian (and societal) ideas of what it meant to be a nor-mal woman. Instead of focusing upon the challenges and satisfactions to be derived from breaking down stereotypes and leading an unconven-tional life, as she herself did, she lent a good bit of her professional prestige to prescribing the traditional roles of wife and mother for the true fulfill-ment of women.[17] The fact that Deutsch was a woman and her best-known work was entitled *The Psychology of Women* gave scientific and per-sonal validity to the psychoanalytic views of women.

Erik Erikson (b. 1902) is an influential psychoanalyst who has also sup-ported an "anatomy is destiny" view for women's development; however, his position does differ from Freud's. His psychosocial-stage theory of human development expands upon Freud's psychosexual formulation but covers the entire life span, focusing upon developmental crises to be solved rather than upon the sexual aspects of development. He acknowl-edges and emphasizes cultural and historical contributions to personality, but has maintained that part of the female anatomy itself, particularly the "inner space" (or womb) exerts powerful effects upon women.[18] In 1968 he wrote:

> Am I saying, then, that "anatomy is destiny"? Yes, it is destiny, insofar as it determines not only the range and configuration of phy-siological functioning and its limitation but also, to an extent, per-sonality configurations. The basic modalities of woman's commit-ment and involvement naturally also reflect the ground plan of her body.[19]

Erikson saw the filling of the inner space as the goal of female development and the emptiness of it as the source of women's despair. And the self-identity of a woman revolves around the man she marries, rather than coming from her own interests and achievements. Erikson wrote, "I think that much of a young woman's identity is already defined in her kind of attractiveness and in the selective nature of her search for the man (or men) by whom she wishes to be sought."[20] And later he argued, "Woman-hood arrives when attractiveness and experience have succeeded in selecting what is to be admitted to the welcome of the inner space 'for keeps.'"[21]

How did these particular psychoanalytic views of woman's true nature affect individual women? Even though only a relatively small percentage of women have ever undergone psychoanalysis, the influence of psychoanalytic thought on Western culture since the early part of this century has been considerable. It has provided a prescription for what it was to be a feminine woman, which includes a number of fairly negative traits, as well as firmly establishing that a woman's goal in life is to marry and have children. With the general acceptance of psychoanalytic theory, norms were established that could have caused individual women (and others) to doubt or question their own normality when they did not conform to the standard. It has also provided labels, often confused as explanations, for aspects of women's behaviour. For example, it is often said that a woman who is beaten by a spouse and stays with him is masochistic. This type of labelling focuses upon the individual, who in this case is a victim, and gives her the responsibility for the fact that someone else is abusing her. Professionals as well as lay people blame female victims for their victimization because they "know" from psychoanalytic theory that women are subconsciously masochistic by nature.

Two other aspects of psychoanalytic theory that have had particularly negative consequences for individual women are Freud's assertions that, first, the normal, mature female sexual orgasm is vaginal rather than clitoral, and, second, that the girl comes to desire a baby from her father as a result of penis envy. Freud's views on the mature female sexual response were dominant until the publication of the careful work of Masters and Johnson in 1966 provided convincing evidence that the clitoris is the primary organ for female orgasm.[22] Before that time, if a woman reported to a doctor or therapist that she did not experience an orgasm during intercourse, she was often told that she was rejecting her femininity and was labelled as frigid. The diagnosis comes directly from Freudian theory and again focuses upon woman's nature rather than upon the interaction between sexual partners. If she did not experience orgasm in intercourse she must be unconsciously (if not consciously) rejecting her feminine role. It is likely that many women who did not report their lack of orgasm simply thought of themselves as frigid.

Freud saw the girl on her way to normal femininity transferring her attachment to her father and wishing for a baby from him. This aspect of the theory developed as a result of the fact that Freud was told by almost all of his female patients that they had been seduced by their fathers.[23] However, when Freud did publicly claim in 1896[24] that infantile sexual experiences figured in the cause of hysteria (a form of emotional disturbance manifested in paralysis, blindness, or other disturbance without a physical cause), his finding was not well received by the Vienna scientific community. Subsequently he reversed his position and claimed that the reports of seduction were fantasies, and he incorporated these fantasies into his theory as a normal part of development. Our awareness today of the prevalence of the sexual abuse of children emphasizes the enormity of Freud's actions – and those of generations of therapists since – in denying that reported sexual abuse actually took place. [25]

Although the psychoanalytic view of women dominated psychology until the early 1970s, Stephanie Shields has reminded us that the psychology of women as it was extrapolated from sex-differences research did have an active pre-Freudian past. [26] In a pioneering article that appeared in 1975, she showed how science in the last half of the nineteenth and the first third of the twentieth centuries played handmaiden to social values and provided 'legitimate' evidence for cataloguing the 'innate' but complementary differences in male and female nature. The 'woman question' entered North American psychology with the incorporation of evolutionary theory into the practice of psychology in the late nineteenth century. The theme of this biological theory as it was applied to the social sciences revolved around the evolutionary supremacy of the Caucasian male. The supplementary, subordinate role of the female was seen as part of this development. Psychological research was directed towards firmly establishing that differences did exist between women and men, and it concluded that the bases for these differences were biological in origin. It is very instructive to see how the social beliefs were reflected in the work of individual scientists dedicated to providing evidence for the naturalness of women's inferior position in society through research on the female brain, the variability hypothesis (individual differences particularly as they related to intellectual ability), and maternal instinct. It is also instructive to read that some women psychologists were critiquing this work at the time and pointing out that environmental and social factors provided explanations for observed differences. Shields quotes Helen Thompson Wooley's 1910 appraisal of the quality of research being done on sex differences: "There is perhaps no field aspiring to be scientific where flagrant personal bias, logic martyred in the cause of supporting a prejudice, unfounded assertions, and even sentimental rot and drivel, have run riot to such an extent as here." [27]

Freudian views on the nature of women were easily accepted by a profession whose thrust in research on women had been to establish their biological inferiority to men and to understand their position in society as a result of natural rather than cultural factors. Although psychologists claimed to base their conclusions on facts, they accepted as fact those things that supported their beliefs. Psychoanalysis, with its comprehensive description of and prescription for the psychology of women, reinforced the conclusions of the earlier sex-difference research and provided a parsimonious explanation of such differences.

Not all psychoanalysts ascribed to Freud's emphasis on biology as the prime determinant of personality development. Some did take issue with his analyses of normal female development. These analysts' views, however, did not receive the kind of popular attention afforded Freudian interpretations. Their positions are not regularly discussed in introductory psychology texts, and it was not until psychology of women texts[28] began to appear in the 1970s that undergraduate students were systematically exposed to the ideas of Karen Horney and Clara Thompson.

Karen Horney (1885-1952) was trained as a Freudian analyst and initially saw her work falling within the framework of Freudian theory. She, however, aspired to eliminate the fallacies of Freudian thought, which she believed had their roots in his mechanistic, biological orientation. She thought that female psychology was based on lack of confidence and an overemphasis on the love relationship, but she saw these as having little to do with the anatomy of the female sex organs and much more to do with a woman's interactions within her social environment. As early as 1926 she pointed out that earlier versions of the psychology of women had been considered only from the point of view of men and actually represented a deposit of the desires and disappointments of men.[29] Unfortunately, from her point of view, women had adapted to the wishes of men and accepted that adaptation to represent their true nature.

Horney also showed how the views of Freudian theory on feminine development mirrored those of the young boy as he becomes conscious of his own genitals as well as those of the little girl. Horney accepted the prevalence of several of the feminine qualities described by Freud, but questioned his interpretation of them. She argued, for instance, that the cultural prescriptions for and restrictions on women were responsible for behaviour that was seen as masochistic. By the end of her career Horney had broken completely with the Freudian school of psychoanalysis and embraced a vision of the person (female or male), "whose best energies are affirmative strivings toward knowledge, toward developing spiritual powers and moral courage, toward achievement in all areas, toward the full use of intellect and imagination."[30] Although Horney claimed to have developed a general theory of development, it has recently been argued that she, too, created a theory that reflected her own gendered and cultural experiences.[31]

Clara Thompson (1893-1958) was a psychoanalyst whose work from the beginning emphasized the importance for personal development of interactions with others rather than biological attributes. As an admirer and a friend of Karen Horney, she was concerned with the Freudian views on the psychology of women. She did not question Freud's observations, but pointed out that he saw female development only from a male perspective and overgeneralized from what he observed in his own culture to all women. Writing in the 1940s and 1950s, she emphasized the importance of cultural pressures on molding the behaviours and beliefs of women. She not only reinterpreted various Freudian concepts in cultural rather than anatomical terms, but also wrote very perceptively on topics such as working women, female sexuality, and cultural pressures in the psychology of women.[32]

Both Horney and Thompson challenged Freudian interpretations of women's nature as well as the beliefs about women prevalent at the time. Although both of them were active and influential as writers and analysts, their ideas did not make their way into the popular culture and were not seen as a threat or a corrective to the views about women that dominated psychology and psychiatry (both were also psychiatrists). The *Zeitgeist* (spirit of the times) was such that interpretations challenging the androcentric (male-centred) prescriptions for women were not considered seriously, if they were heard at all.

Women had achieved the vote in many Western countries by the time Horney and Thompson were writing, and it was widely believed that the franchise would lead to a righting of many of the wrongs that women experienced. But it was not until the 1960s and 1970s, when the far-reaching effects of the present women's movement had begun to sensitize segments of society to the continued, general oppression of women, that voices critical of androcentricity in psychology began to be heard – even in nations that prided themselves upon their liberal ideals of individual freedom. In 1969, when Naomi Weisstein's article "Woman as Nigger" appeared, there were women psychologists who were beginning to recognize the role that their discipline – not out of malicious intent but through uncritical acceptance of the beliefs in women's inferior nature – had in maintaining and adding to the oppression of women. After the publication of this article a concerted critique of psychology's treatment of women began. This critique, which continues today, is extensive and includes analyses of the methods and the knowledge-base of psychology as well as its practices as a profession.

The Feminist Critique

At the centre of the feminist critique is the realization that psychology is an androcentric discipline. Androcentrism is reflected throughout the discipline, from its research topics, through its language and methods, to its implementation of knowledge in practice. Although Horney and Thompson had identified the male focus as a problem in the psychology of women, it was not until the early 1970s that this bias began to be systematically investigated and exposed. At the same time, women psychologists began to organize in order to further the development of the psychology of women and to lobby for changes within the discipline. They have met with a fair amount of success, and the changes within psychology over the past twenty-five years have been impressive.[33]

One of the far-reaching effects of the androcentric bias of psychology is the assumption that the model for human behaviour is the white male human being. Using the male as the standard against which females are compared has had many consequences. A few of these are the development of theories of human behaviour that are more descriptive of the lives of white men than of women, the valuing of characteristics that are traditionally attributed to men and the devaluing of those attributed to women, and the use of a double standard in evaluating behaviour based on the gender of the individual.

Some general theories of life span or adult development are based exclusively on the experiences of white men. This fact, however, is not always salient in the naming and/or describing of the theories. For example, it has become increasingly obvious that the developmental paths followed by women and men in most cultural and racial groups are different primarily because of women's family responsibilities. Middle-class women, for example, are more apt to compromise their own career opportunities for the sake of their husbands' careers and their children's needs than are men. Most theories of human development have not included such considerations and, consequently, do not provide a framework for understanding the experiences of a majority of women.

Similarly there are a number of social-psychological theories of social interaction that are based on an image of the rugged male individualist striving towards his goals and fulfilling his own needs. When studies have subsequently been done to test the implications of these theories, those individuals who showed behaviour that expressed concern for others, for example, were seen as not fitting the model, and, consequently, were evaluated negatively.[34]

The consequence of using the white male as the prototypical human being is that theories of human behaviour may reflect the experiences of such men, but not necessarily of women (or men of other cultural groups). When measured against this male standard, women are often found to be deviant or aberrant. And individuals who do not measure up to the standard are often seen as less worthy or valuable than those who do meet the standard. Similarly, the characteristics of that deviant individual or group of individuals are also devalued. This devaluing of the female was reflected in Freud's theory (there it was attributed to her lack of a penis) and is common in society in general.

The realization that women were absent from male-based theories of human behaviour resulted in early feminist research attempts to add women to existing theories. One area that generated a great deal of work in the late 1960s and early 1970s was achievement motivation. Achievement, as it is generally understood, has traditionally been associated much more with men than with women. Very often women who achieved in the traditional sense of the term were considered failures as women if they were not also wives and mothers. Matina Horner's realization that women were absent from the considerable literature on achievement motivation led her to the discovery of what she called "fear of success." (She defined fear of success as a relatively stable personality characteristic, most apt to be shown by intellectually competent women. It was reflected in the expectation of some negative consequences, such as rejection or the threat to one's femininity as a result of being successful.) The work of Horner and many others provided an extensive analysis of the changing factors that influence and/or inhibit achievement strivings and behaviour and was part of much early research on the topic of women and achievement.[35]

Androcentrism also permeates the language of sex-difference research and is reflected in the differing attributions made for the same behaviour shown by men and by women. Sex-difference research predated Freud's views on femininity and was directed towards establishing scientifically that women had evolved as mothers and as helpmates to men rather than as their social, economic, and political equals. At the beginning of the current feminist movement, there were a number of common assumptions about the cognitive and behavioural ways in which men and women differed from each other. In most cases it was assumed not only that these differences had a biological or natural basis, but also that this was the way it should be and that it was up to parents to foster these sex-based tendencies.[36]

A further consequence of accepting these 'established differences' was that those behaviours or characteristics commonly attributed to boys were implicitly and explicitly seen as 'better' than those behaviours or characteristics attributed to girls. For example, on the average, girls from adolescence on show higher scores on verbal tasks than do boys, while boys, on the average, show higher scores on mathematical tasks. (It should be noted that when talking about sex differences, one is talking about differences between the means [averages] of scores for groups of girls and boys [or women and men]. There are always some boys who score at or near the girls' mean and vice versa. There are usually bigger differences among the girls [or boys] than there are between the means for the two groups.) Although both mathematical and verbal skills are important aspects of cognitive functioning, some psychologists have minimized verbal abilities, even ascribing them to extensive prior practice rather than to intellect.[37]

In the early 1970s, Eleanor Maccoby and Carol Jacklin examined a large number of studies that tested for sex differences in motivation, social behaviour, and intellectual ability. They concluded that there were only four areas (aggression, verbal, mathematical, and visual-spatial abilities) where one could confidently conclude that there were average differences between males and females. All of the other differences reported in the literature were seen to either have no support or to be inadequately tested.[38] Despite the smallness of the average sex differences found, research looking at differences between the sexes – particularly in terms of the functioning and/or structure of the brain – continues and is deemed to be of general interest, as demonstrated in the early 1990s when *Time* magazine ran a cover story on such research entitled "Sizing up the Sexes."[39]

There have been and continue to be feminist critiques of sex-difference research,[40] and certainly not all feminists or other researchers agree on the interpretation of the results or on the value of continued effort in this area. The critiques of the work begun in the 1970s echoed the point made by women psychologists early in the century, as well as by Horney and Thompson: that is, there is no need to resort to biological or anatomical factors to explain psychological or behavioural differences between men and women – factors traditionally used as the basis for denying women a full role in the public life of society. The experiences of and expectations for girls and boys from birth on are so great that socialization and cultural factors provide ample reason for any number of differences measured in childhood, adolescence, or adulthood. Parents' expectations for their own and others' infants are so tied up with gender that it is impossible to eliminate this source of influence on a developing person.[41] And schools, churches, and media consciously and unconsciously perpetuate stereotypes of what is appropriate behaviour for boys and for girls. Consideration of many aspects of the sex-difference research leads to the conclusion that there are more similarities than differences between the behaviours of women and men and that women's lives today, like those of men, are characterized by diversity rather than by similarity.[42] However, within the group of feminist researchers most active in this area of scholarship there are two divergent views. One emphasizes the similarities between the sexes and is based on quantitative research, while the other focuses upon the differences between the sexes as a result of their socialization and makes more use of qualitative analyses. (The latter work will be discussed later in this chapter.)

The tendency to hold stereotypical beliefs about individuals based upon their sex or gender[43] leads to a double standard in making judgements about people, which can have very serious consequences. A number of experimental studies and much everyday experience demonstrate that the same behaviour or description of a situation is judged differently depending upon the gender of the person being judged. That is, the explanation given for the behaviour is determined more by whether a man or a woman is (or is believed to be) the actor than by the behaviour itself. One of the early demonstrations of this tendency was by Philip Goldberg.[44] His study showed that female students judged the quality of a written article higher when they believed the writer was a man than when they thought the *same* article was written by a woman. Other studies have shown a differential judgement based on gender in a wide variety of situations.[45] As more women achieve in areas that were almost exclusively male less than thirty years ago, experimental results show a weakening of these effects. Yet people still have little trouble recognizing the differential attributions for a businessman and a businesswoman resulting from the same kind of behaviour. For example, while he is seen as good on details, she's picky; he's confident, and she's conceited; he stands firm, but she's impossible to deal with; or he climbed the ladder of success, but she slept her way to the top. Behaviour that earns him praise is the source of criticism and condemnation for her.

The realization that gender is a powerful organizing concept can often help women understand the negative reactions of others towards them, which they may have initially interpreted as being their own fault. That is, independent women, who are characterized as being aggressive, pushy individuals, may internalize these attributions and see them as evidence of a personality flaw. In reality, however, any act of independence or expression of their own view would be seen by some as inappropriate female behaviour and therefore negative. A further consequence of such stereotyping has been that women are not judged as individuals with strengths and weaknesses, but as women who do not and should not fit the male norm still prevalent in society.

Psychologists continue to make attributions on the basis of what is seen as gender appropriate. Furthermore, as Naomi Weisstein pointed out in her influential 1969 article, psychologists have a history of focusing upon individual personality characteristics as the *cause* of behaviour, rather than looking to the very important psychosocial environment within which a person is situated. Weisstein claimed that psychology's focus upon "the individual" was an important factor in psychology's ignorance of what women are really like.

The importance of context (which includes expectations) for understanding and predicting human behaviour has been well documented in psychology.[46] Yet it was not until the current feminist critique of psychology began that we became fully aware of how women, particularly as wives and mothers, were 'scapegoated' by psychologists. That is, the view of women as primarily wives and mothers was translated into their having full responsibility for the success of their marriages and of their children's development. When things went wrong in either of these areas, women were often seen as not trying hard enough or as possessing personality characteristics that had detrimental effects upon others. For instance, the expressions 'maternal deprivation' and 'schizophrenogenic mother' are integrated into the psychological literature and focus attention on mothers as the cause of a host of their children's problems, including schizophrenia.[47] There are no parallel terms for fathers, and the use of the terms alone is often assumed to explain the problems, with no further considerations necessary.

Mother-blaming is a common phenomenon, as a 1985 and a 1988 examination of major clinical and family therapy journals, respectively, demonstrated.[48] It was found that mothers' activity was blamed for a wide variety of their children's problems and forms of psychopathology by both female and male therapists, while fathers' activity was cited much less often as a causative factor. Mothers have also been blamed for condoning or driving their husbands to incest.[49] Wives who stay with battering husbands are still often believed both to be showing their masochistic tendencies and to be partly responsible for the beatings they receive.[50] Certainly there are situations in which the actions of women have been injurious to and/or problematic for their children, husbands, and themselves. But, too often, wives and mothers have been held responsible for actions of husbands and problems of children *because* they are women, a view that ignores not only the circumstances within which the interactions take place but also the others involved in the interactions. These assumptions about women and their roles have influenced (and continue to influence) the kind of treatment women receive from psychotherapists.

Even psychotherapists who reject psychoanalytic theory have accepted and been influenced by society's expectations (which are, in turn, influenced by Freudian thought) of what constitutes the appropriate adult female role. Since the early 1970s there have been a number of significant criticisms of psychiatry and psychotherapy, particularly of their effects on women.[51] These analyses have emerged from the stories of women who have turned to the helping professions (psychiatry, psychology, and social work) for aid with problems in living, only to have their complaints turned into symptoms of sickness, ignored, and/or used against them, or to be told that they themselves are the problem. Others with real physical problems have been treated as if they were "hysterical" women, whose symptoms are in their heads.

A recurring theme in these analyses is that the continued acceptance by helping professionals of the stereotypes of what it means to be a woman has led them to serve as enforcers of social control rather than as therapeutic agents. Women's problems have often been compounded and aggravated by their therapists' failure to recognize that social expectations, institutions, and interactions, rather than individual personality dynamics, are at the base of their complaints. Phyllis Chesler was one of the first to launch an all-encompassing indictment of psychiatry and its treatment of women in her pioneering and popular book *Woman and Madness*. In addition to naming those responsible for the history of abuse of power in the name of therapy, Chester also suggested the kinds of changes needed to develop a new psychology of women. Others have added to the critique she initiated and are actively engaged in providing therapy informed by feminist consciousness. A concrete effect of such efforts has been the acceptance of guidelines for non-sexist therapy/counselling with women by the Canadian Psychological Association (CPA).

An examination of these guidelines reveals the kinds of abuses women have been subjected to in the name of therapy. It also provides a clear demonstration of how Freudian ideas and social and cultural stereotypes of women have been ingrained in therapy. The guidelines are as follows:

1. The therapist/counsellor is willing to help the woman client to explore alternative life options in addition to the culturally defined gender role. Besides marriage and motherhood, he or she acknowledges the importance of other activities in both creating and solving women's problems.

2. The therapist/counsellor realizes that women do not bear the total responsibility for the success of marriage and for childrearing.

3. The therapist/counsellor recognizes the existence of social bias against women, and explores with the client the possibility that her problems may be based on society's definition of women's role rather than entirely within herself.

4. While respecting the right of the therapist/counsellor to determine the appropriate therapeutic strategy for a client, he or she is sensitive to and avoids the use of theoretical concepts that serve to reinforce the female stereotype of dependency and passivity, or to limit the woman's personal development.

5. The therapist/counsellor avoids interpreting psychological problems that occur at times of biological change in a woman's life, e.g. – childbirth, menopause – solely in terms of her reproductive/biological functioning.

6. The therapist/counsellor avoids the use of language implying sex

bias, especially sexist jokes and the use of labels derogatory or demeaning to women.

7. The therapist/counsellor recognizes physical violence and sexual abuse as crimes, and does not encourage the woman client to submit to them, to accept their legitimacy, or to feel guilty about being a victim. The therapist actively acknowledges that there is no provocation that justifies resorting to physical or sexual violence.

8. The therapist/counsellor recognizes a woman client's right to have a fully adult role in the therapist-client relationship, without guidance from or deference to a man, and helps her achieve such a role.

9. The therapist/counsellor considers the sexual activity of the client without employing a "double standard" based on gender.

10. The therapist/counsellor does not treat the woman client as a sex object.[52]

Although making therapy/counselling non-sexist for *all* clients should be a necessary condition for any therapy, feminists do not believe that being non-sexist is enough. They consciously incorporate their feminist beliefs into their practice and employ specific strategies in their work with women clients. Judith Myers Avis has identified a number of strategies used by feminist therapists.[53] They include such things as deliberate efforts to reduce the hierarchy of therapist and client; an emphasis and focus on the client's strengths; an avoidance of diagnostic tests and labels; the use of therapeutic contracts that give women more control over their own therapy; the use of social and sex-role analyses to help women understand the impact of social, cultural, and socialization factors upon their lives; the teaching of skill building, stress management, and assertiveness; and working with women in groups to provide support, break down isolation, and increase awareness of the commonality of women's problems and their relation to cultural/social roles and constraints.

Others have pointed out that feminist therapy must be viewed as a perspective that allows for a different way of seeing, understanding, and making connections, rather than as a technique in and of itself. That is, feminist therapy is not another school of therapy but is an approach to therapy that acknowledges the humanity and personal power of both the client and the therapist. The therapist works in a co-operative manner, sharing aspects of her experience rather than remaining aloof while probing and prescribing. Feminist therapists can work within the general framework of a single approach or may be eclectic and use insights and techniques from a number of different kinds of therapy.

In addition to the feminists who provide counselling/therapy in private practice or in private or public hospitals, clinics, or various social agencies, others are developing self-help groups for women outside of the institutionalized helping professions. These self-help groups are founded on the belief that a group of people with a common goal can help and support each other in dealing with problems in living.[54] Feminists have made some important advances in getting their criticisms heard, setting non-sexist guidelines in place, and providing therapy that expands and supports the options of the clients. Yet much of the training and practice of counsellors/therapists does not take into account the contributions that feminists have made in this area.[55]

Another important feminist contribution to psychology has been the critique of the experimental method – the method by which scientific psychology defines itself. Although many psychologists use methods such as questionnaires, interviews, case studies, surveys, and naturalistic observations to gather data, the controlled experiment has been the method most valued by academic psychology. This method provides a way of systematically manipulating a limited number of stimuli or variables while controlling most other factors in the experimental situation. It is believed to be the only truly scientific means by which the *cause* of a particular behaviour can be established. Feminists (and others) have pointed out that the isolation of the individual in the controlled laboratory, stripped of his/her context, greatly limits the usefulness of what is learned.

In spite of the critiques of this aspect of the method, psychologists continue to depend upon this context-stripping methodology, which represents the view that the individual must and can be understood out of context.[56] Although some feminists believe that the experimental method has only limited usefulness in advancing our knowledge of human behaviour, others do *not* reject it outright. They recognize that it will continue to be, and in some cases should be, used and thus are concerned that researchers become aware of and recognize the potentialities for sexism at all stages of the research process. In addition to feminist research, their efforts are directed towards eliminating sexism from all scholarly work regardless of the research method used and towards the recognition that all methods can be used in a feminist manner.[57]

Although there is no one feminist research methodology advocated by feminist psychologists, there are a variety of considerations that inform feminist research into the psychology of women. These considerations include: (1) the acceptance that *all* research is value-laden and influenced by the beliefs and experiences of the researcher;[58] (2) an attempt to be non-sexist at each stage of the research process, from the asking of questions through to the generalization of results; (3) a respect for the subjects of the research, who may be treated more as collaborators in the research than as objects to be studied; (4) the recognition that the understanding and interpretation of the psychological phenomena require an interdisciplinary approach with attention to the social, biological, and political context; and (5) the realization of the potential social and political misuses of the research.[59]

The experiences of women are the starting point for research directed towards expanding our knowledge of the psychology of women; thus much of the data in this evolving field are qualitative rather than quantitative in nature. That is, instead of developing a highly structured questionnaire, where individuals' answers are tallied, in-depth interviews often form the basis for beginning to explore an area of concern to women. It is from this immersion in what participants have said that patterns emerge that begin to provide insights into both the commonalities and the diversities in women's experiences. This kind of qualitative work is seen by some to be the hallmark of feminist research,[60] while others argue that feminists have to use a variety of research methodologies and cannot limit themselves to a single approach. This latter group points out that once the qualitative work has been done, it is necessary to test the implications from that work by using more structured, quantitative methods.

New Directions in the Psychology of Women

The knowledge-base of the psychology of women has grown enormously since the late 1960s and continues to expand and evolve. Women's perceived experiences of all facets of their lives constitute the starting point for theoretical and empirical work in this area, with diversity characterizing the questions asked, the methods of investigation chosen, and the analyses of issues offered. It is now possible to see trends as well as some pitfalls in feminist research in psychology. Some of the concepts and directions of the pioneering work in the development of a new psychology of women have been seen, in retrospect, to have the same characteristics, such as blaming mothers or the victim and focusing upon the individual, that were points of feminist criticism of psychology in general.[61] The continuing development of our understanding of female psychology influences, and is influenced by, feminist scholarship in other areas and is itself continuously informed by the growing consciousness of what it means to be a woman. In broad terms, the development of new scholarship can be traced from a stage where attempts were made to add more information on women to psychology's knowledge-base, through a stage of demonstrating the bias and falsity of the accepted wisdom on women, to a stage of focusing upon women's experiences and attributions and learning more about them from a gynocentric (female-centred) position.[62] Although these trends in scholarship are quite evident, it should be realized that research at all stages is still being done and adding to what we are learning about women. It should also be kept in mind that much of what is being learned is not static, but changes as the social, economic, and political contexts of society change. And it must be remembered that factors such as class, race, ethnicity, and sexual preference affect women's experiences. Although there is no fully formulated woman-based theory of personality,[63] there is an ever-growing amount of information on the psychological aspects of women's lives from birth through to late adulthood.

From the description of the psychoanalytic view of the psychology of women, it might be assumed that feminists would reject all psychoanalytic interpretations as useless. Some do find that "assumptions about the inherent inferiority of women are embedded in the very core of psychoanalytic theory" and no amount of tinkering can rehabilitate it.[64] Thus, Hannah Lerman does not believe that psychoanalytic theory is useful for the development of a woman-based theory of personality or for understanding the experiences of women generally. Other feminists disagree and have developed analyses that utilize insights from psychoanalytic theory.[65]

Perhaps one of the most ambitious attempts to show how psychoanalysis is relevant to our present-day understanding of the psychology of women was made by Juliet Mitchell.[66] She argues persuasively that Freud's theory provides an analysis of the human condition in a patriarchal society. She points out that psychoanalysis does not deal with biology but with the conscious and unconscious ways we think about biological facts. And she shows how a Freudian analysis, with its emphasis on the unconscious and infantile sexuality, provides a fuller understanding of women's inferior role and the feminine personality than does an analysis based on cultural conditioning alone. Mitchell (like others who use a psychoanalytically grounded analysis to understand women's situation today) does acknowledge that future cultural changes will be reflected in changed thoughts and attitudes. That is, there is a recognition that the description of human development provided by Freud is not universal as he claimed, but dependent upon the kind of society within which the individual lives. The psychoanalytic interpretations do, according to Mitchell, show how the realities of patriarchy influence development. A more egalitarian society, for example, where both parents nurture and rear children, would lead to different mental representations.

The fact that women bear and rear children has long been recognized as a barrier to their full participation in society. Recent adaptations of Freudian theory have explored other consequences of women's mothering and reached the conclusion that a system of parenting in which both men and women actively parent is necessary if sexual inequality is to be eliminated.[67] Nancy Chodorow's thought-provoking adaptation of Freudian theory to explain the pervasiveness of mothering by women claims,

"Women are prepared psychologically for mothering through the developmental situation in which they grow up, and in which women have mothered them."[68] Her analysis assumes that mothers sense a oneness and continuity with daughters, which enhances and extends the mother-child relationship for girls. The differences, however, that mothers feel with their sons lead to the growing separation from them. Consequently, boys develop a more differentiated self and experience a growing curtailment of their emphatic tie with their mothers. (This approach focuses upon and provides an explanation for a major difference between the way the two sexes react in the world rather than upon their similarities.) Chodorow sees the fact that women mother as a major feature of a sex-gender system, which leads to sexual inequality as we know it. Among other consequences of women's mothering are the creation of a psychology of male domination, a fear of women in men, and the division of the social world into unequally valued domestic and public spheres.[69] (Chodorow's analysis has received a great deal of attention by feminists, particularly those who are not psychologists, but it has also been criticized by some as mother-blaming.) As a result of her analysis of women's mothering and its consequences, Chodorow advocates a change in the present system in which parenting is primarily the responsibility of mothers.

Many other feminists have also concluded that such a change is necessary. They have arrived at this point, however, through analyses of social institutions and the experiences of women, rather than through psychoanalytic insights. (Susan McDaniel offers one such analysis from a sociological perspective in her chapter on the changing family and the impact of feminism on women's lives.) Many women are going to continue to want to have children, and more and more mothers of preschool children are going to be in the work force. The ideal situation of most mothers and fathers sharing more equally in the nurturing and care of their children is certainly not very near at hand. But issues and problems around motherhood and child care will remain important for some time and in the lives of most women.

Let us consider next a group of women, lesbians, who have been greatly marginalized by society and psychology. With a psychology of women directed towards heterosexual attraction, marriage, and motherhood (as was Freudian psychology), lesbianism was seen as pathological and those who engaged in such behaviours were seen as sick. The feminist and the gay movements have led to a greater recognition of lifestyles that consciously reject the "compulsory heterosexuality"[70] that dominates most if not all societies today. Feminist lesbians are producing an impressive body of knowledge on lesbian existence and identity, which has become a growing part of the disciplinary as well as interdisciplinary literature on women. The recent work produced by lesbian scholars on lesbian issues in psychology is providing lesbians as well as non-lesbians with information, analyses, and theoretical formulations on lesbianism that simply did not exist earlier.

Historically, lesbians (like male homosexuals) have been subject to severe penalties ranging from death to imprisonment to social ostracism for their rejection of heterosexuality. Until December 1973 homosexuality was classified as a mental disorder by the American Psychiatric Association. In a review essay of social-science research looking at lesbian identity and community, Susan Krieger argued:

> The shift that has occurred in the past twenty years may be described as one that moves us from thinking about lesbianism in terms of deviance, narrowness, simple causation, isolated occurrence, and fixed nature to thinking of it in terms of normality, diversity, multiple influence, social context, choice and change.[71]

In her review of the literature Krieger found very little treatment of lesbianism before 1960, but what she did find was based on medical, psychiatric, or psychoanalytic expertise and depicted lesbians as pathological, that is, as sick, perverted, deviant, narcissistic, or masochistic. The influences of Freudianism and cultural myths of normality are clearly evident in the assumptions of these studies. In the late 1950s and early 1960s, work began to appear that challenged the pathological models and suggested that lesbianism was a lifestyle choice closely linked with a sense of personal identity. Krieger asserts that the best of the recent studies published since the mid-1970s views lesbianism as a product of multiple influences, looks at the similarities between lesbians and other women, and considers the lesbian individual in a social context. It also views lesbianism as a matter of total personality identity rather than primarily a sexual condition. The story Krieger hears being told in the social-science literature on lesbianism over the past twenty years is: "Once we were sick and now we are well."[72]

Although psychology of women texts, courses, and conferences do increasingly include consideration of lesbian issues, lesbians often find themselves feeling invisible as the general issues in these contexts focus on "concerns of women with regard to men and the patriarchy. . . . Virtually all of these issues affect lesbians too, but they are experienced in a different context because lesbians use women, not men, as a reference point."[73] Some lesbians have suggested that lesbian psychology should be seen as the core of the psychology of women, because "It permits us to view woman in her 'purest' form, that is, as untainted by the patriarchy as possible."[74] Such a view, it is believed, would lead to the building of entirely new models of how women relate in the world.

Along with the explorations of lesbian existence which include consideration of identity, relationships, family, and community, lesbian academics are also pointing out how the institutionalization of heterosexuality dictates not only sexual behaviour but many other areas of our lives.[75] This assumption that heterosexuality is the norm affects lesbians and homosexuals in much the same fashion that androcentrism affects women. Certainly a gynocentric psychology of women must not only include lesbian existence as a valid choice, but also recognize, study, and attempt to understand the diversity of lesbian experiences. At the same time, it must consciously work against a heterosexist ideology that influences all levels of human interaction.[76]

Revaluing Women's Qualities

As we saw in the discussion of androcentrism in research, psychologists (and society) have tended to value characteristics such as rationality and independence, which are associated with men, and devalue attributes such as emotionality and dependence, which are often associated with women.

Some of the early work in the new psychology of women seemed to be directed towards showing that with proper socialization and training girls could be more like boys. Even the early important work on androgyny seemed to lead to the conclusion that 'masculine' traits were still the important ones to have.[77] But a different focus, which emphasizes the differences between women and men, appeared with the work of Jean Baker Miller.[78] Miller, a psychiatrist, draws on a rich background of clinical practice for examples but centres her analysis on the forces that she believes affect all women by virtue of their being women. For example, she points out that women, in their subservient position to men, have been assigned the tasks of providing for bodily needs and comforts as well as the basic emotional connections between individuals. Miller suggests that these tasks, which men have seen as humanity's 'lowest needs,' may well be humanity's 'highest necessities.' From their socialization and adult experiences, women have learned a great deal more about men than men often know about themselves, and they have learned how to survive with men. As subordinates they have been allowed to express human qualities such as vulnerability, weakness, helplessness, and emotionality, which are experienced by all people but whose expression is often denied to men. In a male-dominated culture, these characteristics are not valued, but Miller argues that being able to accept and deal with these aspects of human life are, in fact, *strengths* that women have developed and that humanity needs. Other strengths she attributes to women are their ability to work co-operatively and to be creative in their continual struggle to create a new concept of personhood. She argues that women's strength is also reflected in the organization of their sense of self around being able to make and then to maintain affiliations and relationships with others. This very important aspect of women's being has been recognized by others and seen to be centrally representative of women's experience and values. As such, it may well characterize a gynocentric psychology of women.[79]

Although caring for others and being aware of their needs and feelings have been, and continue to be, generally devalued by society, Carol Gilligan, like Miller, argues that caring is a source of human strength. Gilligan, a psychologist, was involved in teaching a course on moral development at Harvard with Lawrence Kohlberg, the developer of an influential theory on the stages of human moral development. This theory, however, was based on work done exclusively with boys and men. In Kohlberg's theory, the highest stage of moral judgement is reached when an individual judges moral issues on the basis of self-chosen principles and standards of justice based on universal ethical principles and on the ideals of reciprocity and human equality. Most people do not reach this stage, but remain at the stage below this one, where an individual decides moral issues on the basis of maintaining social order (level 4) or being concerned about the needs and concerns of others (level 3).[80] Gilligan's very influential and pioneering work in the area of women's moral development began when she noticed that more women than men were dropping the course she was teaching with Kohlberg. In following up on this observation, she interviewed several of the dropouts and discovered that some of the moral conflicts being experienced by these women did not fit Kohlberg's moral development framework.

She began a series of studies to explore concepts of self and morality and experiences of conflict and choice. In her interviews she heard what she calls a 'different voice' from the one emphasized in Kohlberg's work. Although she says the different voice is not gender-specific, in her work she traces it primarily through what women have to say. The dominant themes of the two different voices she heard are those of responsibilities (care) and rights (justice), which are heard most clearly in the voices of women and men, respectively. (Gilligan's studies epitomize the work in sex-differences research that focuses on the differences rather than the similarities between women and men.) Gilligan argues that caring for others is a source of human moral strength. Rather than being a lower step on the hierarchy of moral development, caring, she argues, exists *beside* justice, with moral judgements depending upon the context of the moral problem.[81]

In addition to making audible and revaluing women's voices, Gilligan's research method – using intensive interviews and asking people how they defined moral problems, what experiences they construed as moral conflicts, and asking them to resolve moral dilemmas – clearly provides a model of a feminist research methodology. That is, the participants' experiences and perceptions inform, direct, and provide the context and data for understanding the process of making moral decisions. This qualitative approach to exploring areas in which not a great deal is known is being used very fruitfully by feminist psychologists to augment our knowledge of women's lives and experiences. (It is this aspect of Gilligan's work that Lorraine Code finds especially innovative in her discussion of *In a Different Voice* in the chapter on feminist theory.) Gilligan and her colleagues have continued their work to study the development of the two moral voices and the sense of self that appears correlated with them. Their research with children, adolescents, and adults (both female and male) is providing a mapping of the moral domain that challenges existing theories of development. As well they have been involved in a project on the development of girls that has a practical end in attempting actively to help girls weather the crises occasioned by adolescence.[82]

Other researchers using a co-operative method similar to that of Gilligan and her colleagues employed an intensive interview/case study approach with "disadvantaged and forgotten women," who are seldom represented in academic research, as well as with more privileged women. The purpose of the study was "to explore with women their experience and problems as learners and knowers as well as to review their past histories for concepts of the self and relationships with others."[83]

From the portions of the interviews that were designed to elicit information on the women's assumptions about the nature of truth, knowledge, and authority, the researchers grouped women's perspectives on knowing into five major categories. That is, they identified five different ways that the women in their study experienced themselves as knowing. Then they went back to the interviews and provided the context for each of the women in the various categories. The five categories of knowing identified in the study are: (1) silence, a state in which the woman experiences herself as mindless and voiceless, and at the mercy of external authority; (2) received knowledge a position in which the woman cannot create knowledge on her own but can receive and reproduce knowledge from external authorities; (3) subjective knowledge, a state from which truth and knowledge are conceived of as personal, private, and subjectively known; (4) procedural knowledge, a position in which women are invested in learning and applying objective procedures for obtaining and communicating knowledge; and (5) constructed knowledge, a position from which all knowledge is viewed as contextual, with women experiencing themselves as creators of knowledge, and valuing both subjective and objective strategies for knowing.[84] The analyses of women's ways of knowing using the words and experiences of women are extremely rich, insightful, and moving. The researchers also provide suggestions for educators on how to help women develop their own voices as they learn. They argue that these authentic voices will develop:

> if they [educators] emphasize connection over separation, understanding and acceptance over assessment, and collaboration over debate; if they accord respect to and allow time for the knowledge that emerges from first hand experience; if instead of imposing their own expectations and arbitrary requirements, they encourage students to evolve their own patterns of work based on the problems they are pursuing.[85]

Psychologists and researchers are learning a great deal from listening to women's voices and hearing what it is *they* are saying about their ways of being and doing. At the same time, they are also recognizing the value of women's concern for and connectedness with others and seeing it for the strength it is both for themselves and for their societies. New directions will continue to be charted in the psychology of women, and some of the earlier ones will be abandoned. But at this time the basis of a psychology of women, which is also *for* women, seems to have been firmly established.

Conclusion

Psychology has progressed a great deal since 1969, when Naomi Weisstein asserted that psychology does not know what women are really like, what they need, and what they want. At that time psychoanalytic theory still provided a description of and prescription for women's development based on the fact that they differed anatomically from men. This very restricting formulation, which provided a 'scientific' explanation for myths about women, has been and continues to be very influential. Other psychological research on women over the decades has, consciously or unconsciously, reinforced the views that women were inferior, aberrant, sick, and/or the cause of a number of problems experienced by their husbands or children. Over the years, voices have been raised against psychology's prevailing views on women, but it was not until the 1970s that the feminist critique of psychology, its methods, and its practices began to be heard and translated into concrete policy changes and practices. In the 1970s a new psychology of women began to evolve out of the feminist critique of psychology, which has also begun to transform many of the other subfields of psychology. Research on women, feminist psychoanalytic reinterpretations of many aspects of women's lives, and debunking psychology's beliefs about women are all part of the knowledge-base of what we now call the psychology of women. But for many feminist psychologists the goal is not only to construct a gynocentric psychology of women that is firmly grounded in the diversity of women's lived experiences, but also to transform psychology itself to more fully represent human experience.[86]

There has been a great deal learned from and about women in the last twenty-five years, and much of the activity of feminist psychologists has had an impact on psychology generally, as discussed in a recent issue of the *Psychology of Women Quarterly* dedicated to an evaluation of women's heritage in psychology.[87] Although much has been accomplished in a relatively short time, a continuing challenge is to maintain the momentum and make audible the voices of women, in addition to those of men, in constructing a psychology that represents the experiences of both halves of the human experience.

Joanna B. Boehnert

NOTES

1. Naomi Weisstein, "Woman as Nigger," *Psychology Today* 3, no.5 (1969), 20.
2. Sigmund Freud was the creator of the psychoanalytic method by which earlier memories, wishes, and fears hidden from memory are made conscious. He also formed a "school" around this method that attracted many students, several of whom subsequently broke with Freud and established their own schools of psychoanalysis.
3. *Psychoanalytic therapists* emphasize the importance of childhood experience in determining personality structures and the power of mental events to determine human behaviour. Their therapy thus focuses upon recovering these events from the unconscious mind. *Humanistic therapists* assume that individuals have great potential for growth, creativity, and spontaneity and are free to make choices. These therapists focus upon present behaviour and the individual's ability to change aspects of her/his life. There are more than a hundred different varieties of psychotherapy, each with its own program of treatment and outcome goals.
4. A description of the theory can be found in most introductory psychology textbooks, but the original formulation is in Sigmund Freud, *Three Essays on the Theory of Sexuality* (1905) (New York: Avon Books, 1965).
5. Sigmund Freud, "Femininity," in *The Standard Edition of the Complete Psychological Works of Sigmund Freud*, Vol. XXII (London: Hogarth Press, 1964), 125.
6. Ibid., 128.
7. Freud did discuss two other possible, but abnormal, outcomes for girls. First, she might have such envy for the penis (and dissatisfaction with her clitoris) that she is led to repress all sexual impulses, thus leading to neurotic problems later in life. And second, her refusal to accept that she has been castrated can lead to a masculinity complex. The fantasy of being a man might then lead to homosexuality and compel her to act as a man. Ibid., 126.
8. Ibid., 134. Freud also goes on to say, "We also regard women as weaker in their social interests and as having less capacity for sublimating their instincts than men."
9. Ibid., 132. Two other articles by Freud that deal specifically with female development are "Some Psychological Consequences of the Anatomical Distinction between the Sexes" (1925) and "Female Sexuality" (1931) in *Collected Papers*, Vol.5 (New York: Basic Books, 1959), 186-197; 252-272.
10. Marcia Westkott, *The Feminist Legacy of Karen Horney* (New Haven, Conn.: Yale University Press, 1986), 5.
11. Elisabeth Young-Bruehl, *Anna Freud: A Biography* (Toronto: Summit Books, 1988). In the early days of psychoanalysis the analysing of family members, friends, and associates was accepted, but later it was not. Ibid., 114.
12. Ibid., 125.

13. Ibid., 124-126.

14. The term was used by Phyllis Chesler, *Women and Madness* (New York: Avon, 1972), 72.

15. Helene Deutsch, *The Psychology of Women: A Psychoanalytic Interpretation*, Vol.1 (New York: Bantam, 1944), 195. She said about this definition, it "indicates a function, expresses something positive, and can satisfy the feminists among us who often feel that the term 'feminine passivity' has derogatory implications."

16. Ibid., 245-285.

17. *See*: Paul Roazen, *Helene Deutsch: A Psychoanalyst's Life* (Garden City, N.Y.: Anchor Press, 1985).

18. Erickson describes the inner space as "internal organs, with vestibular access, leading to statically expectant ova." "Womanhood and the Inner Space," in Erik H. Erikson, *Identity: Youth and Crisis* (New York: Norton, 1968), 271. Erikson developed this concept from a study done with children creating play constructions. A recent study seriously challenges the concept and the results of the earlier study. See Paula J. Caplan, "Erikson's Concept of Inner Space: A Data-Based Reevaluation," *American Journal of Orthopsychiatry* 49, no.1 (1979), 100-108.

19. Erikson, "Womanhood and the Inner Space," 285.

20. Ibid., 283.

21. Ibid.

22. W.H. Masters and V.E. Johnson, *Human Sexual Response* (Boston: Little Brown, 1966).

23. Freud, "Femininity," 120.

24. Sigmund Freud, "The Aetiology of Hysteria," (1920) in Freud, *Collected Papers* (1) (New York: Basic Books, 1959), 183-219. Interestingly, in this article Freud did not once name fathers as the perpetrators.

25. Discussions of Freud's suppression of the truth of the sexual seduction of children is included in Florence Rush, *The Best Kept Secret: Sexual Abuse of Children* (Englewood Cliffs, N.J.: Prentice-Hall, 1980), 80-104, and is the focus of Jeffrey M. Masson, *The Assault on Truth: Freud's Suppression of the Seduction Theory* (New York: Penguin, 1985). In Canada, estimates are that 54 per cent of females under the age of eighteen have been sexually assaulted. See Alanna Mitchell, "Child Sexual Assault," in Connie Guberman and Margie Wolfe, eds., *No Safe Place: Violence against Women and Children* (Toronto: Women's Press, 1985).

26. Stephanie Shields, "Functionalism, Darwinism, and the Psychology of Women: A Study in Social Myth," *American Psychologist* 30, no.1 (1975), 739-754.

27. Ibid., 739.

28. See, for example, Sue Cox, *Female Psychology: The Emerging Self*, 2nd ed. (New York: St. Martin's Press, 1981); Juanita H. Williams, *Psychology of*

Women: Behavior in a Biosocial Context, 3rd ed. (New York: Norton, 1987); Irene H. Frieze, Jacquelynne E. Parsons, Paula B. Johnson, Diane N. Ruble, and Gail L. Zellman, *Women and Sex Roles: A Social Psychological Perspective* (New York: Norton, 1978). Two Canadian contributions to the area are Esther R. Greenglass, *A World of Difference: Gender Roles in Perspective* (Toronto: John Wiley & Sons, 1982); and Hilary M. Lips and Nina L. Colwill, *The Psychology of Sex Differences*(Englewood Cliffs, N.J.: Prentice-Hall, 1978).

29. Karen Horney, "The Flight from Womanhood," in *Feminine Psychology* (New York: Norton, 1973), 54-70.

30. Williams, *Psychology of Women*, 77.

31. Westkott, *Feminist Legacy of Karen Horney*, 5.

32. Clara M. Thompson, *On Women* (New York: New American Library, 1971).

33. For example, the Canadian Psychological Association (CPA) set up a task force in 1975. Its "Report of the Task Force on the Status of Women in Canadian Psychology," *Canadian Psychological Review* 18, no.1 (1977), contained almost a hundred recommendations, many of which have been implemented. In 1976 an interest group on women and psychology was formed, which became a section of the CPA in 1980. In 1980, Guidelines for Therapy and Counselling with Women were introduced. A committee on the status of women was made a standing committee of the CPA board of directors to implement the task force recommendations, and a psychologist's guide to the conduct of non-sexist research was published and approved by several CPA bodies.

34. See Jeri D. Wine, "Models of Human Functioning: A Feminist Perspective," *International Journal of Women's Studies* 8, no. 2 (1985), 183-192.

35. Matina S. Horner "Toward an Understanding of Achievement Related Conflicts in Women," in Rhoda K. Unger and Florence L. Denmark, eds., *Woman: Dependent or Independent Variable?* (New York: Psychological Dimensions, 1975). *See also*: David W. Tresemer, *Fear of Success* (New York: Plenum, 1977); and Martha T.S. Mednick, Sandra S. Tangri, and Lois W. Hoffman, eds., *Woman and Achievement: Social and Motivational Analyses* (New York: John Wiley & Sons, 1975).

36. *See*: Haim G. Ginott, *Between Parent and Child: New Solutions to Old Problems* (New York: Macmillan, 1965), 167-177.

37. Cited by Olga E. Favreau, "Sex Bias in Psychological Research," *Canadian Psychological Review*, 18, no.1 (1977), 56-65.

38. Eleanor E. Maccoby and Carol N. Jacklin, *The Psychology of Sex Differences* (Stanford, Cal.: Stanford University Press, 1974). They provide a summary of their results in Eleanor E. Maccoby and Carol N. Jacklin, "Myth, Reality and Shades of Gray: What We Know and Don't Know about Sex Differences," *Psychology Today* 8, no.7 (1974), 109-112.

39. Christine Gorman, "Sizing up the Sexes," *Time*, January 20, 1992, 36-43.

40. For example, see Paula J. Caplan, Gail M. MacPherson, and Patricia Tobin,

"Do Sex-Related Differences in Spatial Abilities Exist? A Multilevel Critique with New Data," *American Psychologist* 40, no. 7 (1985), 786-799.

41. An interesting *Nova* program called "The Pinks and the Blues" from the early 1980s provides a wealth of information on this issue. A good discussion is included in Greenglass, *A World of Difference*, 33-46. See also Jeffrey Z. Rubin, Frank J. Provenzano, and Zella Luria, "The Eye of the Beholder: Parents' Views on Sex of Newborns," *American Journal of Orthopsychiatry* 44, no.4 (1974), 512-519.

42. In her review of the sex-differences literature included in her CPA presidential address, Sandra Pyke concluded, "The bottom line with respect to the study of sex differences might well be: never has so much been said by so many about so little." S.W. Pyke, "Confessions of a Reluctant Ideologist," *Canadian Psychology* 23, no. 3 (1982), 125-134. One of the four themes around which Margaret W. Matlin, *The Psychology of Women* (New York: Holt, Rinehart and Winston, 1987) has written her text is: "Women show a wide range of variation from each other in their psychological characteristics, their life choices, and their responses to biological events."

43. The terms "sex" and "gender" are often used interchangeably, but those who attempt to make a distinction between them use "sex" to refer to the biologically based categories of male and female and "gender" to refer to the psychological features associated with the biological events.

44. P.A. Goldberg, "Are Women Prejudiced Against Women?" *Transaction* 5, no. 5 (1968), 28-30.

45. *See*: Inge K. Broverman, Donald M. Broverman, Frank E. Clarkson, Paul S. Rosenkrantz, and Susan R. Vogel, "Sex-Role Stereotypes and Clinical Judgments of Mental Health," in Unger and Denmark, *Woman: Dependent or Independent Variable? See also*: Chapter 3 in Kay Deux, *The Behavior of Women and Men* (Monterey, Cal.: Brooks/Cole, 1976).

46. *See*: Stanley Milgram, *Obedience to Authority: An Experimental View* (New York: Harper Colophon, 1974). For the influence of expectations on behaviour, *see* R. Rosenthal, *Experimenter Effects in Behavioral Research* (New York: Appleton-Century Crofts, 1966).

47. The term "maternal deprivation" was introduced into the literature in 1966 by John Bowlby. *See*: Barbara Ehrenreich and Deidre English, *For Her Own Good: 150 Years of the Experts' Advice to Women* (New York: Anchor Press, 1979). "Schizophrenogenic mother" was first used by Frieda Fromm-Reichmann and was cited by Loren R. Mosher and John G. Gunderson, "Special Report: Schizophrenia, 1972," in David Rosenhan and Perry London, *Theory and Research in Abnormal Psychology*, 2nd ed. (Toronto: Holt, Rinehart and Winston, 1975).

48. Paula J. Caplan and Ian Hall-McCorquodale, "Mother-Blaming in Major Clinical Journals," *American Journal of Orthopsychiatry* 55, no.3 (1985), 345-353; and Cathryn Haig, "Mother-Blaming in Major Family Therapy

Journals: A Content Analysis," unpublished M.A. thesis (University of Guelph), 1988.

49. In the introductory psychology textbook *Psychology Today: An Introduction,* 5th ed. (New York: Random House, 1983), 405, and the same text, 6th ed., (1986), 342, the mother is implicated in incest because of her inability to fulfill the wife role or her failure to stop the incest.

50. For a discussion of some of the consequences of this belief, *see* Paula J. Caplan, *The Myth of Women's Masochism* (New York: E.P. Dutton, 1985).

51. *See*: Chesler, *Women and Madness*; Dorothy E. Smith and Sara J. David, eds., *Women Look at Psychiatry* (Vancouver: Press Gang, 1975); Helen Levine, "The Personal is Political: Feminism and the Helping Professions," in Geraldine Finn and Angela Miles, eds., *Feminism in Canada: From Pressure to Politics* (Montreal: Black Rose Books, 1982); P. Susan Penfold and Gillian A. Walker, *Women and the Psychiatric Paradox* (Montreal: Eden Press, 1983).

52. "Guidelines for Therapy and Counselling with Women," *Canadian Psychology* 21, no. 4(1980), 185-186.

53. Judith M. Avis, "Deepening Awareness: A Private Study Guide to Feminism and Family Therapy," *Journal of Psychotherapy and the Family* 3, no.4 (1988), 13-46.

54. Some of the books written by those who have pioneered in this movement are: Hogie Wyckoff, *Solving Problems Together* (New York: Grove Press, 1980); Sheila Ernst and Lucy Goodison, *In Our Own Hands: A Book of Self-Help Therapy* (London: The Women's Press, 1985); and Women's Counselling Referral and Educational Centre, *A Handbook for Women Starting Groups* (Toronto: WCREC, 1984).

55. In the mid-1980s I audited a graduate course in feminist issues in counselling and psychotherapy. I was surprised to learn that the material we read and discussed was totally new for most of the students. A majority of them claimed that such ideas were never mentioned in their other counselling courses or in their work settings.

56. *See*: Mary B. Parlee, "Psychology and Women," *Signs: Journal of Women in Culture and Society* 5, no.1 (1979), 121-133.

57. *See*: Margrit Eichler, *The Double Standard: A Feminist Critique of Feminist Social Science* (London: Croom Helm, 1980); Cannie Stark-Adamec and Meredith Kimball, "Science Free of Sexism: A Psychologist's Guide to the Conduct of Nonsexist Research," *Canadian Psychology* 25, no. 1 (1984), 23-34; Margrit Eichler and Jeanne Lapointe, *On the Treatment of the Sexes in Research* (Ottawa: SSHRC, 1985); Margrit Eichler, *Non-Sexist Research Methods: A Practical Guide* (Boston: Allen & Unwin, 1988); and Letitia Anne Peplon and Eva Conrad, "Beyond Nonsexist Research: The Perils of Feminist Methods in Psychology," *Psychology of Women Quarterly* 13, no. 4 (1989), 379-400.

58. Some feminists point out that knowledge cannot be value-free and also argue that it cannot be objective. Others believe that value-freedom can be separated from objectivity and that feminists *must* aim for objectivity in their research. See Eichler, *Non-Sexist Research Methods*, 11-14.

59. *See*: Meredith M. Kimball, "Developing a Feminist Psychology of Women: Past and Future Accomplishments," *Canadian Psychology* 27, no.3 (1986), 248-259.

60. *See*: Jeri D. Wine "Gynocentric Values and Feminist Psychology," in Finn and Miles, eds., *Feminism in Canada*; and Liz Stanley and Sue Wise, *Breaking Out: Consciousness and Feminist Research* (London: Routledge and Kegan Paul, 1983).

61. *See*: Wine, "Gynocentric Values."

62. Ibid., 74-79.

63. *See*: Hannah Lerman, "From Freud to Feminist Personality Theory: Getting Here from There," *Psychology of Women Quarterly* 10, no. 1(1986), 1-18.

64. Ibid., 6.

65. Two other writers, not discussed here, who fall into this group are: Dorothy Dinnerstein, *The Mermaid and the Minotaur: Sexual Arrangements and Human Malaise* (New York: Harper Colophon, 1976); and Evelyn F. Keller, *Reflections on Gender and Science* (New Haven, Conn.: Yale University Press, 1985).

66. Juliet Mitchell, *Psychoanalysis and Feminism: Freud, Reich, Laing and Women* (New York: Vintage Books, 1974).

67. Dinnerstein's book is one of these but the more influential analysis was provided by Nancy Chodorow, *The Reproduction of Mothering: Psychoanalysis and the Sociology of Gender* (Berkeley: University of California Press, 1978).

68. Chodorow, *The Reproduction of Mothering*.

69. Ibid., 218-219.

70. The term was introduced by Adrienne Rich, "Compulsory Heterosexuality and Lesbian Existence," *Signs: A Journal of Women in Culture and Society* 5, no.4(1980), 631-660.

71. Susan Krieger, "Lesbian Identity and Community: Recent Social Science Literature," *Signs: A Journal of Women in Culture and Society* 8, no.1(1982), 91-108 (95).

72. Ibid., 93.

73. Boston Lesbian Psychologies Collective, *Lesbian Psychologies: Explorations and Challenges* (Urbana: University of Illinois Press, 1987), 1-2.

74. Ibid., 12.

75. See: *Resources for Feminist Research/ Documentation sur la recherche feministe*, 19, nos. 3 & 4(1990). The theme for the issue is confronting heterosexuality.

76. Jeri D. Wine, "Toward a Feminist Standpoint for Psychology," paper presented at Association for Women in Psychology conference, New York City, 1985.

77. See: Sandra L. Bem, "The Measurement of Psychological Androgyny," *Journal of Consulting and Clinical Psychology* 42, no. 2(1974), 155-162; and Pyke, "Confessions of a Reluctant Ideologist."

78. Jean B. Miller, *Toward a New Psychology of Women*, 2nd ed. (Boston: Beacon Press, 1986).

79. Wine talks of relationality, which she says "refers to consciousness of the necessary interdependence of human beings, to a sense of connectedness to others, to awareness of one's embeddedness in human, social and historical contexts, to the maximization of well-being for all persons, and to commitment to nonviolence." In "Gynocentric Values."

80. Lawrence Kohlberg, "The Child as a Moral Philosopher," *Psychology Today* 2, no. 4(1968), 24-30.

81. Carol Gilligan, *In a Different Voice: Psychological Theory and Women's Development* (Cambridge, Mass.: Harvard University Press, 1982), and "Why Should a Woman be More like a Man?" *Psychology Today* 16, no. 6(1982), 68-77. For criticisms of the work see Linda K. Kerber, Catherine G. Greeno and Eleanor E. Maccoby, Zella Luria, Carol B. Stack, and Carol Gilligan, "On *In a Different Voice*: An Interdisciplinary Forum," *Signs: A Journal of Women in Culture and Society* 11, no. 2(1986), 304-333.

82. Carol Gilligan, Janice Victoria Ward, and Jill McLean Taylor, eds., *Mapping the Moral Domain* (Cambridge, Mass.: Harvard University Press, 1988); and Francine Prose, "Confident at 11, Confused at 16," *New York Times Magazine,* January 7, 1990, 22-25, 37-38, 40, 45-46.

83. Mary F. Belenky, Blythe M. Clinchy, Nancy R. Goldberger, and Jill M. Tarule, *Women's Ways of Knowing: The Development of Self, Voice, and Mind* (New York: Basic Books, 1986), 11.

84. Ibid., 15.

85. Ibid., 229. The terms "connection" and "separation" in the quote refer to how the individual comes to know the "truth" about something. For a connected knower, the truth or understanding emerges from putting oneself into the other's position and developing an understanding from immersion in, for example, the play or the problem. There is a relationship of care between the knower and what is to be known. The individual who is a separated knower learns the impersonal procedures for establishing the truth, that is, learns the rules for how things are done in a particular subject-area. Universities typically emphasize separated learning.

86. Martha T. Mednick, "Currents and Futures in American Feminist Psychology: State of the Art Revisited," *Psychology of Women Quarterly* 15, no. 4(1991), 611-621.

87. Agnes N. O'Connell and Nancy Felipe Russo, eds., "Women's Heritage in Psychology: Origins, Development, and Future Directions," *Psychology of Women Quarterly* 15, no. 4(1991).

SUGGESTED READINGS

Adams, Mary Louise, Helen Lenskyj, Philinda Masters, and Melanie Randell, eds., "Confronting Heterosexuality," *Resources for Feminist Research/Documentation sur la Recherche Feministe* 19, nos. 3&4 (1990), whole issue.

Belenky, Mary Field, Blythe McVicker Clinchy, Nancy Rule Goldberger, and Jill Mattuck Tarule, *Women's Ways of Knowing: The Development of Self, Voice, and Mind.* New York: Basic Books, 1986.

Boston Lesbian Psychologies Collective, ed., *Lesbian Psychologies: Explorations & Challenges.* Urbana: University of Illinois, 1987.

Caplan, Paula J., *The Myth of Women's Masochism.* New York: E.P. Dutton, 1985.

Gilligan, Carol, Janice Victoria Ward, and Jill McLean Taylor, eds., *Mapping the Moral Domain.* Cambridge, Mass: Harvard University Press, 1988.

Miller, Jean Baker, *Toward a New Psychology of Women,* 2nd ed. Boston: Beacon Press, 1986.

O'Connell, Agnes N., and Nancy Felipe Russo, eds., "Women's Heritage in Psychology: Origins, Development, and Future Directions," *Psychology of Women Quarterly* 15, no. 4 (1991), whole issue.

Penfold, P. Susan, and Gillian A. Walker, *Women and the Psychiatric Paradox.* Montreal: Eden Press, 1983.

Stark-Adamec, Cannie, and Meredith Kimball, "Science Free of Sexism: A Psychologist's Guide to the Conduct of Nonsexist Research," *Canadian Psychology* 25, no.1 (1984), 23-34.

Chapter Fourteen

Assisted Reproduction: The Social Issues

≈≈≈≈≈≈≈≈≈≈≈≈≈≈≈≈≈≈≈≈≈≈≈≈≈≈≈≈≈≈≈≈≈≈≈≈

Women's dominant role in the reproduction of the species is the source of both their power and their powerlessness. Reproductive autonomy – the ability and right to control fertility – is fundamental to women's health and well-being. Reproductive technologies can empower or disempower women, depending on how they are used and on the social context in which they are used.

Reproductive technology is a very broad term. It can refer to something as simple and user-controlled as a diaphragm and to technologies as complex and physician-controlled as *in vitro* fertilization. Most reproductive technologies fall within three basic categories: those that inhibit the development of new life, those that monitor the development of new life, and those that involve the creation of new life. Those involved in the inhibition of new life are the most familiar: birth control, sterilization, and abortion. Medical advances in the monitoring of new life are more recent and involve techniques such as ultrasound, amniocentesis, chorionic villi sampling, foetal monitoring, and foetal surgery.[1]

Developments in both of these spheres – in the inhibition of new life and the monitoring of new life – have a tremendous impact on women's reproductive autonomy. Foetal surgery, for example, creates a situation where, potentially, the foetus still in a woman's uterus can be defined as a patient separate from the carrying mother. The capacity to monitor, 'correct,' and artificially sustain foetal life at increasingly earlier stages of pregnancy may, in practice, work against the individual mother's reproductive autonomy. Ruth Hubbard documents two instances in the United States where women were forced to undergo Caesarian sections through a court order.[2] The checkered health record of the Pill and I.U.D. further illustrates the extent to which the technological 'hope chest' for reproductive autonomy and choice may become a 'Pandora's box' under the prevailing social, economic, political, and medical conditions. The central question is not simply choice, but choice for whom, and under what conditions? And from what range of alternatives?

Feminist efforts in relation to reproduction have largely been devoted to ensuring women's right to avoid unwanted pregnancies and the right to plan and space pregnancies. The availability of safe and effective birth control and equal access to legal abortion have been major concerns for feminists in the past two decades.[3] More recently, the right to control the conditions of birth and the right to have access to midwives have emerged as feminist issues. All of these remain important arenas for feminist analysis and action. However, even before these issues are resolved, we are moving into an era that has and will continue to have an unprecedented impact on women's reproductive choice. The developments in the realm of assisted reproduction, those involved in the creation of new life, are the central concerns of this chapter.[4]

Artificial insemination, sperm banks, preconception contracts, *in vitro* fertilization, and related techniques including freezing of sperm, ova, and embryos are some of the developments in the field of assisted reproduction. This is a field of very rapid medical advances; fifteen years ago these techniques would have been considered to be the stuff of science fiction. Although the reporting of many of these techniques has moved beyond the medical journals to front-page news coverage, the actual procedures and the implications of their development are sometimes difficult to grasp. The media tend to sensationalize their coverage and label every new form of conception as 'test-tube.' An authentic 'test-tube' baby would require conception, gestation, and birth to occur completely outside of a woman's body; the technical term for this is 'ectogenesis.' The technology for an authentic 'test-tube' baby has yet to be fully developed, although it may not be too far off in the future. The media's inaccurate description of current procedures, however, has sown the seeds for its public reception.

Reproductive choice, once limited to concerns about avoiding or planning pregnancies, is an issue that takes on new meaning through the use of assisted reproduction procedures. New dilemmas, choices, and responsibilities accompany their introduction into society. As Lorraine Code notes in her discussion of radical feminists' concern with sexuality and reproduction, Shulamith Firestone, a radical-feminist theorist in the early 1970s, proclaimed pregnancy "barbaric" and "the freeing of women from the tyranny of their reproductive biology by every means available" as the first among other structural imperatives for women's freedom.[5] Although Firestone was not lacking in imagination, she did not foresee the complexity and depth of women's role as mothers and its links with both women's strengths and weaknesses, power and powerlessness. In concert with the issues surrounding freedom from motherhood, feminists must now analyse and understand the need to mother expressed by women who will utilize these technologies.

There is a striking absence of social and psychological research on the impact of infertility on either women or men, and infertile women argue that their plight has not been of concern to feminists.[6] Infertility is very simply the inability to reproduce oneself biologically. In the past, the discovery that a wife was 'barren' constituted grounds for divorce; and it currently elicits public sympathy as well as social stigma. The quest for fertility through assisted reproduction, which is taxing emotionally, physically, and sometimes financially, testifies to the strength of women's desire for motherhood despite few publicly sanctioned rewards for this role in our culture. Increased participation in the paid labour force and the opening of opportunities for women to enter professions, limited as they may be, have not eradicated motherhood's centrality to women's identity and self-esteem. The social reasons for this are complex: family pressures, full adult status, gender identity, and the importance of biological continuity or lineage are some of the factors that induce women (and men) to seek fertility through these costly measures. "It hurts to be infertile," as Barbara Menning states in her defence of *in vitro* fertilization.[7]

Before we can fully comprehend the implications of these procedures for women and for society in general, it is important to understand what they actually involve, who will use them, and for what reasons. Ultimately they will have an impact on all women, although they are currently used only by a small number. These technologies definitely do provide the opportunity for some women to bear children who perhaps otherwise could not do so. But they also close down some choices while introducing new pressures and dilemmas for women. A woman confronted with infertility today will feel the pressure to pursue every possible avenue to overcome or circumvent her or her partner's infertility. As with the prenatal diagnostic techniques of amniocentesis and ultrasound, which have become commonplace for many 'high-risk' women, the mere availability of various reproductive technologies may foreclose the option of *not* using them. Furthermore, the causes of infertility may be ignored because they can be bypassed technologically.

Infertility is estimated to affect up to 15 per cent of couples and is considered to be on the increase. At present, approximately one-third of all cases of infertility are attributed to women, one-third are attributed to men, and one-third are either unexplained or shared by both partners. In Canada, infertility is defined as one year of attempting to achieve pregnancy without success. The definition of fertility varies culturally; in France, for example, the definition is five years of unsuccessful attempts to achieve pregnancy. The definition of infertility itself, therefore, is socially defined and structured. Currently, assisted reproduction technologies are used only to assist couples who have fertility problems, or, in some instances, for women without a male procreative partner. However, the potential exists for these technologies to be used for other reasons. For example, a woman or couple might hire another woman to bear her or their child for a number of reasons – for convenience, economic reasons, or simply to avoid the discomforts and health concerns of pregnancy.[8]

As well as the prevalence of infertility, a number of social factors indicate that the demand for these procedures is assured and will likely increase.[9] These include: the decline in availability of children for adoption (particularly healthy white babies, and because of the difficulties and costs of international adoption); the strong emphasis in our culture on having genetically related children (which is possible with some of these technologies but not with others); late childbearing, which sometimes incurs fertility problems; the use of permanent contraceptive methods such as vasectomies or tubal ligations by individuals who later change their mind about childbearing;[10] and the increase in genetic counselling, which may forewarn potential parents about possible genetic defects in their offspring. In addition, the increase in single women who want to be mothers and in lesbian couples who want children without contact with a male promises to increase the demand for some procedures such as donor insemination.

Technically there are two major categories of assisted reproduction technologies: artificial insemination and *in vitro* fertilization. A fundamental technical difference between these two procedures is that artificial insemination is potentially a very simple procedure not necessarily requiring medical assistance. Artificial insemination simply replaces sexual intercourse, and fertilization occurs within the body. In *in vitro* fertilization, conception occurs outside a woman's body in a petri dish (*in vitro* is latin for "in glass"). For each of these two categories there are several different procedures, and in some cases they overlap and are used together. Preconception contracts, for example, might use a simple version of artificial insemination, but this is an entirely different social arrangement from donor insemination, which usually involves lawyers and physicians. It is useful to explain and analyse each procedure individually.

Artificial Insemination

Artificial insemination is the oldest, least visible, and most widespread of what we now call assisted reproduction technologies. It is arguable, given the simplicity of the procedure, whether it is appropriate to call artificial insemination a technology since it is very simply a replacement for sexual intercourse. Semen, obtained through masturbation, is inserted into a woman's vagina at the time of her ovulation. Sometimes a small cap or diaphragm-like device is used to keep the semen in place. Although most artificial insemination takes place in clinical settings, the simplicity of the procedure makes it possible for women to inseminate themselves without the assistance of physicians. Self-insemination groups, who organize the transfer of sperm from donors to women, are springing up in many countries, including Canada.[11] Since conception, gestation, and birth occur through natural processes (or as 'naturally' as pregnancies that occur through sexual intercourse), the term 'artificial' is slightly misleading. Kathleen Lahey argues, for example, that a more appropriate term is 'alternative insemination.'[12]

There are three types of artificial insemination: artificial insemination by husband or male partner (AIH), donor insemination (DI), and artificial insemination combined (AIC).[13] Artificial insemination with a husband's or partner's sperm might be used in a variety of different situations, such as when the male partner's sperm count is low or when he is undergoing treatment that might damage his sperm – such as chemotherapy. The sperm may be concentrated and treated with chemicals to increase its fertility, or frozen and stored for future use. In other instances, the female partner's cervical mucous may be reacting to her husband's sperm; to bypass the cervix, sperm is placed in the uterus. In these cases, in which a medical condition is being overcome, AIH is a treatment for infertility. In other cases, reasons for use may be socially motivated – such as its use after sperm has been treated for sex selection. In donor insemination, because the man who donates the sperm is not the woman's partner, many more complex psychological and social issues are raised. It is for these reasons that DI has had such a surprisingly long but quiet history.

Donor insemination is not a new procedure: the first recorded instance of DI occurred in the United States in 1884. When a local merchant and his wife were unable to conceive a child, they requested help from a Philadelphia physician, Dr. William Pancoast. After testing both the husband and the wife, the doctor concluded that the husband was infertile. While the woman was anaesthetized, Dr. Pancoast and some of his medical students decided to inseminate the woman with the sperm of "the best looking member of the medical class."[14] The woman became pregnant, but she was never informed about the procedure by her husband or Dr. Pancoast. Twenty-five years later, in 1909, a physician, presumably the former "best looking member of the medical class," wrote an article for a medical journal and exposed the whole incident, arousing an enormous debate in medical journals about the ethics of the procedure. Opponents of the procedure argued that it was against the laws of God and nature; that the use of another man's sperm was adulterous; that the legitimacy of the child was questionable; and that the procedure was dishonest and immoral.

Advocates perceived the possibility of improving the quality of the species (an early form of eugenics) and argued that the source of sperm was irrelevant. [15] Over one hundred years later, we have yet to resolve some of these dilemmas. The Roman Catholic church, for example, still considers donor insemination to be adulterous. Furthermore, the issue of secrecy is unresolved and the eugenic potential of DI remains problematic.

Because there is no regulation or monitoring of artificial insemination, its incidence is unknown. Estimates for the early 1980s in Canada range from 1,500 to 6,000 babies born a year through donor insemination alone. Since these estimates were made several years ago and do not include women inseminating themselves outside of clinical settings, the numbers are probably conservative. In the United States a recent survey estimates that in 1986-87, 172,000 women underwent artificial insemination with a resulting 35,000 births for AIH and 30,000 births for DI. [16] Other estimates put the total population of DI offspring at over one million. [17]

Donors are solicited from a variety of sources. A common assumption is that most donors are medical students or medical personnel, but an exploratory study of participants in donor insemination indicates a broader spectrum, varying from postal workers to accountants. [18] Donors are usually paid about $15-$75 for time and expenses, which has led George Annas to argue that sperm donors are more accurately called sperm vendors. [19] In Canada we do not pay blood donors, and there is evidence to indicate that the quality of blood is lower in countries where blood is bought and sold. [20] Payment for reproductive capacities becomes even more problematic when we look at the practice of preconception contracts. The risk of individuals conceived through DI meeting and marrying a half-sibling (unknown to each other as such) increases with the number of DI children produced by each donor. Guidelines generally suggest that donors should father no more than ten children. However, there are frequently poor adherence to professional guidelines and no method of enforcement. As well, poor record-keeping practices and inadequate follow-up procedures make it impossible to monitor the number of pregnancies, births, and the linkages between recipients and donors. One donor in an exploratory study estimated that he had donated approximately 240 times, suggesting that he would have more than ten biological children through DI.

Similarly, with the screening of donors for sexually transmitted diseases including HIV (which may result in AIDS), guidelines are rigorous but not all practising DI physicians will adhere to the guidelines. A 1987 U.S. survey reports haphazard screening of donors. Less than one-half of the physicians surveyed tested donors for HIV antibodies, one out of four did not screen for infertility, and one out of five did not screen for sexually transmitted diseases. [21] There has been no survey of Canadian DI practitioners;

however, at least two women have been infected with HIV through donor sperm. In a precedent-setting case, one woman successfully sued the physician for negligence for not informing her of the risk of acquiring HIV through the insemination. [22]

With donor insemination, the structure of the practice informs us about our attitudes towards it. Although the specifics may vary from physician to physician, the most common practice (which is supported by most legal, medical, and ethical reports) is that donors and recipients remain unknown to each other. Anonymity, it is argued, is essential to avoid emotional complications, to ensure "the stability of the family and the welfare of the child." [23] The fear that conflicting emotional ties might arise if anonymity is not protected is based on the assumption that biologically linked individuals may develop curiosity or other feelings about each other that could threaten the coherence of the family unit created through DI. For example, DI offspring may become interested in the identity of their biological father, the DI mother might become curious about the man who is the biological father of her DI child, or the infertile husband may feel threatened by the sperm donor who was able to impregnate his wife when he was unable to. Consequently, the couple or woman usually have no information about the donor, and the donor is usually not told whether a pregnancy or birth has occurred. Usually there is an attempt to 'match' the physical characteristics of the sperm donor to the DI mother's partner (if present) or to herself. Women using self-insemination (outside of clinical settings) may choose to know or not to know their donors.

This issue of anonymity, in itself, is a momentous shift in reproductive relations. Although neither marriage nor parenthood has always been based on individual choice – our choices are socially structured in any event – neither to know nor to choose the biological father of one's child is an unprecedented social act. In the case of donor insemination, physicians are choosing the reproductive partner, the man who will be the biological 'father' of a DI mother's child.

The practice of DI is surrounded by secrecy, anonymity, and the confidentiality of the doctor-patient relationship. Most physicians advise the parents that there is no reason to tell the children or any other family members about the child's origins through DI. In this respect, DI anonymity is reminiscent of early adoption practice. Unlike adoption, however, DI anonymity provides the possibility to heterosexual couples of 'passing' as biologically linked parents. Single or lesbian DI mothers usually have to explain their child's origin in some way. The explanation of DI may be preferable to the assumption of a 'one night stand.' There is collusion among participants in the procedure to protect the social father and the couple from the stigma of male infertility as well as an attempt to protect the child from feeling 'different.' However, problems arise for a variety of reasons. In some instances the offspring of DI find out about their origins, and usually not under the best of circumstances. As with most secrets, it is most likely to be divulged during periods of emotional stress and conflict such as marital crises, divorce, or death.

In the United States there are already two groups called Donor's Off-spring and HOPE that are asserting their right to know the other half of their biological heritage. This is generally a problem because there is no legal responsibility for the physician to keep records linking the donor, recipient(s), and offspring. Even when records are kept, they are defined as medical records; hence they are the exclusive property of the physicians. In addition, sperm donors participate in DI on the understanding that their identities will remain anonymous. There are, as yet, no laws to protect the participants in DI except in Quebec, where the child is legally considered to be affiliated with the social father, and in the Yukon, where donors are protected from possible legal suits by offspring or recipients. In 1985 the Ontario Law Reform Commission undertook a major study of the legal problems posed by assisted reproduction and proposed amendments to legislation. However, despite the fact that its study purports to protect the "best interests of the child," the report agrees with most other reports in viewing donor anonymity as essential to the success of the procedure. Some individuals conceived through DI may have no interest in knowing the identity of their biological father. However, given the current increase in genetic counselling, access to medical information on sperm donors may be considered important by some, and increasingly so by recipients.

Secrecy about a procedure as significant as this can be experienced as a burden. Among the married DI mothers who participated in an explorat-ory study,[24] those who adhered to secrecy all experienced a cost in keeping the donor insemination secret. Although generally described by respon-dents as 'liveable,' feelings of isolation, a desire to know about the experi-ence of other DI recipients, and painful reminders (usually through com-ments about the physical resemblance of their DI children) were reported. The majority, however, found that secrecy was not feasible and were faced with difficult questions about who, how, and when to tell about their use of DI. For example, one woman's husband had been institutionalized (for mental illness) shortly after the birth of their DI son. Under stress, she quickly told friends and family that her husband was not the 'real' father. Her son (aged eight at the time of the interview) was now asking questions about this unknown, but somehow 'real' father. Understandably, she was confused and frightened by her son's interest in knowing more about his biological father and was uncertain whether any information could be obtained.

In medical literature, DI is described as a treatment for male infertility. It does not, however, cure infertility but circumvents it through the use of another man's sperm. Ironically, but not surprisingly, it is the fertile woman who becomes the patient. Despite the simplicity of the procedure, when it is practised in clinical settings it is frequently accompanied by other medical procedures to increase efficiency and the success rate. The presumably fertile woman may undergo a series of tests to ensure that she is fertile and that sperm is not 'wasted' on a woman with her own fertility problems. These tests can include hysterosalpingograms (a procedure in which dye is injected into the fallopian tubes and uterus), endometrial biopsies, drugs to regulate her ovulation, and possibly drugs to sustain her pregnancy. Several DI mothers in my study described the testing as the worst part. In addition, the insemination itself was described as difficult. Finding a physician, arranging to take time off work, and co-ordinating the schedules of up to four individuals (donor, if fresh sperm is used; partner, if present; mother; and physician) to ovulation time was consistently reported as stressful. If pregnancy was not achieved within a few months, the pressure and stress were described as intolerable. Women who choose to inseminate themselves outside of clinical settings avoid additional medical procedures. Yet all DI mothers share the legal and social ambiguities arising from this shift in reproductive relations.

Preconception Contracts

Preconception contracts are what is popularly referred to as "surrogate motherhood" – a misnomer since "surrogate" means substitute and the so-called "surrogate" is the biological mother of the child. A preconception contract is a much more socially visible procedure than is donor insemination. This is partially because paternity is a less visible event than maternity. It is also a more controversial social arrangement because biological motherhood is a more complex and involved relationship than biological fatherhood. Physiologically, fatherhood (in DI) involves sperm donation, and motherhood (in preconception contracts) involves nine months gestation in which a relationship develops with the baby-to-be. Preconception contracts have captured the attention of the media more than any other assisted reproduction technology. This arrangement is generally used by couples when the wife is infertile. The husband's sperm is used to artificially inseminate a woman (the contractual mother) who agrees (contractually) to surrender the child at birth and who is generally paid a fee for her 'services.' The method has the potential, however, to be used by anyone willing and able to pay a woman to bear a child for them for any reason.

Several questions are raised by the practice of preconception contracts. It is somewhat reminiscent of wet-nursing, when poor working-class women were used to provide breast milk for babies of wealthier women.

By logical extension, it sets the groundwork for some women to become breeders for others – with some contractual mothers being more highly valued according to prevailing standards of beauty or intelligence. Margaret Atwood's novel *The Handmaid's Tale* provides a dystopian vision of this possibility. Indeed, as Shelagh Wilkinson argues in her chapter, Atwood, in *The Handmaid's Tale,* is describing the ultimate patriarchal control of women's sexuality, and, hence, of their reproductive capacities.

Preconception contracts began as an organized practice in the mid-1970s.[25] So far, there are no organized preconception services in Canada. However, media reports indicate that these services do exist as an underground practice, and that Canadians are participating in preconception arrangements (both as contractual mothers and commissioning couples) through U.S. organizations. A 1988 U.S. study reports that fifteen organizations provide the services and concludes that about six hundred arrangements have occurred to date. The report estimates that a typical contract involves a $10,000 fee for the 'contractual mother' and an additional $20,000 to $30,000 for living expenses, medical expenses, and attorney's fees. In these situations about one dollar in four is estimated actually to go to the woman carrying the child.[26] However alarmed we may be at the idea of women bearing children for a fee, it is the lawyers who are making a profit from this practice.

In contrast to donor insemination, the recipients of preconception services generally pick their contractual mother out of a catalogue and may have contact with her during the pregnancy. (This varies according to the particular organization.) There has been a mixed response from the feminist community about preconception contracts, but whatever the response it has been strongly stated. On the one hand it is argued that it is exploitation, similar to prostitution or concubinage, and that the contractual mother is acting as a "surrogate wife" to the biological father. On the other hand some feminists have said, "Why not? Isn't it about time that women were paid for their reproductive labour?" Most paid work for women remains low-status, low-paid, and with little opportunity for advancement. The fee of $10,000 – although less than the minimum wage if calculated on an hourly basis – is still a substantial amount of money, which could alter the short-term economic circumstances of a person's life. Additionally, some contractual mothers say it provides "all the magic of pregnancy" without the responsibility of rearing a child.

To separate themselves emotionally from the child they will surrender at birth, the contractual mothers describe themselves as 'vehicles' or 'vessels.' Nevertheless, there is frequently a grief reaction (called 'transient grief') after the child is given up to the contracting couple or individual. There are already self-help groups for contractual mothers, organized to provide support after the child is surrendered. One writer posed as a contractual mother applicant to gain insight into the workings of one organization from the contractual mother's perspective. Her documentation of the experience is chilling.[27] She reports the inadequacy of screening procedures (medical and psychological), how she was discouraged from seeking independent counsel, and, in short, the company's complete control over the contractual mother.

Although it remains unclear as to what extent these arrangements are enforceable in Canada, contracts potentially divest the contractual mother of her rights over her body throughout the terms of the contract. Interventions include extensive controls over diet, lifestyle, and activities. In 1987 in the United States a contractual mother was charged with a misdemeanour for taking drugs during her pregnancy. The contractual mother may also be required to undergo medical procedures such as ultrasound or amniocentesis to ensure a 'quality product.' If the foetus is discovered to be 'defective' she may be asked to undergo an abortion late in the pregnancy and forfeit the majority or all of her fee. There is also the question of what happens if the contractual mother decides that she does not want to give up the child. In current adoption practice, the birth-mother usually has a period of approximately two weeks after birth to make her final decision. There have already been several instances of contractual mothers changing their minds about surrendering the child after birth. In addition, since the ideal contractual mother is married with children of her own, the effect of the arrangement on other family members such as her other children, husband (or partner), and parents is crucial, but remains unknown.

In the New Jersey case of Baby M, the issues that emerged exemplify the dilemmas inherent in contractual mother arrangements. The contractual mother, Mary Beth Whitehead, *did* change her mind about giving up her baby. The contracting father, William Stern, decided to fight for custody in the courts, and he won – although the case later went on to an appeal in a higher court. The trial went on for months and was reported in detail in several media. At the time of the contract, Mary Beth Whitehead was married, a full-time homemaker, and mother of two children; her husband was a sanitation worker. Despite Whitehead's initial claim that she entered the agreement because her sister was unable to conceive and she felt "empathy for childless couples who were infertile," the $10,000 must be regarded as a substantial sum for this single-income, working-class family. The Sterns, the contracting couple, were earning an estimated $90,000 between them – William Stern as a biochemist, and Elizabeth Stern as a paediatrician.

The arrangement was transparently class-bound. It is difficult, if not impossible, to imagine wealthy women having babies, fee or no fee, for poorer couples. Beyond the obvious, however, this case was loaded with class issues that stem directly from having or not having money but are less apparent than the capacity to pay $10,000 for someone to bear a child. The Sterns' money also bought them knowledge, respectability, and an excellent lawyer. They never gave a press conference without their lawyer present, and throughout this highly volatile and emotional case they projected a public image as controlled, sensible, and cool. In stark contrast, Mary Beth Whitehead 'spilled her guts' to the media, appeared 'hysterical,' 'out of control,' and hot-headed. She looked 'crazy' – that is, she looked like an unfit parent. The Sterns 'looked good' – that is, like fit parents. The Sterns might well have been equally hysterical in the privacy of their home but had the 'good sense' not to damage their public image.

The outcome of the case was predetermined in another dimension, as well. Mary Beth Whitehead cared for her baby for the first four months of her life and named her Sara. The Sterns named her Melissa. When the judge ordered temporary custody to the Sterns (four months after birth and for the duration of the extended trial), the court named the child Baby 'M.' Why 'M'? Why not Baby 'S' or more neutrally Baby 'J'? As George Annas points out, temporary custody orders almost always become permanent orders.[28] The Sterns had this temporary decision on their side from the beginning of the trial.

As well as the custody of the child, at issue in this case was the enforceability of contractual-mother contracts. At the request of William Stern, Mary Beth Whitehead signed a contract that required her to undergo amniocentesis – she did this against her own and her doctor's wishes – and to have an abortion if the foetus were deemed by the physician to be "physiologically abnormal" or determined by tests to be "genetically or congenitally abnormal." If she had conceived an "abnormal" child and aborted, she would have received $1,000. If she had refused to abort, Stern's obligation to her would have "ceased forthwith." Judge Sorkow's decision that this contract was valid and binding confirms the North American belief that 'a deal is a deal,' even when it clearly contravenes social values and legislation against exchange of money for body parts or human beings. Trafficking in humans was outlawed with slavery. The stipulation that Whitehead, like any other contractual mother, would receive her $10,000 only upon delivery of a healthy newborn eliminates any doubt about whether payment is for 'services' or for the 'product' – and the product is a child.

Finally, the manipulation of maternal ideology that accompanies the practice of preconception contracts and this specific legal precedent is of particular interest. The very success of the procedure is dependent on women conceiving, gestating, and relinquishing their children without any messy emotions like attachment, bonding, affection, and/or love. Yet these are precisely the qualities generally required of women to be good mothers; women who leave their child(ren) wear this century's scarlet letter. One mother's virtue, in other words, is another mother's crime. The signing of preconception contracts is a practice that challenges these values, and it is precisely these values that were re-examined, reneged, and tossed out as outmoded and a 'mistake' in the New Jersey courtroom. Mental health experts, some of whom had written passionately in the 1950s about the importance of maternal bonding, were called to the stand to testify that maternal bonding was really non-existent or not that important after all. Whitehead was reported to play patty-cake incorrectly with her daughter and also (incorrectly) gave Sara teddy-bears rather than pots and pans to play with.

The entire trial was the stuff of a best-seller, and several books as well as a television movie emerged after the case was over. Many dramatic scenes were revealed: Whitehead handing her baby out the back window to her husband when the Sterns arrived with the police; Whitehead fleeing to Florida with her baby; the police breaking into her mother's home there and delivering the child back to the Sterns; Stern taping telephone calls from Whitehead in which she threatens to commit suicide and take her child with her; Whitehead's ten-year-old daughter begging the police to be taken away instead of her little sister. Sara/Melissa was passed back and forth between her biological mother and biological father and will be labelled for life as a "surrogate" child. The 'best interests' of this child have already been violated, although her own response to her origins will be unknown for years to come.

In February 1988 the decision by the higher court, the Supreme Court of New Jersey, was reported. Chief Justice Robert Wilentz overturned all aspects of the earlier court's ruling with the exception of the custody ruling. Most significantly, this ruling, which will likely have an impact in other jurisdictions, rules that the contract between Whitehead and Stern was illegal because it violated the state's adoption laws concerning payment for a child. As reported in the press: "'This is the sale of a child, or at the very least, the sale of a mother's right to her child, the only mitigating factor being that one of the purchasers is the father,' the court said."[29]

Another version of preconception contracts involves IVF and embryo transfer (ET), with the "contractual mother" carrying a child genetically unrelated to her. This procedure allows the commissioning couple to preserve their genetic tie to the child and sever the genetic tie of the carrying mother. The "contractual mother," who is the gestational/biological mother but not the genetic mother, becomes a vessel to carry the child for the couple. As might be expected, there is already a U.S. case in which the biological mother changed her mind and decided to keep the child she carried for the commissioning couple. The egg and sperm of the commissioning couple were fertilized *in vitro* and the embryo implanted in the "contractual mother."

The possibility of using IVF, embryo transfer, and a preconception contract arrangement to have a child creates a situation with enormous social and ethical complexity. Although it would seem impossible to make Mary Beth Whitehead's situation any more complex, Anna Johnson's case raises even more issues.[30] Anna Johnson of Los Angeles, a single welfare mother of a three-year old, agreed to carry, birth, and surrender a child to Mark and Cristina Calvert, an insurance underwriter and a registered nurse respectively. To the issue of class, which remains similar to the Mary Beth Whitehead case, is added the issue of race. Anna Johnson is a woman of black, Native American, and Irish heritage. Mark Calvert is Caucasian and his wife Cristina is from the Philippines. To further complicate the psychological dynamics of the case, Johnson had apparently suffered two miscarriages and a stillbirth – information she withheld from the Calverts. The judge decided that the Calverts should have sole custody of the child and commented that Johnson was a 'genetic stranger' to her child.

The question of who is the mother, raised so poignantly in the Baby M case, becomes even more complex with IVF and embryo transfer. Theoretically, it could be even more complex with a third woman as an egg donor. What counts and for how much: genetics? biology? or contracts? Not surprisingly, some countries, such as France, have decided to ban preconception contracts altogether.

In Vitro Fertilization and Related Techniques

In the IVF method of assisted conception, the process moves firmly into the hands of physicians. IVF involves very sophisticated medical technology and medical expertise. The process for recipients is stressful, invasive, and financially and emotionally draining. What most people do not know when the media report with awe the birth of another IVF child is that the success rate is very low. An additional problem is that success rates may be presented in a way that disguises the low rates, such as giving "pregnancy rates" rather than how many couples have a child through this method – the "take-home baby rate." One Canadian study that presents careful results reports a pregnancy rate of 26.1 per cent and a take-home baby rate of 15 per cent.[31] Other estimates of Canadian clinics range from 3 per cent to 13 per cent.[32] The history of IVF is short, with the first successful IVF child having been born in Britain in 1978. Nevertheless, this is definitely a growth industry within the medical profession. There are already fifteen or so IVF clinics in Canada, all of them with very long waiting lists, indicating the prevalence of infertility and the willingness of couples to undergo invasive and uncertain medical treatment to achieve their own genetically linked children.

IVF was initially used when the problem of infertility was on the part of the woman, usually because her fallopian tubes were blocked. Its use has been expanded to couples where the male partner has a low sperm count. Linda Williams, in a preliminary study of IVF candidates, also found IVF being used as a diagnostic tool to define further the source of infertility.[33]

In contrast to artificial insemination, this procedure is not simple. The first step is the retrieval or 'harvesting' of the eggs (note the language of animal husbandry, where all of these techniques were first developed), which involves taking drugs to stimulate egg production, daily blood tests, pelvic examinations, and ultrasound. Then, usually, because drugs have been used to stimulate the ovaries to produce more than one egg at a time, between two to six eggs are removed surgically through a laparoscopy.[34] In the second step, the eggs and sperm (usually the woman's partner's sperm, but not necessarily) are joined in a culture dish, where fertilization may or may not take place. If fertilization does take place, the third step is the transfer of the fertilized eggs into the woman's uterus in the hope that implantation and pregnancy will ensue. Usually more than one fertilized egg is transferred to increase the possibilities of implantation. This is why IVF births frequently involve twins, triplets, or quintuplets. Fertilized eggs, technically referred to as *concepti,* may also be frozen and stored for future use by the genetic mother or another woman.

A more recent technique, very similar to IVF and ET, is called GIFT (gamete intrafallopian transfer) and can be used with women with at least one functioning fallopian tube. In this procedure, eggs are removed in the same way as with IVF but are then combined with sperm in a catheter threaded into the fallopian tube. Fertilization then occurs naturally in the woman's body – in the fallopian tube. The success rates for this procedure are reportedly much higher than with IVF – as high as 30 to 35 per cent. However, as with IVF a broad range of success rates is reported.[35]

Another version of GIFT is ZIFT, in which the egg and sperm are fused to form a zygote (hence zygote intrafallopian transfer) before transfer into the body. Other more experimental techniques include the freezing of embryos, freezing of eggs, and the micromanipulation of sperm. That is, when several embryos are available for transfer (more than three or four), rather than implant all of them, some are frozen for future use to reduce the risk of multiple pregnancies. Although this method was still considered experimental in 1988, sixty children had been born in Australia and Europe using frozen embryos.[36] When the technique of freezing eggs is perfected it will most likely supplant the freezing of embryos in order to avoid the ethical issues of freezing an already fertilized egg. Like men who are currently able to store their sperm, women who face a loss of fertility due to pelvic disease, surgery, radiation, or chemotherapy will be able to freeze their eggs for future use. The eggs could be used for themselves or for another woman.

The final technique, the micromanipulation of sperm into ova, which is still experimental, is used when a man has a low sperm count, a lot of abnormal sperm, or sperm that do not move very well (non-motile). It could also be used for sex selection. In this procedure a sperm cell is injected into an egg. In one type of micromanipulation, sperm is inserted under the egg's outer membrane with a fine glass needle. In another type the egg's outer member is etched chemically to create an opening for sperm penetration. Because these are fertilizations that could not occur otherwise, the consequences of the procedures are as yet unknown.

There are a number of medical, legal, and governmental reports that attempt to identify and resolve the problems raised by the use of all these procedures.[37] In Canada a Royal Commission has been appointed to study the issues.[38] However, we still know very little about who actually uses the technologies and what their experiences are. The legal questions alone raised by these technologies are overwhelming.[39] There is currently a wealth of legal literature that identifies the problems and attempts to resolve them. But the resolution of legal issues will not entirely settle the social problems created by the use of the procedures. Since most of these procedures are still in experimental stages, much is unknown about their short-term or long-term social implications. However, at least four social issues can be identified: the further medicalization of the reproductive process; the impact on family; the commercialization of reproductive capacities; and the potential eugenic uses of assisted reproduction technologies.

Medicalization

Among the most obvious social processes involved in the use of assisted reproduction technologies is the further medicalization of women's reproductive experience. Although reproduction requires the biological contribution of both sexes, it is notable that all of these technologies involve women becoming patients, even in the case of DI, where the woman is presumably fertile. Medicalization, as explained by Wendy Mitchinson in her chapter, is the expansion of medical expertise and influence into previously non-medical arenas of society. The medicalization of women's reproductive experience is an ongoing social process. The introduction of assisted reproduction technologies is not a bold leap into Huxley's Brave New World. Rather, it is a significant furthering of already existing social trends. The medical profession is already very involved in making decisions about reproductive matters, including the choice and distribution of most birth control methods, prenatal and postnatal care, and birthing, all of which increasingly involve reproductive technologies. The development of assisted reproduction technologies may be perceived as a logical (but extreme) extension of the 'planned parenthood' mentality pervasive in our culture. The further involvement of the medical profession provided by the development of assisted reproduction raises new questions about control and about responsibility and influence. In short, these new techniques precipitate a host of social consequences, which reflect, in a heightened manner, already existing social forces.

Society has always attempted to regulate who has sexual intercourse with whom, where, and under what conditions. Informal and sometimes formal sanctions govern sexual behaviour according to, for example, age, race, religion, class, and marital status. Before the development of assisted reproduction, conception occurred through the private, intimate interaction of two individuals – sexual intercourse between a man and a woman. All of these technologies separate the act of sexual intercourse from reproduction. This fact in itself is not necessarily problematic. However, with the exception of self-insemination, assisted reproduction technologies as practised in clinical settings move conception out of the private and into the public realm. Members of the medical profession, in other words, are now deciding who will have access to these services and, therefore, who will or will not become parents. This is not a realm of decision-making for which physicians are trained. Furthermore, the movement of conception into the public realm raises the question of whether every individual has a fundamental right to procreate and whether this right includes access to these services. The potential for discrimination exists on the grounds of class (those who can afford to pay for these services), race, marital status, and sexual preference. Most physicians will presumably attempt to uphold the cultural standard that a heterosexual couple provides the best possible parents for a child.

Family Structure

The diversity of current Canadian family structures has been documented by Margrit Eichler[40] and is discussed by Susan McDaniel in her chapter in this book. Few Canadian families conform to the presumed cultural norm of a married heterosexual couple who rear their biological offspring to adulthood. Nevertheless, the image and norm of the family persist as a normative structure. When we use the term 'parent,' we generally assume that the biological and social components of the role merge in one person.

Exceptions to this are families formed through adoption, foster-parent-hood, and step-parenting. In these situations, the term 'parent' is modified by an additional descriptor indicating some deviation from the presumed cultural norm. With adoption, for example, biological parents are referred to as birth parents and social parents are referred to as adoptive parents.

Assisted reproduction technologies make possible further diversity in family configurations. This assortment of parental roles is reflected in the current linguistic and conceptual confusion in describing these roles. With DI, fathering is split into two roles: the generally unknown biological father (sperm donor) and the social or rearing father. This family configuration presumes that the recipients are a heterosexual couple. If the DI mother is single there will be no rearing or social father. If she is part of a lesbian couple, then the second parent will be another mother (a co-mother) who is not biologically linked to the child. The biological father is in all cases the possibly unknown sperm donor.

The role of 'mother' – traditionally the genetic, uterine, and social mother of a child – is potentially fragmented into six different roles through the use of one or a combination of assisted reproduction technologies: (1) an egg donor – a woman who provides an egg but does not carry or rear the child; (2) a uterine mother – a woman who provides the gestational environment for a child who is not hers genetically, and who will not rear the child; (3) an egg and uterine mother (popularly referred to as a "surrogate" mother or contractual mother) – a woman who is the biological mother, but who will not rear the child (a situation somewhat analogous to a birthmother who gives up a child for adoption at birth); (4) a uterine and social mother – a woman who is the recipient of an egg donation; (5) an egg (or genetic) and social mother – a woman whose fertilized (*in vitro*) egg is carried by another woman who returns the child after birth; and (6) a social mother, not genetically related to the child – the recipient of a preconception contract arrangement. This situation is similar to that of an adoptive mother or stepmother or any woman who raises children to whom she is not genetically related. An even more complex picture emerges when we consider that each of the individuals involved may marry, divorce, and remarry – possibly even several times. Although not all of these roles are socially unprecedented, the manner in which they are created is new. The full implications of this fragmentation of women's reproductive and mothering experience have yet to be realized.

A child conceived through a combination of these procedures could potentially have five parents: two fathers and three mothers. The two fathers are the sperm donor or biological father and the social father. The three possible mothers are the egg donor, the uterine mother, and the

mother who rears the child (the social mother). Again, these family con-
stellations are based on the presumption that the recipients are a
heterosexual couple. Even more possibilities emerge when the recipients
are single or in lesbian couples.

The practice of freezing eggs, sperm, or embryos, technically referred
to as 'cryopreservation,' further complicates our common understanding
of the process of reproduction. Conception, for example, could occur in a
petri dish in Australia. The embryo could be frozen, stored, and trans-
ported to Canada, where it could be implanted in a woman who (if pregnancy is successful) could give birth to a child, conceived many years earlier, to whom she has no genetic ties and whose genetic parents may no
longer be alive. These possibilities alter both our temporal and geographical assumptions about the boundaries of the reproductive process, as well
as the common cultural assumption that the parents of a child are genetically linked.

The rights and responsibilities of gamete (sperm or egg) donors, uterine donors, contractual mothers, and social parents can be legislated. Yet
the image of the family as both socially and biologically linked is strong in
our culture. The consequences for participants in assisted reproduction
procedures, people who are linked solely through biological ties, is
unknown. The feelings, for example, of a woman who provides an egg, her
uterus, or both (as in the case of preconception contracts) to create a child
she may not be involved with rearing are unstudied. In instances in which
contractual mothers change their minds about relinquishing their child,
some develop a relationship similar to that of an aunt, and others, depending upon the policy of the agency, have no contact with the child after
birth. The feelings of the infertile wife in a couple who utilize a contractual
mother are also largely unknown. She may feel jealous of her husband's
'surrogate wife,' who can fulfill his need for his own biological child, or the
two women may develop a close relationship if the arrangement is successful. A woman who donates an egg for another woman who will carry and
rear a child takes on a role somewhat similar to that of a sperm donor.[41]
The potential exists, therefore, for women to 'father' children by providing only genetic material, as do men who donate sperm or biological
fathers who do not assist in rearing their offspring.

Research on children who are adopted indicates that they frequently
desire information about their biological heritage and may search for their
biological parents in order to complete their sense of identity. Individuals
conceived through one or a variety of assisted reproduction procedures
that disassociate their biological and social parentage may react similarly.
If accurate records are kept linking biologically related individuals, and
if participants have access to these records (both of which factors are
questionable at this time), the bureaucratic and social consequences are

formidable. Other issues include the unknown responses of other family members, such as the biological grandparents of DI or preconception contracts (the parents of the donor or contractual mother), aunts, uncles, and siblings of children in both the recipient and donor families.

The success of families created through assisted reproduction rests, to some extent, not on the technologies themselves but on our capacity as a society to redefine what constitutes family. In concert with other changes in family forms, assisted reproduction technologies challenge the sanctity and increasingly mythological image of the biologically linked nuclear family as normative. If the emphasis on the blood-tied nuclear family persists, it is likely that a preference will develop for technologies that preserve the genetic links of parents and offspring wherever possible. This emphasis could result in the use of more expensive and invasive methods over simpler, less costly procedures. For example, in the case of a male with a low sperm count, IVF or the micromanipulation of sperm may be used instead of DI to preserve the genetic link, and when donor gametes are employed they will probably be used on an anonymous basis. The issues are complex and volatile; the consequences are unknown.

Commercialization

Sperm donors are paid approximately $15-$75 each ejaculate, contractual mothers are paid about $10,000, and egg donors in the United States have been paid up to $1,200. Putting a price tag on reproductive capacities has profound social implications. The children created through these technologies will eventually become adults, and they will have to come to terms with their origins. They may feel special and particularly wanted, or they may feel like a commodity, bought and sold. In either case, their creation through a commercial transaction is likely to influence their identities and is potentially stigmatizing.

There are partial social precedents for payment in relation to body parts, organs, and blood, and in spite of legal restriction baby-selling does exist. Insurance companies do establish a 'price' for the loss of an arm, leg, or other body parts. However, all of these analogies are limited because there is a crucial distinction between the maintenance of a life already in existence, the loss of a body part, the use of women's bodies for sexual services, and the payment for reproductive capacities involved in the creation of new life. The result in the last case is a new human being accompanied by new social roles for family members and, consequently, new social responsibilities. Commercialization of reproductive capacities, therefore, although not totally unprecedented, is similar to the issue of medicalization in that it furthers already existing social trends.

Commodification entails a process of evaluating and assessing a human activity or the product of a human activity according to current market forces. It also disguises the presence of the human being involved in the labour required to produce the product. Treating reproductive capacities as commodities commercializes and brings market values and processes into a realm that has previously been immune to these influences.

Eugenics

The final area of concern is the issue of eugenics, the practice of selective breeding intended to 'perfect' the human species. It is generally distinguished by two different methods: positive eugenics and negative eugenics. Positive eugenics is the attempt to increase the number of children born with 'good' characteristics; negative eugenics is the attempt to reduce the number of children born with 'bad' characteristics. An obvious problem arises in deciding what is valued as good or bad, and who is to make these decisions.

At first glance, negative eugenics would seem to be a worthwhile project. Increasingly, genetic screening can detect carriers of diseases such as Huntington's chorea, muscular dystrophy, and cystic fibrosis. Decreasing the incidence of these agonizing diseases would seem socially advantageous; however, grey areas abound. Activists in the rights for the disabled movement have pointed out that screening or aborting for 'defects' further devalues individuals considered by society to be 'defective.'[42] One particularly contentious area is the use of prenatal diagnostic techniques such as ultrasound, chorionic biopsy, or amniocentesis to identify the sex of a foetus, followed by an abortion if the sex does not accord with parental preference. Viola Roggencamp documents the incidence of this phenomenon in India, where female foetuses are overwhelmingly aborted.[43] Closer to home, a U.S. physician has set up a highly controversial clinic in Vancouver for exactly these purposes.[44]

Although the extent of this practice is unknown in Western industrialized countries, we can speculate that wherever males are valued more highly than females, female foetuses would be aborted more frequently. Research on parental sex preferences overwhelmingly indicates a preference for male over female offspring, a view held more frequently by men than women, and particularly in relation to first-borns.[45] The desire for a child of a particular sex might in itself be sexist and could potentially institutionalize sexism at a new level because, for example, first-borns are known to be high achievers. Other concerns include alterations in the sex ratio, with fewer females born than males. The consequences of this possibility can only be speculated about and include feminist concerns about gynocide.[46]

Preconception sex-selection techniques are an example of 'positive' eugenics. These are less invasive methods than postconception techniques and usually involve theories about the timing of intercourse with ovulation or the separation of X- and Y-bearing spermatozoa.[47] What was once the substance of folklore is increasingly the subject of scientific study. A U.S. company has marketed a package called "GenderChoice," available over the counter in drugstores, which the manufacturer claims has an 85 per cent success rate. The product relies on the position of sexual intercourse and the proximity of conception to a woman's ovulation time to predict the sex of a child.

The most extreme example of positive eugenics is the existence in the United States of a Nobel Prize Winner sperm bank from which women or couples of 'superior' intellectual capacities can order sperm. Contractual mothers and gamete donors may be chosen for socially valued traits perceived as genetically inherited. The underlying assumption is that genetics are the key factor in determining personality traits or capacities such as intelligence, athletic abilities, or musical talents. Australian IVF physicians are already claiming that children conceived through IVF are superior to those conceived 'normally.'[48] Statements such as these ignore the obvious influence of environment, including the particular treatment and care these very much wanted children most likely receive from their parents.

The twentieth century has seen the rise of experts advising women how to rear perfect children.[49] Assisted reproduction technologies provide the opportunity for a different level of 'quality control' in the parenting process. Similarly, prenatal diagnostic techniques provide information about a foetus previously unavailable before birth. On the basis of this knowledge a woman in her fifth month of pregnancy may have to choose whether to have an abortion or carry to term and give birth to a child she knows will be disabled – in a society that devalues the 'imperfect.' This instance of choice posed by the new reproductive technologies is a burden carried largely by individual women.

The commercialization of reproductive capacities is inextricably linked to eugenic issues. Through commercialization, the child becomes a commodity, the recipient parents become consumers, and gamete donors and contractual mothers become suppliers. Damaged or defective 'products' – babies who are not 'perfect' – will likely be unacceptable to the consumer. In a preconception contract in 1981, a handicapped child was rejected by both the contracting (presumably) biological father and by the contractual mother. Eventually, a paternity test proved the contractual mother's husband to be the biological father (this destroyed any validity the contract might have had), and the contractual mother and her husband agreed to keep the child. Other problematic instances are bound to arise in the future.

Social policy already lags far behind these rapidly developing medical advances. As the technologies become more sophisticated, the social problems they pose can become more complex – although, in some instances, advances do eliminate earlier difficulties.[50] Medical control over these technologies is already well established and is solidified by recommendations in government reports. Because it is unlikely that a technology will be withdrawn once it has been introduced, all of the technologies are probably here to stay, at least until further technological developments replace them. In cultivating a critical approach to new reproductive technologies, we must consider the point that already scarce health resources are being utilized to develop these technologies. As a result it appears that fewer health resources are being channelled into research concerning the causes of infertility.

As with any new social process or technology, we are granted an opportunity, through analysing these technologies, to rethink and reorganize some of our most deeply embedded assumptions. Consequently, the alterations in our traditional assumptions about parenting facilitated by assisted reproduction may have a hidden blessing. They have the potential to make us reflect on, and enhance our understanding of, the meaning and task of parenting. Over the generations parenting has, after all, been one of the principal influences in the reproduction of gender relations.

Rona Achilles

NOTES

1. *Ultrasound* involves the use of high-frequency sound waves to produce an image of the foetus (or other body parts) on a video screen. Increasingly, particularly in urban centres, it is used routinely in prenatal care and presumed to be safe, although no long-term follow-up studies have been undertaken. *Amniocentesis* is a prenatal diagnostic technique used to detect certain chromosomal abnormalities (such as Down's syndrome). A needle is inserted into the abdomen of a pregnant woman to extract a sample of the amniotic fluid. Amniocentesis, which cannot be used until the second trimester of pregnancy, is becoming a standard practice for women over the age of thirty-five. It can also be used to detect the sex of the foetus. *Chorionic villi sampling* (CVS), or chorionic biopsy, is a newer, still experimental method of prenatal diagnosis to detect foetal abnormalities; it can also be used to detect the sex of the foetus. A sample of foetal cells is removed through the pregnant woman's cervix. CVS can be performed in the first trimester of pregnancy and the results are obtainable more quickly than with amniocentesis. *Foetal monitoring* is a method of measuring the foetal heartbeat during pregnancy or labour. *Foetal surgery* is a form of micro-surgery to correct foetal defects within the womb.

2. Ruth Hubbard, "The Fetus as Patient," MS, October 1982.

3. *See:* Angus McLaren and Arlene Tigar McLaren, *The Bedroom and the State: The Changing Practices and Politics of Contraception and Abortion in Canada, 1880-1980* (Toronto: McClelland and Stewart, 1986) for a historical view of the politics of contraception and abortion in Canada.

4. The typology of reproductive technologies suggested here – the inhibition, monitoring, and creation of new life – is useful to distinguish the variety of reproductive technologies currently available. It is important to note, however, that they are frequently used in combination with each other and are not necessarily distinct. For example, women who conceive through IVF, AI, or surrogate motherhood arrangements may utilize diagnostic techniques such as amniocentesis, ultrasound, or chorionic villi sampling, as may women who conceive 'normally.' The focus of the chapter on assisted reproduction is a pragmatic one because of limitations of space. However, other developments, such as the routine use of amniocentesis for women over the age of thirty-five, are also important issues in considering the new choices available to women in their reproductive and mothering roles.

5. Shulamith Firestone, *The Dialectic of Sex: The Case for Feminist Revolution* (New York: Bantam Books, 1970).

6. See, for example, Jan Rehner, *Infertility: Old Myths New Meanings* (Toronto: The Second Story Press, 1989).

7. Barbara Menning, "In Defense of In Vitro Fertilization," in Helen B. Holmes, Betty B. Hoskins, and Michael Gross, eds., *The Custom-Made Child?* (New Jersey: Humana Press, 1981), 263-267.

8. For example, in the "Baby M" trial in 1987 the counsel for a surrogate mother attempted to reassert her custody rights on the basis that the contracting mother was avoiding pregnancy for minor or convenience concerns.

9. Furthermore, the causes of infertility may be socially rooted to some extent in occupational health hazards, environmental pollution, food additives, and the use of specific drugs such as DES and devices such as I.U.D.S.

10. A vasectomy is a simple medical procedure in which the vas deferens is cut so that sperm cannot mix with seminal fluid. It can be done in a doctor's office with a local anaesthetic. Tubal ligations are more complex procedures (there are several methods) in which the fallopian tubes are blocked or cut so that the sperm and egg cannot join. Usually a general anaesthetic is employed.

11. For further information on self-insemination *see*: Nancy Adamson, "Self-Insemination," *Healthsharing* 6, no. 4 (1985), 8-9; Francie Hornstein, "Children By Donor Insemination: A New Choice For Lesbians," in Rita Arditti, Renate Duelli Klein, and Shelley Minden, eds., *Test-Tube Women: What Future for Motherhood?* (London: Routledge & Kegan Paul, 1984), 382-390; Gillian E. Hanscombe and Jackie Forster, *Rocking the Cradle* (London: Peter Owen, 1981); Cheri Pies, *Considering Parenthood: A Workbook for Lesbians* (San Francisco: Spinster's Ink, 1985); Susan Robinson and H.F. Pizer, *Having a Baby Without a Man* (New York: Simon & Shuster, 1985); Joy Schulenberg, *Gay Parenting* (Garden City, N.J.: Anchor Press, 1985); Kathleen Lahey, "Alternative Insemination: Facing the Conceivable Options," *Broadside* 8, no. 1 (1986), 8-10.

12. Kathleen Lahey, "Reproduction, Male Technology and 'Lifestyle' Conflicts: The Lesbian Challenge," paper presented at the Sixth National Biennial Conference of the National Association of Women and the Law, February 1985.

13. *See*: Menning, "In Defense of In Vitro Fertilization," for a description of treatments for infertility that are utilized before artificial insemination is attempted.

14. A.T. Gregoire and Robert C. Mayer, "The Impregnators," *Fertility and Sterility* 16, no. 1 (1965), 130-134.

15. Ibid.

16. Office of Technology Assessment (OTA), Congress of the United States, *Artificial Insemination: Practice in the United States* (Washington: U.S. Government, 1988).

17. Elizabeth Noble, *Having Your Baby by Donor Insemination* (Boston: Houghton Mifflin, 1987.)

18. Rona Achilles, "The Social Meanings of Biological Ties: A Study of Participants in Artificial Insemination by Donor," Ph.D. dissertation, University of Toronto, 1986.

19. George Annas, "Fathers Anonymous: Beyond the Best Interests of the Sperm Donor," *Child Welfare* 60, no. 3 (1981), 161-174.

20. Richard Titmuss, *The Gift Relationship* (London: Allen & Unwin, 1970).

21. OTA, *Artificial Insemination Practice.*

22. Robert Matas, "Court Awards $883,000 to HIV-infected Woman," *The Globe and Mail*, November 21, 1991, A.1.

23. Ontario Law Reform Commission, *Report on Human Artificial Reproduction and Related Matters* (1985), 103. The Commission was requested by Attorney General Roy McMurtry to "inquire into and consider the legal issues relating to the practice of human artificial insemination, including 'surrogate mothering' and transplantation of fertilized ova to a third party . . . [and] report on the range of alternatives for resolution of any legal issues that may be identified." The legal issues suggested in the terms of reference for the report included: "(1) The legal status and legal rights of the child and the safeguards for protecting the best interests of the child. (2) The legal rights and legal duties of each biological parent. (3) The legal rights and legal duties of the spouse, if any, of each biological parent. (4) The nature and enforceability of agreements relating to artificial insemination and related practices. (5) The nature and enforceability of agreements respecting the custody of the child. (6) The legal rights and liabilities of medical and other personnel involved in performing artificial insemination and other related practices. (7) The legal procedures for establishing and recognizing the biological parentage of the children born as a result of these practices. (8) The applicability of present custody and adoption laws in such cases. (9) The availability of information to identify the child and the parties involved. (10) Such medical and related evidence as may have a bearing on the legal issues raised in these cases."

24. A research project carried out by the author in the mid-1980s. The DI mothers who participated in the study included women who were married at the time of insemination, single women, and lesbian couples. Single or lesbian DI mothers consistently adopted an attitude about openness about their DI child(ren)'s origins. The absence of a male partner made it impossible for them to attempt to conform to the conventional image of the family.

25. Anecdotal evidence suggests that women bore children for other women long before the practice became organized and a profit-making enterprise for lawyers and physicians.

26. Office of Technology Assessment (OTA), Congress of the United States, *Infertility: Medical and Social Choices* (Washington: Government of the United States, 1988).

27. Susan Ince, "Inside the Surrogate Industry," in Arditti, Duelli Klein, and Minden, eds., *Test-Tube Women*, 382-390.

28. Annas, "Fathers Anonymous."

29. Robert Hanley, "Surrogate Deals For Mothers Held Illegal in Jersey," *The New York Times*, February 4, 1988, 1, 14.

30. The information for this section on the Anna Johnson case is taken from an article by Juliet Guichon, *The Ottawa Citizen*, April 7, 1991, E. 1.

31. A.A. Yuzpe et al., "Rates and Outcome of Pregnancies Achieved in the First Four Years of an In Vitro Fertilization Program," *Canadian Medical Association Journal* 140 (1989), 167-172. Cited by H. Bryant, *The Infertility Dilemma* (Ottawa: The Canadian Advisory Council on the Status of Women, 1990), 13.

32. A. Pappert, "Success Rates Quoted by In Vitro Clinics Not What They Seem," *The Globe and Mail*, February 6, 1988, A.3.

33. Linda S. Williams, "Who Qualifies for In Vitro Fertilization? A Sociological Examination of the Stated Admittance Criteria of Three Ontario IVF Programs," paper presented to the Canadian Sociology and Anthropology Association, 1986.

34. A laparoscopy is a surgical procedure requiring a general anaesthetic; eggs are suctioned out through a fiberoptic tube.

35. Anne Mullens, *Missed Conceptions* (Toronto: McGraw-Hill Ryerson, 1990), 273.

36. OTA, *Infertility*.

37. In Canada, the following reports are available: *Artificial Insemination,* Ninth Report of the Royal Commission on Family and Children's Law, Government of British Columbia, 1975; *Status of Children,* University of Alberta, 1976; *Tentative Proposals for a Human Artificial Insemination Act,* Law Reform Commission of Saskatchewan, 1981; *Storage and Utilization of Human Sperm,* Health and Welfare Canada, 1981; *Report on Human Artificial Reproduction and Related Matters,* Ontario Law Reform Commission, 1985. For the United States, *see*: Ethics Committee of the American Fertility Society, "Ethical Considerations of the New Reproductive Technologies," *Fertility and Sterility* 46, no. 3 (1986). For Britain, *see*: The Warnock Report on Human Fertilization and Embryology, *A Question of Life* (Oxford: Blackwell, 1985).

38. The Royal Commission on New Reproductive Technologies had not reported at the time of writing. Its mandate was to "inquire into and report on current and potential medical and scientific developments related to new reproductive technologies, considering in particular their social, ethical, health, research, legal and economic implications and the public interest, recommending what policies and safeguards should be applied . . ."

39. Yet to be clarified are the legal rights and responsibilities of all the participants in artificial reproduction. Traditionally, rights and responsibilities for offspring are assigned to biological parents unless otherwise legislated, as with, for example, adoption. In the practice of DI, the husband of the DI mother is named on the birth certificate as the father of the child, although the sperm donor is the biological father. Further complications arise from the biological and socially defined differences between maternity and paternity. Is an egg donation, for example, the legal equivalent of a sperm donation? What rights do gamete (egg or sperm) donors have over their genetic material? Who 'owns' the extra embryos that are not implanted? Can physicians, lawyers, or surrogate organizations be liable for inadequate screening procedures or

'damaged goods'? For a discussion of these and other legal issues, *see*: Ontario Law Reform Commission, *Report on Human Artificial Reproduction*.

40. Margrit Eichler, *Families in Canada Today* (Toronto: Gage, 1983).

41. The procedure for an egg donation is much more medically invasive than sperm donation, but it is possible that women simply donate extra eggs removed during the initial phase of IVF. In *The Mother Machine* (New York: Harper & Row, 1985), Gena Corea points out that egg 'donations' might occur unknown to some women during surgery.

42. *See*: Anna Finger, "Claiming Our Bodies: Reproductive Rights and Disabilities," in Arditti, Duelli Klein, and Minden, eds., *Test-Tube Women*.

43. *See*: Jalna Hamner, "Sex Predetermination, Artificial Insemination and the Maintenance of Male-Dominated Culture," in Helen Roberts, eds., *Women, Health and Reproduction* (London: Routledge & Kegan Paul, 1984).

44. Kathleen Kenna, "Couples Wanting Only Boys Flock to MD for Gender Test," *The Toronto Star*, December 10, 1990, B.1, B.3.

45. Nancy Williamson, *Sons or Daughters? A Cross-Cultural Study of Parental Preferences* (Beverly Hills, Cal.: Sage Publications, 1976); Nancy Williamson, "Sex Preferences, Sex Control, and the Status of Women," *Signs: A Journal of Women in Culture and Society* 1, no. 4 (1976), 847-862; Nancy Williamson, "Parental Preference and Sex Control," *Population Bulletin* 33, no. 1 (1978).

46. *See*: Neil G. Bennett, ed., *Sex Selection of Children* (New York: Academic Press, 1983).

47. *See*: Hamner, "Sex Predetermination," for a more complete discussion of these methods.

48. Fiona Whitlock, "Test-tube Babies are Smarter and Stronger," *The Australian*, May 17, 1984.

49. Barbara Ehrenreich and Deirdre English, *For Her Own Good: 150 Years of the Experts' Advice to Women* (New York: Anchor Books, 1978).

50. As in the example of egg freezing, which will eliminate the more problematic practice of freezing embryos but will create its own problems.

SUGGESTED READINGS

Arditti, Rita, Renate Duelli Klein, and Shelley Minden, eds., *Test-Tube Women: What Future for Motherhood?* London: Routledge & Kegan Paul, 1984.

Baruch, Elaine Hoffman, ed., *Embryos, Ethics and Women's Rights.* New York: Harrington Park Press, 1987.

Bennett, Neil G., ed., *Sex Selection of Children.* New York: Academic Press, 1983.

Corea, Gena, *The Mother Machine.* New York: Harper & Row, 1985.

Corea, Gena, Renate Duelli Klein, Jalna Halma, Helen B. Holmes, Betty Hoskins, Madhu Kishwar, Janice Raymond, Robyn Rowland, and Roberta Steinbacher, *Man-Made Woman: How New Reproductive Technologies Affect Women.* Bloomington: Indiana University Press, 1987.

Holmes, Helen B., Betty Hoskins, and Michael Gross, *The Custom-Made Child? Women-Centered Perspectives.* New Jersey: Humana Press, 1981.

McLaren, Angus, and Arlene Tigar McLaren, *The Bedroom and the State: The Changing Practices and Politics of Contraception and Abortion in Canada, 1880-1980.* Toronto: McClelland & Stewart, 1986.

Mullens, Anne, *Missed Conceptions, Overcoming Infertility.* Toronto: McGraw-Hill Ryerson, 1990.

Office of Technology Assessment (OTA), Congress of the United States, *Infertility: Medical and Social Choices.* Washington: Government of the United States. 1988.

Overall, Christine, *Ethics and Human Reproduction: A Feminist Analysis.* Boston: Allen and Unwin, 1987.

Overall, Christine, ed., *The Future of Human Reproduction.* Toronto: The Women's Press, 1989.

Ratcliff, Kathryn Strother, ed., *Healing Technology.* Ann Arbor: The University of Michigan Press, 1989.

Roberts, Helen, ed., *Women, Health, and Reproduction.* London: Routledge & Kegan Paul, 1981.

Rothman, Barbara Katz, *The Tentative Pregnancy.* New York: Penguin, 1987.

Spallone, Patricia, and Deborah Lynn Steinberg, eds., *Made to Order: The Myth of Reproductive and Genetic Progress.* New York: Pergamon Press, 1987.

Special issue, "Women and Reproduction," *Canadian Journal of Women and the Law* 1, no. 2 (1986).

Stanworth, Michelle, ed. *Reproductive Technologies: Gender, Motherhood and Medicine.* Minneapolis: University of Minnesota Press, 1987.

Notes on Contributors

≈≈≈≈≈≈≈≈≈≈≈≈≈≈≈≈≈≈≈≈≈≈≈≈≈≈≈≈≈≈≈≈≈≈≈≈≈≈≈

RONA ACHILLES is the Coordinator of Family Planning Research in the Department of Public Health, City of Toronto. She is also an Assistant Professor, status only, in the Department of Behavioural Science, Faculty of Medicine, at the University of Toronto. She has written extensively on women's health issues, particularly those related to the new reproductive technologies. She also worked as a consultant for the Royal Commission on New Reproductive Technologies.

BEVERLEY BAINES is Co-coordinator of the Women's Studies Program in the Faculty of Arts and Science at Queen's University, where she has been a member of the Faculty of Law since 1974. She has taught courses on women and the law, feminist jurisprudence, human rights, property law, and public law. Her research interests include feminist pedagogy, women's Charter-based rights, the political representation of women, and a feminist perspective on constitutional law.

NAOMI BLACK is Professor of Political Science at York University, where she has been teaching since 1965, and has served as Women's Studies Co-ordinator (Faculty of Arts) and Adviser to the President on the Status of Women. She has published on international relations theory, foreign policy, feminist theory and methodology, and women's organizations. Publications include *Canadian Women: A History* (1985, co-authored as part of the Women's History Collective) and *Social Feminism* (1984).

JOANNA B. BOEHNERT has degrees from Lake Erie College, the State University of Iowa, and the University of Toronto. She is an Associate Professor of Psychology and Co-ordinator of the Women's Studies Program at the University of Guelph. Her professional interests include the enhancement of teaching effectiveness and the psychology of women.

SANDRA BURT teaches political science at the University of Waterloo, where she has also served as the first co-ordinator of Women's Studies (1979-80) and Associate Dean for Graduate Studies in the Faculty of Arts (1990-92). Her research interests include feminist women's groups, Canadian public policy, and feminist methodologies.

LORRAINE CODE is Professor of Philosophy at York University. In addition to numerous articles on epistemology and feminist philosophy, she is the author of *Epistemic Responsibility* (1987) and *What Can She Know? Feminist Theory and the Construction of Knowledge* (1991); and co-editor of *Feminist Perspectives: Feminist Essays on Method and Morals.*

LINDSAY DORNEY teaches English at the University of St. Jerome's College at the University of Waterloo. She is a former Director of Women's Studies at the University of Waterloo, and has long devoted her energies to feminist issues in literature and criticisms, in pedagogy, in environmental and social conditions affecting Canadian women, and women and development.

JANE ERRINGTON teaches history at the Royal Military College in Kingston, Ontario. She is the author of *The Lion, the Eagle and Upper Canada* (1987), which was awarded the Albert Corey prize, and has completed an illustrated history of Kingston. She is currently working on a manuscript on women and work in Upper Canada.

PAULINE GREENHILL is Associate Professor and Co-ordinator of Women's Studies at the University of Winnipeg in Manitoba. DIANE TYE is a Social Science and Humanities Research Council of Canada Post Doctoral Fellow in Canadian Studies at Mount Allison University in Sackville, New Brunswick. They are currently collaborating on an interdisciplinary book of collected essays, tentatively titled *Undisciplined Women: The (Dis)place(ment) of Female Traditional Culture in Canada.*

SUSAN A. MCDANIEL is a Professor of Sociology at the University of Alberta. She is the author of two books, *Social Problems Through Conflict and Order* (1982, with Ben Agger) and *Canada's Aging Population* (1986), as well as numerous articles and book chapters on aging, the family, and women. She was Canada's first Thérèse Casgrain Research Fellow in 1987-88.

MICHÈLE MARTIN is assistant professor at Télé-université, Université du Québec. In addition to various articles on women and communication, she is the author of *Hello Central? Gender, Technology and Culture in the Development of Telephone Systems* (1991) and of *Communication et médias de masse* (1991).

WENDY MITCHINSON is a Professor of History at the University of Waterloo. Her research is focused on the medical treatment of women. In 1988-89 she was the Hannah Visiting Professor at McMaster University, and she is the 1993 recipient of the Thérèse Casgrain Research Fellowship.

ROXANA NG immigrated to Canada in 1970. She has been active in immigrant women's organizing since 1976. She received her Ph.D in 1984 and teaches sociology at the Ontario Institute for Studies in Education. She writes in the areas of race and gender relations, community-state relations, and anti-racist and feminist pedagogy.

SALLY WEAVER is a political anthropologist who teaches at the University of Waterloo. She undertakes research in Canadian Indian and Australian aboriginal policy.

SHELAGH WILKINSON is University Professor at York University, where she lectures in the departments of Humanities and Women's Studies at Atkinson College. She is the Founding Director of the York Centre for Feminist Research/Centre de recherches féministes; and editor and publisher of *Canadian Woman Studies/Les cahiers de la femme.* She lectures internationally on feminist literary studies, Canadian women writers, and processes of developing women's studies in universities. She has four granddaughters who give her much joy.

INDEX

Heterosexuality, as compulsory, 41, 439, 473, 474, *see also* Lesbian women, Sexuality
History, women's, 59-60
Hobbes, Thomas, 26
Hollingsworth, Margaret, 378-79
Holmes, Joan, 123
Homestead Act (1878), 214
Horner, Matina, 464
Horney, Karen, 461, 462, 463
Hospitalières, 61
House of Commons, 80, 81, 170, 228
Housework, 16, 39, 289, 292-96, *see also* Domestic service
Housing, 73, 74, 103, 105, 112, 123, 125, 141
Human Rights Act, 103, 141, 224
Humour, 315-16, 327

Immigrant women: and housework, 292-96; and labour-force participation, 12, 288-92, 297-300; and racism, 280, 288, 291, 299, 300; and sponsorship, 284; and training, 285-87; writing by, 341, 374
Immigrant Women of Saskatchewan, 300
Immigrant Women's Centre (Toronto), 300
Immigration policy, 105, 279, 281-84, 291, 293, 298, 302 n8
In vitro fertilization, 501-3
Incest, 164, 191, 213, 271-72, 357, 358, 435, 467
Indian Association of Alberta, 100, 101
Indian Rights for Indian Women (IRIW), 100, 101, 102, 104, 113
Industrialization, 12, 25, 29, 61, 68, 70, 71, 73, 82, 85, 215, 293, *see also* Factory work
Infant mortality, 218, 398
Inferiority, female, 23-24, 37, 50, 164, 178, 227, 245, 249, 452, 456, 460, 462, 472
Infertility, 14, 439, 490-91, 492, 494, 495, 496, 501, 502, 506, 510, 512 n9
Insanity, 401, 405, 411-12, 414
INTERCEDE, 297, 299, 300
International Women's Day, 32
International Women's Year, 196, 197, 300
Inuit Tapirisat of Canada (ITC), 131, 268
Inuit women, 92, 131, 319, 327-28
Inuit Women's Association, 131
Irigaray, Luce, 46

Jameson, Anna, 340

Jamieson, Alice, 252, 257
Jamieson, Kathleen, 104
Janzen and Govereau v. Platy Enterprises, 271
Jean, Michèle, 185, 186, 187

Kamboureli, Smaro, 373-74
Kane, Marilyn, 121
Kirkland-Casgrain, Claire, 229
Kodish, Debora, 323
Kogawa, Joy, 374
Kollontai, Alexandra, 32
Kreps, Bonnie, 165
Kristeva, Julia, 45-46

L'Heureux-Dubé, Claire, 169, 270, 272
La bonne parole, 182-85, 186, 187, 188, 189, 204, 205
Laberge-Colas, Réjane, 158
Labour-force participation, of women, 10, 14, 15, 29, 67-68, 70-71, 81-82, 152, 159, 184, 215-16, 220, 427-432, *see also* Immigrant women
Lacan, Jacques, 45
Lalonde, Marc, 234
LaMarsh, Judy, 159
Langstaff, Annie Macdonald, 246-47, 250-51, 252, 255, 257
Langton, Anne, 339
Language, and gender difference, 45-46, 190, 359
Lapointe, Jeanne, 160
Lasnier, Michèlle, 194-95, 196, 198, 200, 201, 210 n90
LaTour, Madame, 319
Laurence, Margaret, 347, 351-52, 358, 364, 377
Lavallee, R. v., 271
Lavell, Jeannette Corbiere, 96, 97-98, 99, 100, 260, 261
Law: and biological determinism, 24; and minimum wage, 82, 217; and personhood, 80, 89, 243, 246-58; and property, 63, 78, 82, 169, 214; Bill C-31, 115-24, 127-28, 138 n163, 139 n164, 140 n188, 140 n192; Bill C-47, 111-15, 124; family, 163, 169
League of Women's Rights, 80
Legal Education and Action Fund (LEAF), 270
Legal profession, admission of women into, 72, 243, 246-53
Les têtes de pioche, 165, 182, 183, 185-88, 193, 205